John Willis and Ben Hodges
THEATRE WORLD®

Volume 60
2003–2004

APPLAUSE
THEATRE & CINEMA BOOKS

THEATRE WORLD
Volume 60

Art direction Mark Lerner
Cover and interior design Pearl Chang

ISBN (hardcover) 1-55783-650-7
ISBN (paperback) 1-55783-651-5
ISSN 1088-4564

Applause Theatre & Cinema Books
19 West 21st Street, Suite 201
New York, NY 10010
Phone: (212) 575-9265
Fax: (212) 575-9270
Email: info@applausepub.com
Internet: www.applausepub.com

Applause books are available through your local bookstore, or you may order at
www.applausepub.com or call Music Dispatch at 800-637-2852

Sales & Distribution
North America:
    Hal Leonard Corp.
    7777 West Bluemound Road
    P. O. Box 13819
    Milwaukee, WI 53213
    Phone: (414) 774-3630
    Fax: (414) 774-3259
    Email: halinfo@halleonard.com
    Internet: www.halleonard.com
Europe:
    Roundhouse Publishing Ltd.
    Millstone, Limers Lane
    Northam, North Devon EX 39 2RG
    Phone: (0) 1237-474-474
    Fax: (0) 1237-474-774
    Email: roundhouse.group@ukgateway.net

In Memory of **ZAN VAN ANTWERP** & **CHARLIE GRANT**

July 8, 1934 – February 26, 2005   June 28, 1926 – June 28, 2005

Without their steadfast encouragement of the associate editor for the past eight years, this series would not have continued to be published.

Their unwavering and enthusiastic support of the arts and artists in all respects was surpassed only by their inspirational devotion to one another and those they loved. They will forever be remembered and honored by the editors of these volumes, as well as by all who were lucky enough to have known them.

CONTENTS

PAST EDITOR   Daniel Blum (1945–1963)

EDITOR   John Willis (1964–present)

ASSOCIATE EDITOR   Ben Hodges (1998–present)

ACKNOWLEDGEMENTS:

Assistant Editors: Scott Denny, Victoria Gueli, Lucy Nathanson, Zachary David Palmer, Rachel Werbel;
Assistant: John Sala; **Staff Photographers:** Henry Grossman, Aubrey Reuben, Michael Riordan, Laura Viade,
Michael Viade, Jack Williams; **Applause Books Staff:** Brian Black, Pearl Chang, Haley Pierson.

SPECIAL THANKS:

New York and regional theatre press agents, publicists and photographers, all of whom continue to be largely
responsible for the production of this publication, Michael Messina and Kay Radtke at Applause Theatre and Cinema
Books, Stanley Ackert and Gersen, Blakeman, and Ackert, LLP, Robert Rems, Epitacio Arganza, The New York Innovative
Theatre Awards staff: Jason Bowcutt, Shay Gines, and Nick Micozzi, Sue Cosson, Susan Cosson, Michael Che,
Jason Cicci and Monday Morning Productions, The Learning Theatre, Inc. staff: Tim Deak and Kim Spanjol; Robert Dean
Davis, Carol and Nick Dawson, Jaime deRoy, Diane Dixon, Jeutan Dobbs and the Roundabout Theatre Company,
Patricia Elliott, Nicole Falack, Ben Feldman and Epstein, Levinsohn, Bodine, Hurwitz, & Weinstein, LLP, Emily
Feldman, Peter Filichia, Yvonne Gahareb, Leigh Giroux and Dumler and Giroux, LLP, Allison Graham, Helen Guditis and
the Broadway Theater Institute, Brad Hampton, Harry Haun, Laura Hanson, Al and Sherry Hodges, Richard Michael
Henderson, Sr. and Patricia Lynn Henderson, Richard Michael Henderson, Jr. and Jennifer Henderson, Doug Holmes,
the staff of the Otterbein College Department of Theatre & Dance, including Jeanne Augustus, Craig Johnson,
Katie Robbins, Dennis Romer, Fred J. Thayer, Dean Jo Ann Van Sant and Ed Vaughan, Gretchen, Aaron, Eli, and
Max Kerr, Howard Kissel, David Lowry, Tom Lynch and Barry Monush, Dr. Cecelia McCarton and the staffs of the
McCarton Center and the McCarton School, Kati Meister, Virginia Moraweck, Matthew Murray, Bob Ost and Theater
Resources Unlimited, Kathie Packer, Angie and Drew Powell, Ricochet, LLC staff: Ric Wanetik, David Hagans, Steven
Gelston, Kim Jackson and Mollie Levin, Carolyn, David, and Glenna Rapp, Frank Scheck, Michael Sommers,
Susan Stoller, Renee and Bob Tobin, Kate, Laura, Anna and Eric Tobin, Wilson Valentin, Frederic B. Vogel and the
Commercial Theater Institute, Doug Watt, Sarah and Bill Willis, Walter Willison, Jack Williams, Barbara Dewey
and the University of Tennessee at Knoxville, Linda Winer, Shane Wolters, Belinda Yong.

HIGHLIGHTS

AVENUE Q
Left: John Tartaglia and Princeton
Below: Stephanie D'Abruzzo and Lucy the Slut

PHOTOS BY CAROL ROSEGG AND NICK REUCHEL

LITTLE SHOP OF HORRORS
Left: Hunter Foster

PHOTO BY PAUL KOLNIK

ASSASSINS
Below: The Company

PHOTO BY JOAN MARCUS

THE BOY FROM OZ
Hugh Jackman
PHOTOS BY JOAN MARCUS

HENRY IV
Right: Richard Easton, Michael Hayden
PHOTO BY PAUL KOLNIK

KING LEAR
Below: Domini Blythe, Lucy Peacock, Christopher Plummer
PHOTO BY JOAN MARCUS

TABOO
Euan Morton

FIDDLER ON THE ROOF
Left: Randy Graff
Below: Alfred Molina
PHOTOS BY CAROL ROSEGG

CAT ON A HOT TIN ROOF
Ned Beatty, Ashley Judd
PHOTO BY JOAN MARCUS

WICKED
Kristin Chenoweth, Idina Menzel
PHOTO BY JOAN MARCUS

BOMBAY DREAMS
Left, Top: Ayesha Dharker (center) and the Company
Left, Below: Ayesha Dharker

PHOTOS BY JOAN MARCUS

GOLDA'S BALCONY
Above: Tovah Feldshuh

PHOTO BY AARON LEICHTE

FROZEN
Swoosie Kurtz

CAROLINE, OR CHANGE
Chandra Wilson, Tonya Pinkins
PHOTO BY MICHAEL DANIEL

A RAISIN IN THE SUN
Sanaa Lathan, Alexander Mitchell, Phylicia
Rashad, Sean Combs, Audra McDonald
PHOTO BY JOAN MARCUS

WONDERFUL TOWN

Above: Jennifer Westfeldt, Donna Murphy

PHOTO BY PAUL KOLNIK

TRUMBO

Left: Nathan Lane

PHOTO BY JOAN MARCUS

ANNA IN THE TROPICS
Priscilla Lopez
PHOTO BY JOAN MARCUS

BROADWAY

Productions that opened **June 1, 2003 – May 31, 2004**

Michael Boatman, Christopher Denham, Danny Glover

Christopher Denham, Danny Glover

Michael Boatman, Danny Glover   PHOTOS BY JOAN MARCUS

MASTER HAROLD...AND THE BOYS

Roundabout Theatre Company revival of the play by Athol Fugard. Artistic Director, Todd Haimes; Managing Director, Ellen Richard; Executive Director of External Relations, Julia C. Levy; Lonny Price, Director; Scenery, John Lee Beatty; Costumes, Jane Greenwood; Lighting, Peter Kaczorowski; Sound, Brian Ronan; Casting, Jim Carnahan, Mele Nagler; Production Stage Manager, Jay Adler; Stage Manager, Debra Acquavella; Press, Boneau/Bryan-Brown, Adrian Bryan-Brown, Matt Polk, Amy Dinnerman. Opened at the Royale Theatre, June 1, 2003*

Danny Glover

Cast

Sam **Danny Glover**
Willie **Michael Boatman**
Hally **Christopher Denham**

Understudies: Daryl Edwards (Sam, Willie); Bobby Steggert (Hally)

Time: 1950. Place: St. Georges Park Tea Room, Port Elizabeth, South Africa. A play presented without intermission.

*Closed July 13, 2003

BIG RIVER:
THE ADVENTURES OF HUCKLEBERRY FINN

Roundabout Theatre Company presentation of the Deaf West Theatre revival of the Musical with Book by William Hauptman; Music and Lyrics by Roger Miller; Adapted From the novel by Mark Twain. Artistic Director, Todd Haimes, Managing Director, Ellen Richard; Executive Director of External Affairs for Roundabout Theatre Company, Julia C. Levy; Artistic Director, Ed Waterstreet; Producing Director for Deaf West Theatre, Bill O'Brien, In Association with Center Theatre Group/Mark Taper Forum. Directed and Choreographed by Jeff Calhoun; Scenery, Ray Klausen; Costumes, David R. Zyla; Lighting, Michael Gilliam; Sound, Peter Fitzgerald; Music Direction and Special Music Arrangements, Steven Landau; Music Coordinator, John Miller; Associate Director and Choreographer, Coy Middlebrook; Casting Jim Carnahan; Production Stage Manager, Peter Hanson; Press, Boneau/Bryan-Brown, Adrian Bryan-Brown, Matt Polk, Jessica Johnson. Opened at the American Airlines Theatre, July 24, 2003*

Cast

Mark Twain; Voice of Huck **Daniel Jenkins**
Huckleberry Finn **Tyrone Giordano**
Jim **Michael McElroy**
Tom Sawyer **Michael Arden**
Widow Douglas ; Voice of Sally **Gina Ferrall**
Miss Watson; Sally **Phyllis Frelich**
Mary Jane Wilkes; Voice of Miss Watson;
 Voice of Joanna Wilkes; **Melissa van der Schyff**
Judge Thatcher; Harvey Wilkes; Silas; First Man **Iosif Schneiderman**
Ben Rogers; Puppeteer; Andy; Ronald Robinson;
 Voice of Young Fool; Voice of Sherrif Bell **Scott Barnhardt**
Jo Harper; Lafe; Donald Robinson **Rod Keller**
Dick Simon; Hank; Young Fool; Sheriff Bell **Ryan Schlecht**
Voice of Dick Simon; Voice of Harvey Wilkes;
 Voice of Hank; Second Man **Drew McVety**
Pap; Duke **Troy Kotsur**
Pap; King; Voice of Silas **Lyle Kanouse**
Joanna Wilkes **Alexandria Wailes**
Preacher; Doctor; Voice of Judge; Voice of Duke;
 Voice of First Man **Walter Charles**
Alice; Voice of Alice's Daughter; Slave **Gwen Stewart**
Alice's Daughter; Slave **Christina Ellison Dunams**

Ensemble: Michael Arden, Gina Ferrall, Phyllis Frelich, Iosif Schneiderman, Scott Barnhardt, Rod Keller, Ryan Schlecht, Drew McVety, Troy Kotsur, Lyle Kanouse, Alexandria Wailes, Walter Charles, Gwen Stewart, Christina Ellison Dunams

Understudies: Drew McVety (Mark Twain, Voice of Huck); Guthrie Nutter (Huckleberry Finn); Catherine Brunell (Widow Douglas, Voice of Sally, Mary Jane Wilkes, Voice of Miss Watson, Voice of Joanna Wilkes, Joanna Wilkes, Ensemble); Alexandria Wailes (Miss Watson, Sally, Ensemble); David Aron Damane (Jim); Rod Keller (Tom Sawyer, Ensemble); Kevin Massey (Ben Rogers, Puppeteer, Andy, Ronald Robinson, Voice of Young Fool, Voice of Sheriff Bell, Jo Harper, Lafe,

Christina Ellison Dunams, Gwen Stewart PHOTOS BY JOAN MARCUS

Donald Robinson, Ensemble); Guthrie Nutter (Dick Simon, Hank, Young Fool, Sheriff Bell, Judge Thatcher, Harvey Wilkes, Silas, First Man, Ensemble); Ryan Schlecht (Pap, Duke, Ensemble); George McDaniel (Pap, Kink, Voice of Silas, Voice of Dick Simon, Voice of Harvey Wilkes, Voice of Hank, Second Man, Preacher, Doctor, Voice of Judge, Voice of Duke, Voice of First Man, Ensemble)

Orchestra: Steven Landau, conductor, piano; Gordon Titcomb, banjo, guitar, dobro, mandolin, harmonica; Greg Utzig, guitar, dobro, banjo, mandolin; Cenovia Cummins, fiddle, mandolin; Dave Phillips, acoustic bass; Frank Pagano, percussion; dulcimer.

Musical Numbers: Overture, Do You Wanna Go To Heaven?, We Are the Boys, Waitin' for the Light to Shine, Guv'ment, I, Huckleberry, Me, Muddy Water, The Crossing, River in the Rain, When the Sun Goes Down in the South, Entr'acte, The Royal Nonesuch, Worlds Apart, Arkansas, How Blest We Are, You Oughta Be Here With Me, Leavin's Not the Only Way to Go, Waitin' for the Light to Shine (Reprise), Free At Last, Muddy Water (Reprise)

*Closed September 21, 2003

Daniel Jenkins, Michael McElroy, Troy Kotsur, Tyrone Giordano, Lyle Kanouse

Jordan Gelber, Natalie Venetia Belcon, Nicky, Rick Lyon (behind Nicky), Princeton, John Tartaglia, Jennifer Barnhart, Kate Monster, Rod, Stephanie D'Abruzzo, Ann Harada   PHOTO BY CAROL ROSEGG

AVENUE Q

Transfer of the Off-Broadway Musical with Book by Jeff Whitty; Music and Lyrics by Robert Lopez and Jeff Marx. Produced by Kevin McCollum, Robyn Goodman, Jeffrey Seller, Vineyard Theatre and The New Group. Director, Jason Moore; Choreography, Ken Roberson; Scenery, Anna Louizos; Costumes, Mirena Rada; Lighting, Howell Binkley; Sound, Acme Sound Partners; Orchestrations, Music Supervision and Arrangements, Stephanie Oremus; Music Direction and Incidental Music, Mr. Adler; Music Coordination, Michael Keller; Associate Producers, Sonny Everett, Walter Grossman, Morton Swinsky; Casting, Cindy Tolan; Production Stage Manager, Evan Ensign; Press, Sam Rudy Media Relations, Sam Rudy, Robert Lasko. Opened at the Golden Theatre, July 31, 2003*

Cast

Princeton; Rod **John Tartaglia**
Brian **Jordan Gelber**
Kate Monster; Lucy; Others **Stephanie D'Abruzzo**
Nicky; Trekkie Monster; Bear; Others **Rick Lyon**
Christmas Eve **Ann Harada**
Gary Coleman **Natalie Venetia Belcon**
Mrs. T.; Bear; Others **Jennifer Barnhart**
Ensemble **Jodi Eichelberger, Peter Linz**

Rick Lyon, Trekkie Monster, Jennifer Barnhart   PHOTO BY NICK REUCHEL

(CONTINUED FROM PREVIOUS PAGE)

Stephanie D'Abruzzo, Lucy the Slut PHOTO BY NICK REUCHEL

Princeton, John Tartaglia, Kate Monster, Stephanie D'Abruzzo PHOTO BY CAROL ROSEGG

Understudies: Jodi Eichelberger, Peter Linz (Princeton, Rod); Peter Linz (Brian); Jennifer Barnhart, Aymee Garcia (Kate Monster, Lucy, Others); Jodi Eichelberger, Peter Linz (Nicky, Trekkie Monster, Bear, Others); Aymee Garcia (Mrs. T, Bear, Others); Erin Quill (Christmas Eve); Carmen Ruby Floyd (Gary Coleman)

Orchestra: Gary Adler, conductor, keyboard; Mark Hartman, associate conductor, keyboard; Maryann McSweeney, bass; Brian Koonin, guitar; Patience Higgins, reeds; Michael Croiter, drums.

Musical Numbers: Avenue Q Theme, What Do You Do With a BA in English?/It Sucks to be Me, If You Were Gay, Purpose, Everyone's a Little Bit Racist, The Internet Is for Porn, Mix Tape, I'm Not Wearing Underwear Today, Special, You Can Be as Loud as the Hell You Want (When You're Makin' Love), Fantasies Come True, My Girlfriend, Who Lives in Canada, There's a Fine, Fine Line, There Is Life Outside Your Apartment, The More You Ruv Someone, Schadenfreude, I Wish I Could Go Back to College, The Money Song, For Now

Time: The present. Place: An outer borough of New York City. Musical presented in two acts.

*Still playing May 31, 2004

Rick Lyon, Nicky, Jennifer Barnhart PHOTO BY NICK REUCHEL

Rod, John Tartaglia PHOTO BY CAROL ROSEGG

LITTLE SHOP OF HORRORS

Revival of the Musical with Book and Lyrics by Howard Ashman; Music by Alan Menken; based on the film by Roger Corman. Produced by Marc Routh, Richard Frankel, Thomas Viertel, Steven Baruch, James D. Stern, Douglas L. Meyer, Rick Steiner/John and Bonnie Osher, Simone Genatt Haft, in Association with Frederic H. Mayerson, Amy Danis/Mark Johannes. Director, Jerry Zaks; Choreography, Kathleen Marshall; Scenery, Scott Pask; Costumes, William Ivey Long; Lighting, Donald Holder; Sound, T. Richard Fitzgerald; Puppet Design, The Jim Henson Company, Martin P. Robinson; Orchestrations, Danny Troob; Music Direction, Mr. Aronson; Vocal Arrangements, Robert Billig; Music Supervision and Arrangements, Michael Kosarin; Music Coordinator, John Miller; Associate Producers, HoriPro/Tokyo Broadcasting System, Clear Channel Entertainment, Endgame Entertainment, Zemiro, Morton Swinsky/Michael Fuchs, Judith Marinoff Cohn, Rhoda Mayerson; Casting, Bernard Telsey Casting; Production Stage Manager, Karen Armstrong, Stage Manager, Adam John Hunter; Press, Barlow-Hartman Public Relations, John Barlow, Michael Hartman, Jeremy Shaffer. Opened at the Virginia Theatre, October 2, 2003*

Carla J. Hargrove, DeQuina Moore, Trisha Jeffrey

Hunter Foster, Kerry Butler

Douglas Sills, Hunter Foster

Cast

Chiffon **DeQuina Moore**
Crystal **Trisha Jeffrey**
Ronnette **Carla J. Hargrove**
Mushnick **Rob Bartlett**
Audrey **Kerry Butler**
Seymour **Hunter Foster**
Orin; Others **Douglas Sills**
Voice of Audrey II **Michael-Leon Wooley**
Prologue Voice **Don Morrow**

Audrey II Manipulation: Martin P. Robinson, Antony Asbury, Bill Remington, Matt Vogel

Ensemble: Anthony Asbury, Bill Remington, Martin P. Robinson, Douglas Sills, Michael-Leon Wooley, Matt Vogel

Audrey II, Hunter Foster PHOTOS BY PAUL KOLNIK

Carla J. Hargrove, DeQuina Moore, Trisha Jeffrey

Rob Bartlett, Hunter Foster

(CONTINUED FROM PREVIOUS PAGE)

Understudies: Ta'Rea Campbell (Chiffon, Crystal, Ronnette); Ray DeMattis (Mushnik); Michael James Leslie (Voice of Audrey II); Jonathan Rayson (Seymour, Orin, Others); Jessica Snow Wilson (Audrey)

Orchestra: Henry Aronson, Conductor, keyboard; John Samorian, Associate Conductor, keyboard; John Benthal, guitar, mandolin; Steve Gelfand, bass; Tom Murray, Matt Hong, woodwinds; Tony Kadleck, Dave Spier, trumpet; David Yee, percussion; Rich Mercurio, drums

Musical Numbers: Little Shop of Horrors, Downtown (Skid Row), Da-Doo, Grow for Me, Ya Never Know, Somewhere That's Green, Closed for Renovation, Dentist!, Mushnik and Son, Git It, Now (It's Just the Gas), Call Back in the Morning, Suddenly Seymour, Suppertime, The Meek Shall Inherit, Sominex/Suppertime (Reprise), Somewhere That's Green (Reprise), Finale: Don't Feed the Plants

Time: 1950s. Place: Greenwich Village, New York City. Musical presented in two acts.

*Still playing May 31, 2004

Kerry Butler, Hunter Foster

DeQuina Moore, Trisha Jeffrey, Carla J. Hargrove PHOTOS BY PAUL KOLNIK

GOLDA'S BALCONY

Transfer from Off-Broadway of the solo performance piece by William Gibson. Produced by Manhattan Ensemble Theatre, David Fishelson, Roy Gabay, Randall L. Wreghitt, Jerry and Cindy Benjamin, Cheryl and Philip Milstein, Jerome L. Stern, David and Sylvia Steiner; Director Scott Schwartz; Scenery, Anna Louizos; Costumes, Jess Golstein; Lighting, Howell Binkley; Sound and Music, Mark Bennett; Projections, Batwin and Robin Productions; Assistant Director, Nell Balaban; Dramaturg, Aaron Leichter; Associate Producers, Lynne Peyser, Stephen Herman, Zev Guber, Dede Harris/Ruth Hendel/Sharon Karmazin/Morton Swinsky, James E. Sparnon, Sandra Garner; Production Stage Manager, Charles M. Turner III; Press, Richard Kornberg and Associates, Richard Kornberg, Rick Miramontez, Don Summa, Tom D'Ambrosio, Carrie Friedman. Opened at the Helen Hayes Theatre, October 15, 2003*

Cast
Golda Meir **Tovah Feldshuh**

A solo performance piece presented without intermission.

*Still playing as of May 31, 2004

Tovah Feldshuh

Tovah Feldshuh   PHOTOS BY AARON LEICHTERS

THE BOY FROM OZ

Musical with Book by Martin Sherman, Original Book by Nick Enright; Book and Lyrics by Peter Allen and others. Produced by Ben Gannon and Robert Fox; Director, Philip Wm. McKinley; Choreography, Joey McKneely; Scenery, Robin Wagner; Costumes, William Ivey Long; Lighting, Donald Holder; Sound, Acme Sound Partners; Wig and Hair, Paul Huntley; Orchestrations, Michael Gibson; Music Coordinator, Michael Keller; Dance Music Arrangements, Mark Hummel; Music Direction, Incidental Music and Vocal Arrangements, Mr. Vaccariello; Casting, Dave Clemmons Casting, Joseph McConnell; Production Stage Manager, Eileen F. Haggerty; Stage Manager, Richard C. Rauscher; Press, Boneau/Bryan-Brown, Adrian Bryan-Brown, Jackie Green, Joe Perrotta. Opened at the Imperial Theatre, October 16, 2003*

Hugh Jackman and the Company

Jarrod Emmick, Hugh Jackman, Michael Mulheren

Cast

Peter Allen **Hugh Jackman**
Boy (Young Peter) **Mitchel David Federan**
Marion Woolnough **Beth Fowler**
Dick Woolnough **Michael Mulheren**
Chris Bell **Timothy A. Fitz-Gerald**
Judy Garland **Isabel Keating**
Mark Herron **John Hill**
Liza Minnelli **Stephanie J. Block**
Trio **Colleen Hawks**, **Tari Kelly**, **Stephanie Kurtzuba**
Greg Connell **Jarrod Emick**
Dee Anthony **Michael Mulheren**

Standby: Hugh Jackman (Kevin Spirtas)

Ensemble: Leslie Alexander, Brad Anderson, Kelly Crandall, Naleah Dey, Nicholas Dromard, Timothy A. Fitz-Gerald, Christopher Freeman, Tyler Hanes, Colleen Hawks, John Hill, Pamela Jordan, Tari Kelly, Stephanie Kurtzuba, Heather Laws, Brian J. Marcum, Jennifer Savelli, Matthew Stocke.

Understudies: John Hill (Peter Allen); P.J. Verhoest (Boy [Young Peter]); Leslie Alexander (Marion Woolnough); Matthew Stocke (Dick Woolnough); Stephanie Kurtzuba, Heather Laws (Judy Garland);

Hugh Jackman PHOTOS BY JOAN MARCUS

Stephanie J. Block, Hugh Jackman, Isabel Keating

Tari Kelly, Heather Laws (Liza Minnelli); Brad Anderson, John Hill, Kevin Spirtas (Greg Connell)

Swings: Todd Anderson, Jessica Hartman

Orchestra: Patrick Vaccariello, conductor; Jim Laev, associate conductor, keyboards; Sylvia D'Avanzo, concertmaster, Victor Heifets, Fritz Krakowski, Wende Namkung, Cecelia Hobbs Gardner, Nina Evtuhov, violin; Mairi Dorman, Vivian Israel, cello; Cary Potts, bass; J McGreehan, guitar; Ted Nash, Ben Kono, Ken Dybisz, Don McGreen, reeds; Jeff Kievit, lead trumpet; Tino Gagliardi, Earl Gardner, trumpet; Clint Sharman, Randy Andros, trombone; Mark Berman, keyboard; Dan McMillan, percussion; Brian Brake, drums

Isabel Keating, Hugh Jackman

Hugh Jackman and the Company

Musical Numbers: Overture, The Lives of Me, When I Get My Name in Lights, When I Get My Name in Lights (Reprise), Love Crazy, Waltzing Matilda, All I Wanted Was the Dream, Only an Older Woman, Best That You Can Do, Don't Wish Too Hard, Come Save Me, Continental American, She Loves to Hear the Music, Quiet Please, There's a Lady on Stage, Not the Boy Next Door, Bi Coastal, If You Were Wondering, Sure Thing Baby, Everything Old Is New Again, Everything Old Is New Again (Reprise), Love Don't Need a Reason, I Honestly Love You, You and Me, I Still Call Australia Home, Don't Cry Out Loud, Once Before I Go, I Go to Rio

Time: 1950s–1990s. Place: Australia, Hong Kong and New York. Musical presented in two acts.

*Still playing May 31, 2004

John Lithgow, Ben Chaplin

THE RETREAT FROM MOSCOW

By William Nicholson. Produced by Susan Quint Gallin, Stuart Thompson, Ron Kastner, True Love Productions, Mary Lu Roffe and Jam Theatricals; Director, Daniel Sullivan; Scenery, John Lee Beatty; Costumes, Jane Greenwood; Lighting, Brian MacDevitt; Music and Sound, John Gromada; Associate Producer, McGhee Entertainment Inc.; Casting, Daniel Swee; Production Stage Manager, Roy Harris; Stage Manager, Denise Yaney; Press, Barlow-Hartman Public Relations, John Barlow, Michael Hartman, Wayne Wolfe. Opened at the Booth Theatre, October 23, 2003*

Cast

Edward **John Lithgow**
Jamie **Ben Chaplin**
Alice **Eileen Atkins**

Standbys: Edmond Genest (Edward), Mark Saturno (Jamie), Sandra Shipley (Alice)

Time: Present. Place: England. A play presented in two acts.

*Closed February 29, 2004

Eileen Atkins, John Lithgow PHOTOS BY JOAN MARCUS

SIX DANCE LESSONS IN SIX WEEKS

By Richard Alfieri. Produced by Rodger Hess, Marcia Seligson, Entpro Plays Inc., Carolyn S. Chambers, Sight Sound and Action Ltd., Brantley M. Dunaway, Judy Arnold and Patricia Greenwald; Directed by Arthur Allan Seidelman; choreography, Kay Cole; scenery, Roy Christopher; costumes, Helen Butler; lighting, Tom Ruzika; sound, Philip G. Allen; associate producers, Marilyn Gilbert, Nathan Rundlett, Etelvina Hutchins, Scottie Held and Joseph M. Eastwood; casting, Cindi Rush Casting; production stage manager, Jim Semmelman; stage manager, Marci Glotzer; press, Boneau/Bryan-Brown, Adrian Bryan-Brown, Jackie Green, Susanne Tighe, Juliana Hannett. Opened at the Belasco Theatre, October 29, 2003*

Cast

Lily Harrison **Polly Bergen**
Michael Minetti **Mark Hamill**

Standbys: Kathleen Doyle (Lily Harrison), Joseph Kolinski (Michael Minetti)

Time: The present. Place: Lily Harrison's condo in St. Petersburg Beach, Florida. A play presented in two acts.

*Closed November 23, 2003

Polly Bergen, Mark Hamill

Mark Hamill, Polly Bergen PHOTOS BY CAROL ROSEGG

Idina Menzel, William Youmans

Christopher Fitzgerald, Michelle Federer

WICKED

Musical with Book by Winnie Holzman; Music and Lyrics by Stephen Schwartz; Based on a novel by Gregory Maguire. Produced by Marc Platt, Universal Pictures, The Araca Group, Jon B. Platt and David Stone; Director, Joe Mantello; Choreography, Wayne Cilento; Scenery, Eugene Lee; Costumes, Susan Hilferty; Lighting, Kenneth Posner; Sound, Tony Meola; Projections, Elanie J. McCarthy; Special Effects, Chic Silber; Flying Sequences, Paul Rubin/ZFX Inc.; Wigs and hair, Tom Watson; Orchestrations, William David Brohn; Music Arrangements, Alex Lacamoire and Stephen Oremus; Music Direction, Mr. Oremus; Music Coordinator, Michael Keller; Dance Arrangements, James Lynn Abbott; Executive Producers, Marcia Goldberg and Nina Essman; Casting, Bernard Telsey Casting; Production Stage Manager, Steven Beckler; Stage Manager, Erica Schwartz; Press, The Publicity Office, Bob Fennell, Marc Thibodeau, Michael S. Borowski. Opened at the Gershwin Theatre, October 30, 2003*

Idina Menzel, Kristin Chenoweth

Cast

Glinda **Kristin Chenoweth**
Witch's Father **Sean McCourt**
Witch's Mother **Cristy Candler**
Midwife **Jan Neuberger**
Elphaba **Idina Menzel**
Nessarose **Michelle Federer**
Boq **Christopher Fitzgerald**
Madame Morrible **Carole Shelley**
Doctor Dillamond **William Youmans**
Fiyero **Norbert Leo Butz**
Ozian Official **Sean McCourt**
The Wonderful Wizard of Oz **Joel Grey**
Chistery **Manuel Herrera**

Ensemble: Ioana Alfonso, Ben Cameron, Cristy Candler, Kristy Cates, Melissa Bell Chait, Marcus Choi, Kristoffer Cusick, Kathy Deitch, Melissa

Kristin Chenoweth, Norbert Leo Butz, and the Company

Carole Shelley, Joel Grey PHOTOS BY JOAN MARCUS

Fahn, Rhett G. George, Manuel Herrera, Kisha Howard, LJ Jellison, Sean McCourt, Corrine McFadden, Jan Neuberger, Walter Winston Oneil, Andrew Palermo, Andy Pellick, Michael Seelbach, Lorna Ventura, Derrick Williams

Standby for Ms. Menzel: Eden Espinosa

Understudies: Melissa Bell Chait (Glinda), Kristy Cates (Elphaba), Kristoffer Cusick (Fiyero), Sean McCourt (The Wonderful Wizard of Oz, Doctor Dillamond), Jan Neuberger; Lorna Ventura (Madame Morrible), Andrew Palermo (Boq), Cristy Candler; Eden Espinosa (Nessarose)

Swings: Kristen Leigh Gorski, Mark Myars

Idina Menzel, Kristin Chenoweth

Orchestra: Stephen Oremus, conductor; Alex Lacamoire, associate conductor, piano, synthesizer; Christian Hebel, concertmaster; Victor Schultz, violin; Kevin Roy, viola; Dan Miller, cello; Konrad Adderly, bass; Greg Skaff, guitar; John Moses, clarinet, soprano sax; John Campo, bassoon, baritone sax, clarinet; Tuck Lee, oboe; Helen Campo, flute; Jon Owens, lead trumpet; Tom Hoyt, trumpet; Dale Kirkland, Douglas Purviance, trombone; Theo Primis, Kelly Dent, French horn; Paul Loesel, David Evans, keyboard; Ric Molina, Andy Jones, percussion; Gary Seligson, drums; Laura Sherman, harp

Musical numbers: No One Mourns the Wicked, Dear Old Shiz, The Wizard and I, What Is This Feeling?, Something Bad, Dancing Through Life, Popular, I'm Not That Girl, One Short Day, A Sentimental Man, Defying Gravity, No One Mourns the Wicked (Reprise), Thank Goodness, The Wicked Witch of the East, Wonderful, I'm Not That Girl (Reprise), As Long as You're Mine, No Good Deed, March of the Witch Hunters, For Good, Finale

Musical presented in two acts.

*Still playing May 31, 2004

CAT ON A HOT TIN ROOF

Revival of the play by Tennessee Williams. Produced by Bill Kenwright; Director, Anthony Page; Scenery, Maria Bjornson; Costumes, Jane Greenwood; Lighting, Howard Harrison; Sound, Christopher Cronin; Music, Neil McArthur; Casting, Pat McCorkle; Production Stage Manager, Susie Cordon; Stage Manager, Allison Sommers; Press, Philip Rinaldi Publicity, Philip Rinaldi, Barbara Carroll. Opened at the Music Box, November 2, 2003*

Cast

Margaret **Ashley Judd**
Brick **Jason Patric**
Mae **Amy Hohn**
Grooper **Michael Mastro**
Big Mama **Margo Martindale**
Reverend Tooker **Patrick Collins**
Big Daddy **Ned Beatty**
Doctor Baugh **Edwin C. Owens**
Lacey **Alvin Keith**
Brightie **Starla Benford**
Nursemaid **Jo Twiss**
Buster **Charles Saxton**
Dixie **Isabella Mehiel**
Trixie **Pamela Jane Henning**
Polly **Muireann Phelan**
Sonny **Zachary Ross**

Standby: Ted Koch (Brick)

Understudies: Kelly McAndrew (Margaret, Mae), Edwin C. Owens (Big Daddy), Jo Twiss (Big Mama), Ted Koch (Grooper, Reverend Tooker), Patrick Collins (Doctor Baugh), Alvin Keith (Brightie)

Time: Mid-1950s. Place: A bed-sitting room and section of the gallery of a plantation home in the Mississippi Delta. A play presented in three acts.

*Closed March 7, 2004

Amy Hohn, Ashley Judd, Jason Patric

Ned Beatty, Ashley Judd

Margo Martindale, Ashley Judd, Ned Beatty PHOTOS BY JOAN MARCUS

THE VIOLET HOUR

The Manhattan Theatre Club presentation of the play by Richard Greenberg; Artistic Director, Lynne Meadow; Executive Producer, Barry Grove; Director, Evan Yionoulis; Scenery, Christopher Barreca; Costumes, Jane Greenwood; Lighting, Donald Holder; Sound, Scott Myers; Special Effects, Gregory Meeh; Casting, Nancy Piccione, David Caparelliotis; Production Stage Manager, Ed Fitzgerald; Stage Manager, James FitzSimmons; Press, Boneau/Bryan-Brown, Chris Boneau, Jim Byk, Aaron Meier; Opened at the Biltmore Theatre, November 6, 2003*

Cast

Gidger **Mario Cantone**
Rosamund Plinth **Dagmara Dominczyk**
Denis McCleary **Scott Foley**
John Pace Seavering **Robert Sean Leonard**
Jessie Brewster **Robin Miles**

Understudies: Eisa Davis (Jessie Brewster), Robert L. Devaney (John Pace Seavering, Denis McCleary, Gidger), Heather Mazur (Rosamund Plinth)

Scott Foley, Dagmara Dominczyk

Time: April 1, 1919. Place: An office in a Manhattan tower. A play presented in two acts.

*Closed December 21, 2003

Dagmara Dominczyk, Scott Foley, Robert Sean Leonard   PHOTOS BY JOAN MARCUS

THE CARETAKER

Roundabout Theatre Company revival of the play by Harold Pinter. Todd Haimes artistic director; Ellen Richard managing director, Julia C. Levy executive director of external relations; Director, David Jones; Scenery, John Lee Beatty; Costumes, Jane Greenwood; Lighting, Peter Kaczorowski; Sound, Scott Lehrer; Casting, Jim Carnahan; Production Stage Manager, Matthew Silver; Stage Manager, Leslie C. Lyter; Press, Boneau/Bryan-Brown, Adrian Bryan-Brown, Matt Polk, Jessica Johnson. Opened at the American Airlines Theatre, November 9, 2003*

Cast

Mick **Aidan Gillen**
Aston **Kyle MacLachlan**
Davies **Patrick Stewart**

Standbys: Karl Kenzler (Mick, Aston), Julian Gamble (Davies)

Time: A winter night, the next morning and two weeks later. Place: A house in west London. A play presented in three acts.

*Closed January 4, 2004

Patrick Stewart

Kyle MacLachlan, Aidan Gillen, Patrick Stewart PHOTOS BY JOAN MARCUS

John Leguizamo

SEXAHOLIX...A LOVE STORY

Solo performance by John Leguizamo. Revival of the solo performance piece by John Leguizamo. Produced by Tate Entertainment Group; Director, Peter Askin; Press, Bill Evans and Associates, Jim Randolph. Opened at the Broadway Theatre, November 11, 2003*

*Closed December 7, 2003

John Leguizamo PHOTOS BY JOAN MARCUS

TABOO

Musical with Book by Charles Busch; adapted from the original Book by Mark Davies; Music and Lyrics by Boy George; Produced by Rosie O'Donnell and Adam Kenwright; Director, Christopher Renshaw; Choreography, Mark Dendy; Scenery, Tim Goodchild; Costumes, Mike Nicholls, Bobby Pearce; Lighting, Natasha Katz; Sound, Jonathan Deans; Hair and Makeup, Christine Bateman; Fight Direction, Rick Sordelet; Additional Composition, Mr. Frost; Orchestrations, Steve Margoshes; Additional Music, John Themis, Richie Stevens; Music Supervision and Arrangements, John McDaniel; Music Direction, Mr. Howland; Music Coordinator, Michael Keller; Associate Producer, Daniel MacDonald, Lori E. Seid, Michael Fuchs; Casting, Bernard Telsey Casting; Production Stage Manger, Peter Wolf; Stage Manager, Karen Moore; Press, Barlow-Hartman Public Relations, John Barlow, Michael Hartman, Bill Coyle, Rob Finn. Opened at the Plymouth Theatre, November 13, 2003*

Raúl Esparza

Cast

Big Sue **Liz McCartney**
Philip Sallon **Raúl Esparza**
George **Euan Morton**
Nicola **Sarah Uriarte Berry**
Marilyn **Jeffrey Carlson**
Marcus **Cary Shields**
Leigh Bowery **George O'Dowd**

Ensemble: Jennifer Cody, Dioni Michelle Collins, Brooke Elliott, Felice B. Gajda, William Robert Gaynor, Curtis Holbrook, Jennifer K. Mrozik, Nathan Peck, Alexander Quiroga, Asa Somers, Denise Summerford, Gregory Treco

Standbys: Donnie R. Keshawarz (Philip Sallon, Leigh Bowery)

George O'Dowd and the Company

Understudies: Dioni Michelle Collins, Brooke Elliott (Big Sue); Asa Somers, Gregory Treco (George); Lori Holmes, Jennifer K. Mrozik, Denise Summerford (Nicola); Alexander Quiroga, Gregory Treco (Marilyn); William Robert Gaynor (Marcus)

Orchestra: Jason Howland, conductor, keyboard; Daniel A. Weiss, associate conductor, second keyboard, second guitar; Sean Carney, violin; Arthur Dibble, viola; Ted Mook, cello; David Kuhn, bass; Kevan Frost, guitar; Charles Pillow, reeds; Chris Jago, drums.

Musical Numbers: Freak/Ode to Attention Seekers, Stranger in This World, Safe in the City, Dress to Kill, Genocide Peroxide, I'll Have You All, Sexual Confusion, Pretty Lies, Guttersnipe, Love Is a Question Mark, Do You Really Want to Hurt Me, Church of the Poison Mind/Karma Cameleon, Everything Taboo, Talk Amongst Yourselves, The Fame Game, See Through You, Ich Bin Kunst, Petrified, Out of Fashion, Il Adore, Come on in From the Outside

Time: 1980s. Place: An abandoned warehouse that housed the club Taboo, and other places in and around London. Musical presented in two acts.

*Closed February 8, 2004

Liz McCartney PHOTOS BY JOAN MARCUS

ANNA IN THE TROPICS

By Nilo Cruz; Produced by Roger Berlind, Daryl Roth, Ray Larsen, in association with Robert G. Bartner; Director, Emily Mann; Scenery, Robert Brill; Costumes, Anita Yavich; Lighting, Peter Kaczorowski; Sound, Dan Moses Scheier; Casting, Bernard Telsey Casting; Production Stage Manager, Cheryl Mintz; Stage Manager, Joshua Halperin; Press, Barlow Hartman Public Relations, John Barlow, Michael Hartman, Wayne Wolfe. Opened at the Royale Theatre, November 16, 2003*

Cast

Eliades **John Ortiz**
Santiago **Victor Argo**
Cheché **David Zayas**
Marela **Vanessa Aspillaga**
Conchita **Daphne Rubin-Vega**
Ofelia **Priscilla Lopez**
Juan Julian **Jimmy Smits**
Palomo **John Ortiz**

Understudies: Jason Manuel Olazabal (Eliades, Santiago, Cheche, Juan Julian)

Time: 1929. Place: Ybor City in Tampa, Florida. A play presented in two acts.

*Closed February 22, 2004

John Ortiz, Jimmy Smits, David Zayas

John Ortiz, Daphne Rubin-Vega PHOTOS BY JOAN MARCUS

THE OLDEST LIVING CONFEDERATE WIDOW TELLS ALL

Solo performance piece by Martin Tahse; based on the novel by Allan Gurganus; Produced by Elliot Martin, Jane Bergère, Morton Swinsky, Ruth Hendel and Everett King; Director, Don Scardino; Scenery, Allen Moyer; Costumes, Jane Greenwood; Lighting, Kenneth Posner; Sound, Peter Fitzgerald; Projections, Wendall K. Harrington; Production Stage Manager, Dianne Trulock; Press, Richard Kornberg and Associates, Tom D'Ambrosio. Opened at the Longacre Theatre, November 17, 2003*

Cast

Lucy Marsden **Ellen Burstyn**

*Closed November 17, 2003

Ellen Burstyn PHOTOS BY JOAN MARCUS

LAUGHING ROOM ONLY

Musical revue with Book by Dennis Blair and Digby Wolfe; Music and Lyrics by Doug Katsaros; Additional Material by Jackie Mason; Produced by Jyll Rosenfeld, Jon Stoll, James Scibelli, in association with Sidney Kimmel, John Morgan and The Helen Hayes Theatre Company; Director, Robert Johanson; Choreography, Michael Lichtefeld; Scenery, Michael Anania; Costumes, Thom Heyer; Lighting, Paul D. Miller; Sound, Peter Hylenski; Orchestrations, Mr. Katsaros; Music Direction and Vocal Arrangements, Joseph Baker; Dance Arrangements, Ian Herman; Assistant Director, Jayme McDaniel; Associate Choreographer, Joe Bowerman; Casting, Norman Meranus; Production Stage Manager; C. Randall White. Opened at the Brooks Atkinson Theatre, November 19, 2003*

Darrin Baker, Jackie Mason, Cheryl Stern   PHOTO BY PAUL UNDERSINGER

Cast
Jackie Mason
Darrin Baker
Robert Creighton
Ruth Gottschall
Cheryl Stern
Barry Finkel

Standbys: Michael Gruber, Danette Holden

Musical presented in two acts.

*Closed November 30, 2003

HENRY IV

Lincoln Center Theatre revival of the play by William Shakespeare; Adapted by Dakin Matthews; Artistic Director, André Bishop; Executive Producer, Bernard Gersten; Director, Jack O'Brien; Scenery, Ralph Funicello; Costumes, Jess Goldstein; Lighting, Brian MacDevitt; Music and Sound, Mark Bennet; Special Effects, Gregory Meeh; Fight Direction, Steve Rankin; Associate Director, Matt August; Dramaturg, Mr. Matthews; Stage Manager, Michael Brunner; Press, Philip Rinaldi Publicity, Philip Rinaldi, Barbara Carroll. Opened at the Vivian Beaumont Theatre, November 20, 2003*

Richard Easton, Michael Hayden

Cast

King Henry IV **Richard Easton**
Henry ("Hal"), Prince of Wales **Michael Hayden**
John of Lancaster **Lorenzo Pisoni**
Chief Justice Warwick **Dakin Matthews**
Earl of Westmoreland **Tyrees Allen**
Thomas Percy, Earl of Worcester **Byron Jennings**
Earl of Northumberland **Terry Beaver**
Lady Northumberland **Dana Ivey**
Henry Percy ("Hotspur") **Ethan Hawke**
Lady Percy **Audra McDonald**
Owen Glendower **Dakin Matthews**
Sir Richard Vernon **Peter Jay Fernandez**
Edmund Mortimer **Scott Ferrara**
Lady Mortimer **Anastasia Barzee**
Lord Hastings **Stevie Ray Dallimore**
Archbishop of York **Tom Bloom**
Earl of Douglas **C.J. Wilson**
Sir John Falstaff **Kevin Kline**
Poins **Steve Rankin**
Pistol **David Manis**
Nym **Ty Jones**
Bardolph **Stephen DeRosa**
Mistress Quickly **Dana Ivey**
Doll Tearsheet **Genevieve Elam**
Francis **Aaron Krohn**

The Company

Ralph **Jed Orlemann**
Justice Shallow **Jeff Weiss**
Justic Silence **Tom Bloom**
Davy **Jed Orlemann**

Ensemble: Christine Marie Brown, Albert Jones, Ty Jones, Lucas Caleb Rooney, Daniel Stewart Sherman, Corey Stoll, Baylen Thomas, Nance Williamson, Richard Ziman

Understudies: Dakin Matthews (King Henry IV); Lorenzo Pisoni (Henry ["Hal"]; Prince of Wales); David Manis (Sir John Falstaff); Scott Ferrara (Henry Percy ["Hotspur"], Stevie Ray Dallimore (Poins; Thomas Percy; Earl of Worcester; Earl of Westmoreland); Richard Ziman (Glendower; Archbishop of York); Nance Williamson (Lady Northumberland; Mistress Quickly); Stephen DeRosa (Shallow, Silence); Albert Jones (Nym); Christine Marie Brown (Lady Percy; Doll Tearsheet; Lady Mortimer; Davy); Peter Jay Fernandez (Earl of Northumberland); Jed Orlemann (John of Lancaster); Baylen Thomas (Edmund Mortimer; Lord Hastings); Aaron Krohn (Bardolph); C.J. Wilson (Pistol); Lucas Caleb Rooney (Earl of Douglas); Ty Jones (Sir Richard Vernon)

Time: 1403. Place: England. A play presented in three acts.

*Closed January 18, 2004

Michael Hayden, Kevin Kline, and the Company PHOTOS BY PAUL KOLNIK

WONDERFUL TOWN

Revival of the Musical with Book by Joseph Fields and Jerome Chodorov; Music by Leonard Bernstein; Lyrics by Betty Comden and Adolph Green; based on the play My Sister Eileen by Messrs. Fields and Chodorov, and on stories by Ruth McKenney. Produced by Roger Berlind and Barry and Fran Weissler, in association with Edwin W. Schloss, Allen Spivak, Clear Channel Entertainment and Harvey Weinstein. Directed and Choreographed by Kathleen Marshall; Scenery, John Lee Beatty; Costumes, Martin Pakledinaz; Lighting, Peter Kaczorowski; Sound, Lew Mead; Orchestrations, Don Walker; Music Direction and Vocal Arrangements, Mr. Fisher; Music Coordinator, Seymour Reed Press; Assistant Director, Marc Bruni; Associate Choreographer, Daniel H. Posener; Executive Producer, Alecia Parker; Production Stage Manager, Peter Hanson; Stage Managers, Kimberly Russel, Maximo Torres; Press, The Pete Sanders Group, Pete Sanders, Glenna Freedman, Jim Mannino. Opened at the Al Hirschfeld Theatre, November 23, 2003*

Donna Murphy, Cadets

Cast

Tour Guide **Ken Barnett**
Appopolous **David Margulies**
Officer Lonian **Timothy Shew**
Wreck **Raymond Jaramillo McLeod**
Helen **Nancy Anderson**
Violet **Linda Mugleston**
Speedy Valenti **Stanley Wayne Mathis**
Eileen Sherwood **Jennifer Westfeldt**
Ruth Sherwood **Donna Murphy**
Italian Chef **Vince Pesce**
Italian Waiter **Rick Faugno**
Drunks **David Eggers, Devin Richards**
Strange Man **Ray Wills**
Frank Lippencott **Peter Benson**
Robert Baker **Gregg Edelman**
Associate Editors **Ken Barnett, Ray Wills**
Mrs. Wade **Randy Danson**
Kid **Mark Price**
Chick Clark **Michael McGrath**

David Margulies, Donna Murphy, Jennifer Westfeldt

Shore Patrolman **Ray Wills**
Cadets: David Eggers, Rick Faugno, Vince Pesce, Mark Price, Devin Richards, J.D. Webster
Policemen: Ken Barnett, David Eggers, Vince Pesce, Devin Richards, J.D. Webster, Ray Wills

Greenwich Villagers: Ken Barnett, Joyce Chittick, Susan Derry, David Eggers, Rick Faugno, Lorin Latarro, Linda Mugleston, Tina Ou, Vince Pesce, Mark Price, Devin Richards, Angela Robinson, Megan Sikora, J.D. Webster, Ray Wills

Understudies: Linda Mugleston (Ruth Sherwood, Mrs. Wade); Nancy Anderson, Susan Derry (Eileen Sherwood); Matthew Shepard (Officer Lonian); David Eggers (Drunk); Ray Willis (Strange Man); Randy Donaldson (Speedy Valenti); Joyce Chittick (Helen)

Swings: Randy Donaldson, Stephanie Fredricks, Lisa Mayer, Matthew Shepard

Michael McGrath, Jennifer Westfeldt, Peter Benson PHOTOS BY PAUL KOLNIK

The Company

(CONTINUED FROM PREVIOUS PAGE)

Orchestra: Rob Fisher, conductor, Rob Berman, alternate conductor; Leslie Stifelman, associate conductor, piano; Marilyn Reynolds, Christoph Franzgrote, Rebekah Johnson, Lisa Matricardi, Masako Yanagita, violin; Jill Jaffe, Crystal Garner, viola; Diane Barere, Lanny Paykin, cello; Lou Bruno, bass; Steven Kenyon, Lino Gomez, Fred DeChristofaro, Edward Salkin, John Winder, woodwinds, Stu Satalof, David Trigg, David Gale, Ron Tooley, trumpet; Jack Gale, Jason Jackson, Jack Schatz, trombone; David Ratajczak, drums and percussion.

Musical Numbers: Overture, Christopher Street, Ohio, Conquering New York, One Hundred Easy Ways, What a Waste, Ruth's Story Vignettes, A Little Bit in Love, Pass the Football, Conversation Piece, A Quiet Girl, A Quiet Girl (Reprise), Conga!, Conga! (Reprise), My Darlin' Eileen, Swing, Ohio (Reprise), It's Love, Ballet at the Village Vortex, Wrong Note Rag, Finale

Time: 1935. Place: New York City. Musical presented in two acts.

*Still playing May 31, 2004

Gregg Edelman, Donna Murphy PHOTOS BY PAUL KOLNIK

I AM MY OWN WIFE

Transfer of the Off-Broadway solo performance piece by Doug Wright. Produced by Delphi Productions, in association with Playwrights Horizons; Director, Moisés Kaufman; Scenery, Derek McLane; Costumes, Janice Pytel; Lighting, David Lander; Sound, Andre J. Pluess and Ben Sussman; Production Stage Manager, Nancy Harrington; Press, Richard Kornberg and Associates, Richard Kornberg, Don Summa, Tom D'Ambrosio. Opened at the Lyceum Theatre, December 3, 2003*

Cast

Charlotte von Mahlsdorf   **Jefferson Mays**

Time: The Nazi Years; the Communist Years. Place: Various locations in the U.S. and Germany. A solo performance piece presented in two acts.

*Still playing May 31, 2004

Jefferson Mays

Jefferson Mays   PHOTO BY JOAN MARCUS

NEVER GONNA DANCE

Musical with Book by Jeffrey Hatcher; Music by Jerome Kern; Lyrics by Dorothy Fields, Oscar Hammerstein II, Otto Harbach, Johnny Mercer, Ira Gershwin, Bernard Dougall, P.G. Wodehouse, Jimmy McHugh and Edward Laska; based on the RKO Pictures film *Swing Time* and a story by Erwin Gelsey. Produced by Weissberger Theatre Group/Jay Harris, Edgar Bronfman Jr., James Walsh, Ted Hartley/RKO Pictures, Harvey Weinstein; Director, Michael Greif, Choreography, Jerry Mitchell; Scenery, Robin Wagner; Costumes, William Ivey Long; lighting, Paul Gallo; Sound, Acme Sound Partners; Orchestrations, Harold Wheeler; Music Direction and Vocal Arrangements, Robert Billig; Song Arrangements, James Sampliner; Dance Music Arrangements, Zane Mark; Music Coordinator, John Miller; Associate Director, Leigh Silverman; Associate Choreographer, Jodi Moccia; Casting, Bernard Telsey Casting; Production Stage Manager, Kristen Harris; Stage Manager, Michael John Egan; Press, Boneau/Bryan-Brown, Adrian Bryan-Brown, Amy Jacobs, Juliana Hannett. Opened at the Broadhurst Theatre, December 4, 2003*

Cast

The Charms **Roxane Barlow, Sally Mae Dunn, Jennifer Frankel**
Lucky Garnett **Noah Racey**
Mr. Chalfont **Philip LeStrange**
Margaret Chalfont **Deborah Leamy**
A Minister **Kirby Ward**
Mabel Pritt **Karen Ziemba**
Penny Carroll **Nancy Lemenager**
Alfred J. Morganthal **Peter Gerety**
Mr. Pangborn **Peter Bartlett**
Major Bowes **Ron Orbach**
Miss Tattersall **Julie Connors**
Ricardo Romero **David Pittu**
The Rome-Tones **Julio Agustin, Jason Gillman, T. Oliver Reed**
Spud **Eugene Fleming**
Velma **Deidre Goodwin**
Dice Raymond **Timothy J. Alex**
Waitresses **Sally Mae Dunn, Jennifer Frankel, Ipsita Paul**
A Construction Worker **Kirby Ward**

Ensemble: Julio Agustin, Timothy J. Alex, Roxane Barlow, Julie Connors, Sally Mae Dunn, Jennifer Frankel, Jason Gillman, Greg Graham, Kenya Unique Massey, Ipsita Paul, T. Oliver Reid, Kirby Ward, Tommar Wilson

Understudies: Jason Gillman, Greg Graham (Lucky Garnett); Nili Bassman, Deborah Leamy (Penny Carroll); Sally Mae Dunn, Jennifer Frankel (Mabel Pritt); Ron Orbach, Kirby Ward (Alfred J. Morganthal); Julio Agustin, Philip LeStrange (Mr. Pangborn); Julio Agustin, Timothy J. Alex (Ricardo Romero); Julie Connors (Margaret Chalfont); Timothy J. Alex, Kirby Ward (Mr. Chalfont); Timothy J. Alex, Kirby Ward (Major Bowes); T. Oliver Reid, Tommar Wilson (Spud); Kenya Unique Massey, Ipsita Paul (Velma)

Swings: Nili Bassman, Ashley Hull, Denis Jones, Tony Yazbeck

Peter Gerety, Karen Ziemba PHOTO BY JOAN MARCUS

Orchestra: Robert Billig, conductor; James Sampliner, associate conductor, keyboard; Howard Joines, assistant conductor, percussion; Mineko Yajima, concertmaster, James Tsao, Jonathan Dinklage, Claire Chan, violin; Sarah Carter, cello; Benjamin Franklin Brown, bass; Chuck Wilson, Rick Heckman, Mark Thrasher, reeds; Don Downs, John Chudoba, trumpet; Keith O'Quinn, Michael Boschen, trombone; Russell Rizner, French horn; Zane Mark, keyboard; Dean Sharenow, drums

Musical Numbers: Dearly Beloved, Put Me to the Test, I Won't Dance, Pick Yourself Up, Pick Yourself Up (Reprise), Who?, I'm Old Fashioned, She Didn't Say Yes, She Didn't Say No, The Song is You, The Way You Look Tonight, Waltz in Swing Time, Shimmy With Me, A Fine Romance, I'll Be Hard to Handle, I Got Love, The Most Exciting Night, Remind Me, Never Gonna Dance, Dearly Beloved/I Won't Dance (Reprise)

Time: 1936. Place: Punxsutawney, Pennsylvania; New York City. Musical presented in two acts.

*Closed February 15, 2004

DROWNING CROW

Manhattan Theatre Club production of the play by Regina Taylor; adapted from *The Seagull* by Anton Chekhov. Artistic Director, Lynne Meadow; Executive Producer, Barry Grove; Director, Marion McClinton; Choreography, Ken Roberson; Scenery, David Gallo; Costumes, Paul Tazewell; Lighting, Ken Billington; Sound, Dan Moses Schreier; Music, Daryl Waters; Projections, Wendall K. Harrington; Production Stage Manager, Diane DiVita; Stage Manager, Cynthia Kocher; Press, Boneau/Bryan-Brown, Chris Boneau, Jim Byk, Aaron Meier. Opened at the Biltmore Theatre, February 19, 2004*

Cast
Yak **Peter Macon**
Okra **Baron Vaughn**
Constantine Trip (C-Trip) **Anthony Mackie**
Simon **Curtis McClarin**
Mary Bow **Tracie Thoms**
Peter Nicholas **Paul Butler**

Anthony Mackie

Hannah Jordan **Aunjanue Ellis**
Eugene Dawn **Roger Robinson**
Paula Andrea Bow **Stephanie Berry**
Sammy Bow **Stephen McKinley Henderson**
Josephine Nicholas Ark **Alfre Woodard**
Jackie **Ebony Jo-Ann**
Robert Alexander Trigor **Peter Francis James**

Understudies: Caroline Clay (Josephine Nicholas Ark, Paula Andrea Bow, Jackie); Joseph Edward (Robert Alexander Trigor, Simon, Yak, Okra); Peter Macon (Constantine Trip [C-Trip]); Tiffany Thompson (Hannah Jordan, Mary Bow); Ronald Wyche (Peter Nicholas, Sammy Bow, Eugene Dawn)

Time: The present. Place: Gullah Islands, South Carolina. A play presented in two acts.

*Closed April 4, 2004

Alfre Woodard   PHOTOS BY JOAN MARCUS

Molly Ephraim, Sally Murphy, Lea Michele, Alfred Molina, Laura Michelle Kelly, Tricia Paoluccio

The Bottle Dancers

Marsha Waterbury, Nancy Opel, Joy Hermalyn

Sally Murphy, John Cariani

FIDDLER ON THE ROOF

Revival of the Musical with Book by Joseph Stein; Music by Jerry Bock, Lyrics by Sheldon Harnick; Based on stories by Sholom Aleichem. Produced by James L. Nederlander, Stewart F. Lane/Bonnie Comley, Harbor Entertainment, Terry Allen Kramer, Bob Boyett/Lawrence Horowitz, Clear Channel Entertainment; Director, David Leveaux, Director; Choreography, Jerome Robbins; Scenery, Tom Pye; Costumes, Vicki Mortimer; Lighting, Brian MacDevitt; Sound, Acme Sound Partners; Flying Sequences, ZFX Inc.; Wigs and Hair, David Brian Brown; Orchestrations, Don Walker, Larry Hochman; Music Coordinator, Michael Keller; Musical Staging, Jonathan Butterell; Music Direction, Kevin Stites; Production Stage Manager, David John O'Brien; Stage Manager, Jenny Dewar; Press, Barlow-Hartman Public Relations, John Barlow, Michael Hartman, Wayne Wolfe. Opened at the Minskoff Theatre, Februrary 26, 2004.*

Cast

Teyve **Alfred Molina**
Golde **Randy Graff**
Tzeitel **Sally Murphy**
Hodel **Laura Michelle Kelly**
Chava **Tricia Paoluccio**
Shprintze **Lea Michele**
Bielke **Molly Ephraim**
Yente, the Matchmaker **Nancy Opel**
Lazar Wolf **David Wohl**
Rabbi **Yusef Bulos**
Mordcha **Philip Hoffman**
Avram **Mark Lotito**
Jakov **David Rossmer**
Chaim **Bruce Winant**
Shandel **Barbara Tirrell**
Mirala **Marsha Waterbury**
Fredel **Rita Harvey**
Rivka **Joy Hermalyn**
Motel **John Cariani**
Perchik **Robert Petkoff**
Mendel **Chris Ghelfi**
Yussel **Enrique Brown**
Yitzuk **Randy Bobish**
Label **Jeff Lewis**
Shloime **Francis Toumbakaris**
Anya **Melissa Bohon**
Surcha **Haviland Stillwell**
Nachum, the Beggar **Tom Titone**
Fiddler **Nick Danielson**
Boy **Michael Tommer**
Boy (alt.) **Sean Curley**
Constable **Stephen Lee Anderson**
Fyedka **David Ayers**
Sasha **Johnathan Sharp**
Vladek **Stephen Ward Billeisen**
Vladimir **Keith K. Ühl**
Boris **Craig Ramsay**
Grandma **Haviland Stillwell**
Fruma Sarah **Joy Hermalyn**
Onstage clarinetist **Andrew Sterman**

Bottle Dancers: Randy Bobish, Enrique Brown, Chris Ghelfi, Jeff Lewis, Francis Toumbakaris

Understudies: Peter Hoffman, Mark Lotito (Teyve); Barbara Tirrell, Marsha Waterbury (Golde); Joy Hermalyn, Barbara Tirrell (Yente, the Matchmaker); Rita Harvey, Gina Lamparella (Tzeitel); Rita Harvey, Haviland Stillwell (Hodel); Melissa Bohon, Lea Michele (Chava); Melissa Bohon, Haviland Stillwell (Shprintze, Bielke); Jeff Lewis, David Rossmer (Motel); David Rossmer, Randy Bobish (Perchik); Stephen Ward Billeisen, Jonathan Sharp (Fyedka); Philip Hoffman, Mark Lotito (Lazar Wolf); Mark Lotito, Bruce Winant (Constable); Antoine Silverman, David Rossmer (Fiddler); Tom Titone, Bruce Winant (Rabbi); Randy Bobish, Roger Rosen (Mendel); Tom Titone, Bruce Winant (Mordcha); Tom Titone, Roger Rose (Avram); Gina

Laura Michelle Kelly, Robert Petkoff PHOTOS BY CAROL ROSEGG

Lamparella (Surcha, Fruma Sarah); Sean Curley, David Best (Boy)

Swings: Gina Lamparella, Roger Rosen, Gustavo Wons

Orchestra: Kevin Stites, Conductor; Charles duChateau, Associate Conductor, cello; Martin Agee, concertmaster; Cenovia Cummins, Conrad Harris, Heidi Stubner, Antoine Silverman, violin; Debra Shufelt, Maxine Roach, viola; Peter Sachon, cello; Peter Donovan, bass; Greg Utzig, guitar, mandolin, lute; Brian Miller, flute; Andrew Sterman, Martha Hyde, flute, clarinet; Matthew Dine, oboe; Marc Goldberg, bassoon; Wayne duMaine, lead trumpet; Tim Schadt, Joseph Reardon, trumpet; Lisa Albrecht, trombone, euphonium; Larry DiBello, Peter Schoettler, French horn; Elaine Lord, accordian, celeste; Billy Miller, drums, percussion

Musical Numbers: Tradition, Matchmaker, If I Were a Rich Man, Sabbath Prayer, To Life, Miracle of Miracles, Tevye's Dream, Sunrise, Sunset, Now I Have Everything, Do You Love Me?, Topsy-Turvy, Far From the Home I Love, Chavaleh, Anatevka

Time: 1905. Place: Anatvka, Russia. Musical presented in two acts.

*Still playing May 31, 2004

KING LEAR

Lincoln Center Theatre Production of the play by William Shakespeare. Artistic Director, André Bishop; Executive Producer, Bernard Gersten; in association with the Stratford Festival of Canada; Director, Jonathan Miller; Scenery, Ralph Funicello; Costumes, Clare Mitchell; Lighting, Robert Thomson; Music, Berthold Carriere; Sound, Scott Anderson; Casting, Daniel Swee; Stage Manager, Brian Scott; Press, Philip Rinaldi Publicity, Barbara Carroll. Opened at the Vivian Beaumont Theatre, March 4, 2004*

Cast

King Lear **Christopher Plummer**
Goneril **Domini Blythe**
Regan **Lucy Peacock**
Cordelia **Claire Jullien**
Duke of Albany **Ian Deakin**
Duke of Cornwall **Stephen Russell**
Earl of Kent **Benedict Campbell**
Earl of Gloucester **James Blendick**
Edgar **Brent Carver**
Edmund **Geraint Wyn Davies**
Fool **Barry MacGregor**
King of France **Paul O'Brien**
Duke of Burgundy **Guy Paul**
Oswald **Brian Tree**
Curan **Eric Sheffer Stevens**
Cornwall's Servants **David Furr, Christopher McHale, Jay Edwards**
Old Man **Leo Lyden**
Doctor **William Cain**
Captain **David Furr**
Herald **Quentin Maré**

Ensemble: Caroline Bootle, Jay Edwards, David Furr, Douglas Harmsen, Leo Leyden, Matt Loney, Quentin Mare, Christopher McHale, Andy Prosky, Christopher Randolph, Brian Sgambati, Eric Sheffer Stevens, Baylen Thomas, Susan Wilder

Understudies: Benedict Campbell (King Lear); Stephen Russell (Earl of Kent); Brian Tree (Fool); William Cain (Earl of Gloucester, Old Man); Paul O'Brien (Duke of Albany); Guy Paul (Duke of Cornwall); Christopher McHale (Doctor, [one of] Cornwall's Servants); Quentin Mare (Edmund); Caroline Bootle (Cordelia); Susan Wilder (Goneril, Regan); Christopher Randolph (King of France); Douglas Harmsen (Edgar); Andy Prosky (Oswald); Eric Sheffer Stevens (Duke of Burgundy); Matt Loney (Curan, Herald); Baylen Thomas (Captain, [one of] Cornwall's Servants)

A play presented in two acts.

*Closed April 18, 2004

Christopher Plummer

Domini Blythe, Lucy Peacock, Christopher Plummer

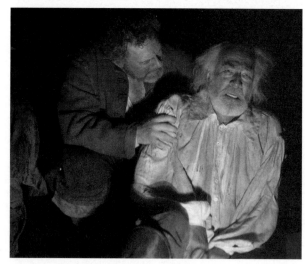

Benedict Campbell, Christopher Plummer PHOTOS BY JOAN MARCUS

TWENTIETH CENTURY

Roundabout Theatre Company revival of the play by Ben Hecht and Charles MacArthur; based on a play by Charles Bruce Millholland; adapted by Ken Ludwig. Artistic Director, Todd Haimes; Managing Director, Ellen Richard; Executive Director of External Affairs, Julia C. Levy; Director, Walter Bobbie; Scenery, John Lee Beatty; Costumes, William Ivey Long; Lighting, Peter Kaczorowski; Sound, Acme Sound Partners; Casting, Jim Carnahan, Mele Nagler; Production Stage Manager, James Harker; Stage Manager, Leslie C. Lyter; Press, Boneau/Bryan-Brown, Adrian Bryan-Brown, Matt Polk, Jessica Johnson. Opened at the American Airlines Theatre, March 25, 2004*

Alec Baldwin, Dan Butler, Anne Heche, Julie Halston, Tom Aldredge

Anne Heche

Cast

Anita Highland **Kellie Overbey**
Dr. Grover Lockwood **Jonathan Walker**
Porter **Robert M. Jiménez**
Matthew Clark **Tom Aldredge**
Owen O'Malley **Dan Butler**
Conductor **Terry Beaver**
Ida Webb **Julie Halston**
Oscar Jaffe **Alec Baldwin**
Lily Garland **Anne Heche**
George Smith **Ryan Shively**
Beard **Stephen DeRosa**
Detective **Patrick Boll**
Max Jacobs **Stephen DeRosa**

Ensemble: Patrick Boll, Todd Cerveris, Darian Dauchan, Bill English, Virginia Louise Smith

Understudies: Patrick Boll (Oscar Jaffe); Virginia Louise Smith (Lily Garland, Ida Webb, Anita Highland); Todd Cerveris (Owen O'Malley, Dr. Grover Lockwood, Beard); Robert M. Jimenez (Matthew Clark, Conductor); Bill English (George Smith, Detective); Darian Dauchan (Porter)

Time: October 1938. Place: Aboard the Twentieth Century Limited. A play presented in two acts.

*Still playing May 31, 2004

Alec Baldwin, Anne Heche PHOTOS BY JOAN MARCUS

Barbara Cook

BARBARA COOK'S BROADWAY!

Solo performance by Barbara Cook. Lincoln Center Theatre Production, Artistic Director, André Bishop; Executive Producer, Bernard Gersten; Music Direction and Arrangement, Wally Harper; Stage Manager, Mahlon Kruse; Press, Philip Rinaldi, Barbara Carroll. Opened at the Vivian Beaumont Theatre, March 28, 2004*

Performed by Barbara Cook, with Wally Harper (piano) and Richard Sarpola (bass)

A solo performance piece presented without intermission.

*Closed April 18, 2004

Barbara Cook, Wally Harper PHOTO BY RAHAV SEGEV

SLY FOX

Revival of the play by Larry Gelbart; based on *Volpone* by Ben Jonson. Produced by Julian Schlossberg, Roy Furman, Ben Sprecher, Michael Gardner, Jim Fantaci, Cheryl Lachowicz, Christine Duncan and Nelle Nugent, By Arrangement with Andrew Braunsberg; Director, Arthur Penn; Scenery, George Jenkins and Jesse Poleshuck; costumes, Albert Wolsky; Lighting, Phil Monat; Sound, T. Richard Fitzgerald and Carl Casella; Fight Direction, B.H. Barry; Associate Producers, Aaron Levy, Jill Furman, Debra Black, Peter May; Casting, Stuart Howard and Amy Schecter; Production Stage Manager, Marybeth Abel; Stage Manager, Bryan Landrine; Press, The Publicity Office, Bob Fennell, Marc Thibodeau, Michael S. Borowski. Opened at the Ethel Barrymore Theatre, April 1, 2004*

Bob Dishy, Rene Auberjonois, Bronson Pinchot

Peter Scolari, Elizabeth Berkley

Cast

Simon Able **Eric Stoltz**
Sly's servants **Jeremy Hollingworth, Charles Antalosky, Linda Halaska**
Foxwell J. Sly **Richard Dreyfuss**
Lawyer Craven **Bronson Pinchot**
Jethro Crouch **René Auberjonois**
Abner Truckle **Bob Dishy**
Miss Fancy **Rachel York**
Mrs. Truckle **Elizabeth Berkley**
Crouch's servant **Jason Ma**
Captain Crouch **Nick Wyman**
Chief of Police **Peter Scolari**
1st Policeman **Robert LaVelle**
2nd Policeman **Gordon Joseph Weiss**
3rd Policeman **Jeff Talbott**
Court Clerk **Professor Irwin Corey**
Judge **Richard Dreyfuss**

Understudies: Jeremy Hollingworth (Simon Able); Peter Scolari, Gordon Joseph Weiss (Abner Truckle); Professor Irwin Corey, Charles Antalosky (Jethro Couch); Linda Halaska (Mrs. Truckle, Miss Fancy); Robert LaVelle (Captain Crouch); Peter Scolari, Gordon Joseph Weiss (Lawyer Craven); Charles Antalosky, Gordon Joseph Weiss (Chief of Police); Charles

Rene Auberjonois, Rachel York

Antalosky (Court Clerk); Jeff Talbott, Jason Ma (1st Policeman, 2nd Policeman, 3rd Policeman); Jeff Talbott (2nd Policeman, Crouch's servant, [one of] Sly's servants, Bailiff)

Time: A day in the late 1800s. Place: San Francisco. A play presented in two acts.

*Still playing May 31, 2004

Eric Stoltz, Richard Dreyfuss, Bronson Pinchot PHOTOS BY CAROL ROSEGG

MATCH

By Stephen Belber; Produced by the Araca Group, East of Doheny Theatricals, Chase Mishkin, In Association With Ray and Kit Sawyer, Carol Grose; Director, Nicholas Martin; Scenery, James Noone; Costumes, Michael Krass; Lighting, Brian MacDevitt; Sound, Kurt Kellenberger and Jerry Yager; Fight Direction, Rick Sordelet; Associate Producers, Clint Bond Jr., Edward Nelson; Casting, Bernard Telsey Casting; Production Stage Manager, Andrea "Spook" Testani; Stage Manager, Stephen M. Kaus; Press, Boneau/Bryan-Brown, Adrian Bryan-Brown, Jackie Green, Joe Perrotta. Opened at the Plymouth Theatre, April 8, 2004*

Cast

Toby **Frank Langella**
Mike **Ray Liotta**
Lisa **Jane Adams**

Understudies: Malcolm Ingram (Toby); Karl Bury (Mike); Alexandra Neil (Lisa)

Time: The present. Place: Upper Manhattan. A play presented in two acts.

*Closed May 23, 2004

Jane Adams, Frank Langella, Ray Liotta

Ray Liotta, Frank Langella PHOTOS BY JOAN MARCUS

SIXTEEN WOUNDED

By Eliam Kraiem. Produced by Jujamcyn Theatres, Producers Four and Robert G. Bartner, In Association With Debra Black, Lisa Vioni, Michael Watt; Director, Garry Hynes; Scenery and Costumes, Francis O'Connor; Lighting, James F. Ingalls; Music and Sound, John Gromada; Special Effects, Gregory Meeh; Fight Direction, Thomas Schall; Associate Producers, Jerry Meyer, Patrick Catullo; Casting, Jay Binder, Jack Bowdan; Production Stage Manager, David Hyslop; Stage Manager, Deirdre McCrane; Press, Barlow-Hartman Public Relations, John Barlow, Michael Hartman, Bill Coyle, Andrew Snyder. Opened at the Walter Kerr Theatre, April 15, 2004*

Cast

Hans **Judd Hirsch**
Sonya **Jan Maxwell**
Mahmoud **Omar Metwally**
Nora **Martha Plimpton**
Ashraf **Waleed F. Zuaiter**

Understudies: Martin Rayner (Hans); Natacha Roi (Sonya, Nora); Waleed F. Zuaiter, Jonathan Hova (Mahmoud); Waleed F. Zuaiter (Jonathan Hova)

Time: 1992–1994. Place: A bakery in Amsterdam. A play presented in two acts.

*Closed April 25, 2004

Waleed F. Zuaiter, Omar Metwally

Martha Plimpton, Omar Metwally, Judd Hirsch PHOTOS BY JOAN MARCUS

Michael Cerveris

Denis O'Hare, Michael Cerveris, James Barbour, Becky Ann Baker

ASSASSINS

Roundabout Theatre Company revival of the Musical with Book by John Weidman; Music and Lyrics by Stephen Sondheim. Artistic Director, Todd Haimes; Managing Director, Ellen Richard; Executive Director of External Relations, Julia C. Levy; Director, Joe Mantello; Choreography, Jonathan Butterell; Scenery, Robert Brill; Costumes, Susan Hilferty; Lighting, Jules Fisher and Peggy Eisenhauer; Casting, Jim Carnahan; Production Stage Manager, William Joseph Barnes; Stage Manager, Jon Krause; Press, Boneau/Bryan-Brown, Adrian Bryan-Brown, Matt Polk, Jessica Johnson. Opened at Studio 54, April 22, 2004*

Cast

Propietor **Marc Kudisch**
Leon Czolgosz **James Barbour**
John Hinckley **Alexander Gemignani**
Charles Guiteau **Denis O'Hare**
Giuseppe Zangara **Jeffrey Kuhn**
Samuel Byck **Mario Cantone**
Lynette "Squeaky" Fromme **Mary Catherine Garrison**
Sara Jane Moore **Becky Ann Baker**
John Wilkes Booth **Michael Cerveris**
Balladeer **Neil Patrick Harris**
David Herold **Brandon Wardell**
Emma Goldman **Anne L. Nathan**
James Blaine **James Clow**
President James Garfield **Merwin Foard**
Billy **Eamon Foley**
President Gerald Ford **James Clow**
Lee Harvey Oswald **Neil Patrick Harris**

Ensemble: James Clow, Merwin Foard, Eamon Foley, Kendra Kassebaum, Anne L. Nathan, Brandon Wardell

Understudies: Kendra Kassebaum (Lynette "Squeaky" Fromme); James Clow (John Wilkes Booth, Charles Guiteau); Merwin Foard (Leon Czolgosz, Samuel Byck, Propietor); Brandon Wardell (John Hinckley, Balladeer, Giuseppe Zangara)

Swings: Ken Krugman, Sally Wilfert, Chris Peluso

Alexander Gemignani, Becky Ann Baker, Jeffrey Kuhn, Michael Cerveris, Neil Patrick Harris, Mario Cantone, Mary Catherine Garrison, Denis O'Hare, James Barbour

Orchestra: Paul Gemignani, conductor; Nicholas Michael Archer, associate conductor, keyboard; Paul Ford, keyboard; Dennis Anderson, flute, piccolo, clarinet, soprano sax, harmonica; Andrew Shreeves, oboe, English horn, piccolo, clarinet, alto sax; Scott Schachter, clarinet, flute, piccolo, bass clarinet, E-flat clarinet, tenor sax; Mark Thrasher, bassoon, clarinet, baritone sax; Dominic Derasse, trumpet, cornet; Phil Granger, trumpet, flugelhorn; Ronald Sell, French horn; Bruce Eidem, trombone, euphonium; Scott Kuney guitar, banjo, mandolin; John Beal, bass, electric bass; Larry Lelli, drums, percussion

Musical Numbers: Everybody's Got the Right, The Ballad of Booth, How I Saved Roosevelt, Gun Song, The Ballad of Czolgosz, Unworthy of Your Love, The Ballad of Guiteau, Another National Anthem, Something Just Broke, Everybody's Got the Right

Musical presented without intermission.

*Still playing May 31, 2004

The Company PHOTOS BY JOAN MARCUS

JUMPERS

Revival of the play by Tom Stoppard. Produced by Boyett Ostar Productions, Nederlander Presentations Inc., Freddy DeMann, Jean Doumanian, Stephani McClelland, Arielle Tepper, in association with the National Theatre of Great Britain; Director, David Leveaux; Choreography, Aidan Treays; Scenery, Vicki Mortimer; Costumes, Nicky Gillibrand; Lighting, Paule Constable; Sound, John Leonard for Aura; Music, Corin Buckeridge; Music Coordinator, Michael Keller; Associate Director, Matt Wilde; Casting, Jim Carnahan; Production Stage Manager, Arthur Gaffin; Stage Manager, Laurie Goldfeder; Press, Boneau/Bryan-Brown, Adrian Bryan-Brown, Jim Byk, Juliana Hannett. Opened at the Brooks Atkinson Theatre, April 25, 2004*

Cast
Dorothy **Essie Davis**
Secretary **Eliza Lumley**
Crouch **John Rogan**
George **Simon Russell Beale**
Archie **Nicky Henson**
Bones **Nicholas Woodeson**
Greystoke; Jumper **Michael Hollick**
McFee; Jumper **Hillel Meltzer**

Jumpers: Michael Arnold, Andrew Asnes, Clark Scott Carmichael, Tom Hildebrand, Don Johanson, Joseph P. McDonnell

Standbys: John Curless (George); Crista Moore (Dorothy, Secretary); Tony Carlin (Archie); Julian Gamble (Bones, Crouch)

Swings: Karl Christian, Aaron Vexler

Orchestra: Tim Weil, conductor, keyboards; James Saporito, drums; Richard Sarpola, bass.

A play presented in two acts.

*Still playing May 31, 2004

Essie Davis, Simon Russell Beale

Essie Davis PHOTOS BY HUGO GLENDINNING

Sanaa Lathan, Alexander Mitchell, Phylicia Rashad, Sean Combs, Audra McDonald

A RAISIN IN THE SUN

Revival of the play by Lorraine Hansberry. Produced by David Binder, Vivek J. Tiwary, Susan Batson, Carl Rumbaugh, Ruth Hendel, Jayne Baron Sherman, Dede Harris, in Association with Arielle Tepper, Barbary Whitman, Cynthia Stroum; Director, Kenny Leon; Scenery, Thomas Lynch; Costumes, Paul Tazewell; Lighting, Brian MacDevitt; Sound, T. Richard Fitzgerald; Music, Dwight Andrews; Associate Producers, Brian Savelson, Hal Goldberg; Casting, James Calleri; Production Stage Manager, Michael Brunner; Stage Manager, Narda Alcorn; Press, The Publicity Office, Bob Fennell, Marc Thibodeau, Michael S. Borowski. Opened at the Royale Theatre, Opened April 26, 2004*

Phylicia Rashad, Audra McDonald, Sanaa Lathan

Cast

Ruth Younger **Audra McDonald**
Travis Younger **Alexander Mitchell**
Walter Lee Younger **Sean Combs**
Beneatha Younger **Sanaa Lathan**
Lena Younger **Phylicia Rashad**
Joseph Asagai **Teagle F. Bougere**
George Murchison **Frank Harts**
Karl Lindner **David Aaron Baker**
Bobo **Bill Nunn**
Moving Men **Lawrence Ballard, Billy Eugene Jones**

Time: 1950s. Place: Chicago's Southside. A play presented in two acts.

*Still playing May 31, 2004

Audra McDonald, Sean Combs PHOTOS BY JOAN MARCUS

BOMBAY DREAMS

Musical with Book by Meera Syal and Thomas Meehan; Music by A.R. Rahman; Lyrics by Don Black; Based on an idea by Shekhar Kapur and Andrew Lloyd Webber. Produced by Waxman Williams Entertainment and TGA Entertainment; In Association With Denise Rich and Ralph Williams, Scott Prisand and Danny Seraphine, Harold Thau/Max Cooper/Judy Arnold and Brantley Dunaway, Independent Presenters Network; Director, Steven Pimlott; Choreography, Anthony Van Laast and Farh Khan; Scenery and Costumes, Mark Thompson; Lighting, Hugh Vanstone; Sound, Mick Potter; Fight Direction, J. Steven White; Music Direction, Dance Music Arrangement, James L. Abbott; Additional Musical Arrangements, Christopher Nightingale; Music Supervision, arrangements, orchestrations, Paul Bogaev; Music Coordinator, Michael Keller; Associate Directors, Lucy Skilbeck, Thomas Caruso, Associate Choreographers, Lisa Stevens, Nichola Treherne; Executive Producer, Waxwill Theatrical Division; Associate Producers, Sudhir Vaishnav, The Entertainment Partnership, Alexander Fraser, Ken Denison; Casting, Tara Rubin Casting; Production Stage Manager, Bonnie L. Becker; Press, Barlow-Hartman Public Relations, John Barlow, Michael Hartman, Jeremy Shaffer. Opened at the Broadway Theatre, April 29, 2004*

Cast

Akaash **Manu Narayan**
Eunuchs (Hijira) **Ron Nahass, Bobby Pestka, Darryl Semira, Kirk Torigoe**
Ram **Mueen Jahan Ahmad**
Salim **Aalok Mehta**
Shanti **Madhur Jaffrey**
Sweetie **Sriram Ganesan**
Munna **Neil Jay Shastri**
Munna (alternate performances) **Tanvir Gopal**
Hard Hats **Suresh John, Gabriel Burrafato**
Vikram **Deep Katdare**
Priya **Anisha Nagarajan**
Madan **Marvin L. Ishmael**
Pageant Announcer **Zahf Paroo**

Manu Narayan, Anisha Nagarajan PHOTOS BY JOAN MARCUS

Sriram Ganesan, Manu Narayan, and the Company

Rani **Ayesha Dharker**
Policemen **Zahf Paroo, Gabriel Burrafato**
Shaheen **Jolly Abraham**
Kitty DaSouza **Sarah Ripard**
Movie Sweetie **Darryl Semira**
Movie Shanti **Anjali Bhimani**
Movie Akaash **Zahf Paroo**
Wedding Qawali Singers **Gabriel Burrafato, Ian Jutsun, Zahf Paroo**

Ensemble: Jolly Abraham, Mueen Jahan Ahmad, Aaron J. Albano, Celine Alwyn, Anjali Bhimani, Shane Bland, Gabriel Burrafato, Wendy Calio, Tiffany Michelle Cooper, Sheetal Gandhi, Krystal Kiran Garib, Tania Marie Hakkim, Dell Howlett, Suresh John, Ian Jutsun, Miriam Laube, Aalok Mehta, Ron Nahass, Michelle Nigalan, Zahf Paroo, Danny Pathan, Bobby Pestka, Kafi Pierre, Sarah Ripard, Darryl Semira, Kirk Torigoe

Understudies: Aaron J. Albano, Zahf Paroo, Danny Pathan (Akaash), Krystal Kiran Garib, Sheetal Gandhi, Michelle Nigalan (Priya), Jolly Abraham, Anjali Bhimani, Sarah Ripard (Rani), Shane Bland, Darryl Semira (Sweetie), Anjali Bhimani, Sarah Ripard (Shanti), Gabriel Burrafato, Zahf Paroo (Vikram), Mueen Jahan Ahmad, Suresh John, Ian Jutsun (Madan), Tanvir Gopal, Neil Jay Shastri (Munna)

Swings: Rommy Sandhu, Lisa Stevens, James R. Whittington, Nicole Winhoffer

Orchestra: James L. Abbott, conductor; Dan Riddle, associate conductor; Sylvia D'Avanzo, concertmaster; Sean Carney, Nina Evtuhov, Pauline Kim, Ming Yeh, violin; Liuh-Wen Ting, Arthur Dibble, viola; Ted Mook, Roger Shall, cello; Randy Landau, bass; Anders Bostrom, flute; Charles Pillow, oboe, English horn; Adam Ben-David, Dan Riddle, Ann Gerschefski, keyboard; Deep Singh, David Sharma, percussion; Ray Grappone, drums

Musical Numbers: Overture: Salaa'm Bombay, Bollywood, Love's Never Easy, Lovely, Lovely Ladies, Bhangra, Shakalaka Baby, I Could Live Here, Is This Love?, Famous, Love's Never Easy (Reprise), Chaiyya Chaiyya, How Many Stars?, Salaa'm Bombay (Reprise), Hero, Ganesh Procession, Theh Journey Home, Wedding Qawali

Musical presented in two acts.

*Still playing May 31, 2004

Chandra Wilson, Tonya Pinkins

Tonya Pinkins, Harrison Chad   PHOTOS BY MICHAEL DANIEL

CAROLINE, OR CHANGE

Transfer of the Public Theatre's Off-Broadway Musical with Book and Lyrics by Tony Kushner; Music by Jeanine Tesori. Produced by Carole Shorenstein Hays, HBO Films, Jujamcyn Theatres, Freddy DeMann, Scott Rudin, Ruth Hendel/Elisabeth Morten/Cheryl Wiesenfeld, Fox Theatricals/Jennifer Manocherian/Jane Bergère, Roger Berlind, Clear Channel Entertainment, Joan Cullman, Greg Holland/Scott E. Nederlander, Margo Lion, Daryl Roth, Frederick Zollo, Jeffrey Sine, In Association With The Public Theatre; Director, George C. Wolfe; Choreography, Hope Clarke; Scenery, Riccardo Hernández; Costumes, Paul Tazewell; Lighting, Jules Fisher and Peggy Eisenhauer; Sound, Jon Weston; Hair, Jeffrey Frank; Orchestrations, Rick Bassett, Joseph Joubert, Buryl Red; Music Supervision, Kimberly Grigsby; Music Direction, Linda Twine; Music Coordinator, John Miller; Casting, Jordan Thaler, Heidi Griffiths; Production Stage Manager, Rick Steiger; Stage Manager, Lisa Dawn Cave; Press, Boneau/Bryan-Brown, Chris Boneau, Amy Jacobs, Juliana Hannett. Opened at the Eugene O'Neill Theatre, May 2, 2004*

(CONTINUED FROM PREVIOUS PAGE)

Cast

Caroline Thibodeaux **Tonya Pinkins**
The Washing Machine **Capathia Jenkins**
The Radio **Tracy Nicole Chapman, Marva Hicks, Ramona Keller**
Noah Gellman **Harrison Chad**
The Dryer **Chuck Cooper**
Grandma Gellman **Alice Playten**
Grandpa Gellman **Reathel Bean**
Rose Stopnick Gellman **Veanne Cox**
Stuart Gellman **David Costabile**
Dotty Moffett **Chandra Wilson**
The Moon **Aisha de Haas**
The Bus **Chuck Cooper**
Emie Thibodeaux **Anika Noni Rose**
Jackie Thibodeaux **Leon G. Thomas III**
Joe Thibodeaux **Marcus Carl Franklin**
Mr. Stopnick **Larry Keith**

Standbys: Adriane Lenox (Caroline Thibodeaux); Ledisi (The Washing Machine); Shannon Antalan, Vanessa A. Jones, Brandi Chavonne Massey, Ledisi (The Radio); Sy Adamowsky (Noah Gellman); Milton Craig Nealy (The Bus); Sue Goodman (Grandma Gellman, Rose Stopnick Gellman); Donald Grody (Grandpa Gellman); Adam Heller (Stuart Gellman); Vanessa A. Jones (Dotty Moffett); Vanessa A. Jones (The Moon); Shannon Antalan (Emie Thibodeaux); Chevon Rutty (Jackie Thibodeaux, Joe Thibodeaux); Donald Grody (Mr. Stopnick)

Orchestra: Linda Twine, conductor; Matthew Sklar, associate conductor, keyboard; Paul Woodiel, Christopher Cardona, violin; David Creswell, viola; Anja Wood, cello; Steve Bargonetti, guitar; Benjamin Franklin Brown, bass; Paul Garment, Stephen Wisner, reeds; John Clancy, Shane Shanahan, percussion

Musical Numbers: Washer/Dryer, Cabbage, Long Distance, Moon Change, Duets, The Bleach Cup, Ironing, The Chanukah Party, The Twenty-Dollar Bill, Aftermath, Lot's Wife, How Long Has This Been Going On?

Time: November–December 1963. Place: Lake Charles, Louisiana. Musical presented in two acts.

*Still playing May 31, 2004

Tonya Pinkins, Harrison Chad

Brían F. O'Byrne, Swoosie Kurtz

FROZEN

Transfer of the Off Broadway play by Bryony Lavery. Produced by MCC Theatre (Robert LuPone, Bernard Telsey, William Cantler, John G. Schultz), Harold Newman, Frederick Zollo/Nicholas Paleologos and Jeffrey Sine, Roy Garbay, Lorie Cowen Levy and Beth Smith, Peggy Hill, Thompson H. Rogers, Morton Swinsky/Michael Filerman/Ruth Hendel, Spring Sirkin/Marianne Mills/Jim Baldassare, Darren Bagert; Director, Doug Hughes; Scenery, Hugh Landwehr; Costumes, Catherine Zuber; Lighting, Clifton Taylor; Music and Sound, David Van Tieghem; Fight Direction, Rick Sordelet; Associate Producers, Edmund and Mary Fusco; Production Stage Manager, James FitzSimmons; Casting, Bernard Telsey Casting; Press, Boneau/Bryan-Brown, Chris Boneau, Adriana Douzos. Opened at the Circle in the Square, May 4, 2004*

Cast
Agnetha **Laila Robins**
Nancy **Swoosie Kurtz**
Ralph **Brían F. O'Byrne**
Guard **Sam Kitchin**

A play presented in two acts.

*Still playing May 31, 2004

Swoosie Kurtz PHOTO BY JOAN MARCUS

Phyllis Frelich, André De Shields

James Naughton, Heather Tom PHOTOS BY PAUL KOLNIK

PRYMATE

By Mark Medoff. Produced by Michael Parva, Chase Mishkin, Leonard Soloway, In Association With Debra Black; Director, Edwin Sherin; Choreography, Andre De Shields; Scenery, Robert Steinberg; Costumes, Colleen Muscha; Lighting, Jeff Nellis; Sound, Michael Smith; Fight Direction, Paul Steger; Associate Producer, Steven W. Wallace; Production Stage Manager, Peter Wolfe; Stage Manager, Andrea O. Saraffian; Press, The Pete Sanders Group. Opened at the Longacre Theatre, May 5, 2004*

Cast

Graham **André De Shields**
Esther **Phyllis Frelich**
Avrum **James Naughton**
Allison **Heather Tom**

Understudies: Kathyrun Finch (Allison); Jackie Roth (Esther); Ronald Wyche (Graham)

A play presented without intermission.

*Closed May 8, 2004

Marc Salem

MARC SALEM'S
MIND GAMES ON BROADWAY

Solo performance by Marc Salem. Produced by Delphi Productions; Press, Richard Kornberg and Associates. Opened at the Lyceum Theatre; May 24, 2004

A solo performance piece presented without intermission.

*Still playing May 31, 2004

SIGHT UNSEEN

Manhattan Theatre Club revival of the play by Donald Margulies; Artistic Director, Lynne Meadow; Executive Producer, Barry Grove; Director, Daniel Sullivan; Scenery, Douglas W. Schmidt; Costumes, Jess Goldstein; Lighting, Pat Collins; Music and Sound, John Gromada; Casting, Nancy Piccione and David Caparelliotis; Production Stage Manager, Roy Harris; Stage Manager, Denise Yaney; Press, Boneau/Bryan-Brown, Chris Boneau, Jim Byk, Aaron Meier. Opened at the Biltmore Theatre, May 25, 2004

Cast

Jonathan Waxman **Ben Shenkman**
Nick **Byron Jennings**
Patricia **Laura Linney**
Grete **Ana Reeder**

Understudies: J. Anthony Crane (Jonathan Waxman), Paul DeBoy (Nick), Kate Forbes (Patricia, Grete)

Time: 1991; 1976; 1974. Place: Norfolk and London, England; Brooklyn and Upstate New York. A play presented in two acts.

*Still playing May 31, 2004

Ben Shenkman, Ana Reeder

Ben Shenkman, Laura Linney PHOTO BY JOAN MARCUS

Productions from past seasons that **played through this season**

Taylor Dane

Adam Pascal, Heather Headley

Heather Headley, members of the Company PHOTOS BY JOAN MARCUS

AIDA

Music, Elton John; Lyrics, Tim Rice; Book, Linda Woolverton, Robert Falls, David Henry Hwang; Suggested by the opera; Director, Robert Falls; Choreography, Wayne Cilento; Set/Costumes, Bob Crowley; Lighting, Natasha Katz; Sound, Steve C. Kennedy; Music Producer and Musical Direction, Paul Bogaev; Music Arrangements, Guy Babylon, Paul Bogaev; Orchestrations, Steve Margoshes, Guy Babylon, Paul Bogaev; Casting, Bernard Telsey; Production Stage Manager, Clifford Schwartz; Cast Recording, Buena Vista; Presented by Hyperion Theatricals (Peter Schneider and Thomas Schumacher); Press, Chris Boneau–Adrian Bryan-Brown/Jackie Green, Steven Padla. Previewed from February 25, 2000; Opened in the Palace Theatre on Thursday, March 23, 2000*

Cast
Amneris **Sherie René Scott** †1
Radames **Adam Pascal** †2
Aida **Heather Headley** †3
Mereb **Damian Perkins** †4
Zoser **John Hickok** †5
Pharaoh **Daniel Oreskes**
Nehebka **Schele Williams**
Amonasro **Tyrees Allen**

Ensemble: Robert M. Armitage, Troy Allan Burgess, Franne Calma, Bob Gaynor, Kisha Howard, Tim Hunter, Youn Kim, Kyra Little, Kenya Unique Massey, Corinne McFadden, Phineas Newborn III, Jody Ripplinger, Raymond Rodriguez, Eric Sciotto, Samuel N. Thiam, Jerald Vincent, Schele Williams, Natalia Zisa

Understudies: Robert M. Armitage (Pharaoh); Troy Allen Burgess (Zoser); Franne Calma (Amneris); Kelli Fournier (Amneris); Bob Gaynor (Radames); Tim Hunter (Mereb); Kyra Little (Nehebka); Phineas Newborn III (Mereb); Raymond Rodriguez (Radames); Eric Sciotto (Radames); Endalyn Taylor-Shellman (Nehebka); Samuel N. Thiam (Amonasro); Jerald Vincent (Amonasro); Schele Williams (Aida)

Standbys: Neal Benari (Pharaoh, Zoser); Thursday Farrar (Aida)

Swings: Chris Payne Duprè, Kelli Fournier, Timothy Edward Smith, Endalyn Taylor-Shellman

Musical Numbers: Every Story Is a Love Story, Fortune Favors the Brave, The Past Is Another Land, Another Pyramid, How I Know You, My Strongest Suit, Enchantment Passing Through, The Dance of the Robe, Not Me, Elaborate Lives, The Gods Love Nubia, A Step Too Far, Easy as Life, Like Father Like Son, Radames' Letter, Written in the Stars, I Know the Truth

Musical presented in two acts. The action takes place in Egypt. Winner of 2000 Tony Awards for Original Score, Actress in a Musical (Heather Headley), Scenic Design, and Lighting Design.

*Still playing May 31, 2004
†Succeeded by: 1. Taylor Dane, Idina Menzel, Felicia Finley, Mandy Gonzalez, Lisa Brescia 2. Richard H. Blake, Will Chase 3. Maya Days, Simone, Saycon Sembloh, Toni Braxton, Michelle Williams, Deborah Cox 4. Delisco, Eric LaJuan Summers 5. Donnie Kehr, Micky Dolenz

BEAUTY AND THE BEAST

Music, Alan Menken; Lyrics, Howard Ashman, Tim Rice; Book, Linda Woolverton; Director, Robert Jess Roth; Orchestrations, Danny Troob; Musical Supervision/Vocal Arrangements, David Friedman; Musical Director/Incidental Arrangements, Michael Kosarin; Choreography, Matt West; Set, Stan Meyer; Costumes, Ann Hould-Ward; Lighting, Natasha Katz; Sound, T. Richard Fitzgerald; Hairstylist, David H. Lawrence; Illusions, Jim Steinmeyer, John Gaughan; Prosthetics, John Dods; Fights, Rick Sordelet; Cast Recording, Walt Disney Records; General Manager, Dodger Productions; Production Supervisor, Jeremiah J. Harris; Company Manager, Kim Sellon; Stage Managers, James Harker, John M. Atherlay, Pat Sosnow, Kim Vernace; Presented by Walt Disney Productions; Press, Chris Boneau/Adrian Bryan-Brown, Amy Jacobs, Steven Padla. Previewed from Wednesday, March 9, 1994; Opened in the Palace Theatre on Monday, April 18, 1994*

Cast

Enchantress **Wendy Oliver**
Young Prince **Harrison Beal**
Beast **Terrance Man** †1
Belle **Susan Egan** †2
Lefou **Kenny Raskin** †3
Gaston **Burke Moses** †4
Three Silly Girls **Paige Price, Sarah Solie Shannon, Linda Talcott**
Maurice **Tom Bosley** †5
Cogsworth **Heath Lamberts** †6
Lumiere **Gary Beach** †7
Babette **Stacey Logan** †8
Mrs. Potts **Beth Fowler** †9
Chip **Brian Press**
Madame de la Grande Bouche **Eleanor Glockner**
Monsieur D'Arque **Gordon Stanley**
Prologue Narrator **David Ogden Stiers**
Townspeople/Enchanted Objects: Joan Barber, Roxane Barlow, Harrison Beal, Michael-Demby Cain, Kate Dowe, David Elder, Merwin Foard, Gregory Garrison, Jack Hayes, Kim Huber, Elmore James, Rob Lorey, Patrick Loy, Barbara Marineau, Joanne McHugh, Anna McNeely, Bill Nabel, Wendy Oliver, Vince Pesce, Paige Price, Sarah Solie Shannon, Gordon Stanley, Linda Talcott, Wysandria Woolsey

Musical Numbers: Overture, Prologue (Enchantress), Belle, No Matter What, Me, Home, Gaston, How Long Must This Go On?, Be Our Guest, If I Can't Love Her, Entr'acte/Wolf Chase, Something There, Human Again, Maison des Lunes, Beauty and the Beast, Mob Song, The Battle, Transformation, Finale

Musical presented in two acts. An expanded, live action version of the 1992 animated film Musical with additional songs. *Beauty and the Beast* was the winner of 1994 Tony for Best Costume Design.

*Still playing May 31, 2004. The production moved to the Lunt-Fontanne Theatre on November 12, 1999.

Andrea McArdle, Steve Blanchard PHOTO BY EDUARDO PATINO

†Succeeded by: 1. Jeff McCarthy, Chuck Wagner, James Barbour, Steve Blanchard, Jeff McCarthy, Steve Blanchard 2. Sarah Uriarte Berry, Christianne Tisdale, Kerry Butler, Deborah Gibson, Kim Huber, Toni Braxton, Andrea McArdle, Sarah Litzsinger, Jamie-Lynn Sigler, Sarah Litzsinger, Megan McGinnis, Christy Carlson Romano 3. Harrison Beal, Jamie Torcellini, Jeffrey Howard Schecter, Jay Brian Winnick, Gerard McIsaac, Brad Aspel, Steve Lavner, Aldrin Gonzalez 4. Marc Kudisch, Steve Blanchard, Patrick Ryan Sullivan, Christopher Sieber, Chris Hoch, Grant Norman 5. MacIntyre Dixon, Tom Bosley, Kurt Knudson, Timothy Jerome, J.B. Adams, Jamie Ross 6. Peter Bartlett, Robert Gibby Brand, John Christopher Jones, Jeff Brooks 7. Gary Beach, Lee Roy Reams, Patrick Quinn, Gary Beach, Meshach Taylor, Patrick Page, Paul Schoeffler, Patrick Page, Bryan Batt, Rob Lorey, David DeVries 8. Pamela Winslow, Leslie Castay, Pam Klinger, Louisa Kendrick, Pam Klinger 9. Cass Morgan, Beth Fowler, Barbara Marineau, Beth Flower, Cass Morgan, Alma Cuervo

CHICAGO

Music, John Kander; Lyrics, Fred Ebb; Book, Mr. Ebb, Bob Fosse; Script Adaptation, David Thompson; Based on the play by Maurine Dallas Watkins; Original Production Directed and Choreographed by Bob Fosse; Director, Walter Bobbie; Choreography, Ann Reinking in the style of Bob Fosse; Music Director, Rob Fisher; Orchestrations, Ralph Burns; Set, John Lee Beatty; Costumes, William Ivey Long; Lighting, Ken Billington; Sound, Scott Lehrer; Dance Arrangements, Peter Howard; Cast Recording, RCA; General Manager, Darwell Associates and Maria Di Dia; Company Manager, Scott A. Moore; Stage Managers, Clifford Schwartz, Terrence J. Witter; Presented by Barry & Fran Weissler in association with Kardana Productions; Press, Pete Sanders/Helen Davis, Clint Bond Jr., Glenna Freedman, Bridget Klapinski. Previewed from Wednesday, October 23, 1996; Opened in the Richard Rodgers Theatre on Thursday, November 14, 1996*

Cast

Velma Kelly **Bebe Neuwirth** †1
Roxie Hart **Anne Reinking** †2
Fred Casely **Michael Berresse**
Sergeant Fogarty **Michael Kubala**
Amos Hart **Joel Grey** †3
Liz **Denise Faye**
Annie **Mamie Duncan-Gibbs**
June **Mary Ann Lamb**
Hunyak **Tina Paul**
Mona **Caitlin Carter**
Matron "Mama" Morton **Marcia Lewis** †4
Billy Flynn **James Naughton** †5
Mary Sunshine **D. Sabella** †6
Go-To-Hell-Kitty **Leigh Zimmerman**
Harry **Rocker Verastique**
Aaron **David Warren-Gibson**
Judge **Jim Borstelmann**
Martin Harrison; Doctor **Bruce Anthony Davis**
Court Clerk **John Mineo**
Juror **Michael Kubala**

Understudies/Standbys: Michael Berresse (Billy Flynn); Mamie Duncan-Gibbs (Matron); Nancy Hess (Roxie Hart, Velma Kelly); J. Loeffelholz (Mary Sunshine); John Mineo (Amos Hart)

Musical Numbers: All That Jazz, Funny Honey, Cell Block Tango, When You're Good to Mama, Tap Dance, All I Care About, A Little Bit of Good, We Both Reached for the Gun, Roxie, I Can't Do It Alone, My Own Best Friend, Entr'acte, I Know a Girl, Me and My Baby, Mister Cellophane, When Velma Takes the Stand, Razzle Dazzle, Class, Nowadays, Hot Honey Rag, Finale

A new production of the 1975 Musical in two acts. This production is based on the staged concert presented by City Center Encores. The action takes place in Chicago, late 1920s. Winner of 1997 Tony Awards for Revival of a Musical, Leading Actor in a Musical (James Naughton), Leading Actress in a Musical (Bebe Neuwirth), Direction of a Musical, Choreography, and Lighting.

Brent Barrett and the Merry Murderesses PHOTO BY CAROL ROSEGG

For original Broadway production with Gwen Verdon, Chita Rivera, and Jerry Orbach, see *Theatre World* Vol. 32.

*Still playing May 31, 2004. Moved to the Shubert Theatre on February 12, 1997. Moved to the Ambassador Theatre on January 29, 2003.
†Succeeded by: 1. Nancy Hess, Ute Lemper, Bebe Neuwirth, Ruthie Henshall, Mamie Duncan-Gibbs, Bebe Neuwirth, Donna Marie Asbury, Sharon Lawrence, Vicki Lewis, Jasmine Guy, Bebe Neuwirth, Donna Marie Asbury, Deidre Goodwin, Vicki Lewis, Deidre Goodwin, Anna Montanero, Deidre Goodwin, Donna Marie Asbury, Roxane Carrasco, Deidre Goodwin, Stephanie Pope, Roxane Carraasco, Caroline O'Connor, Brenda Braxton, Deidre Goodwin, Reva Rice, Brenda Braxton, Pia Dowes, Brenda Braxton 2. Marilu Henner, Karen Ziemba, Belle Calaway, Charlotte d'Amboise, Sandy Duncan, Belle Calaway, Charlotte d'Amboise, Belle Calaway, Nana Visitor, Petra Nielsen, Nana Visitor, Belle Callaway, Denise Van Outen, Belle Calaway, Amy Spanger, Belle Calaway, Tracy Shayne, Melanie Griffith, Charlotte d'Amboise, Bianca Marroquin, Gretchen Mol, Charlotte d'Amboise 3. Ernie Sabella, Tom McGowan, P.J. Benjamin, Ernie Sabella, P.J. Benjamin, Tom McGowan, P.J. Benjamin, Ray Bokhour, P.J. Benjamin, Rob Bartlett, P.J. Benjamin 4. Roz Ryan, Marcia Lewis, Roz Ryan, Marcia Lewis, Roz Ryan, Marcia Lewis, Jennifer Holliday, Marcia Lewis, Roz Ryan, Michele Pawk, Alix Korey, B.J. Crosby, Angie Stone, Carmille Saviola, Debbie Gravitte, Roz Ryan 5. Gregory Jbara, Hinton Battle, Alan Thicke, Michael Berresse, Brent Barrett, Robert Urich, Clarke Peters, Brent Barrett, Chuck Cooper, Brent Barrett, Chuck Cooper, George Hamilton, Eric Jordan Young, Ron Raines, George Hamilton, Michael C. Hall, Destan Owens, Taye Diggs, Billy Zane, Kevin Richardson, Clarke Peters, Gregory Harrison, Brent Barrett, Patrick Swayze, James Naughton, Norm Lewis, Christopher Sieber, Tom Wopat 6. J. Loeffelholz, R. Bean, A. Saunders, J. Maldonado, R. Bean, A. Saunders, R. Bean, M. Agnes, D. Sabella, R. Bean

The Company PHOTO BY JOAN MARCUS

42ND STREET

Music, Harry Warren; Lyrics, Al Dubin; Book, Michael Stewart, Mark Bramble; Based on a Novel by Bradford Ropes; Director, Mark Bramble; Musical Staging/New Choreography, Randy Skinner; Musical Director, Todd Ellison; Musical Adaptation/Arrangements, Donald Johnston; Orchestrations (original), Philip J. Lang; Set, Douglas W. Schmidt; Costumes, Roger Kirk; Lighting, Paul Gallo; Sound, Peter Fitzgerald; Hair/Wigs, David H. Lawrence; Company Manager, Sandra Carlson; General Manager, Robert C. Strickstein, Sally Campbell Morse; Production Stage Manager, Frank Hartenstein; Stage Manager, Karen Armstrong; Casting, Jay Binder; Original Direction/Dances, Gower Champion; Presented by Dodger Theatricals, Joop Van Den Ende and Stage Holding; Press, Chris Boneau–Adrian Bryan-Brown/Susanne Tighe, Amy Jacobs, Adriana Douzos. Previewed from Wednesday, April 4, 2001; Opened in the Ford Center for the Performing Arts on Wednesday, May 2, 2001*

Cast

Andy Lee **Michael Arnold**
Maggie Jones **Mary Testa**
Bert Barry **Jonathan Freeman**
Mac **Allen Fitzpatrick**
Phyllis **Catherine Wreford**
Lorraine **Megan Sikora**
Diane **Tamlyn Brooke Shusterman**
Annie **Mylinda Hull**
Ethel **Amy Dolan**
Billy Lawlor **David Elder**
Peggy Sawyer **Kate Levering** †1
Oscar **Billy Stritch**
Julian Marsh **Michael Cumpsty** †2
Dorothy Brock **Christine Ebersole** †3
Abner Dillon **Michael McCarty**
Pat Denning **Richard Muenz**
Waiters **Brad Aspel, Mike Warshaw, Shonn Wiley**
Thugs **Allen Fitzpatrick, Jerry Tellier**
Doctor **Allen Fitzpatrick**

Ensemble: Brad Aspel, Becky Berstler, Randy Bobish, Chris Clay, Michael Clowers, Maryam Myika Day, Alexander de Jong, Amy Dolan, Isabelle Flachsmann, Jennifer Jones, Dontee Kiehn, Renée Klapmeyer, Jessica Kostival, Keirsten Kupiec, Todd Lattimore, Melissa Rae Mahon, Michael Malone, Jennifer Marquardt, Meredith Patterson, Darin Phelps, Wendy Rosoff, Megan Schenck, Kelly Sheehan, Tamlyn Brooke Shusterman, Megan Sikora, Jennifer Stetor, Erin Stoddard, Yasuko Tamaki, Jonathan Taylor, Jerry Tellier, Elisa Van Duyne, Erika Vaughn, Mike Warshaw, Merrill West, Shonn Wiley, Catherine Wreford

Understudies/Standbys: Brad Aspel (Andy Lee, Bert Barry); Becky Berstler (Annie); Randy Bobish (Andy Lee); Amy Dolan (Annie, Maggie Jones); Allen Fitzpatrick (Abner Dillon, Pat Denning); Renée Klapmeyer (Diane); Jessica Kostival (Dorothy Brock); Richard Muenz (Julian Marsh); Meredith Patterson (Peggy Sawyer); Darin Phelps (Doctor, Mac, Thug); Erin Stoddard (Lorraine, Peggy Sawyer); Jerry Tellier (Julian Marsh, Pat Denning); Elisa Van Duyne (Phyllis); Luke Walrath (Doctor, Mac, Thug); Shonn Wiley (Billy Lawlor)

Musical Numbers: Overture, Audition, Young and Healthy, Shadow Waltz, Go into Your Dance, You're Getting to Be a Habit with Me, Getting Out of Town, Dames, Keep Young and Beautiful, Dames, I Only Have Eyes for You (not in orig production), We're in the Money, Keep Young and Beautiful (not in orig production), Entr'acte, Sunny Side to Every Situation, Lullaby of Broadway, Getting Out of Town, Montage, About a Quarter to Nine, With Plenty of Money and You (not in orig. production), Shuffle Off to Buffalo, 42nd Street, Finale

A revival of the original 1980 Musical presented in two acts. The action takes place in New York City and Philadelphia, 1933. *42nd Street* was the winner of 2001 Tony Awards for Best Revival/Musical and Best Actress in a Musical (Christine Ebersole). For original Broadway production with Jerry Orbach and Tammy Grimes, see *Theatre World* Vol. 37.

Variety tallied 11 favorable, 1 mixed, and 4 negative reviews. *Times* (Brantley): "…premature revival…a faded fax of the last musical staged by the fabled Gower Champion…" *News* (Kissel) "…loaded with talent. And you know it as soon as the curtain rises on 24 pairs of tap-dancing feet." *Post* (Barnes): "…cast with exquisite care…everyone is superb…" *Variety* (Isherwood): "…gaudy, relentless production…pays tribute to the Gower Champion original…"

*Still playing May 31, 2004
†Succeeded by 1. Meredith Patterson, Kate Levering, Nadine Isenegger, 2. Michael Dantuono, Tom Wopat, Patrick Ryan Sullivan, Patrick Cassidy, 3. Beth Leavel, Shirely Jones

HAIRSPRAY

Musical with Book by Mark O'Donnell and Thomas Meehan; Music, Marc Shaiman; Lyrics, Marc Shaiman, Scott Wittman; Producers, Margo Lion, Adam Epstein, the Baruch-Viertel-Routh-Frankel Group, James D. Stern/Douglas L. Meyer, Rick Steiner, Frederic H. Mayerson, SEL and GFO, New Line Cinema, in association with Clear Channel Entertainment, Allan S. Gordon, Elan V. McAllister, Dede Harris, Morton Swinsky, John and Bonnie Osher; Director, Jack O'Brien, Choreography, Jerry Mitchell; Scenery, David Rockwell; Costumes, William Ivey Long; Lighting, Kenneth Posner; Sound, Steve C. Kennedy; Orchestrations, Harold Wheeler, Music Direction, Lon Hoyt, Music Coordinator, John Miller, Assistant Director, Matt Lenz, Associate Choreographer, Michele Lynch; Associate Producers, Rhoda Mayerson, the Aspen Group, Daniel C. Staton; Casting, Bernard Telsey Casting; Production Stage Manager, Steven Beckler; Stage Manager, J. Philip Bassett; Press, Richard Kornberg and Associates, Richard Kornberg, Don Summa, Tom D'Ambrosio, Carrie Friedman. Opened at the Neil Simon Theatre, August 15, 2002*

Cast

Tracy Turnblad **Marissa Jaret Winokur** †1
Corny Collins **Clarke Thorell** †2
Amber Von Tussle **Laura Bell Bundy** †3
Brad **Peter Matthew Smith**
Tammy **Hollie Howard**
Fender **John Hill**
Brenda **Jennifer Gambatese**
Sketch **Adam Fleming**
Shelley **Shoshana Bean**
IQ **Todd Michel Smith**
Lou Ann **Katharine Leonard**
Link Larkin **Matthew Morrison** †4
Prudy Pingleton; Gym Teacher; Matron **Jackie Hoffman**
Edna Turnblad **Harvey Fierstein** †5
Penny Pingleton **Kerry Butler** †6
Velma Von Tussle **Linda Hart** †7
Harriman F. Spritzer; Principal; Mr. Pinky; Guard **Joel Vig**
Wilbur Turnblad **Dick Latessa**
Seaweed J. Stubbs **Corey Reynolds** †8
Duane **Eric Anthony**
Gilbert **Eric Dysart**
Lorraine **Danielle Lee Greaves**
Thad **Rashad Naylor**
The Dynamites **Kamilah Martin, Judine Richard, Shayna Steele**
Little Inez **Danelle Eugenia Wilson** †9
Motormouth Maybelle **Mary Bond Davis**

Denizens of Baltimore: Eric Anthony, Shoshana Bean, Eric Dysart, Adam Fleming, Jennifer Gambatese, Danielle Lee Greaves, John Hill, Jackie Hoffman, Hollie Howard, Katharine Leonard, Kamilah Martin, Rashad Naylor, Judine Richard, Peter Matthew Smith, Todd Michel Smith, Shayna Steele, Joel Vig

Onstage Musicians: Matthew Morrison, guitar; Linda Hart, keyboard; Joel Vig, glockenspiel; Kerry Butler, harmonica

Understudies: Eric Anthony (Seaweed J. Stubbs); Shoshana Bean (Tracy Turnblad, Velma Von Tussle); Eric Dysart (Seaweed J. Stubbs); Adam Fleming (Jul 18, 2002–Feb 8, 2004) (Link Larkin); Jennifer Gambatese (Penny Pingleton); Danielle Lee Greaves (Motormouth Maybelle); David Greenspan (Edna Turnblad, Wilbur Turnblad); Katy Grenfell (Tracy Turnblad); John Hill (Corny Collins, Link Larkin); Jackie Hoffman (Velma Von Tussle); Hollie Howard (Amber Von Tussle, Penny Pingleton); Katharine Leonard (Amber Von Tussle); Kamilah Martin (Motormouth Maybelle); Judine Richárd (Little Inez); Peter Matthew Smith (Corny Collins); Shayna Steele (Little Inez); Joel Vig (Edna Turnblad, Wilbur Turnblad)

Orchestra: Lon Hoyt, conductor, keyboard; Keith Cotton, associate conductor, keyboard; Seth Farber, assistant conductor, keyboard; David Spinozza, Peter Calo, guitars; Francisco Centeno, electric bass; Clint de Ganon, drums; Walter "Wally" Usiatynski, percussion; David Mann, Dave Rickenberg, reeds; Danny Cahn, trumpet; Birch Johnson, trombone; Rob Shaw, Carol Pool, violins; Sarah Hewitt Roth, cello

Musical Numbers: Good Morning Baltimore, The Nicest Kids in Town, Mama, I'm a Big Girl Now, I Can Hear the Bells, (The Legend of) Miss Baltimore Crabs, The Madison, The Nicest Kids in Town (Reprise), Welcome to the '60s, Run and Tell That, Big, Blond and Beautiful, The Big Dollhouse, Good Morning Baltimore, Timeless to Me, Without Love, I Know Where I've Been, Hairspray, Cooties, You Can't Stop the Beat

Time: 1962. Place: Baltimore. Musical presented in two acts.

*Still playing May 31, 2004
†Succeeded by: 1. Kathy Brier, Carly Jibson 2. Jonathan Dokuchitz 3. Tracy Jai Edwards 4. Richard H. Blake 5. Michael McKean 6. Jennifer Gambatese, Brooke Tansley, Jennifer Gambatese 7. Barbara Walsh 8. Chester Gregory II 9. Aja Maria Johnson

Marissa Janet Winokur, Matthew Morrison PHOTO BY PAUL KOLNIK

THE LION KING

Music, Elton John; Lyrics, Tim Rice; Additional Music/Lyrics, Lebo M, Mark Mancina, Jay Rifkin, Julie Taymor, Hans Zimmer; Book, Roger Allers and Irene Mecchi adapted from screenplay by Ms. Mecchi, Jonathan Roberts and Linda Woolverton; Director, Julie Taymor; Choreography, Garth Fagan; Orchestrations, Robert Elhai, David Metzger, Bruce Fowler; Music Director, Joseph Church; Set, Richard Hudson; Costumes, Julie Taymor; Lighting, Donald Holder; Masks/Puppets, Julie Taymor, Michael Curry; Sound, Tony Meola; Vocal Arrangements/Choral Director, Lebo M; Cast Recording, Disney; Company Manager, Steven Chaikelson; Stage Manager, Jeff Lee; Presented by Walt Disney Theatrical Productions (Peter Schneider, President; Thomas Schumacher, Executive VP); Press, Chris Boneau–Adrian Bryan-Brown/Jackie Green, Patty Onagan, Colleen Hughes. Previewed from Wednesday, October 15, 1997; Opened in the New Amsterdam Theatre on Thursday, November 13, 1997*

Cast

Rafiki **Tsidii Le Loka** †1
Mufasa **Samuel E. Wright** †2
Sarabi **Gina Breedlove** †3
Zazu **Geoff Hoyle** †4
Scar **John Vickery** †5
Young Simba **Scott Irby-Ranniar**
Young **Nala Kajuana Shuford**
Shenzi **Tracy Nicole Chapman** †6
Banzai **Stanley Wayne Mathis** †7
Ed **Kevin Cahoon** †8
Timon **Max Casella** †9
Pumbaa **Tom Alan Robbins**
Simba **Jason Raize** †10
Nala **Heather Headley** †11

Ensemble Singers: Eugene Barry-Hill, Gina Breedlove, Ntomb'khona Dlamini, Sheila Gibbs, Lindiwe Hlengwa, Christopher Jackson, Vanessa A. Jones, Faca Kulu, Ron Kunene, Anthony Manough, Philip Dorian McAdoo, Sam McKelton, Lebo M, Nandi Morake, Rachel Tecora Tucker

Ensemble Dancers: Camille M. Brown, Iresol Cardona, Mark Allan Davis, Lana Gordon, Timothy Hunter, Michael Joy, Aubrey Lynch II, Karine Plantadit-Bageot, Endalyn Taylor-Shellman, Levensky Smith, Ashi K. Smythe, Christine Yasunaga

Understudies/Swings: Kevin Bailey (Scar); Eugene Barry-Hill (Mufasa); Camille M. Brown (Sarabi); Kevin Cahoon (Timon, Zazu); Alberto Cruz Jr. (Young Simba); Sheila Gibbs (Rafiki); Lana Gordon (Shenzi); Lindiwe Hlengwa (Nala, Rafiki); Tim Hunter (Simba); Christopher Jackson (Simba); Vanessa A. Jones (Sarabi, Shenzi); Jennifer Josephs (Young Nala); Sonya Leslie (Nala); Philip Dorian McAdoo (Banzai, Mufasa, Pumbaa); Danny Rutigliano (Pumbaa, Timon, Zazu); Levensky Smith (Banzai); Frank Wright II

Musical Numbers: Circle of Life, Morning Report, I Just Can't Wait to Be King, Chow Down, They Live in You, Be Prepared, Hakuna Matata, One by One, Madness of King Scar, Shadowland, Endless Night, Can You Feel the Love Tonight, King of Pride Rock/Finale

Sheila Gibbs PHOTO BY JOAN MARCUS

Musical presented in two acts. Winner of 1998 Tony Awards for Best Musical, Direction of a Musical, Scenic Design, Costume Design, Lighting and Choreography.

*Still playing May 31, 2004
†Succeeded by: 1. Thuli Dumakude, Sheila Gibbs, Nomvula Dlamini, Tshidi Manye 2. Alton Fitzgerald White 3. Meena T. Jahi, Denise Marie Williams, Meena T. Jahi, Robyn Payne 4. Bill Bowers, Robert Dorfman, Tony Freeman, Adam Stein, Jeffrey Binder 5. Tom Hewitt, Derek Smith, Patrick Page 6. Vanessa S. Jones, Lana Gordon, Marlayna Sims 7. Keith Bennett, Leonard Joseph, Curtiss I' Cook, Rodrick Covington 8. Jeff Skowron, Jeff Gurner, Timothy Gulan, Thom Christopher Warren, Enrique Segura 9. Danny Rutigliano, John E. Brady, Danny Rutigliano 10. Christopher Jackson, Josh Tower 11. Mary Randle, Heather Headley, Bashirrah Cresswell, Sharon L. Young, Rene Elise Goldsberry, Kissy Simmons

MAMMA MIA!

Book by Catherine Johnson; Music and Lyrics, Benny Andersson, Björn Ulvaeus, some songs with Stig Anderson; Director, Phyllida Lloyd; Sets and Costumes, Mark Thompson; Lighting, Howard Harrison; Sound, Andrew Bruce, Bobby Aitken; Choreography, Anthony Van Laast; Musical Supervision, Martin Koch; Musical Direction, David Holcenberg; Musical Coordination, Michael Keller; Associate Director, Robert McQueen; Associate Choreographer, Nichola Treherne; Produced by Judy Craymer, Richard East and Björn Ulvaeus for LittleStar, in association with Universal Casting, Tara Rubin; Press, Boneau/Bryan-Brown, Adrian Bryan-Brown, Steven Padla, Jackie Green, Karalee Dawn. Opened at the Winter Garden Theatre October 18, 2001*

Orchestra: David Holcenberg, conductor, keyboard; Rob Preuss, associate music director, keyboard 3; Steve Marzullo, keyboard 2; Myles Chase, keyboard 4; Doug Quinn, guitar 1; Jeff Campbell, guitar 2; Paul Adamy, bass; Gary Tillman, drums; David Nyberg, percussion

Musical Numbers: Chiquitita, Dancing Queen, Does Your Mother Know?, Gimme! Gimmie! Gimmie!, Honey, Honey, I Do, I Do, I Do, I Do, I Have a Dream, Knowing Me Knowing You, Lay All Your Love on Me, Mamma Mia, Money Money Money, One of Us, Our Last Summer, Slipping Through My Fingers, S.O.S., Super Trouper, Take a Chance on Me, Thank You For the Music, The Name of the Game, The Winner Takes All, Under Attack, Voulez-Vous

Musical presented in two acts. Time: A wedding weekend. Place: A tiny Greek island. Songs of the 1970s group ABBA strung together in a story of baby boomer wistfulness and a girl's search for her unknown father.

*Still playing May 31, 2004
†Succeeded by: 1. Jenny Fellner 2. Jeanine Morick, Tamara Bernier 3. Harriett D. Foy 4. Dee Hoty 5. Richard Binsley, Michael Winther 6. Adam LeFevre 7. John Hillner, David W. Keeley, John Hillner

Ken Marks, David W. Keeley, Dean Nolen

Cast

Sophie Sheridan **Tina Maddigan** †1
Ali **Sara Inbar**
Lisa **Tonya Doran**
Tanya **Karen Mason** †2
Rosie **Judy Kaye** †3
Donna Sheridan **Louise Pitre** †4
Sky **Joe Machota**
Pepper **Mark Price**
Eddie **Michael Benjamin Washington**
Harry Bright **Dean Nolan** †5
Bill Austin **Ken Marks** †6
Sam Carmicheal **David W. Keeley** †7
Father Alexandrios **Bill Carmichael**

Understudies: Meredith Akins (Lisa); Leslie Alexander (Tanya); Stephan Alexander (Pepper); Kim-E J. Balmilero (Ali); Robin Baxter (Rosie); Brent Black (Bill Austin, Sam Carmichael); Tony Carlin (Bill Austin, Harry Bright, Sam Carmichael); Bill Carmichael (Harry Bright); Meghann Dreyfuss (Sophie Sheridan); Jon-Erik Goldberg (Pepper); Somer Lee Graham (Sophie Sheridan); Kristin McDonald (Ali); Adam Monley (Sky); Chris Prinzo (Eddie); Peter Matthew Smith (Eddie, Sky); Yuka Takara (Lisa); Marsha Waterbury (Donna Sheridan, Rosie, Tanya)

Karen Mason, Louise Pitre, Judy Kaye PHOTOS BY JOAN MARCUS

MOVIN' OUT

Dance Musical by Billy Joel; Music and Lyrics by Billy Joel; Conception by Twyla Tharp; Producers, James L Nederlander, Hal Luftig, Scott E. Nederlander, Terry Allen Kramer, Clear Channel Entertainment, Emanuel Azenberg; Director and Choreographer, Twyla Tharp; Scenery, Santo Loquasto; Costumes, Suzy Benzinger; Lighting, Donald Holder; Sound, Brian Ruggles, Peter Fitzgerald; Additional Music Arrangements and Orchestrations, Stuart Malina; Music Coordinator, John Miller; Assistant Director and Choreographer, Mr. Wise; Casting, Jay Binder Casting, Sarah Prosser; Production Stage Manager, Tom Barlett; Stage Manager, Kim Vernace; Press, Barlow-Hartman, Michael Hartman, John Barlow, Bill Coyle. Opened at the Richard Rodgers Theatre, October 24, 2002*

Cast

Eddie **John Selya**
Brenda **Elizabeth Parkinson** †1
Tony **Keith Roberts** †2
Judy **Ashley Tuttle** †3
James **Benjamin G. Bowman** †4
Sergeant O'Leary; Drill Sergeant **Scott Wise**
Piano; Lead Vocals **Michael Cavanaugh**

Ensemble: Mark Arvin, Karine Bageot, Alexander Brady, Holly Cruikshank, Ron DeJesus, Melissa Downey, Pascale Faye, Scott Fowler, David Gomez, Rod McCune, Jill Nicklaus, Rika Okamoto

Wednesday and Saturday Matinees

Eddie **William Marrie**
Brenda **Holly Cruikshank**
Tony **David Gomez**
Judy **Dana Stackpole**
James **Benjamin G. Bowman**
Sergeant O'Leary; Drill Sergeant **Scott Wise**
Piano; Lead Vocals **Wade Preston**

Ensemble: Mark Arvin, Karine Bageot, Alexander Brady, Holly Cruikshank, Ron Dejesus, Melissa Downey, Pascale Faye, Scott Fowler,

The Company PHOTOS BY JOAN MARCUS

John Selya

David Gomez, Rod McCune, Jill Nicklaus, Rika Okamoto

Understudies: Andrew Allagree (Eddie); Karine Bageot (Brenda); Alexander Brady (James); Holly Cruikshank (Brenda); Ron DeJesus (Tony); Scott Fowler (James); David Gomez (Tony); William Marrie (Eddie); Meg Paul (Judy); Lawrence Rabson (Eddie); Dana Stackpole (Judy); John J. Todd (Sergeant O'Leary).

Swings: Andrew Allagree, Aliane Baquerot; Laurie Kanyok, William Marrie, Meg Paul, Lawrence Rabson, Dana Stackpole, John J. Todd

Orchestra: Micahel Cavanaugh, piano, lead vocals; Tommy Byrnes, leader, guitar; Wade Preston, keyboard; Dennis DelGaudio, guitar; Greg Smith, bass; Chuck Burgi, drums; John Scarpulla, lead sax, percussion; Scott Kreitzer, sax; Barry Danielian, trumpet; Kevin Osborne, trombone, whistler, vocals

Musical Numbers: It's Still Rock and Roll to Me, Scenes from an Italian Restaurant, Movin' Out (Anthony's Song), Reverie (Villa D'Este), Just the Way You Are, For the Longest Time, Uptown Girl, This Night, Summer, Highland Falls, Waltz #1 (Nunley's Carousel), We Didn't Start the Fire, She's Got A Way, The Stranger, Elegy (The Great Peconic), Invention in C Minor, Angry Young Man, Big Shot, Big Man on Mulberry Street, Captain Jack, Innocent Man, Pressure, Goodnight Saigon, Air (Dublinesque), Shameless, James, River of Dreams, Keeping the Faith, Only the Good Die Young, I've Loved These Days, Scenes from an Italian Restaurant (Reprise)

Time: 1960s. Place: Long Island, New York. Musical presented in two acts.

*Still playing May 31, 2004
†Succeeded by: 1. Nancy Lemenager 2. Ian Carney, Keith Roberts 3. Mabel Modrono 4. Kurt Froman

Howard McGillin PHOTO BY JOAN MARCUS

THE PHANTOM OF THE OPERA

Music, Andrew Lloyd Webber; Lyrics, Charles Hart; Additional Lyrics, Richard Stilgoe; Book, Mr. Stilgoe, Mr. Lloyd Webber; Director, Harold Prince; Musical Staging/Choreography, Gillian Lynne; Orchestrations, David Cullen, Mr. Lloyd Webber; Based on the novel by Gaston Leroux; Design, Maria Björnson; Lighting, Andrew Bridge; Sound, Martin Levan; Musical Direction/Supervision, David Caddick; Conductor, Jack Gaughan; Cast Recording (London), Polygram/Polydor; Casting, Johnson-Liff & Zerman; General Manager, Alan Wasser; Company Manager, Michael Gill; Stage Managers, Steve McCorkle, Bethe Ward, Richard Hester, Barbara-Mae Phillips; Presented by Cameron Mackintosh and The Really Useful Theatre Co.; Press, Merle Frimark, Marc Thibodeau. Previewed from Saturday, January 9, 1988; Opened in the Majestic Theatre on Tuesday, January 26, 1988*

Cast

The Phantom of the Opera **Michael Crawford** †1
Christine Daae **Sarah Brightman** †2
Christine Daae (alt.) **Patti Cohenour** †3
Raoul, Vicomte de Chagny **Steve Barton** †4
Carlotta Giudicelli **Judy Kaye**
Monsieur Andre **Cris Groenendaal**
Monsieur Firmin **Nicholas Wyman**
Madame Giry **Leila Martin**

Ubaldo Piangi **David Romano**
Meg Giry **Elisa Heinsohn**
Monsieur Reyer **Peter Kevoian**
Auctioneer **Richard Warren Pugh**
Porter; Marksman **Jeff Keller**
Monsieur Lefevre **Kenneth H. Waller**
Joseph Buquet **Philip Steele**
Don Attilio **George Lee Andrews**
Passarino **George Lee Andrews**
Slave Master **Luis Perez**
Flunky; Stagehand **Barry McNabb**
Marksman **Jeff Keller**
Policeman **Charles Rule**
Page **Candace Rogers-Adler**
Porter; Fireman **William Scott Brown**
Wardrobe Mistress; Confidante **Mary Leigh Stahl**
Princess **Rebecca Luker**
Madame Firmin **Beth McVey**
Innkeeper's Wife **Jan Horvath**
Ballet Chorus of the Opera Populaire **Irene Cho**, **Nicole Fosse**, **Lisa Lockwood**, **Lori MacPherson**, **Dodie Pettit**, **Catherine Ulissey**

Understudies: George Lee Andrews (Monsieur André, Monsieur Firmin); William Scott Brown (Ubaldo Piangi); Cris Groenendaal (Raoul); Jan Horvath (Carlotta Guidicelli); Jeff Keller (Phantom of the Opera); Peter Kevoian (Monsieur André, Monsieur Firmin); Rebecca Luker (Christine Daaé); Barry McNabb (Slave Master); Beth McVey (Carlotta Guidicelli); Dodie Pettit (Meg Giry); Richard Warren Pugh (Ubaldo Piangi); Mary Leigh Stahl (Madame Giry); Olga Talyn (Madame Giry); Catherine Ulissey (Meg Giry)

Swings: Frank Mastrone, Alba Quezada

Musical Numbers: Think of Me, Angel of Music, Little Lotte/The Mirror, Phantom of the Opera, Music of the Night, I Remember/Stranger Than You Dreamt It, Magical Lasso, Notes/Prima Donna, Poor Fool He Makes Me Laugh, Why Have You Brought Me Here?/Raoul I've Been There, All I Ask of You, Masquerade/Why So Silent?, Twisted Every Way, Wishing You Were Somehow Here Again, Wandering Child/Bravo Bravo, Point of No Return, Down Once More/Track Down This Murderer, Finale

Musical presented in two acts with nineteen scenes and a prologue. The action takes place in and around the Paris Opera House, 1881–1911. Winner of 1988 Tony Awards for Best Musical, Leading Actor in a Musical (Michael Crawford), Featured Actress in a Musical (Judy Kaye), Direction of a Musical, Scenic Design, and Lighting Design. The title role has been played by Michael Crawford, Timothy Nolen, Cris Groenendaal, Steve Barton, Jeff Keller, Kevin Gray, Marc Jacoby, Marcus Lovett, Davis Gaines, Thomas J. O'Leary, Hugh Panaro, and Howard McGillin.

*Still playing May 31, 2004
†Succeeded by: 1. Thomas James O'Leary, Hugh Panaro, Howard McGillin, Brad Little, Howard McGillin, Hugh Panaro, Howard McGillin, Hugh Panaro 2. Sandra Joseph, Adrienne McEwan, Sarah Pfisterer, Elizabeth Southard, Lisa Vroman, Sandra Joseph 3. Adrienne McEwan, Sarah Pfisterer, Adrienne McEwan, Lisa Vroman, Adrienne McEwan, Julie Hanson 4. Gary Mauer, Jim Weitzer, Michael Shawn Lewis, John Cudia, Jim Weitzer, John Cudia

Matthew Broderick and the Company PHOTO BY PAUL KOLNIK

THE PRODUCERS

Music and Lyrics, Mel Brooks; Book, Mr. Brooks, Thomas Meehan; Based on the 1967 film. Director and Choreography, Susan Stroman; Director, Patrick S. Brady; Musical Arrangements/Supervision, Glen Kelly; Orchestrations, Douglas Besterman, Larry Blank (uncredited); Musical Director/Vocal Arrangements, Patrick S. Brady; Set, Robin Wagner; Costumes, William Ivey Long; Lighting, Peter Kaczorowski; Sound, Steve Canyon Kennedy; Hair and Wigs, Paul Huntley; General Manager, Richard Frankel/Laura Green; Company Manager, Kathy Lowe; Production Stage Manager, Steven Zweigbaum; Stage Manager, Ira Mont; Cast Recording, Sony; Casting, Johnson-Liff Associates; Advertising, Serino Coyne, Inc.; Presented by Rocco Landesman, SFX Theatrical Group, The Frankel-Baruch-Viertel-Routh Group, Bob and Harvey Weinstein, Rick Steiner, Robert F.X. Sillerman and Mel Brooks, in association with James D. Stern/Douglas L. Meyer; Press, John Barlow–Michael Hartman/Bill Coyle, Shellie Schovanec. Previewed from Wednesday, March 21, 2001; Opened in the St. James Theatre on Thursday, April 19, 2001*

Cast

The Usherettes **Bryn Dowling, Jennifer Smith**
Max Bialystock **Nathan Lane** †1
Leo Bloom **Matthew Broderick** †2
Hold-me Touch-me **Madeleine Doherty**
Mr. Marks **Ray Wills**
Franz Liebkind **Brad Oscar** †3
Carmen Ghia **Roger Bart** †4
Roger De Bris **Gary Beach** †5

Bryan; Judge; Jack Lepidus **Peter Marinos**
Scott; Guard; Donald Dinsmore **Jeffry Denman**
Ulla **Cady Huffman** †6
Lick-me Bite-me **Jennifer Smith**
Shirley; Kiss-me Feel-me; Jury Foreman **Kathy Fitzgerald**
Kevin; Jason Green; Trustee **Ray Wills**
Lead Tenor **Eric Gunhus**
O'Rourke; Baliff **Abe Sylvia**
O'Riley **Matt Loehr**
O'Houlihan **Robert H. Fowler**

Ensemble: Jeffry Denman, Madeleine Doherty, Bryn Dowling, Kathy Fitzgerald, Robert H. Fowler, Ida Gilliams, Eric Gunhus, Kimberly Hester, Naomi Kakuk, Matt Loehr, Peter Marinos, Angie L. Schworer, Jennifer Smith, Abe Sylvia, Tracy Terstriep, Ray Wills

Understudies: Jim Borstelmann (Franz Liebkind, Roger De Bris); Jeffry Denman (Franz Liebkind, Leo Bloom); Ida Gilliams, Angie L. Schworer (Ulla); Jamie LaVerdiere (Carmen Ghia, Leo Bloom); Brad Musgrove (Carmen Ghia, Roger De Bris); Brad Oscar (Max Bialystock, Roger De Bris); Ray Wills (Max Bialystock)

Swings: Jim Borstelmann, Adrienne Gibbons, Jamie LaVerdiere, Brad Musgrove, Christina Marie Norrup

Musical Numbers: Opening Night, The King of Broadway, We Can Do It, I Wanna Be a Producer, In Old Bavaria, Der Guten Tag Hop Clop, Keep It Gay, When You Got It Flaunt It, Along Came Bialy, Act One Finale, That Face, Haben Sie Gehoert das Deutsche Band?, You Never Say "Good Luck" On Opening Night, Springtime for Hitler, Where Did We Go Right?, Betrayed, 'Til Him, Prisoners of Love, Leo and Max, Goodbye!

Musical comedy presented in two acts. The action takes place in New York City, 1959. Winner of 2001 Tony Awards for Best Musical, Best Score, Best Book of a Musical, Best Actor in a Musical (Nathan Lane), Best Featured Actor in a Musical (Gary Beach), Best Featured Actress in a Musical (Cady Huffman), Best Director/Musical, Best Choreography, Best Sets, Best Costumes, Best Lighting, Best Orchestrations

Variety tallied 18 favorable and 1 mixed review. *Times* (Brantley): "...the real thing: a big Broadway book musical that is so ecstatically drunk on its powers to entertain that it leaves you delirious, too....Mr. Lane and Mr. Broderick...have the most dynamic stage chemistry since Natasha Richardson met Liam Neeson in *Anna Christie*..." *News* (Kissel): "Nathan Lane does his funniest work in years...Matthew Broderick sings and dances with suitably for-lorn charm...No new musical in ages has offered so much imagination, so much sheer pleasure." *Post* (Barnes): "...a cast-iron, copper-bottomed, super-duper, mammoth old-time Broadway hit." *Variety* (Isherwood): "...the material is inherently terrific. But Brooks and his collaborators go further, capitalizing on the new medium in ways that add immensely to its appeal...the first Broadway smash of the new century."

*Still playing May 31, 2004
†Succeeded by: 1. Henry Goodman, Brad Oscar, Lewis J. Stadlen, Fred Applegate, Nathan Lane, Brad Oscar 2. Steven Weber, Roger Bart, Don Stephenson, Matthew Broderick, Roger Bart 3. John Treacy Egan, Peter Samuel, John Treacy Egan 4. Sam Harris, Brad Musgrove 5. John Treacy Egan, Gary Beach 6. Sarah Cornell, Angie L. Schworer

RENT

Music/Lyrics/Book by Jonathan Larson; Director, Michael Greif; Arrangements, Steve Skinner; Musical Supervision/Additional Arrangements, Tim Weill; Choreography, Marlies Yearby; Original Concept/Additional Lyrics, Billy Aronson; Set, Paul Clay; Costumes, Angela Wendt; Lighting, Blake Burba; Sound, Kurt Fischer; Cast Recording, Dreamworks; General Management, Emanuel Azenberg, John Corker; Company Manager, Brig Berney; Stage Managers, John Vivian, Crystal Huntington; Presented by Jeffrey Seller, Kevin McCollum, Allan S. Gordon, and New York Theatre Workshop; Press, Richard Kornberg/Don Summa, Ian Rand; Previewed from Tuesday, April 16, 1996; Opened in the Nederlander Theatre on Monday, April 29, 1996*

Manley Pope, Loraine Velez PHOTO BY JOAN MARCUS

Cast

Roger Davis **Adam Pascal** † 1
Mark Cohen **Anthony Rapp** †2
Tom Collins **Jesse L. Martin** †3
Benjamin Coffin III **Taye Diggs** †4
Joanne Jefferson **Fredi Walker** †5
Angel Schunard **Wilson Jermaine Heredia** †6
Mimi Marquez **Daphne Rubin-Vega** †7
Maureen Johnson **Idina Menzel** †8
Mark's Mom; Alison; Others **Kristen Lee Kelly**
Christmas Caroler; Mr. Jefferson; Pastor; Others **Byron Utley**
Mrs. Jefferson; Woman with Bags; Others **Gwen Stewart**
Gordon; The Man; Mr. Grey; Others **Timothy Britten Parker**
Steve; Man with Squeegee; Waiter; Others **Gilles Chiasson**
Paul; Cop; Others **Rodney Hicks**
Alexi Darling; Roger's Mom; Others **Aiko Nakasone**

Understudies: Yassmin Alers (Maureen Johnson, Mimi Marquez); Gilles Chiasson (Mark Cohen, Roger Davis); Darius de Haas (Angel Schunard, Benjamin Coffin III, Tom Collins); Shelley Dickinson (Joanne Jefferson); David Driver (Mark Cohen, Roger Davis); Rodney Hicks (Benjamin Coffin III); Kristen Lee Kelly (Maureen Johnson); Mark Setlock (Angel Schunard); Simone (Joanne Jefferson, Mimi Marquez); Byron Utley (Tom Collins)

Swings: Yassmin Alers, Darius de Haas, Shelley Dickinson, David Driver, Mark Setlock, Simone

Musical Numbers: Tune Up, Voice Mail (#1–#5), Rent, You Okay Honey?, One Song Glory, Light My Candle, Today 4 U, You'll See, Tango: Maureen, Life Support, Out Tonight, Another Day, Will I?, On the Street, Santa Fe, We're Okay, I'll Cover You, Christmas Bells, Over the Moon, La Vie Boheme/I Should Tell You, Seasons of Love, Happy New Year, Take Me or Leave Me, Without You, Contact, Halloween, Goodbye Love, What You Own, Finale/Your Eyes

Musical presented in two acts. The action takes place in New York City's East Village. Winner of 1996 Tony Awards for Best Musical, Best Original Score, Best Book of a Musical and Featured Actor in a Musical (Wilson Jermaine Heredia). *Rent* passed its 2,000th Broadway performance during this season. Tragedy occurred when the 35-year-old author, Jonathan Larson, died of an aortic aneurysm after watching the final dress rehearsal of his show on January 24, 1996.

*Still playing May 31, 2004
†Succeeded by: 1. Norbert Leo Butz, Richard H. Blake (alt.), Manley Pope, Sebastian Arcelus, Ryan Link, Jeremy Kushnier 2. Jim Poulos, Trey Ellett, Matt Caplan, Joey Fatone, Matt Caplan 3. Michael McElroy, Rufus Bonds Jr., Alan Mingo Jr. Mark Leroy Jackson, Mark Richard Ford 4. Jacques C. Smith, Stu James, D'Monroe 5. Gwen Stewart, Alia Leon, Kenna J. Ramsey, Danielle Lee Greaves, Natalie Venetia Belcon, Myiia Watson-Davis, Merle Dandridge, Kenna J. Ramsey, Merle Dandridge 6. Wilson Cruz, Shaun Earl, Jose Llana, Jai Rodriguez, Andy Señor, Jai Rodriguez, Andy Señor 7. Marcy Harriell, Krysten Cummings, Maya Days, Loraine Velez, Karmine Alers, Krystal L. Washington, Melanie Brown 8. Sherie René Scott, Kristen Lee Kelly, Tamara Podemski, Cristina Fadale, Maggie Benjamin, Cristina Fadale, Maggie Benjamin

THOROUGHLY MODERN MILLIE

Book by Richard Morris and Dick Scanlan; Based on the Story and Screenplay by Richard Morris (Universal Pictures production); Director, Michael Mayer; Sets, David Gallo; Lighting, Donald Holder; Costumes, Martin Pakledinaz; Sound, Jon Weston; New Music, Jeanine Tesori; New Lyrics, Dick Scanlan; Choreography, Rob Ashford; Orchestrations, Doug Besterman, Ralph Burns; Music Coordination, John Miller; Casting, Jim Carnahan; Produced by Michael Leavitt, Fox Theatricals, Hal Luftig, Stewart F. Lane, James L. Nederlander, Independent Presenters Network, Libby Adler Mages/Marian Glick, Dori Berinstein/Jennifer Manocherian, Dramatic Forces, John York Noble, Whoopi Goldberg; Associate Producers, Mike Isaacson, Kristin Caskey, Clear Channel Entertainment; Press, Barlow-Hartman Public Relations, John Barlow, Michael Hartman, Jeremy Shaffer. Opened at the Marquis Theatre April 18, 2002*

Cast

Millie Dillmount **Sutton Foster** †1
Ruth **Megan Sikora**
Gloria **JoAnn M. Hunter**
Rita **Jessica Grové**
Alice **Alisa Klein**
Ethel Peas **Joyce Chittick**
Cora **Catherine Brunell**
Lucille **Kate Baldwin**
Mrs. Meers **Harriet Harris** †2
Miss Dorothy Brown **Angela Christian** †3
Ching Ho **Ken Leung**
Bun Foo **Francis Jue**
Miss Flannery **Anne L. Nathan** †4
Mr. Trevor Graydon **Marc Kudisch** †5
Speed Tappists **Casey Nicholaw, Noah Racey**
The Pearl Lady **Roxane Barlow**
Jimmy Smith **Gavin Creel** †6
The Letch **Noah Racey**
Officer **Casey Nicholaw**
Muzzy Van Hossmere **Sheryl Lee Ralph** †7
Kenneth **Brandon Wardell**
Mathilde **Catherine Brunell**
George Gershwin **Noah Racey**
Dorothy Parker **Julie Connors**
Rodney **Aaron Ramey**
Dishwashers **Aldrin Gonzalez, Aaron Ramey, Brandon Wardell**
Muzzy's Boys **Gregg Goodbrod, Darren Lee, Dan LoBuono, John MacInnis, Noah Racey, T. Oliver Reid**
Daphne **Kate Baldwin**
Dexter **Casey Nicholaw**
New Modern **Jessica Grové**

Ensemble: Kate Baldwin, Roxane Barlow, Catherine Brunell, Joyce Chittick, Julie Connors, David Eggers, Gregg Goodbrod, Aldrin Gonzalez, Jessica Grové, Amy Heggins, JoAnn M. Hunter, Alisa Klein, Darren Lee, Dan LoBuono, John MacInnis, Casey Nicholaw, Noah Racey, Aaron Ramey, T. Oliver Reid, Megan Sikora, Brandon Wardell

Understudies: Kate Baldwin (Miss Dorothy Brown); Catherine Brunell (Millie Dillmount); Julie Connors (Miss Flannery); Gregg Goodbrod (Mr. Trevor Graydon); Jessica Grové (Miss Dorothy Brown); Susan Haefner (Millie Dillmount, Miss Flannery); JoAnn M. Hunter (Bun Foo); Francis Jue (Ching Ho); Darren Lee (Bun Foo, Ching Ho); Aaron Ramey (Jimmy Smith, Mr. Trevor Graydon); Brandon Wardell (Jimmy Smith)

Orchestra: Michael Rafter, conductor, music director; Lawrence Goldberg, associate conductor and piano; Charles Descarfino, assistant conductor, percussion; Lawrence Feldman, Walt Weiskopf, Dan Willis, Allen Won, woodwinds; Craig Johnson, Brian O'Flaherty, Glenn Drewes, trumpet; Larry Farrell, Jeff Nelson, trombone; Brad Gemeinhardt, French horn; Belinda Whitney, Eric DeGioia, Laura Oatts, Karl Kawahara, Mary Whitaker, violin; Stephanie Cummins, Anik Oulianine, cello; Emily Mitchell, harp; Ray Kilday, bass; Jack Cavari, guitar; Warren Odze, drums

Musical Numbers: Not For the Life of Me, Thoroughly Modern Millie, How the Other Half Lives, The Speed Test, They Don't Know, The Nuttycracker Suite, What Do I Need With Love?, Only in New York, Jimmy, Forget About the Boy, I'm Falling in Love With Someone, I Turned the Corner, Muqin, Long As I'm Here With You, Gimme Gimme

Musical presented in two acts. Time: 1920s. Place: New York City. Based on a 1967 movie about a kid from Kansas who struggles to survive amid adversity in the big city. Winner of six Tony Awards, 2002: Best Actress, Featured Actress, Choreography, Musical, Orchestrations, Costumes.

*Still playing May 31, 2004
† Succeeded by: 1. Susan Egan 2. Delta Burke, Terry Burrell, Dixie Carter 3. Emily Rozek, Jessica Grové 4. Liz McCartney 5. Christopher Sieber, Kevin Earley 6. Christian Borle 7. Leslie Uggams

Sheryl Lee Ralph PHOTO BY JOAN MARCUS

Productions from past seasons that **closed during this season**

CABARET
Below: Gina Gershon
2,777 performances
Opened March 19, 1998
Closed January 4, 2004
PHOTO BY JOAN MARCUS

A DAY IN THE DEATH OF JOE EGG
Left: Victoria Hamilton, Eddie Izzard
69 performances
Opened April 3, 2003
Closed June 1, 2003
PHOTO BY JOAN MARCUS

ENCHANTED APRIL
Left: Elizabeth Ashley
143 performances
Opened April 29, 2003
Closed August 31, 2003
PHOTO BY CAROL ROSEGG

GYPSY
Below left: Tammy Blanchard
451 performances
Opened May 1, 2003
Closed May 30, 2004
PHOTO BY JOAN MARCUS AND T. CHARLES ERICSON

LA BOHÊME
Above: Chloe Wright
228 performances
Opened December 8, 2003
Closed June 29, 2003
PHOTO BY SUE ADLER

LONG DAY'S JOURNEY INTO NIGHT
Below: Brian Dennehy, Vanessa Redgrave
117 performances
Opened May 6, 2003
Closed August 31, 2003
PHOTO BY JOAN MARCUS

THE LOOK OF LOVE
Left: Shannon Jones, Janine La Manna, Rachelle Rak
49 performances
Opened May 4, 2003
Closed June 15, 2003
PHOTOS BY JOAN MARCUS

MAN OF LA MANCHA
Above: Brian Stokes Mitchell
304 performances
Opened December 5, 2002
Closed August 31, 2003
PHOTO BY JOAN MARCUS

NINE
Above: Mary Stuart Masterson, Antonio Banderas, Jane Krakowski
285 performances
Opened April 10, 2003
Closed December 14, 2003
PHOTO BY JOAN MARCUS

THE PLAY WHAT I WROTE
Left: Hamish McColl, Sean Foley, Tobey Jones
89 performances
Opened March 30 2003
Closed June 15, 2003
PHOTO BY JOAN MARCUS

SALOME
Left: David Strathairn, Marisa Tomei
40 performances
Opened April 30, 2003
Closed June 12, 2003
PHOTO BY JOAN MARCUS

SAY GOODNIGHT, GRACIE
Above: Frank Gorshin
354 performances
Opened October 10, 2002
Closed August 24, 2003
PHOTO BY CAROL ROSEGG

TAKE ME OUT
Left: The Company
355 performances
Opened February 27, 2003
Closed January 4, 2004
PHOTO BY JOAN MARCUS

URINETOWN
Left: The Company
965 performances
Opened September 20, 2001
Closed January 18, 2004
PHOTO BY JOAN MARCUS

A YEAR WITH FROG AND TOAD
Below: Jay Goede, Mark Linn-Baker
73 performances
Opened April 13, 2003
Closed June 15, 2003
PHOTO BY ROB LEVINE

OFF-BROADWAY

Productions that opened **June 1, 2003 – May 31, 2004**

THE PRINCE AND THE PAUPER

Revival of the Musical with Book by Bernie Garzia and Ray Roderick; Music by Neil Berg; Lyrics by Neil Berg, Bernie Garzia and Ray Roderick; based on the novel by Mark Twain. Produced by Leftfield Productions, Marian Lerman Jacobs; Director, Ray Roderick; Scenery, Dana Kenn; Costumes, Samantha Fleming; Lighting, Eric T. Haugen; Sound, One Dream Sound; Fight Direction, Rick Sordelet; Associate Producer, Douglas N. Wall; Casting, Dave Clemmons; Press, Cromarty and Company, Peter Cromarty. Opened at the Lamb's Theatre, June 4, 2003*

Cast

Lady Edith; Karyn **Leslie Castay**
Tom Canty (The Pauper) **Jimmy Dieffenbach**
Miles; Charlie; Patch **Robert Evan**
Lady Jane; Jamie **Allison Fischer**
Annie; Floozy; Baker's Wife **Amy Goldberger**
Prince Edward **Dennis Michael Hall**
Father Andrew; Pike **James Hindman**
Hermit; Dresser **Roland Rusinek**
Hugh Hendon; Stache **Wayne Schroder**
John Canty; King Henry; Castle Cook **Dan Sharkey**
Mary Canty; Maggie **Sally Wilfert**

Musical presented in two acts.

*Closed August 31, 2003

FAIRY TALES OF THE ABSURD

Untitled Theatre Company #61 presentation of a collection of three short plays: *Tales for Children* and *To Prepare a Hard Boiled Egg* by Eugene Ionesco and *One Head Too Many* by Edward Einhorn. Originally presented as part of both the Ionesco Festival and the 2001 New York International Fringe Festival. Director, Edward Einhorn; Producer, David A. Einhorn; Puppet design/Stage Manager, Berit Johnson; Scenery, Michelle Malavet; Costumes, Carla Gant; Lighting, Gregg Carville; Music and Sound, William Sullivan Niederkorn; Opened at Theatre 80 St. Marks Place, June 12, 2003*

Performed by John Blaylock, Peter B. Brown, Ian W. Hill, Uma Incrocci, Celia Montgomery.

Three short plays presented without intermission.

*Closed June 29, 2003

Dennis Michael Hall, Jimmy Dieffenbach in *The Prince and the Pauper* PHOTO BY CAROL ROSEGG

Uma Incrocci (seated), Ian Hill, Peter Brown, John Blaylock, Celia Montgomery in *Fairy Tales of the Absurd* PHOTO BY EDWARD EINHORN

Jason Wiles, Henry Afro-Bradley in *Safe* PHOTOS BY MANU BOYER

SAFE

Broadsword Productions and the Imua! Theatre Company production of the play by Anthony Ruivivar and Tony Glazer; Artistic Director, Kaipo Schwab; Associate Producer, Coby Bell; Director, Anthony Ruivivar; Scenery, Antje Ellerman; Costumes, Este Stanley; Lighting, Shawn K. Kaufman; Sound; Mark Bruckner; Fight Director, Robert Tuftee; Original Music, Mark Bruckner, Misha Lepetich, Anthony Ruivivar; Production Stage Manager, Jenna Gottlieb; Production Manager, Michael Kemp; Casting, Stephanie Holbrook; Press, Shirley Herz Associates. Opened at the Jose Quintero Theatre, June 14, 2003*

Cast
Truss **Jason Wiles**
Oakley **Henry Afro-Bradley**
Feliz **Carlin Glynn**
Sabine **Yvonne Jung**
Ryan **Coby Bell**

A play presented in two acts.

*Closed July 17, 2003

Henry Afro-Bradley, Jason Wiles, Carlin Glynn, Yvonne Jung, Coby Bell in *Safe*

MACK THE KNIFE...
THE LIFE AND MUSIC OF BOBBY DARIN

Musical revue by Chaz Esposito and James Haddon. Produced by Splish Splash Productions; Director, Chaz Esposito; Scenery, Martin Machitto; Lighting and Sound, John Pappas; Music Direction and Arrangements, James Haddon; Press, KPM Associates, Kevin P. McAnarney, Grant Lindsey. Opened at the Theatre at St. Peter's, June 22, 2003*

Performed by Chaz Esposito, with Music by Larry Frenock.

Musical Numbers: Splish Splash, Dream Lover, Beyond the Sea, Things, You're the Reason I'm Living, If I Were a Carpenter, Mack the Knife, others

Musical revue presented in two acts.

*Closed August 10, 2003

THE IMPORTANCE OF BEING EARNEST

The Aquila Theatre Company Revival of the play by Oscar Wilde. Producing Artistic Director, Peter Meineck; Director, Robert Richmond; Scenery, Robert Richmond and Peter Meineck; Lighting, David Dunford; Production Stage Manager, Allegra Libonati; Press, The Pete Sanders Group. Opened at the Baruch Performing Arts Center, June 29, 2003*

Cast
Algernon Moncrieff **Guy Oliver-Watts**
John (Jack) Worthing **Richard Willis**
Lady Bracknell **Alex Webb**
Hon. Gwendolen Fairfax **Cameron Blair**
Miss Prism **Renata Friedman**
Cecily Cardew **Lindsay Rae Taylor**
Lane, Manservant, Rev. Canon Chasuble **Andrew Schwartz**
Merriman, Butler **Ryan Conarro**

A play presented in two acts.

*Closed August 3, 2003

HENRY V

The Public Theatre revival of the play by William Shakespeare. Producer, George C. Wolfe; Executive Director, Mara Manus; Director, Mark Wing-Davey; Choreography, David Neumann; Scenery, Mark Wendland; Costumes, Gabriel Berry; Lighting, David Weiner; Sound, Acme Sound Partners; Music, John Gromada; Casting, Jordan Thaler, Heidi Griffiths; Production Stage Manager, Lisa Porter; Press, Carol R. Fineman, Elizabeth Wehrle. Opened at the Delacorte Theatre in Central Park, July 15, 2003*

Nicole Leach, Liev Schreiber in *Henry V*   PHOTO BY MICHAL DANIEL

Cast

Chorus; Sir Thomas Grey; John Bates **Steven Rattazzi**
King Henry, the Fifth **Liev Schreiber**
Duke of Clarence **Ryan McCarthy**
Duke of Gloucester **David Flaherty**
Duke of Exeter **Daniel Oreskes**
Earl of Westmoreland; Bardolph;
  Duke of Burgandy **Tom Alan Robbins**
Archbishop of Canterbury; Montjoy **David Costabile**
Bishop of Ely; Captain Fluellen; Queen Isabel **Peter Gerety**
Early of Cambridge; Duke of Orleans;
  Captain Morris **Mark Gerald Douglas**
Lord Scroop **Gregory Derelian**
Nym; Earl of Grandpre **Dan Moran**
Pistol **Bronson Pinchot**
Nell Quickly; Alice **Mercedes Herrero**
Captain Gower; Charles the Sixth **Martin Rayner**
Captain Jamy; Monsieur Le Fer **Orlando Pabotoy**
Louis, the Dauphin **Ryan Shively**
Princess Katherine **Nicole Leach**
Charles Delabreth; Michael Williams **Adam Dannheisser**
Duke of Bourbon **Colman Domingo**
Governor of Harfleur **Jon Dolton**
French Messenger **Gbenga Akinnagbe**
Alexander Court **Mike Strickland**
Queen Elizabeth **Arie Thompson**

A play presented in two acts.

*Closed August 10, 2003

CAPITOL STEPS: BETWEEN IRAQ AND A HARD PLACE

Musical revue by Bill Strauss, Elaina Newport and Mark Eaton. Produced by Eric Krebs and Capitol Steps; Director, Bill Strauss, Elaina Newport and Mark Eaton; Scenery, R.J. Matson; Costumes, Ms. Payne; Lighting, Krista Martocci; Sound, Jill B.C. DuBoff; Music Director, Ken Lundie; Press, Jeffrey Richards Associates, Irene Gandy, Alana O'Brien, Eric Sanders. Opened at the John Houseman Theatre, July 19, 2003*

Performed by Bill Strauss, Elaina Newport, Mike Carruthers, Kevin Corbett, Morgan Duncan, Ann Johnson, Linda Rose Payne, Jack Rowles, Bari Sedar, Tracey Stephens, Mike Thornton, Mike Tilford, Jamie Zemarel.

Musical revue presented in two acts.

*Closed August 31, 2003

The Company in *Capitol Steps: Between Iraq and a Hard Place*   PHOTO BY RICHARD TERMINE

EDGE

Solo performance piece by Paul Alexander. Produced by Daryl Roth; Director, Paul Alexander; Costumes, Gabrielle Hammil; Lighting, Joe Levasseur; Sound, Dennis Michael Keefe; Production Stage Manager, Leslie Anne Pinney; Press, Barlow-Hartman Public Relations, John Barlow, Michael Hartman. Opened at the DR2 Theatre, July 21, 2003*

Cast
Sylvia Plath **Angelica Torn**

A play presented in two acts. Time: February 11, 1963. Place: Sylvia Plath's London flat.

*Closed September 20, 2003

Brenda Withers, Mindy Kaling in *Matt and Ben* PHOTOS BY JASON LINDBERG

THAT DAY IN SEPTEMBER

Solo performance piece by Artie Van Why. Produced by Carolyn Rossi Copeland Productions and Marie B Corporation, In Association With The Lamb's Theatre Company; Director, Richard Masur; Scenery, Marjorie Bradley Kellogg; Lighting, Ann G. Wrightson; Sound, Jake Hall; Stage Manager; Robert Ross Parker. Opened at the Lamb's Theatre, July 23, 2003*

Performed by Artie Van Why.

*Closed August 31, 2003

SERENADE THE WORLD: THE MUSIC AND WORDS OF OSCAR BROWN JR.

Musical revue conceived and produced by Eric Krebs; Director, Stephen Henderson; Opened at the John Houseman Theatre Center, July 29, 2003*

Performed by Genovis Albright and the Oscar Brown Trio

Musical review performed in two parts.

*Closed August 30, 2003

MATT AND BEN

By Mindy Kaling and Brenda Withers. Produced by Victoria Lang and Pier Paolo Piccoli, Stephen Pevner and Jason Hsaio; Director, David Warren; Scenery, James Youmans; Costumes, Anne Sung; Lighting, Jeff Croiter; Sound, Fitz Patton; Production Stage Manager, Jana Lynn; Associate Producers, Josh Wood and Wendy Smith; Management, Martian Entertainment, Inc.; Press, Keith Sherman & Associates. Opened at P.S. 122, August 7, 2003*

Cast
Matt (Damon) **Mindy Kailing**
Ben (Affleck) **Brenda Withers**
Replacement Cast: Quincy Tyler Bernstine (Ben) and Jennifer R. Morris (Matt) March 25, 2003

A play presented without intermission.

*Closed May 15, 2004

THE LOVE-HUNGRY FARMER

Irish Repertory Theatre revival of the solo performance piece by Des Keogh; based on the writings of John B. Keane. Artistic Director, Charlotte Moore; Producing Director, Ciarán O'Reilly; Director, Charlotte Moore; Costumes, David Toser; Lighting, Sean Farell; Production Stage Manager, Andrew Theodorou; Press, Barlow-Hartman Public Relations, Joe Perrotta. Opened at the Irish Repertory Theatre Mainstage August 7, 2003*

Cast
John Boscoe McLean **Des Keogh**

*Closed September 28, 2003

PLAYING BURTON

Irish Repertory Theatre and Redbranch Productions presentation of a solo performance piece by Mark Jenkins. Artistic Director, Charlotte Moore; Production Director, Ciarán O'Reilly; Director, Mark Jenkins; Scenery and Lighting, Mark Hankla; Costumes, David Toser; Sound, Dan Donnelly; Press, Barlow-Hartman Public Relations, Joe Perrotta. Opened and the Irish Repertory Theatre Downstairs space August 14, 2003*

Performed by Brian Mallon.

*Closed September 14, 2003

CARNIVAL KNOWLEDGE

A stage production by Todd Robbins. Produced by Dana Matthow in association with The Presley Theatre Company; Director, Kirsten Sanderson; Stage Banner Art, Johnny Meah; Lighting, Tyler Micoleau; Press Representative, Media Blitz; Opened at the SoHo Playhouse, August 17, 2003*

Performed by Todd Robbins, Shannon Morrow, Little Jimmy, Twistina, Madame Electra, Pythonia, The Flying Ebola Brothers, Zanitra, Olga Hess.

A theatrical experience featuring carnival and circus sideshow acts.

*Still playing May 31, 2004

Ron Bohmer, Marc Kudisch, Leah Hocking in *The Thing About Men* PHOTO BY CAROL ROSEGG

Todd Robbins, Little Jimmy, Shannon Morrow in *Carnival Knowledge* PHOTO BY RICHEY FAHEY

THE THING ABOUT MEN

Musical with Book and Lyrics by Joe DiPietro; Music by Jimmy Roberts. Based on the screenplay *Men* by Doris Dörrie. Produced by Jonathan Pollard, Bernie Kukoff and Tony Converse, In Association With James Hammerstein Productions; Director, Mark Clements; Choreography, Rob Ashford; Scenery, Richard Hoover; Costumes, Gregory Gale; Lighting, Ken Billington; Sound, Jon Weston; Orchestrations, Bruce Coughlin; Music Director, Lynne Shankel; Music Coordinator, John Miller; Associate Producers, Gregory Taft Gerard, Karen Jason; Casting, Cindy Rush; Production Stage Manager, Debra Acquavella; Press, Richard Kornberg and Associates, Richard Kornberg, Tom D'Ambrosio. Opened at the Promenade Theatre, August 27, 2003*

Cast
Tom **Marc Kudisch**
Sebastian **Ron Bohmer**
Lucy **Leah Hocking**
Man **Daniel Reichard**
Woman **Jennifer Simard**
Understudies: Carter Calvert (Lucy, Woman); Daniel Cooney, Graham Rowat (Tom, Sebastian, Man)

Orchestra: Lynee Shankel, conductor, keyboard; Victoria Paterson, violin; Peter Sachon, cello, percussion; Christopher Miele, reeds.

Musical Numbers: Oh, What a Man, No Competiton for Me, Opportunity Knocking, Free, Easy Guy, Take Me Into You, Lucy the Greatest Friend, Downtown Bohemian Slum, You Will Never Get Into This Restaurant, Me, Too, One-Woman Man, Take Me Into You (Reprise), Highway of Your Heart, The Road to Lucy, Make Me a Promise, Thomas, New, Beautiful Man, I Can't Have It All (Finale)

Musical presented in two acts.

*Closed February 15, 2004

Gordon MacDonald, Nathan Lane in *Trumbo*

TRUMBO

By Christopher Trumbo; based on the letters of Dalton Trumbo. Produced by Claudia Catania and The Westside Theatre; Director, Peter Askin; Scenery, Loy Arcenas; Lighting, Jeff Croiter, Sound and Music, John Gromada; Video, Dennis Diamond; Associate Producer, Terry Byrne; Casting, Margery Simkin; Production Stage Manager, Arabella Powell; Press, The Publicity Office, Bob Fennell. Opened at the Westside Theatre Downstairs, September 4, 2003*

Cast
Dalton Trumbo **Nathan Lane**
Christopher Trumbo **Gordon MacDonald**

A play presented without intermission.

*Closed January 18, 2004

BERKSHIRE VILLAGE IDIOT

Solo Performance piece by Michael Isaac Connor. Produced by David S. Singer and Jennifer Manocherian; Director, Barry Edelstein; Scenery, Derek McLane; Lighting, Russell H. Champa; Sound, John Gromada; Press, Barlow-Hartman Public Relations, Michael Hartman, Jeremy Shaffer. Opened at the The Zipper Theatre, September 7, 2003*

Performed by Michael Isaac Connor.

A performance piece presented without intermission. Time: 1970s. Place: Berkshire Village.

*Closed January 18, 2004

Gordon MacDonald in *Trumbo* PHOTOS BY JOAN MARCUS

DUTCH HEART OF MAN

By Robert Glaudini; Produced by LAByrinth Theatre Company, Director, Charles Goforth; Scenery, Narelle Sissons; Lighting, Jason Kantrowitz; Sound, Elizabeth Rhodes; Costumes, Mimi O'Donnell; Production Stage Manager, Jane Llynn; Stage Manager, Richard A. Hodge; Opened at the Susan Stein Shiva Theatre at the Public Theatre, September 16, 2003*

Cast
Florence **Maggie Bofill**
Momma; Marty's Mom **Maggie Burke**
Marty **David Deblinger**
Phyllis **Wilemina Olivia Garcia**
Costumer #2; Bananas/Chef **Scott Hudson**
Dutch **Salvatore Inzerillo**
Customer #1/ Mrs. Stamen **Portia**

A play performed in two acts.

*Closed October 19, 2003

PORTRAITS

By Jonathan Bell; Produced by Vincent Curcio; Director, Mark Pinter; Scenery, Andrew Knapp; Costumes, Charles Schoonmaker; Lighting, Aaron Meadow; Sound, Raymond D. Shilke; Music, Joshua Pearl; Casting, Jay Binder Casting, Jack Bowdan; Production Stage Manager, Kimothy Cruse; Stage Manager, Alden Fulcomer; Press, The Pete Sanders Group, Pete Sanders, Glenna Freedman, Jim Mannino. Opened at the Union Square Theatre, September 21, 2003*

Cast
Andrew **Christopher Coucill**
Betty **Darrie Lawrence**
Daniel **Victor Slezak**
Arifa **Anjali Bhimani**
John **Matte Osian**
Ruth **Roberta Maxwell**
Nancy **Dana Reeve**

Understudies: Erika LaVonn (Nancy, Arifa); Matt Loney (Andrew, Daniel, John); Susanne Marley (Betty, Ruth)

A play presented without intermission. Time: Post-September 11, 2001. Place: New York and other locations.

*Closed October 5, 2003.

A ROOSTER IN THE HENHOUSE

Solo performance piece by John O'Hern. Produced by Ohoby Productions; Director, Mark S. Graham; Lighting, Greg MacPherson; Production Stage Manager, Jennifer G. Birge; Press, Origlio Public Relations, Tony Origlio. Opened at the Lion Theatre, September 21, 2003*; Reopened at the Kirk Theatre, October 8, 2003**

Performed by John O'Hern.

A play presented without intermission.

*Closed October 4, 2003
**Closed October 25, 2003

Dana Reeve, Roberta Maxwell in *Portraits* PHOTO BY JOAN MARCUS

CUPID AND PSYCHE

Musical with Book and Lyrics by Sean Hartley; Music by Jihwan Kim; Presented by The Imagination Company; Director, Timothy Childs; Choreographer, Devanand Janki; Scenery, David Swayze; Costumes, Christine Darch; Lighting, Aaron J. Mason; Musical Director, Peter Yarin; Musical Supervisor & Additional Arrangements, Edward G. Robinson; Stage Manager, Scott Fagant; Press, Springer/Chicoine PR, Joe Trentacosta. Opened at the John Houseman Studio Theatre, September 24, 2003*

Cast
Venus **Laura Marie Duncan**
Cupid **Barrett Foa**
Psyche **Deborah Lew**
Mercury **Logan Lipton**

Pianists: Peter Yarin, Jihwan Kim

Musical presented without intermission.

*Closed October 26, 2003

Barrett Foa, Deborah Lew in *Cupid and Psyche* PHOTO BY AARON J. MASON

OMNIUM GATHERUM

By Theresa Rebeck and Alexandra Gersten-Vassilaros. Produced by Robert Cole, Joyce Johnson, In Association With Jujamcyn Theatres, Charles Flateman/Kerrin Behrend; Director, Will Frears; Scenery, David Rockwell; Costumes, Junghyun Georgia Lee; Lighting, Jules Fisher and Peggy Eisenhauer; Sound, Vincent Olivieri; Casting, Bernard Telsey Casting; Production Stage Manager, Jane Grey; Stage Manager, Sid King; Press, Richard Kornberg and Associates, Richard Kornberg, Don Summa, Rick Miramontez, Carrie Friedman, Tom D'Ambrosio. Opened at The Variety Arts Theatre, September 25, 2003*

Cast
Suzie **Kristine Nielsen**
Roger **Phillip Clark**
Lydia **Jenny Bacon**
Julia **Melanna Gray**
Khalid **Edward A. Hajj**
Terence **Dean Nolen**
Jeff **Joseph Lyle Taylor**
Mohammed **Amir Arison**

A play performed without intermission.

*Closed November 30, 2003

Marian Seldes in *Beckett/Albee*

ROUNDING THIRD

By Richard Dresser. Produced by Eric Krebs, Ted Tulchin, Robert G. Bartner, Chase Mishkin, Jerry Frankel, In Association With M. Kilburg Reedy; Director, John Rando; Scenery, Derek McLane; Lighting, F. Mitchell Dana; Sound, Jill B.C. DuBoff; Music, Robert Reale; Fight Direction, Rick Sordelet; Casting, Barry Moss; Production Stage Manager, Jack Gianino; Stage Manager, Babette Roberts; Press, Jeffery Richards Associates. Opened at the John Houseman Theatre, October 7, 2003*

Cast
Michael **Matthew Arkin**
Don **Robert Clohessy**

A play presented in two acts. Time: The present. Place: A baseball field.

*Closed December 7, 2003.

BECKETT/ALBEE

Collection of one-acts by Samuel Beckett and Edward Albee. Produced by Elizabeth Ireland McCann, Daryl Roth, Roger Berlind, Terry Allen Kramer, Scott Rudin, Nick Simunek, In Association With Robert G. Bartner; Director, Lawrence Sacharow; Scenery and costumes, Catherine Zuber; Lighting, Michael Chybowski; Sound, Mark Bennett and Ken Travis; Casting, James Calleri; Production Stage Manager, Charles Means; Press, Shirley Herz Associates, Shirley Herz, Sam Rudy, Kevin P. McAnarney, Robert Lasko, Val Sherman. Opened at Century Center for the Peforming Arts, October 9, 2003*

Cast
Not I by Samuel Beckett
Mouth **Marian Seldes**
Auditor **Peter Kybart**
A Piece of Monologue by Samuel Beckett
Speaker **Brian Murray**
Footfalls by Samuel Beckett
May **Marian Seldes**
Woman's Voice **Delphi Harrington**
Counting the Ways by Edward Albee
She **Marian Seldes**
He **Brian Murray**

Standby: Peter Kybart for Brian Murray

A play presented in two acts.

*Closed January 4, 2004

THE TWO NOBLE KINSMEN

The Public Theatre revival of the play by William Shakespeare and John Fletcher. Producer, George C. Wolfe; Executive Director, Mara Manus; Director, Darko Tresnjak; Scenery, David P. Gordon; Costumes, Linda Cho; Lighting, Robert Wierzel; Sound, Michael Creason; Fight Direction, DeeAnn Weir; Associate Producer, Steven Tabakin; Casting, Jordan Thaler, Heidi Griffiths; Production Stage Manager, Francesca Russell; Press, Carol R. Fineman, Elizabeth Wehrle. Opened in Martinson Hall, October 19, 2003*

Cast
ATHENIANS
Theseus **Sam Tsoutsouvas**
Pirithous **Tyrone Mitchell Henderson**
Hippolyta **Opal Alladin**
Emilia **Doan Ly**
Jailer **Jonathan Fried**
Wooer **Liam Craig**
Jailer's Daughter **Jennifer Ikeda**
Waiting Woman **Candy Buckley**
Countrymen **Candy Buckley**, **Jonathan Fried**, **Liam Craig**
Doctor **Candy Buckley**
THEBANS
Arcite **David Harbour**
Palamon **Graham Hamilton**
Queens **Candy Buckley**, **Jonathan Fried**, **Liam Craig**
GODS
Valerius **Jonathan Fried**
Mars **Sam Tsoutsouvas**
Venus **Jennifer Ikeda**
Diana **Opal Alladin**

A play presented in two acts.

*Closed November 9, 2003

Brian Murray in *Beckett/Albee* PHOTOS BY CAROL ROSEGG

LISTEN TO MY HEART: THE SONGS OF DAVID FRIEDMAN

Musical revue with Music and Lyrics by David Friedman; additional Lyrics by Scott Barnes, Robin Boudreau, Deborah Brevoort, Clarissa Dane, Kathie Lee Gifford, Peter Kellogg, Alix Korey, Portia Nelson, Muriel Robinson, Barbara Rothstein. Produced by Victoria Lang, Pier Paolo Piccoli and William P. Suter; Directed by Mark Waldrop; Scenery, Michael Anania; Costumes, Markas Henry; Lighting and Sound, Matt Berman; Associate Producer, Carol Cogan Savitsky; Casting, Alan Filderman; Production Stage Manager, Matt Berman. Opened at Upstairs at Studio 54 on October 23, 2003*

Performed by Allison Briner, Joe Cassidy, David Friedman, Michael Hunsaker, Alix Korey, Anne Runolfsson.

Musical revue presented in two acts.

*Closed December 7, 2003

David Friedman, Anne Runolfsson, Alix Korey, Joe Cassidy, Michael Hunsaker, Allison Briner in *Listen to My Heart: The Songs of David Friedman* PHOTO BY ROBERT ZASH

NOBODY DON'T LIKE YOGI

Solo performance piece by Thomas Lysaght. Produced by Don Gregory; Director, Paul Linke; Scenery and Costumes, Tony Walton; Lighting, Ken Billington; Sound, Tony Melfa; Stage Manager, John Handy; Press, Bill Evans and Associates, Bill Evans, Jim Randolph. Opened at the Lamb's Theatre, October 26, 2003*

Cast

Yogi Berra **Ben Gazzara**

A solo performance piece presented without intermission. Time: Opening day, 1999. Place: The players' clubhouse in Yankee Stadium.

*Closed January 18, 2004

HAMLET

The New 42nd Street presentation of the Theatre de la Jeune Lune revival of the play by William Shakespeare; Adapted by Paddy Hayter with Theatre de la Jeune Lune. Artistic Directors, Barbra Berlovitz, Steven Epp, Vincent Gracieux, Robert Rosen, Dominique Serrand; Director, Paddy Hayter; Scenery, Fredericka Hayter; Costumes, Sonya Berlovit; Lighting, Marcus Dilliard; Music and Music Direction, Eric Jensen; Stage Manager, Andrea C. Hendricks; Press, Lauren Daniluk. Opened at the New Victory Theatre, October 26, 2003*

Cast

Claudius **Vincent Gracieux**
Gertrude **Barbra Berlovitz**
Hamlet **Steven Epp**
Ghost **Vincent Gracieux**
Polonius **Luverne Seifert**
Laertes **Stephen Cartmell**
Ophelia **Sarah Agnew**
Horatio **Jason Lambert**
Osric **Kevin Bitterman**
Priest **Kristopher Lencowski**
Marcellus **Joel Spence**
Bernardo **Kristopher Lencowski**
Francisco **Kevin Bitterman**
Gravediggers **Joel Spence, Luverne Seifert**
Player King **Joel Spence**
Players and Chorus **Company**

Musicians: Eric Jensen, keyboard; Elizabeth Karges, cello

A play presented in two acts.

*Closed November 2, 2003

Ben Gazzara in *Nobody Don't Like Yogi* PHOTO BY ALEX OTTAVIANO

AMERICAN STORAGE

Broken Watch Theatre Company production of a play by Edward Allan Baker; Artistic Director and Director, Drew DeCorleto; Executive Director, Leo Lauer; Scenery, J. Wiese; Costumes, Jito-Min Lee; Lighting, Christien Methot; Sound, Derek Holbrook; Stage Manager, Heather Prince; Press, Springer/Chicoine, Joe Trentacosta. Opened at the Kirk Theatre, November 3, 2003*

Cast
Howard **Stephen Brumble Jr.**
Allie **Teresa L. Goding**
Bry **Andrew J. Hoff**
Rollie **Leo Lauer**

A play presented in two acts.

*Closed November 23, 2003

PRIVATE JOKES, PUBLIC PLACES

By Oren Safdie. Produced by Steven Chaikelson, Donny Epstein, Ergo Entertainment, Avram C. Freedberg, Yeeshai Gross, Elie Landau and Brannon Wiles; Director, Maria Mileaf; Scenery, Neil Patel; Costumes, Laurie Churba; Lighting, Jeff Croiter; Casting, Cindy Tolan; Production Stage Manager, Tom Taylor; Press, Sam Rudy Media Relations, Sam Rudy; Robert Lasko. Opened at the Theatre at the Center for Architecture, November 5, 2003*

Cast
William **Anthony Rapp**
Margaret **M.J. Kang**
Colin **Geoffrey Wade**
Erhardt **Sebastian Roché**

A play presented without intermission.

*Closed February 22, 2004.

Anthony Rapp, Geoffrey Wade, M.J. Kang, Sebastian Roché in *Private Jokes, Public Places* PHOTO BY CAROL ROSEGG

Stephen Brumble Jr. (down center), Leo Lauer, Andrew J. Hoff, Teresa L. Goding in *American Storage* PHOTO BY DOUBLE WIDE

LYPSINKA! AS I LAY LIP-SYNCHING

Solo Performance piece by John Epperson. Produced by Phil Ciasullo Conrad, Jeanette Finch-Walton, Tweed Theatreworks, In Association With Margaret Cotter; Director, Kevin Malony; Scenery and Lighting, Mark T. Simpson; Costumes, Bryant Hoven; Sound, Brett Jarvis; Wig Design, Mitch Ely; Press, The Publicity Office, Bob Fennell, Michael S. Borowski. Opened at the Minetta Lane Theatre, November 5, 2003*

Cast

Lypsinka **John Epperson**

A solo performance piece presented without intermission.

*Closed December 21, 2003

FAME ON 42ND STREET

Musical with Book by José Fernandez; Music by Steve Margoshes; Lyrics by Jacques Levy; Based on the MGM Studios film developed by David De Silva. Produced by Richard Martini, Allen Spivak and Joop van den Ende/Dodger Stage Holding, By Arrangement With the Father Fame Foundation; Director, Drew Scott Harris; Choreography, Lars Bethke; Scenery, Norbert U. Kolb; Costumes, Paul Tazewell; Lighting, Ken Billington; Sound, Christopher K. Bond; Music Direction, Eric Barnes; Music Coordinator, John Monaco; Associate Producers, Larry Magid, Adam Spivak, Lee Marshall, Joe Marsh; Casting, Stuart Howard and Amy Schecter; Production Stage Manager, Christopher K. Bond; Stage Manager, Inga Pedersen; Press, Boneau/Bryan-Brown, Adrian Bryan-Brown; Susanne Tighe, Adriana Douzos. Opened at the Little Shubert Theatre, November 11, 2003*

Cast

Nick Piazza **Christopher J. Hanke**
Serena Katz **Sara Schmidt**
José (Joe) Vegas **Jose Restrepo**
Carmen Diaz **Nicole Leach**
Mabel Washington **Q. Smith**
Grace "Lambchops" Lamb **Jenna Coker**
Miss Ester Sherman **Cheryl Freeman**
Schlomo Metzenbaum **Dennis Moench**
Tyrone Jackson **Shakiem Evans**
Mr. Myers **Peter Reardon**
Ms. Greta Bell **Nancy Hess**
Mr. Sheinkopf **Gannon McHale**
Goodman "Goody" King **Michael Kary**
Iris Kelly **Emily Corney**

Ensemble: Angela Brydon, Alexis Carra, Ryan Christopher Chotto, David Finch, David Garcia, Jesse Nager, Jennifer Parsinen, Dawn Noel Pignuola, Eduardo Rioseco, Enrico Rodriguez, Danita Salamida, Erika Weber.

Understudies: Eduardo Rioseco (Nik Piazza); Alexis Carra, Erika Weber (Serena Katz); Enrico Rodriguez, David Finch (Jose [Joe] Vegas); Erika

John Epperson in *Lypsinka! As I Lay Lip-Synching* PHOTO BY ROSALIE O'CONNOR

Weber (Carmen Diaz); Danita Salamida (Mabel Washington); Danita Salamida (Grace "Lambchops" Lamb); Nancy Hess (Miss Ester Sherman); David Finch (Schlomo Metzenbaum); Jesse Nager (Tyrone Jackson); David Finch (Mr. Myers); Danita Salamida, Erika Weber (Ms. Greta Bell); Peter Reardon (Mr. Sheinkopf); David Finch (Goodman "Goody" King); Alexis Carra (Iris Kelly)

Swings: David Finch, Jesse Nager, Danita Salamida, Erika Weber

Orchestra: Eric Barnes, conductor, first keyboard; Lynn Crigler, associate conductor, second keyboard; Edward Hamilton, guitar; Vincent Fay, electric bass; Matthew Taylor, reeds; Joseph Giorgianni, trumpet; Bryan Johnson, trombone; David Tancredi, drums

Musical presented in two acts. Time: 1980–84. Place: New York's High School for the Performing Arts.

*Still playing May 31, 2004

Nicole Leach and the Company in *Fame on 42nd Street* PHOTO BY CAROL ROSEGG

MY BIG GAY ITALIAN WEDDING

A comedy by Anthony Wilkinson; General Mangement by Martian Entertainment Inc., Jamie Cesa, Carl D. White, Tom Smedes; Director, Peter Rapanaro; Associate Director Teresa Anne Cicala; Choreography, Joseph Ritsch; Musical Director, Robert Levulis; Scenery, John Kenny; Costumes, Chris March; Lighting, Aaron Copp; Stage Manager, Zsa Zsa Fa; Press, Spin Cycle, Ron Lasko. Opened at The Actors' Playhouse, November 14, 2003*

Cast
Anthony **Anthony Wilkinson**
Andrew **Bill Fisher**
Joseph **Joe Scanio**
Maria **Meredith Cullen**
Carmela **Maria Nazzaro**
Father Rosalia **JC Alvarez**
Mario **Nick Scarnati**
Gregorio **Vincent Briguccia**
Wedding guests: **Brett Douglas, Michael Batelli, Lorenzo Cambriello, Joseph Cirillo, Amanda Minker, Perryn Pomatto, Antony Raymond, Donna Ross, Rocco Parente, Kevin T. Moore, Yvonne Roen, Concetta Maria Aliotta, Melanie Maras, Joe Grimaldi, Laura Gaspari, Carla-Marie Mercun**

A play presented in two acts.

*Still playing May 31, 2004

The Company in *My Big Fat Gay Italian Wedding* PHOTO BY NIGEL TEARE

GOLF: THE MUSICAL

A new Musical revue by Michael Roberts; Producer, Eric Krebs; Director and Choreographer, Christopher Scott; Scenery, James Joughin; Costumes, Bernard Grenier; Lighting, Aaron Spivey; Musical Director, Ken Lundie; General Manager, Jonathan Shulman; Production Stage Manager, Brenda Arko; Stage Manager, Jake Witlen; Casting, Stephanie Klapper; Press, Terence Womble and Jeffrey Kurtz. Opened at the John Houseman Theatre Studio A, November 19, 2003*

Performed by Joel Blum, Trisha Rapier, Christopher Sutton, Sal Viviano.

Musicans: Ken Lundie, piano, Rachel Kaufman, piano

Musical Numbers: A Show About Golf, The History of Golf, Who Plays Celebrity Golf?, Scratch Golfer, Plaid, The Golfer's Psalm, Tiger Woods, A Great Lady Golfer, Let's Bring Golf to the Gulf, My Husband's Playing Around, The Golfing Museum, The Road to Heaven, No Blacks, No Chicks, No Jews, The Ballad of Casey Martin, Pro Shop Polyphony, Golf's Such a Naughty Game, Presidents and Golf, The Beautiful Time, I'm Going Golfing Tomorrow

Musical revue presented in two acts.

*Closed April 4, 2004

Joel Blum, Christopher Sutton, Trisha Rapier, Sal Viviano in *Golf: The Musical* PHOTO BY BRUCE GLIKAS

WOMEN ON FIRE

Cherry Lane Theatre presentation of the performance piece by Irene O'Garden. Artistic Director, Angelina Fiordellisi; Director, Mary B. Robinson; Scenery and Costumes, Michael Krass; Lighting, Pat Dignan; Sound, Bart Fasbender; Production Stage Manager, Misha Siegel-Rivers. Opened at the Cherry Lane Theatre, November 19, 2003*; Reopened January 7, 2004**

Performed by Judith Ivey.

A solo performance piece presented without intermission.

*Closed December 21, 2003
**Closed February 8, 2004

Judith Ivey in *Women on Fire* PHOTO BY CAROL ROSEGG

OUR SINATRA: A MUSICAL CELEBRATION

Revival of the Musical revue by Eric Comstock, Hilary Kole and Christopher Gines. Produced by Jack Lewin; Director, Kurt Stamm, with Richard Maltby Jr.; Lighting, Jeff Nellis; Press, Origlio Public Relations, Tony Origlio, Martine Sainvil. Opened at Birdland, November 20, 2003*

Performed by Hilary Kole, Tony DeSare, Adam James.

*Closed March 14, 2004

Eric Comstock, Hilary Kole, Christopher Gines in *Our Sinatra* PHOTO BY JOAN MARCUS

CAROLINE, OR CHANGE

The Public Theatre presentation of the Musical with Book and Lyrics by Tony Kushner; Music by Jeanine Tesori. Director, George C. Wolfe; Choreography, Hope Clarke; Scenery, Riccardo Hernández; Costumes, Paul Tazewell; Lighting, Jules Fisher and Peggy Eisenhauer; Sound, Jon Weston; Hair, Jeffrey Frank; Orchestrations, Rich Bassett, Joseph Joubert; Buryl Red; Music Supervision, Kimberly Grigsby; Music Direction, Linda Twine; Associate Producers, Peter DuBois, Steven Tabakin; Casting, Jordan Thaler, Heidi Griffiths; Production Stage Manager, Rick Steiger; Stage Manager, Lisa Dawn Cave; Press, Carol R. Fineman, Elizabeth Wehrle. Opened in the Newman Theatre, November 30, 2003*

Cast

Caroline Thibodeaux **Tonya Pinkins**
The Washing Machine **Capathia Jenkins**
The Radio **Tracy Nicole Chapman**, **Marva Hicks**, **Ramona Keller**
Noah Gellman **Harrison Chad**
The Dryer **Chuck Cooper**
Grandma Gellman **Alice Playten**
Grandpa Gellman **Reathel Bean**
Rose Stopnick Gellman **Veanne Cox**

Stuart Gellman **David Costabile**
Dotty Moffett **Chandra Wilson**
The Moon **Adriane Lenox**
The Bus **Chuck Cooper**
Emmie Thibodeaux **Kevin Ricardo Tate**
Joe Thibodeaux **Marcus Carl Franklin**
Mr. Stopnick **Larry Keith**

Orchestra: Linda Twine, conductor; Antoine Silverman, Chris Cardona, violin; David Creswell, viola; Anja Wood, cello; Paul Garment, first reed; Stephen Wisner, second reed; Steve Bargonetti, guitar; Peter Donovan, bass; Ed Alstrom, piano; John Clancy, Shane Shanahan, percussion.

Musical Numbers: Washer/Dryer, Cabbage, Long Distance, Moon Change, Duets, The Bleach Cup, Ironing, The Chanukah Party, The Twenty-Dollar Bill, Aftermath, Lot's Wife, How Long Has This Been Going On?, Epilogue

Musical presented in two acts. Time: November–December 1963. Place: Lake Charles, Louisiana.

*Closed February 1, 2004

Ramona Keller, Marva Hicks, Tracy Nicole Chapman in *Caroline, or Change*

DUET

By Otho Eskin; Presented by The Villar-Hauser Theatre Development Fund; Director, Ludovica Villar-Hauser; General Manager, George Elmer; Scenery, Mark Symczak; Costumes, Christopher Lione; Lighting, Doug Filomena; Composer and Sound, Dewey Dellay; Opened at The Greenwich Street Theatre, December 4, 2003*

Cast

Sarah Bernhardt **Laura Esterman**
Eleonora Duse **Pamela Payton-Wright**
Gabriel D'Annuncio/Various Men **Robert Emmet Lunney**

A play presented without intermission.

*Closed February 1, 2004

Tonya Pinkins in *Caroline, or Change* PHOTOS BY MICHAL DANIEL

Laura Esterman, Pamela Payton-Wright in *Duet* PHOTO BY RAINER FEHRINGER

Phylicia Rashad, Erika Alexander, Damon Gupton in *The Story* PHOTO BY MICHAEL DANIEL

THE STORY

The Public Theatre Presentation of the play by Tracey Scott Wilson. Producer, George C. Wolfe; Executive Director, Mara Manus; In Association With the Long Wharf Theatre (Artistic Director, Gordon Edelstein; Managing Director, Michael Stotts); Director, Loretta Greco; Scenery, Robert Brill; Costumes, Emilio Sosa; Lighting, James Vermeulen; Sound and Music, Robert Kaplowitz; Associate Producers, Peter DuBois, Steven Tabakin; Casting, Jordan Thaler, Heidi Griffiths; Production Stage Manager, Buzz Cohen; Stage Manager, Damon W. Arrington; Press, Carol R. Fineman, Elizabeth Wehrle. Opened in the Anspacher Theatre, December 10, 2003*

Cast

Yvonne **Erika Alexander**
Jeff; Tim Dunn **Stephen Kunken**
Pat **Phylicia Rashad**
Neil **Damon Gupton**
Jessica Dunn **Sarah Grace Wilson**
Detective; Ensemble **Michelle Hurst**
Carla; Ensemble **Kalimi Baxter**
Reporter/Ensemble **Susan Kelechi Watson**
Latisha **Tammi Clayton**

A play presented in two acts. Time: The present. Place: The newsroom of a large daily paper and locations around a city.

*Closed December 21, 2003

ROAD HOUSE: THE STAGE PLAY

Transfer of the Off Off Broadway play, officially titled *Road House: The Stage Version Of The Cinema Classic That Starred Patrick Swayze, Except This One Stars Taimak From The 80's Cult Classic "The Last Dragon" Wearing A Blond Mullet Wig.* Produced by Publicity Outfitters and Tanya Bershadsky, in association with Andrea Ciannavei, Paul Smithyman, and the Barry Z Show; Director, Timothy J. Haskell; Fight Choreography, Taimak Guarriello; Scenery, Paul Smithyman; Costumes and Chorgeography, Rebeca Ramirez; Lighting, Angela Sierra; Sound, Rachelle Anthes and Nick Arens; Musical Arrangement, Mark Cannistraro; Wigs, Hugh Dill; Stage Manager, Parys LeBron; Press, Publicity Outfitters, Timothy J. Haskell. Opened at the Barrow Street Theatre, December 12, 2003*

Performed by Taimak Guarriello, Giuseppe "Ago" Agostaro, Jamie Benge, Christopher Joy, Harry Listig, Lucia Burns, Kellie Arens, Nick Arens, Laura Baggett, Ago, Rolando Zuniga, Rachael Roberts, Brian Kantrowitz.

A play presented without an intermission.

*Closed February 8, 2004

Taimak Guarriello, Giuseppe "Ago" Agostaro in *Road House: The Stage Play* PHOTO BY GABE EVANS

SHOLOM ALEICHEM—NOW YOU'RE TALKING!

Solo performance piece by Saul Reichlin; Based on the stories of Sholom Aleichem. Produced by Lone Star Theatre, LLC. Opened at the DR2 Theatre, December 14, 2003*

Performed by Saul Reichlin.

*Closed February 4, 2004

ADDICTED...A COMEDY OF SUBSTANCE

Solo performance piece by Mark Lundholm. Produced by Clear Channel Entertainment; Director, Bob Balaban; Scenery, Walt Spangler; Lighting, Paul Miller; Sound, Randy Hansen and Duncan Robert Edwards; Executive Producer, Jennifer Costello, Clint Mitchell; Associate Producer, Erin McMurrough; Press, Barlow-Hartman Public Relations; Michael Hartman, Jeremy Shaffer, Dayle Gruet. Opened at the Zipper Theatre, December 14, 2003*

Performed by Mark Lundholm.

A solo performance piece presented without intermission.

*Closed March 21, 2004

(front) Joanne Bogart, Lovette George, (back) Craig Fols, Eric Rockwell in *The Musical of Musicals: The Musical!* PHOTO BY CAROL ROSEGG

THE MUSICAL OF MUSICALS: THE MUSICAL!

York Theatre Company presentation of the Musical with Book by Eric Rockwell and Joanne Bogart; Music by Eric Rockwell; Lyrics by Joanne Bogart. Artistic Director, James Morgan; In Association With Musicals Tonight!; Director and Choreographer, Pamela Hunt; Scenery, James Morgan; Costumes, John Carver Sullivan; Lighting, Mary Jo Dondlinger; Production Supervisor, Scott Dela Cruz; Production Stage Manager, Dan Zittlel; Casting, Norman Meranus; Press, Cohn Davis Bigar Communications, Helene Davis, Dan Dutcher. Opened at the Theatre at St. Peter's, December 16, 2003*

Cast

Big Willy; Billy; William; Bill; Villy **Craig Fols**
June; Jeune; Junie Faye; Junita; Juny **Lovette George**
Jidder; Jitter; Mr. Jitters; Phantom Jitter; Jütter **Eric Rockwell**
Mother Abbey; Abby; Auntie Abby; Abigail Von Schtarr; Fraulein Abby **Joanne Bogart**

Musical presented in two acts.

*Closed January 25, 2004

Stephen Quint, Richard Holmes in *H.M.S. Pinafore* PHOTO BY LEE SNIDER

A VERY MERRY UNAUTHORIZED CHILDREN'S SCIENTOLOGY PAGEANT

Transfer of the Off-Off-Broadway Musical; Conceived and Directed by Alex Timbers; Text and Music, Kyle Jarrow; Producer, Aaron Lemon-Strauss; Stage Manager, Bailie Slevin; Production Designer, Jennifer Rogien; Lighting, Samantha Trepel; Production Supervisor, Ronnie Tobia; Assistant Director, David Kilpatrick. Presented by Les Freres Corbusier, Mr. Lemon-Strauss, Executive Director; Ms. Rogien, Executive Producer; Mr. Timbers, Artistic Director. Opened at the John Houseman Theatre, December 21, 2003*

Performed by Seamus Boyle, Spenser Lee Carrion-O'Driscoll, Alison Stacy Klein, Joshua Marmer, Max Miner, Stephanie Favoreto Queiroz, Daren Watson, Emma Whitfield, Sophie Whitfield, Jordan Wolfe.

Musical presented without intermission.

*Closed January 4, 2004

IOLANTHE

New York Gilbert and Sullivan Players production of the revival of the operetta with Book by W.S. Gilbert; Music by Arthur Sullivan. Artistic Director, Albert Bergeret; Director, Albert Bergeret; Scenery, Jack Garver; Costumes, Gail J. Wofford; Lighting, Sally Small; Press, Cromarty and Company; Peter Cromarty. Opened at City Center, January 9, 2004*

Cast

Lord Chancellor **Stephen O'Brien**
Fairy Queen **Melissa Parks**
Phyllis **Kimilee Bryant**
Lord Mountararat **Richard Holmes**
Private Willis **Ross Crutchlow**

An operetta presented in two acts.

*Closed January 11, 2004

H.M.S. PINAFORE

New York Gilbert and Sullivan Players production of the revival of the operetta with Book by W.S. Gilbert; Music by Arthur Sullivan. Artistic Director, Albert Bergeret; Direction and Scenery, Albert Bergeret; Costumes, Gail J. Wofford; Lighting, Sally Small; Press, Cromarty and Company, Peter Cromarty. Opened at City Center, January 16, 2004*

Cast

Sir Joseph Porter **Stephen Quint**
Captain **Keith Jurosko/Richard Holmes**
Josephine **Kimilee Bryant**
Ralph Rackstraw **Michael Harris**

An operetta presented in two acts.

*Closed January 18, 2004

THE MIKADO

New York Gilbert and Sullivan Players production of the revival of the operetta with Book by W.S. Gilbert; Music by Arthur Sullivan. Artistic Director, Albert Bergeret; Direction and Scenery, Albert Bergeret; Costumes, Gail J. Wofford; Lighting, Sally Small; Press, Cromarty and Company, Peter Cromarty. Opened at City Center, January 23, 2004*

Cast

Mikado **Keith Jurosko**
Yum-Yum **Laurelyn Watson**
Katisha **Melissa Parks**
Nanki-Poo **Michael Harris**
Ko-Ko **Stephen Quint**

An operetta presented in two acts.

*Closed January 25, 2004

Barry Mann, Cynthia Weil in *They Wrote That?* PHOTO BY JOAN MARCUS

AGAMEMNON

Aquila Theatre Company presentation of a play by Aeschylus, translated by P.W. Meineck. Director and Scenery, Robert Richmond and Peter Meineck; Costumes, Theoni V. Aldredge; Lighting, Peter Meineck; Music, Anthony Cochrane, Movement, Robert Richmond; Dramaturg, Helen Foley; Stage Manager, Francesca Russell; General Manager, Nate Terracio; Opened at the John Jay College Theatre, February 12, 2004*

Cast

Aegisthus **Marco Barricelli**
Watchman/Elder of Argos **Louis Butelli**
Elders of Argos **David Adkins, Matthew Lewis,**
Nicholas Kepros, Thomas Schall, Alex Webb
Clytemnestra **Olympia Dukakis**
Soldier/Elder of Argos **John Sierros**
Agamemnon **Louis Zorich**
Cassandra **Miriam Laube**
Women of Argos **Gillian Claire Chadsey, Toni Melaas,**
Magin Schantz
Iphigenia **Carris Guild**
Guards **Ray Cisara, Jay Painter**

A play presented without intermission.

*Closed February 22, 2004

THEY WROTE THAT?

Musical revue with Music by Barry Mann; Lyrics by Cynthia Weil. Produced by CTM Productions and James B. Freydberg; Director, Richard Maltby Jr.; Scenery, Neil Patel; Costumes, Laurie Churba; Lighting, Heather Carson; Sound, Peter Fitzgerald; Musical Staging, Kurt Stamm; Casting, Dave Clemmons Casting; Production Stage Manager, James Latus; Boneau/Bryan-Brown, Chris Boneau, Jackie Green. Opened at the McGinn/Cazale Theatre, February 5, 2004*

Performed by Barry Mann and Cynthia Weil, with Deb Lyons, Moeisha McGill, Jenelle Lynn Randall.

Orchestra: Fred Mollin, conductor, guitar; Steve Tarshis, electric guitar; Paul Ossola, upright and electric bass; Charlie Giordano, second keyboard; Denny McDermott, drums, percussion.

Musical Numbers: You've Lost That Lovin' Feeling, Sometimes When We Touch, We've Gotta Get Out of this Place, Here You Come Again, Blame It on the Bossa Nova, Make Your Own Kind of Music, Who Put the Bomp, On Broadway, Just Once, Don't Know Much, He's So Shy, Running With the Night, Walkin' in the Rain, Love How You Love Me, others

Musical revue presented without intermission.

*Closed March 14, 2004

Max Morath in *Max Morath: Ragtime and Again*   PHOTO BY DIANE FAY SKOMARS

MAX MORATH: RAGTIME AND AGAIN

The York Theatre Company presentation of the solo performance piece by Max Morath. Artistic Director, James Morgan; Director, Robert Marks; Scenery, Max Morgan; Lighting, Mary Jo Dondlinger; Production Stage Manager, Jay McLeod; Press, Cohn Davis Bigar Communciations, Helen Davis. Opened at the Theatre at St. Peter's, February 8, 2004*

Performed by Max Morath.

A solo performance piece presented in two acts.

*Closed March 14, 2004

Sarah Jones in *Sarah Jones' bridge and tunnel* PHOTO BY BRIAN MICHAEL THOMAS

ROULETTE

Ensemble Studio Theatre production of the play by Paul Weitz. Artistic Director, Curt Dempster; Executive Director, Susann Brinkley; Director, Trip Cullman; Scenery, Takeshi Kata; Costumes, Alejo Vietti; Lighting, Greg MacPherson; Sound, Aural Fixation; Music, Michael Friedman; Production Stage Manager, Lori Ann Zepp; Press, David Gersten and Associates. Opened at the John Houseman Theatre February 18, 2004*

Cast

Jon **Larry Bryggman**
Virginia **Ana Gasteyer**
Jock **Shawn Hatosy**
Enid **Leslie Lyles**
Jenny **Anna Paquin**
Steve **Mark Setlock**

A play presented in two acts.

*Closed March 14, 2004

SARAH JONES' BRIDGE AND TUNNEL

Solo performance piece by Sarah Jones. Produced by Meryl Streep and the Culture Project, In Association With Robert Dragotta, Jayson Jackson, Michael Alden, Eric Falkenstein, Marcia Roberts, Jean Kennedy Smith, Tom Wirtshafter; Director, Tony Taccone; Scenery, Blake Lethem; Lighting, Alexander V. Nichols; Sound, DJ Rekha and Chris Meade; Assistant Director, Steve Colman; Stage Manager, Annie Brown; Press, Origlio Public Relations, Tony Origlio, Martine Sainvil. Opened at 45 Bleecker, February 19, 2004.

Performed by Sarah Jones.

A solo performance piece presented without intermission.

MAGIC HANDS FREDDY

By Arje Shaw. Produced by Dana Matthow, Steve Alpert and Kenneth Greiner; Director, Rebecca Taylor; Scenery and Lighting, Jason Sturm; Costumes, Yvonne De Moravia; Stage Manager, Adam Grosswirth; Press, Keith Sherman & Associates, Brent Olberman. Opened at the Soho Playhouse, February 19, 2004*

Cast

Freddy **Michael Rispoli**
Calvin **Ralph Macchio**
Maria **Antionette LaVecchia**
Sal; Others **Ed Chemaly**

Understudies: Matthew Boston (Calvin); Michele Melland (Maria); Steve Scionti, Matt Servitto (Freddy)

A play presented in two acts.

*Closed May 2, 2004

Michael Rispoli, Ralph Macchio in *Magic Hands Freddy* PHOTO BY CAROL ROSEGG

Shannon Cochran, Michael Cullen in *Bug* PHOTO BY GABE EVAN

BUG

By Tracy Letts. Produced by Scott Morfee, Amy Danis and Mark Johannes, In Association With Planetearth Partners: Director, Dexter Bullard; Scenery, Lauren Helpern; Costumes, Kim Gill; Lighting, Tyler Micoleau; Sound, Brian Ronan; Fight Direction, J. David Brimmer; Production Stage Manager, Richard A. Hodge; Press, Publicity Outfitters, Timothy Haskell, Tanya Bershadsky. Opened at the Barrow Street Theatre, February 29, 2004

Cast

Agnes White **Shannon Cochran**
R.C. **Amy Landecker**
Peter Evans **Michael Shannon**
Jerry Goss **Michael Cullen**
Dr. Sweet **Reed Birney**

Understudies: Allyn Burrows, Dee Pelletier

A play presented in two acts.

THE MOONLIGHT ROOM

Transfer of the Off Off Broadway play by Tristine Skyler. Produced by Arielle Tepper and Freddy DeMann, in Association with Solecist Productions; Director, Jeff Cohen; Scenery, Marion Williams; Costumes, Kim Gill; Lighting, Scott Bolman; Sound, Laura Grace Brown; Production Stage Manager, Michael V. Mendelson; Press, Carol Fineman Publicity, Carol R. Fineman, Leslie Baden. Opened at the Beckett Theatre, March 1, 2004*

Cast

Sal **Laura Breckenridge**
Joshua **Brendan Sexton II**
Mrs. Kelly **Kathryn Layng**
Mr. Wells **Lawrence James**
Adam **Mark Rosenthal**

A play presented in two acts. Time: Present. Place: A New York hospital.

*Closed May 2, 2004

Jason Scott Campell and the Company in *Ministry of Progress* PHOTO BY RAHAV SEGEV

MINISTRY OF PROGRESS

Musical with Book by Kim Hughes; Music and Songs by John Beltzer, Sara Carlson, Philip Dessinger, Ted Eyes, Alex Forbes, Kathy Hart, Kim Hughes, Gary Levine, Christian Martirano, Jeremy Schonfeld, Tony Visconti; Based on a radio play by Charles Morrow. Produced by Terry E. Schnuck. Director, Kim Hughes; Scenery, Adriana Serrano; Costumes, Fabio Toblini; Lighting, Jason Kantrowitz; Sound, Michael G. Ward; Orchestrations and Music Direction, Christian Martirano; Press, The Jacksina Company, Judy Jacksina, Debra Page. Opened at the Jane Street Theatre, March 4, 2004*

Performed by Jason Scott Campbell, Brian J. Dorsey, Tyne Firmin, Gary Maricheck, Jennifer McCabe, Maia Moss, Julie Reiber, Stacey Sargeant, Richard E. Waits, Christian Whelan.

Musical presented without intermission.

*Closed March 28, 2004

COOKIN'

Transfer of the Off-Off-Broadway performance piece by Seung Whan Song. Produced by PMC Production Company Ltd., Kwang Ho Lee, Seung Whan Song, The Broadway Asia Company, Simone Genatt Haft, Marc Routh, In Association With Zemiro, Morton Swinsky/Michael Fuchs, Amy Danis/Mark Johannes; Director, Seung Whan Song; Scenery, Dong Woo Park; Costumes, Hee Joo Kim; Lighting, Hak Young Kim; Sound, Hyun Park; Fight Direction, Jame Guan; Assistant Directors, Won Hae Kim, Seung Yong You; Executive Producer, Sunny Oh; Associate Producer, Jong Heon Kim; Casting, Lynne Taylor-Corbett; Production Stage Manager, Mark Willoughby; Press, Barlow-Hartman Public Relations, John Barlow, Jeremy Shaffer, Dayle Gruet. Opened at the Minetta Lane Theatre, March 7, 2004*

Performed by Kang Il Kim, Won Hae Kim, Bum Chan Lee, Chu Ja Seo, Ho Yeoul Sul, Hyung Suk Jung, Ji Won Kang, Young Hoon Kim, Sung Min Lee.

A performance piece presented without intermission.

*Still playing May 31, 2004

SWEENEY TODD

New York City Opera revival of the Musical with Book by Hugh Wheeler; Music and Lyrics by Stephen Sondheim; From an Adaptation by Christopher Bond. General and Artistic Director, Paul Kellogg; Executive Producer, Sherwin M. Goldman; Music Director, George Manahan; Director, Arthur Masella; Based on Harold Prince's production; Choreography, Larry Fuller; Scenery, Eugene Lee; Costumes, Franne Lee; Lighting, Ken Billington; Sound, Abe Jacob; Orchestrations, Jonathan Tunick; Music Direction, George Manahan; Press, Richard Kornberg and Associates. Opened at the New York State Theatre, March 9, 2004*

Cast
Anthony Hope **Keith Phares**
Sweeney Todd **Mark Delavan, Timothy Nolen** (alt.)
Beggar Woman **Judith Blazer**
Mrs. Lovett **Elaine Paige, Myrna Paris** (alt.)
Judge Turpin **Walter Charles**
The Beadle **Roland Rusinek**
Johanna **Sarah Coburn**
Tobias Ragg **Keith Jameson**
Pirelli **Andrew Drost**
Jonas Fogg; Birdseller **William Ledbetter**

Musical presented in two acts.

*Closed March 28, 2004

Cookin'   PHOTO BY JOAN MARCUS

EMBEDDED

The Public Theatre presentation of The Actors' Gang production of the play by Tim Robbins; With Reportage by John Simpson (BBC), Alan Feure (*The New York Times*), Robert Fisk (*The Independent*), Martha Gellhorn. Producer, George C. Wolfe; Executive Director, Mara Manus; Director, Tim Robbins; Scenery, Richard Hoover; Costumes, Yasuko Takahara; Lighting, Adam H. Greene; Sound, David Robbins; Masks, Erhard Stiefel; Projections, Elaine J. McCarthy; Associate Producers, Peter DuBois, Steven Tabakin; Casting, Jordan Thaler, Heidi Griffiths; Production Stage Manager, Samantha Jane Robson; Press, Carol R. Fineman, Elizabeth Wehrle. Opened at the Newman Theatre, March 14, 2004*

Cast
Sarge, Cove, Journalist **Brian T. Finney**
Maryanne, Gwen, Woof **Kate Mulligan**
June, Kitten Kattan **Toni Torres**
Monk, Journalist **Ben Gain**
Jen's Dad, Dick, Buford T., Journalist **Steven M. Porter**
Jen-Jen Ryan, Journalist **Kaili Hollister**
Jen's Mom, Amy, Woof **Lolly Ward**
Gondola, Journalist **Riki Lindhome**
Rum-Rum, Chip Webb **Brian Powell**
Pearly White, Stringer **Andrew Wheeler**
Colonel, Announcer **V.J. Foster**
Perez, Camera Kid **J.R. Martinez**
Lieutenant, Journalist **Mark Lewis**

A play presented without intermission. Time: October 2002–June 2003. Place: Various locations in the US, Kuwait and Iraq.

*Closed March 28, 2004

Karla DeVito, Robby Benson in *Open Heart* PHOTO BY CAROL ROSEGG

MY KITCHEN WARS

By Dorothy Lyman; Adapted from Betty Fussell's memoir. Produced by Robin Strasser and Beverly Penberthy; Director, Elinor Renfield; Scenery, George H. Landry; Lighting, Ji-youn Chang; Sound, Melissa Sweeney; Music Direction, Bill Cunliffe; Press, The Pete Sanders Group, Glenna Freedman, Jim Mannino. Opened at the 78th Street Theatre Lab, March 17, 2004*

Performed by Dorothy Lyman and Melissa Sweeney.

A play presented without intermission.

*Closed May 1, 2004

Andrew Wheeler in *Embedded* PHOTO BY MICHAL DANIEL

OPEN HEART

Cherry Lane Theatre production of a Musical by Robby Benson. Director, Matt Williams; Musical Direction, Kevin Farrell; Choreograper, Luis Perez; Scnery, Michael Brown; Costumes, Ann Hould-Ward; Lighting, Ken Billington; Sound, Aural Fixation; Media Design, Batwin & Robin Productions. Opened at The Cherry Lane Theatre, March 17, 2004*

Performed by Robby Benson, Karla DeVito, Stan Brown.

Musical presented without intermission.

*Closed April 25, 2004

Jane Milmore, Billy Van Zandt in *Silent Laughter* PHOTO BY CAROL ROSEGG

SILENT LAUGHTER

By Billy Van Zandt and Jane Milmore. Produced by Carolyn Rossi Copeland, In Association With The Lamb's Theatre Company; Director, Billy Van Zandt; Scenery, Dan Kenn; Costumes, Cynthia Nordstrom; Lighting, Richard Winkler; Production Stage Manager, Thom Schilling. Opened at the Lamb's Theatre, March 18, 2004*

Cast
Ruth **Jane Milmore**
Billy **Billy Van Zandt**
Billy's Pal **Glenn Jones**
Lionel Drippinwithit **John Gregorio**
Sarge **Art Neill**

Ensemble: James Darrah, Jim Fitzpatrick, Ken Jennings, Megan Byrne, Ed Carlo

Time: 1917. A play presented in two parts.

*Closed April 11, 2004

Yeardley Smith in *More* PHOTO BY CAROL ROSEGG

MORE

Solo performance piece by Yeardley Smith. Produced by Kevin Schon; Director, Judith Ivey; Scenery, Loy Arcenas; Costumes, John Schneeman; Lighting, Beverly Emmons; Sound, David Meschter; Production Stage Manger, Neil Krasnow; Press, Sam Rudy Media Relations. Opened at the Union Square Theatre, March 22, 2004*

Performed by Yeardley Smith.

A solo performance piece presented without intermission.

*Closed April 18, 2004

JOHNNY GUITAR

Musical with Book by Nicholas van Hoogstraten; Music by Joel Higgins and Martin Silvestri; Lyrics by Joel Higgins; Based on the Republic Entertainment film and the novel by Roy Chanslor. Produced by A Definite Maybe Productions and Mark H. Kress, In Association With Victoria Lang and Pier Paolo Piccoli and The Century Center for Performing Arts; Director, Joel Higgins; Choreography, Jane Lanier; Scenery, Van Santvoord; Costumes, Kaye Voyce; Lighting, Ed McCarthy; Sound, Laura Grace Brown; Arrangements, Steve Wright; Music Direction, James Mironchik; Associate Director, Ian Belton; Associate Producers, Sarah Brokus, Jeffrey Kent; Casting, Stephanie Klapper; Production Stage Manager, Matthew Lacey; Press, The Karpel Group, Bridget Klapinski, Josh Rosenzweig. Opened at the Century Center for the Performing Arts, March 23, 2004*

Cast
Vienna; Title Singer **Judy McLane**
Johnny Guitar **Steve Blanchard**
Sam; Ned **Grant Norman**
Tom; Bart; Carl **David Sinkus**
Eddie; Hank; Jenks **Jason Edwards**
Emma Small **Ann Crumb**
Mr. McIvers **Ed Sala**
The Dancin' Kid **Robert Evan**
Turkey; Western Singer **Robb Sapp**

Understudies: Kevin Kraft, Kristie Dale Sanders

Musicians: James Mironchik, Conductor-Keyborad; Steve Bartosik, Drums; Steve Court, Bass; John Putnam, Guitar

Musical Numbers: Johnny Guitar, Let It Spin, A Smoke and A Good Cup o' Coffee, Branded a Tramp, In Old Santa Fe, What's in It for Me?, Who Do They Think They Are?, Welcome Home, Johnny Guitar (reprise), Tell Me a Lie, The Gunfighter, We've Had Our Moments, Bad Blood, Johnny Guitar (reprise)

Musical presented in two acts.

*Closed May 16, 2004

Ann Crumb, Judy McLane in *Johnny Guitar* PHOTO BY JOAN MARCUS

Dan Lauria, Bill Dawes in *Ears on a Beatle* PHOTO BY CAROL ROSEGG

FROM DOOR TO DOOR

By James Sherman. Produced by Morton Wolkowitz and Chase Mishkin; Director, Joe Brancato; Scenery, Tony Straiges; Costumes, Ingrid Maurer; Lighting, Jeff Nellis; Sound, Johnna Doty; Casting, Alan Filderman; Production Stage Manager, Barclay Stiff; Press, The Pete Sanders Group, Pete Sanders, Glenna Freedman. Opened at the Westside Theatre Downstairs, March 24, 2004*

Cast
Bessie **Anita Keal**
Deborah **Sarah McCafrey**
Mary **Suzanne Toren**

Understudies: Kathryn Competatore (Deborah); Susan Moses (Bessie, Mary)

A play presented without intermission. Time: 1939 to the present.

*Still playing May 31, 2004

Lisa Kron, Jayne Houdyshell in *Well* PHOTO BY MICHAL DANIEL

EARS ON A BEATLE

By Mark St. Germain. Produced by Daryl Roth, Debra Black and Leon Wildes; Director, Mark St. Germain; Scenery, Eric Renschler; Costumes, David C. Woolard; Lighting, Daniel Ordower; Sound, Randy Hansen; Projections, Carl Casella; Production Stage Manager, Brian Maschka; Press, Sam Rudy Media Relations, Sam Rudy. Opened at the DR2 Theatre, March 28, 2004*

Cast
Howard Ballantine **Dan Lauria**
Daniel McClure **Bill Dawes**

A play presented without intermission. Time: 1970s. Place: New York City.

*Still playing May 31, 2004

Sarah McCafrey, Anita Keal, Suzanne Toren in *From Door to Door* PHOTO BY CAROL ROSEGG

WELL

The Public Theatre production of the play by Lisa Kron. Producer, George C. Wolfe; Executive Director, Mara Manus; Director, Leigh Silverman; Scenery, Allen Moyer; Costumes, Miranda Hoffman; Lighting, Christopher Akerlind; Sound, Jill B.C. DuBoff; Associate Producers, Peter DuBois, Steven Tabakin; Casting, Jordan Thaler, Heidi Griffiths; Production Stage Manager, Martha Donaldson; Press, Carol R. Fineman, Elizabeth Wehrle. Opened in Martinson Hall, March 28, 2004*

Performed by Lisa Kron, Kenajuan Bentley, Saidah Arrika, Ekulona, Jayne Houdyshell, Joel Van Liew, Welker White.

A play presented without intermission.

*Closed May 16, 2004

THE MARIJUANA-LOGUES

By Arj Barker, Doug Benson and Tony Camin. Produced by Ideal Entertainment Group and Magic Arts and Entertainment. Director, Jim Millan; Scenery and Lighting, Gregory Allen Hirsch; Sound, Michael G. Ward; Press, The Karpel Group; Bridget Klapinski, Billy Zavelson. Opened at the Actors' Playhouse, March 30, 2004*

Performed by Arj Barker, Doug Benson, Tony Camin.

A play presented without intermission.

*Still playing May 31, 2004

HANNAH AND MARTIN

Epic Theatre Center presentation of a play by Kate Fodor. Director, Ron Russell; Scenery, Nathan Heverin; Costumes, Margaret E. Weedon; Lighting, Elizabeth Gaines; Production Stage Manager, Bryan Scott Clark; Press, Richard Kornberg & Associates. Opened at the Manhattan Ensemble Theatre, March 31, 2004*

Cast
Hannah Arendt **Melissa Freedman**
Martin Heideggar **David Strathairn**
Karl Jaspers **George Morfogen**
Elfride Heideggar **Laura Hicks**
With: Teri Lamm, Brandon Miller, Sandra Shipley, James Willert

A play presented in two acts.

*Closed April 18, 2004

MRS. FARNSWORTH

A Flea Theatre presentation of a new play by A.R. Gurney. Director, Jim Simpson; Scenery, Kyle Chepulis; Costumes, Claudia Brown; Lighting, Brian Aldous; Stage Manager, Jennifer Noterman. Opened at the Flea Theatre, April 7, 2004*

Cast
Mrs. Farnsworth **Sigourney Weaver**
Mr. Farnsworth **John Lithgow**
Gordon **Danny Burstein**
Amy **Kate Benson**
Rick **Fernando Gambaroni**
Janet **Tarajia Morrell**

A play presented without intermission.

*Closed May 8, 2004

Arj Barker, Doug Benson, Tony Camin in *The Marijuana-Logues* PHOTO BY JOAN MARCUS

Martin Moran in *The Tricky Part* PHOTO BY JOAN MARCUS

John Lithgow, Sigourney Weaver in *Mrs. Farnsworth* PHOTO BY FABRICE TROMBERT

THE TRICKY PART

Solo performance piece by Martin Moran. Produced by James B. Freydberg, CTM Productions, Wendy vanden Heuvel and Sharon Rosen, In Association With True Love Productions; Director, Seth Barrish; Scenery, Paul Steinberg; Costumes, Laurie Churba; Lighting, Heather Carson; Production Stage Manager, Tom Taylor; Press, Boneau/Bryan-Brown, Chris Boneau, Susanne Tighe. Opened at the McGinn/Cazale Theatre, April 12, 2004*

Performed by Martin Moran.

A solo performance piece presented without intermission.

*Closed May 30, 2004

Ntare Guma Mbaho Mwine in *Biro*   PHOTO BY MICHAEL DANIEL

BIRO

The Public Theatre production of the solo performance peice by Ntare Guma Mbaho Mwine. Producer, George C. Wolfe; Executive Producer, Mara Manus; Director, Peter DuBois; Scenery, Riccardo Hernández; Lighting, Chad McArver; Sound, Acme Sound Partners; Projections, Peter Nigrini; Casting, Jordan Thaler, Heidi Griffiths; Production Stage Manager, Damon W. Arrington; Press, Carol R. Fineman, Elizabeth Wehrle. Opened in LuEster Hall, April 18, 2004*

Cast
Biro **Ntare Guma Mbaho Mwine**

A solo performance piece presented without intermission.

*Closed May 9, 2004

Paige Price, Jim Walton, Shannon Lewis in *Chef's Theatre: A Musical Feast*

CHEF'S THEATRE: A MUSICAL FEAST

Musical revue conceived by Marty Bell and Joe Allegro; Songs by Lynn Ahrens and Stephen Flaherty, Andrew Lippa, Marcy Heisler, Zina Goldrich. Produced by West Egg Entertainment, Marty Bell, Greg Smith and Stephen Fass, Clear Channel Entertainment; Director, Stafford Arima; Choreography, Casey Nicholaw; Scenery, Beowulf Boritt; Costumes, Debbie Cheretun; Lighting, Ben Stanton; Sound, Peter Hylenski; Production Stage Manager, Dana Williams; Executive Producer, Joe Allegro. Opened at the Supper Club, April 14, 2004*

Performed by: Lynn Ahrens, Jason Robert Brown, Michael Cavanaugh, Stephen Flaherty, Marcy Heisler, Mylinda Hull, Lauren Kennedy, Shannon Lewis, Janine LaManna, Andrew Lippa, Julia Murney, Kelli O'Hara, Adam Pascal, Michele Pawk, Billy Porter, Paige Price, Alice Ripley, Daphne Rubin-Vega, Kate Shindle, Jim Walton, Zina Goldrich

Chefs: Todd English, Tom Valenti, Tyler Florence, Mary Sue Milliken, Susan Feniger, Michael Lomonaco, Michael Romano, Rick Moonen

Sommeliers: Josh Wesson, Andrea Immer, Steve Olsen

Musical review and performance piece presented in two acts.

*Closed May 18, 2004

Chef Todd English, Paige Price in *Chef's Theatre: A Musical Feast*   PHOTOS BY CAROL ROSEGG

TOXIC AUDIO IN LOUDMOUTH

By Toxic Audio. Produced by Eric Krebs and the John Houseman Theatre Center, In Association With Castle Talent Inc. and M. Kilburg Reedy. Director, René Ruiz; Scenery and Lighting, Peter R. Feuchtwanger; Costumes, David Brooks; Sound, John A. Valines III; Press, Terence Womble, Alan Miller. Opened at the John Houseman Theatre, April 18, 2004*

Performed by Jeremy James, Shalisa James, René Ruiz, Paul Sperrazza, Michelle Mailhot-Valines.

Musical performance piece presented without intermission.

*Still playing May 31, 2004

Jeremy James, Rene Ruiz, Shalisa James, Michelle Mailhot-Valines, Paul Sperrazza in *Toxic Audio in Loudmouth* PHOTO BY CAROL ROSEGG

BARE: A POP OPERA

Musical with Book by John Hartmere Jr. and Damon Intrabartolo; Music by Damon Intrabartolo; Lyrics by John Hartmere Jr.. Produced by Dodger Stage Holding and Jack Grossbart/Marc Schwartz; Director, Kristin Hanggi; Choreography, Sergio Trujillo; Scenery, David Gallo; Costumes, David C. Woolard; Lighting, Mike Baldassari; Sound, Domonic Sack; Associate Producers, William M. Apfelbaum, Amanda Dubois; Casting Dave Clemmons Casting; Production Stage Manager, Phyllis Schray; Press, Boneau/Bryan-Brown, Adrian Bryan-Brown, Jim Byk, Aaron Meier. Opened at the American Theatre of Actors, April 19, 2004*

Cast
Peter **Michael Arden**
Zach **Mike Cannon**
Lucas **Adam Fleming**
Kyra **Kearran Giovanni**
Ivy **Jenna Leigh Green**
Jason **John Hill**
Claire **Kaitlin Hopkins**
Nadia **Natalie Joy Johnson**
Matt **Aaron Lohr**
Priest **Jim Price**
Rory **Lindsay Scott**
Diane **Kay Trinidad**

Swings/Understudies: Romelda T. Benjamin, Isaac Calpito, Sasha Allen, Scott Allgauer

Orchestra: Damon Intrabartolo, conductor, keyboard; Jesse Vargas, assistant conductor, keyboard; David Madden, acoustic guitar, keyboard; Kyle Smith, acoustic guitar, electric guitar; Adam Countryman, bass; Kevin Rice, drums, percussion

Jenna Leigh Green, John Hill in *Bare: A Pop Opera*

Michael Arden, John Hill in *Bare: A Pop Opera*

The Company in *Bare: A Pop Opera* PHOTOS BY JOAN MARCUS

Musical Numbers: Epiphany, You and I, Role of a lifetime, Auditions, Love, Dad, Wonderland, A Quiet Night at Home, Best Kept Secret, Confession, Portrait of a Girl, Birthday, Bitch!, One Kiss, Are You There?, 911! Emergency!, Reputation Stain'd, Ever After, Spring, One, Wedding Bells, In the Hallway, Touch My Soul, See Me, Warning, Pilgrim's Hands, God Don't Make No Trash, All Grown Up, Promise, Cross, Two Households, Queen Mab, Bare, A Glooming Peach, Absolution, No Voice

Musical presented in two acts.

*Closed May 27, 2004

THE NORMAL HEART

The Public Theatre presentation of the Worth Street Theatre Company revival of the play by Larry Kramer. Producer, George C. Wolfe; Executive Director, Mara Manus; Director, David Esbjornson; Scenery, Eugene Lee; Costumes, Jess Goldstein; Lighting, Ken Billington; Sound, Tony Meola; Casting, Stuart Howard; Amy Schecter, Mark Simon; Production Stage Manager, Thom Gates; Press, Carol Fineman Publicity; Carol R. Fineman, Leslie Baden, Meghan Zaneski. Opened in the Anspacher Theatre, April 21, 2004*

Cast

Ned Weeks **Raúl Esparza**
Craig Donner, Grady, Examining Doctor, Orderly **Paul Whitthorne**
Micky Marcus **Fred Berman**
David, Hiram Keebler, Examing Doctor, Orderly **Jay Russell**
Dr. Emma Brookner **Joanna Gleason**
Bruce Niles **Mark Dobies**
Felix Turner **Billy Warlock**
Ben Weeks **Richard Bekins**
Tommy Boatwright **McCaleb Burnett**

A play presented in two acts. Time: July 1981–May 1984. Place: Various locations in New York City.

*Still playing May 31, 2004

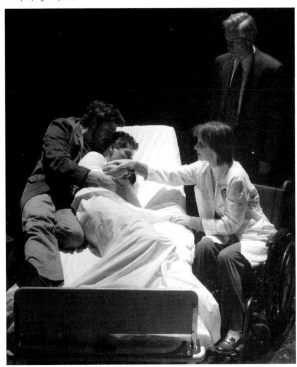

Raul Esparza, Billy Warlock, Joanna Gleason, Richard Bekins in *The Normal Heart*
PHOTO BY CAROL ROSEGG

GUINEA PIG SOLO

The Public Theatre presentation of the LAByrinth Theatre Company production of the play by Brett C. Leonard; Based on *Woyzeck* by Georg Büchner. Producer, George C. Wolfe; Executive Director, Mara Manus; Director, Ian Belton; Scenery, Andromache Chalfant; Costumes, Kaye Voyce; Lighting, Paul Whitaker; Sound, Fitz Patton; Fight Direction, David Anzuelo; Production Stage Manager, Rachel N. Facher; Press, Carol R. Fineman, Elizabeth Wehrle. Opened in the Shiva Theatre, May 9, 2004*

Cast

Linda **Kim Director**
Junior **Alexander Flores**
Doctor **Robert Glaudini**
Gary **Stephen Adly Guirgis**
John **Jason Manuel Olazabal**
José Solo **John Ortiz**
Charlie **Richard Petrocelli**
Nikki; Receptionist **Portia**
Vivian **Judy Reyes**

A play presented in two acts. Time: The present. Place: New York City.

*Still playing May 31, 2004

THE JOYS OF SEX

Musical by Melissa Levis and David Weinstein; Music by David Weinstein; Lyrics by Melissa Levis. Produced by Ben Sprecher, William P. Miller, Kenneth D. Greenblatt and Benjamin C. Singer; Director, Jeremy Dobrish; Choreography, Lisa Shriver; Scenery, Neil Patel; Costumes, David C. Woolard; Lighting, Donald Holder; Sound, T. Richard Fitzgerald; Music Direction, Steven Ray Watkins; Orchestrations and Arrangements, David Weinstein; Production Stage Manager, Katherine Lee Boyer; Press, The Publicity Office, Bob Fennell, Marc Thibodeau, Michael S. Borowski. Opened at Variety Arts Theatre, May 12, 2004*

Cast

Howard Nolton; Irving **Ron Bohmer**
Brian Shapiro; Others **David Josefsberg**
Stephs Nolton; Others **Stephanie Kurtzuba**
April Jones; Others **Jenelle Lynn Randall**

Musical Numbers: The Joy of Sex, "O" No, Cup of Sugar, Intercourse on the Internet, The First Time, One Night Stand, In the Parlor Be a Lady, Twins, In Our Fantasy, Kinks, The Vault, The Three-Way, Pandora's Box, Free the Tiger, I Need It Bad, Fantasy Come True, Not Too Nice, Making Love With You, The Joys of Sex (Reprise)

Musical presented without intermission.

*Still playing May 31, 2004

John Ortiz in *Guinea Pig Solo*   PHOTO BY CAROL ROSEGG

Jenelle Lynn Randall, Ron Bohmer, Stephanie Kurtzuba in *The Joys of Sex*

Ron Bohmer, David Josefsberg, Stephanie Kurtzuba, Jenelle Lynn Randall in *The Joys of Sex* PHOTOS BY CAROL ROSEGG

THE TWO AND ONLY

Atlantic Theatre Company production of the solo performance piece by Jay Johnson. Artistic Director, Neil Pepe; In Association with Roger Allen Gindi, Stewart F. Lane and Bonnie Comley, Dan Whitten, Herbert Goldsmith Productions, WetRock Entertainment; Director, Murphy Cross and Paul Kreppel; Scenery, Beowulf Boritt; Lighting, Clifton Taylor; Sound, David Gotwald; Music, Michael Andreas; Production Stage Manager, Lori Ann Zepp; Press, Bill Evans and Associates, Jim Randolph. Opened May 13, 2004*

Performed by Jay Johnson.

A solo performance piece presented without intermission.

*Still playing May 31, 2004

Squeaky, Jay Johnson in *The Two and Only*

Darwin, Jay Johnson in *The Two and Only*

Nevermore, Jay Johnson in *The Two and Only* PHOTOS BY CAROL ROSEGG

HERE LIES JENNY

Musical revue by Roger Rees; Produced by Maria Di Dia, Kathryn Frawley, Hugh Hayes, Martin Platt and The Zipper Theatre; Music by Kurt Weill; Lyrics by Bertolt Brecht, Roger Fernay, Ira Gershwin, Jehuda Halevi, Langston Hughes, Alan Jay Lerner, Maurice Margre, Ogden Nash, Franz Werfel, Kurt Weill; Director, Roger Rees; Choreography, Ann Reinking; Music Direction and Supervision, Leslie Stifelman; Scenery, Neil Patel; Costumes, Kay Voyce; Lighting, Frances Aronson; Sound, Tony Meola; Stage Manager, Adam Grosswith; Marketing, HHC Marketing; Press Representative, Barlow-Hartman. Opened at the Zipper Theatre, May 27, 2004 *

Cast:

Jenny **Bebe Neuwirth**
Jim **Greg Butler**
George **Shawn Emamjomeh**
John **Ed Dixon**
The Piano Player **Leslie Stifelman**

Shawn Emamjomeh, Bebe Neuwirth, Ed Dixon, Greg Butler

Bebe Neuwirth

Musical Numbers: A Boy Like You, Army Song, Barbara's Song, Berlin im Licht-Song, Bilbao Song, Children's Game, Don't Be Afraid, In meinem Garten, In our Childhood's Bright Endeavor, Je ne t'aime pas, Marterl, Oh Heavenly Salvation, Pimps Ballad, Saga of Jenny, Song of Ruth, Song of the Big Shot, Stranger Here Myself, Surabaya Johnny, Susan's Dream, The Tale of the Soldier's Wife, Youkali: Tango Habanera

Musical revue presented without intermission.

*Still playing May 31, 2004

Greg Butler, Bebe Neuwirth, Shawn Emamjomeh

Bebe Neuwirth, Greg Butler, Shawn Emamjomeh PHOTOS BY CAROL ROSEGG

Productions from past seasons that **played through this season**

DE LA GUARDA: VILLA VILLA

Created/Directed by Pichon Baldinu and Diqui James; Music/Musical Director, Gabriel Kerpel; Presented by Kevin McCollum, Jeffrey Seller, David Binder, Daryl Roth; Press, Richard Kornberg/Don Summa; Opened in the Daryl Roth Theatre on Tuesday, June 9, 1998*

Cast
Valerie Alonso
Pichon Baldinu
Gabriela Barberio
Martin Bauer
Mayra Bonard
Carlos Casella
Fabio D'Aquila
Julieta Dentone
Rafael Ferro
Ana Frenkel
Alejandro Garcia
Diqui James
Tomas James
Gabriel Kerpel
Maria Ucedo

A performance art presented (in an old bank) without intermission. "Villa Villa" translates roughly, as "by the seat of your pants."

*Still playing May 31, 2004

De La Guarda: Villa Villa

THE DONKEY SHOW

Created and Directed by Diane Paulus and Randy Weiner. Conception, Mr. Weiner; Set, Scott Pask; Costumes, David C. Woolard; Lighting, Kevin Adams; Sound, Brett Jarvis; Specialty Dances, Maria Torres; Stage Manager, Jim Atens; Press, Karpel Group/Bridget Klapinski, Brian Carmody; Judy Jacksina/Aryn DeKaye, Molly Shaffer; Presented by Jordan Roth; Opened August 10, 1999, at Club El Flamingo*

Cast
Oberon, club owner **Rachel Benbow Murdy**
Tytania, disco-diva girlfriend **Anna Wilson**
Rollerena, Puck on Roller Skates **Roman Pietrs**
Helen, in love with Dimitri **Jordin Ruderman**
Dimitri, in love with Mia **Emily Hellstrom**
Mia, beloved of Sander **Rachel Benbow Murdy**
Sander, beloved of Mia **Anna Wilson**
Vinnie 1, a rude mechanical **Jordin Ruderman**
Vinnie 2, a rude mechanical **Emily Hellstrom**
Mustard Seed, Tytania's Fairy **Oscar Estevez**
Cob Web, Tytania's Fairy **Luke Miller**
Moth, Tytania's Fairy **Dan Cryer**
Peasebottom, Tytania's Fairy **Quinn**
Rico Suave, bouncer **Orlando Santana**
Disco Lady **Barbara Resstab**
DJ Hernando Pacheski **Kevin Shand**

Musical Numbers: A Fifth of Beethoven, Also Sprach Zarathustra, Car Wash, Dance with Me, Disco Circus, Don't Leave Me This Way, I Love the Nightlife, Never Knew Love Like This Before, I'm Your Boogie Man, Knock on Wood, Ring My Bell, Salsation, That's the Way of the World, You Sexy Thing, We Are Family

A disco adaptation of Shakespeare's *A Midsummer Night's Dream* performed in a dance club.

*Still playing May 31, 2004

FORBIDDEN BROADWAY: 20TH ANNIVERSARY CELEBRATION

Created, Written and Directed by Gerard Alessandrini. Co-director, Philip George; Costumes, Alvin Colt; Set, Bradley Kaye; Musical Director/Pianist, Brad Ellis; Choreographer, Philip George; Consultant, Pete Blue; General Manager, Jay Kingwell; Stage Manager, Jim Griffith; Cast Recordings, DRG; Presented by John Freedson, Harriet Yellin, Jon B. Platt; Press, Pete Sanders/Glenna Freedman; Opened at the Douglas Fairbanks Theatre February 7, 2002*

Cast
Donna English
Michael West
Ben Evans
Valerie Fagan

Current program includes: Selections from *Mamma Mia!*, *The Producers*, *Aida*, *The Lion King*, *Chicago*, *Les Misérables*

Performed in two acts. The twentieth anniversary edition of the long-running revue which first Premiered in 1982.

*Still playing May 31, 2004

I LOVE YOU, YOU'RE PERFECT, NOW CHANGE

Music and Arrangements by Jimmy Roberts; Lyrics and Book by Joe DiPietro. Director, Joel Bishoff; Musical Director, Tom Fay; Set, Neil Peter Jampolis; Costumes, Candice Donnelly; Lighting, Mary Louise Geiger; Sound, Duncan Edwards; Cast Recording, Varese Sarabande; Production Supervisor, Matthew G. Marholin; Stage Manager, William H. Lang; Presented by James Hammerstein, Bernie Kukoff, Jonathan Pollard; Press, Bill Evans/Jim Randolph; Previewed from July 15, 1996; Opened in the Westside Theatre/Upstairs on Friday, August 1, 1996*

Cast
Jordan Leeds †1
Robert Roznowski †2
Jennifer Simard †3
Melissa Weil †4

Musical Numbers: Cantata for a First Date, Stud and a Babe, Single Man Drought, Why Cause I'm a Guy, Tear Jerk, I Will Be Loved Tonight, Hey There Single Guy/Gal, He Called Me, Wedding Vows, Always a Bridesmaid, Baby Song, Marriage Tango, On the Highway of Love, Waiting Trio, Shouldn't I Be Less in Love with You?, I Can Live with That, I Love You You're Perfect Now Change

A two-act Musical revue for hopeful heterosexuals. On January 7, 2001, the production played its 1,848th performance and became the longest running Musical revue in Off-Broadway history (besting *Jacques Brel Is Alive and Well and Living in Paris*).

Andrea Chamberlain, Marylee Graffeo, Jordan Leeds, Adam Hunter in *I Love You, You're Perfect, Now Change* PHOTO BY CAROL ROSEGG

*Still playing May 31, 2004
†Succeeded by: 1. Danny Burstein, Adam Grupper, Gary Imhoff, Adam Grupper, Jordan Leeds, Bob Walton, Jordan Leeds, Darrin Baker, Danny Burstein, Jordan Leeds 2. Kevin Pariseau, Adam Hunter, Sean Arbuckle, Frank Baiocchi, Colin Stokes 3. Erin Leigh Peck, Kelly Anne Clark, Andrea Chamberlain, Lori Hammel, Andrea Chamberlain, Amanda Watkins, Karyn Quackenbush, Marissa Burgoyne, Andrea Chamberlain, Karyn Quackenbush, Sandy Rustin, Andrea Chamberlain 4. Cheryl Stern, Mylinda Hull, Melissa Weil, Evy O'Rourke, Marylee Graffeo, Cheryl Stern, Marylee Graffeo, Janet Metz, Anne Bobby, Janet Metz

MENOPAUSE: THE MUSICAL

Book and Lyrics by Jeannie Linders. Director, Kathleen Lindsay; Sets, Jesse Poleshuck; Lighting, Michael Gilliam; Costumes, Martha Bromelmeier; Sound, Johnna Doty; Musical Direction, Corinne Aquilina; Production Stage Manager, Christine Catti; Producers, Mark Schwartz and TOC Productions; in association with Brent Peek; Press, Shirley Herz Associates; Opened at Theatre Four on April 4, 2002*

Cast
Power Woman **Joy Lynn Matthews**
Soap Star **Mary Jo McConnell** †1
Earth Mother **Joyce Presutti** †2
Iowa Housewife **Carolanne Page**

Understudies: Nancy Slusser, Wanda Houston

Orchestra: Jane Zieonka, piano, keyboard; Diana Herald, drums; Audry Perry, bass guitar

Musical presented without intermission. The action takes place in Bloomingdale's department store, in the present.

*Still playing May 31, 2004
†Succeeded by: 1. Sally Ann Swarm 2. Lynn Eldredge

Carolanne Page, Lynn Eldredge, Joy Lynn Matthews, Sally Ann Swarm in *Menopause: The Musical* PHOTOS BY JOAN MARCUS

Carolanne Page, Joy Lynn Matthews, Sally Ann Swarm, Lynn Eldredge in *Menopause: The Musical* PHOTOS BY CAROL ROSEGG

The Company of *Naked Boys Singing!* PHOTO BY JOAN MARCUS

NAKED BOYS SINGING!

By Stephen Bates, Marie Cain, Perry Hart, Shelly Markham, Jim Morgan, David Pevsner, Rayme Sciaroni, Mark Savage, Ben Schaechter, Robert Schrock, Trance Thompson, Bruce Vilanch, Mark Winkler. Conceived and Directed by Robert Schrock; Choreography, Jeffry Denman; Musical Direction/Arrangements, Stephen Bates; Set/Costumes, Carl D. White; Lighting, Aaron Copp; Stage Manager, Christine Catti; Presented by Jamie Cesa, Carl D. White, Hugh Hayes, Tom Smedes, Jennifer Dumas; Press, Peter Cromarty; Previewed from Friday, July 2, 1999; Opened in the Actors' Playhouse on Thursday, July 22, 1999*

Cast
Glenn Allen †1
Jonathan Brody †2
Tim Burke †3
Tom Gualtieri †4
Daniel C. Levine †5
Sean McNally †6
Adam Michaels †7
Trance Thompson †8

Musical Numbers: Gratuitous Nudity, Naked Maid, Bliss, Window to Window, Fight the Urge, Robert Mitchum, Jack's Song, Members Only, Perky Little Porn Star, Kris Look What You've Missed, Muscle Addiction, Nothin' but the Radio on, The Entertainer, Window to the Soul, Finale/Naked Boys Singing!

Musical revue presented in two acts.

*Still playing May 31, 2004
†Succeeded by: 1. Timothy Connell, Eric Dean Davis, Trevor Richardson 2. Richard Lear, David Macaluso, Steven Spraragen 3. Patrick Boyd, William DiPaola, Scott McLean, Kristopher Kelly, Ryan Lowe 4. Frank Galgano, Jeffrey Todd 5. Gavin Esham, George Livergood 6. Billy Briggs, Robert McGown, John Serchrist, Trevor Southworth, Cannon Starnes, Gregory D. Stockbridge, Luis Villabon 7. Patrick Herwood, Timothy John 8. Stephan Alexander, Brian M. Golub, Eric Potter

PERFECT CRIME

By Warren Manzi. Director, Jeffrey Hyatt; Set, Jay Stone, Mr. Manzi; Costumes, Nancy Bush; Lighting, Jeff Fontaine; Sound, David Lawson; Stage Manager, Julia Murphy; Presented by The Actors Collective in association with the Methuen Company; Press, Debenham Smythe/Michelle Vincents, Paul Lewis, Jeffrey Clarke; Opened in the Courtyard Playhouse on April 18, 1987*

Cast

Margaret Thorne Brent **Catherine Russell**
Inspector James Ascher **Michael Minor**
W. Harrison Brent **Don Leslie** †1
Lionel McAuley **Chris Lutkin** †2
David Breuer **Patrick Robustelli**

Understudies: Lauren Lovett (Females); J.R. Robinson (Males)

A mystery presented in two acts. The action takes place in Windsor Locks, Connecticut.

*Still playing May 31, 2004. After opening at the Courtyard Playhouse, the production transferred to the Second Stage, 47th St. Playhouse, Intar 53 Theatre, Harold Clurman Theatre, Theatre Four, and currently, The Duffy Theatre.
†Succeeded by: 1. Peter Ratray 2. Brian Hotaling

James Farrell, Catherine Russell in *Perfect Crime* PHOTO BY JOE BLY

STOMP

Created and Directed by Luke Cresswell and Steve McNicholas. Lighting, Mr. McNicholas, Neil Tiplady; Production Manager, Pete Donno; General Management, Richard Frankel/Marc Routh; Presented by Columbia Artists Management, Harriet Newman Leve, James D. Stren, Morton Wolkowitz, Schuster/Maxwell, Galin/Sandler, and Markley/Manocherian; Press, Chris Boneau/Adrian Bryan-Brown, Jackie Green, Bob Fennell; Previewed from Friday, February 18, 1994; Opened in the Orpheum Theatre on Sunday, February 27, 1994*

Cast

Taro Alexander
Morris Anthony
Maria Emilia Breyer
Marivaldo Dos Santos
Mindy Haywood
Raquel Horsford
Stephanie Marshall
Keith Middleton
Jason Mills
Mikel Paris
Raymond Poitier
Ray Rodriguez Rosa
R.J. Samson
Henry W. Shead Jr.
Mario Torres
Davi Vieira
Sheilynn Wactor
Fiona Wilkes

An evening of percussive performance art. The ensemble uses everything but conventional percussion to make rhythm and dance.

*Still playing May 31, 2004

TUBES

Created and Written by Matt Goldman, Phil Stanton, Chris Wink. Director, Marlene Swartz and Blue Man Group; Artistic Coordinator, Caryl Glaab; Artistic/Musical Collaborators, Larry Heinemann, Ian Pai; Set, Kevin Joseph Roach; Costumes, Lydia Tanji, Patricia Murphy; Lighting, Brian Aldous, Matthew McCarthy; Sound, Raymond Schilke, Jon Weston; Computer Graphics, Kurisu-Chan; Stage Manager, Lori J. Weaver; Presented by Blue Man Group; Press, Manuel Igrejas; Opened at the Astor Place Theatre on Thursday, November 7, 1991*

Cast

Matt Goldman
Phil Stanton
Chris Wink
Succeeding Cast Members: Chris Bowen, Michael Cates, Wes Day, Jeffrey Doornbos, Gen. Fermon Judd Jr., Matt Goldman, John Grady, Colin Hurd, Randall Jaynes, Michael Rahhal, Matt Ramsey, Pete Simpson, Phil Stanton, Pete Starrett, Steve White, Chris Wink

An evening of performance art presented without intermission.

*Still playing May 31, 2004.

Productions from past seasons that **closed during this season**

BARBRA'S WEDDING
Left: John Pankow, Julie White
101 performances
Opened March 5, 2003
Closed June 15, 2003
PHOTO BY JOAN MARCUS

BARTENDERS
Below: Louis Mustillo
228 performances
Opened November 22, 2002
Closed July 6, 2003
PHOTO BY STEFAN HAGEN

BOOBS! THE MUSICAL
(THE WORLD ACCORDING TO RUTH WALLIS)
Left: Rebecca Young, Bob Hunt
304 performances
Opened May 19, 2003
Closed February 8, 2004
PHOTO BY CAROL ROSEGG

CAVEDWELLER (not pictured)
30 performances
Opened May 8, 2003
Closed June 1, 2003

THE EXONERATED (not pictured)
608 performances
Opened October 10, 2002
Closed March 7, 2004

GOLDA'S BALCONY (not pictured)
116 performances
Opened March 26, 2003
Closed July 13, 2003

HANK WILLIAMS: LOST HIGHWAY (not pictured)
132 performances
Opened March 26, 2003
Closed July 20, 2003

HUMBLE BOY
Above: Jared Harris
57 performances
Opened May 18, 2003
Closed July 6, 2003
PHOTO BY JOAN MARCUS

I AM MY OWN WIFE (not pictured)
80 performances
Opened May 27, 2003
Closed August 3, 2003

THE LAST SUNDAY IN JUNE
Left: Susan Pourfar, David Turner, Donald Corren, Arnie Burton
103 performances
Opened April 9, 2003
Closed July 6, 2003
PHOTO BY ROBERT CAREY

OUR LADY OF 121ST STREET

Left: Melissa Feldman,
Portia, Liza Colón-Zayas
166 performances
Opened March 6, 2003
Closed July 27, 2003
PHOTO BY JOAN MARCUS

TALKING HEADS

Below: Kathleen Chalfant
177 performances
Opened April 6, 2003
Closed September 7, 2003
PHOTO BY CAROL ROSEGG

TEA AT FIVE

Left: Kate Mulgrew
127 performances
Opened March 9, 2003
Closed July 13, 2003
PHOTO BY CAROL ROSEGG

WRITER'S BLOCK
Left: Skip Sudduth, Paul Reiser
54 performances
Opened May 15, 2003
Closed June 6, 2003
PHOTO BY CAROL ROSEGG

I AM MY OWN WIFE (not pictured)
80 performances
Opened May 27, 2003
Closed August 3, 2003

ZANNA, DON'T
Right: The Company
112 performances
Opened March 20, 2003
Closed June 29, 2003
PHOTO BY JOAN MARCUS

Company Series

ABINGDON THEATRE COMPANY

ELEVENTH SEASON

Jan Buttram and Pamela Paul; Co-Artistic Directors; Samuel Bellinger, Managing Director

BEYOND RECOGNITION by John Petrick. Director, Kate Bushmann; Scenery, Michael Schweikart; Costumes, Ingrid Maurer; Lighting, David Castaneda; Fight Director, Rick Sordelet; Stage Manager, Olivia Tsang; Production Manager; Peter Brouwer; Cast: Christopher Burns (Andrew), Michael Goduti (Josh), David Valcin (Mark), Grant James Vargas (Kevin)

A play presented in two acts; June Havoc Theatre; October 17–November 9, 2003; 24 performances

THE PAGANS by Ann Noble. Director, Stephen Hollis; Scenery, James Wolk; Costumes, Wade Laboissonniere; Lighting, David Castaneda; Fight Director, Rick Sordelet; Props, Shannon Flynn; Technical Director, Peter Brouwer; Stage Manager, Olivia Tsang; Production Manager, Kim Sharp; Cast: Victoria Adams (Anna Leigh), Mark Alhadeff (Bobby Quinn), Frank Anderson (Thomas Riordan), Nora Chester (Margaret Riordan), Christopher Drescher (Tadhg Riordan), Rachel Fowler (Danaan O'Doherty), Susanne Marley (Frances Dorcey), Steven Rishard (Michael Riordan),

A play presented in two acts; June Havoc Theatre; March 3–21, 2004; 24 performances

Michael Goduti in *Beyond Recognition* PHOTO BY KIM T. SHARP

Mark Alhadeff, Steven Rishard in *The Pagans* PHOTO BY CAROL ROSEGG

ATLANTIC THEATRE COMPANY

NINETEENTH SEASON

Neil Pepe, Artistic Director

THE NIGHT HERON by Jez Butterworth. Director, Neil Pepe; Scenery, Walt Spangler; Costumes, Laura Bauer; Lighting, Tyler Micoleau; Sound, Scott Myers; Production Stage Manager, Darcy Stephens; Production Manager, Kurt Gardner; General Manager; Ryan Freeman; Press Representative, Boneau/Bryan-Brown—Chris Boneau, Susanne Tighe and Joe Perrotta; Cast: Chris Bauer (Wattmore), Clark Gregg (Griffin), Mary McCann (Bolla), Damian Young (Neddy), Jordan Lange (Royce), Joe Stipek (Boy), Jim Frangione (Dougal)

A play presented in two acts; October 7—November 9, 2003; 56 performances

Clark Gregg, Chris Bauer, Mary McCann in *The Night Heron* PHOTO BY CAROL ROSEGG

FRAME 312 by Keith Reddin. Director, Karen Kohlhaas; Scenery, Walt Spangler; Costumes, Mimi O'Donnell; Lighting, Robert Perry; Sound, Scott Myers; Production Stage Manager, Amy Patricia Stern; Production Manager, Kurt Gardner; Dramaturg, Christian Parker; Casting, Bernard Telsey Casting; Press, Boneau/Bryan-Brown—Chris Boneau, Susanne Tighe and Joe Perrotta; Cast: Mary Beth Peil (Lynette), Larry Bryggman (Graham), Maggie Kiley (Margie/Marie/Doris), Ana Reeder (Stephanie), Mandy Siegfried (Lynette circa 1960), Greg Stuhr (Tom/Roy/Agent Barry, Conductor)

A play presented in two acts; December 11, 2003–January 11, 2004; 48 performances

Mandy Siegfried, Larry Bryggman in *Frame 312*

SEA OF TRANQUILITY by Howard Korder. Director, Neil Pepe; Scenery, Santo Loquasto; Costumes, Kaye Voyce; Lighting, David Weiner; Sound, Scott Myers; Original Music, David Yazbek; Fight Director, Rick Sordelet; Production Stage Manager, Janet Takami; Production Manager, Kurt Gardner; General Manager, Melinda Berk; Casting, Bernard Telsey Casting; Press, Boneau/Bryan-Brown- Chris Boneau, Susanne Tighe and Joe Perrotta; Cast: Dylan Baker (Ben), Patricia Kalember (Nessa), Betsy Aidem (Phyllis), Heidi Armbruster (Astarte), Liz Elkins (Kat), Jason Fuchs (Josh), Jordan Lange (Barry/Johanssen), Lizbeth Mackay (Adele/Ashley)

A play presented in two acts; February 25–March 28, 2004; 56 performances

Greg Stuhr, Larry Bryggman, Mandy Siegfried in *Frame 312* PHOTOS BY CAROL ROSEGG

Patricia Kalember, Dylan Baker in *Sea of Tranquility* PHOTO BY CAROL ROSEGG

BROOKLYN ACADEMY OF MUSIC

FOUNDED IN 1861

Alan H. Fishman, Chairman of the Board; Karen Brooks Hopkins, President; Joseph V. Melillo, Executive Producer

Jonas Malmsjö, Pernilla August, Jan Malmsjö in *Ghosts* PHOTO BY STEPHANIE BERGER

GHOSTS by Henrik Ibsen, presented by the Royal Dramatic Theatre of Sweden; translated and adapted by Ingmar Bergman. Director, Ingmar Bergman; Scenery, Göran Wassberg; Costumes, Anna Bergman; Lighting, Pierre Leveau; Press, Sandy Sawotka; Melissa Cusick, Fatima Kafele, Tamara McCaw, Kila Packett; Cast: Pernilla August (Mrs. Helene Aliving), Jonas Malmsjö (Osvald Alving), Jan Malmsjö (Pastor Manders), Örjan Ramberg (Jacob Engstrand), Angela Kovacs (Regine Engstrand)

Revival of a play presented in two acts; Harvey Theatre; June 10–14, 2003; 5 performances

PERICLES by William Shakespeare, presented by Theatre for a New Audience. Director, Bartlett Sher; Scenery and Lighting, Christopher Akerlind; Costumes, Elizabeth Caitlin Ward; Sound and Music, Peter John Still; Dramaturg, Ben Nadler; Production Stage Manager, Judith Schoenfeld; Press, Sandy Sawotka, Fatima Kafele, Eva Chien, Tamara McCaw, Jennifer Lam; Cast: Brenda White (Gower, Lychorida), Christopher McCann (Antiochus, Pericles); Tim Hopper (Pericles, Lysimachus), Julyana Soelistyo (Daughter of Antiochus, Marina), Graham Winton (Thaliard,

Julyano Soelistyo, Christopher McCann, Tim Hopper in *Pericles* PHOTO BY RICHARD TERMINE

Leonine), Philip Goodwin (Helicanus, Cerimon), Robert LuPone (Cleon, Pandar), Kristine Nielsen (Dionyza, Bawd), Andrew Weems (Simonides, Boult), Linda Powell (Thais), Ensemble: Glenn Flesher, Bruce Turk, Albert Jones, Paul Niebanck

Revival of a play presented in two acts; Harvey Theatre; February 17–22, 2004; 10 performances

A MIDSUMMER NIGHT'S DREAM by William Shakespeare, presented by the Watermill Theatre/Propeller Theatre. Director, Edward Hall; Scenery and Costumes, Michael Pavelka; Lighting, Ben Ormerod; Music, Tony Bell, Dugald Bruce-Lockhart, Jules Werner; Dramaturg, Roger Warren; Press, Sandy Sawotka, Fatima Kafele, Eva Chien, Tamara McCaw, Jennifer Lam; Cast: Tony Bell (Bottom), Dugald Bruce-Lockhart (Lysander), Sam Callis (Titania), Alasdair Giles (Fairy), Robert Hands (Helena), Barnaby Kay (Oberon), Vincent Leigh (Demetrius, Snout), Jonathan McGuinness (Hermia, Snug), Chris Myles (Quince, Egeus), Simon Scardifield (Puck, Starveling), Jules Werner (Flute)

Revival of a play presented in two acts; Harvey Theatre; March 16–28, 2004; 14 performances

Simon Scardifield, Barnaby Kay in *A Midsummer Night's Dream* PHOTO BY RICHARD TERMINE

HOMEBODY/KABUL by Tony Kushner, presented by the Steppenwolf Theatre Company and Center Theatre Group/Mark Taper Forum. Director, Fran Galati; Scenery, James Schuette; Costumes, Mara Blumenfeld; Lighting, Christopher Akerlind; Sound and Music, Joe Cerqua; Fight Direction, Thomas Schall; Assistant Director, Kappy Kilburn; Casting, Amy Lieberman, Erica Daniels; Press, Sandy Sawotka, Fatima Kafele, Eva Chien, Tamara McCaw, Jennifer Lam; Cast: Linda Edmond (The Homebody), Ali Reza (Dr. Quri Shah), Aasif Mandvi (Mullah Ali Aftar Durranni), Reed Birney (Milton Ceiling), Maggie Gyllenhaal (Priscilla Ceiling), Bill Camp (Quang Twistleton), Rahul Gupta (Munkrat, Border Guard), Firdous Bamji (Khwaja Aziz Mondanabosh), Dariush Kashani (Zai Garshi), Rita Wolf (Woman in Burqa, Mahala); Ensemble: Rod Gnapp, Laura Kachergus, Kamal Maray, Arian Moayed, Michelle Morain, Diana Simonzadeh

Revival of a play presented in three acts; Harvey Theatre; May 11–30, 2004; 21 performances

CITY CENTER ENCORES!

ELEVENTH SEASON

Judith E. Daykin, President and Executive Director, Jack Viertel, Artistic Director

CAN-CAN Book by Abe Burrows; Music and Lyrics by Cole Porter; Concert Adaptation by David Lee. Director, Lonny Price; Choreography, Melinda Roy; Scenery, John Lee Beatty; Costumes, Toni-Leslie James; Lighting, Kenneth Posner; Sound, Scott Lehrer; Music Director, Michael Kosarin; Casting, Jay Binder; Production Stage Manager, Jeffrey M. Markowitz; Press, Barlow-Hartman Public Relations, John Barlow, Bill Coyle; Cast: Patti LuPone (La Mome Pistache), Michael Nouri (Judge Aristide Forestier), Reg Rogers (Boris Adzinidzinadze), Charlotte d'Amboise (Claudine), Paul Schoeffler (Hilaire Jussac), Caitlin Carter (Celestine), David Constabile (Theophile), Michael Goldstrom (Etienne), David Hibbard (Hercule), Mary Ann Lamb (Marie), Solange Sandy (Gabrielle), Robert Wersinger (Apache Dancer), Eli Wallach (Judge Paul Barriere)

A concert version of the Musical presented in two acts; City Center; February 12–15, 2004; 5 performances

PARDON MY ENGLISH Book by Herbert Fields and Morrie Ryskind; Music by George Gershwin; Lyrics by Ira Gershwin; Adapted by David Ives. Director, Gary Griffin; Choreography, Rob Ashford; Scenery, John Lee Beatty; Costumes, Martin Pakledinaz; Lighting, Ken Billington; Sound, Scott Lehrer; Production Stage Manager, Karen Moore; Cast: Brian d'Arcy James (Golo Schmidt, Michael Bramleigh), Emily Skinner (Gita Gobel), Jennifer Laura Thompson (Frieda Bauer), Rob Bartlett (Herman Bauer), Don Stephenson (Dickie Carter), Tom Alan Robbins (Dr. Adolph Steiner), Felicia Finley (Magda), Kein Carolan (Sergeant Schultz), Lee Zarrett (Katz)

A concert version of the Musical presented in two acts; City Center; March 25–28, 2004; 5 performances

Patti LuPone, Michael Nouri in *Can-Can* PHOTO BY JOAN MARCUS

William Robert Gaynor and the Company in *Bye Bye Birdie* PHOTO BY JOAN MARCUS

BYE BYE BIRDIE Book by Michael Stewart; Music by Charles Strouse; Lyrics by Lee Adams. Director, Jerry Zaks; Choreography, Casey Nicholaw; Scenery, John Lee Beatty; Costumes, William Ivey Long; Lighting, Ken Billington; Sound, Peter Fitzgerald; Casting, Jay Binder; Production Stage Manager, Karen Moore; Press, Barlow-Hartman Public Relations, John Barlow, Bill Coyle, Andrew Snyder; Cast: Karen Ziemba (Rosie Alvarez), Daniel Jenkins (Albert Peterson), William Robert Gaynor (Conrad Birdie), Walter Bobbie (Mr. MacAfee), Doris Roberts (Mae Peterson), Keith Nobbs (Hugo Peabody), Jessica Grové (Kim Macafee), Victoria Clark (Mrs. MacAfee), William Ullrich (Randolph MacAfee)

A concert version of the Musical presented in two acts; City Center; May 6–10, 2004; 5 performances

Emily Skinner, Brian d'Arcy James in *Pardon My English* PHOTO BY JOAN MARCUS

CLASSIC STAGE COMPANY

THIRTY-SIXTH SEASON

Barry Edelstein and Brian Kulick, Artistic Directors, Anne Tanaka, Producing Director

SAVANNAH BAY by Marguerite Duras; translated by Barbara Bray. Director, Les Waters; Scenery, Myung Hee Cho; Costumes, Ilona Somogyi; Lighting, Robert Wierzel; Sound, Darron L. West; General Manager, Reed Ridgely; Production Stage Manager, Rachel J. Perlman; Production Manager, Ian Tresselt; General Manager, Lisa Barnes; Casting, Vince Liebhart/Tom Alberg; Press Representative, The Publicity Office; Cast: Kathleen Chalfant (Madeleine), Marin Ireland (Young Woman)

A play presented in two acts; June 11–29, 2003; 33 performances

RATTHE FIRST LOOK FESTIVAL OCTOBER 1–12, 2003

THE JEW OF MALTA by Christopher Marlowe; Director, Brian Kulick; Cast: Ron Liebman; October 1, 2003

ARDEN OF FAVERSHAM by Anonymous; Director, Erica Schmidt; Cast: Frances McDormand; October 3, 2003

VOLPONE by Ben Jonson; Director, Michael Sexton; Cast: F. Murray Abraham; October 8, 2003

RICHARD III by William Shakespeare; Director, Barry Edelstein; Cast: John Turturro, Julianna Margulies; Lynn Cohen; Brian Keane; Ronald Guttman; Peter Jacobson; Daniel Oreskes; James Joseph O'Neill; Phyllis Somerville, Stephen Barker Turner; October 10–12, 2003

One night only staged reading and workshop productions of rarely seen classics

THE MYSTERIES adapted by Dario Fo, Mikhail Bulgakov, Tony Harrison and Borislav Pekic from the Wakefield and York Cycles. Director, Brian Kulick; Scenery, Mark Wendland; Costumes, Mattie Ulrich; Lighting, Kevin Adams; Sound, Darron L. West; Casting, James Calleri and Alaine Alldaffer; Production Stage Manager, Gillian Duncan; Production Manager, B.D. White; General Manager, Lisa Barnes; Press Representative, The Publicity Office; Cast: Bill Buell, Mario Campanaro, Michael Potts, Carme Roman, John Rothman, Jennifer Roszell, Michael Stuhlbarg, Sam Tsoutsouvas, Chandler Williams

A play presented in two acts; January 22–February 15, 2004; 40 performances

ANTIGONE: AS PLAYED & DANCED BY THREE FATES ON THE WAY TO BECOMING THREE GRACES by Mac Wellman; Produced in conjunction with Big Dance Theatre. Director, Paul Lazar; Choreography and Musical Staging, Annie-B Parson; Music, Cynthia Hopkins; Scenery, Joanne Howard; Costumes, Claudia Stephens; Lighting, Jay Ryan; Sound, Jane Shaw and Annie-B Parson; General Manager, Lisa Barnes; Press Representative, The Publicity Office; Cast: Nancy Ellis, Molly Hickok; Leroy Logan, Dierdre O'Connell, Rebecca Wisocky

A play with dance and Music presented in two acts; Classic Stage Company; May 2–23, 2004; 26 performances

Kathleen Chalfant, Marin Ireland in *Savannah Bay* PHOTO BY DIXIE SHERIDAN

Michael Potts, Mario Campanaro in *The Mysteries* PHOTO BY DIXIE SHERIDAN

IRISH REPERTORY THEATRE

SIXTEENTH SEASON

Ciarán O'Reilly, Producing Director; Charlotte Moore, Artistic Director

THE COLLEEN BAWN by Dion Boucicault. Director, Charlotte Moore; Scenery, James Morgan; Costumes, Linda Fisher; Lighting, Brian Nason; Sound, Zachary Williamson; Press, Barlow-Harman; Cast: Paul Vincent Black (Myles-na-Coppaleen), James Cleveland (Fiddler), Terry Donnelly (Sheelah), Laura James Flynn (Anne Chute), George Heslin (Kyrle Daly), John Keating (Father Tom), Colin Lane (Mr. Corrigan), Declan Mooney (Kyrle Daly), Heather O'Neill (Eily O'Connor), Ciaran O'Reilly (Danny Mann), Caroline Winterson (Mrs. Corrigan)

A play presented in two acts; October 19–November 30, December 17–28, 2003; 62 performances

Declan Mooney, Laura James Flynn in *The Colleen Bawn* PHOTO BY CAROL ROSEGG

CHRISTMAS WITH TOMMY MAKEM Director, Charlotte Moore; December 4, 2003; Cast: Tommy Makem, Rory Makem

A performance of holiday songs, dances, and poems; December 4–28, 2003; 14 performances

EDEN by Eugene O'Brien. Director, John Tillinger; Scenery and Costumes, Klara Zieglerova; Lighting, Howell Binkley; Production Stage Mananger, Colette Morris; Cast: Ciarán O'Reilly (Billy), Catherine Byrne (Breeda)

A play presented in two acts; February 1–March 21, 2004; 72 performances

Melissa Errico, Malcom Gets in *Finian's Rainbow* PHOTO BY CAROL ROSEGG

FINIAN'S RAINBOW Musical with Book by E.Y. Harburg and Fred Saidy; Music by Burton Lane; Lyrics by E.Y. Harburg; Adapted by Charlotte Moore. Director, Charlotte Moore; Choreography, Barry McNabb, Music Director/Orchestrations/Vocal Arrangements, Mark Hartman; Associate Musical Director, Mark Janas; Scenery, James Morgan; Costumes, David Toser; Lighting, Mary Jo Dondlinger; Production Stage Manager, Jennifer O'Byrne; Stage Manager, Pamela Brusoski; Press, Shirley Herz Associates, Shirley Herz and Val Sherman; Cast: Mark Aldrich (Buzz Collins/Company), Melissa Errico* (Sharon McLonergan), Jonathan Freeman (Finian McLonergan), Malcolm Gets** (Og, a leprechaun), Jonathan Hadley (Sheriff/Mr. Shears/Company), Eric Jackson (Howard/Gospeleer/Company), Jayne Ackley Lynch (Company), Kimberly Dawn Neumann (Susan Mahoney), John Sloman (Senator Rawkins), David Staller (Narrator/Mr Robust), Joacquin Stevens (Henry/Gospeleer/Company), Max von Essen*** (Woody Mahoney), Terri White (Maid/Gospeleer/Company)

*Replaced by Kerry O'Malley May 11
**Replaced by Chad Kimball June 1, 2004
***Replaced by Kevin Kern June 8, 2004

Musical presented in two acts; Irish Repertory Theatre Mainstage; April 15–July 11, 2004; 106 performances

Catherine Byrne in *Eden* PHOTO BY CAROL ROSEGG

JEAN COCTEAU REPERTORY

THIRTY-THIRD SEASON

David Fuller, Producing Artistic Director

THE THREEPENNY OPERA Musical with Book and Lyrics by Bertolt Brecht; Music by Kurt Weill; Adapted by Marc Blitzstein. Director, David Fuller; Musical Director, Charles Berigan; Scenery, Roman Tatarowicz; Costumes, Joanne Haas; Lighting, Giles Hogya; Stage Manager, Allen Hale; Press, David J. Gersten; Cast: Natalie Ballesteros (Lucy Brown), Harris Berlinsky (Reverend Kimball/Smith the Constable), Danny Dempsey (Readymoney Matt), Eileen Glenn (Molly), Abe Goldfarb (Tiger Brown), Angus Hepburn (J.J. Peachum), Kate Holland (Betty), Brian Lee Huynh (Crookfinger Jake), Marlene May (Mrs. Peachum), Sara Mayer (Coaxer), Timothy McDonough (Walt Dreary), Joey Piscopo (Filch), Elise Stone (Jenny), Amy Lee Williams (Polly Peachum), Chad A. Suitts (Macheath)

Musical presented in two acts; Bouwerie Lane Theatre; September 7–November 23, 2003; 46 performances

Elise Stone in *Lysistrata* PHOTO BY GERRY GOODSTEIN

LYSISTRATA by Aristophanes; Conceived, Translated and Adapted by David Lee Jiranek. Director, David Fuller; Original Music and Sound, Guy Sherman; Scenery, James Wolk; Costumes, Margaret McKowen; Lighting, David Kniep; Sound, Aural Fixation; Production Stage Manager, Allison Smith; Press, David J. Gersten; Cast: Elise Stone (Lysistrata), Eileen Glenn (Calonice), Amanda Jones (Myrrhine), Marlene May (Scythianess#1/Nicodice), Carolyn Ratteray (Scythianess#2/Stratyllis), Jolie Garrett (Lampito/Spartan Herald/Reconciliaiton), Brian Lee Huynh (Boeotia/Scythian #2), Allen Hale (Corinthia/Spartan Ambassador), Angus Hepburn (Strymodorus), Michael Surabian (Philurgus), Harris Berlinsky (Probolous), Abe Goldfarb (Sycthian #1/Cinesias)

A play presented in two acts; Bouwerie Lane Theatre; October 24, 2003–February 5, 2004; 41 performances

(CONTINUED ON NEXT PAGE)

Chad A. Suitts in *The Threepenny Opera* PHOTO BY GERRY GOODSTEIN

(CONTINUED FROM PREVIOUS PAGE)

DONA ROSITA THE SPINSTER by Frederico Garcia Lorca; Adapted by Gwynne Edwards. Director, Ernest Johns; Scenery, Roman Tatarowicz; Costumes, Margaret McKowen; Lighting, David Kniep; Sound and Music, Charles Berigan; Choreographer, Schellie Archbold; Production Stage Manager, Amanda Kadrmas; Press, David Gersten; Cast: Craig Smith (Uncle), Eileen Glenn (Housekeeper), Elise Stone (Aunt), Amanda Jones (Dona Rosita), Danaher Dempsey (Nephew/Workman), Amy Lee Williams (Manola/1st Ayola), Sara Mayer (Manola/2nd Spinster), Carolyn Ratteray (Manola/2nd Ayola), Natalie Ballesteros (1st Spinster), Marlene May (Mother of Spinsters), Michael Surabian (Mr. X/Don Martin), Timothy McDonough (Youth)

A play presented in two acts; Bouwerie Lane Theatre; December 19–April 4, 2004; 35 performances

THE WILD DUCK by Henrik Ibsen; Translated by Rolf Fjelde. Director, Eve Adamson; Scenery, Robert Klingelhoefer; Costumes, Margaret McKowen and Joel Ebarb; Lighting, Eve Adamson; Sound and Music, Ellen Mandel; Production Stage Manager, Dan Zisson; Press, David Gersten; Cast: Bill

Amanda Jones, Danaher Dempsey in *Dona Rosita The Spinster* PHOTO BY JOSHUA JOHN FRACHISEUR

Bairbairn (Haakon Werle), Chad Suitts (Gregors Werle), Eileen Glenn (Mrs. Sorby), Tim Morton (Lieutenant Ekdal), Michael Surabian (Hjalmar Ekdal), Angela Madden (Gina Ekdal), Erin Scanlon (Hedvig), Harris Berlinsky (Doctor Relling/Guest), Danaher Dempsey (Molvik/Guest), Dan Zisson (Guest), Sara Jeanne Asselin (Servant), Allen Hale (Servant)

A play presented in two acts, Bouwerie Lane Theatre, February 29–May 20, 2004; 36 performances

THE BOURGEOIS GENTLEMAN by Molière; translated by Rod McLucas. Director, Rod McLucas; Scenery, Robert Martin; Costumes, Robin I. Shane; Lighting, Wendy Luedtke; Music, Raphael Crystal; Production Stage Manager, Alison Smith; Press, David Gersten; Cast: Sara Jeanne Asselin (The Troupe), Natalie Ballesteros (The Troupe), Pascal Beauboeuf (Cleonte), Danaher Dempsey (Coviello), Bill Fairbairn (Dorante), Allen Hale (The Troupe), Kristina Klebe (Dorimene), Marlene May (Madame Jourdan), Sara Mayer (Lucile), Timothy McDonough (The Troupe), Ralph Petrarca (The Troupe), Carolyn Ratteray (The Maid), Lindsey White (The Troupe), Angus Hepburn (Mousieur Jourdan)

A play presented in two acts, Bouwerie Lane Theatre; April 25–June 6, 2004; 33 performances

Kristina Klebe, Marlene May, Angus Hepburn in *The Bourgeois Gentleman*
PHOTO BY GERRY GOODSTEIN

Jan Maxwell, Kala Savage, Jonathan Hadary in *A Bad Friend* PHOTO BY JOAN MARCUS

Warona Seane, John Kani, Esmeralda Bihl in *Nothing But the Truth* PHOTO BY PAUL KOLNIK

LINCOLN CENTER THEATRE

NINETEENTH SEASON

André Bishop, Artistic Director; Bernard Gersten, Executive Producer

A BAD FRIEND by Jules Feiffer; Director, Jerry Zaks; Scenery, Douglas Stein; Costumes, William Ivey Long; Lighting, Paul Gallo; Sound, Aural Fixation; Projections, Jan Hartley; Casting, Daniel Swee; Stage Manager, Thom Widmann; Press, Philip Rinaldi Publicity, Philip Rinaldi, Barbara Carroll; Cast: Mark Feuerstein (Uncle Morty), Kala Savage (Rose), Larry Bryggman (Emil), Jan Maxwell (Naomi), Jonathan Hadary (Shelly), David Harbour (Fallon), Peter Rini (Radio Voice); Understudies: Peter Rini (Uncle Monty, Fallon), Terry Layman (Emil, Shelly), Blyth Auffarth (Rose), Shelley Williams (Naomi)

A play presented in two acts; Mitzi E. Newhouse Theatre; June 9–July 27, 2003; 56 performances

NOTHING BUT THE TRUTH by John Kani; Director, Janice Honeyman; Scenery and Costumes, Sarah Roberts; Lighting, Mannie Manim; Stage Manager, Thom Widmann; Press, Philip Rinaldi Publicity, Philip Rinaldi, Barbara Carroll; Cast: Esmeralda Bihl (Mandisa MacKay), John Kani (Sipho Makhaya), Warona Seane (Thando Makhaya)

A play presented in two acts; Mitzi E. Newhouse; December 7, 2003–January 18, 2004; 48 performances

BIG BILL by A.R. Gurney; Director, Mark Lamos; Scenery, John Lee Beatty; Costumes, Jess Goldstein; Lighting, Rui Rita; Sound, Scott Stauffer; Stage Manager, Fredric H. Orner; Casting, Cindy Tolan and Daniel Swee; Press, Philip Rinaldi, Barbara Carroll; Cast: John Michael Higgins (William T. Tilden II), David Cromwell (Umpire, Judge, Others), Steven Rowe (Herb, Maddox, Others), Margaret Welsh (Mary Garden, Suzanne Lenglen, Others), Alex Knold (Student, Ball Boy, Others), Michael Esper (Pete, Ball Boy, Others), Donal Thoms-Cappello (Jimmy, Ball Boy, Others), Jeremiah Miller (Arthur, Ball Boy, Others); Understudies: Jack Koenig (William T. Tilden II), Michael Hammond (Umpire, Judge, Herb, Maddox, Others), Wendy Rich Stetson, Mercedes Herrero (Mary Garden, Suzanne Lenglen, Others), Gideon Banner (Student, Pete, Jimmy, Arthur, Ball Boy, Others), Donal Thoms-Cappello (Student), Jeremiah Miller (Pete), Michael Esper (Jimmy), Alex Knold (Arthur)

A play presented without intermission; Mitzi E. Newhouse; February 22–March 16, 2004; 97 performances

MCC THEATRE

EIGHTEENTH SEASON

Robert LuPone and Bernard Telsey, Artistic Directors; William Cantler, Associate Artistic Director; John Schultz, Executive Director

INTRIGUE WITH FAYE by Kate Robin; Director, Jim Simpson; Scenery, Riccardo Hernandez; Costumes, Fabio Toblini; Lighting, Robert Wierzel; Sound and Original Music, Fabian Obispo; Video Design, Dennis Diamond; Director of Photography, Tom Houghton; Production Stage Manager, Stacy P. Hughes; Production Manager, B.D. White; Casting, Bernard Telsey Casting; Press, Boneau/Bryan-Brown-Chris Boneau and Adriana Douzos; Cast: Julianna Margulies (Lissa); Benjamin Bratt (Kean); video appearances by Michael Gaston (Male Client), Craig Bierko (Frank), Jenna Lamia (Tina), Gretchen Mol (Faye), Swoosie Kurtz (Woman), Tom Noonan (Man)

A play presented in two acts, Acorn Theatre, June 11–July 16, 2003; 56 performances

Seana Kofoed, Paul Fitzgerald in *Bright Ideas* PHOTO BY DIXIE SHERIDAN

BRIGHT IDEAS by Eric Coble; Director, John Rando; Scenery, Rob Odorisio; Costumes, Gregory Gale; Lighting, James Vermeulen; Hair and Wigs, Darlene Dannenfelser; Sound and Original Music, Fabian Obispo; Fight Direction, Rick Sordelet; Production Stage Manager, Anna Saggesse; Production Manager, B.D. White; Casting, Bernard Tesley Casting; Press, Boneau/Bryan-Brown-Chris Boneau and Adriana Douzos; Cast: Orlagh Cassidy (Denise/Cate/Miss Caithness/Mom #2/Ms. Malcolm); Colman Domingo (Ross/Steward/Mr. Angus/Bix), Paul Fitzgerald (Joshua Bradley), Seana Kofoed (Genevra Bradley), Linda Marie Larson (Lynzie/Mrs. Heath/Mrs. Menteith/Mrs. Lenox/Mom #1)

A play presented in two acts; East 13th Street Theatre; November 12–December 7, 2003; 48 performances

FROZEN by Bryony Lavery; Director, Doug Hughes; Scenery, Hugh Landwehr; Costumes, Catherine Zuber; Lighting, Clifton Taylor; Music and Sound, David Van Tieghem; Fight Direction, Rick Sordelet; Dialect Coach, Stephen Gabis; Production Stage Manager, James FitzSimmons; Production

Benjamin Bratt, Julianna Margulies in *Intrigue with Faye* PHOTO BY DIXIE SHERIDAN

Manager, B.D. White; Casting, Bernard Telsey Casting; Press, Boneau/Bryan-Brown-Chris Boneau and Adriana Douzos; Cast: Swoozie Kurtz (Nancy), Brían F. O'Byrne (Ralph), Laila Robins (Agnetha), Sam Kitchin (Guard)

A play presented in two acts; East 13th Street Theatre; March 18–April 10, 2004; 49 performances. Transferred to Broadway April 28th, opened May 4 at Circle in the Square. (See *Broadway Productions That Opened This Season* in this volume)

THE DISTANCE FROM HERE by Neil LaBute; Director, Michael Greif; Scenery, Louisa Thompson; Costumes, Angela Wendt; Lighting, JamesVermuelen; Additional Music and Sound, Robert Kaplowitz; Fight Direction, Rick Sordelet; General Manager, Barbara L. Auld; Production Stage Manager, Joel Rosen; Production Manager, B.D. White; Casting, Bernard Telsey Casting; Press, Boneau/Bryan-Brown-Chris Boneau and Adriana Douzos; Cast: Amelia Alvarez (Girl), Ian Brennan (Employee/Boy), Josh Charles (Rich), Melissa Leo (Cammie), Logan Marshall-Green (Tim), Anna Paquin (Shari), Alison Pill (Jenn), Mark Webber (Darrell)

A play presented in two acts; The Duke Theatre on 42nd Street; May 6–June 5, 2004; 53 performances

Mark Webber, Logan Marshall-Green in *The Distance From Here* PHOTO BY DIXIE SHERIDAN

MANHATTAN THEATRE CLUB

THIRTY-SECOND SEASON

Lynne Meadow, Artistic Director; Barry Grove, Executive Producer

LAST DANCE By Marsha Norman; Director, Lynne Meadow; Scenery, Loy Arcenas; Costumes, Ann Roth; Lighting, Duane Schuler; Sound, Bruce Ellman; Music, Jason Robert Brown; Casting, David Caparelliotis, Nancy Piccione; Production Stage Manager, James FitzSimmons; Press, Boneau/Bryan-Brown, Chris Boneau, Jim Byk, Aaron Meier; Cast: Heather Goldenhersh (Georgeanne), Lorenzo Pisoni (Cab), David Rashe (Randall), JoBeth Williams (Charotte)

A play presented without intermission; City Center Stage II; June 3–July 6, 2003; 40 performances

Susan Pourfar, Jennifer Dundas, Lisa Emery, John Curless in *Iron* PHOTO BY JOAN MARCUS

IRON By Rona Munro; Director, Anna D. Shapiro; Scenery and Costumes, Mark Wendland; Lighting, Kevin Adams; Sound, Bruce Ellman; Casting, David Caparelliotis, Nancy Piccione; Production Stage Manager, Alex Lyu Volckhausen; Press, Boneau/Bryan-Brown, Chris Boneau, Jim Byk, Aaron Meier; Cast: John Curless (Guard 1), Jennifer Dundas (Josie), Lisa Emery (Fay), Susan Pourfar (Guard 2)

A play presented in two acts; City Center Stage II; October 21–December 28, 2003; 80 performances

ROSE'S DILEMMA By Neil Simon; Director, Lynne Meadow; Scenery, Thomas Lynch; Costumes, William Ivey Long; Lighting, Pat Collins; Sound, Bruce Ellman; Wigs, Paul Huntley; Production Stage Manager, Robert Witherow; Press, Boneau/Bryan-Brown, Chris Boneau, Jim Byk, Aaron Meier; Cast: Patricia Hodges (Rose Steiner), David Aaron Baker (Gavin Clancy), Geneva Carr (Arlene Moss), John Cullum (Walsh McLaren)

A play presented in two acts; City Center Stage I; December 18, 2003–February 1, 2004; 54 performances

J. Smith-Cameron, Richard Masur, Andrew Katz in *Sarah, Sarah* PHOTO BY JOAN MARCUS

SARAH, SARAH By Daniel Goldfarb; Director, Mark Nelson; Scenery, James Noone; Costumes, Michael Krass; Lighting, Howell Binkley; Sound and Music, Scott Killian; Production Stage Manager, Jennifer Rae Moore; Stage Manager, Julie C. Miller; Press, Boneau/Bryan-Brown, Chris Boneau, Jim Byk, Aaron Meier; Cast: Andrew Katz (Arthur "Artie" Grosberg, Miles), Richard Masur (Vicent, Arthur Grosberg), Lori Prince (Rochelle Bloom, Maggie), J. Smith-Cameron (Sarah Grosberg, Jeannie Grosberg)

City Center Stage II; March 30, 2004; 72 performances

BETWEEN US By Joe Hortua; Director, Christopher Ashley; Scenery, Neil Patel; Costumes, Jess Goldstein; Lighting, Christopher Akerlind; Sound, Darron L. West; Casting, Nancy Piccione, David Caparelliotis; Production Stage Manager, Kelley Kirkpatrick; Stage Manager, Robyn Henry; Press, Boneau/Bryan-Brown, Chris Boneau, Jim Byk, Aaron Meier; Cast: Kate Jennings Grant (Sharyl), David Harbour (Joel), Daphne Rubin-Vega (Grace), Bradley White (Carlo); Understudies: Heather Lea Anderson (Sharyl, Grace), Wayne Maugans (Joel, Carlo)

City Center Stage I; April 20–May 27, 2004; 48 performances

Kate Jennings Grant, David Harbour, Bradley White, Daphne Rubin-Vega in *Between Us*
PHOTO BY JOAN MARCUS

MINT THEATRE COMPANY

ELEVENTH SEASON

Jonathan Bank, Artistic Director

THE DAUGHTER-IN-LAW by D.H. Lawrence; Director, Martin L. Platt; Scenery, Bill Clarke; Costumes, Holly Poe Durbin; Lighting, Jeff Nellis; Production Stage Manager, Samone Weissman; Graphic Design, Jude Dvorak; Dialect Coach, Amy Stoller; Casting, Sharron Bower; Press, David Gersten & Associates; Cast: Mikel Sarah Lambert (Mrs. Gascoyne), Jodie Lynne McClintock (Mrs. Purdy), Angela Reed (Minnie), Peter Russo (Joe/Cabman), Gareth Saxe(Luther)

A play presented in two acts; June 15–October 26, 2003; 145 performances

FAR AND WIDE (DAS WEITE LAND) by Arthur Schnitzler; Adapted by Jonathan Bank; Director, Jonathan Bank; Scenery, Vicki R. Davis; Costumes, Theresa Squire; Lighting, Josh Bradford; Sound, Stefan Jacobs; Translation Advisor, Peter Snyder; Production Stage Managers, Douglas Shearer and Allison Deutsch; Graphic Design, Jude Dvorak; Press, David Gersten & Associates; Cast: Kate Arrington/ Victoria Mack (Erna Wahl), Kelly AuCoin/ Rob Breckinridge (Demeter Stanzides,/Hiker), Ezra Barnes (Doctor Franz Mauer), Lisa Bostnar (Genia Hofreiter), Lee Bryant (Anna Meinhold-Aigner), Anne-Marie Cusson (Frau Wahl), Joshua Decker (Otto von Aigner), Kurt Everhart (Rosenstock), Ken Kliban (Doctor von Aigner), Peter Reznikoff/ Allen Lewis Rickman (Natter/Serknitz), Hans Tester (Friedrich Hofreiter), Matthew Wilkas/ Matt Opatrny (Paul Kreindl), Katie Firth/ Pilar Witherspoon (Adele)

Return engagement of a play presented in two acts; September 18, 2004–January 1, 2004; 110 performances

MILNE AT THE MINT

THE TRUTH ABOUT BLAYDS and **MR. PIM PASSES BY** by A.A. Milne; Director, Jonathan Bank; Scenery, Sarah Lambert; Costumes, Theresa Squire; Lighting, Mark T. Simpson; Sound, Jared Coseglia; Stage Manager, Samone B. Weissman; Production Manager, Helena Webb; Casting, Sharron Bower; Press, David Gersten & Associates. Cast: Lisa Bostnar, Jack Davidson, Kristin Griffith, James Knight, Katie Lowes, Victoria Mack, Jack Ryland, Stephen Schnetzer

Two full-length plays presented in repertory; March 2–May 23, 2004. *The Truth About Blayds*—52 performances; *Mr Pim Passes By*—33 performances

Gareth Saxe, Angela Reed in *The Daughter-In-Law* PHOTO BY RICHARD TERMINE

Lisa Bostnar, Hans Tester in *Far and Wide (Das Weite Land)* PHOTO BY RICHARD TERMINE

Lisa Bostnar, Jack Ryland in *The Truth About Blayds* PHOTO BY RICHARD TERMINE

NATIONAL ACTORS THEATRE

TWELFTH SEASON

Tony Randall, Artistic Director

THE PERSIANS by Aeschylus; adapted by Ellen McLaughlin; Executive Producer, Manny Kanditis; Managing Dirctor, Fred Walker; Director, Ethan McSweeny; Scenery, James Noone; Costumes, Jess Goldstein; Lighting, Kevin Adams; Music and Sound, Michael Roth; Projections, Marilys Ernst; Production Stage Manager, James Latus; Stage Manager, Cyrille Blackburn; Press, Springer/Chicoine Public Relations, Gary Springer, Joe Trentacosta; Cast: John DeVries, Ed Dixon, Herb Foster, Michael Potts, Henry Stram, Henry Strozier, Charles Turner (Counsellors), Roberta Maxwell (Attosa), Brennan Brown (Herald), Len Cariou (Darius) Michael Stuhlbarg (Xerxes). Musicians: Greg Byer (percussion), Mairi Dorman (cello), David Shively (percussion). Attendants: Christina Dunham, Ben Lebish, Mike Horowitz, Yueni Zander

A play presented in one act; Michael Schimmel Center for the Arts; June 10–June 29, 2003; 29 performances

RIGHT YOU ARE by Luigi Pirandello; Translated by Eric Bentley; Director, Fabrizio Melano; Scenery, James Noone; Lighting, Kirk Bookman; Costumes, Noel Taylor; Sound, Richard Fitzgerald; Cast: Yolande Bavan (Signora Cini), Brennan Brown (Signor Ponza), Fred Burrell (The Governor), Edmund C. Davys, Mireille Enos (Dina), Herb Foster, Penny Fuller (Amalia Aggazzi), Peter Ganim (Police Commissioner), Jurian Hughes (Signora Sirelli), Addie Johnson, Florencia Lozano (Signora Ponza), Peter Maloney (Signor Sirelli), Natalie Norwick (Signora Nenni, u/s Signora Cini), Tony Randall (Lamberto Laudisi), Henry Strozier (Councillor Agazzi), Maria Tucci (Signora Frola)

A play presented in two acts; Michael Schimmel Center for the Arts; December 7–21, 2003; 27 performances

Michael Stuhlbarg (seated), Charles Turner, Jon DeVries, Herb Foster, Henry Stram, Henry Strozier, Michael Potts, Ed Dixon in *The Persians* PHOTO BY CAROL ROSEGG

Mireille Enos, Tony Randall, Jurian Hughes in *Right You Are* PHOTO BY CAROL ROSEGG

Kristen Johnston, Lili Taylor in *Aunt Dan and Lemon* PHOTO BY CAROL ROSEGG

NEW GROUP

EIGHTH SEASON

Scott Elliott, Artistic Director; Geoffrey Rich, Executive Director; Ian Morgan, Associate Artistic Director

AUNT DAN AND LEMON by Wallace Shawn; Director, Scott Elliott; Scenery, Derek McLane; Cosutmes, Eric Becker; Lighting, Jason Lyons; Sound, Ken Travis; General Manager, Jill Bowerman; Production Supervisor, Peter R. Feuchtwanger; Production Stage Manager, Valerie A. Peterson; Press, The Karpel Group, Briget Klapinski/Billy Zavelson; Cast: Kristen Johnston (Aunt Dan), Lili Taylor (Lemon), Marcia Stephanie Blake (Flora), Isaac De Bankolé (Andy), Liam Craig (Freddy), Melissa Errico (Mother), Carlos Leon (Raimondo), Emily Cass McDonnell (June), Brooke Sunny Moriber (Mindy), Maulik Pancholy (Marty), Stephen Park (Jasper), Bill Sage (Father)

A play presented in two acts; Acorn Theatre; December 18, 2003–March 27, 2004; 107 performances

ROAR by Betty Shamieh; Director, Marion McClinton; Scenery, Beowulf Boritt; Costumes, Mattie Ullrich; Lighting, Jason Lyons; Sound, Ken Travis; Production Stage Manager, Valerie A. Peterson; Press, The Karpel Group, Bridget Klapinski/Billy Zavelson; Cast: Annabella Sciorra (Hala), Sarita Choudhury (Karema), Sherri Eldin (Irene), Joseph Kamal (Ahmed), Daniel Oreskes (Abe)

A play presented in two acts; Harold Clurman Theatre; April 7–May 8, 2004; 55 performances

NEW YORK THEATRE WORKSHOP

TWENTY-FOURTH SEASON

James C. Nicola, Artistic Director; Lynn Moffat, Managing Director

FLESH AND BLOOD By Peter Gaitens; adapted from the novel by Michael Cunningham; Director, Doug Hughes; Scenery, Christine Jones; Costumes, Paul Tazewell; Lighting, Scott Zielinski; Sound and Music, David Van Tieghem; Production Stage Manager, Charles Means; Press, Richard Kornberg and Associates, Richard Kornberg, Don Summa; Cast: Martha Plimpton (Zoe, Jamal's Daughter), Airrion Dugan (Jamal, Levon), Sean Dugan (Ben, Joel), John Sierros (Constantine Stassos), Peter Gaitens (Billy), Peter Frechette (Harry, Cody, Matt), Jeff Weiss (Cassandra), Patricia Buckley (Magda, Rosemary, Trancas, Charlotte), Jessica Hecht (Susan), Cherry Jones (Mary Stassos), Chris McGarry (Todd, Mr. Fleming, Ted, Nick, Foster, Officer)

A play presented in two acts; July 16–August 24, 2003; 45 performances

Jeff Weiss, Cherry Jones in *Flesh and Blood* PHOTO BY JOAN MARCUS

FLOW Off-Off Broadway transfer of the solo performance piece by Will Power; Director, Danny Hoch; Scenery, David Ellis; Costumes, Gabriel Berry; Lighting, Sarah Sidman; Music Director, Ms. Reborn; Production Stage Manager, Timothy R. Semon; Press, Richard Kornberg and Associates, Richard Kornberg, Don Summa; Cast: Will Power, with DJ Reborn

A play presented without intermission; September 5–October 5, 2003; 33 performances

THE BEARD OF AVON By Amy Freed; Director, Doug Hughes; Scenery, Neil Patel; Costumes, Catherine Zuber; Lighting, Michael Chybowski; Sound and Music, David Van Tieghem; Production Stage Manager, Judith Schoenfeld; Press, Richard Kornberg and Associates, Richard Kornberg, Don Summa; Cast: Timothy Doyle (Minstrel, Walter Fitch, Earl of Derby, Player), James Gale (Richard Burbage, Lord Walsingham), Kate Jennings Grant (Anne Hathaway), Mark Harelik (Edward De Vere), Tom Lacy (Old Colin, Lord Burleigh, Lucy, Player), Alan Mandell (Henry Condel, Sir Francis Bacon), Tim Blake Nelson (William Shakespeare), David Schramm (John Heminge), Justin Schultz (Geoffrey Dunderbread, Lady Lettice), Jeffy Whitty (Henry Wriothesly, Player), Mary Louise Wilson (Queen Elizabeth)

A play presented in two acts; November 18–December 21, 2003; 40 performances

Mary Louise Wilson, James Gale, Justin Schultz, Tim Blake Nelson in *The Beard of Avon*
PHOTO BY JOAN MARCUS

VALHALLA By Paul Rudnick; Director, Christopher Ashley; Choreography, Daniel Pelzig; Scenery, Thomas Lynch; Costumes, William Ivey Long; Lighting, Kenneth Posner; Sound, Mark Bennett; Production Stage Manager, Sarah Bittenbender; Press, Richard Kornberg and Associates, Don Summa; Cast: Scott Barrow (Henry Lee Stafford, Helmut, Singer), Candy Buckley (Queen Marie, Margaret Avery, Princess Enid, Natalie Kippelbaum), Sean Dugan (James Avery), Peter Frechette (King Ludwig), Samantha Soule (Sally Mortimer, Princess Sophie, Princess Patricia, Marie Antoinette, Anne Avery), Jack Willis (Footman, Otto, Pfeiffer, Princess Ursula, Rev. Howesbury, Sergeant)

A play presented in two acts; February 5–March 21, 2004; 54 performances

J. Kyle Manzay in *Light Raise the Roof*   PHOTO BY JOAN MARCUS

LIGHT RAISE THE ROOF By Kia Corthron; Director, Michael John Garcés; Scenery, Narelle Sissons; Costumes, Gabriel Berry; Lighting, Ben Stanton; Sound, Robert Kaplowitz; Production Stage Manager, Shelli Aderman; Press, Richard Kornberg and Associates, Richard Kornberg, Don Summa; Cast: Moe Moe Alston (Em), Robert Beitzel (Zekie), Caroline Stefanie Clay (Arnell, Others), Romi Dias (Toddo's Wife, Others), Royce Johnson (Toddo, Others), Mia Katigbak (Mai), J. Kyle Manzay (Free), Chris McKinney (Cole), Andres Munar (Boy, Others), April Yvette Thompson (Bebbie), Collen Werthmann (Marmalade, Others)

A play presented in two acts; May 20–June 13, 2004; 50 performances

PAN ASIAN REPERTORY THEATRE

TWENTY-SEVENTH SEASON

Tisa Chang, Artistic Producing Director

LEGACY CODES by Cherylene Lee; Director, Ron Nakahara; Scenery, Eric Lowell Renschler; Costumes, Ingrid Maurer; Lighting, Victor En Yu Tan; Sound, Christopher Plummer; Press, Max Eisen. November 5, 2003; Cast: Bonnie Black (Diane Fortier), Lindsey Gates (Minna Fortier), Wai Ching Ho (Ming Liu), Scott Klavan (Richard Fortier), Jackson Loo (Erling Liu), Les J.N. Mau (Dr. Tai Liu)

A play presented in two acts; West End Theatre; November 5–23, 2003; 26 performances

Lindsey Gates, Jackson Loo in *Legacy Codes* PHOTO BY CORKY LEE

KWATZ! by Ernest Abuba; Director, Tisa Chang; Scenery, Kaori Alkazawa; Costumes, Carol Pelletier; Lighting, James F. Primm II; Sound, Michael Mittelsdorf; Stage Manager, Elis C. Arroyo; Press, Audrey Ross; Cast: Arthur T. Acuña (Dorje), John Baray (Drupka Kunley/10th Panchen Lama/Monk/ Surgical Team/5th Column/A Reporter), John Chou (Man/Nagapoi Ngawang Jigme/Tsering/Surgical Team/5th Column/A Reporter/Young Boy/Chinese Soldier/A Reporter), Tran T. Thuc Hanh (Bride/Surgical Team/ 5th Column/A Reporter), Rosanne Ma (Nun/Lover/Surgical Team/5th Column/A Reporter), Tom Matsusaka (The Interrogator/Father/Surgical Team/5th Column/A Reporter), Shigeko Suga (Mother/Surgical Team/5th Column/A Reporter/ Young Boy's Mother)

A play presented in one act; West End Theatre; March 24–April 11, 2004; 28 performances

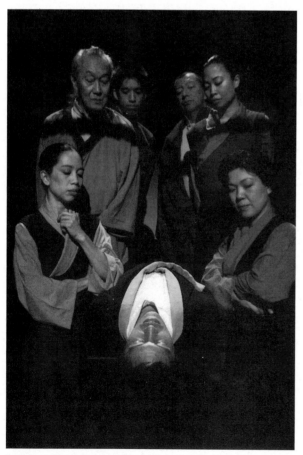

(front) Tran T. Thuc Hanh, Arthur T. Acuna, Shigeko Suga, (back) Tom Matsusaka, John Chou, John Baray, Rosanne Ma in *Kwatz!* PHOTO BY CORKY LEE

PEARL THEATRE COMPANY

TWENTIETH SEASON

Shepard Sobel, Artistic Director

THE RIVALS by Richard Brinsley Sheridan; Director, Robert Neff Williams; Scenery, Sarah Lambert; Costumes, Frank Champa; Lighting and Sound, Stephen Petrilli; Production Stage Manager, Dale Smallwood; General Manager, Amy Kaiser; Press, Codie K. Fitch; Cast: Celeste Ciulla (Lucy), Dominic Cuskern (Bob Acres/Thomas), Dan Daily (Lucius O'Trigger), Robert Hock (Sir Anthony Absolute), Sean McNall (Captain Jack Absolute), Christopher Moore (Faulkland), Edward Seamon (Fag) , Carol Schultz (Mrs. Malaprop), Rachel Botchan (Lydia Languish), Eunice Wong (Julia), Patrick Toon (David)

A play presented in two acts; Theatre 80 St. Marks Place; September 21– December 6, 2004; 43 performances

THE MERCHANT OF VENICE by William Shakespeare; Director, Shepard Sobel; Scenery, Sarah Lambert; Costumes, Sam Fleming; Lighting, Stephen Petrilli; Sound, Sara Bader; Production Stage Manager, Lisa Ledwich; General Manager, Amy Kaiser; Press, Codie K. Fitch; Cast: Dan Daily (Antonio), Cornell Womack (Salerio), Jason Ma (Solanio), Scott Whitehurst (Bassanio), Sean McNall (Lorenzo), Christopher Moore (Gratiano), Celeste Ciulla (Portia), Rachel Botchan (Nerissa), Patrick Toon (Stephano) , Dominic Cuskern (Shylock) , Calli Sarkesh (Morroco/ Jailer), Andy Prosky (Launcelot Gobbo/Arragon), Edward Seamon (Old Gobbo/Tubal/Duke), Edward Griffin (Leonardo), Eunice Wong (Jessica)

A play presented in two acts; Theatre 80 St. Marks Place; November 2– December 7, 2003; 36 performances

Sean McNall, Rachel Botchan in *The Rivals* PHOTO BY CODIE K. FITCH

Dominic Cuskern in *The Merchant of Venice* PHOTO BY CODIE K. FITCH

PERSIANS by Aeschylus; Director, Shepard Sobel; Scenery, Sarah Lambert; Costumes, Devon Painter; Lighting, Stephen Petrilli; Composer, Andy Teirstein; Movement, Alice Teirsten; Dramaturge, Prof. Tamara Green; Production Stage Manager, Dale Smallwood; General Manager, Amy Kaiser; Press, Codie K. Fitch; Cast: Joanne Camp (Atossa), Robert Hock (Darius), Sean McNall (Xerxes), Scott Whitehurst (Messenger)

A play presented in two acts; Theatre 80 St. Marks Place; January 11– February 8, 2004; 33 performances

Scott Whitehurst in *Persians* PHOTO BY MATTHEW SHANE COLEMAN

(CONTINUED FROM PREVIOUS PAGE)

DOUBLE INFIDELITY by Marivaux; Adapted by Oscar Mandel; Director, Beatrice Terry; Scenery, Sarah Lambert; Costumes, Liz Covey; Lighting, Stephen Petrilli; Sound, Walter Trarbach; Production Stage Manager, Lisa Ledwich; General Manager, Amy Kaiser; Press, Codie K. Fitch; Cast: Rachel Botchan (Sylvia), Scott Whitehurst (Prince), Christopher Moore (Arlequin), Celeste Ciulla (Flaminia), Dominic Cuskern (Trivelin), Sean McNall (Lord), Allison Nichols (Lisette)

A play presented in two acts; Theatre 80 St. Marks Place; February 22–March 21, 2004; 36 performances

Robert Hock in *When We Dead Awaken* PHOTO BY CODIE K. FITCH

Rachel Botchan, Scott Whitehurst in *Double Infidelity* PHOTO BY CODIE K. FITCH

WHEN WE DEAD AWAKEN by Henrik Ibsen; Translated by Rolf Fjelde; Director, Benno Haenel; Scenery, Sarah Lambert; Costumes, Barbara A. Bell; Lighting, Stephen Petrilli; Sound, Jane Shaw; Production Stage Manager, Dale Smallwood; General Manager, Amy Kaiser; Press, Codie K. Fitch; Cast: Rachel Botchan (Maia), Joanne Camp (Irene), Robert Hock (Rubek), Scott Whitehurst (Ulfhejm), Dominic Cuskern (Manager), Katherine Gansell (Nun)

A play presented in two acts; Theatre 80 St. Marks Place; April 4–25, 2004; 31 performances

PLAYWRIGHTS HORIZONS

THIRTY-THIRD SEASON

Tim Sanford, Artistic Director; Leslie Marcus, Managing Director; William Russo, General Manager

BAD DATES Solo performance piece by Theresa Rebeck; Director, John Benjamin Hickey; Scenery, Derek McLane; Costumes, Mattie Ullrich; Lighting, Frances Aronson; Sound, Bruce Ellman; Casting, James Calleri; Production Stage Manager, Megan Scheid; Press, The Publicity Office, Bob Fennell, Marc Thibodeau, Michael S. Borowski, Candi Adams; Cast: Julie White (Haley)

A solo performance piece presented without intermission; Peter Jay Sharp Theatre; June 15–July 6, 2003; 33 performances

Heather Graham, Jesse J. Perez, Hamish Linklater in *Recent Tragic Events* PHOTOS BY JOAN MARCUS

Julie White in *Bad Dates* PHOTO BY CAROL ROSEGG

RECENT TRAGIC EVENTS By Craig Wright; Director, Michael John Garcés; Scenery, Adam Stockhausen; Costumes, Elizabeth Hope Clancy; Lighting, Kirk Bookman; Sound and Music, Scott Myers; Casting, James Calleri; Production Stage Manager, Shelli Aderman; Press, The Publicity Office, Bob Fennell, Michael S. Borowski; Cast: Heather Graham (Waverly), Hamish Linklater (Andrew), Jesse J. Perez (Ron), Colleen Werthmann (Nancy), Kalimi Baxter (Stage Manager)

A play presented in two acts; September 28–October 12, 2003; 17 performances

WILDER Musical by Erin Cressida Wilson, Jack Herrick and Mike Craver; Director, Lisa Portes; Choreography, Jane Comfort; Scenery and Costumes, G.W. Mercier; Lighting, Jane Cox; Sound, Tom Morse; Music Direction, Jack Herrick; Associate Producer, Ira Weitzman; James Calleri, Casting; Renée Lutz, Production Stage Manager; Press, The Publicity Office, Bob Fennell, Marc Thibodeau, Michael S. Borowski; Cast: Mike Craver (Mike), John Cullum (Old Wilder), Jack Herrick (Jack), Lacey Kohl (Jessie, Melora), Jeremiah Miller (Wilder)

Musical presented without intermission; Peter Jay Sharp Theatre; October 26–November 14, 2003; 21 performances

(CONTINUED ON NEXT PAGE)

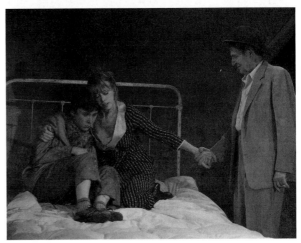

Jeremiah Miller, Lacey Kohl, John Cullum in *Wilder* PHOTO BY JOAN MARCUS

(CONTINUED FROM PREVIOUS PAGE)

JUVENILIA By Wendy MacLeod; Director, David Petrarca; Scenery, Michael Yeargan; Costumes, Martin Pakledinaz; Lighting, Mark McCullough; Sound, Rob Milburn and Michael Bodeen; Casting, James Calleri; Production Stage Manager, David Sugarman; Stage Manager, Barclay Stiff; Press, the Publicity Office, Bob Fennell, Michael S. Borowski; Cast: Ian Brennan (Henry), Aubrey Dollar (Meredith), Luke MacFarlane (Brodie), Erica N. Tazel (Angie)

A play presented in two acts; December 7–21, 2003; 17 performances

Luke MacFarlane, Ian Brennan, Aubrey Dollar, Erica N. Tazel in *Juvenilia*

Rosemarie DeWitt, Daniel Eric Gold, Lee Pace, Ana Reeder, Rob Campbell, Mary Shultz in *Small Tragedy* PHOTOS BY JOAN MARCUS

SMALL TRAGEDY By Craig Lucas; Director, Mark Wing-Davey; Scenery, Douglas Stein; Costumes, Marina Draghici; Lighting, Jennifer Tipton; Sound and Music, John Gromada; Casting, James Calleri; Production Stage Manager, Thom Widmann; Press, The Publicity Office, Bob Fennell, Marc Thibodeau, Michael S. Borowski, Jeremy Hooper; Cast: Ana Reeder (Jen), Mary Shultz (Paola), Rob Campbell (Nathaniel), Daniel Eric Gold (Christmas), Lee Pace (Hakija), Rosemarie DeWitt (Fanny)

A play presented in two acts; March 11–28, 2004; 22 performances

Bess Wohl, Tyler Francavilla, Peter Strauss, Will McCormack in *Chinese Friends*

CHINESE FRIENDS By Jon Robin Baitz; Director, Robert Egan; Scenery, Santo Loquasto; Costumes, Laura Bauer; Lighting, Donald Holder; Sound and Music, Obadiah Eaves; Fight Direction, Joseph Travers; Casting, James Calleri; Production Stage Manager, James Latus; Press, The Publicity Office, Bob Fennell, Marc Thibodeau, Michael S. Borowski; Cast: Peter Strauss (Arthur Brice), Tyler Francavilla (Ajax), Will McCormack (Stephan), Bess Wohl (Alegra)

A play presented in two acts; May 27–June 13, 2004; 22 performances

PRIMARY STAGES

NINETEENTH SEASON

Casey Childs, Executive Producer; Andrew Leynse, Artistic Director

STRICTLY ACADEMIC by A.R. Gurney; Director, Paul Benedict; Scenery, James Noone; Costumes, Laura Crow; Lighting, Deborah Constantine; Production Stage Manager, Pamela Singer; Press, Barlow-Hartman, John Barlow/Rob Finn

> **THE PROBLEM** Cast: Susan Greenhill (Wife), Keith Reddin (Husband)

> **THE GUEST LECTURER** Cast: Remy Auberjonois (Hartley), Susan Greenhill (Mona), Keith Reddin (Fred)

Two one-act plays presented with intermission, Primary Stages 45th Street Theatre; October 21–November 30, 2003; 45 performances

THE STENDHAL SYNDROME by Terrence McNally; Director, Leonard Foglia; Scenery, Michael McGarty; Costumes, David C. Woolard; Lighting, Russell H. Champa; Music and Sound, David Van Tiehem; Projections, Elaine J. McCarthy; Production Stage Manager, Renee Lutz; Production Manager, Lester P. Grant; Casting, Stephanie Klapper; Press, Barlow/Hartman

> **FULL FRONTAL NUDITY** Cast: Isabella Rossellini* (Bimbi), Jennifer Mudge (Lana), Michael Countryman (Hector), Yul Vasqauez (Leo)

> **PRELUDE & LIEBESTOD** Cast: Richard Thomas (Conductor), Isabella Rossellini* (Conductor's Wife), Yul Vasquez (Young Man), Micahael Countryman (Concert Master), Jennifer Mudge (Soprano)

* Maria Tucci replaced Isabella Rossellini for the performances March 28–April 27

Two one-act plays presented with intermission, 59E59 Theatre; February 16–May 12, 2004; 112 performances

Susan Greenhill, Keith Reddin in *Strictly Academic* PHOTO BY JAMES LEYNSE

Robert Hogan (Terry), T.R. Knight (Boy), Caitlin O'Connel (Maureen), Miriam Shor (Sara)

A play presented in two acts; Primary Stages 45th Street Theatre; May 18–June 24, 2004; 45 performances

Isabella Rossellini, Jennifer Mudge in *The Stendhal Syndrome* PHOTOS BY JOAN MARCUS

BOY by Julia Jordon; Director, Joe Calarco; Scenery, Michael Fagin; Costumes, Anne Kennedy; Lighting, Chris Lee; Sound and Original Music, Lindsay Jones; Production Stage Manager, Bonnie Brady; Casting, Stephanie Klapper; Press, Barlow/Hartman; Cast: Kelly AuCoin (Mick),

T.R. Knight, Robert Hogan in *Boy* PHOTO BY JAMES LEYNSE

ROUNDABOUT THEATRE COMPANY

THIRTY-EIGHTH SEASON

Todd Haimes, Artistic Director; Ellen Richard, Managing Director; Julia C. Levy, Executive Director of External Affairs

INTIMATE APPAREL By Lynn Nottage; Director, Daniel Sullivan; Scenery, Derek McLane; Costumes, Catherine Zuber; Lighting, Allen Lee Hughes; Sound, Marc Gwinn; Music, Harold Wheeler; Casting, Mele Nagler; Press, Boneau/Bryan-Brown, Joe Perrotta, Matt Polk, Jessica Johnson. Opened at the Laura Pels Theatre at the Harold and Miriam Steinberg Center for Theatre; Cast: Viola Davis (Esther), Lynda Gravátt (Mrs. Dickson), Russell Hornsby (George), Arija Bareikis (Mrs. Van Buren), Corey Stoll (Mr. Marks), Lauren Velez (Mayme); Understudies: Gwendolyn Mulamba (Esther, Mayme), Edloe Blackwell (Mrs. Dickson), Charles Parnell (George), Nisi Sturgis (Mrs. Van Buren), Darren Goldstein (Mr. Marks)

A play presented in two acts; Laura Pels Theatre; April 11–June 13, 2004; 57 performances

(front) Anjali Bhimani, Lizzy Cooper Davis, Kyle Hall, Louise Lamson; (back) Mariann Mayberry, Christopher Donahue in *The Notebooks of Leonardo da Vinci*

SECOND STAGE THEATRE

TWENTY-FOURTH SEASON

Carol Rothman, Artistic Director; Carol Fishman, Managing Director

THE NOTEBOOKS OF LEONARDO DA VINCI By Mary Zimmerman; based on the work of Leonardo da Vinci; In Association With the Berkeley Repertory Theatre; Director, Mary Zimmerman; Scenery, Scott Bradley; Costumes, Mara Blumenfeld; Based on Designs by Allison Reeds; Lighting, T.J. Gerckens; Sound, Michael Bodeen; Music, Miriam Strum and Michael Bodeen; Production Stage Manager, Cynthia Cahill; Stage Manager, Bethany Ford; Press, Richard Kornberg and Associates, Tom D'Ambrosio, Don Summa, Rick Miramontez, Carrie Friedman; Cast: Anjali Bhimani (Leonardo), Lucia Brawley (Leonardo), Lizzy Cooper Davis (Leonardo), Christopher Donahue (Leonardo), Kyle Hall (Leonardo), Doug Hara (Leonardo), Louise Lamson (Leonardo), Mariann Mayberry (Leonardo), Paul Oakley Stovall (Leonardo)

A play presented without intermission; June 29–August 3, 2003; 41 performances

LIVING OUT By Lisa Loomer; Director, Jo Bonney; Scenery, Neil Patel; Costumes, Emilio Sosa; Lighting, David Weiner; Sound, John Gromada; Production Stage Manager, Pamela Edington; Stage Manager, Kelly Hance; Casting, Tara Rubin Casting; Press, Richard Kornberg and Associates, Richard Kornberg, Tom D'Ambrosio, Don Summa, Rick Miramontez, Carrie Friedman; Cast: Liza Colón-Zayas (Zoila Tezo), Judith Hawking (Wallace Breyer), Kathryn Meisle (Nancy Robin), Zilah Mendoza (Ana Hernandez), Kelly Coffield Park (Linda Billins Farzam), Gary Perez (Bobby Hernandez), Maria Elena Ramirez (Sandra Zavala), Joseph Urla (Richard Robin)

A play presented in two acts; September 30, 2003–November 2, 2003; 40 performances

Viola Davis, Arija Bareikis in *Intimate Apparel* PHOTOS BY JOAN MARCUS

Jonathan Reynolds in *Dinner With Demons*

Judith Hawking, Kathryn Meisle, Kelly Coffield Park in *Living Out* PHOTOS BY JOAN MARCUS

DINNER WITH DEMONS Solo performance piece by Jonathan Reynolds; Scenery, Heidi Ettinger; Lighting, Kevin Adams; Sound, John Gromada; Production Stage Manager, Kelly Hance; Press, Richard Kornberg and Associates, Richard Kornberg, Tom D'Ambrosio; Performed by Jonathan Reynolds

A solo performance peice presented without intermission; December 16, 2003–January 18, 2004; 40 performances

Nicholas Hormann, T. Scott Cunningham, Marsha Mason, Michael Cerveris in *Wintertime*

WINTERTIME By Charles L. Mee; Director, David Schweizer; Choreography, Sean Curran; Scenery, Andrew Lieberman; Costumes, David Zinn; Lighting, Kevin Adams; Sound, Eric Shim; Production Stage Manager, Christine Lemme; Stage Manager, Kelly Hance; Press, Richard Kornberg and Associates, Richard Kornberg, Tom D'Ambrosio; Cast: Tina Benko (Jacqueline), Brienin Bryant (Ariel), Marylouise Burke (Hilda), Michael Cerveris (Francois), T. Scott Cunningham (Edmund), Carmen de Lavallade (Bertha), Christopher Denham (Jonathan), Nicholas Hormann (Frank), Marsha Mason (Maria), Danny Mastrogiorgio (Bob)

A play presented in two acts; March 2–21, 2004; 24 performances

SIGNATURE THEATRE COMPANY

THIRTEENTH SEASON

James Houghton, Artistic Director; Kathryn M. Limpuma, Executive Director

THE HARLEQUIN STUDIES by Bill Irwin; Director, Bill Irwin; Music and Musical Director, Doug Skinner; Choreographer, Lorenzo Pisoni; Scenery, Douglas Stein; Costumes, Catherine Zuber; Lighting, James Vermeulen; Sound, Brett Jarvis; General Manager, Jodi Schoenbrun; Production Stage Manager, Jennifer Rae Moore; Production Manager, Chris Moses; Production Coordinator, Nancy Harrington; Casting, Bernard Telsey Casting; Press, Publicity Office; Cast: Bill Irwin (Harlequin), Marin Ireland (The Girl), John Oyzon (Dream Pantalone), Andrew Pacho (Dream Captain), Rocco Sisto (The Captain), Paxton Whitehead (Pantalone), Steven T. Williams (Dream Harlequin). Musicians: Sean Mc Morris (percussion), Doug Skinner (piano), David Gold (viola/violin)

A play presented in two acts; Peter Norton Space; September 23–November 9, 2003; 74 performances

Doug Skinner, Bill Irwin in *The Regard Evening*

THE REGARD EVENING by Bill Irwin; in collaboration with Doug Skinner, Michael O'Connor and Nancy Harrington; Director, Bill Irwin; Scenery, Douglas Stein; Costumes, Catherine Zuber; Lighting, Nancy Schertler; Sound, Brett Jarvis; Video Design, Dennis Diamond; Puppet Design, Roman Paska; Original Music, Doug Skinner; General Manager, Jodi Schoenbrun; Production Stage Manager, Nancy Harrington; Production Manager, Chris Moses; Press, Publicity Office. Cast: Bill Irwin, Doug Skinner, Michael O'Connor

A play presented in two acts; Peter Norton Space; December 15, 2003– February 1, 2004; 65 performances

MR. FOX: A RUMINATION by Bill Irwin; Director, James Houghton; Scenery, Christine Jones; Costumes, Elizabeth Caitlin Ward; Lighting, James Vermeulen; Sound, Brett Jarvis; Music Direction, Loren Toolajian; Production Stage Manager, Jennifer Grutza; General Manager, Jodi Schoenbrun; Production Manager, Chris Moses; Press, Publicity Office; Cast: Bill Irwin (G.L. Fox, Humpty Clown), Bianca Amato (Columbine, et al.),

Bill Irwin, Marin Ireland in *The Harlequin Studies*

Jason Butler Harner (Harlequin, et al.), Geoff Hoyle (Charlie Fox, et al.), Marc Damon Johnson (George Topack, Freedman Bill), Peter Maloney (Daly, et al.), Richard Poe (Lingard, et al.)

A new play presented in one act; Peter Norton Space; April 13–May 9, 2004; 50 performances

Bill Irwin in *Mr. Fox: A Rumination* PHOTOS BY CAROL ROSEGG

THEATRE FOR A NEW AUDIENCE

TWENTY-FIFTH SEASON

Artistic Director, Jeffrey Horowitz; Managing Director, Dorothy Ryan

THE LAST LETTER Based on the novel *Life and Fate* by Vasily Grossman, Translated by Robert Chandler; Director, Frederick Wiseman; Scenic Design, Douglas Stein; Costume Design, Miranda Hoffman; Lighting Design, Donald Holder; December 11, 2003–January 11, 2004; Cast: Kathleen Chalfant (Anna Semyonovna)

Christopher McCann, Brenda Wehle in *Pericles*

PERICLES by William Shakespeare; Director, Bartlett Sher; Set and Lighting Design, Christopher Akerlind; Costume Design, Elizabeth Caitlin Ward; Sound Design and Music Composition, Peter John Still; February 12–February 28, 2004; Cast: Brenda Wehle (Gower/Lychorida/Diana), Christopher McCann (Antiochus/Poor Man/Pericles, fourteen years later), Tim Hopper (Pericles/Lysimachus), Julyana Soelistyo (Daughter of Antiochus/Marina), Graham Winton (Thaliard/Leonine/Knight of Athens/Gentleman), Glenn Fleshler (Lord/Sailor/1st Fisherman/Waiter/Gentleman/Philemon/1st Pirate), Bruce Turk (Lord/Sailor/2nd Fisherman/ Waiter/Gentleman/ 2nd Pirate), Albert Jones (Lord/Sailor/3rd Fisherman/ Knight of Antioch/ Gentleman/Servant/3rd Pirate), Philip Goodwin (Helicanus/Marshal/ Cerimon), Robert LuPone (Cleon/Pandar), Kristine Nielsen (Dionyza/Bawd), Paul Niebanck (Lord/Sailor/Knight of Sparta/Servant), Andrew Weems (Simonides/Boult), Linda Powell (Thaisa)

Kathleen Chalfant in *The Last Letter* PHOTOS BY GERRY GOODSTEIN, RICHARD TERMINE

ENGAGED by W.S. Gilbert; Director, Doug Hughes; Scenic Design, John Lee Beatty; Costume Design, Catherine Zuber; Lighting Design, Rui Rita; Sound Design, Aural Fixation; April 20–May 16, 2004; Cast: Maggie Lacey (Maggie Macfarlane), David Don Miller (Angus Macalister), Sloane Shelton (Mrs. Macfarlane), John Christopher Jones (Belvawney), Caitlin Muelder (Belinda Treherne), Jeremy Shamos (Cheviot Hill), John Horton (Mr. Symperson), James Gale (Major McGillicuddy), Nicole Lowrance (Minnie Symperson), Danielle Ferland (Parker)

Caitlin Muelder, Jeremy Shamos, Nicole Lowrance in *Engaged*

Christopher Innvar, Daniella Alonso in *Eight Days (Backwards)* PHOTO BY CAROL ROSEGG

29TH STREET REP

FIFTEENTH SEASON

David Mogentale and Tim Corcoran, Artistic Directors

BOLD GIRLS by Rona Munro; Director, Ludovica Villar-Hauser; Scenery, Mark Symczak; Costumes and Graphic Design, Christopher Lione; Lighting, Douglas Cox; Sound and Original Music, Tim Cramer; Production Stage Manager, Cesar Malantic; Additional Original Music, Susan McKeown; Dialect Coach, Steve Gabis; Press, Karen Greco; Cast: Moira MacDonald (Deirdre), Susan Barrett (Marie), Paula Ewin (Nora), Heidi James (Cassie)

A play presented in two acts; September 18–November 1, 2003; 56 performances

IN THE BELLY OF THE BEAST REVISITED by Jack Henry Abbott; Adapted by Adrian Hall. Director, Leo Farley; Scenery, Mark Symczak; Costumes, Christopher Lione; Lighting, Stewart Wagner; Sound Design and Composer, Vera Beren; Slide Photographer, Diane Greene Lent; Production Stage Manager, Will Schmidt; Press, Karen Greco; Cast: James E. Smith (Reader 1), Heidi James (Reader 2), Gordon Holmes (Reader 3), David Mogentale (Jack Henry Abbott)

A play presented in two acts; March 8–April 3, 2004; 36 performances

Penny Fuller, George Grizzard in *Beautiful Child* PHOTO BY CAROL ROSEGG

VINEYARD THEATRE

TWENTY-THIRD SEASON

Douglas Aibel, Artistic Director; Jennifer Garvey-Blackwell, Executive Director; Bardo S. Ramirez, Managing Director

EIGHT DAYS (BACKWARDS) by Jeremy Dobrish; Director, Mark Brokaw; Scenery, Mark Wendland; Costumes, Michael Krass; Lighting, Mary Louise Geirger; Sound, Janet Kalas; Original Music, Lewis Flinn; Production Manager, Kai Brothers/Bridget Markov; Production Stage Manager, Jennifer Rae Moore; Casting, Cindy Tolen; Press, Sam Rudy; General Manager, Rebecca Habel; Cast: Josh Radnor (Jonathan), David Garrison (Weinstein/Izzy), Randy Danson (Gloria/Fortune Teller), Bill Buell (Frank/Kaplan), Daniella Alonso (Consuela/Seleana), Christopher Innvar (Goldberg/Bartender), Barbara Garrick (Stern/Sheila Goldberg)

A play in two acts; June 16–July 5, 2003; 55 performances

Randy Graff, Catherine Kellner, Will McCormack, Enid Graham, Mark Blum in *The Long Christmas Ride Home* PHOTO BY CAROL ROSEGG

THE LONG CHRISTMAS RIDE HOME by Paula Vogel; Director, Mark Brokaw; Scenery, Neil Patel; Costumes, Jess Goldstein; Lighting, Mark McCullough; Original Music & Sound, David Van Tieghem; Projection Design, Jan Hartley; Production Managers, Kai Brothers and Bridget Markov; Production Stage Manager, Michael McGoff; Casting, Cindy Tolan; Press, Sam Rudy; Director of Production, Reed Ridgley; General Manager, Rebecca Habel; Choreography, John Carrafa; Puppetry Concept and Design, Basil Twist; Cast: Mark Blum (Narrator/Man), Randy Graff (Narrator/Woman), Sean Palmer (Minister/Dancer), Catherine Kellner (Rebecca), Enid Graham (Claire), Will McCormack (Stephen), Matthew Acheson, Oliver Dalzell, Erin K. Orr, Marc Petrosino, Sarah Provost, Lake Simons (Puppeteers); Luke Notary (Musician)

A play presented in two acts; November 4–December 7, 2003; 55 performances

BEAUTIFUL CHILD by Nicky Silver; Director, Terry Kinney; Scenery, Richard Hoover; Costumes, Michael Krass; Lighting, David Lander; Original Music & Sound, Obadiah Eaves; Production Manager, Kai Brothers and Bridget Markov; Production Stage Manager, Rachel Perlman; Casting, Cindy Tolan; Press, Sam Rudy; Director of Production, Reed Ridgley; General Manager, Rebecca Habel; Cast: George Grizzard (Harry), Penny Fuller (Nan), Steven Pasquale (Isaac), Alexandra Gersten-Vassilaros (Delia), Kaitlin Hopkins (Dr. Elizabeth Hilton, Victoria's Mother)

A play presented in two acts; February 24–March 28, 2004; 53 performances

WHERE DO WE LIVE? by Christopher Shinn; Director, Christopher Shinn; Scenery, Rachel Hauck; Costumes, Mattie Ullrich; Lighting, David Weiner; Original Music, Storm P; Sound, Jill BC DuBoff; Production Manager Kai Brothers and Bridget Markov; Production Stage Manager, Erika Timperman; Casting, Cindy Tolan; Press, Sam Rudy; Director of Production, Reed Ridgley; General Manager, Rebecca Habel; Cast: Burl Moseley (Shedrick), Luke MacFarlane (Stephen), Emily Bergl (Patricia), Aaron Stanford (Dave, et al.), Jesse Tyler Ferguson (Billy, et al.), Liz Stauber (Lily), Daryl Edwards (Timothy), Aaron Yoo (Leo, Cellist), Jacob Pitts (Tyler)

A play presented in one act; May 11–30, 2004; 48 performances

WOMEN'S PROJECT AND PRODUCTIONS

TWENTY-SIXTH SEASON

Julia Miles, Founder; Loretta Greco, Producing Artistic Director; Georgia Buchana, Managing Director; Marya Cohen, Acting Artistic Director

TOUCH by Toni Press-Coffman; Director, Loretta Greco; Scenery, Michael Brown; Costumes, Jeff Mahshie; Lighting, James Vermeulen; Sound and Original Music, Robert Kaplowitz; Production Stage Manager, Gillian Duncan; Cast: Tom Everett Scott (Kyle), Michele Ammon (Kathleen), Matthew Del Negro (Bennie), Yetta Gottesman (Serena)

A play presented in two acts; Women's Project Theatre; October 9–26, 2003; 23 performances

BIRDY by Naomi Wallace; adapted from the novel by William Wharton; Director, Lisa Peterson; Scenery, Riccardo Hernandez; Costumes, Gabriel Berry; Lighting, Scott Zielinski; Sound, Jill B.C. DuBoff; Original Music, David Van Tieghem; Fight Director, J. Allen Suddeth; Production Stage Manager, Erika Timperman; Casting, Judy Henderson; Dramaturg, Karen Keagle; Press, Bill Evans & Associates, Jim Randolph; Cast: Richard Bekins (Doctor White), Teagle F. Bougere (Renaldi), Zachary Knighton (Young Al), Adam Rothenberg (Sargeant Al Comumbato), Ted Schneider (Birdy), Peter Stadlen (Young Birdy)

A play presented in two acts; Women's Project Theatre; December 2–21, 2003; 24 performances

Liz Stauber, Burl Moseley in *Where Do We Live?* PHOTO BY CAROL ROSEGG

Matthew Del Negro, Yetta Gottesman, Tom Everett Scott, Michelle Ammon in *Touch*
PHOTO BY CAROL ROSEGG

Zachary Knighton, Peter Stadlen in *Birdy* PHOTO BY CAROL ROSEGG

OFF-OFF-BROADWAY

Productions that opened **June 1, 2003 – May 31, 2004**

ABINGDON THEATRE COMPLEX

THE ATTIC by Stephen Gaydos; Director, Paul Zablocki; October 25, 2003; Cast: Michael Szeles, Josh Heine, Meg Howrey, Megan McNulty, Stephanie Weldon

THE KILLER NEWS Musical with Book, Music and Lyrics by Steven P. Reed; Director, Steven P. Reed; December 3, 2003; Cast: Linnea Redfern, Pete Stickel, Alexander Meltsin, Brigitte Beniquez, L.H. "Starborn" Bryant, Shelly Rudolph, Andrew Kletjian, Joseph Emil, W.B. Riggins, Steve Penser, G. Curtis Smith, John Lee, Gillian Fallon, Leighbarry Harvard, Christine Mogle, Miriam Lopez, Michele Burnett, Chris Cotten, George Grauer

A REED IN THE WIND by Joseph P. McDonald; Director, Ernie Martin; January 15, 2004; Cast: Jack Walsh, Aubyn Philabaum, Phil Burke, Kevin Hagan

STATES OF SHOCK by Sam Shepard; Director, Cyndy Marion; February 13, 2004; Cast: Richard Leighton, Diane Shilling, Dee Spencer, Rod Sweitzer, Bill Weeden

ITALIAN-AMERICAN CANTOS by Anthony P. Pennino; Director, Gregory Simmons; April 18, 2004; Cast: Lisa Barnes, Joseph Camardella, Kathleen DeFouw, Suzanne DiDonna, Richard Kohn, Ania Michaels, Jarrod Pistilli, Paul Romanello, Christina Romanello, Joseph Schommer, Tom Walker

HOME AGAIN by Troy Hill; Director, Troy Hill; May 16, 2004; Cast: Cynthia Barnett, Michael Fegley, Rachelle Guiragossian, Gerry Hildebrant, Bryan Michael McGuire, Thomas James O'Leary, Kara Payne

ACCESS THEATRE

THE JOURNEY OF THE FIFTH HORSE by Ronald Ribman; Director, Lise McDermott; August 14, 2003; Cast: Dan Patrick Brady, Denise Dimirjian, Jonas Wadler, Duke York, Kim Clay, Eric Dente, Ledger Free, Fran Barkan, Lou Tally, Michael Boothroyd, Diedre Brennan, Jennifer J. Kats, Daniel Hicks, Robin Goldsmith

FASTER by Jessica Almasy, Rachel Chavkin, Brian Hastert, Tiffany May, Kristen Sieh, Ryan West; inspired by James Gleick's book; Director, Rachel Chavkin; November 20, 2003; Cast: Jessica Almasy, Brian Hastert, Tiffany May, Kristen Sieh, Ryan West

600 DAYS OF PAIN by Gene Perelson and Jamil Ellis; Directors, Gene Perelson and Jamil Ellis; March 11, 2004; Cast: Gene Perelson and Jamil Ellis

James Murtaugh, Rachel Fowler in *The Triangle Factory Fire Project* PHOTO BY CAROL ROSEGG

THE ACTORS COMPANY THEATRE (TACT)

THE MARRIAGE OF BETTE AND BOO by Christopher Durang; Director, Scott Alan Evans; October 18, 2003; Cast: Cynthia Darlow, Cynthia Harris, Greg McFadden, Eve Michelson, James Murtaugh, James Prendergast, Kate Ross, Gregory Salata, Scott Schafer, Jenn Thompson

FATHERS AND SONS by Brian Friel; based on the novel by Ivan Turgenev; Director, Stephen Hollis; November 22, 2003; Cast: Sean Arbuckle, Mary Bacon, Lucas Beck, Jamie Bennett, Lynn Cohen, Francesca Di Mauro, Richard Ferrone, Sam Gregory, John Horton, Kelly Hutchinson, Elizabeth Shepard, David Staller, Ashley West

THE GOOD SOUP (LA BONNE SOUPE) by Felicien Marceau; adapted by Garson Kanin; Director, Kyle Fabel; January 24, 2004; Cast: Delphi Harrington, Margaret Nichols, Gregory Salata, Sean Arbuckle, Nora Chester, Francesca Di Mauro, Simon Jones, Jack Koenig, Darrie Lawrence, Greg McFadden, James Prendergast, Scott Schafer, Kelly Hutchinson, Joel Jones

THE CHALK GARDEN by Enid Bagnold; Director, John Christopher Jones, March 13, 2004; Cast: Mary Bacon, Cynthia Darlow, Francesca Di Mauro, Cynthia Harris; Simon Jones, Darrie Lawrence, Gloria Moore, Nicholas Kepros

THE TRIANGLE FACTORY FIRE PROJECT by Christopher Piehler; Director, Scott Alan Evans; May 14, 2004; Cast: Jamie Bennett, Nora Chester, Francesca Di Mauro, Kyle Fabel, Rachel Fowler, James Murtaugh, Margaret Nichols, Scott Schafer, Kelly Hutchinson, Timothy McCracken

ALTERED STAGES

AN ENOLA GAY CHRISTMAS by Doug Field; Director, Dana Synder; December 4, 2003; Cast: Nan Schmid

AMERICAN THEATRE OF ACTORS

AND THEN THERE WAS NIN by Jennifer Ewing Pierce; Director, Jennifer Ewing Pierce; June 27, 2003; Cast: Joshua Longo, Kalle Macrides, Mikeah Jennings, Khoa Nguyen, Tito Ruiz, Melanie Julian, Ryan Tavlin

CONFESSIONS OF A WONDERBABE by Jennifer Ewing Pierce; Director, Jennifer Ewing Pierce; July 1, 2003; Cast: Ryan Tavlin, Allison McAtee, Laura Winsor Attanasio

THE WOOD DEMON by Anton Chekov; translated by Carol Rocamora; Director, Cynthia Dillon; August 8, 2003; Cast: John Jamiel, Tashya Valdevit, Jeff Winter

DALLIANCE IN VIENNA by Douglas Braverman; Director, Thomas Morrissey; December 4, 2003; Cast: Glenn Lakison, Thomas James O'Leary, Christine Pedi, Lucas Steele, Emily Strang, Melinda Tanner, Ian Tomaschik

ORESTEIA by Aeschylus; January 19, 2004

AGAMEMNON adapted by Erik Nelson; Director, Erik Nelson; Cast: Saori Tsukada, Chris Oden

THE MOURNERS adapted by Yuval Sharon from The Libation Bearers; Director, Yuval Sharon; Cast: Constance Tarbox, Laura Knight, Sara Fraunfelder, Tia Shearer, Layna Fisher, Jonathan Day, Caroline Worra, Jeanne Lehman, Cara Consilvio

EUMENIDES adapted by David Johnston; Director, Kevin Lee Newbury; Cast: Cortney Keim, Beau Allulli, Kath Lichter, Michael Bell, Vivian Manning, Nell Gwynn, Heidi McAllister, Lori Lane Jefferson

PROMISED LAND by Harvey Huddleston; Director, Tom Dybeck; January 30, 2004; Cast: David Mazzeo, Lynne McCollough, Matthew Faber, Danny Rose, Bruce McKinnon, Emily Sproch, Jasmine Goldman

ATLANTIC 453

THE HIDING PLACE by Jeff Whitty; Director, Christian Parker; January 19, 2004; Cast: Kate Blumberg

THE BALD SOPRANO and **THE LESSON** by Eugene Ionesco; translated by Tina Howe; Director, Carl Forsman; April 13, 2004

NEW WORKS: CHANCE FESTIVAL of short plays by Michael Dowling, Jerome Hairston, Jordan Lag, Scott Organ, Kate Moira Ryan; Directors, Ian Morgan, Scott Organ, Anya Saffir, Gary Upton Schwartz, Sarah Stern; May 17, 2004; Casts Included: Kate Blumberg, Jason Cornwell, Gretchen Egolf, Susan Finch, Christopher Innvar, Maggie Kiley, DeAnna Lenhart, Adam Lustick, Jenny Maguire, Greg Stuhr, Ray Anthony Thomas, Charles Tucker

ARS NOVA

JUDY SPEAKS by Mary Birdsong; Director, Gregory Wolfe; August 11, 2003; Cast: Mary Birdsong

THE WAU WAU SISTERS by Tanya Gagné and Adrienne Truscott; Director, Trip Cullman; May 20, 2004; Cast: Tanya Gagné, Adrienne Truscott

AXIS COMPANY

A GLANCE AT NEW YORK by Benjamin A. Baker; Director, Randy Sharp; June 7, 2003; Cast: Wren Arthur, Brian Barnhart, David Crabb, Joe Fuer, Laurie Kilmartin, Sue Ann Molinell, Edgar Oliver, Margo Passalaqua, Jim Sterling, Christopher Swift

USS FRANKENSTEIN by Axis Company; Directors, Randy Sharp, Brian Barnhart, Christopher Swift, Jim Sterling, David Crabb, Edgar Oliver; October 30, 2003

IN TOKEN OF MY ADMIRATION by Axis Company; Director, Randy Sharp; April 22, 2004; Cast: Brian Barnhart, Joe Fuer

BANK STREET THEATRE

THE FISHERMEN OF BEAUDRAIS by Kathleen Rowlands and Joseph Rinaldi; adapted from the screenplay by Ring Lardner Jr. and Dalton Trumbo; Director, Keith Oncale; July 3, 2003; Cast: Matt Conley, Jennifer Lindsey, Richard Simon, Sherry Nehmer, Jennifer Chudy

JANE by S.N. Behrman; Director, Dan Wackerman; October 5, 2003; Cast: Susan Jeffries, Leila Martin, Richard Bekins, Roland Johnson, Chris Kipiniak, Kristina Bell, Matthew DeCapua

JOSH KORNBLUTH'S LOVE AND TAXES by Josh Kornbluth; Director, David Dower; December 8, 2003; Cast: Josh Kornbluth

RIGHT AS ROD by Judd Bloch; Director, Max Williams; February 2, 2004; Cast: Thomas Guiry, Mark Auerbach, John Dohrman, Kathryn Ekblad, Susan-Kate Heaney, Jono Hustis, Carolyn Ladd, Yvonne Lin, Ben Lizza, Seth Michael May, John McAdams, Mike Mosley, Erica Rhodes, Jas Robertson

COUNSELLOR-AT-LAW by Elmer Rice; Director, Dan Wackerman; May 9, 2004; Cast: John Rubinstein, Madeleine Martin, Joseph Martin, D. Michael Berkowitz, Dennis Burke, Beth Glover, Nell Gwynn, James M. Larmer, David Lavine, Mark Light-Orr, Lanie McEwan, Racheline Maltese, Sal Mistretta, Robert O'Gorman, Ginger Rich, Tara Sands, Letty Serra, Brian Taylor, Ashley West

THE BARROW GROUP

SONNETS FOR AN OLD CENTURY by José Rivera; Director, Emory Van Cleve; October 3, 2003; Cast: Tricia Alexandro, Rozie Bacchi, Dawn Bennett, Georgi Cerruti, Corinne Chandler, Monique Gabriela Curnen, Pietro Gonzalez, Kate McCauley, Myles O'Connor, Eric Paeper, Ron Piretti, Michael Cruz Sullivan, Hope Singsen, Martin Van Treuren, Kevin Craig West

LOBBY HERO by Kenneth Lonergan; Director, Donna Jean Fogel; January 23, 2004; Cast: Jacob White, K. Lorrel Manning, Rozie Bacchi, Larry Mitchell

BARUCH PERFORMING ARTS CENTER

TALES OF UNREST: JOSEPH CONRAD ON STAGE OCTOBER 6, 2003

> **ARSAT** by Christine Simpson; adapted from "The Lagoon"; Director, Christine Simpson; Cast: Jojo Gonzalez, Kevin Bartlett, Lydia Gaston, Tim Kang

> **ONE DAY MORE** by Joseph Conrad; adapted from "Tomorrow;" Director, Jonathan Bank; Cast: Mel Gionson, Jojo Gonzalez, Maile Holck, Robert Wu

CONSTELLATIONS by Julie Book; Director, Thomas G. Waites; December 14, 2003; Cast: Stephanie Schweitzer, Ernest Mingione, James Riordan, Charlie Moss, Annie McGovern

KALIGHAT by Paul Knox; Director, Paul Knox; January 25, 2004; Cast: Samir Ajmera, Susham Bedi, Omar Botros, Grainne de Buitlear, Anna Ewing Bull, Geeta Citygirl, Simon Deonarian, Prashant Kumar Gupta, Ranjit Gupte, Poorna Jagannathan, G.R. Johnson, Naheed Khan, Mami Kimura, Rizwan Manji, David Mason, Suneel Mubayi, Nitika Nadgar, Tyler Pierce, Karam Puri, Eliyas Qureshi, Shawn Rajguru, Giuliana Santini, Chandon Donny Sethi, Mukesh Sethi, Reena Shah, Usman Saukat

THE ROARING GIRLE by Thomas Middleton and Thomas Dekker; adapted by Alice Tuan and Melanie Joseph; Director, Melanie Joseph; February 20, 2004; Cast: Okwui Okpokwasili, Harry Hogan, Marissa Copeland, Douglas Rees, John Epperson, Rebecka Ray, Michael Urie, Clove Galilee, Michael Huston, Jodi Lin, Steven Rattazzi, Andrew McGinn, Steve Cuiffo, Mike Caban

THREE SECONDS IN THE KEY by Deb Margolin; Director, Loretta Greco; Cast: Deb Margolin

TRUE WEST by Sam Shepard; Director, Thomas G. Waites; March 3, 2004; Cast: Marlene Wallace, Sarah Jackson, Charlie Moss, Mary A. Sarno

BECKETT THEATRE

FOR PETE'S SAKE! Musical with Book by Randy Conti; Music by Jeffrey Stein; Lyrics by Douglas Farrell; Director, Randy Conti; October 14, 2003; Cast: Kayla Mason, Chrystal Verdichizzi, Ron Carlos, Danny Carroll, Tatyana de Muns, Emily Gildea, Max Edmands Ryan Crimmins, Jaime Gruber, Rebekah Rubenstein, Ashley Kilbride, Joanna Stein, Jade Elkind, Maddie Smith-Spanier, Frank Sansone, Ashlee Bakey, Amy Joscelyn, Ariel Azoff, Elise Tarantina, Dov Rubenstein, Lindsay Michaels, Hillary Goldfarb, Kaela Teilhaber, Tommy Joscelyn, Chenier Lewis, Sean Whiteford, Noah DeBiase, Alix Josefski

OUR FATHERS by Luigi Lunari; Director, Stephen Jobes; Cast: Mica Begnasco, John Wojda

BELT THEATRE

THE NUCLEAR FAMILY by John Gregorio, Stephen Guarino and Jimmy Bennett; Directors, John Gregorio, Stephen Guarino and Jimmy Bennett; September 10, 2003; Cast: John Gregorio, Stephen Guarino and Jimmy Bennett

MAGGIE MAY by Tom O'Brien; Director, Jocelyn Szabo; February 16, 2004; Cast: Christiane Szabo, Ean Sheehy, Ethan Duff, Stephen Bradbury

TOO MUCH LIGHT MAKES THE BABY GO BLIND by Greg Allen; Directed by the Neo-Futurists; April 2, 2004; Cast: Katrina Toshiko, Desiree Burch, Michael Cyril Creighton, Rob Neill, Justin Tolley, Lindsay Brandon Hunter, Chris Dippel, Sarah Levy, Regie Cabico, Molly Flynn

BLUE HERON ARTS CENTER

THE FLU SEASON by Will Eno; Director, Hal Brooks; January 29, 2004; Cast: Matthew Lawler, David Fitzgerald, Andrew Benator, Roxanna Hope, Elizabeth Sherman, Scott Bowman, James Urbaniak

BEE-LUTHER-HATCHEE by Thomas Gibbons; Director, Jim Pelegano; March 14, 2004; Cast: Perri Gaffney, Thomas James O'Leary, Gha'il Rhodes Benjamin, Catherine Eaton, Lance Spellerberg

BOOMERANG THEATRE COMPANY

THE HOT MONTH by Taylor Mac Bowyer; Director, Marc Parees; September 3, 2003; Cast: Ken Bolden, Paul Caiola, Samantha Desz, Pamela Dunlap, Vince Gatton

THE SUBSTANCE OF JOHN by Francis Kuzler; Director, Cailin Heffernan; September 5, 2003; Cast: David Arthur Bachrach, Ronald Cohen, Jason Field, Bram Heidiger, Jennifer Larkin, Aaron Lisman, Ben Masur, Susan Moses, Heather Paradise, Ian Pfister, Stu Richel, Sarah Sutel

KEELY AND DU by Jane Martin; Director, Rachel Wood; September 10, 2003; Cast: Ken Bolden, Catherin Dowling, Peter O'Connor, Karen Sternberg

DAYS OF WINE AND ROSES by J.P. Miller; Director, Rachel Wood; October 3, 2003; Cast: Mac Brydon, Wally Carroll, Ronald Cohen, Philip Emeott, John Flaherty, Margaret A. Flanagan, Andrea Judge, Montgomery Maguire, Victoria Rosen, Paul Schnee, Laura Siner

CAFÉ A GO GO THEATRE

CAFÉ A GO GO Musical by Joe Corcoran and Dan Corcoran; Director, John Hadden; June 5, 2003; Cast: Vin Adinolfi, Jessica Aquino, Jessica Cannon, Wade Fisher, Zachary Gilman, Stacie May Hassler, Matthew Knowland, John-Mark McGaha, Jasika Nicole Pruitt, Stephanie St. Hilaire

CAP 21

THE BARBARA WOLFF MONDAY NIGHT READING SERIES

TOUCH OF RAPTURE by Mary Fenger Gail; Director, Rasa Allan Kazlas; October 27, 2003

BRAIN CHILDREN by Liza Lentini; Director, Melanie Sutherland; November 3, 2003

THE SIEGE OF ENNIS by Eileen O'Leary; Director, Lawrence Arancio; November 10, 2003

LEGACIES by Susan Cameron; Director, David Grillo; November 17, 2003

THE WHISPER OF SAINTS by Mark Scharf; Director, Eliza Ventura; March 22, 2004

AN UNTITLED NEW MUSICAL Musical with Book and Lyrics by Diane Seymour; Music by Steven Schoenberg; Director, Robert Billig; March 29, 2004

SIX OF ONE Musical with Book and Lyrics by Scott Burkell; Music by Paul Loesel; Director, Frank Ventura; April 12, 2004

CENTER STAGE

THE CHALK GARDEN by Enid Bagnold; Director, Terese Hayden; September 24, 2003; Cast: Jaqueline Brookes, Charles Cissel, Emi Fujinami Jones, Robin Long, Roberta MacIvor, Caitlin McDonough-Thayer, Elizabeth Nafpaktitis, Mary Round, James Stevenson

WAITING FOR GODOT by Samuel Beckett; Director, Keith Teller; October 10, 2003; Cast: Jeffrey M. Bender, Paul Molnar, Michael Rhodes, Greg Skura, Noah Longo

SQUARE ONE by Steve Tesich; Director, Allison Eve Zell; December 3, 2003; Cast: Huda Bordeaux, Ethan Perry

MAO ON LINE ONE by Kimberly Megna; Director, Kelly Gillespie; January 16, 2004; Cast: Jeffrey M. Bender, Christy Collier, Natalie Gold, Eric Loscheider, Ellen Shanman, Michael Warner

THE ELIOTS by Lear deBessonet; Director, Lear deBessonet; April 29, 2004; Cast: Julie Kline, Christopher Logan Healy, Lethia Nall, Nate Schenkkan, Ryan West

CHASHAMA

FIRST LIGHT: A FESTIVAL OF NEW SHORT PLAYS
JUNE 12–29, 2003
PROGRAM A

YOUR CALL IS IMPORTANT by Craig Lucas, Director, Marie-Louise Miller

THIS WILL BE THE DEATH OF HIM by David Dewitt; Director, Vernice Miller

THE LONG SHOT by Richard Cottrell; Director, Elaine Morinaro

MERMAIDS ON THE HUDSON by Anastasia Traina; Director, Mary Monroe

LILY OF THE VALLEY by Lisa Humbertson; Director, Erma Duricko

PROGRAM B

CLIMATE by Joe Pintauro; Director, Jude Schanzer

LOVE by Betty Shamieh; Director, Janice Goldberg

INFORMED CONSENT by Paul Knox; Director, Keith Greer

SOOOO SAD by Ty Adams; Director, Barbar Bosch

THE FUQUA, SLONE, REISENGLASS APPRAISAL by Lawrence Harvey Schulman; Director, Guy Giarrizzo

VERT-GALANT by Jon Fraser; Director, Jon Fraser

SLEEPING IN TOMORROW by Duncan Pflaster; Director, Clara Barton Green; October 7, 2003; Cast: Lauren Adler, Sue Berch, Elizabeth Boskey, Wael Haggiagi, Dawn Pollock Jones, Paul Martin Kovic, Ehud Segev, Jason Specland, Sami Zetts

AS I LAY DYING by William Faulkner; adapted by Andrew Grosso; Director, Andrew Grosso; November 11, 2003; Cast: Arthur Aulisi, Lynne Bolton, Drew Cortese, Meg Defoe, Jordan Gelber, Hillary Keegin, Susan O'Connor, Thomas Piper, Lorenzo Pisoni, Tommy Schrider, John Thomas Waite

WE'RE ALL DEAD Musical with Book and Lyrics by Francis Heaney and James Evans; Music by Francis Heaney; Director, James Evans; November 15, 2003; Cast: Jedidiah Cohen, Tom Bartos, Michelle Bialeck, Trisha Gorman, Tate Henderson, Sean P. Doran, Jason St. Sauver, Vanessa Longley-Cook

HIGH HEELS AND RED NOSES by Keith Nelson and Stephanie Monseu; Directors, Michael Preston and Barbara Karger; January 12, 2004; Cast: the Bindlestiff Family Cirkus

MADAMA FORTUNA! by Antonio Rodriguez; Directors, Antonio Rodriguez and Lisa Marie Black-Meller; Cast: Drew Cortese, Aundre Chin, Jenny Penny Curry, Fred Gunsch, Luke Miller, Dalia Farmer, Erel Pilo

THE LADIES by Anne Washburn; Director, Anne Kauffman; February 8, 2004; Cast: Quincy Tyler Bernstine, Jennifer Dundas, Nina Hellman, Jennifer R. Morris, Maria Striar, Alison Weller

CHERRY LANE THEATRE

GRASMERE by Kristina Leach; Director, Joseph Arnold; June 8, 2003; Cast: Darcy Blakesley, Annie Di Martino, Aaron Gordon, Logan Sledge

THREE WEEKS AFTER PARADISE by Israel Horovitz; Director, Jill André; September 11, 2003; Cast: Mel England

LUSCIOUS MUSIC by Matthew Maguire; September 14, 2003; Cast: Veronica Kehoe, Lourdes Martin, Eric Stoltz, Marisa Echeverria, Ray Anthony Thomas, Richard Petrocelli

MOOMTAJ by Michael Weller; Director, Michael Weller; September 15, 2003; Cast: Jane Burd, Michael Emerson, Lisa Emery, Teresa L. Goding, Jonathan Press, Jay O. Sanders

OLD VIC/NEW VOICES SEPTEMBER 17–24, 2003

THE MENTALISTS by Richard Bean; Director, Ari Edelson; Cast: Bill Buell, David Cale

THE DROWNED WORLD by Gary Own; Director, Tyler Marchant; Cast: Chris Diamantopoulos, Jennifer Mudge, Michael Stuhlbarg, Mary Bacon

A LISTENING HEAVEN Torbenn Betts; Director, Erica Schmidt; Cast: Marylouise Burke, Kathleen Chalfant, Allan Corduner, Daniel Gerroll, Deborah Rush, Heather Goldenhersh

PORT by Simon Stephens; Director, Dave Mowers; Cast: Jen Albano, Keith Nobbs, Brennan Brown, Henry Woronicz, Greg McFadden, Kate Blumberg

TONGUES: A READING SERIES NOVEMBER 5–DECEMBER 3, 2003

DAYS ON EARTH by Richard Caliban

PLANET EYES by Erica Schmidt

BULRUSHER by Eisa Davis

KINDRED STRANGERS by David Batan

SUBWAYS AND BEDROOMS by Tasha Ross

PLEASE STOP TALKING by Sam Forman

LUSCIOUS MUSIC by Matthew Maguire

CAPPY'S FIELD by Glyn O'Malley

HEAVEN HILL, NOVA SCOTIA by Graeme Gillis

800 WORDS: THE TRANSMIGRATION OF PHILIP K. DICK by Victoria Stewart

WORDSWORTH by Alexandra Bullen

YOUNG PLAYWRIGHTS FESTIVAL JANUARY 6–FEBRUARY 20, 2004

THICK by Travis Baker

EASTER CANDY by Halley Feiffer

THE VIEW FROM TALL by Caitlin Montanye Parrish

MENTOR PROJECT: PUBLIC READINGS January 12–26, 2004

DOUBLE SOPHIA by Kendra Levin; Mentored by Michael Weller; Director, Hayley Finn

WORDSWORTH by Alexandra Bullen; Mentored by Ed Bullins; Director, Richard Caliban; January 19, 2004

THUNDERBIRD by Joseph Fisher; Mentored by A.R. Gurney; Director, Randy White; January 26, 2004

MENTOR PROJECT: SHOWCASES MARCH 10–MAY 22, 2004

DOUBLE SOPHIA by Kendra Levin; Mentored by Michael Weller; Director, Hayley Finn; Cast: Janine Barris, Flora Diaz, Justin Grace, Kathryn Grody, Scott Klavan, Anna McCarthy, Peter Scanavino

WORDSWORTH by Alexandra Bullen; Mentored by Ed Bullins; Director, Richard Caliban; Cast: Richard Hughes, Michael Reid, chandra thomas, Anne Louis Zachry

THUNDERBIRD by Joseph Fisher; Mentored by A.R. Gurney; Director, Randy White; Cast: Michael Chernus, Tonya Cornelisse, Laura Flanagan, Michael Rudko, Thomas Sadoski, Tamilla Woodard

TONGUES: READING SERIES

FOREST CITY by Bridgette Wimberly; Directed by Marion McClinton; April 5, 2004; Cast: Cecilia Antoinette, Caroline Clay, Wiley Moore, Charles Turner

CHINA CLUB

THE KARAOKE SHOW by Randy Weiner; Directed by Diane Paulus; November 8, 2003; Cast: Rachel Benbow Murdy, Julie Danao, David Diangelo, Aaron Fuksa, Emily Hellstrom, Charles King, Anderson Lim, Derek Mitchell-Giganti, Robert Orosco, Steve Park, Jordin Ruderman, Marc Santa Maria, Jenny Lee Stern, Erin Stutland, Anna Wilson, Well Yang

CLASSICAL THEATRE OF HARLEM

MACBETH by William Shakespeare; Director, Alfred Preisser; July 11, 2003; Cast: Ty Jones, April Yvette Thompson, Arthur French, Leopold Lowe, Lawrence Winslow, De'adre Aziza, Ouonta Beasley, Onyemaechi Aharanwa

DREAM ON MONKEY MOUNTAIN by Derek Walcott; Director, Alfred Preisser; October 3, 2003; Cast: André De Shields, Kim Sullivan, Benton Greene, Jerry Clicquot, Michael Early, Arthur James Soloman, Neil Dawson, Dele, Celli Pitt, De'adre Aziza, Jaime Carrillo, Tracy Jack, Adenrele Ojo, Catherine Jean-Charles, Melanie J-B Charles

MOTHER COURAGE AND HER CHILDREN by Bertolt Brecht; Director, Christopher McElroen; February 6, 2004; Cast: Gwendolyn Mulamba, Oberon K.A. Adjepong, Onyemaechi Lowe, James Miles, Michael C. O'Day, Parris Wittingham, James Rana, Anna Zastrow

TROJAN WOMEN by Euripides; Adapted by Alfred Preisser; Director, Alfred Preisser; April 2, 2004; Cast: Onyemaechi Aharanwa, Tamela Aldridge, Brie Eley, Phyre Hawkins, Zora Howard, Kerisse Hutchinson, Rain Jack, Tracy Jack, Aman Re-Jack, Zainab Jah, Giselle Jones, Ty Jones, Anthony Lalor, Tonya Latrice, Lisa Mitchell, Folake Olowofoyeku, Ron Simons, Damani Varnado, Channie Waites, Robyne Landiss Walker

CLEMENTE SOTO VELEZ CULTURAL CENTER

BALD DIVA! by David Koteles; Director, Jason Jacobs and Jamee Freedus; July 16, 2003

KAROAKE STORIES by Euijoon Kim; Director, Ala Muraoka, August 8, 2003; Cast: Sekiya Billman, Cindy Cheung, Deborah S. Craig, Siho Ellsmore, Mel Gionson, Marcus Ho, Paul H. Juhn, David Jung, Tim Kang, Peter Kim, Evan Lai, Hoon Lee, Marissa Lichwick, Brian Nishii, Eileen Rivera, James Saito, Jonathan Salkin, Jason Schuchman, Kaipo Schwab, Rodney To, Keo Woolford, Aaron Yoo

ROAD HOUSE: THE STAGE PLAY Director, Timothy Haskell; October 30, 2003; Cast: Taimak Guarriello, Jamie Benge, Christopher Joy, Harry Listig, Lucia Burns, Kellie Montanio, Nick Ahrens, Laura Baggett, Ago the Magichef, Rolando Zuniga, Rachel Roberts, Brian Kantrowitz

SONGS FROM COCONUT HILLA FESTIVAL OF NEW WORKS BY LATINO PLAYWRIGHTS MARCH 22–APRIL 4, 2004

> **ADORATION OF THE OLD WOMAN** by José Rivera
>
> **THE OUTSIDE MAN** by Robert Dominguez
>
> **THE WOMEN OF NINE** by Angie Cruz, Cyn Cañel Rossi and Karen Torres
>
> **LEY OF THE LAND** by Fernando Mañon
>
> **ALL SIDES** by Michael J. Narvaez
>
> **TO THE BAGGAGE CLAIM** by Tanya Saracho
>
> **CHAINED DOG** by Robert Santana
>
> **TRANSPLANTATIONS** by Janis Astor del Valle
>
> **FUEGO** by Juan Shamsul Alam
>
> **BLURRING THE LINES** November 3, 2003
>
> **SHARKEY'S NIGHT** by Brian Snapp; Director, Brian Snapp
>
> **BLACKSTOCKING JENKINS** by Eric Michael Kochmer; Director, Emanuel Bocchieri
>
> **I DREAMED OF DOGS** by Eric Michael Kochmer, Director, Ros Peabody

TROILUS AND CRESSIDA by William Shakespeare; Director, Marc Fajer; March 4, 2004; Cast: Kate Benson, Fernando Betancourt, Pascal Beauboeuf, Jennifer Boggs, Damian Buzzerio, Kiebpoli Calnek, Michelle Kovacs, Emily Mitchell, Michael Moore, Andrew Moore

CONNELLY THEATRE

CAN'T LET GO by Keith Reddin; Director, Carl Forsman; June 1, 2003; Cast: Rebecca Luker, Cheyenne Casebier, Glen Fleshler, Brian Hutchinson, Greg Stuhr

LOST Musical with Book by Kirk Wood Bromley; Music by Jessica Grace Wing; Lyrics by Kirk Wood Bromley; Director, Rob Urbinati; September 5, 2003; Cast: Anni Bruno, Youssif Eid, Annemieke Marie Farrow, Molly Karlin, Adam Kemmerer, Ted Malawer, Janell O'Rourke, Timothy Reynolds, Ed Roggenkamp, Jenna Rose, Karin Lili Ruhe, Michael Ruby, John Schumacher, Kelly Spitco, April Vidal, Chanelle Wilson

GOOD MORNING, BILL by P.G. Wodehouse; Director, Carl Forsman; September 25, 2003; Cast: Jeremiah Wiggins, Heidi Armbruster, Nick Toren, Bridget Ann White, Jenny Mercein, John Vennema, David Standish

JULIUS CAESAR by William Shakespeare; Director, Gregory Wolfe; November 9, 2003; Cast: May Birdsong, Gabriel Edelman, Jay Gaussoin, Gail Giovaniello, Tatiana Gomberg, Bill Gorman, Christopher Haas, Kelly Kinsella, Sarah Knowlton, Ax Norman, Kim Patton, Mason Pettit, John Roque, Dan Snow, Justin Steeve, Paula Stevens, Christopher Yates

THE ORWELL PROJECT FEBRUARY 8, 2004

1984 adapted by Alan Lyddiard; Director, Ginevra Bull

ANIMAL FARM Musical adaptation with Book by Peter Hall; Music by Richard Peaslee; Lyrics by Adrian Mitchell; Director, David Travis

FIRST LADY SUITE by Michael John LaChiusa; Director, Jack Cummings III, April 4, 2004; Cast: Sherry D. Boone, Donna Lynne Champlin, Ruth Gottschall, James Hindman, Robyn Hussa, Julia Murney, Mary Beth Peil, Cheryl Stern, Diane Sutherland, Mary Testa

SCHOOL FOR SCANDAL by Richard Brinsley Sheridan; Director, Rebecca Patterson; April 24, 2003; Cast: Lauren Jill Ahrold, Virginia Baeta, Cynthia Brown, Eliza Ladd, Valentina McKenzie, Maureen Porter, Shanti Elise Prasad, Gisele Richardson, Ami Shukla, DeeAnn Weir

DR2 THEATRE

THE LAST RESORT OR FARBLONDJET by Jeremy Kareken; Director, Michael Montel; October 16, 2003; Cast: Ann Talman, Peter Rini, Robert Heller, Polly Lee, David Staller

ANTIGONE by Jean Anouilh; adapted by Lewis Galantiere; Director, Richard Kuranda; October 29, 2003; Cast: Alicia Regan, David Gideon, Rufus Collins, Elle Zalejski, Carolyn Craig, Daryl Stokes

DANCE THEATRE WORKSHOP

O, SAY A SUNSET by Robin Holcomb; based on the writings of Rachel Carson; Director, Nikki Appino; September 24, 2003; Cast: Robin Holcomb, Julie Rawley, Susanna Burney

ABUNDANCE by Marty Pottenger; Director, Marty Pottenger and Steve Bailey; January 8, 2004; Cast: Cary Barker, Herb Downer, Joe Gioco, Thom Rivera, Nikki E. Walker

DILLON'S

CRATCHETT FARM Musical with Book and Lyrics by Al Pailet; Music by Marshall Pailet; Director and choreographer, Jay Duffer; September 5, 2003; Cast: Dennis Moench, Justis Bolding, Hale Appleman, Eric Briarley, Richard True, Dan Vissers, Joanna Young

THE SHOW MIGHT GO ON by David Kosh; Director, Ann Bowen; November 3, 2003; Cast: Frederic J. Bender, Ross Bechsler, Michael Bullrich, Ali Costine, Katherine Dillingham, Aramand Gabriel, Asta Hansen, Raymond Hill, Carl Maguire, Audrey Moore, Cameron Stevens, Dan Stowell

MINIMUM WAGE Musical with Charlie LaGreca and Jeff LaGreca, with Sean Altman; Director, David G. Armstrong; May 7, 2004; Cast: Charlie LaGreca, Jeff LaGreca, Paul Ashley, Chris Carlisle, Brian Depetris, Harold Lieman, Elen Meulener, Paul Romero, Suzanne Slade, Leah Sprecher

THE DIRECTORS COMPANY

ONCE UPON A TIME IN NEW JERSEY Musical with Book and Lyrics by Susan DiLallo, Music by Stephen Weiner; Director, Pat Birch; June 25, 2003; Cast: Erin Annarella, Todd Buonopane, Nick Cavarra, Funda Duval, Alayna Gallo, Brian Munn, Robert Neary, Orfeh, Ginette Rhodes, Melanie Vaughan, Richard Vida, Wayne Wilcox

BAD GIRLS by Joyce Carol Oates; Director, Susana Tubert; November 10, 2003; Cast: Sarah Hyland, Merrit Wever, Anastasia Webb, Deborah LeCoy, David Sims Bishins

THE PAVILION by Craig Wright; Director, Lucie Tiberghien; February 19, 2004; Cast: Jennifer Mudge, Lee Sellars, Paul Sparks

EDGE THEATRE COMPANY

BLACKBIRD by Adam Rapp; Director, Adam Rapp; April 15, 2004; Cast: Mandy Siegfried, Paul Sparks

NOW THAT'S WHAT I CALL A STORM by Ann Marie Healy; Director, Carolyn Cantor; April 26, 2004; Cast: Marylouise Burke, Daniel Ahearn, Guy Boyd, Rebecca Nelson, Ted Schneider, Daniel Talbott

EMERGING ARTISTS THEATRE COMPANY

EATFEST 2003 NOVEMBER 5–23, 2003

BUM STEER by Justin Warner; Director, James Bowcutt; Cast: Kim Crooks, Nick Battiste

SUN TOUCHING by Eric Kaiser; Director, Lauren Jacobs; Cast: Mike Boland, Jeff Branson

'TIL DEATH DO US PART by Jay C. Rehak; Director, Julie Jensen; Cast: Amy Bizjak, Tom Greenman, John Misselwitz, Kara Taitz

UNFINISHED WORK by Edgar Chisholm; Director, Christ Wojyltko; Cast: Jeanine Abraham, Peter Levine

JOB STRIKES BACK by Matt Casarino; Director, JoEllen Notte; Cast: Wynne Anders, Christopher Borg, Ashley Green, Bill Reinking, Christopher Yustin

L-O-V-E by Joan Ross Sorkin; Director, Amy Fiore; Cast: Eric Christie, Ellen Reilly

FRESHLY KILLED DOVES by Jonathan Reuning; Director, Wes Apfel; Cast: Erin Hadley, Bryan McKinley, Vivian Meisner

TRUE LOVE by Chris Wojyltko; Director, Dere Roche; Cast: Aimee Howard, Richard Ezra Zekaria

PRELUDE TO THE FIRST DAY by Ted LoRusso; Director, Sturgis Warner; Cast: Erin Grann, Danielle Quisenberry, Mark Farnsworth, Matt Behan, Jim Ferris

COSMIC GOOFS by Barbara Lindsay; Director, Ian Marshall; Cast: Peter Herrick, Dayna Steinfeld, Casey Weaver

CLAYMONT by Kevin Brofsky; Director, Derek Jamison; February 1, 2004; Cast: Wynne Anders, Jacqueline Barsh, Glory Gallo, Jason Hare, Aimee Howard, Jason O'Connell, Stephen Sherman

EATFEST 2004 MARCH 16–APRIL 4, 2004

THE ONE ABOUT THE RABBI by Mark Lambeck; Director, Troy Miller; Cast: Lavette Gleis, Wayne Henry, Geany Masai

A MESSAGE FOR ANGELA by Jack Rushen; Director, Pamela Rosenberger; Cast: Laura Fois, Tom Greenman, Christopher Michael Todd

A CURTAIN CALL TO ARMS by Matt Casarino; Director, Deb Guston; Cast: Amy Bizjak, Ryan Duncan, Erin Hadley, Peter Herrick, Bryan McKinley, Vivian Meisner, Kim Reed, Bill Reinking, Wayne Temple, Tracee Chimo, Lela Frechett

MARKIE7722 by Alex Lewin; Director, Rebecca Kendall; Cast: Desmond Dutcher, Jason O'Connell, J. Michael Zally

LIGHTS OUT by Cassie Angley; Director, Amy Fiore; Cast: Jessica Calvello, Stephanie Ila Silver, Rochele Tillman, Wynne Anders

3 WOMEN by Michael Edwin Stuart; Director, Dawn Copeland; Cast: Valerie David, Glory Gallo, Robyn Ganeles

PEACHES EN REGALIA by Steven Lyons; Director, Andrew Ronan; Cast: Matt Boethin, Carter Inskeep, Yvonne Roen, Casey Weaver

FEZ

MAKE LOVE by Karen Finley; Director, Lance Cruse; July 13, 2003; Cast: Karen Finley, Chris Tanner, Lance Cruse

ART, LIFE AND SHOW-BIZ by Ain Gordon; Director, Ain Gordon; April 18, 2004; Cast: Helen Gallagher, Lola Pashalinski, Valda Setterfield

59E59

BRITS OFF BROADWAY APRIL 7–JULY 4, 2004

MY ARM by Tim Crouch; Cast: Tim Crouch

SUN IS SHINING by Matt Wilkinson; Director, Matt Wilkinson

THE WOMAN DESTROYED by Simone de Beauvoir; Translated by Diana Quick; Cast: Diana Quick

HEAVENLY by Frantic Assembly

COOKING FOR KINGS by Ian Kelly; Director, Simon Green; Cast: Ian Kelly

ABSOLUTELY FASCINATING by Fascinating Aida

GHOST CITY by Gary Owen; Director, Simon Harris

BERKOFF'S WOMEN/NO FEAR! Perfomed in Rep; Cast: Linda Marlowe

HURRICANE by Richard Dormer; Director, Rachel O'Riordan; Cast: Rachel Dormer

THE STRAITS by Gregory Burke; Director, John Tiffany

Adele Anderson, Dillie Keane, Liza Pulman in *Absolutely Fascinating* PHOTO BY ANDY BRADSHAW

THE FLEA THEATRE

GETTING INTO HEAVEN by Polly Draper; Director, Claire Lundberg; July 2, 2003; Cast: Polly Draper, James Badge Dale, Gretchen Egolf, Barbara Eda-Young, Cooper Pillot

LIKE I SAY by Len Jenkin; Director, Len Jenkin; October 30, 2003; Cast: Oberon K.A. Adjepong, Matthew Dellapina, Paula Ehrenberg, Fernando Gambaroni, Shari Hellman, Lanna Joffrey, Carolinne Messihi, Melissa Miller, Jeffrey Nauman, Jack O'Neill, John Peterson, Jonathan Kells Phillips, Sayra Player, Jerry Zellers

CELLOPHANE by Mac Wellman; Director, Jim Simpson; September 17, 2003; Cast: Oberon K.A. Adjepong, Katie Apicella, Matthew Dellapina, Paula Ehrenberg, Ayse Eldek, Fernando Gabaroni, Lindy Gomez, Sarah Hayon, Lanna Joffrey, Josh Mann, Holly McLean, Jace McLean, Carolinne Messihi, Jeffrey Nauman, John Peterson, Johnathan Kells Phillips, Monica Stith, Sakura Sugihara, Gilbert Vela, Aaron Yoo, Jerry Zellers

POWDER KEG by Dejan Dukovski; Translated by Philip Philipovich; Director, Michelle Malavet; November 10, 2003; Cast: Rafael De Mussa, Randy Ryan, James Nardella, Stacy Rock, Jace McLean

THE PARROT by Paul Zimet and Ellen Maddow; Director, Paul Zimet; January 21, 2004; Cast: Scott Blumenthal, Elizabeth Daniels, Matthew Dellapina, Autum Dornfeld, Kimberly Gambino, Carolyn Goelzer, Paul Iacono, Steven Rosen, Renoly Santiago

THE WANDERER by Dmitry Lipkin; Director, Adam Melnick; March 2, 2004; Cast: Anthony Arkin, Larry Block, Amelia Campbell, Matthew Dellapina, Brian Gottesman, Irma St.Paule, David Warshofsky

DESIGN YOUR KITCHEN by Kate Ryan; Directors, Kate Ryan and Jim Simpson; April 14, 2004

THE LAKE by Gary Winter; Director, Hayley Finn; April 21, 2004; Cast: Jennifer Boggs, Lanna Joffrey, Dan O'Brien, Sayra Player

45 BLEECKER

DON JONNY by Anton Dudley and Jonathan Spottiswoode; Director, Jesse Berger; November 3, 2003

A MAD WORLD, MY MASTERS by Thomas Middleton; Director, Michael Barakiva

THE WITCH OF EDMONTON by Thomas Dekker, John Ford and William Rowley; Director, David Grimm; November 9, 2003; Cast: Morgan Jenness

DANTON'S DEATH by Georg Büchner; Director, Christopher McCann; November 11, 2003

PHAEDRA by Elizabeth Egloff; Director, Jesse Berger; November 16, 2003; Cast: Amy Irving, Ruth Maleczech

KEAN by Jean-Paul Sartre; Director, Eleanor Holdridge; November 18, 2003

THE TRADGEDY OF HAMLET, PRINCE OF DENMARK by Rob Grace; Director, Devon Berkshire; November 21, 2003; Cast: Bradford Louryk, Michael Cyril Creighton, Hannah Bos, Paul Thureen, Phoebe Ventouras, Alexa Scott-Flaherty

THE LIFE OF SPIDERS by Kelly Stuart; Director, Rebecca Holderness; March 19, 2004; Cast: Tuomas Hil, Kathryn Foster, Kevin Kuhlke, Jessma Evans, Christopher Burns, Raïna von Waldenburg, Malinda Walford, Robert Airhart, Kate Kohler Amory, Brendan McCall, Mark Wilson

THE INTERNATIONALIST by Anne Washburn; Director, Ken Rus Schmoll; April 19, 2004; Cast: Mark Shanahan, Heidi Schreck, Gibson Frazier, Kristen Kosmas, Travis York

45TH STREET THEATRE

ANTICIPATING HEAT by Charlotte Winters; Director, Ria Cooper; January 6, 2004; Cast: Devon Berkshire, Erin Logemann, Blake Longacre, Jen Wineman

UN BECOMING by Rick Schweikert; Director, Rick Schweikert and Jeffrey Edward Carpenter; February 11, 2004; Cast: Laura Flanagan, Tami Dixon, Benjamin Moore, David McCamish, Jeffrey Edward Carpenter, Sage Fitzgerald, Naomi Barr

THE JOURNALS OF MIHAIL SEBASTIAN by Mihail Sebastian; adapted by David Auburn; March 23, 2004; Director, Carl Forsman; Cast: Stephen Kunken

GREENWICH STREET THEATRE

THE PITCHFORK DISNEY by Philip Ridley; Director, Kevin Kittle; June 18, 2003; Cast: Victor Villar-Hauser, Tara Denby, James M. Larmer, Aidan Redmond

CHEKHOV'S RIFLE by Alex Ladd; Director, Nolan Haims; September 23, 2003; Cast: Austin Pendleton, Jess Osuna, Craig Bachmann, Veronica Bero, Bridget Flanery, Dawn McGee, George Morafetis

GROUND FLOOR THEATRE

Fat Chance Productions, Inc. and Monday Morning Productions

CLOSET CHRONICLES by Eric R. Pfeffinger; Producers, Jason Cicci, Ben Hodges; Director, Ben Hodges; Scenic Design, David Esler; Costumes, Liz Beckham; Lighting, Juliet Chia; Sound, Dennis Michael Keefe; Production Stage Manager, Karen Munkel; Master Carpenter, Matt Picheco; Prop Design, Casey Kern; Asst. to Producers, Rachel Werbel; Press, Karen Greco Entertainment. A play in two acts. The action takes place in the present, at the Angell family home, located in Cincinnati, Ohio. Opened at the Ground Floor Theatre, October 10–November 2, 2003; Cast: Marilyn Sokol (Nancy), Brandon Malone (George), Emilie Madison (Agatha), Richard Leighton (Ed), Jason Cicci (Dr. Lester Niemark), Ben Hersey (Wes)

Marilyn Sokol, (top to bottom) Ben Hersey, Brandon Malone, Emilie Madison in *Closet Chronicles* PHOTO BY ANTHONY VAN SLYKE

HAROLD CLURMAN THEATRE

THE TRIALS OF MS KATHERINE by Chuck McMahon; Director, George Allison; November 8, 2003; Cast: Janet Dunson, Ruth Miller, Jimmy Dean, Monica Bailey, Cecelia Riddert, Samantha Bilinkas, Stephen Benson, Darren Capozzi, Wilbur Edwin Henry, Joel Nagle

HERE ARTS CENTER

FUSE: THE NYC CELEBRATION OF QUEER CULTURE JUNE 16–JULY 5, 2003

> **LESBIAN PULP-O-RAMA!** by Heather de Michele, Anna Fitzwater, Gretchen M. Michelfeld, Beatrice Terry
>
> **HOLLY'S FOLLY** by Brandon Olson and Chris Tanner
>
> **WEEKENDS AT PED CLUB** by Peter Morris; Director, Joseph Rosswog
>
> **ANDY HOROWITZ'S B.D.F.** by Andy Horowitz
>
> **BAD GIRLS!** by Greg Wolloch and Allison Castillo

GRAVITY ALWAYS WINS by Marc Spitz; Director, Jonathan Lisecki; July 11, 2003; Cast: Jonathan Lisecki, Zeke Farrow, Andersen Gabrych, Philip Littell, Brian Reilly, Alexandra Oliver, Valerie Clift

(front) Dale Soules, (back) Monica Appleby, April Matthis in *Anna Bella Eema*

April Matthis, Dale Soules, Monica Appleby in *Anna Bella Eema* PHOTOS BY CAROL ROSEGG

RANDOM SEXUAL ACTS Short plays by John Lee and Derek Paul Narendra; Director, Ava Clade; August 4–20, 2003; Cast: Natalie Arkus, Kelly Ann Heaney, Brian Parks, Nick Paglino

> **THE PARISAN LOVE STORY** by Derek Paul Narendra
>
> **HONESTY** by John Lee
>
> **THE PROPOSAL** by Derek Paul Narendra
>
> **SPAM, INC.** by John Lee
>
> **LIGHTS, CAMERA, ACTION** by Derek Paul Narendra

MR. GALLICO by Sam Carter; Director, Henry Caplan; August 8, 2003; Cast: Jason Howard, Karl Herlinger, Tate Henderson

BELLY: THREE SHORTS by Alva Rogers; Director, Julia Whitworth; September 9, 2003; Cast: Sherry D. Boone, Myorah B. Middleton, Barbara Pitts, Margi Sharp, Sophia Skiles, Meredith Wright

ANNA BELLA EEMA by Lisa D'Amour and Chris Sidorfsky; Director, Katie Pearl; September 15, 2003; Cast: Monica Appleby, April Matthis, Dale Soules

LESBIAN PULP-O-RAMA IN A VERY PULPY CHRISTMAS by Heather de Michele, Anna Fitzwater, Gretchen M. Michelfeld, Beatrice Terry; December 8, 2003

THESE VERY SERIOUS JOKES by Douglas Langworthy; adapted from Goethe's Faust; Directed by David Herskovits; January 8, 2004; Cast: David Greenspan, Will Badgett, George Hannah, E.C. Kelly, Pun Bandhu, Yuri Skujins, Wayne Scott

THE VIY by Nikolai Gogol; Adapted by Richard Harland Smith; Director, Richard Harland Smith; March 20, 2004; Cast: Stephen Aloi, Jamie Askew, Roy Bacon, Jeff Buckner, Tom Cappadona, Michael Cuomo, Julie Hera, Karl Jeremy Schwartz, Jarrod Spector, Julie Whitney

THE MYSTERY OF THE CHARITY OF JOAN OF ARC by Charles Pèguy; translated by Julian Green; Director, David Herskovits; May 12, 2004; Cast: Daphne Gaines, Jerusha Klemperer, Sophia Skiles

THE IMMIGRANTS' THEATRE PROJECT

LITTLE PITFALL by Markéta Bláhová; translated by Jiri Topel; Director, Marcy Arlin; January 21, 2004; Cast: Mayura Baweja, Oscar de la Fe Colon, Nannette Deasy, Adriana Gaviria, Eileen Rivera, Tzahi Moskovitz

NEW INDIGENOUS VOICES FROM AUSTRALIA
MARCH 17–MAY 18, 2004

CROWFIRE by Jadah Milroy; Director, Kaipo Schwab; Cast: Bryan Andy

YANAGAI! YANAGAI! by Andrea James; Director, Marcy Arlin; Cast: Louise Bennett

BOX THE PONY by Scott Rankin and Leah Purcell

STOLEN by Jane Harrison; Director, Karen Oughtred; Cast: Kylie Belling

CONVERSATIONS WITH THE DEAD by Richard Frankland; Director, Muriel Miguel; Cast: Aaron Pederson

INTAR 53

SMASHING by Brooke Berman; Director, Trip Cullman; October 12, 2003; Cast: David Barlow, Lucas Papaelias, Katharine Powell, Joseph Siravo, Katherine Waterston, Merritt Wever

THE IRONDALE ENSEMBLE PROJECT

OUTSIDE THE LAW by Jim Niesen and the company; Director, Jim Niesen; May 11, 2004; Cast: Danny Bacher, Josh Bacher, Erin Biernard, Terry Greiss, Michael-David Gordon, Jack Lush, Barbara Mackenzie-Wood, Celli Pitt, Damen Scranton, Laura Wickens

JOHN MONTGOMERY THEATRE COMPANY

SAME TRAIN by Levy Lee Simon; Music and Lyrics by Mark Bruckner; Director, Nicki H.J. Stadm; February 7, 2004; Cast: Henry Afro-Bradley, Tamela Aldridge, Nicoye Banks, Thaddeus Daniels, Chris Evans, Indigo Melendez, LaRee Reese, Norman Small Jr.

KIRK THEATRE

TRUST by Gary Mitchell; Director, Erical Schmidt; May 9, 2004; Cast: Ritchie Coster, Fiona Gallagher, Kevin Isola, Colin Lane, Dan McCabe, Declan Mooney, Meredith Zinner

KRAINE THEATRE

DAY OF RECKONING by Melody Cooper; Director, Lorca Peress; April 14, 2004; Cast: Freedom Bailey, Parris Nicole Cisco; Melody Cooper, Michael Kennealy, Alima Lindsey

LARK PLAY DEVELOPMENT CENTER

ANNUAL PLAYWRIGHTS WEEK JUNE 4–7, 2003

MR. AND MRS. G by Jeff Barow; Director, Jim Ashcraft

I'M BREATHING THE WATER NOW by Bash Halow; Director, May Adrales

HUMANS REMAIN by Robin Rice Lichtig; Director, Daniella Topol

SUSPECTS by Joe DiMiceli; Director, Angel David

LINGUA by Roger Williams; Director, Michael Johnson-Chase

THE MOTHERLINE by Chantal Bilodeau; Director, Steven Williford

THREE CHRISTS LIVE by Dan O'Brien; Director, Leah C. Gardiner

THE GRANDMAMA TREE: A FOLKFABLE by Bernard Cummings; Director, Jack Cummings III

WAXING WEST by Saviana Stanescu; Director, Michael Johnson-Chase; September 25, 2003; Cast: Michael Bakkensen, Glynis Bell, Celia Howard, Tom Ligon, Connie Nelson, George Pappas, Wayne Schroder, Jennifer Dorr White

UNDONE by Andrea Thome; Director, Victor Maog; October 30, 2003; Cast: Denia Brache, Victoria Cartagena, Carlo D'Amore, Mateo Gomez, Ernesto Rodriguez, Teresa Yenque

SEX IN OTHER PEOPLE'S HOUSES by Sonia Pabley; Director, Ashok Sinha; April 23, 2004; Cast: Rizwan Manji, Pooja Kumar, Nandita Shenoy, Samir Younis

JAZ and **BIG SHOOT** by Koffi Kwahulé; translated by Chantal Bilodeau; Director, Michael Johnson-Chase; May 18, 2004; Cast: Zabryna Guevara, Wayne Schroder, Sorab Wadia

LION THEATRE

WHITE WIDOW Musical by Paul Dick; Based on Mario Fratti's *Mafia*; Director, Cara Reichel; June 7, 2003; Cast: Patrick Spencer Bodd, Larry Brustofski, Sarah Corey, Michael Day, James Donegan, Dennis D. Driskill, Al Gordon, Matthew Allen Hardy, Gloria Hodes, Ronald Roy Johnson Jr., Elizabeth Kingsley, Rachel Styne, Marina Torres

UNIDENTIFIED HUMAN REMAINS AND THE TRUE NATURE OF LOVE by Brad Fraser; Director, Robert Bella; March 27, 2004; Cast: Diana Ascher, Caroline Cagney, Lauren Castellano, Andrew Frost, Greg Jackson, Joe Stipek, Brandon Thompson

THE END OF YOU by Michael D. Cohen; Director, Sarah Gurfield; May 14, 2004; Cast: PJ Sosko, Poorna Jagannathan

LUCILLE LORTEL THEATRE

SUMMER OF THE SWANS by Julia Jordan, based on the children's book by Betsy Byers; Director, Joe Calarco; July 16–August 20, 2003; Music, Obadiah Eaves; Producer, Theatreworks/USA; Cast: Angela Bullock, John Lloyd Young, Greg Shamie, Dustin Sullivan, Bethany Butler and Kate Wetherhead.

Kate Wetherhead, John Lloyd Young in *Summer of the Swans* PHOTO BY CAROL ROSEGG

MANHATTAN ENSEMBLE THEATRE

THE HUNGER WALTZ by Sheila Callaghan; Director, Olivia Honegger; January 10, 2004; Cast: Susan O'Connor, Kittson O'Neill, Michael Connors, Brent Popolisio, Susan O'Connor

MANHATTAN THEATRE SOURCE

THREE SISTERS by Anton Chekhov; Translated by Boris Kievsky; Director, Andrew Frank; January 7, 2004; Cast: Daryl Boling, Ato Essandoh, Joe Ganem, Hope Garland, Carla Hayes, Jason Howard, Fiona Jones, Clyde Kelley, Boris Kievsky, Neil Maffin, Mitchell Riggs, Carla Tassara, Ben Thomas, Catherine Zambri

THAT WOMAN: REBECCA WEST REMEMBERS by Carl Rollyson, Anne Bobby and Helen Macleod; Director, David Drake; March 6, 2004; Cast: Anne Bobby

SHRINKAGE by Manuel Igrejas; Director, Lory Henning-Dyson; March 31, 2004; Cast: Susan Blackwell, Laura Camien, Jeffrey Doornbos

MA-YI THEATRE COMPANY

WAVE by Sung Rno; Director, Will Pomerantz; March 21, 2004; Cast: Michi Barall, Deborah S. Craig, Ron Domingo, Paul H. Juhn, Patrick McNulty, Aaron Yoo

MAZER THEATRE

A STOOP ON ORCHARD STREET Musical by Jay Kholos; Director, Lon Gary; August 7, 2003; Cast: Edward Anthony, Selby Brown, Lili Corn, Valerie David, Eleni Delopoulos, Daniel Fischer, Lon Gary, Deborah Grausman, Joel Halsted, Kristian Hunter Lazzaro, Stuart Marshall, Sarah Matteucci, David Mendell, Shad Olsen, Jonathan Schneidman, Joseph Spiotta, Scott Steven, Antonia Garza Szilagi, Sharon Taylor, Anne Tonelson, Marlar Weiner, Stephanie Wilberding

MELTING POT THEATRE COMPANY

VANISHING POINT Musical with Book by Liv Cummins and Robert Hartmann; Music, Robert Hartmann; Lyrics by Liv Cummins, Robert Hartmann, and Scott Keys; Director, Michelle Tattenbaum; April 26, 2004; Cast: Alison Fraser, Emily Skinner, Barbara Walsh

MIDTOWN INTERNATIONAL THEATRE FESTIVAL JULY 14–AUGUST 3, 2003

SCHEDULE INCLUDED:

THE COLONEL'S WIFE by Mario Fratti; Director, Roi Escudero; Cast: Roi Escudero, Alex McCord, Michael Earle, Francisco Cantilo, Julio Soler, Paula Wilson

THE REMARKABLE JOURNEY OF PRINCE JEN Musical with Book and Lyrics by Brian Vinero; Music, Seth Weinstein; Based on the novel by Lloyd Alexander; Director, Joel Froomkin

FAVORITE COLORS by Scott R. Ritter; Director, Ernest Abuba

COMPANIONS by Denis McKeown; Director, Jason Grant

NICE GUYS FINISH... by Eric Alter; Director, Rob Sullivan

THE OVERDEVELOPMENT OF SCOTT by Sharon Fogarty; Director, Sharon Fogarty

STAINED GLASS UGLY by Qui Nguyen; Director, Robert Ross Parker

WAITING FOR THE GLACIERS TO MELT by Brian Lane Green

WHO AM I by Rodney E. Reyes; Director, Rodney E. Reyes

WALKING THROUGH THE NIGHT by Haerry Kim; Director, Christopher Petit

THRILL ME: THE LEOPOLD AND LOEB STORY Musical with Book, Music, and Lyrics by Stephen Dolginoff; Director, Martin Charnin

CRIMINAL by Javier Daulte; Director, Gwynn MacDonald

THE $25,000 PYRAMID by Nick Vigorito Jr.; Director, Morgan Doninger; Cast: Damian Vanore, Antony Vitrano, Tim Cinnante, Pete Mele, Michael Bullrich

AMERICAN TREACLE Musical with Book by Bricken Sparacino and Natalie Wilder; Music by Natalie Sparacino, Eric Chercover, Michael Birch and Richard Homan; Lyrics by Bricken Sparacino, Natalie Wilder, Eric Chercover, Michael Birch, Richard Homan

BKC by Matt Schapiro and Brad Webb; Directors, Matt Schapiro and Brad Webb

LILIA! by Libby Skala; Director, Gabriel Barre; Cast: Libby Skala

(GONE WITH) MISS JULIE by Shela Xoregos; Based on a Michael Meyer translation of August Strindberg's *Miss Julie*; Director and Choreographer, Shela Xoregos; Cast: Keith Carter, Kim Gainer, Erin Hunter, Talie Melnyk, Carin Murphy, Gregory Ward

JUST US BOYS by Frank Stancati; Director, Catherine Lamm

THE WINNER: A BROOKLYN FABLE Musical with Book by Inez Basso Glick and Annmarie Fabricatore; Music and Lyrics by Stanley Glick; Director, Ron Nakahara; Cast: Michael Ricciardone, Marnie Baumer, Jeremy Ellison Gadstone

THAT PLAY: A ONE PERSON MACBETH by William Shakespeare; Adapted by Tom Gualtieri and Heather Hill; Director, Heather Hill; Cast: Tom Gualtieri

MINT SPACE

THE HEIRESS adapted by Ruth and Augustus Goetz; based on the novel *Washington Square* by Henry James; Director, Mahayana Landowne; January 14, 2004; Cast: Michael Balsley, Sarah Dandridge, David Gochfeld, Rebecca Hoodwin, James Jacobson, Kelly Ann Moore, Jean Morgan, Dee Pelletier, Michele Tauber

NEIGHBORHOOD PLAYHOUSE

HANDY DANDY by William Gibson; Director, Don Amendolia; December 9, 2003; Cast: Helen Gallagher, Nicolas Surovy

TASTING MEMORIES by Michael Fischetti and Emily Mitchell; Director, Don Amendolia; May 21, 2004; Cast: Michael Fischetti, Don Amendolia, Emily Mitchell and a rotating cast including Rosemary Harris, Kitty Carlisle Hart, Philip Bosco, Tammy Grimes, Alvin Epstein, Richard Easton, Joy Franz, Kathleen Noone, Mel Cobb

NEW VICTORY THEATRE

COOKIN' by Seung Whan Song; Director, Seung Whan Song; September 25, 2003; Cast: Kang Il Kim, Won Hae Kim, Bum Chan Lee, Coo Ja Seo, Jo Yeoul Sul, Hyung Suk Jung, Ji Won Kang, Young Hoon Kim, Sung Min Lee

BUG MUSIC by Don Byron; April 26, 2004; Cast: Don Byron

IDIOTS ADIOS: THE FLAMING IDIOTS May 26, 2004; Cast: Rob Williams, Jon O'Connor, Kevin Hunt

THE NEW YORK CITY HIP-HOP THEATRE FESTIVAL JUNE 3–14, 2003

FLOW by Will Power; Director, Danny Hoch; Cast: Will Power

TILL THE BREAK OF DAWN by Danny Hoch

JACK YA BODY PART 1: STORM'S SOLO FOR TWO by the Rubberband Dance Company

OPEN STREET HYDRANT by Jen Sabel

JACK YA BODY PART 2: OLIVE by the Rubberband Dance Company

BEATBOX: A RAPPERETTA by Tommy Shepherd and Dan Wolf

WORD BECOMES FLESH by Marc Bamuthi

BLOODCLAAT by D'bi Young

MELIC COMPOSED by Lisa Biggs and Tanisha Christie

IN THE HEIGHTS by Lin Manuel-Miranda

SLICK RHYMES by Claudia Alick

MY STARSHIP by Zvi Rosenfeld

TEA by Ben Snyder

SOUNDTRACK CITY by Yuri Lane

SLICE by Kerri Kochanski

CULTURE BANDIT by Vanessa Hidary

BLACK FOLKS GUIDE TO BLACK FOLKS by Hanifah Walidah

BULLETPROOF DELI by Sabela

STAKES IS HIGH by Pattydukes

ANGELA'S MIX TAPE by Eisa Davis

IN THE LAST CAR by MUMs

ROUGH DRAFT OF MY LIFE by tigerlily

REWIND by Greg Beuthin

GIVING UP THE GUN by David Rodriguez

NEW YORK INTERNATIONAL FRINGE FESTIVAL AUGUST 8–24, 2003

SCHEDULE INCLUDED:

ACTS OF CONTRITION by Timothy Nolan; Director, Vincent Marano

AMERICAN FABULOUS by Jeffry Strouth; Adapted by Troy Carson; Director, Jonathan Warman; Cast: Troy Carson

ASHIRA69 (EPISODE #1: CUT TO THE CHASE!) by Paul Sapp; Director, Tina Polzin

BERSERKER by Paul Outlaw; Director, Tanya Kane-Parry

CARESSES by Sergie Belbel; Director, Adam C. Eisenstein

GOD BLESS AMERICANA: THE RETRO VACATION SLIDE SHOW by Charles Phoenix

DEAR CHARLOTTE by Joy Gregory; Director, Joy Gregory and Anthony Byrnes

"BUDDY" CIANCI: THE MUSICAL by Jonathan Van Gieson and Mike Tarantino; Director, Dean Strober

A LIFE IN HER DAY by Hilary Chaplain; Director, Patricia Buckley

PANIC IS NOT A DISORDER by Pat Candaras; Cast: Pat Candaras

FAITH By Eric Sanders; Director, Eric Sanders

STAGGERING TOWARD AMERICA by Rik Reppe; Director, Jack Rowe

BIG GIRL, LITTLE WORLD by Jay Duffer; Director, Jay Duffer

SCALPEL Musical with Book, Music, and Lyrics by D'Arcy Drollinger; Director, John Ficarra

THE IRREPLACEABLE COMMODITY by Michael Minn; Director and Choreographer, Gary Slavin

MO(U)RNING by Adrian Rodriguez; Director, Adrian Blanco

FREEDOM OF SPEECH by Eliza Jane Schneider; Director, Sal Romeo

PALE IDIOT by Kirk Lynn; Director, Laramie Dennis

NEW YORK THEATRE WORKSHOP

James C. Nicola, Artistic director; Lynn Moffat, Managing director

THE ARCHITECTURE OF LOSS BY Julia Cho; Director, Chay Yew; January 11, 2004; Cast: Angel Desai, Mia Katigbak, Jason Lew, Will Marchetti, Matthew Saldivar, Victor Slezak, Eric Wippo

92ND STREET Y

RETURN JOURNEY by Bob Kingdom; Director, Anthony Hopkins; Cast: Bob Kingdom

OHIO THEATRE

ICE FACTORY 2003 SUMMER THEATRE FESTIVAL JULY 9–AUGUST 16, 2003

MOTHER'S LITTLE HELPER by Lenora Champagne; Director, Robert Lyons; Cast: Lenora Champagne

CONQUEST OF THE UNIVERSE by Charles Ludlam; Director, Emma Griffin

FLOP created by Pig Iron Theatre

THE MYOPIA by David Greenspan; Cast: David Greenspan

HATCHED created by SaBooge Theatre

DECEPTION by Jeremy Dobrish; Director, Jeremy Dobrish

MOBY DICK by Herman Melville; Adapted by Julian Rad; Director, Hilary Adams; September 6, 2003; Cast: Christopher Kelly, Michael Berry, Michael Shawn Montgomery, Julian Rad, Antony Ferguson, Joseph Melendez, Eirik Gislason, William Metzo

NO MEAT NO IRONY by Robert Lyons; Director, Robert Lyons; September 29, 2003; Cast: Celia Schaeffer, Jeremy Brisiel

TERROTICA by Wade Bowen; Director, Bard Krumholz; October 23, 2003; Cast: Wade Bowen, Rosaruby Glaberman, Sarah Dey Hirshan, Patricia Skarbinski

DEMON BABY by Erin Courtney; Director, Ken Rus Schmoll; January 9, 2004; Cast: Heidi Schreck, Patrick McNulty, Nina Hellman, Gibson Frazier, Leo Kittay, Polly Lee, Mark Shanahan, Glenn Fleschler

SUPERPOWERS by Jeremy Dobrish; Director, Jessica Davis-Irons; May 1, 2004; Cast: Arthur Aulisi, Jeremy Brisiel, Ryan Bronz, Nina Hellman, Dana Croll Smith, Stan Lachow, Christy Meyer, Margie Stokley

AS I LAY DYING by William Faulkner; Adapted by Andrew Grosso; Director, Andrew Grosso; May 2, 2004; Cast: Arthur Aulisi, Sarah Bellows, Eric Martin Brown, Drew Cortese, Aimee McCormick, Thomas Piper, Tommy Schrider, John Thomas Waite, Amy Laird Webb

ONTOLOGICAL THEATRE

NON-D by Andrew Irons; Director, Jessica Davis-Irons; August 20, 2003; Cast: Emanuele Ancornini, Arthur Aulisi, Sarah Bellows, Jeremy Brisiel, Richard Hamilton Dibella, Jeremy Ellison-Gladstone, Margie Stokley

KING COWBOY RUFUS RULES THE UNIVERSE by Richard Foreman; Director, Richard Foreman; January 15, 2004; Cast: Juliana Francis, Jay Smith, T. Ryder Smith

MY RENAISSANCE FAIRE LADY by Evan Cabnet; Director, Evan Cabnet; Cast: John Forest, Eris V. Migliorini, Corey Patrick, Caleb Scott, Noah Trepanier, Ted Welch

PANTHEON THEATRE

NEW ANATOMIES by Timberlake Wertenbaker; Director, James Marshall; September 10, 2003; Cast: Anny Hopkins; Shawn Kane, Mireya Lucio, Melanie Levy, Lilly Medville

SACRIFICE TO EROS by Frederick Timm; Director, Marc Parees; October 22, 2003; Cast: Pamela Dunlap, Jaime Sanchez, Caesar Samayoa, Don Clark Williams, Eric Jordan Young, Maria Helan Checa

SEASCAPE WITH SHARKES AND DANCER by Don Nigro; Director, Jason Eiland; November 5, 2003; Cast: April Dawn Brown, Jef Cozza

METROPOLITAN OPERAS by Joe Pintauro; Directors, Lisa Melita French, Michael LoPorto, Francisco Solorzano; April 15, 2004; Cast: Jeremy Brena, Gabriel Buentello, AnaMaria Correa, Kendra Leigh Landon, Victoria Malvagno, Keri Meoni, Chiara Montalto, Jay Rivera, Gilberto Ron, Francisco Solorzano, Dedra McCord-Ware

NECROPOLIS by Don Nigro; Director, John DiFusco; May 13, 2004; Cast: Francesca Nina O'Keefe, Jim Thalman

PARADISE THEATRE

PEOPLE DIE THAT WAY by Lisa Ebersole; Director, Lisa Ebersole; February 22, 2004; Cast: Dahl Colson, Lisa Ebersole, Ken Forman, Rhonda Keyser, Monique Vukovic

PELICAN STUDIO THEATRE

THE CURATE SHAKESPEARE AS YOU LIKE IT by Don Nigro; Director, Christopher Thomasson; April 16, 2004; Cast: Christopher Yeatts, Candice Holdorf, Sarah Sutel, Brian J. Carter, Josephine Cashman, Todd Butera, Timothy Roselle

PETER JAY SHARP THEATRE

FIGHTING WORDS by Sunil Kuruvilla; Director, Liz Diamond; February 15, 2004; Cast: Marin Ireland, Jayne Houdyshell, Pilar Witherspoon

PHIL BOSAKOWSKI THEATRE

THE TEMPEST AND RICHARD III by William Shakespeare; Director, Jason Alan Carvell; October 23, 2003

ORESTES by Charles L. Mee; Director, Ellen Beckerman; January 8, 2004; Cast: Margot Ebling, Shawn Fagan, James Saidy

PROSPECT THEATRE COMPANY

THE BELLE'S STRATAGEM by Hanna Cowley; Director, David McCallum; September 27, 2003; Cast: Dorothy Abraham, Robert Bowen Jr., Aysan Çelik, R. Paul Hamilton, Leo Kittay, Damian Long, Kate MacKenzie, Ian Oldaker, Saxon Palmer, Christian Roulleau, Wendy Rich Stetson, Ed Vassallo, Susan Wands

THE HOUSE OF BERNARDA ALBA by Frederico Garcia Lorca; Director, Cara Reichel; January 17, 2004; Cast: Betty Hudson, Giovanna Zaccaro, Jennifer Michele Brown, Danielle Melanie Brown, Sandy York, Roxann Kraemer, Amy Hutchins, Juliet O'Brien, Anna Bullard, Susan Maris, Karen Sternberg, Jennifer Herzog, Jennifer Blood, Suzy Kay, Arlene Love, Dara Seitman, Jennifer McGeorge, Dolores Kenan

THE AFGHANISTAN PROJECT by William Mastrosimone; February 3, 2004; Cast: Christina Gelsone

MAN IS MAN by Bertolt Brecht; Translated by Marcella Nowak; Director, Jackson Gay; April 17, 2004; Cast: Brad Herberllle, Dara Seitzman, Jennifer Bruno, Sarah Elliot, Robyn Ganeles, Matthew Humphreys, Austin Jones, Frank Liotti, Lisa Louttit, Mark Mattek, Nathaniel Nicc-Annan, Paul Paglia, Partricia Spahn, Joe Vena, Marnye Young

LOVELY RHYMES Musical revue by Peter Mills; Director, Cara Reichel; April 22, 2004; Cast: Jason Mills, Tracey Moor, Liz Power, Noah Weisberg

THE PUBLIC THEATRE

George C. Wolfe, Producer; Mara Manus, Executive Director

NEW WORK NOW! FESTIVAL OF NEW PLAY READINGS

DIRTY TRICKS by John Jeter; Director, Margaret Whitton; April 19, 2004

THE ANTIGONE PROJECT by Amy Brenneman, Karen Hartman, Chiori Miyagawa, Lynn Nottage, Sabrina Peck, Caridad Svich; Director, Sabrina Peck; April 26, 2004

WELLSPRING by Ruth Margraff; Director, Elyse Singer; May 3, 2004

NINE PARTS OF DESIRE by Heather Raffo; May 10, 2004

SURFING DNA by Jodi Long; May 17, 2004

OUTLYING ISLANDS by David Grieg; Director, Jo Bonney; May 24, 2004

RATTLESTICK THEATRE

AN EVENING WITH BURTON AND RUSSELL by Arnie Burton and Jay Russel; Director, Shelley Delaney; June 16, 2003; Cast: Arnie Burton and Jay Russell

ST. CRISPIN'S DAY by Matt Pepper; Director, Simon Hammerstein; June 22, 2003; Cast: David Wilson Barnes, Lauren Berst, Lee Blair, Denis Butkus, Alex Draper, Mayhill Fowler, Michael Gladis, Darren Goldstein, Richard Liccardo, Tommy Schrider

FOUR BEERS by David Van Vleck; Director, Roger Danforth; September 29, 2003; Cast: Robert LuPone, Peter Maloney, Lee Wilkof, Guy Boyd, Michael Cullen

FIVE FLIGHTS by Adam Bock; Director, Kent Nicholson, January 19, 2004; Cast: Joanna P. Adler, Jason Butler Harner, Kevin Karrick, Matthew Montelongo, Alice Ripley, Lisa Steindler

RED ROOM

SPECTER by Don Nigro; Director, Michael Kimmel; September 12, 2003

RABBITHEAD by Leora Barish; Director, Nina V. Kerova; November 20, 2003

BALD DIVA! by David Koteles; Director, Jason Jacobs; February 14, 2004; Cast: Tim Cusack, Gerald Marsini, Matthew Pritchard, Terrence Michael McCrossan, Jeffrey James Keyes, Nathan Blew

SHOW WORLD THEATRE CENTER

LYPSINKA! AS I LAY LIP-SYNCHING by John Epperson; Director, Kevin Malony; August 14, 2003; Cast: John Epperson

ST. ANN'S WAREHOUSE

HIROSHIMA MAIDEN by Dan Hurlin; Director, Dan Hurlin; January 14, 2004; Cast: Matthew Acheson, Nami Yamamoto, Dawn Akemi Seito, Lake Simons, Deana Headley, Tom Lee, Kazu Nakamura, Chris Green, Eric Wright, Yoko Myoi, Jeff Berman, Robert Een, Bill Ruyle

ACCIDENTALLY NOSTALGIA by Cynthia Hopkins; Director, DJ Mendel; March 26, 2004; Cast: Cynthia Hopkins, Jim Findlay, Jeff Sugg

SANDE SHURIN THEATRE

BITTER HOMES AND GARDENS by John Benjamin Martin; Director, Donna Castellano; July 24, 2003; Cast: Jordan Auslander, Simcha Borenstein, Barbara Kidd Calvano, Donna Castellano, Carlo Fiorletta, Brian James Grace, Alexis Iacono, Pierre Farrell, Stephen Wheeler

THE SEA by Olafur Haukur Simonarson; Director, Kristina O'Neal; June 13, 2003; Cast: Richard Kohn, Evelyn Page, Simone Lutz, Elizabeth Flynn Jones, Liam Mitchell, Annette Fama Jarred, Brett Michael Dykes, Josh Stein Sapir, Christos Klapsis, Kristina O'Neal, T.J. Zale, Suzanne Levinson, Briana Trautman-Maier

RIFF-RAFF by Laurence Fishburne; Director, Jason Summers; December 11, 2003; Cast: Damien D. Smith, Sean Slater, Ben Rivers

SANFORD MEISNER THEATRE

THE LARK by Jean Anouilh; Adapted by Vanya Cassel Pawson; Director, Vanya Cassel Pawson; November 29, 2003; Cast: Lindsay Halladay, Clay Cockrell, Matt Semrick, Michael Boothroyd, David McCamish, Carlyle Lincoln, Ron Hirt, Peter Whalen, Patrick Mahoney, Silvane Chebance, Max Goldberg, Lino Alvarez, Gloria Garayua

78TH STREET THEATRE LAB

NOTES TO THE MOTHERLAND by Paul Rajeckas and George L. Chieffet; Director, George L. Chieffet; September 21, 2003; Cast: Paul Rajeckas

ALL IS ALMOST STILL by Adam Seelig; Director, Adam Seelig; May 8, 2004; Cast: Billie James, Craig Evans, Lawrence Merritt

STORM THEATRE

THE ROGUERIES OF SCAPIN by Molière; Translated by Jack Clay; Director, Stephen Logan Day; October 1, 2003; Cast: Shay Ansari, Julisa Banbanaste, Dan Berkey, Ashton Crosby, Simon Deonarian, Adriane Erdos, Hugh Brandon Kelly, Kelleigh Miller, Maury Miller, Tim Roberts

NOAH by Andre Obey, Translated by Judith Suther and Earl Clowney; Directors, Peter Dobbins and Arin Arbus; October 1, 2003; Cast: Jennifer Curfman, Bernardo De Paula, Sharon Freedman, Stacey Gladstone, David Huber, Marisa Lee, Peter Mantia, Damon Noland, Viviana L. Rodriguez, Timothy Rosselle, Matt Schuneman, Rolando J. Vargas

SPOKESONG Musical with Book and Lyrics by Stewart Parker; Music by Jimmy Kennedy; Director, Peter Dobbins; February 12, 2004; Cast: Jill Anderson, Colleen Crawford, Ethan Flower, Robin Haynes, Paul Jackel, Michael Mendiola

A MIDSUMMER NIGHT'S DREAM by William Shakespeare; Director, Peter Dobbins; May 24, 2004; Cast: John Riggins, Kate Shindle, Joshua Vasquez, Ethan Flower, Jo Benincasa, Adriane Erdos, Bernardo De Paula, Hugh Brandon Kelly, Geoffrey Warren Barnes II, Joe Sanchez, Eamon Montgomery, Joel C. Roman, Kelleigh Miller

THE TANK

CHOCOLATE IN HEAT: GROWING UP ARAB IN AMERICA by Betty Shamieh; Director, Sam Gold; September 6, 2003; Cast: Betty Shamieh, Piter Fattouche

A VERY MERRY UNAUTHORIZED CHILDREN'S SCIENTOLOGY PAGEANT Conceived and directed by Alex Timbers; Book and Music by Kyle Jarrow; Producer, Aaron Lemon-Strauss, Les Freres Corbusier; December 3, 2003; Cast: Seamus Boyle, Spenser Lee Carrion-O'Driscoll, Alison Stacy Klein, Joshua Marmer, Max Miner, Stephanie Favoreto Queiroz, Daren Watson, Emma Whitfield, Sophie Whitfield and Jordan Wolfe.

THEATRE AT ST. CLEMENT'S

SPRING STORM by Tennessee Williams; Director, Coy Middlebrook; May 9, 2004; Cast: Kristen Cerelli, John Gazzale, David Gideon, Carlin Glynn, Elizabeth Kemp, Krista Lambden, Joe B. McCarthy, Gabe Fazio, Patricia Marie Kelly, Marianne Matthews, Drew McVety, Sylvia Norman, Summer Serafin

THEATRE 54

MASTERBUILDER: REBUILT by Henrik Ibsen; Adapted by Victoria Pero; Director, Victoria Pero; November 8, 2003; Cast: Chris Clavelli, Grant Neale, Emera Felice Krauss, Okwui Okpokwasili, Hilary Spector

LITTLE PITFALL by Markéta Bláhová; Director, Marcy Arlin; January 21, 2004; Cast: Eileen Rivera, Nannette Deasy, Tzahi Moskovitz, Adriana Gaviria, Mayura Baweja, Oscar de la Fe Colon

ORCHIDELIRIUM by Dave Carley; Director, Stephen Wargo; March 25, 2004; Cast: Margaret Norwood, Michael Poignand, Fred Arsenault, Navida Stein

THEATRE 3

UNDER MILK WOOD by Dylan Thomas; Director, Moni Yakim; December 3, 2003; Cast: Jeff Broitman, Phannie Davis, Olivia Goode, John Grimball, Emily Gunyou, Anna Guttormsgard, Jody Hegarty, Nina Millin, Brad Seal, Dan Truman

THE THEATRE-STUDIO

CLASH BY NIGHT by Clifford Odets; Director, Anne Raychel; January 14, 2004; Cast: Jack Fitz, Bob Gallagher, Hilary Howard, Abby Fox, Astrit Ibroci, Douglas Clark Johnson, Joshua Kauffman

TRIAD THEATRE

WHO KILLED WOODY ALLEN? by Dan Callahan, Brendan Connor and Tom Dunn; Directors, Dan Callahan, Brendan Connor and Tom Dunn; December 4, 2003; Cast: Peter Loureir, Brendan Connor, Jillian Dugan, John Mooney, John Shaver, Christopher Wisner

MERCURY: THE AFTERLIFE AND TIMES OF A ROCK GOD by Charles Messina; Director, Charles Messina; January 14, 2004; Cast: Amir Darvish

CIRQUE JACQUELINE by Andrea Reese; Director, Charles Messina; March 17, 2004; Cast: Andrea Reese

LOVE IN GREAT NECK Musical with Book by Tuvia Tenenbom and Maria Lowy; Music and Lyrics by Phil Rubin; Director, Tuvia Tenenbom; May 152 2004; Cast: Joan Fishman, Johnnie Mae, Mario Golden, Diane Quinn, Amitai Kedar

TRILOGY THEATRE

7 BLOW JOBS by Mac Wellman; Director, Phillip Cruise; June 19, 2003; Cast: Phillip Cruise, Robert Lincourt, Madeleine Maby, Edward Miller, Elizabeth Neptune, Billy Steel, Michael Whitney, Travis York

EAT YOUR HEART OUT by Nick Hall; Director, Nancy S. Chu; October 3, 2003; Cast: Marc Diraison, Katie Honaker, David Brainard, Marlene Hamerling, Jim Kane

Varick Boyd, Dan Roach, Keri Meoni in *Styrofoam* PHOTO BY JONATHAN SLAFF

STYROFOAM by Kevin Doyle; Director, Brian Snapp; January 9, 2004; Cast: Dan Roach, Keri Meoni, Varick Boyd, Patrick Shelfski

T. SCHREIBER STUDIO

EASTERN STANDARD by Richard Greenberg; Director, Glenn Krutoff; October 11, 2004; Cast: Michelle Bagwell, Shane Jacobsen, Debbie Jaffe, Andrea Marshall-Money, Jack Reiling, Jason Salmon, Conor T. McNamara, Dian Varisco

BEDROOM FARCE by Alan Ayckbourn; Director, Janis Powell; November 22, 2003; Cast: Dona Abraham, Gwendolyn Brown, Morgan Foxworth, Ed Franklin, Hillary Parker, Todd Reichart, Allyson Ryan, David Shoup

LANDSCAPE OF THE BODY by John Guare; Director, Terry Schreiber; January 29, 2004; Cast: Kimilee Bryant, Albert Insinnia, Joseph Rodriguez, Jessica Allen, Loren Bidner, Francesco Brazzini, Pamela Crofton, Cristina Doikos, James Dunigan, Ian Campbell Dunn, Chriss Lococo, Fred Tumas, Erica Wendal

URBAN STAGES

MORE THAN THIS by Edmund De Santis; Director, Marc Geller; June 15, 2003; Cast: Eric Frandsen, Tracey Gilbert, Christopher H. Matthews, Lucy McMichael, Wendy Walker, Charlotte Hampden, Glenn Kalison, Abby Royle

IN SPITE OF MYSELF by Antoinette LaVecchia; Director, Jesse Berger; September 3, 2003; Cast: Antoinette LaVecchia

ORIGINS OF HAPPINESS by Felix Pire; Director, Angel David; September 6, 2003; Cast: Felix Pire

MUCH ADO ABOUT NOTHING by William Shakespeare; Director, Rebecca Patterson; October 4, 2003; Cast: Lauren Jill Ahrold, Virginia Baeta, Jacqueline Gregg, Gretchen S. Hall, Zainab Jah, Shanti Elise Prasad, Ami Shukla, Carey Urban, DeeAnn Weir

AH, MY DEAR ANDERSEN Fairy Tales by Hans Christian Andersen; Adapted by Aleksey Burago; Director, Aleksey Burago; December 5, 2003; Cast: Snejana Chernova, Marissa Lichwick, Erica Newhouse, Nysheva-Starr

WEIGHTS by Lynn Manning; Director, Robert Egan; January 11, 2004; Cast: Lynn Manning

SUMMIT CONFERENCE by Robert David MacDonald; Director, Kit Thacker; February 7, 2004; Cast: Eric Atheide, Rita Pietropinto, Sarah Megan Thomas

SEVEN RABBITS ON A POLE by John C. Picardi; Director, Frances Hill; April 6, 2004; Cast: Bob Ari, Stephanie Cozart, Linda Cook, Brian Hutchinson, Kahan James, Anthony Veneziale

VITAL THEATRE COMPANY

VITAL SIGNS: NEW WORKS FESTIVAL OCTOBER 30–NOVEMBER 20, 2003

PROGRESS by Al Sjoerdsma; Director, Jeff Griffin

ON THE EDGE by Craig Pospisil; Director, Tom Rowan

WORLD'S LONGEST KISS by Peter Morris; Director, Michael Scheman

GLADIATORS OR KAMIKAZES by Peter Hardy; Director, Randy Baruh

THE RECIPE by D. Lee Miller; Director, Ken Lowstetter

THE GALLERY by Loretta Novick; Director, Cynthia A. Thomas

ARMS AND THE MAN by Erick R. Pfeffinger; Director, David Hilder

AN ACTOR PREPARES by Mark Young; Director, Ari Kreith

FIRST ONE DOWN by Blair Singer; Director, Jesse Berger

YOUNG SISTAS by Lorna Littleway; Director, Sue Lawless

MY WIFE'S COAT by Kellie Overbey; Director, Linda Ames Key

ONE SUNDAY MORNING by Dennis Jones; Director, Mark Hayes

DAR AND BARB by Catherine Allen; Director, Emily Tetzlaff

BLISS by Stephanie Zadravec; Director, Georgi Cerruti

MEDUSA by Steven Christopher Yockey; Director, Bob Cline

PLASTIC by Robert Shaffron; Director, Mary Catherine Burke

MILK IN CHINA by Lisa Rosenthal; Director, Derek Jamison

SUPERHERO by Mark Harvey Levine; Director, Gregory Thorson

A FAMILY MANUAL FOR KWANZAA by Aurin Squire; Director, Kim Kefgen

THE KEEPSAKE by Andrew McCaldon; Director, Claire M. Hewitt

URSA MINOR by Gary Giovannetti; Director, Eric Parness

HIJAB by Monica Raymond; Director, Mahayana Landowne

NATURAL HISTORY by Jennifer Camp; Director, Anton Dudley

WALKERSPACE

THE FLID SHOW by Richard Willett; Director, Eliza Beckwith; November 2, 2003; Cast: Alison Adams, Harley Adams, Katherine Heasley Clarvoe, Kim Donovan, Kate Downing, Suzanna Hay, Laurence Lau, Amy Staats, James Thomas, Chris Wight

ASHES TO ASHES by Harold Pinter; Director, Robert Mann; December 3, 2003; Cast: Gloria Mann Craft, Warren Kelder

SO CLOSE by Marin Gazzaniga; Director, Michael Sexton; May 15, 2004; Cast: John Ellison Conlee, Perri Gaffney, Marin Gazzaniga, Julia Gibson, Daniel Freedom Stewart, Cristine McMudo-Wallis

WHERE EAGLES DARE THEATRE

LILIA! by Libby Skala; Director, Libby Skala; November 3, 2003; Cast: Libby Skala

A ROCKETTE'S TAIL by JoAnna Rush; Director, Walter Willison; November 8, 2003; Cast: JoAnna Rush

WHITE BIRD PRODUCTIONS

COOKING WITH LARD by Cindy D. Hanson and Cheryl Norris; Director, Paul Mullins; March 19, 2004; Cast: Cindy D. Hanson, Cheryl Norris, Lorrie Harrison, Bijou Clinger, Kathryn Dickinson

WINGS THEATRE COMPANY

UNCOVERING EDEN by George Barthel; Director, L.J. Kleeman and Richard Bacon; June 2, 2004; Cast: James A. Walsh, Raymond O. Wagner, Gabrie Rivas, Josh Mertz

JANE EYRE: THE MUSICAL with Book and Lyrics by Rebecca Thompson-Duvall and Kari Skousen; Music by Bill Kilpatrick; Director, Craig Duke; June 27, 2003; Cast: Lilly Kershaw, Gabriel Rivera, Breton Frazier, Edward Harding, Kristin Carter, Maureen Griffin, Alicia Sable, Sydney Sahr, Anna Budinger, Leslie Klug, Leah Landau, Jenny Long, Paul Malamphy, Jay Gould, Peter Previti, Greg Horton, Daniel Hughes, Jason Adamo, Jackson Budinger

TALES FROM THE MANHATTAN WOODS Musical Based On *Die Fledermaus* by Johann Strauss Jr; Adapted by Frederick Stroppel; Book and Lyrics by Frederick Stroppel; Director, Judith Fredricks; November 13, 2003; Cast: Sarah Miller, Shawna Stone, Elizabeth Harman, Melanie Melcher, Kyle Bradford, Linsey Jager, Brian Costello, Frances Jones, Karen Coker, Gideon Dabi, Kevin Kash

VINCENT Musical with Book, Music and Lyrics by Robert Mitchell; Director, Judith Fredricks; February 27, 2004; Cast: Paul Woodson, Mark Campbell, Sarah Marvel Bleasdale, Charles Karel, John Wilmes, Erik Schark, Cristin J. Hubbard, James Gilchrist, Daniel Gurvich, Walter Hartman, Lynne Henderson, Mara Kelly, James LaRosa, Sarah Lilley, James Murphy, Ian Rhodes, Nathan Lee Scherich, Jodie Trappe, Martin Vasquez, Kathleen Devine

SIX DEGREES OF SEPARATION by John Guare; Directors, Louis Reyes Cardenas and Sarah Rosenberg; April 8, 2004; Cast: Ree Davis, Edmond Wilkinson, Bashir Solebo, Brian Tracy, Frank Tamez, Henry Garrett, Amy Johnson, Burke Adams, Peter Monro, Joe Moran, Rocco Lapenna, Valerie Garduno, Louis Reyes Cardenas, Robert Berlin, Daphne Crosby, Marcelo DeOliveira, Lou Mastantuono

AFRICAN NIGHTS by Clint Jefferies; Director, Jeffery Corrick; May 17, 2004; Cast: Antwan Ward, Bekka Lindstrom, Joel Halpern, Sheri Delaine, Karen Stanion, Nick Marcotti, JoHary Ramos, Ed Roggenkamp

THE WOOSTER GROUP

POOR THEATRE based on the work of Jerzy Grotowski, William Forsythe and Max Ernst; Director, Elizabeth LeCompte; February 18, 2004; Cast: Geoff Abbas, J. Reid Farrington, Iver Findlay, Ari Fliakos, Sam Gold, Bozkurt Karasu, Ken Kobland, Christopher Kondek, Margaret Mann, Gabe Maxson, Sheena See, Scott Sheperd, Jennifer Tipton, Kate Valk, Ruud van de Akker

Company Series

ABINGDON THEATRE COMPANY

Jan Buttram and Pamela Paul, Artistic Directors; Samuel J. Bellinger, Managing Director Stage II Productions

BRUNO HAUPTMANN KISSED MY FOREHEAD by John Yearley; Director, James F. Wolk; June 5, 2003; Cast: Pun Bandhu, Lori Gardner, Joel Leffert, Joseph J. Menino, Pamela Paul, Michael Puzzo

THE MAIGINOT LINE by Margaret Hunt; Director, Kent Paul; September 19, 2003

TEXAS HOMOS by Jan Buttram; Director, Melvin Bernhardt; January 23, 2004

GRADUATION DAY by Barton Bishop; Director, Alex Dmitriev; May 14, 2004; Cast: Alice Barden, Stephen Benson, David Holmes, Jacob Lavin, Rachel Alexa Norman

AMAS MUSICAL THEATRE

Donna Trinkoff, Producing Director

FROM MY HOMETOWN Musical with Book by Lee Summers, Ty Stephens and Herbert Rawlings Jr; Music by Lee Summers, Ty Stephens, Will Barrow and Others; Director, Keven Ramsey; June 19, 2003; Cast: Kevin R. Free, André Garner, Rodney Hicks

SEX! THE MUSICAL Musical by David Coffman; Director, Devanand Janki; October 27, 2003

SPIN Musical with Book, Music and Lyrics by M. Kilburg Reedy; Director, Matt Morrow; November 3, 2003

SIX WOMEN WITH BRAIN DEATH Musical with Book by Cheryl Benge, Christy Brandt, Rosanna E. Coppedge, Valerie Fagan, Ross Freese, Mark Houston, Sandee Johnson, Peggy Phar Wilson; Music and Lyrics by Mark Houston; Director, Matt M. Morrow; December 8, 2003

BLACKOUT Musical with Book and Lyrics by Sharleen Cooper Cohen; Music by Debra Barsha; Director, Phillip George; December 4, 2003

BROOKLYN ACADEMY OF MUSIC—
Next Wave Festival

Alan H. Fishman, Chairman of the Board; Karen Brooks Hopkins, President; Joseph V. Melillo, Executive Producer

HENRY IV, PART ONE By William Shakespeare; Director, Richard Maxwell; September 30, 2003; with the New York City Players

THE SOUND OF OCEAN by U Theatre; Director and Choreographer, Liu Ching-Ming; October 7, 2003

BOBRAUSCHENBERGAMERICA by Charles L. Mee; Director, Anne Bogart; October 7, 2003; With the SITI Company

Andre Garner, Rodney Hicks, Kevin R. Free in *From My Hometown* PHOTOS BY JOAN MARCUS

THE NEW YORKERS by Michael Gordon, David Lang and Julia Wolfe; with texts by Lou Reed; Director, Barry Edelstein; October 22, 2003; With Bang on a Can All-Stars, Ethel, Michael Gordon Band, Theo Bleckmann

AINADAMAR Opera with Book by David Henry Hwang; Music by Osvaldo Golijov; Director, Chay Yew; October 28, 2003; Cast: Dawn Upshaw, Tanglewood Music Center Vocal Fellows and Orchestra

THE HANGING MAN by Phelim McDermott; Lee Simpson and Julian Crouch; Directors, Phelim McDermott, Lee Simpson and Julian Crouch; November 4, 2003

ALLADEEN by Keith Khan, Marianne Weems and Ali Zaidi; with text by Martha Baer; Director, Marianne Weems; December 2, 2003

ENSEMBLE STUDIO THEATRE

Curt Dempster, Artistic Director

MARATHON 2003 (SERIES B) JUNE 1–21, 2003

HI THERE, MR. MACHINE by Leslie Ayvazian; Director, Leigh Silverman; Cast: Leslie Ayvazian

THE CHANGING OF THE GUARD by Amy Staats; Director, Mark Roberts; Cast: Julie Leeds, Diana Ruppe, Scotty Bloch

WASHED UP ON THE POTOMAC by Lynn Rosen; Director, Eileen Myers; Cast: Anne Torsiglieri; Sean Sutherland; Maria Thayer; Joan Rosenfels; William Franke

WATER MUSIC by Tina Howe; Director, Pam MacKinnon; Cast: Lizbeth Mackay, Juan Carlos Hernandez, Laura Heisler

WOMAN AT A THRESHOLD BECKONING by John Guare; Director, Will Pomerantz; Cast: Andrew Weems, Miriam Laube, Chris Ceraso, Ted Neustadt, Michael Cullen, Michael Thomas Holmes, India Cooper, Jay Patterson

THICKER THAN WATER: NEW ONE-ACT PLAYS MARCH 4–28, 2004

WATER-BORN by Edith L. Freni; Director, Brian Roff; Cast: Annie McNamara, Michael Szeles

CHARLIE BLAKE'S BOAT by Graeme Gillis; Director, Jamie Richards; Cast: Leo Lauer, Katie Barrett

D.C. by Daria Polatin; Director, R.J. Tolan; Cast: Shana Dowdeswell, Gideon Glick, Joanna Parson

WELCOME BACK, BUDDY COMBS by Ben Rosenthal; Director, Abigal Zealey Bess; Cast: Denny Bess, Diana Ruppe, Jonny Giacalone

FIRST LIGHT 2004 APRIL 9–MAY 3, 2004

TOOTH AND CLAW by Michael Hollinger; Director, Dave P. Moore; Cast: Gloria Biegler, Steven Crossley, Flora Díaz, Jojo Gonzalez, Sebastian LaCause, Ruben Luque, Nathan Perez, Anthony Ruiz, Joaquin Torres, Noel Velez

DAYS OF HAPPINESS by Arthur Giron; Director, David Shookhoff

THE MONKEY ROOM by Kevin Fisher; Director, Mark Roberts

L'ORNITOTERO: THE BIRD MACHINE by Carlo Adinolfi and Renee Phillipi

GUTENBERG: THE MUSICAL by Scott Brown and Anthony King

PARADISE OF EARTHWORMS by David Valdes Greenwood; Director, R.J. Tolan

BLACKFOOT NOTES by Rajendra Ramoon Maharaj; Director, Kirsten Berkman

GIRL SCIENCE by Larry Loebell

TWIN PRIMES by Alex Lewin

THE SEPARATION OF BLOOD by Bridgette Wimberly

THE BONES OF GIANTS by Cheryl L. Davis

PROGRESS IN FLYING by Lynn Rosen

INTAR

Max Ferrá, Michael John Garcés, Producing Artistic Directors

FAITH, HOPE AND CHARITY by Alberto Pedro; translated by Caridad Svich; Director, Max Ferrá; June 5, 2003; Cast: Maria Cellario, Judith Delgado, Dana Manno, Mizan Nunes

THE COOK by Eduardo Machado; Director, Michael John Garcés; November 20, 2003; Cast: Maggie Bofill, Zabryna Guevara, Jason Madera, Jason Quarles, Nilaja Sun

LA MAMA EXPERIMENTAL THEATRE CLUB (ETC)

Ellen Stewart, Founder and Director

CALENDAR OF STONE by Denise Stoklos; Director, Denise Stoklos; June 12, 2003; Cast: Denise Stoklos

MARGA GOMEZ'S INTIMATE DETAILS by Marga Gomez; Director, David Schweizer; June 19, 2003; Cast: Marga Gomez

SWAN by Oleh Lysheha; Translated by Oleh Lysheha and James Brasfield; Director, Virlana Tkacz; June 19, 2003; Cast: Andrew Colteaux, Soomi Kim

TARGET AUDIENCE (THE CODE OF THE WESTERN) by Jim Neu; Director, Keith McDermott; September 19, 2003; Cast: Jim Neu, Deborah Auer, Bill Rice

THE BACCHAE: TORN TO PIECES by Euripides; Director, Susan Fenichell; October 9, 2003; Cast: Ellen McLaughlin, Amy Lee Maguire, Matt Pepper, David Russell, Paul Savas

THE MIDDLE BEAST by Joe Kodeih, Elie Karam and Marc Koheih; Director, Joe Koheih; October 10, 2003; Cast: Marc Kodeih, Elie Karam, Mario Bassil, Jacques Maroun, Taranahsa Wallace

Eve Udesky, Brian Bickerstaff in *Butt-Crack Bingo* PHOTO BY PATRICIA SULLIVAN

FOREIGN AIDS by Pieter-Dirk Uys; October 23, 2003; Cast: Pieter-Dirk Uys

PHILOKTETES by John Jesurun; October 23, 2003; Cast: Jeff Weiss

HO'ICHI, THE EAR LESS by Ryo Onodera; Based on a Japanese ghost fable by Yukumo Koizumi; Directed by Kanako Hiyama; October 23, 2003; Cast: Tom Lee, Lars Preece

CHANG IN A VOID MOON by John Jesurun; Director, John Jesurun; October 31, 2003; Cast: John Hagan, Donna Herman, Ruth Gray, Helena White, Anna Kohler, Sanghi Wagner, Oscar de la Fe Colon; Lisa Herman, Nicky Paraiso, Rebecca Moore, Greg Mehrten, Mary Schultz, Black-Eyed Susan, Ching Valdes-Aran, David Cale

HENRY 5 by William Shakespeare; Adapted by Thadeus Phillips; Director, Tatiana Mallarino; November 3, 2003; Cast: Thadeus Phillips

WORLD WAR NOW OR HOW SEYMOUR GOT HIS GUN OFF by Mark Eisenstein; Director, Tom O'Horgan; November 11, 2003; Cast: Edward Asner, Estelle Parsons, Brian Backer, Charles Baler, Brian Dusseau, Joseph Del Giodice, Bobby Faust, Richard Hirschfeld, Peter Linari, Katarina Oost, Nick Taylor

BUTT-CRACK BINGO by Jack Bump; Director, David Soul; November 13, 2003; Cast: Brian Bickerstaff, Jeff Biehl, Danny Camiel, Alien Comic (Tom Murrin), Laura Flanagan, Gibson Fraiser, Laura Kindred, April Sweeney, Conrad Rheims, Eve Udesky

Donna Herman in *Chang in a Void Moon* PHOTO BY DONNA CORT

(CONTINUED ON NEXT PAGE)

(CONTINUED FROM PREVIOUS PAGE)

RAMAYANA 2K3 by Robert A. Prior; Director, Robert A. Prior; November 20, 2003; Cast: Fabulous Monsters Performance Group

THE GOOD FAITH: 1940–1990 Musical with Book, Music, and Lyrics by Harold Dean James; Director, Harold Dean James; November 20, 2003; Cast: Paul Albe, Jamie Leigh Allen, Jason Blaine, Daniel Clymer, Erika Dioniso, Linus Gelber, Grant Machan, Joe Matheson, Gheree O'Bannon, Rachel Ponce, Christiane Szabo, Christa Victoria, Cezar Williams

GLAMOUR, GLORY AND GOLD by Jackie Curtis; Director, Joe Preston; December 4, 2003; Cast: D'Arcy Drollinger, Clayton Dean Smith, Janine Kyanko, John Patrick Kelly, Laverne Cox, Bryan Safi, Boris Kievsky, Christopher Ross

Jason Blaine (center) in *The Good Faith: 1940–1990* PHOTO BY LINDA OBUCHOSKA

WOZA ALBERT! by Percy Mtwa, Mbongeni Ngema, Barney Simon; Directed by Lucky Ngema; December 16, 2003; Cast: Patrick Ssenjovu, Lucky Ngema

THE BROTHERS KARAMOZOV, PART II by Fyodor Dostoyevsky; Adapted by Alexander Harrington; Director, Alexander Harrington; January 2, 2004; Cast: Gary Andrews, Steven L. Barron, Anthony Cataldo, Stafford Clark-Price, J. Anthony Crane, Alessio Franko, Antony Hagopian, Jim Iseman III, Danielle Langlois, Christopher Lukas, J.M. McDonough, Chris Meyer, Winslow Mohr, George Morafetis, Peter Oliver, Jennifer Opalcz, Margo Skinner, Yaakov Sullivan, Sorrel Tomlinson, Svetlana Yankovskaya

OUT AT SEA and **STRIPTEASE** by Slawomir Mrozek; Out at Sea Translated by Amiel Melnick and Asha Oniszczuk; Striptease Translated by Lola Gruenthal; Director, Paul Bargetto; January 4, 2004; Cast: Cornel Gabara, Troy Lavallee, Paul Todaro, Nora Laudani

LINAS IS KINSKI by Linas Phillips; Director, Linas Phillips; January 8, 2004; Cast: Linas Phillips, Larissa Dooley, Jim Fletcher

DEFENSES OF PRAGUE by Sophia Murashkovsky; Director, Leslie Lee; January 22, 2004; Cast: Walter Krochmal, Nicolas Mongiardo-Cooper; Angelica Ayala, Nina Savinsky, Julie Saad, Vina Less, Maria Hurdle, Chris Alonzo, Dan Kastoriano, Maya Levy, Gary Andrews, Malia Miller, Channie Waites, Robert Eggards, Meghan Andrews, Erin Lehy

Sorrel Tomlinson, J. Anthony Crane in *The Brothers Karamazov, Part II*

Gary Andrews, J. Anthony Crane in *The Brothers Karamazov, Part II* PHOTOS BY JONATHAN SLAFF

(front) Walter Krochmal, Svetlana Yankovsky, (above) Maria Hurdle in *Defenses of Prague*
PHOTO BY JONATHAN SLAFF

LAST SUPPER by Lars Norén; Translated by Martia Lindholm-Gochman; Director, Zishan Ugurlu; January 22, 2004; Cast: Raina von Waldenburg, Tullan Holmqvist; Dan Illian; Olle Agelii

KLUB KA: THE BLUES LEGEND by James V. Hatch and Suzanne Noguere; Director, Tisch Jones; February 5, 2004; Cast: Kevin "B.F." Burt, Janice Bishop, Michael Kachingwe; Frankie Cordero, Emily Happe, Eric Forsythe, Cary Gant, Christa Victoria, Amy Olson, Dara Bengelsdorf, Yaritza Pizarro, Rod Bladel, Sean Christopher Lewis

ODYSSEY: THE HOMECOMING by Theodora Skipitares; Director, Theodora Skipitares; February 12, 2004; Cast: Michael Kelly, Chris Maresca, Alisa Mello, Bernadette Witzack, Bronwyn Bittetti, Amanda Villalobos

EXPIRATION DATE by Abla Khoury; Director, Abla Khoury; February 12, 2004; Cast: Zishan Ugurlu, Abla Khoury, Kajla Sai, Patrick Ssenjovu, Chris Wild, Sara Galassini, Denise Greber, Federico Restrepo

THE WARRIOR'S SISTER by Virlana Tkacz, Sayan Zhambalov and Erhena Zhambalov; Director, Virlana Tkacz, Sayan Zhambalov, Erhena Zhambalov; March 6, 2004; Cast: Sayan Zhambalov, Erhena Zhambalov, Victor Zhalsaov, Bayarto Endonov, Eunice Wong, Andrew Coltreaux, Hettiene Park, Meredith Wright

ANCHORPECTORIS by Gerald Thomas; Director, Gerald Thomas; March 6, 2004; Cast: Nikki Alikakos, George Bartenieff, Chantal Bushelle, Sonia Elaine Butler, Sean P. Doran, Fabiana Guglielmetti, Kate Holland, Josh Mann, Stephen Nisbet, Kila Packett, Stacey Raymond, Tom Walker

HOUSE/BOY 2004 by Nicky Paraiso; Director, Ralph B. Peña; April 22, 2004; Cast: Nicky Paraiso

THE LIFE AND DEATH OF TOM THUMB THE GREAT Adapted from the book by Henry Fielding; Music by Brendan Connelly; Directed by Brooke O'Harra; May 13, 2004; Cast: Brian Bickerstaff, Suli Holum, Matthew Stadelmann, Mary Regan, Cecile Evans, David B. Gould, Lula Graves, Lauren Brown, Tatiana Pavela, Matt Shapiro, Matt Berger, Juliana Sanderson

THE CODE OF THE WESTERN RIDES AGAIN by Jim Neu; Directed by Keith McDermott; May 13, 2004; Cast: Jim Neu; Deborah Auer, Bill Rice

THE LIFE AND TIMES OF LEE HARVEY OSWALD by Vít Horejš; Directed by Vít Horejš; May 27, 2004; Cast: Deborah Beshaw, Michelle Beshaw, David Friend, Vít Horejš; Ron Jones, Sarah Lafferty, Theresa Linnihan, Emily Wilson, Benjamin Caron

Adrienne Woodard, Emily Happe, Amy Olson in *Klub Ka, The Blues Legend*

Kevin "B.F." Burt, Emily Happe in *Klub Ka: The Blues Legend* PHOTOS BY REGGIE MORROW

LINCOLN CENTER FESTIVAL 2003

Nigel Redden, Director

THE ANGEL PROJECT by Deborah Warner; Director, Deborah Warner; July 8, 2003

MYTHOS by Rina Yerushalmi; Translated by Aharon Shabtai and Shimon Buzaglo; Directed by Rina Yerushalmi; July 8, 2003; Cast: Titina K. Assefa, Noa Barkai, Gal Barzilay, Maya Ben Avraham, Ruthie Ben-Efrat, Avraham Cohen, Barak Gonen, Emmanuel Hannon, Michal Kalman, Yehuda Lazarovich, Noa Raban, Yousef Sweid, Karin Tepper, Yoav Yeffet

PANSORI FIVE SOLO KOREAN EPICS.

> **HEUNGBOGA**; July 16, 2003; Cast: Kim Soo-yeon

> **SUGUNGGA**; July 17, 2003; Cast: Cho Tong-dal

> **SIMCHEONGGA**; July 18, 2003; Cast: Kim Young-ja

> **JEOOKBYEOKGA**; July 19, 2003; Cast: Kim Il-goo

> **CHUNHYANGGA**; July 20, 2003; Cast: Ahn Suk-sun

THE ORPHAN OF ZHAO Based on the play by Ji Juan-Xiang; English adaptation by David Greenspan; Director, Chen Shi-Zheng; July 19, 2003; Cast: David Patrick Kelly, Rob Campbell, William Youmans, Jenny Bacon

MABOU MINES

Lee Breuer, Sharon Fogarty, Ruth Maleczech, Frederick Neumann, Tony O'Reilly, Artistic Directorate

DOLLHOUSE by Henrik Ibsen; Adapted by Lee Breuer; Director, Lee Breuer; November 19, 2003; Cast: Mark Povinelli, Maude Mitchell, Kristopher Medina, Honora Ferguson, Ricardo Gil, Lisa Harris, Tate Katie Mitchell, Zachary Houppert Nunns, Matthew Forker, Sophie Forker

NEW DRAMATISTS

Todd London, Artistic Director; Joel K. Ruark, Executive Producer

TEATRO MARIA by Lonnie Carter; Director, Loy Arcenas; June 23, 2003; Cast: Michael Stuhlbarg, Celia Howard, Bree Elrod, Charles Randall, Michael Matthis, April Matthis, John Wernke

MOVE by Brooke Berman; Director, Randy White; June 26, 2003; Cast: Dee Pelletier, Josh Hecht, Marin Ireland, Michael Chernus, Michael Stuhlbarg

INFINITUDE by Sung Rno; Director, Linsay Firman; June 26, 2003; Cast: Paul H. Juhn, Sue Jean Kim, Michi Barall, Tom Lee, Andy Pang, C. S. Lee

SICK AGAIN by Gordon Dahlquist; Director, Randy White; June 30, 2003; Cast: Scott Bryer, Laura Flanagan, Patrick McNulty, Melinda Wade

NEW RESIDENT EVENT SEPTEMBER 8, 2003

> **DARK YELLOW** by Julia Jordan; Cast: Paul Sparks, Isaac Maddow-Zimet

> **A TEXAS CAROL** by Daniel Alexander Jones; Cast: Cindy Creekmore, Gretchen Lee Krich, Ana Parea, Randolph Curtis Rand, T. Ryder Smith

> **CUSTOMS** by Michael John Garcés; Director, Sturgis Warner; Cast: Lourdes Martin, Andres Mudor, Matthew Maguire

> **APPARITION** by Anne Washburn; Director, Linsay Firman; Cast: T. Ryder Smith, Scott Blumenthal

> **A MONOLOGUE** by Gary Sunshine; Director, Trip Cullman; Cast: Glenn Fitzgerald

> **THE HOLY MOTHER OF HADLEY NEW YORK** by Barbara Wiechmann; Cast: Gretchen Lee Krich, Matthew Macguire

> **PAINTED SNAKE IN A PAINTED CHAIR** by Ellen Maddow; Cast: Diane Beckett, Lizzie Olesker, Ellen Maddow, Randolph Curtis Rand, Gary Brownlee

PLACES PLEASE: ACT ONE by Warren Kliewer; Director, Cliff Goodwin; September 16, 2003; Cast: Michèle LaRue

BLASTED by Sarah Kane; Director, Jon Schumacher; September 16, 2003; Cast: Marin Ireland, Michael Cumpsty, Gareth Saxe, Rachel Aronson

LEAVING ITALY by Sybil Patten; Director, Randy White; September 9, 2003; Cast: Jess Wexler, Charles H. Hyman, Johnny Giacalone, Dee Pelletier

THREE CONTINENTS by Catherine Filloux; Director, Jean Randich; September 22, 2003; Cast: Larissa Kiel, Rich Canzano, Yusef Bulos, Taylor Mac Bowyer, Angel Desai

THE BARBARA BARONDESS MCLEAN FESTIVAL

ANON by Kate Robin; Director, Melissa Kievman; September 29, 2003; Cast: Katy Selverstone, Josh Hamilton, Beth Lincks, Charlotte Colavin, Bill Buell, Mia Barron, Lindsey Gates, Joanna Liao, Melinda Wade, Vanessa Aspillaga, Liz Douglas, Keli Garrett, Sarah Trelease, Eisa Davis

MESSALINA by Gordon Dahlquist; Director, David Levine; September 30, 2003; Cast: John McAdams, Laura Flanagan, Daria Polatin, Lee Tergesen, Molly Powell, Bill Dawes

SIBERIA by Diana Son; October 3, 2003; Cast: Kevin Carroll, Rick Holmes, Geoffrey Molloy, Sonnie Brown, Jessica Hecht, KJ Sanchez

THE DEVIL'S PLAYGROUND by Doug Wright; October 6, 2003; Cast: Michael Tisdale, Jefferson Mays, Edward Hibbert, Kristine Nielsen, Stacie Morgain Lewis, Susan Lyons, Laura Heisler, Jack Ferver, Christopher Evan Welch

BOBBY M by Edwin Sanchez; October 7, 2003; Cast: Lorenzo Laboy, David Ayers, Mireille Enos, Roderick Hill, Julie Halston, Alvaro Mendoza, Michelle Rios, Jon Schumacher

SANDERMANIA by Sander Hicks; Director, Mahayana Landowne; October 8, 2003; Cast: Jenny Weaver, Joey Liao, Dan O'Brien, Roderick Hill, Ron Riley, Nick Colt

FALLING PETALS by Ben Ellis; Director, Steve Cosson; October 20, 2003; Cast: Alicia Goranson, Ted Schneider, Mandy Siegfried; Lynne McCollough, Buzz Bovshow

SLEEPER by Justin Boyd; Director, Hayley Nutt; October 21, 2003; Cast: Charles Parnell, Dan O'Brien, Yvonne Woods, Yusef Bulos

FROZEN by Bryony Lavery; Director, Anne Kauffman; October 23, 2003; Cast: Ken Marks, Barbara Eda-Young, Karen Young, Sergei Burbank

PERDITA GRACIA by Caridad Svich; Director, Debbie Saivetz; October 27, 2003; Cast: April Matthis, Ellen Lancaster, Nilaja Sun, Alfredo Narciso, Ed Vassallo, Chris Wells, Flaco Navaja, Olivia Oguma, Lorenzo Laboy, Andres Munar

PLAYTIME

MY FIRST RADICAL by Rogelio Martinez; Director, Michael Sexton; November 13, 2003; Cast: Carlo Alban, Laura Jo Anderson, Chris De Oni, Ed DeSoto, Matthew Maguire, Joseph Goodrich

WELLSPRING by Ruth Margraff; Director, Jean Randich; November 14, 2003; Cast: Piter Fattouche, Lanna Joffrey, Ed Vassallo, Dawn Saito, Jennifer Gibbs, Akili Prince

BREAKFAST, LUNCH AND DINNER by Luis Alfaro; Director, Dim Rubinstein; November 14, 2003; Cast: Saidah Arrika Ekulona, Michael Potts, Yvette Ganier, Leslie Elliard

THE STREET OF USEFUL THINGS

by Stephanie Fleischmann; Director, Linsay Firman; November 17, 2003; Cast: Jenny Sterlin; Patrick Husted, Molly Powell, Emily Donahoe, Franca Barchiesi, Judith Lightfoot Clarke

SMOKE AND MIRRORS by Joseph Goodrich; Director, Nick Faust; November 17, 2003; Cast: Andrew Guilarte, Graham Brown, Elzbieta Czyzewska, Matthew Morgan, John McAdams, Dale Soules, Angel Desai

MOLOCH AND OTHER DEMONS by Jason Grote; Director, Alex Correia; December 1, 2003; Cast: Kate Benson, Jeff Biehl, Michael Chernus, Patch Darragh, Michael Milligan

UNTILWEFINDEACHOTHER by Brooke Berman; Director, Carolyn Cantor; December 4, 2003; Cast: Naama Potok, Michael Chernus, Josie Whittlesey, David Barlow, Seth Herzog, Dana Fisher, Blythe Zava

YALE PLAYWRIGHTS FESTIVAL DECEMBER 12, 2003

BURIED HISTORY AND A SPLASH OF NUTMEG IN MILK by Sarah Fornia; Director, Daniella Topol; Cast: Mark Blum, Geraldine Librandi, Mia Barron, Heather Mazur, Michael Goldstrom, Nicole Lowrance, Ching Valdes-Aran, Ron Crawford

LAST OF THE CHATTERBOX WOLVES by Rolin Jones; Director, Kim Rubinstein; Cast: Jeanine Serralles, Clark Middleton, Greg Steinbruner, Brad Heberlee, Judith Hawking, Mia Barron

BANDITOS by Jami O'Brien; Directed by Trip Cullman; Cast: Heather Mazur, Joanna P. Adler, Siobhan Mahoney, Ching Valdes-Aran, Michael Chernus, Matthew Humphreys, Mark Blum, Lucas Papaelias, Tim Acito

AND JESUS MOONWALKS ON THE MISSISIPI and **DANCE THE HOLY GHOST** by Marcus Gardley; Director, Seret Scott; Cast: Kevin Carroll, Cherise Boothe, Barbara Pitts, Rony Clanton, Graham Brown, Ebony Jo-Ann

PLAYGROUND WORKSHOP

AMAZING by Brooke Berman; Director, Ethan McSweeny; December 18, 2003; Cast: Lucas Papaelias, Mandy Siegfried, Michael Chernus, Marin Ireland

THE LOST BOYS OF SUDAN by Lonnie Carter; Director, Peter Brosius; December 19, 2003; Cast: Akili Prince, Teagle F. Bougere, April Matthis, Michael Rogers, Forrest McClendon, Mike Hodge, Jill Kotler, Keith Davis

THE MIDNIGHT TEA, OR THE PUZZLING MAPS OF BESSEMER SHANKS by Glen Berger; Director, Allison Narver; December 19, 2003; Cast: Ann Arvia, Elyas Khan, Michelle Federer, Maria Thayer, David Ranson, Shelly Watson, Timothy Reynolds, Jesse Pennington

ROME by Herman Farrell; Director, Herman Farrell; January 8, 2004; Cast: Akili Prince, Alice Haining, Rob Campbell, Jen Ryan, Joseph Urla

PLASTICINE by Vassily Sigarev; Director, Jon Schumacher; January 20, 2004; Cast: Luke MacFarlane, John Gallagher, Susan Ferrara, Laura Marks, Ken Marks, Alex Napier, Laura Kindred, Jeff Biehl, Matt Kalman, Flora Diaz

(CONTINUED ON NEXT PAGE)

(CONTINUED FROM PREVIOUS PAGE)

FIREFACE by Marius von Mayenburg; Director, Jon Schumacher; February 10, 2004; Cast: Elise Santora, Jon Krupp, June Raphael, Thomas Sadoski, Aaron Stanford

RAW BOYS by Dael Orlandersmith; Director, Blanka Zizka; February 11, 2004; Cast: Paul Vincent Black, John Keating, Colin Lane, Kathleen Doyle

MADAME KILLER by Honour Kane and Diana Kane; Music by Paul Loesel; Director, Linsay Firman; February 23, 2004; Cast: Aedin Moloney, Jill Gascoine, Jan Leslie Harding, Okwui Okpokwasili, Thomas Schall, Derek Lucci

THE NAME by Jon Fosse; Director, Jon Schumacher; February 24, 2004; Cast: Christy Meyer, Jeffrey Scott Green, Kate Wetherhead, Mia Katigbak, Keith Randolph Smith, Thomas Sadoski

BELIZE by Paul Zimet; Music by Ellen Maddow; March 16, 2004; Cast: Eisa Davis, John Keating, T. Ryder Smith, Tina Shepard, Marjorie Johnson, Will Badgett, Connie Winston, Steven Rosen, Scott Blumenthal, Steven Rattazzi, Carolyn Goelzer, Blue Gene Tyranny

IN THE NAME OF BOB by Jono Hustis; March 23, 2004; Cast: Julien Schwab, Ali Walsh, Eric Miller

MARY BETH by Matthew Kirsch; Director, Joanna P. Adler; April 2, 2004; Cast: Carla Briscoe, Matthew Stadelmann, Jenna Stern, Steven Rattazzi, Greg Stuhr, John Seitz

THRUSH by Caridad Svich; April 5, 2004; Cast: Jeffrey Frace, Kristi Casey, Alfredo Narciso, Heidi Schreck, Chris Wells, Alexandra Oliver

AUTODELETE://BEGINNING DUMP OF PHYSICAL MEMORY// by Honour Kane; Music by Eve Beglarian; Director, Leigh Silverman; April 5, 2004; Cast: Honour Kane, Paul Vincent Black, David Greenspan, Alejandro Morales, Andy Phelan, Warren Elgort, John C. Russell

MARIA KIZITO by Erik Ehn; April 7, 2004; Cast: Djola Branner, Laurie Carlos, Sandra DeLuca, Robbie McCauley, Stacey Robinson, Rhonda Ross, Vinie Burrows, Eisa Davis

BLURRING SHINE by Zakiyyah Alexander; Director, Daniel Banks; April 12, 2004; Cast: Danny Johnson, Archie Ekong, Kevin Carroll, Charles Anthony Burks, Charles Parnell

BELTED BLUE, BLEEDING YELLOW by Qui Nguyen; Director, Victor Maog; April 12, 2004; Cast: Pun Bandhu, Ben Wang, Mary Kickel

THINGS BEYOND OUR CONTROL by Jesse Kellerman; Director, Ted Sod; April 19, 2004; Cast: Jan Leslie Harding, Elise Santora, Edward A. Hajj, Jonathan Hogan, George Oliphant, Ed Vassallo, Elizabeth Canavan, Michael Esper, Dan Domingues

PHOTOGRAPHS OF A BLACK MAN ON DISPLAY by Rogelio Martinez; Director, Leigh Silverman; April 20, 2004; Cast: Dylan Baker, Kenajuan Bentley, Greg Bratman, Laura Breckenridge, Airrion Doss, Steven Rattazzi

MEASURE FOR PLEASURE OR THE HAPPINESS OF PURSUIT by David Grimm; Director, David Grimm; April 26, 2004; Cast: Michael Stuhlbarg, John Steitz, Michael Tisdale, Justin Schultz, Laura Esterman, Dale Soules, Tamsi Hollo, Jesse Bernstein

MARY PEABODY IN CUBA by Anne Garcia-Romero; Director, Leah C. Gardiner; April 27, 2004; Cast: Mia Barron, Felix Solis, Guy Boyd, Kate Wetherhead, Mateo Gomez

MORNINGS AT MANGANO'S by Stacie Vourakis; Director, Randy White; April 28, 2004; Cast: Kathryn Foster, Charlotte Colavin, Andrew Zimmerman, Lynn Cohen, Ronald Cohen, James Himelsbach, Bruce MacVittie

WET by Liz Duffy Adams; Music by Cliff Caruthers; Director, Liz Duffy Adams; May 3, 2004; Cast: Isabel Keating, Elisa Terrezas, Sarah Lord, Sean Owens, George De La Pena, Daniel Breaker, Lee Rosen, Linda Jones

SILENT CONCERTO by Andrew Morales; Director, Scott Ebersold; April 28, 2004; Cast: Susan O'Connor; Ivan Quintanilla, Lee Rosen

THE LONG SEASON by Chay Yew; Music by Fabian Obispo; Director, Peter DuBois; May 4, 2004; Cast: Orville Mendoza, Rona Figueroa, Jose Llana, Francis Jue

GIBRALTAR by Octavio Solis; Director, Liz Diamond; May 17, 2004; Cast: Adriana Sevan, Jason Manuel Olazábal, Charles Parnell, Brian Keane, June Ballinger, Lucia Brawley, Charles H. Hyman, Peggy Scott

ROSE OF CORAZON by Keith Glover; Director, Ed Herendeen; May 18, 2004; Cast: Ceasar Samayoa, Michael Flanigan, Joey Collins, Anney Giobbe, Arielle Jacobs, Christianne Tisdale

TONGUE-TIED AND DUTY FREE by James Nicholson; Director, Sturgis Warner; May 20, 2004; Cast: Yetta Gottesman, Steven Boyer, Jason Pugatch, Danielle Quisenberry, Karl Herlinger, Mercedes Herrero, Sam Gunclear

NEW FEDERAL THEATRE

Woodie King Jr., Producing Director

DISS DISS AND DISS DAT Musical with Book by Rajendra Ramoon Maharaj and Woodie King Jr.; Music and Lyrics and by Funke Natives; Director and choreographer, Rajendra Ramoon Maharaj; November 2, 2003; Cast: Du Kelly, Amber Efe, Haninibal, McKenzie Frye, Rodney Gilbert, Bryan Taronne Jones, Sharifa LaGuerre, Ayana Wiles-Bey, Jonathan Anderson

GREAT MEN OF GOSPEL by Elizabeth Van Dyke; Director, Elizabeth Van Dyke; March 10, 2004; Cast: Richard Bellazzin, Jeff Bolding, Ralph Carter, Cliff Terry, Gary E. Vincent, Montroville C. Williams

WAITIN' 2 END HELL by William A. Parker; Director, Woodie King Jr.; May 27, 2004; Cast: O.L. Duke, Trish McCall, Eric McLendon, Elica Funastu, Marcus Naylor, Ron Scott, Thyais Walsh

PERFORMANCE SPACE 122

Mark Russell, Artistic Director

TRAGEDY IN 9 LIVES Musical by Karen Houppert; Music by Aaron Maxwell and Alexander MacSween; Director, Stephen Nunns; July 13, 2003; Cast: Juliana Francis, T. Ryder Smith, James "Tigger" Ferguson, Laura Flanagan, Chris Mirto, Chris Spencer Wells

LIFE INTERRUPTED by Spalding Gray; October 5, 2003; Cast: Spalding Gray

TO MY CHAGRIN by Peggy Shaw; Director, Lois Weaver; October 2, 2003; Cast: Peggy Shaw, Vivian Stoll

WHAT EVER: AN AMERICAN ODYSSEY IN EIGHT ACTS by Heather Woodbury; Director, Dudley Saunders; September 4, 2003; Cast: Heather Woodbury

HOUSE OF NO MORE by Caden Manson and Jemma Nelson; Director, Caden Manson; January 8, 2004; Cast: Rebecca Sumner Burgos, Ebony Hatchett, Heather Litter, Amy Miley, Ned Stresen-Reuter

INSTRUCTIONS FOR FORGETTING by Tim Echells; Director, Tim Echells; January 8, 2004; Cast: Tim Echells

PUERTO RICAN TRAVELING THEATRE

Miriam Colón Valle, Founder and Producer

2003 FESTIVAL OF NEW PLAY READINGS JUNE 2–30, 2003

POWER HOUSE by Fred Crecca

CONFESSIONS OF A P.K. by Henry Guzman

THE COURTSHIP OF DIDEROT by María Elena Torres

GONE FISHIN'—WON'T BE BACK by Harding Robert de los Reyes

SIN PARADISE by George Joshua

WELCOME TO MARGARET'S WORLD by Oscar A. Colón

A SIMPLE GIFT by T. Cat Ford

WHEN JOHNNY COMES MARCHING HOME by Noemi Martínez

LATE BLOOMING ROSES by Allen Davis III

BESSIE, THE BUTCHER OF PALM BEACH by Allen Davis III; Director, William Koch; March 31, 2004; Cast: Miriam Cruz, Denia Brache, Alicia Kaplan, Fred Valle

Christina Kirk in *Suitcase*

Colleen Werthmann in *Suitcase*

Christina Kirk in *Suitcase* PHOTOS BY DAVID GOCHFELD

Thomas Jay Ryan, Christina Kirk in *Suitcase*

SOHO REP

Daniel Aukin, Artistic director, Alexandra Conley, Executive director

SUITCASE by Melissa James Gibson; Director, Daniel Aukin; January 24, 2004; Cast: Christina Kirk, Thomas Jay Ryan, Jeremy Shamos, Colleen Werthmann

THE APPEAL by Young Jean Lee; Director, Young Jean Lee; April 9, 2004; Cast: Maggie Hoffman, Michael Portnoy, Pete Simpson, James Stanley

THEATRE FOR THE NEW CITY

Crystal Field, Executive Director

TULIPS AND CADAVERS by Jimmy Camicia; Director, Jimmy Camicia; March 18, 2004; Cast: Jimmy Camicia, Crystal Field, Craig Meade

THE FIST by Misha Shulman; Director, Michael E. Rutenberg; March 25, 2004; Cast: Misha Shulman, Bob Adrian, Judith Jablonka, Mark Brill, Anna Tsiriotakis, Don Lauer, Guy Yanay, Reed Young

ELAINA VANCE'S LAST DANCE by Stacy Presha; Director, Carmen Matthis; April 2, 2004; Cast: Dorothi Fox, Arthur French, Johnnie Mae, Bershan Shaw

NOSSIG'S ANTICS by Lazarre Seymour Simckes; Director, Crystal Field; April 25, 2004; Cast: Stuart Rudin, Mira Rivera, Robert Fitzsimmons, Robert Vaquero, Aesha Waks, Lei Zhou

RITE OF RETURN by Victoria Linchon; Director, Victoria Linchon; April 29, 2004; Cast: Sanaz Mozafarian, Vittoria Setta, Jana Zenadeen, Mohamed Djellouli, A. Michael Elian, Anity Wlody, Frank Shkreli

THEATRE TEN TEN

Judith Jarosz, Producing Artistic Director

ALLS WELL THAT ENDS WELL (The Trials of Helena de Narbonne) by William Shakespeare; Director, Lynn Marie Macy; February 6, 2004; Cast: Glen J. Beck, Craig Brown, Addie Brownlee, Dan Callaway, Derek Devareaux, Elizabeth Fountain, Michael Gnat, Paula Hoza, Colleen Piquette, Teresa Principe, Duncan Rogers, Laura Standley, Ellen Turkelson

IOLANTHE, OR THE PEER (NOBLEMAN) AND THE PERI (FAIRY) by Gilbert and Sullivan; Director, Judith Jarosz; April 30, 2004; Cast: Jacquelyn Baker, Kelly Cooper, Frederick Hamilton, Greg Horton, Nicholas Mongiardo-Cooper, Lisa Riegel, Morgan Sills, David Tillistrand, Ruth Weber, Christiane Young, Sarah Zeitler

Stuart Rudin in *Nossig's Antics* PHOTO BY JONATHAN SLAFF

WORKSHOP THEATRE

Jerry Less, Artistic Director

THE TRIAL OF KLAUS BARBIE by Fred Pezzulli, Directed by Manfred Bormann; June 1–14, 2003; Cast: Burt Edwards, Noel Farmer, Mack Harrell, Allan Knee, Natalie Mosco, Patricia O'Connell, G.W. Reed, Flavio Romeo, Virginia Roncetti, Macha Ross, Linda Sheridan

CONVERSATION WITH A KLEAGLE by Rudy Gray, Directed by Stacy Waring; July 31–August 16, 2003; Cast: Steve Aronson, Antonio Charity, Mark A. Daly, Todd Davis, Charley Gartman, Willie Ann Gissendanner, Eric Moreland, Ronald Rand, Doug Stone

OPERAPLAY by Rick Eisenberg, Directed by Steven Petrillo; September 5–27, 2003; Cast: John D'Arcangelo, Peter Farrell, Dee Dee Friedman, Catherine LaValle, Gerrianne Raphael

FIVE O'CLOCK by Richard Brockman, Directed by Mirra Bank; October 6–25, 2003; Cast: Liz Amberly, Manfred Bormann, Jed Dickson, Jake Robards, Linda Sheridan, Dena Tyler

SKIN DEEP by Jon Lonoff, Directed by Marc Raphael; November 6–22, 2003; Cast: Jed Dickson, Michele Foor, Jim Ligon, Tracy Newirth

A MIDSUMMER NIGHT'S DREAM by William Shakespeare, Directed by Carol Bennett Gerber; December 4–20, 2003; Cast: Erin Carrero, Alexandra Devin, Chad Deverman, Letty Ferrer, Marc Geller, Charles E. Gerber, Michael Jankowitz, Shaniqua Jeffries, Jennifer Jiles, Andy Laird, Kathy Gail MacGowan, Bob Manus, Jennifer Kathryn Marshall, Naomi Martinez, David Mead, Sandy Moore, Natalia C. Paulino, G.W.Reed, Roger Stude, Shade Vaughn

CHEMISTRY LAB by Ben Alexander, Directed by Jerry Less; February 5–21, 2004; Cast: Matthew Armstrong, Peter Esmond, Anne Richardson, Ivan Sandomire, Regina Taufen, LB Williams

THE BARKSDALE CONFESSION by William C. Kovacsik, Directed by Richard Kent Green; February 11–March 6, 2004; Cast: Jeff Paul, Larry Sharp, Dena Tyler

THE PHILOSOPHER'S JOKE by Scott C. Sickles, Directed by David Lenchus; February 18–March 13, 2004; Cast: Tom Berdik, Lori Faiella, Dee Dee Friedman, Timothy Scott Harris, Michael McEachran, David Mead, Gail Thomas

HENRY IV PARTS ONE AND TWO by William Shakespeare, Adapted and Directed by Jerry Less; March 18, 2004; Cast: Munro M. Bonnell, Richard Kent Green, Brian C. Homer, Jennifer Kathryn Marshall, Brian Tom O'Connor, Mark Thornton, Dana Watkins, Stage Manager: Lillian Minnich

GRACELAND by Donald Steele, Directed by David M. Pincus; April 15–May 8, 2004; Cast: Ellen Dolan, Mark Hofmaier, Johnin E. Reade, Nicole Taylor

WORTH STREET THEATRE COMPANY

THE MOONLIGHT ROOM by Tristine Skyler; Director, Jeff Cohen; November 3, 2003; Cast: Laura Breckenridge, Brendan Sexton III, Kathryn Layng, Lawrence James, Mark Rosenthal

PROFESSIONAL REGIONAL COMPANIES

A CONTEMPORARY THEATRE (ACT)

Seattle, Washington
THIRTY-NINTH SEASON

Kurt Beattie, Artistic Director; Susan Trapnell, Managing Director

ABSURD PERSON SINGULAR by Alan Ayckbourn; Directed by Jeff Steitzer; Scenic Design by Don Yanik; Costume Design by Rose Pederson; Lighting Design by Rick Paulsen; Sound Design by Dominic CodyKramers; July 11–August 3, 2003; Cast: Julie Briskman (Jane); Liz McCarthy (Eva); Marianne Owen (Marion); Larry Paulsen (Sidney); Michael Winters (Ronald); R. Hamilton Wright (Geoffrey)

THE GOAT, OR WHO IS SYLVIA? by Edward Albee; Directed by Warner Shook; Scenic Design by Michael Olich; Costume Design by Frances Kenny; Lighting Design by Mary Louise Geiger; Sound Design by Eric Chappelle; July 25–August 17, 2003; Cast: Cynthia Mace (Stevie); Brian Kerwin (Martin); Frank Corrado (Ross); Ian Fraser (Billy)

A MOON FOR THE MISBEGOTTEN by Eugene O'Neill; Directed by Kurt Beattie; Scenic Design by Shelley Henze Schermer; Costume Design by Deb Trout; Lighting Design by Geoff Korf; Sound Design by Dominic CodyKramers; September 5–28, 2003; Cast: Jeanne Paulsen (Josie Hogan); David Gehrman (Mike Hogan); Sean G. Griffin (Phil Hogan); John Procaccino (James Tyrone, Jr.); Galen Joseph Osier (T. Stedman Harder)

OMNIUM-GATHERUM by Theresa Rebeck and Alexandra Gersten-Vassilaros; Directed by Jon Jory; Scenic Design by Robert Dahlstrom; Costume Design by Marcia Dixcy Jory; Lighting Design by Greg Sullivan; Lighting Design by Eric Chappelle; October 10–November 2, 2003; Cast: Kent Broadhurst (Terence); David Drummond (Jeff); Timothy Evans (Server); Cynthia Jones (Julia); Joseph Kamal (Khalid); Eddie Levi Lee (Roger); Dennis Mosley (Mohammed); Mari Nelson (Lydia); Marianne Owen (Suzie)

THE SYRINGA TREE by Pamela Gien; Directed by Larry Moss; Produced by Matt Salinger: Scenic Design by Kenneth Foy; Lighting Design by Steven B. Mannshardt; Sound Design by Tony Suraci; October 31–November 23, 2003; Cast (in rotation): Gin Hammond (Elizabeth); Eva Kaminski (Elizabeth)

A CHRISTMAS CAROL by Charles Dickens; Adapted by Gregory A. Falls; Directed by Kurt Beattie; Music Composed and Conducted by Adam Stern; Scenic Design by Shelley Henze Schermer; Costume Design by Deb Trout; Lighting Design by Michael Wellborn; Sound Design by Dominic Cody Kramers; Original Sound Design by Steven M. Klein; Music Director Eric Chappelle; Choreographer Wade Madsen; November 28–December 27, 2003; Cast: Eric Ray Anderson (Bob Cratchit, Jonathan); Erica Badgeley (Martha Cratchit, Dancer); Casey Cassinelli (Turkey Boy, Undertaker's Assistant, Singing Thief); Deanna Companion (Spirit 1, Party Guest); Philip Davidson (Scrooge (in rotation)); David Drummond (Fred, Robin Crusoe, Dick, Bread Lady, Spirit 3); Mary Jane Gibson (Belle, Niece, Charwoman); Kit Harris (Mrs. Fezziwig, Mrs. Dilber, Sister, Sugar Plum Seller); AnnieRose Kafer (Elizabeth Cratchit, Lil Fezziwig, Want); Emma Kelley (Belinda Cratchit, Fan); Charles Leggett (Spirit 2, Gentleman, Ragpicker); Tallis Moore (Young Scrooge, Charles Cratchit); Terry Edward Moore (Scrooge (in rotation)); Galen Joseph Osier (Middle Scrooge, Topper, Businessman, Beggar); Javin Reid (Tiny Tim, Ignorance); Morgan Rowe (Mrs. Cratchit, Elizabeth); Vincent Norton Scott (Peter Cratchit, Master Fezziwig); Tom Spiller (Mr. Fezziwig, Old Joe, Gentleman, Grocer); Brian Thompson (Jacob Marley, Poor May, Party Guest, Businessman); Jane May (Female Understudy); Justin Alley (Male Understudy)

FORTIETH SEASON

LIFE: A GUIDE FOR THE PERPLEXED Book by Paul Magid, Music by Mark Ettinger, Lyrics by Howard Jay Patterson; Directed by Michael Preston; Scenic Design by Bliss Kolb and Jessica Dodge; Costume Design by Carolyn Keim; Lighting Design by David Hutson; Sound Design by Mark Ettinger; February 21–March 21, 2004; The Flying Karamazov Brothers: Paul Magid, Howard Jay Patterson, Mark Ettinger, Roderick Kimball

BLACK COFFEE by Agatha Christie; Directed by Kurt Beattie; Scenic Design by Matthew Smucker; Costume Design by Carolyn Keim; Lighting Design by Christopher Reay; Sound Design by Dominic CodyKramers; April 13–May 2, 2004; Cast: Laurence Ballard (Sir Claud Amory); Ian Bell (Inspector Japp); Alan Bryce (Dr. Graham/Constable); Emily Cedergreen (Barbara Amory); Frank Corrado (Dr. Carelli); Susan Corzatte (Miss Caroline Amory); Jim Gall (Richard Amory); Mary Jane Gibson (Lucia Amory); Tim Liese (Edward Raynor); David Pichette (Hercule Poirot); Brian Thompson (Tredwell); R. Hamilton Wright (Captain Hastings)

ALKI by Eric Overmyer (World Premiere); Directed by Kurt Beattie; Scenic & Projection Design by Scott Weldin; Projection Co-design by Martin Christoffel; Costume design by Deb Trout; Lighting Design by Geoff Korf; Sound Design by Dominic CodyKramers; Adam Stern, Composer; June 4–27, 2004; Cast: Justin Alley (John Johnson, ensemble), Suzanne Bouchard (Woman in Green, ensemble), Julie Briskman (Remedios, ensemble); Deborah Fialkow (Alberta, ensemble); Mary Jane Gibson (Sally, ensemble); Ray Gonzalez (Preacher Rowe, ensemble); Douglas Moening (Smitty, ensemble); Todd Jefferson Moore (Bad Otter, ensemble), Marianne Owen (Hannah Gynt, ensemble); David Pichette (Mysterious Stranger, ensemble); Jonah Von Spreecken (Ugly Boy, ensemble); Michael Winters (King of the Haints, ensemble); R. Hamilton Wright (Peer Gynt)

ENCHANTED APRIL by Matthew Barber from the novel by Elizabeth von Arnim; Directed by Warner Shook; Scenic Design by Robert A. Dahlstrom; Costume Design by Frances Kenny, Lighting Design by Mary Louise Geiger; Composer and Sound Design by Michael Roth; July 16–August 8, 2004; Cast: Suzanne Bouchard (Rose Arnott); Julie Briskman (Lotty Wilton); Deborah Fialkow (Caroline Bramble); Suzy Hunt (Mrs. Graves); Marianne Owen (English Maid/Costanza); David Pichette (Mellersh Wilton); Michael Winters (Frederick Arnott); R. Hamilton Wright (Antony Wilding)

(CONTINUED ON NEXT PAGE)

(CONTINUED FROM PREVIOUS PAGE)

JUMPERS by Tom Stoppard; Directed by Jeff Steitzer; Scenic Design by Matthew Smucker; Costume Design by Marcia Dixcy Jory; Lighting Design by Alex Berry; Sound Design by Dominic Cody Kramers; Music Directed by Richard Gray; August 27–September 19, 2004; Cast: Matt Bariletti (Jumpers/Tarzan); Julie Briskman (Secretary); Ky Dobson (Jumper); Elizabeth Erber (Jumper); Richard Gray (Jumper); Sean G. Griffin; (Crouch); Cassidy Katims (Jumper); Ian Lindsay (Jumper/McFee); John Patrick Lowrie (Bones); David Pichette (George Moore); Erika Rolfsrud (Dotty); R. Hamilton Wright (Archie)

GOOD BOYS by Jane Martin: Directed by Jon Jory; Scenic Designer Carey Wong; Costume Design by Marcia Dixcy Jory; Lighting Design by Greg Sullivan; Sound Design by Chris R. Walker; September 24–October 17, 2004; Cast: Thomas Jefferson Byrd (Thomas Thurman); Jeffrey Hayenga (James Erskine); Dennis Mosley (Marcus Thurman); Michael Scott (Ethan Thurman); Adam Western (Corin Thurman)

FICTION by Steven Dietz; Directed by Steven Dietz; Scenic Design by Scott Weldin; Costume Design by Carolyn Keim; Lighting Design by Rick Paulsen; Sound Design by Eric Chappelle; October 22–November 14, 2004; Cast: Suzanne Bouchard (Linda Waterman); Emily Cedergreen (Amanda Drake); John Procaccino (Michael Waterman)

ALLEY THEATRE

Houston, Texas

FIFTY-SEVENTH SEASON

Artistic Director, Gregory Boyd; Managing Director, Paul Tetreault

SHERLOCK HOLMES by William Gillette; Director, Gregory Boyd; Scenic Design, Vincent Mountain; Costume Design, Fabio Toblini; Lighting Design, Rui Rita; Sound Design, Rob Milburn and Michael Bodeen; October 10–November 2, 2003; Cast: Josie de Guzman (Madge Larrabee), David Born (Benjamin Forman), Paul Hope (James Larrabee), John Tyson (Sidney Prince), Elizabeth Heflin (Alice Faulkner), Julie Krohn (Terese), Todd Waite (Sherlock Holmes), Philip Lehl (Alfred Bassick), James Black (Professor Moriarty), Tony Oller (Billy), Jeffrey Bean (Dr. Watson), James Belcher (Jim Craigin, Parsons), Daniel Magill (Thomas Leary, Count Von Stalburg), Timothy Wrobel (Lightfoot McTague), Charles Krohn (Sir Edward Leighton), Bettye Fitzpatrick (Woman on the street)

FULLY COMMITTED by Becky Mode; Director, Rob Bundy; Scenic Design, Kevin Rigdon; Costume Design, Andrea Lauer; Lighting Design, Kevin Rigdon; Sound Design, Ryan Rumery; October 17–November16, 2003; Cast: Jamison Stern (Sam and others)

James Black, Jeffrey Bean in *Twelfth Night* or *What You Will* PHOTO BY T. CHARLES ERICKSON

A CHRISTMAS CAROL, A GHOST STORY OF CHRISTMAS by Charles Dickens; Director and Adaptation by Stephen Rayne; Scenic Design, Douglas W. Schmidt; Costume Design, Esther Marquis; Lighting Design, Rui Rita; Sound Design, Malcolm Nicholls; November 28–December 28, 2003; Cast: James Belcher (Ebenezer Scrooge), Bettye Fitzpatrick (Miss Goodleigh, Mrs. Dilber), Philip Lehl (Bob Cratchit), Paul Hope (Coutts, Fezziwig), Jeffrey Bean (Marley, Old Joe), Charles Krohn (Priest), Jovan Jackson (Ghost of Christmas Future, Labourer, Fezziwig Guest), Todd Waite (Fred), David Rainey (Poor Man, Ghost of Christmas Present), Sarah Prikryl (Ghost of Christmas Past, Mrs. O'Mally), Sigali Hamberger (Moll, Miss 1, Fred's Sister, Poor Woman), David Born (Undertaker, Fezziwig Guest, Fred Guest), Anne Quackenbush (Miss Bumble, Miss 3, Mrs. Fred), Fritz Dickman (Phizz, Belle's Husband, Fezziwig Guest), Julia Krohn (Belle, Martha), Shelley Calene-Black (Mrs. Cratchit, Mrs. Fezziwig), Richard Carlson (Topper), K. Todd Freeman (Deedles), Richard Ramsey (Royal Exchange, Turkey Boy)

PROOF by David Auburn; Director, James Black; Scenic Design, Kevin Rigdon; Costume Design, Andrea Lauer; Lighting Design, Michael Lincoln; Sound Design, John Gromada; January 9–February 1, 2004; Cast: John Tyson (Robert), Elizabeth Bunch (Catherine), Chris Hutchison (Hal), Robin Terry (Claire)

TOPDOG/UNDERDOG by Suzan-Lori Parks; Director, Amy Morton; Scenic Design, Loy Arcenas; Costume Design, Nan Cibula-Jenkins; Lighting Design, Kevin Rigdon; Sound Design, Rob Milburn and Michael Bodeen; January 16–February 15, 2004; Cast: K. Todd Freeman (Booth), David Rainey (Lincoln)

TWELFTH NIGHT or **WHAT YOU WILL** by William Shakespeare; Director, Gregory Boyd; Scenic Design, Kevin Rigdon; Costume Design, Fabio Toblini; Lighting Design, Chris Parry; Sound Design, Rob Milburn and Michael Bodeen; February 20–March 14, 2004; Cast: Todd Waite (Orsino), Philip Lehl (Valentine, Fabian), Josie de Guzman (Viola), Charles Krohn (Captain, Priest), James Black (Sir Toby Belch), Kimberly King (Maria), John Tyson (Sir Andrew Aguecheek), Jeffrey Bean (Feste), Elizabeth Heflin (Olivia), Paul Hope (Malvolio), James Belcher (Antonio), Daniel Magill (Sebastian), Richard Ramsey (First Officer), Timothy Wrobel (Second Officer), Livia Bornigia (Gentlewoman)

LIFE (X) 3 by Yasmina Reza; Translated by Christopher Hampton; Director, Pam MacKinnon; Scenic Design, Kevin Rigdon; Costume Design, Linda Ross; Lighting Design, John Ambrosone; Sound Design, Joe Pino; March 26–April 18, 2004; Cast: Jeffrey Bean (Henry), Elizabeth Heflin (Sonia), Kimberly King (Inez), Todd Waite (Hubert), Loren Thornton (Child)

OUR LADY OF 121ST STREET by Stephen Adly Guirgus; Director, James Black; Scenic Design, Tony Rosenthal; Costume Design, Mara Blumenfeld; Lighting Design, Michael Lincoln; March 19–April 18, 2004; Cast: James Belcher (Victor), Pablo Bracho (Balthazar), Alex Morris (Rooftop), Charles Krohn (Father Lux), Adrian Porter (Flip), Philip Lehl (Gail), Alice Gatling (Inez), Patricia Duran (Norca), Luis Galindo (Edwin), Ezequiel Guerra, Jr. (Pinky), Shelley Calene-Black (Marcia), Michelle Edwards (Sonia)

A FUNNY THING HAPPENED ON THE WAY TO THE FORUM by Burt Shevelove and Larry Gelbart; Music and Lyrics by Stephen Sondheim; Director, Gregory Boyd; Scenic Design, Vincent Mountain; Costume Design, Constance Hoffman; Lighting Design, John Ambrosone; Sound Design, Ray Nardelli; May 14–June 6, 2004; Cast: John Tyson (Pseudolus), Philip Lehl, Ezequiel Guerra Jr., Eric Brandon Mota (The Proteans), Charles Krohn (Senex), Jennie Welch (Domina), Todd Waite (Hero), Jeffrey Bean (Hysterium), James Black (Lycus), Melissa H. Pritchett (Panacea), Cora M. Campbell (Tintinabula), Brooke E. Wilson (Vibrata), Laura Scott (Gymnasia), Mary Sharon Komarek, Patricia Salvo (The Geminae), Elizabeth Heflin (Philia), James Belcher (Erronius), Paul Hope (Miles Gloriosus)

AMERICAN CONSERVATORY THEATER

San Francisco, California
THIRTY-SEVENTH SEASON

Artistic Director, Carey Perloff; Executive Director, Heather Kitchen

MAINSTAGE SEASON PRODUCTIONS AT THE GEARY THEATER

LES LIAISONS DANGEREUSES by Choderlos de Laclos; Director and Adaptation by Giles Havergal; Scenic Design, Kate Edmunds; Costume Design, Deborah Dryden; Lighting Design, Rui Rita; Sound Design, Garth Hemphill; September 11–October 12, 2003; Cast: Joan MacIntosh (Madame), Lise Bruneau (Marquise de Merteuil), Marco Barricelli (Vicomte de Valmont), Libby West (Madame de Tourvel), Elizabeth Raetz (Cécile de Volanges), Neil Hopkins (Chevalier Danceny), Anthony Fusco (Ensemble), Lauren Grace (Ensemble), Michele Leavy (Ensemble), Scott Nordquist (Ensemble), Patrick Sieler (Ensemble), Taylor Valentine (Ensemble)

(CONTINUED ON NEXT PAGE)

Marco Barricelli, Lise Bruneau in *Les Liasons Dangereuses*   PHOTO BY KEVIN BERNE

The Company in *A Funny Thing Happened on the Way to the Forum*   PHOTO BY T. CHARLES ERICKSON

(CONTINUED FROM PREVIOUS PAGE)

WAITING FOR GODOT by Samuel Beckett; Director, Carey Perloff; Scenic Design, J. B. Wilson; Costume Design, Beaver Bauer; Lighting Design, Russell H. Champa; Sound Design, Garth Hemphill; October 17–November 16, 2003; Cast: Steven Anthony Jones (Pozzo), Gregory Wallace (Estragon), Peter Frechette (Vladimir), Frank Wood (Lucky), Lawrence Papale/Jonathan Rosen (Boy)

A CHRISTMAS CAROL by Charles Dickens; Adaptation by Dennis Powers and Laird Williamson; Director, Craig Slaight; Original Director, Laird Williamson; Scenic Design, Robert Blackman; Costume Design, Robert Morgan; Additional Costumes and Design Supervision, David F. Draper; Lighting Design, Peter Maradudin; Music, Lee Hoiby; Original Lyrics, Laird Williamson; Sound Design, Garth Hemphill; Music Director, Peter Maleitzke; November 29–December 24, 2003; Cast: Alec Page (Boy Caroler, Cabin Boy, Boy in the Street), Tommy A. Gomez (Dickens, Ghost of Christmas Present), Steven Anthony Jones (Scrooge), Jud Williford (Bob Cratchit), Stephanie Weeks (Charitable Gentlewoman, Fezziwig Guest, Beth), Margaret Schenck (Charitable Gentlewoman, Mrs. Fezziwig, Caroler), Jeff Galfer (Fred, Businessman), Davis Duffield (Carol Seller, Christmas Eve Walker, Young Scrooge, Caroler), Isadora Epstein (Carol Seller, Belinda Cratchit), Maren Vick (Carol Seller, Celebrant), Nicholas Perloff-Giles (Sled Boy, Ned Cratchit), Kai Young (Sled Boy, Ignorance), Jeff Tittiger (Sled Boy, Toy Bear), David McKenna (Sled Boy, Toy Monkey), James Donovan Finnie II (Sled Boy, Tiny Tim Cratchit), Kira Blaskovich (Woman in the Street, Belle Cousins, Miner's Family), Imaide Steverango (Daughter of Woman in the Street, Sally Cratchit), Miranda Carlin-Swain (Beggar Girl, Toy Clown, Want), Julianna Cressman (Beggar Girl, Toy Ballerina), David Valdez (Wood Carrier, Mistletoe Carrier, Fezziwig Guest, Caroler), Brian Keith Russell (Christmas Eve Walker, Mr. Fezziwig, Helmsman), Ka-Ling Cheung (Christmas Eve Walker, Fezziwig Guest, Martha Cratchit), Adriean Delaney (Christmas Eve Walker, Fezziwig Guest, Ted, Ghost of Christmas Future), Andrew Fleischer (Christmas Eve Walker, Peter Cratchit), Stacey Jenson (Christmas Eve Walker, Fezziwig Guest, Meg, Mrs. Dilber), D.J. Lapite (Christmas Eve Walker, Chainbearer, Dick Wilkins, Caroler, Businessman), Lisa McCormick (Christmas Eve Walker, Fezziwig Guest, Mary), Robert Seitelman (Christmas Eve Walker, Fezziwig Guest, Topper, Businessman), Nicholas Dominick Sweeney (Christmas Eve Walker, Chainbearer, Jack, Old Joe), Marilee Talkington (Christmas Eve Walker, Mrs. Cratchit), Nicholas Taber (Christmas Eve Walker, Boy Scrooge, Celebrant), Molly Fehr (Christmas Eve Walker, Little Fan, Toy Cat), Rhonnie Washington (Marley's Ghost, Miner, Businessman), Erik Heger (Ghost of Christmas Past, Caroler, Businessman), Crystal Noelle (Wife of Christmas Past, Miner's Wife, Mrs. Filcher), Daniel Patrick Kennedy (Son of Past, Miner's Family), Devon Hadsell (Daughter of Past, Miner's Family)

A DOLL'S HOUSE by Henrik Ibsen; Translation by Paul Walsh; Director, Carey Perloff; Scenic Design, Annie Smart; Costume Design, Sandra Woodall; Lighting Design, David Finn; Sound Design, Garth Hemphill; Composer, Karl Fredrik Lundeberg; January 8–February 8, 2004; Cast: René Augesen (Nora Helmer), Stephen Caffrey (Torvald Helmer), Joan Harris-Gelb (Kristine Linde), James Carpenter (Dr. Rank), Gregory Wallace (Nils

Anthony Zerbe, Roscoe Lee Brown in *Behind the Broken Words* PHOTO BY KEVIN BERNE

Krogstad), Griffin and Louise Wurzelbacher/Austin Greene and Tobi Jane Moore (Ivar and Emmy Helmer), Joy Carlin (Nanny), Zehra Berkman (A Maid)

LEVEE JAMES by S. M. Shephard-Massat; Director, Israel Hicks; Scenic Design, Loy Arcenas; Costume Design, Michael J. Cesario; Lighting Design, Nancy Schertler; Sound Design, Garth Hemphill; February 13–March 14, 2004; Cast: Rosalyn Coleman (Lily Grace Hoterfield), Steven Anthony Jones (Wesley Slaton), Gregory Wallace (Fitzhugh Marvin)

THE TIME OF YOUR LIFE by William Saroyan; Director, Tina Landau; Scenic Design, G. W. Mercier; Costume Design, James Schuette; Lighting Design, Scott Zielinski; Original Music and Sound Design, Rob Milburn and Michael Bodeen; March 25–May 2, 2004; Cast: Darren Barrerre/Gabriel Kenney (Newsboy), Jeff Perry (Joe), Robert Ernst (The Armenian), Rod Gnapp (The Drunk), Yasen Peyankov (Nick), Ramiz Monsef (Willie), Patrick New (Tom), Mariann Mayberry (Kitty Duval), Guy Adkins (Harry), Darragh Kennan (Dudley), Don Shell (Wesley), Cathleen Riddley (Lorene), Lawrence MacGowan (Blick), Joan Harris-Gelb (Mary L.), Guy Van Swearingen (Krupp), Andy Murray (McCarthy), Margaret Schenck (Society Lady), Howard Witt (Kit Carson), Kyra Himmelbaum (Elsie), Tom Blair (Society Man), Kira Blaskovich (Ensemble), Jenn Wagner (Ensemble), T. Edward Webster (Ensemble), Jud Williford (Ensemble)

A MOTHER by Constance Congdon; Director, Carey Perloff; Scenic Design, Ralph Funicello; Costume Design, Beaver Bauer; Lighting Design, James F. Ingalls; Sound Design, Garth Hemphill; May 13–June 13, 2004; Cast: Olympia Dukakis (Vassa Petrovna Zheleznova), Marcia Pizzo (Anna), Reg Rogers (Semyon), John Keating (Pavel), Margaret Schenck (Natalya), René Augesen (Liudmila), Tom Mardirosian (Prokhor Zheleznov), Louis Zorich (Mikhail Vassilyev), Jeri Lynn Cohen (Lipa)

THE GOOD BODY by Eve Ensler; Director, Peter Askin; Scenic Design, Robert Brill; Costume Design, Susan Hilferty; Lighting Design, Kevin Adams; Original Music & Sound Design, David Van Tieghem; Video Design, Wendall K. Harrington; June 24–July 25, 2004; Cast: Eve Ensler

OTHER PRODUCTIONS AT THE GEARY THEATER

BEHIND THE BROKEN WORDS by Roscoe Lee Browne & Anthony Zerbe; November 19–November 23, 2003; Cast: Roscoe Lee Browne, Anthony Zerbe

BOLD & BRASSY BLUES; December 27–December 31, 2003; Cast: Sandra Reaves-Phillips, Lacy Darryl Phillips, Marishka Shanice Phillips

TSCHAIKOWSKY (AND OTHER RUSSIANS); February 29–March 14, 2004; Cast: Mark Nadler

AN EVENING WITH CAROL CHANNING; April 11–April 12, 2004; Cast: Carol Channing

PROFESSIONAL PRODUCTION AT ZEUM THEATER

YŌHEN by Philip Kan Gotanda; Director, Seret Scott; Scenic Design, David Ledsinger; Costume Design, Callie Floor; Lighting Design, Alexander Vladimir Nichols; Sound Design, Cliff Caruthers; September 6-27, 2003; Cast: Steven Anthony Jones (James), Dian Kobayashi (Sumi)

A.C.T. CONSERVATORY PRODUCTIONS AT ZEUM THEATER

KORCZAK'S CHILDREN by Jeffrey Hatcher; Director, Domenique Lozano; Lighting Design, Kimberly Scott; Sound Design, j.j. Bergovoy; August 21–August 30, 2003; Cast: Matthew Moore (Janusz Korczak), Naomi Frank, Barclay Iversen, Sonja Dale, Bailey Hopkins, Alison Kinzy, Ann O'Hare, Miranda Swain, Alanna Pinell, Alexandra Pinell, Will Sultan, Janice Amaya, Elizabeth Behrs, Ryan Campos, David Ebong, Remy Jewell, Charlie Locke, Brooke Bundy, Alex Hersler, Chase Maxwell, Maxie Pulliam, Billy Cirocco, Daniel Kennedy, Montana Mirandilla, Jay Wineroth, Timothy Smith-Stewart, Paul Hoffert

A MIDSUMMER NIGHT'S DREAM by William Shakespeare; Director, Giles Havergal; Scenic Design, Yank Frances; Costume Design, Callie Floor; Lighting Design, Kimberly J. Scott; October 9–October 23, 2003; Cast: Kira Blaskovich (Tom Snout), Ka-Ling Cheung (Philostrate), Adriean Delaney (Oberon), Davis Duffield (Robin Starveling), Andrew Fleischer (Francis Flute), Jeffrey Galfer (Lysander), Erik Heger (Egeus), Stacey Jenson (Helena), D. J. Lapité (Demetrius), Lisa McCormick (Puck), Crystal Noelle McCreary (Hippolyta), Robert Seitelman (Nick Bottom), Nicholas Sweeney (Theseus), Marilee Talkington (Titania), David Valdez (Peter Quince), Stephanie Weeks (Hermia), Jud Williford (Snug)

WAR DADDY by Jim Grimsley; Director, W. D. Keith; Scenic Design, Rachel Lawton; Costume Design, Malia Miyashiro and Katy Simola; Lighting Design, Kimberly J. Scott; Sound Design, j. j. Bergovoy; November 13–November 22, 2003; Cast: Hannah Finnie, Aidan O'Reilly, Max Mosher, Jacob Gordon, Gus Heagerty, Brooke Bundy, Lauren Klingman, Lili Weckler, Adde Bigelow, Stephen Cirillo, Charles Filipov, Joshua Schell, Aurora Simcovich, Alexandra Steinman, Ian Budd Wolff, Morgan Green

THE MASTER AND MARGARITA by Mikhail Bulgakov; Adaptation and Director, Adrian Giurgea; Scenic Design, Danila Korogodsky; Costume Design, Callie Floor; Lighting Design, Kimberly J. Scott; Sound Design, j. j. Bergovoy; February 26–March 13, 2004; Cast: Jeff Galfer (Woland), Jud Williford (The Master), Crystal Noelle (Margarita), D. J. Lapité (Pontius Pilate), Kira Blaskovich (Ensemble), Ka-Ling Cheung (Ensemble), Adriean Delaney (Ensemble), Andrew Fleischer (Ensemble), Erik Heger (Ensemble), Stacey Jenson (Ensemble), Lisa McCormick (Ensemble), Rob Seitelman (Ensemble), Nicholas Dominic Sweeney (Ensemble), Marilee Talkington (Ensemble), David Valdez (Ensemble), Stephanie Weeks (Ensemble)

GRAY'S ANATOMY by Jim Leonard; Director, Craig Slaight; Costume Design, Callie Floor; Lighting Design, Kimberly Scott; March 19–March 28, 2004; Cast: Jacob Gordon (Galen P. Gray), Laelena Brooks, Della Duncan, Emma Fasler, Charles Filipov, Hannah Finnie, Nathalie Gorman, Emily Iscoff Daigian, Martine Moore, Julien Inclan, Julia Mattison, Joshua Schell, Aurora Simcovich

LADIES OF THE CANYON: THE MUSIC OF JONI MITCHELL; Director, Craig Slaight; Musical Director, Krista Wigle; Scenic Design, Dean Shibuya; Lighting Design, Kimberly J. Scott; June 4–June 19, 2004; Cast: Dillan Arrick, Adde Bigelow, Hannah Finnie, Lucia Grahamjones, Sarah Grandin, Emily Iscoff-Daigian, Scout Katovich, Julia Mattison, Rachel Rubenstein, Charlotte Ubben

Dian Kobayashi, Steven Anthony Jones in *Yōhen* PHOTO BY KEVIN BERNE

ARDEN THEATRE COMPANY

Philadelphia, Pennsylvania
SIXTEENTH SEASON

Artistic Director, Terrence J. Nolen; Managing Director, Amy L. Murphy

CAFÉ PUTTANESCA Music and lyrics by Michael Ogborn; book by Terrence J. Nolen and Michael Ogborn; Director, Terrence J. Nolen; Musical Director, Vince DiMura; Scenic Design, Bob Phillips; Costume Design, K.J. Gilmer; Lighting Design, James Leitner; Sound Design, Nick Rye; September 11–November 2, 2003; Cast: Tony Braithwaite (The Owner), Tracie Higgins (The Duchess), Mary Martello (The Baroness), Kristin Purcell (The Cook), Jilline Ringle (The Marquesa)

ROSENCRANTZ AND GUILDENSTERN ARE DEAD by Tom Stoppard; Director, Aaron Posner; Scenic Design, David P. Gordon; Costume Design, Rosemarie McKelvey, Lighting Design, John Stephen Hoey; Sound Design, Karin Graybash; October 9–November 9, 2003; Cast: Jon L. Egging (Hamlet), Scott Greer (Guildenstern), Jefferson Haynes (Alfred, Guard), Dave Jadico (Tragedian, Guard), Mary McCool (Ophelia, Tragedian), Paul Meshejian (Claudius, Tragedian), Ian Merrill Peakes (Rosencrantz), Hayden Saunier (Gertrude, Tragedian), Lee Sellars (The Player), H. Michael Walls (Polonius, Tragedian)

SIDEWAYS STORIES FROM WAYSIDE SCHOOL by Louis Sachar; Adaptation by John Olive; Director, Whit MacLaughlin; Scenic Design, Nick Embree; Costume Design, Richard St. Clair; Lighting Design, Thomas C. Hase; Sound and Video Design, Jorge Cousineau; December 10, 2003–January 15, 2004 Cast: Ben Dibble (Louis), Christina Gianaris (Bebe), Maggie Lakis (Leslie), Joshua Lamon (Myron), Marcia Saunders (Mrs. Gorf/Sammy/Mr. Pickle/Miss Valooosh/Mr. Gorf), Catharine K. Slusar (Ms. Jewls), Dionne Stone (Rondi), Steven Wright (Dameon)

PROOF by David Auburn; Director, James J. Christy; Scenic Design, Lewis Folden; Costume Design, Alison Roberts; Lighting Design, Jerold R. Forsyth; Sound Designer, Jorge Cousineau; January 22–March 21, 2004; Cast: Bev Appleton (Robert), Alexandra Geis (Catherine), Christie Parker (Claire), Geoff Sobelle (Hal)

TOOTH AND CLAW by Michael Hollinger; Director, Terrence J. Nolen; Scenic Design, James Kronzer; Costume Design, Anne Kennedy; Lighting Design, Michael Philippi, Sound Design, Jorge Cousineau; March 11–April 11, 2004; Cast: David Grillo (Carlos), Donald Grody (Malcolm), Susan McKey (Schuyler), Alvaro Mendoza (Mendoza, Ensemble), Marcos Muniz (Park Official, Ensemble), Elvis O. Nolasco (Tito, Ensemble), Tlaloc Antonio Rivas (Pedro, Ensemble), Al D. Rodriguez (Gonzalo); Shirley Roeca (Ana), Paco Tolson (Jorge, Ensemble)

Mary Martello in *Café Puttanesca* PHOTO BY MARK GARVIN

FRANKLIN'S APPRENTICE by Laurie Brooks; Director, Aaron Posner; Scenic Design, Daniel Conway; Costume Design, Alison Roberts; Lighting Design, James Leitner; Sound Design, Karin Graybash; April 20–May 22, 2004; Cast: Charlotte Ford (Sally Franklin), Kate Eastwood Norris (Debbie Franklin), Steve Pacek (William Franklin), Ian Merrill Peakes (Ben Franklin), Eric Antonio Sáez (John, The Apprentice), Buck Schirner (Spencer), Brian A. Wilson (Rev. Rickersley)

Joshua Lamon, Marcia Saunders in *Sideways Stories From Wayside School* PHOTO BY MARK GARVIN

HARD TIMES by Charles Dickens; Adaptation by Heidi Stillman; Director, Heidi Stillman; Scenic Designer, Daniel Ostling; Costume Designer, Mara Blumenfeld; Lighting Design, Brian Sidney Bembridge; Sound Design/Composers, Andre Pluess and Ben Sussman; May 27–June 27, 2004; Cast: Eva Barr (Mrs. Sparsit, Stephen's Wife, Pufflerumpus), Larry Distasi (Stephen, Sleary), Laura Eason (Rachael, Mrs. Gradgrind, Scherezade), Raymond Fox (Gradgrind, Slackbridge, Sissy's Father), Tony Hernandez (Bitzer, Amore), Lauren Hirte (Sissy), Louise Lamson (Louisa), Ceal Phelan (Mrs. Pegler), Philip R. Smith (Mr. Harthouse, Mr. M'Choakumchild, Kidderminster), Troy West (Mr. Bounderby), Matt Zeigler (Tom)

ARENA STAGE

Washington, DC

FIFTY-THIRD SEASON

Artistic Director, Molly Smith; Executive Director, Stephen Richard

IN THE FICHANDLER:

SHAKESPEARE IN HOLLYWOOD by Ken Ludwig; Director, Kyle Donnelly; Scenic Design, Thomas Lynch; Costume Design, Jess Goldstein; Lighting Design, Nancy Schertler; Sound Design, Susan R. White; September 12–October 19, 2003; Cast: Ellen Karas (Louella Parsons), Robert Prosky (Max Reinhardt), David Fendig (Dick Powell), Rick Foucheux (Jack Warner), Michael Skinner (Daryl), Alice Ripley (Lydia Lansing), Casey Biggs (Oberon), Emily Donahoe (Puck), Maggie Lacey (Olivia Darnell), Everett Quinton (Will Hays), Hugh Nees (Joe E. Brown), Adam Richman (Jimmy Cagney), Bethany Caputo (Ensemble), Scott Graham (Ensemble), Eric Jorgensen (Ensemble), Robert McClure (Ensemble)

CAMELOT Book and Lyrics by Alan Jay Lerner, Music by Frederick Loewe, Director, Molly Smith; Scenic Design, Kate Edmunds; Costume Design, Paul Tazewell; Lighting Design, John Ambrosone; Sound Design, Timothy M. Thompson; November 20–January 4, 2003; Cast: James Soller/ Barndon Thane Wilson (Young Arthur/Tom of Warwick), J. Fred Shiffman (Merlyn/Pellinore), Steven Skybell (Arthur), Kate Suber (Guenevere), Christianne Tisdale (Nimue/Morgan Le Fey), Stephen F. Schmidt (Sir Dinadan/Ensemble), Kevin M. Burrows (Sir Lionel/Ensemble), Micheal L. Forrest (Sir Sagramore/Ensemble), Lawrence Brimmer (Sir Bliant/Ensemble), Parker Esse (Sir Colgrevance/Ensemble), Jeffrey Luke (Sir Timur Khan/Ensemble), Vic DiMonda (Sir Castor/Ensemble), J. Edward Lucas (Sir Olatungi/Ensemble), Peggy Yates (Lady Anne/Ensemble), Deanna Harris (Lady Catherine/Ensemble), Jennifer Anderson (Lady Sybil/Ensemble), Michelle Liu Coughlin (Lady Lui, Ensemble), Zoie Morris (Lady Anaya/Ensemble), Eduardo Placer (Clarius/Ensemble), Anthony Aloise (Darius/Ensemble), Matt Bogart (Lancelot), Bev Appleton (Squire Dap/Ensemble), Jack Ferver (Mordred), Debra Buonaccorsi (Swing), Gabriel Veneziano (Swing)

A MAN'S A MAN by Bertolt Brecht, translated by Gerhard Nellhaus; Director, Enikö Eszenyi; Scenic Design, Karl Eigsti; Costume Design, Ilona Somogyi; Lighting Design, Nancy Schertler; Sound Design, David Madox, Dwayne Nitz; February 5–March 7, 2004; Cast: Valerie Leonard (Leocadia Begbick), Zachary Knower (Galy Gay), Jane Beard (Galy Gay's Wife), Michael Hogan (Uriah Shelley), James Ludwig (Jesse Mahoney), Michael Mandell (Jeraiah Jip), David Fendig (Polly Baker), C.S. Lee (Mr. Wang), Eduardo Placer (Mah Sing), Tim Artz (Charles Fairchild), Ryan Clardy (Soldier), James O. Dunn (Soldier), David Maddox (Soldier/Musician), Dwayne Nitz (Soldier/Musician)

SEÑOR DISCRETION HIMSELF by Frank Loesser; Director, Charles Randolph-Wright; Scenic Design, Thomas Lynch; Costume Design, Emilio Sosa; Lighting Design, Michael Gilliam; Sound Design, Timothy M. Thompson; April 9–May 23, 2004; Cast: Doreen Montalvo (Curandera),

Shawn Elliott (Pancito), Tony Chiroldes (Father Francisco), Carlos Lopez (Father Manuel), Robert Almodovar (Father Orlando), Margo Reymundo (Carolina), Elena Shaddow (Lupita), Ivan Hernandez (Martin), John Bolton (Hilario), Diego Prieto (Josè), Eduardo Placer (Jimenez), Steven Cupo (Cantiñero), Lynnette Marrero (La India Maria), Laura-Lisa (Aerialist), Rayanne Gonzales (Old Woman), Deanna Harris (Dolores), Venny Carranza (Inspector Garcia)

IN THE KREEGER:

PROOF by David Auburn; Director, Wendy C. Goldberg; Scenic Design, Michael Brown; Costume Design, Anne Kennedy; Lighting Design, Allen Lee Hughes; Sound Design, Timothy M. Thompson; October 9–October 23, 2003; Cast: Michael Rudko (Robert), Keira Naughton (Catherine), Barnaby Carpenter (Hal), Susan Lynskey (Claire)

CROWNS by Regina Taylor; director, Regina Taylor, adapted from the book by Michael Cunningham and Craig Marberry, Co-Produced with Alliance Theatre and The Goodman Theatre; Scenic Design, Riccardo Hernandez; Costume and Hat Design, Emilio Sosa; Lighting Design, Scott Zielinski; Sound Design, Darron L. West; December 18–February 14, 2004; Cast: John Steven Crowley (Preacher/Man), Desire DuBose (Yolanda), Tina Fabrique (Mother Shaw), Gail Grate (Wanda), Lynda Gravatt (Mabel), Karan Kendrick (Jeanette), Bernardine Mitchell (Velma)

YELLOWMAN by Dael Orlandersmith; Director, Tazewell Thompson; Scenic Design, Donald Eastman; Costume Design, LeVonee Lindsay; Lighting Design, Robert Wierzel; Sound Design, Fabian Obispo; March 11–April 18, 2004, Cast: Laiona Michelle (Alma), Howard W. Overshown (Eugene)

ORPHEUS DESCENDING by Tennessee Williams; Director, Molly Smith; Scenic Design, Bill C. Ray; Costume Design, Linda Cho; Lighting Design, Michael Gilliam; Sound Design, Eric Shim; Lyrics, Jack Cannon; May 20–June 27, 2004; Cast: Kate Kiley (Beulah Binnings), Rena Cherry Brown (Dolly Hamma), Bruce M. Holmes (Pee Wee/Man), Paul Morella (Dog Hamma/David Cutrere), Kate Goehring (Carol Cutrere), Linda High (Eva Temple/Nurse Porter), Anne Stone (Sister Temple/Opal Ritter), Frederick Strother (Uncle Pleasant), Matt Bogart (Val Xavier), Janice Duclos (Vee Talbott), Chandler Vinton (Lady Torrance), J. Fred Shiffman (Jabe Torrance), Delaney Williams (Sheriff Talbott)

Christianne Tisdale and the Company in *Camelot* PHOTO BY SCOTT SUCHMAN

ARKANSAS REPERTORY THEATRE

Little Rock, Arkansas
TWENTY-EIGHTH SEASON

Producing Artistic Director, Robert Hupp; General Manager, Mike McCurdy

THE SPITFIRE GRILL by James Valcq (Music and Book) and Fred Alley (Lyrics and Book); Based on the film by Lee David Zlotoff; Director, Robert Hupp; Musical Director, Michael Heavner; Scenic Designer, Mike Nichols; Costume Designer, Yslan Hicks; Lighting Designer, Joshua Williamson; Sound Designer, M. Jason Pruzin; Musical Staging, Ron Hutchins; Production Manager, Rafael Colon Castanera; Stage Manager, Kathy Snyder; September 5–28, 2003; Cast: Stacey Oristano (PercyTalbot), Ashton Byrum (Sheriff Joe Sutter), Victoria Boothby (Hannah Ferguson), David Benoit (Caleb Thorpe), Audrey Lavine (Effy Krayneck), Jessica Wright (Shelby Thorpe), Tom Kagy (The Visitor)

ALL MY SONS by Arthur Miller; Director, Eve Adamson; Scenic Designer, Mike Nichols; Costume Designer, Margaret A. McKowen; Lighting Designer, James Japhy Weideman; Sound Designer, M. Jason Pruzin; Production Manager, Rafael Colon Castanera; Stage Manager, Kathy Snyder; October 24–November 9, 2003; Cast: Joseph Graves (Joe Keller), JoAnn Johnson (Kate Keller), Jason O'Connell (Chris Keller), Jessica Henson (Ann Deever), Joseph E. Murray (George Deever), Joseph J. Menino (Dr. Jim Bayliss), Karen Case Cook (Sue Bayliss), Drake Mann (Frank Lubey), Amy Elizabeth Sabin (Lydia Lubey)

CINDERELLA by Richard Rodgers (Music) and Oscar Hammerstein II (Book and Lyrics); Director, Brad Mooy; Choreographer, Ron Hutchins; Musical Director, Eric Alsford; Scenic Designer, Alan Donahue; Costume Designer, Robert A. Pittenridge; Lighting Designer, Andrew Meyers; Sound Designer, M. Jason Pruzin; December 5, 2003–January 4, 2004; Cast: Allison Spratt (Cinderella), Dan Callaway (Prince), Maureen Sadusk (Godmother), Lisa McMillan (Stepmother), Alexandra Kolb (Joy), Dierdre Friel (Portia), Raissa Katona Bennett (Queen), Larry Daggett (King), Jay Brian Winnick (Herald), Michael Busillo (Adult Ensemble), Nicole Capri (Adult Ensemble), Edgar Contreras (Adult Ensemble), Caroline Holt (Adult Ensemble), William B. Hubert II (Adult Ensemble), Amber C. Irvin (Adult Ensemble), Paula Isbell (Adult Ensemble), Michael M. Mallard (Adult Ensemble), Eric T. Mann (Adult Ensemble), James Sheldon (Adult Ensemble), James Sheldon (Adult Ensemble), Ragan Renteria (Adult Ensemble), Amy Elizabeth Sabin (Adult Ensemble), Kimberly Scott (Adult Ensemble), Lise Ashley Strigel (Adult Ensemble), James Thweatt (Adult Ensemble), Nicholas Willson (Adult Ensemble) Sydney Alman (Youth Ensemble), Alex Bush (Youth Ensemble), Sarah Clagett (Youth Ensemble), Rachel Flowers (Youth Ensemble), Cameren Kvaternick (Youth Ensemble), Rachel Madigan (Youth Ensemble), Michelle McCain (Youth Ensemble), Caroline McCormick (Youth Ensemble), Karrah Peden (Youth Ensemble), Molly Rosenthal (Youth Ensemble), Anna Robbins (Youth Ensemble), Jackson Stewart (Youth Ensemble), Allison Traylor (Youth Ensemble), Mary Katelin Ward (Youth Ensemble)

Allison Spratt in *Cinderella* PHOTO BY BENJAMIN KRAIN

GOD'S MAN IN TEXAS by David Rambo; Director, Robert Hupp; Scenic Designer, Mike Nichols; Costume Designer, Olivia Koach; Lighting Designer, James Japhy Weideman; Sound Designer, Darin F. Karnes; Production Manager, Rafael Colon Castanera; Stage Manager, Julie Stemmler; January 23–February 15, 2004; Cast: David Alford (Dr. Jeremiah (Jerry) Mears), Warren Hammack (Dr. Philip Gottschall), Brian Webb Russell (Hugo Taney)

ROMEO & JULIET by William Shakespeare; Director, Robert Hupp; Fight Choreographer, D.C. Wright; Scenic Designer, Mike Nichols; Costume Designer, Margaret A. McKowen; Lighting Designer, Andrew Meyers; Sound Designer, M. Jason Pruzin;Original Music Composed and Arranged by Ellen Mandel; Production Manager, Rafael Colon Castanera; Stage Manager, Kathy Snyder; March 12–April 4, 2003; Cast: Amber C. Irvin (Chorus, Servant), Jay Sullivan (Benvolio), Michael Stewart Allen (Tybalt), Brian Webb Russell (Capulet), Joy Jones (Lady Capulet), Bordon Hallowes (Montague, Friar John), Nicholas Wilson (Servant to Montague, Servingman, Officer, Apothecary, Captain of the Watch), Dan Snow (Escalus), Shannon Michael Wamser (Romeo), Justin Gibbs (The County Paris), Michele Tauber (Nurse), Anne W. Griffin (Juliet), Stafford Clark-Price (Mercutio), John Nagle (Friar Laurence), Michael M. Mallard (Peter, Balthasar), Matthew Millikin (First Watchman)

THE SECOND CITY; Director, Marc Warzecha; Music Director, Chad Krueger; Stage Manager, Lee Brackett; April 13–25, 2004; Cast: Brendan Dowling, Ithamar Enriquez, Jenny Hagel, Niki Lindren, Angel Sudik, Mark Swaner

DREAMGIRLS by Tom Eyen (Book and Lyrics) and Henry Krieger (Music); Director, Rajendra Ramoon Maharaj; Co-Choreographer, Ron Hutchins; Musical Director, Charles Creath; Scenic Designer, Mike Nichols; Costume Designer, Daryl Harris; Lighting Designer, Kathy A. Perkins; Sound Designer, M. Jason Pruzin; Wig Designer, Robert A. Pittenridge; Stage Manager, Julie Stemmler; June 11–July 11, 2004; Cast: Marla Ricks (Young Effie), Sydney McClain (Young Deena), Tia Woods (Young Lorrell), Paula Isbell (Stepp Sister, Les Styles, D.J.), Llyweyla Rawlins (Stepp Sister, Les Styles, Ms. Morgan), Ayana Wiles-Bey (Stepp Sister, Les Styles, Edna Burke), Carly Hughes (Charlene, Michelle Morris), Ragan Rene Renteria (Joann), Shirley Tripp (Marty), Raun Ruffin (Curtis Taylor, Jr.), McKenzie Frye (Deena Jones), Amber Efé (Lorrell Robinson), Roberta Thomas (Effie Melody White), Steve Broadnax (Master of Ceremonies, Tru-Tone, Frank, Jerry Norman, Tuxedo), Steven J. Young (Tiny Joe Dixon, D.J.), Korey Jackson (C.C.), Anthony Magee (Little Albert, Tuxedo), Christian Stewart Carter (Tru-Tone, Tuxedo, Dwight, Security Guard), Rodney Gilbert (Tru-Tone, Wayne, Carl, Tuxedo), Daryl DeLance Minefee (Tru-Tone, Tuxedo), Byron Glenn Willis (Jimmy Early), Kelsey B.H. Newman (Young Michelle, Magic), Gary Carlson (Dave, Stage Manager), Pamela Crane (Sweetheart), Ragan Rene Renteria (Sweetheart), Charles Creath (Brian)

ASOLO THEATRE

Sarasota, Florida
FORTY-FIFTH SEASON

Artistic Director, Howard J. Millman; Managing Director, Linda M. DiGabriele

THE CRUCIBLE by Arthur Miller; Director, Isa Thomas; Scenic Design, Steven Rubin; Costume Design, Catherine King; Lighting Design, James D. Sale; Sound Design, Matthew Parker; October 31, 2003–February 21, 2004; Cast: David Breitbarth (Reverend Samuel Parris), Tara Caruso (Betty Parris), Gale Fulton Ross (Tituba), Merideth Maddox (Abigail Williams), Ayla Ocasio (Susanna Wallcott), Katherine Michelle Tanner (Mrs. Ann Putman), Dean Anthony (Thomas Putman), Luciann LaJoie (Mercy Lewis), Lauren Orkus (Mary Warren), Patrick James Clarke (John Proctor), Sharon Spelman (Rebecca Nurse), John Sterling Arnold (Giles Corey), Douglas Jones (Reverend John Hale), Devora Millman (Elizabeth Proctor), Dan Higgs (Francis Nurse), David Downing (Ezekiael Cheever), Gabriel V. Ortiz (Marshal Herrick), David S. Howard (Judge Hawthorn), Bradford Wallace (Deputy-Governor Danforth), Kylie Sophie Fitch (Esther), Carolyn Zaput (Sarah Good), Francisco Lozano (Hopkins)

THE ROAD TO RUIN by Thomas Holcroft, adapted by Eberle Thomas; Director, Eberle Thomas; Scenic Design, Michael Lasswell; Costume Design, Vicki S. Holden; Lighting Design, James D. Sale; Sound Design, Matthew Parker; November 7, 2003–February 22, 2004; Cast: Bradford Wallace (Mr. Dornton), Dan Higgs (Smythe), John Sterling Arnold (Mr. Sulky), Gabriel V. Ortiz (Harry), Brian Graves (Jack Milford), Luciann LaJoie (Sophie Freelove), Katherine Michelle Tanner (Jenny), Heather Corwin (Mrs. Ledger), Sharon Spelman (The Widdow Warren), Francisco Lozano (Charles Goldfinch), Peter Neil Nason (The Sheriff's Officer), Dean Anthony (Mr. Mincing), Douglas Jones (Mr. Silky), Michael DeSantis (Jacob), Clement Valentine (The Hosier)

THE MILLIONAIRESS by George Bernard Shaw; Director, Paul Weidner; Scenic Design, Steven Rubin; Costume Design, Vicki S. Holden; Lighting Design, James D. Sale; Sound Design, Matthew Parker; November 14, 2003–April 2, 2003; Cast: Carolyn Michel (Epifania Ognisanti Di Parerga), Douglas Jones (Mr. Julius Sagamore), Patrick James Clarke (Alastair Fitzfassenden), Devora Millman (Patricia Smith), David Breitbarth (Adrian Blenderbland), David S. Howard (The Old Man), Sharon Spelman (The Old Woman), Brian Graves (The Manager), Bradford Wallace (Egyptian Doctor)

MURDER BY MISADVENTURE by Edward Taylor; Director, Barbara Redmond; Scenic Design, Jeffrey W. Dean; Costume Design, B.G. FitzGerald; Lighting Design, James D. Sale; Sound Design, Matthew Parker; November 29, 2003–January 11, 2004; Cast: David Breitbarth (Harold Kent), Carolyn Michel (Emma Kent), Patrick James Clark (Paul Riggs), Stephen Johnson (Inspector Egan)

I'M NOT RAPPAPORT by Herb Gardner; Director, Howard J. Millman; Scenic Design, Jeffrey W. Dean; Costume Design, Vicki S. Holden; Lighting Design, James D. Sale; Sound Design, Matthew Parker; January 23–May 22, 2004; Cast: David S. Howard (Nat), David Downing (Midge), Dean Anthony (Danforth), Merideth Maddox (Laurie), Francisco Lozano (The Cowboy), Brian Graves (Gilley), Carolyn Michel (Clara)

NOEL COWARD AT THE CAFÉ DE PARIS by Will Stutts; January 28–February 22, 2004; Cast: Mr. Will Stutts (Sir Noel Coward)

THE DIARY OF ANNE FRANK by Frances Goodrich and Albert Hackett; Director, Howard J. Millman; Scenic Design, Jeffrey W. Dean; Costume Design, Catherine King; Lighting Design, James D. Sale; Sound Design Matthew Parker; March 12–May 23, 2004; Cast: David Breitbarth (Mr. Frank), Katherine Michelle Tanner (Miep), Carolyn Michel (Mrs. Van Daan), Bradford Wallace (Mr. Van Daan), Andrew Foster (Peter Van Daan), Devora Millman (Mrs. Frank), Kate Goldman (Margot Frank), Lauren Orkus (Anne Frank), David S. Howard (Mr. Kraler), Dean Anthony (Mr. Dussel)

HAY FEVER by Noel Coward; Director, Gil Lazier; Scenic Design, Steven Rubin; Costume Design, Vicki S. Holden; Lighting Design, James D. Sale; Sound Design, Matthew Parker; March 19–May 22, 2004; Cast: Sharon Spelman (Judith Bliss), Patrick James Clarke (David Bliss), Luciann LaJoie (Sorel Bliss), Brian Graves (Simon Bliss), Heather Corwin (Myra Arundel), Douglas Jones (Richard Greatham), Merideth Maddox (Jackie Coryton), Gabriel V. Ortiz (Sandy Tyrell), Jan Wallace (Clara)

FREE AND CLEAR by Robert Anderson; Director, Eberle Thomas; Scenic Design, Jeffrey W. Dean; Costume Design, Catherine King, Lighting Design, James D. Sale; Sound Design, Matthew Parker; May 6–30, 2004; Cast: Polly Holliday (Sarah Morrison), John Krich (John), Bryan Barter (Larry), Bryant Mason (Jack)

BARTER THEATRE

Abingdon, Virginia
SEVENTY-FIRST SEASON

Producing Artistic Director, Richard Rose

FULLY COMMITTED by Becky Mode; Director, John Hardy; Scenic Designer, Cheri Prough Devol; Costume Designer, Lynae Vandermeulen; Lighting Designer, Trevor Maynard; Sound Designer, Bobby Beck; Stage Manager, John Keith Hall; Assistant Stage Manager, John Hardy; Dialect Coach, Karen Sabo; Barter Stage II, February 12–April 17, 2004; Cast: Mike Ostroski (Sam, Mrs. Vandevere, The Sheik's Right-Hand Man, Mrs. Winslow, Bryce, Midwestern Secretary, Carolann Rosenstein-Fishburn, Stephanie, Oscar, Mrs. Watanabe, Bob, Chef, Sam's Dad, Jerry Miller, Jean-Claude, Bell Atlantic Recording Woman, Sexy Recorded Voice, Curtis, Dominick Veccini, Mrs. Sebag, Hector, Mrs. Buxbaum, Mr. Decoste, Mr. Zagat, Laryngitis Guy, Judith Rush, Depressed Secretary, Paramount Lady, Steven, Gloria Hathaway, Jean-Claude's Wife, Smarmy man, Nancy, Rick from Carson Aviation, AT&T Operator, Mr. Inoue, Dr. Ruth Westheimer)

PUMP BOYS & DINETTES Conceived and written by John Foley, Mark Hardwick, Debra Monk, Cass Morgan, John Schimmel, Jim Wann; Director, Karen Sabo; Musical Director, WM. Perry Morgan; Scenic Designer, Cheri Prough Devol; Costume Designer, Lynae Vandermeulen; Lighting Designer, Trevor Maynard; Sound Designer, Bobby Beck; Stage Manager, John Keith Hall; Assistant Stage Manager, Connie M. Silver; Barter Stage II, February 26–August 14, 2004; Cast: Melissa Davidson (Rhetta), Kimberly Mays (Prudie), Derek Davidson (Jim), Gil Braswell (Jackson), WM. Perry Morgan (L.M., *Bass*), James Hollingsworth (Eddie, *Piano*)

ARSENIC & OLD LACE by Joseph Kesselring; Director, Katy Brown; Scenic Designer, Cheri Prough Devol; Costume Designer, Amanda Aldridge; Lighting Designer, E. Tonry Lathroum; Sound Designer, Bobby Beck; Stage Manager, Karen N. Rowe; Barter Theatre, March 5–May 22, 2004; Cast: Evalyn Baron (Abby Brewster), John Hardy (The Rev. Dr. Harper, Lieutenant Rooney), John Hedges/Rick McVey (Teddy Brewster), Roger Dean Grubb (Officer Brophy), Titus Oxley (Officer Klein), Mary Lucy Bivins (Martha Brewster), Seana Hollingsworth (Elaine Harper), Nicholas Piper (Mortimer Brewster), Brandon Roberts (Mr. Gibbs, Officer O'Hara, Mr. Witherspoon), Eugene Wolf (Johnathan Brewster), Peter Yonka (Dr. Einstein)

DEATH OF A SALESMAN by Arthur Miller; Director, Richard Rose; Scenic Designer, Daniel Ettinger; Costume, Amanda Aldridge; Lighting Designer, E. Tonry Lathroum; Sound Designer, Bobby Beck; Stage Manager, Karen N. Rowe; Barter Theatre, March 17–May 22, 2004; Cast: Eugene Wolf (Willy Loman), Mary Lucy Bivins (Linda), Nicholas Piper (Biff), Peter Yonka (Happy), Brandon Roberts (Bernard), Karen Sabo (The Woman), John Hedges (Charley), Michael Poisson (Uncle Ben), John Hardy (Howard Wagner), Titus Oxley (Stanley), Evalyn Baron *Recorded* (Operator Voice), Seana Hollingsworth (Miss Forsythe)

THE ODD COUPLE by Neil Simon; Director, Evalyn Baron; Scenic Designer, Cheri Prough Devol; Costume Designer, Amanda Aldridge; Lighting Designer, Trevor Maynard; Sound Designer, Bobby Beck; Properties Designer, Helen Stratakes; Technical Director, Mark J. Devol; Stage Manager, John Keith Hall; Barter Stage II, April 29–August 15, 2004; Cast: Mike Ostroski (Speed), Gill Braswell (Murray), Frank Green (Roy), Scot Atkinson (Vinnie), John Hedges (Oscar Madison), Michael Poisson (Felix Unger), Elizabeth P. McKnight (Gwendolyn Pigeon), Kimberly Mays (Cecily Pigeon)

GIRL OF MY DREAMS Music by Peter Ekstrom, Lyrics by Steven Hayes and Peter Ekstrom, Book and Additional Lyrics by David DeBoy; Director, John Hardy; Musical Director, WM. Perry Morgan; Assistant Musical Director/Conductor, James Hollingsworth; Choreographer, Amanda Aldridge; Tap choreography, Chris Boyd; Scenic Designer, Dale Jordan; Costume Designer, Amanda Aldridge; Lighting Designer, Dale Jordan; Orchestrations & Arrangements, Barry Levitt; Additional Orchestrations & Arrangements, James Hollingsworth; Sound Designer, Bobby Beck; Properties Designer, Helen Stratakes; Stage Manager, Karen N. Rowe; Assistant Stage Manager, Connie M. Silver; Dance Captain, Derek Davidson; Musicians, WM. Perry Morgan (Bass), James Hollingsworth (Keyboards), Matthew Frederick (Trumpet), Jay Oberfeitinger (Percussion); Barter Theatre, May 28–September 5, 2004; Cast: Eugene Wolf (Grandad), Seana Hollingsworth (Laurie), Chris Boyd (Ben Piper), Julia Megan Sullivan (Effie Lawrence), Karen Sabo (Cindy Hawthorne), Peter Yonka/Mike Ostroski (Phil Gold), Nicholas Piper (Freddy Gillette), Derek Davidson (Luke Wheeler), Stephanie Holladay (Olive Finer), Amber Wiley (Edna Smith)

FIRST BAPTIST OF IVY GAP by Ron Osborne; Director, Richard Rose; Scenic Designer, Dale Jordan; Costume Designer, Amanda Aldridge; Lighting Designer, Dale Jordan; Sound Designer, Bobby Beck; Properties Designer, Helen Stratakes; Stage Manager, John Keith Hall; Barter Theatre, June 9–August 28, 2004; Cast: Alice White (Luby), Seana Hollingsworth (Olene), Karen Sabo (Mae Ellen), Mary Lucy Bivins (Edith), Elizabeth P. McKnight (Sammy), Evalyn Baron (Vera)

TWO CAN PLAY by A.J. Carothers, based on *Harry and Mary* by Robert Thomas Noll and Edward Walsh; Director, John Hardy; Scenic Designer, Cheri Prough Devol; Costume Designer, Amanda Aldridge; Lighting Designer, Rose Nuchims; Sound Designer. Bobby Beck; Properties Designer, Helen Stratakes; Technical Director, Mark J. Devol; Stage Manager, John Keith Hall; Dramaturge, John Hardy; Barter Stage II, August 19–August 29, 2004; Cast: Gary Collins (Harry), Joyce Bulifant (Mary)

SLEUTH by Anthony Shaffer; Director, John Hardy; Set Designer, Cheri Prough Devol; Costume Designer, Karen Brewster; Lighting Designer, Cheri Prough Devol; Sound Designer, Bobby Beck; Properties Master, Helen Stratakes; Technical Director, Mark J. Devol; Stage Manager, Karen Rowe; Barter Stage II, September 3–November 14, 2004; Cast: John Hedges (Andrew Wyke), Peter Yonka (Milo Tindle), Paul Snedeker (Inspector Doppler), Daniel K. Lindsey (Detective Sergeant Trarrant), Mark Treadway (Police Constable Higgs)

GYPSY Book by Arthur Laurents, Music by Jule Styne, Lyrics by Stephen Sondheim, Suggested by the memoirs of Gypsy Rose Lee, Original Production by David Merrick & Leland Hayward, Entire production originally directed and choreographed by Jerome Robbins; Director, Richard Rose; Choreographer, Amanda Aldridge; Music Director, James Hollingsworth; Assistant Musical Director, WM. Perry Morgan; Additional Arrangements, James Hollingsworth; Additional Orchestrations, Peter Yonka; Set Designer, Daniel Ettinger; Costume Designer, Amanda Aldridge; Lighting Designer, Trevor Maynard; Sound Designer, Bobby Beck; Dance Captain, Seana Hollingsworth; Properties Master, Helen Stratakes; Technical Director, Mark J. Devol; Stage Manager, John Keith Hall; Musicians, James Hollingsworth (Piano), Matthew Frederick (Trumpet), Bill Medearis (Trombone), Phil Reed (Percussion); Barter Theatre, September 10–Novmber 20, 2004; Cast: Scot Atkinson (Uncle Jocko, Rich Man in Car, Webber, Kringelein, Cigar, Phil), Frank Green (George, Hotel Border, Electra), Harry Land (Arnold, Young Tulsa), Jessie Nunley (Balloon Girl, Young LA), Wesley Brillhart (Boy in Costume, Young Yonkers), Mary Lucy Bivins (Stage Mother, Hotel Border, Tessie Tura, Renee) Elizabeth P. McKnight (Stage Mother, Hotel Border, Miss Cratchit, Marjorie May, Minsky's Show Girl), Wendy C. Mitchell (Stage Mother, Angie, Thelme, Minsky's Show Girl), Christie Wilson/Stephanie Demaree (Baby Louise), Jessica Presnell/Mackenzie Demaree (Baby June), Evalyn Baron (Rose), Mike Ostroski (Pop, Boy Scout, Back of Cow, Mr. Goldstone, Pastey), Derek Davidson (Boy Scout, Yonkers, Front end of Cow, Minsky's Show Girl), Gwen Edwards (Boy Scout, Waitress, Dolores), Michael Poisson (Herbie), Stephanie Holladay (Louise), Karen Sabo (June), Ben Mackel (Tulsa), Seana Hollingsworth (LA, Agnes, Minsky's Show Girl), Ryane Nicole Studivant (Hotel Border, Mazeppa)

THE HUNCHBACK OF NOTRE DAME by Rick Whelan, from the original novel by Victor Hugo; Director, Richard Rose; Original Music and Musical Score, Peter Yonka; Set Designer, Cheri Prough Devol; Costume Designer, Amanda Aldridge; Lighting Designer, Trevor Maynard; Sound Designer, Bobby Beck; Make-Up Designer, Karen Brewster; Properties Master, Helen Stratakes; Technical Director, Mark J. Devol; Stage Manager, John Keith Hall; Fight Captain, Mike Ostroski; Barter Theatre, September 22–November 20, 2004; Cast: Mike Ostroski (Archdeacon Dom Claude Frollo), Frank Green (Quasimodo), Seana Hollingsworth (La Esmeralda), John Hardy (Clopin), Michael Poisson (Arrut, One-Legged Man, Judge Henry Poteau, Citizen, Barbedienne, a Priest), Stephanie Holladay (Djali), Scot Atkinson (Citizen, Jahen, Lame Man on Car, Chaperone, Matheus, Sergeant, a Priest, Soldier), Matt Greenbaum (Citizen, Guillaume, Woman with Baby, Monsieur Torterue, Executioner's Man, Soldier), Amelia Ampuero (Citizen, Diane, Beggar, Paquette), Gwen Edwards (Citizen, Colombe, Palsied, Woman with Baby), Ben Mackel (Citizen, Poussepain, Constable, Old Man, Clerk, Suitor, Charmolue), Wendy C. Mitchell (Citizen, Old Woman Pulling Cart, Paquette's Mother, Fleur-de-Lys Gondelaurier, a Priest), Ryane Nicole Studivant (Citizen, Blind Woman, Woman with Baby, Falourdel), Mary Lucy Bivins (Gudule), Peter Yonka (Phoebus de Chateaupeurs)

THIS IS OUR HOUSE! by Peter Coy; Director, Evalyn Baron; Set Designer, Cheri Prough Devol; Costume Designer, Melissa Davidson; Lighting Designer, Cheri Prough Devol; Sound Designer, Bobby Beck; Stage Manager, Karen Rowe; Barter Stage II, September 29–November 13, 2004; Cast: Derek Davidson (Asa), Elizabeth P. McKnight (Dory), Karen Sabo (Holly), John Hedges (Franz)

A MODERN CHRISTMAS CAROL Adapted by Richard Rose from Dickens *A Christmas Carol,* with traditional Christmas carols and additional songs by Nicholas Piper; Director, Richard Rose; Musical Director, James Hollingsworth; Dramaturges, Kathy Brown and Derek Davidson; Scenic Designer, Cheri Prough Devol; Costume Designer, Roland Guidry; Lighting Designer and Special Effects, Trevor Maynard; Video and Sound Design, Bobby Beck; Stage Manager, John Keith Hall; Barter Theatre, November 26–December 30, 2004; Cast: John Hardy (Mr. S), Elizabeth P. McKnight (Voice of MS Enterprises, 1950s Couple, Nurse, Michele, Woman Caller, an Elf, Part of a Farm Couple, Molly, Business Person #3), Karen Sabo (Cratchit, Mother, Mrs. Blevins, Woman with Baby), Mike Ostroski (Man Out of Work, 1950s Couple, Doctor, an Elf, Part of a Seafaring Couple, Peter, Business Person #1, Janitor), John Hedges (J.M., Man Caller, an Elf, Soldier, Hospital worker), Jared Foster/Harry Land (Boy Singing a Carol, Little Tim, an Elf, Ignorance), Michael Poisson (News Reporter, Past (an Auditor), Miner, Business Person #2, Old Joe, Michele's Husband), Derek Davidson (Nephew, Father), Anita Ostrovsky/Annie Grace Surber (Sara, Fan, an Elf, Want), Frank Green (Phil (a Rotarian), Part of a Farm Couple, Miner, Solider, Future (an angel)), Seanna Hollingsworth (Mrs. Thropic (Junior League), 1950s Couple, Older fan, Jody C., an Elf, Part of a Seafaring Couple, Gretchen, Housekeeper), Peter Yonka (1950s Couple, Samuel Blevins, Present (a Santa), a Worker, Hospital Worker)

WISE WOMEN by Ron Osborne, Original Wise Women Theme compose by Peter Yonka; Director, Evalyn Baron; Scenic Designer, Tim Bruneau; Costume Designer, Amanda Aldridge; Lighting Designer, Craig Zemsky; Sound Designer, Bobby Beck; Stage Manager, Karen N. Rowe; Barter Stage II, November 23–December 23, 2004; Cast: Mary Lucy Bivins (Florence), Gwen Edwards (Rose), Stephanie Holladay (Sarah Ruth), Amelia Ampuero (Jiggs), Scot Atkinson (Donnie), Matt Greenbaum (Howard)

BERKELEY REPERTORY THEATRE

Berkeley, California
THIRTY-SIXTH SEASON

Artistic Director, Tony Taccone; Managing Director, Susan Medak; Associate Artistic Director, Les Waters

THE NOTEBOOKS OF LEONARDO DA VINCI adapted by Mary Zimmerman; Director, Mary Zimmerman; Scenic Design, Scott Bradley; Costume Design, Mara Blumenfeld (based on the original designs by Allison Reeds); Lighting Design, T.J. Gerckens; Sound Designer, Michael Bodeen; Original Music, Miriam Sturm and Michael Bodeen; Stage Manager, Cynthia Cahill; Assistant Stage Manager, Michael Suenkel; September 5–October 19, 2003; Cast: Lucia Brawley (Leonardo), Jane Cho (Leonardo), Lizzy Cooper Davis (Leonardo), Christopher Donahue (Leonardo), Kyle Hall (Leonardo), Doug Hara (Leonardo), Mariann Mayberry (Leonardo), Paul Oakley Stovall (Leonardo) Co-production with Second Stage Theatre

CONTINENTAL DIVIDE by David Edgar; Director, Tony Taccone; Scenic & Projection Design, William Bloodgood; Costume Design, Deborah M. Dryden; Lighting & Projection Design, Alexander V. Nichols; Sound Design, Jeremy J. Lee; Composer, *Mothers Against*, Todd Barton; Dramaturgs, Lue Morgan Douthit, Douglas Langworthy, Luan Schooler; Associate Director, Randy White; Casting Director, Amy Potozkin; Stage Manager, Michael Suenkel; Assistant Stage Manager, Kimberley Jean Barry; November 6–December 28, 2003; Cast of *Mothers Against*: Tony DeBruno (Mitchell Vine), Michael Elich (Don D'Avanzo), Bill Geisslinger (Sheldon Vine), Robynn Rodriguez (Connie Vine), Susannah Schulman (Lorianne Weiner), Vilma Silva (Caryl M Marquez), Derrick Lee Weeden (Vincent Baptiste), Christine Williams (Deborah Vine); Cast of *Daughters of the Revolution*: Tony DeBruno (Arnie, Ira, Eddie, Mitchell), Michelle Duffy (Abby, Beth, Branflake), Michael Elich (Bill Troy, Zee, Don D'Avanzo), Bill Geisslinger (Ted, Jimmy, Nighthawk, Sheldon Vine), Marielle Heller (Dana, Nancy, Trina, Aquarius), Lorri Holt (Blair Lowe), Terry Layman (Michael Bern), Craig W. Marker (Jack, Darren, Sam, No Shit), Jacob Ming-Trent (Jools, J.C., Rainbow, Bob L LeJeune), Robynn Rodriguez (Elaine, Ash, Connie Vine), Susannah Schulman (Lorianne Weiner, Firefly), Vilma Silva (Kate, Therese, Yolande, Hoola Hoop), Melissa Smith (Rebecca McKeene), Derrick Lee Weeden (Kwesi Ntuli), Christine Williams (Ryan, Pat, Snowbird) Presented in association with Oregon Shakespeare Festival

YELLOWMAN by Dael Orlandersmith; Director, Les Waters; Scenic & Costume Design, Annie Smart; Lighting Designer, James F. Ingalls; Dramaturg, Nicole Galland; Dialect Coach, Lynne Soffer; Stage Manager, Cynthia Cahill; Casting Director, Amy Potozkin; January 23–March 7, 2004 (extended through March 14); Cast: Deidrie N. Henry (Alma), Clark Jackson (Eugene) Presented in association with Lorraine Hansberry Theatre

GHOSTS translated by Rick Davis and Brian Johnston from the play by Henrik Ibsen; Director, Jonathan Moscone; Scenic Design, Neil Patel; Costume Design, Meg Neville; Lighting Design, Scott Zielinski; Sound Designer, Jake Rodriguez; Dramaturg, Nicole Galland; Stage Manager, Kimberly Mark Webb; Assistant Stage Manager, Michael Suenkel; Casting, Amy Potozkin, Janet Foster; February 27–April 11, 2004; Cast: Emily Ackerman (Regina Engstrand), James Carpenter (Pastor Manders), Davis Duffield (Osvald Alving), Ellen McLaughlin (Mrs. Helene Alving), Brian Keith Russell (Jakob Engstrand)

THE MYSTERY OF IRMA VEP by Charles Ludlam; Director, Les Waters; Scenic and Costume Design, Annie Smart; Lighting Design, Robert Wierzel; Original Music & Sound, Peter Golub; Dramaturg, Nicole Galland; Stage Manager, Elisa Guthertz; Casting, Amy Potozkin, Paul Fouquet; April 9–May 23, 2004; Cast: Arnie Burton (Nicodemus Underwood, Lady Enid Hillcrest, Alcazar, Pev Amri), Erik Steele (Jane Twisden, Lord Edgar Hillcrest, an Intruder)

MASTER CLASS by Terrence McNally; Director, Moisés Kaufman; Scenic Design, Mark Wendland; Costume Design, Lydia Tanji; Lighting Design, David Lander; Sound Design, Jon Gottlieb; Music Director, Gary Sheldon; Dramaturg, Nicole Galland; Dialect Coach, Lynne Soffer; Stage Manager, Michael Suenkel; Assistant Stage Manager, Nicole Dickerson; Casting, Amy Potozkin, Alan Filderman; May 21–July 18, 2004 (extended through July 25); Cast: Kevin Paul Anderson (Tenor–Tony), Sherry Boone (Second Soprano–Sharon), Donna Lynne Champlin (First Soprano–Sophie), Rita Moreno (Maria Callas), Owen Murphy (Stagehand), Cheree A. Sager (Young Maria), Michael Wiles (Accompanist–Manny)

21 DOG YEARS: DOING TIME @ AMAZON.COM by Mike Daisey; Director/Stage Manager, Jean-Michele Gregory; Lighting Design, Jim Cave; Production Manager, Madelyn Mackie; Production Assistant, Rebecca Helgeson; June 10–July 2, 2004 (extended through July 24); Cast: Mike Daisey

CAPITAL REPERTORY THEATRE

Albany, New York
TWENTY-THIRD SEASON

Producing Artistic Director, Maggie Mancinelli-Cahill; Managing Director, Jeff Dannick

COWGIRLS Conceived by Mary Murfitt; Book by Betsy Howie; Music & Lyrics by Mary Murfitt Director, Eleanor Reissa; Scenic Design, James Noone; Costume Design, Isabel Rubio; Lighting Design, Traci Klainer; Sound Design, Christopher St. Hilaire; July 11–August 23, 2003; Cast: Rhonda Coullet (Jo Carlson), Mary Ehlinger (Rita), Mimi Bessette (Lee), Mary Murfitt (Mary Lou), Amy Jordan (Mo), Julie Rowe (Mickey)

DR. FAUSTUS by Christopher Marlowe; freely adapted by Jeff Clinkenbeard & Maggie Mancinelli-Cahill; Director, Maggie Mancinelli-Cahill; Scenic Design, Michael Blau; Costume Design, Natasha Landau; Lighting Design, Rachel Budin; Sound Design, Steve Stevens ; September 19–October 18, 2003; Cast: Wynn Harmon (Doctor John Faustus), Tom Martin (Wagner), Nancy Ann Chatty (Good Angel, Scholar, Duchess), Jeff Clinkenbeard (Bad Angel, Scholar, Duke), Leah Hennessy (Valdes, Lucifer, Helen of Troy), Wally Valenti (Rafe), Justin Tracy (Cornelius, Beelzebub, Benvolio), Sam House (Mephistopheles)

THE SWEEPERS by John C. Picardi; Director Frances W. Hill; Scenic Design, Roman J. Tatarowicz; Costume Design, Kevin Brainerd; Lighting Design, Annmarie Duggan; Sound Design, Jane Shaw; November 14–December 14, 2003; Cast: Lori Wilner (Mary DeGrazio), Brigitte Viellieu-Davis (Dotty Larnino), Carole Healey (Bella Cichinelli-MaCarthy), Matthew Montelongo (Sonny McCarthy-Cichinelli), Karen Foletti (Stephanie Cozart),

JACQUES BREL IS ALIVE & WELL & LIVING IN PARIS Production conception, English lyrics & additional music by Eric Blau & Mort Shuman, Based on Jacques Brel's lyrics & commentary, Music by Jacques Brel; Director, Gordon Greenberg; Scenic Design, Rob Bissinger; Costume

Rhonda Coullet (standing), Mary Murfitt, Mimi Bessette, Mary Ehlinger in *Cowgirls*

Design, Natasha Landau; Lighting Design, Traci Klainer; Sound Design, Christopher St. Hilaire; January 9–February 8, 2004; Cast: Don Brewer (Man #1), Lisa Capps (Woman #1), Gay Marshall (Woman #2), Jay Montgomery (Man #2)

CRUMBS FROM THE TABLE OF JOY by Lynn Nottage; Director, Laura Margolis; Scenic Design, Harry Feiner; Costume Design, Barbara Bell; Lighting Design, Stephen Quandt; Sound Design, Jane Shaw; February 27–April 3, 2004; Cast: Chanda Hartman (Ernestine Crump), Erin Cherry (Ermina Crump), Ron Scott (Godfrey Crump), Melissa Maxwell (Lily Ann Green), Stina Nelson (Gerte Schulte Crump)

FUDDY MEERS (IN REP WITH ROUNDING THIRD) by David Lindsay-Abaire; Director, Elysa Marden; Scenic Design, Donald Eastman; Costume Design, Denise Dygert; Lighting Design, Deborah Constantine; Sound Design, Christopher St. Hilaire; April 23–May 29, 2004; Cast: Bernadette Quigley (Claire), Gregory Northrop (Richard), Aaron Northrup (Kenny), Chris Hutchison (Limping Man), Eileen Schuyler (Gertie), Jeffrey M. Bender (Millet), Karen Cash (Heidi)

ROUNDING THIRD (IN REP WITH FUDDY MEERS) by Richard Dresser; Director, Maggie Mancinelli-Cahill; Scenic Design, Donald Eastman; Costume Design, Denise Dygert; Lighting Design, Deborah Constantine; Sound Design, Christopher St. Hilaire; April 23–June 12, 2004; Cast: Chris Hutchison (Don), Jeffrey M. Bender (Michael)

Carole Healey, Lori Wilner, Brigitte Viellieu-Davis in *Sweepers* PHOTOS BY JOE SCHUYLER

CENTERSTAGE

Baltimore, Maryland
FORTY-FIRST SEASON

Artistic Director, Irene Lewis; Managing Director, Michael Ross

MISALLIANCE by George Bernard Shaw; Director, Irene Lewis; Scenic Design, Tony Straiges; Costume Design, Candice Donnelly; Lighting Design, Mimi Jordan Sherin; Sound Design, David Budries; Production Dramaturg, Gavin Witt; October 3–November 2, 2003; Cast: Trent Dawson (Johnny Tarleton), Andrew Weems (Bentley Summerhays), Stacy Ross (Hypatia Tarleton), Patricia O'Connell (Mrs. Tarleton), George Morfogen (Lord Summerhays), Peter Van Norden (Mr. John Tarleton), Eric Sheffer Stevens (Joey Percival), Natalija Nogulich (Lina Szczepanowska), Carson Elrod (Gunner)

A.M. SUNDAY by Jerome Hairston; Director Marion McClinton; Scenic Design, David Gallo; Costume Design, David Burdick; Lighting Design, Donald Holder; Sound Design, Shane Rettig; Production Dramaturg, James Magruder; November 13–December 14, 2003; Cast: Massimo Angelo Delogu, Jr. or Sylk (Denny), Ray Anthony Thomas (R.P.), Johanna Day (Helen), JD Williams (Jay), Robyn Simpson (Lorie)

THE MISER by Molière, translation and adaptation by James Magruder; Director David Schweizer; Scenic Design, Riccardo Hernandez; Costume Design, David Zinn; Lighting Design, Russell H. Champa; Sound Design/Composer, Mark Bennett; Production Dramaturg, Gavin Witt; January 9–February 8, 2004; Cast: Dan Cordle (La FlÉche/Commissioner), Christian Corp (Mariane), Trent Dawson (ValÈre), June Gable (Frosine), Ian Gould (Brindavoine), Kate Guyton (Elise), Jonathan Hammond (Master Jacques), Tom Mardirosian (Harpagon), John Ramsey (MaÔtre Simon/Dame Claude/Signeur Anselme), Jake Riggs (La Merluche), Charles Daniel Sandoval (Cléante), José Miguel Cueto (Violinist)

SWEENEY TODD music and lyrics by Stephen Sondheim, book by Hugh Wheeler; Directed by Irene Lewis; Music Director/Orchestrator, Milton Granger; Choreography, Willie Rosario; Scenic Design, John Conklin; Costume Design, Catherine Zuber; Lighting Design, Mimi Jordan Sherin; Sound Design, David Budries; Production Dramaturg, James Magruder; February 20–April 11, 2004; Cast: Rebecca Baxter (Beggar Woman), James E. Bonilla or Reed Cahill Vicchio (Boy), Maria Couch (Johanna), Ron DeStefano (Tobias Ragg), Ed Dixon (Judge Turpin), Michael Brian Dunn (Pirelli/Fogg), Osborn Focht (Ensemble), Nicole Halmos (Ensemble), Jay Lusteck (Ensemble), Nora Mae Lyng (Mrs. Lovett), Joseph Mahowald (Sweeney Todd), Mary Jo McConnell (Ensemble), Wayne W. Pretlow (The Beadle), Aaron Ramey (Anthony Hope), Rebecca Robbins (Ensemble), Alecia Robinson (Ensemble), Stephen F. Schmidt (Ensemble)

SPEED-THE-PLOW by David Mamet; Director Daniel Fish; Scenic Design Andrew Lieberman; Costume Design, Kaye Voyce; Lighting Design, Jane Cox; Sound Design, Amy C. Wedel; Production Dramatrug, Dylan Southard; April 2–May 2, 2004; Cast: David Chandler (Bobby Gould), Vincent Guastaferro (Charlie Fox); Lindsay Campbell (Karen)

PICNIC by William Inge; Director Irene Lewis; Scenic Design, Scott Bradley; Costume Design, David Burdick; Lighting Design, D.M. Wood; Sound Design, Martin Desjardins; Choreography, Ken Roberson; Production Dramaturg, Madeleine Oldham; May 14–June 20, 2004; Cast: Tana Hicken (Helen Potts), Leo Kittay (Hal Carter); Kristen Sieh (Millie Owens); Josh Heine (Bomber); Anne Bowles (Madge Owens); Linda Gehringer (Flo Owens); Kristine Nielsen (Rosemary Sydney); Eric Sheffer Stevens (Alan Seymour); Ann Talman (Irma Kronkite); Finnerty Steeves (Christine Schoenwalder); Kevin McClarnon (Howard Bevans)

Rebecca Baxter, Joseph Mahowald in *Sweeney Todd* PHOTO BY RICHARD ANDERSON

THE CLEVELAND PLAYHOUSE

Cleveland, Ohio
EIGHTY-EIGHTH SEASON

Artistic Director, Peter Hackett; Managing Director, Dean R. Gladden

2 PIANOS, 4 HANDS by Ted Dykstra & Richard Greenblatt; Director, Bruce K. Sevy; Scenic Design, Scott Weldin; Lighting Design, Jane Spencer; Costume Design, Kish Finnegan; Sound Design, Brian Jerome Peterson; Stage Manager, Corrie E. Purdum; September 23–October 19, 2003; Cast: Mark Anders (Ted), Carl J. Danielsen (Richard)

FOREST CITY by Bridgette A. Wimberly; Director, Seth Gordon; Scenic Design, Beowulf Boritt; Lighting Design, Derek Duarte; Costume Design, Myrna Colley-Lee; Resident Sound Designer, Robin Heath; Composer, Michael Wimberly; Stage Manager, John Godbout; Casting Agency, Elissa Myers/Paul Fouquet Casting; October 21–November 16, 2003; Cast: Johnny Lee Davenport (John Taylor (JT)), Caroline S. Clay (Sandra Mae Taylor), Margaret Ford-Taylor (Mother Taylor), Wiley Moore (Dr. Michael Thomas), Count Stovall (Clarence), Sterling X. Scruggs and Wyatt W. Scruggs (Benny)

PLAID TIDINGS A SPECIAL HOLIDAY EDITION OF FOREVER PLAID by Stuart Ross; Director, Stuart Ross; Musical Director, Pianist, Brad Ellis; Associate Director, Understudy for all roles, Robert Randle; Scenic Design, Neil Peter Jampolis; Costume Design, Debra Stein; Lighting Design, Jane Reisman; Resident Sound Designer, Robin Heath; Stage Manager, Corrie E. Purdum; Original Sound Designer, Frederick W. Boot; November 18–December 21, 2003; Cast: Jody Ashworth (Smudge), Jonathan Brody (Sparky), Scot Fedderly (Frankie), Randy Rineck (Jinx)

NEIL SIMON'S THE DINNER PARTY by Neil Simon; Director, Peter Hackett; Scenic Design, Vicki Smith; Costume Design, David Kay Mickelson; Lighting Design, William H. Grant III; Resident Sound Designer, Robin Heath; Stage Manager, John Godbout; Casting Agency, Elissa Myers/Paul Fouquet Casting; January 6–February 1, 2004; Cast: David Brummel (Andre), Cynthia Darlow (Gabrielle), Mary Gen Fjelstad (Mariette), Keven Hogan (Claude), Steve McCue (Albert), Derdriu Ring (Yvonne)

VINCENT IN BRIXTON by Nicholas Wright; Director, Seth Gordon; Scenic and lighting Design, Kent Dorsey; Costume Design, David Kay Mickelson; Resident Sound Designer, Robin Heath; Stage Manager, Corrie E. Purdum; Casting Agency, Elissa Myers/Paul Fouquet Casting; February 10–March 7, 2004; Cast: Beth Dixon (Ursula Loyer), Simon Kendall (Vincent van Gogh), Virginia Donohoe (Eugenie Loyer), Patrick Jones (Sam Plowman), Emily Frazier Klingensmith (Anna van Gogh)

THE UNDERPANTS adapted by Steve Martin; Director, Peter Hackett; Scenic Design, Bill Clarke; Costume Design, Kristine A. Kearney; Lighting Design, Richard Winkler; Resident Sound Designer, Robin Heath; Stage Manager, John Godbout; Casting Agency, Elissa Myers/Paul Fouquet Casting; March 2–28, 2004; Cast: Chaz Mena (Theo Maske), Tanya Clarke (Louise Maske), Johanna Morrison (Gertrude Deuter), Sam Gregory (Frank Versati), Brad Bellamy (Benjamin Cohen), Ronald Thomas Wilson (Klinglehoff), Rich Sommer (The King)

FAR AWAY by Caryl Churchill; Director, Peter Hackett; Scenographer: Scenic, Costume, and Lighting Design, Pavel Dobrusky; Resident Sound Designer, Robin Heath; Composer, Larry Delinger; Choreographer, Ronald Thomas Wilson; Stage Manager, Corrie E. Purdum; March 30–April 25, 2004; Cast: Cat Maddox (Joan), Matthew Joslyn (Todd), Derdriu Ring (Harper), Angela Holecko (Young Joan)

COOKIN' AT THE COOKERY: THE MUSIC & TIMES OF ALBERTA HUNTER by Marion J. Caffey; Director-Choreographer, Marion J. Caffey; Musical Supervision and Arrangements, Danny Holgate; Assistant Director, Roumel Reaux; Musical Director, Conductor, Pianist, William Foster McDaniel; Scene and Lighting Design, Dale F. Jordan; Costume Design, Marilyn A. Wall; Wigmaker/Hair Design, Bettie O. Rogers; Resident Sound Designer, Robin Heath; Stage Manager, John Godbout; Casting Agency, Elissa Myers/Paul Fouquet Casting; April 27–May 30, 2004; Cast: Gail Nelson (Alberta Hunter), Carla Woods (The Narrator)

CINCINNATI PLAYHOUSE IN THE PARK

Cincinnati, Ohio
FORTY-FOURTH SEASON

Producing Artistic Director, Edward Stern; Executive Director, Buzz Ward

MY FAIR LADY book and lyrics by Alan Jay Lerner, music by Frederick Loewe, adapted from George Bernard Shaw's play and Gabrial Pascal's motion picture *Pygmalion*; Director, Susan V. Booth; Choreographer, Daniel Pelzig; Musical Director, Steven Gross; Set Design, Michael Philippi; Costume Design, Linda Roethke; Lighting Design, Dawn Chiang; Dialect Coach, Rocco Dal Vera; September 2–October 3, 2003; Cast: Neal Benari (Henry Higgins), Keith Howard (Busker, George, Higgins' Butler, Zoltan Karpathy and Vendor), Howard Kaye (Busker, Selsey Man, Harry, Charles, The Royal Footman and Vendor), Jeffrey Kuhn (Busker, Hoxton Man, Jamie, Higgins' Footman, Lord Boxington, Lord Tarrington and Vendor), Russell Leib (Colonel Pickering), Crista Moore (Eliza Doolittle), Alan Souza (Freddy Eynsford-Hill), Rebecca Spencer (Mrs. Eynsford-Hill, Busker, Higgins' Maid, Angry Woman, Servant, Lady Tarrington, Queen of Transylvania and Mrs. Higgins' Maid), Linda Stephens (Mrs. Higgins and Mrs. Pearce), Peter Van Wagner (Alfred P. Doolittle)

ONE world premiere by Joseph McDonough; Director, Edward Stern; Set Design, Joseph P. Tilford; Costume Design, Elizabeth Covey; Lighting Design, Thomas C. Hase; Composer, Douglas Lowry; Dialect Coach, Rocco Dal Vera; September 27–October 26, 2003; Cast: Anney Giobbe (Emily), Tim Altmeyer (Kyle), Henny Russell (Jill)

METAMORPHOSES by Mary Zimmerman, based on the myths of Ovid; Director, Mary Zimmerman; Staged by Eric Rosen; Set Design, Daniel Ostling; Costume Design, Mara Blumenfeld; Lighting Design, T.J. Gerckens; Sound Design, Andre Pluess and Ben Sussman; Composer, Willy Schwarz; October 21–November 21, 2003; Cast: Cherise Boothe (Alcyone and Others), Sun Mee Chomet (Myrrha and Others), Joe Dempsey (Erysichthon and Others), Anne Fogarty (Eurydice and Others), Antony Hagopian (Vertumnus and Others), Andrew Long (Midas and Others), James McKay (Phaeton and Others), Manu Narayan (Orpheus and Others), Lisa Tejero (Therapist and Others), Tamilla Woodard (Aphrodite and Others)

ALWAYS...PATSY CLINE written and originally directed by Ted Swindley; Director, Frazier W. Marsh; Music Director, Scott Kasbaum; Set Design, Paul Owen; Costume Design, Delmar L. Rinehart, Jr.; Lighting Design, Tony Penna; November 8, 2003–January 18, 2004; Cast: Molly Andrews (Patsy), Adale O'Brien (Louise)

A CHRISTMAS CAROL by Charles Dickens, adapted by Howard Dallin; Director, Michael Evan Haney; Set Design, James Leonard Joy; Costume Design, David Murin; Lighting Design, Kirk Bookman; Sound Design and Composer, David B. Smith; Musical Director, Rebecca N. Childs; Choreographer, Dee Anne Bryll; December 3–December 30, 2003; Cast: Joneal Joplin (Ebenezer Scrooge), Stephen Skiles (Mr. Cupp, Percy and Rich Father at Fezziwig's), Rashaad Ernesto Green (Mr. Sosser, Dick Wilkens,

Topper and Man with Shoe Shine), Bruce Cromer (Bob Cratchit and Schoolmaster Oxlip), Jake Storms (Fred), Gregory Procaccino (Jacob Marley and Old Joe), Dale Hodges (Ghost of Christmas Past, Rose and Mrs. Peake), Alec Shelby Bowling (Boy Scrooge, Boy at Fezziwig's and Bootblack), Ali Breneman (Fan, Guest at Fezziwig's and Streets), Mark Mineart (Mr. Fezziwig and Ghost of Christmas Present), Amy Warner (Mrs. Fezziwig, Patience and Streets), Jeremiah Wiggins (Young and Mature Scrooge and Ghost of Christmas Future), Angela Lin (Belle and Catherine Margaret), Regina Pugh (Mrs. Cratchit and Laundress), Thomas Langlois (Peter Cratchit, Gregory and Apprentice at Fezziwig's), Theresa White (Belinda Cratchit, Guest at Fezziwig's and Streets), K. McKenzie Miller (Martha Cratchit, Guest at Fezziwig's and Streets), Lucas Clark (Tiny Tim), Iriemimen Oniha (Rich Caroler, Maid at Fezziwig's and Streets), Jim Ward (Rich Caroler and Accountant at Fezziwig's), Amber K. Browning (Poor Caroler and Rich Wife at Fezziwig's), John Hashop (Poor Caroler, Tailor at Fezziwig's, Man with Pipe and Streets), Nathan Robbins (Matthew, Rich Son at Fezziwig's and Ignorance), Aaron Mayo (Charles, Apprentice at Fezziwig's, George and Streets), Megan Zink (Want, Guest at Fezziwig's and Streets), Marie Howey (Guest at Fezziwig's, Mrs. Dilber and Streets), Jodie Beerman (Scrubwoman at Fezziwig's and Streets), Keven Kaddi (Constable at Fezziwig's, Poulterer and Streets), Michael Mihm (Lawyer at Fezziwig's, Undertaker and Streets)

GOING GONE world premiere by Karen Hartman; Director, Michael Bloom; Set Design, Klara Zieglerova; Costume Design, Susan E. Mickey; Lighting Design, Nancy Schertler; Sound Design, Geoff Zink; January 13–February 13, 2004; Cast: Tony Hoty (Harry Hartman), Maureen Silliman (Mama), Laura Heisler (Maidle), Todd Gearhart (Hank the Hero and Voiceover), Jared Gertner (Hanky), David Ian Dahlman (Attendant), Jeff DeMaria (Attendant), Jeffrey Groh (Attendant), Michael Joseph Thomas Ward (Attendant)

THE DRAWER BOY by Michael Healey; Director, Michael Evan Haney; Set Design, Ursula Belden; Costume Design, John P. White; Lighting Design, Tony Penna; Sound Design, Andrew Hopson; February 7–March 7, 2004; Cast: John Thomas Waite (Angus), Brian Ibsen (Miles), William McNulty (Morgan)

BLUE by Charles Randolph-Wright, music by Nona Hendryx, lyrics by Nona Hendryx and Charles Randolph-Wright; Director, Kenny Leon; Music Director, Dwight Douglas Andrews; Set Design, Marjorie Bradley Kellogg; Costume Design, Susan E. Mickey; Lighting Design, Tom Sturge; Sound Design, Marc Gwinn; March 2–April 2, 2004; Cast: Yusef Miller (Reuben Clark), Denise Burse (Peggy Clark), Darnell Smith, Jr. (Young Reuben and Baby Blue), Kevyn Morrow (Blue Williams), Rashad J. Anthony (Samuel Clark III), Tinashe Kajese (LaTonya Dinkins), Peter Jay Fernandez (Samuel Clark, Jr.), Brenda Thomas (Tillie Clark)

HIDING BEHIND COMETS world premiere by Brian Dykstra; Director, Michael Evan Haney; Set Design, Kevin Rigdon; Costume Design, Gordon DeVinney; Lighting Design, David Lander; Sound Design, Chuck Hatcher; Fight Director, Drew Fracher; March 20–April 18, 2004; Cast: Christian Conn (Troy), Jacqueline van Biene (Honey), Erica Schroeder (Erin), Dan Moran (Cole)

MISTER ROBERTS by Thomas Heggen and Joshua Logan; Director, Edward Stern; Set Design, Paul Shortt; Costume Design, Kristine Kearney; Lighting Design, Peter E. Sargent; Fight Director, Drew Fracher; April 25–May 28, 2004; Cast: John Ahlin (Chief Johnson), Bill Doyle (Lieutenant Roberts), Joneal Joplin (Doc), Gary McGurk (Dowdy), Robert Elliott (The Captain), Jim Holdridge (Insigna), Mark Mineart (Mannion), Josh Renfree (Lindstrom), Andre Marrero (Stefanowski), Matthew Francisco Morgan (Wiley), Greg McFadden (Ensign Pulver), Geoffrey Molloy (Dolan), Christopher Gottschalk (Gerhart), Cristin Mortenson (Lieutenant Ann Girard), John Hashop (Shore Patrol Officer), A. Jackson Ford (Military Policeman), Mike Mihm (Shore Patrolman), David Ian Dahlman (Sailor), John Graham (Sailor), Keven Kaddi (Sailor), Ryan Mills (Sailor)

SING HALLELUJAH! conceived by Worth Gardner and Donald Lawrence; Director, Worth Gardner; Musical Director, Donald Lawrence; Set Design, Joseph P. Tilford; Costume Design, Gordon DeVinney; Lighting Design, Kirk Bookman; May 15–June 27, 2004; Cast: Erica Bratton-McCollough, Anitra Castleberry, Russell Hinton, Candy West, DeWayne L. Woods

Candy West in *Sing Hallelujah!* PHOTO BY SANDY UNDERWOOD, JERRY NAUNHEIM, JR.

CLARENCE BROWN THEATRE

Knoxville, Tennesee
THIRTIETH SEASON

Artistic Director, Blake Robison; Managing Director, Thomas Cervone

THE DRESSER by Ronald Harwood: Director, Gerald Freedman; Scenic Design, John Ezell; Costume Design, Bill Black, Lighting Design, Beverly Emmons; Sound Design, Mike Ponder; August 26–September 11; Cast: John Cullum (Sir), JD Cullum (Norman), Carol Mayo Jenkins (Her Ladyship), Bonnie Gould (Madge), Alecia White (Irene), J.T. Waite (Geoffrey Thornton), Robin Chadwick (Mr. Oxenby), David Brian Alley (Gloucester, Albany, Gentleman), T. Anthony Marotta (Kent), Dan Owenby (Electrician), Greg Congleton (Knight 1), Donald Thorne (Knight 2)

ANNA KARENINA by Leo Tolstoy: Director, Blake Robison; Scenic Design, Marianne Custer; Costume Design, Marianne Custer, Lighting Design, Kenton Yeager; Sound Design, Mike Ponder; October 7–24; Cast: Connan Morrissey (Anna), John Feltch (Levin), T. Anthony Marotta (Stiva), Erin O'Leary (Dolly, Countess, Governess), Tracie Merrill (Kitty), Jeremy Holm (Vronsky), Terry Weber (Karenin), Sally Wood (Princess, Agatha, Widow), David Brian Alley (Nikola, Petritsky, Priest, Bailiff), Ben Croisdale (Seriozha)

INTO THE WOODS Music and Lyrics by Stephen Sondheim, Book by James Lapine. Director, Terry Silver-Alford; Scenic Design, Christopher Pickart; Costume Design, Amanda Jenkins, Lighting Design, Weston Wilkerson; Sound Design, Mike Ponder; November 5–20; Cast: John Forrest Ferguson (Narrator, Mysterious Man), Harmony Livingston (Cinderella), Jay Schaad (Jack), Nancy Dinwiddie (Jack's Mother), Jon Levenson (Baker), Morgan Scott (Baker's Wife), Crystal Stroupe (Cinderella's Stepmother), Joan Williams (Florinda), Kaitlin Steer (Lucinda), Dan Owenby (Cinderella's Father), Mary Alice Skalko (Little Red Ridinghood), Shawn Farrar (Witch), Sara Cravens (Cinderella's Mother, Granny, Giant), Shana Hammett (Rapunzel), Bill Piper (Rapunzel's Prince), Charlie Effler (Cinderella's Prince, Wolf), Zach England (Steward)

THE ODD COUPLE by Neil Simon: Director, Charlie Hensley; Scenic Design, Marty Lynch; Costume Design, Felia Katherine, Lighting Design, Patrick Mihalik; Sound Design, Mike Ponder; Jan. 27–Feb. 12; Cast: Ed Kershen (Speed), Harrison Long (Murray), James E. Halter (Roy), John Thomas Waite (Vinnie), John Forrest Ferguson (Oscar Madison), Terry Weber (Felix Ungar), Connan Morrissey (Gwendolyn Pigeon), Ericka Kreutz (Cecily Pigeon)

(CONTINUED ON NEXT PAGE)

(CONTINUED FROM PREVIOUS PAGE)

METAMORPHOSES by Mary Zimmerman: Director, Joseph Haj; Scenic Design,Clinton O'Dell; Costume Design, Clinton O'Dell, Lighting Design, Keith Kirkland; Sound Design, Mike Ponder; Feb. 25–Mar. 12; Cast: John Cullum (Sir), JD Cullum (Norman), Carol Mayo Jenkins (Her Ladyship), Bonnie Gould (Madge), Alecia White (Irene), J.T. Waite (Geoffrey Thornton), Robin Chadwick (Mr. Oxenby), David Brian Alley (Gloucester, Albany, Gentleman), T. Anthony Marotta (Kent), Dan Owenby (Electrician), Greg Congleton (Knight 1), Donald Thorne (Knight 2)

ALL THE WAY HOME adapted from *James Agee* by Tad Mosel: Director: Paul Barnes; Scenic Design, Carl Tallent; Costume Design, Nicole Jescinth Smith, Lighting Design, Kenton Yeager; Sound Design, Mike Ponder; April 7–23; Cast: Ben Croisdale (Rufus Follet), Christiane Frith (Boy), Jacob Hodges (Boy) Caitlin Kennedy (boy), Andrew Wolfe (Boy), Jed Diamond (Jay Follet), Connan Morrissey (Mary Follet) Harrison Long (Ralph Follet) Shawn Farrar (Sally Follet) Donald Thorne (John Henry Follet) Nancy Dinwiddie (Jessie Follet) Benjamin Frith (Jim Wilson) Bonnie Gould (Aunt Sadie Follet) Janice Stanton (Great-Great-Granmaw) Dee Maaske (Catherine Lynch) Carol Mayo Jenkins (Aunt Hannah Lynch) John Forrest Ferguson (Joel Lynch) Fisher Neal (Andrew Lynch) Dan Owenby (Father Jackson)

COURT THEATRE

Chicago, Illinois
FORTY-NINTH SEASON

Artistic Director, Charles Newell; Executive Director, Diane Claussen

THE SOUND OF A VOICE An Opera by Philip Glass. Libretto by David Henry Hwang. Music by Philip Glass. Directed by Robert Woodruff. Produced in association with American Repertory Theatre. Scenic Designer, Robert Israel; Costume Designer, Kasia Walicka Maimone; Lighting Designer, Beverly Emmons; Production Dramaturg, Ryan McKittrick; Stage Manager, Laxmi Kumaran; Assistant Stage Manager, Lesley Anne Stone; September 25–November 2, 2003; Cast: Janice Felty (Woman), Suzan Hanson (Hanako), Eugene Perry (Kenji Yamamoto), Herbert Perry (Man). Musicians: Susan Gall (Flute), Chase Pamela Morrison (Cello), Tina Keitel (Percussion), Min Xiao-Fen (Pipa)

JAMES JOYCE'S THE DEAD Book by Richard Nelson. Music by Shaun Davey. Lyrics conceived and adapted by Richard Nelson and Shaun Davey. Directed by Charles Newell. Music Direction by Doug Peck. Scenic Designer, Brian Bembridge; Costume Designer, Linda Rothke; Lighting Designer, Joel Moritz; Sound Designer, Bruce Holland; Choreographer, Mark Howard; November 24 2003–January 4, 2004; Cast: Chrsta Buck (Lily), McKinley Carter (Mary Jane), Christopher Cordon (Freddy Malins), Deanna Dunagan (Aunt Julia Morkan), Neil Friedman (Mr. Browne), Robert Adelman Hancock (Michael), Kimberly Irion (Rita, Young Julia), Carey Peters (Molly Ivors), John Reeger (Gabriel Conroy), Paula Scrofano (Gretta Conroy), Penny Slusher (Mrs. Malins), Stephen Wallem (Bartell D'Arcy), Ann Stevenson Whitney (Aunt Kelley Morkan). Orchestra: Martine Benmann (Cello), Marie Micol Bennett (Flute), Tim Meade (Guitar), Eugenia Wie (Violin)

GUYS AND DOLLS Based on a story and characters of Damon Runyon. Music and Lyrics by Frank Loesser. Book by Jo Swerling & Abe Burrows. Directed by Charles Newell. Music Direction by Doug Peck. Scenic Designer, John Culbert, Costume Designer, Rachel Anne Healy; Lighting Designer, Michelle Habeck; Sound Designer, Joshua Horvath; Dramaturg, Rachel Shteir; Associate Scenic Designer, Jack Magaw; Dialect Coach, Matt Harding; Stage Manager, Laxmi Kumaran; Assistant Stage Manager, Ellen Hay; January 22–March 28, 2004; Cast: Daniel Allar (Big Jule), Lance Stuart Baker (Harry the Horse), Kelsey Collins (Mimi, Agatha), Ben Dicke (Rusty Charlie), Jeff Dumas (Nicely Nicely Johnson), Don Forston (Arvide), Neil Friedman (Benny Southstreet), Heidi Kettenring (Miss Adelaide), Susan Moniz (Sarah Brown), David New (Sky Masterson), Scott Parkinson (Nathan Detroit), Duane Sharp (Lt. Brannigan), Tina Thuerwatcher (General Cartwright). Musicians: Mike Combopiano (Trumpet), Geoffrey Lowe (Upright Bass), Robert Reddrick (Drums)

FRAÜLEIN ELSE Translated and Adapted by Francesca Faridany. From the novella by Arthur Schnitzler. Directed by Lucy Smith Conroy. Scenic Designer, Michael Brown; Costume Designer, Jaqueline Firkins; Lighting Designer, Michelle Habeck; Co-Sound Designers/ Composers, Joshua Horvath and Ray Nardelli; Stage Manager, Christine D. Freedburg; Assistant Stage Manager, Sara Gammage; April 22–May 16, 2004; Cast: Thomas J. Cox (Porter), Linda Gillum (Cissy), Ned Noyes (Paul), Roderick Peeples (Herr von Dorsday), Paula Scrofano (Mother), Whitney Sneed (Else)

CYRANO Conceived and Directed by Jim Lasko and Charles Newell. From a new rhymed verse translation by Mickle Maher. Based on the play Cyrano de Bergerac by Edmond Rostand. Co-produced by Court Theatre and Redmoon Theater. Scenic Designer, Stephanie Nelson; Costume Designer, Tatjana Radsic; Lighting Designer, John Culbert; Co-Sound Designers/Composers, Andre Pleuss and Ben Sussman; David Christopher Krause (Artistic Engineer); Scott Pondrom (Prop and Object Designer); Shoshanna Utchenik (Puppet Designer), Sarah Gubbins (Dramaturg); Stage Manager, Laxmi Kumaran; Assistant Stage Manager, Stephenie Moser; Presented at the Museum of Contemporary Art, May 20–June 27, 2004; Cast: Lance Stuart Baker (De Guiche), Andrew Burlinson (Ensemble), Chaon Cross (Roxane), Laura T. Fisher (LeBret), Allen Gilmore (Cyrano), Alison Halstead (Ragueneau), Vanessa Stalling (Ensemble), Jay Whittaker (Christian)

DALLAS THEATER CENTER

Dallas, Texas
FORTY-FIFTH SEASON

Artistic Director, Richard Hamburger; Managing Director, Mark Hadley

HAMLET by William Shakespeare; Director, Richard Hamburger; Scenic Design, Klara Zieglerova; Costume Design, Ilona Somogyi; Lighting Design, Marcus Doshi; Sound Design, Fitz Patton; Fight Director, Thomas Schall; Dramaturg/Text Consultant, Margaret Loft. September 10–October 11, 2003; Cast: Jason Butler Harner (Hamlet); Shawn Elliott (Claudius); Caitlin O'Connell (Gertrude); Michael Kevin (Ghost of Hamlet's father); Ross Bickell (Polonios); Chuck Huber (Laertes); Karron Graves (Ophelia); Billy Eugene Jones (Horatio); Regan Adair (Rosencrantz); Jakie Cabe (Guildenstern); William Harper (Marcellus); Matthew Stephen Tompkins (Fortinbras); Michael Kevin (Player King); Chuck Huber (Player Queen); Matthew Stephen Tompkins (Lucianus); Chamblee Ferguson (Osric); Ross Bickell (A Gravedigger); Matthew Stephen Tompkins (A Priest); Regan Adair, Jakie Cabe, William Harper, Blair Mitchell, Joey Oglesby, Wm. Paul Williams (Soldiers/Servants)

THE GLASS MENAGERIE by Tennessee Williams; Director, Claudia Zelevansky; Scenic Design, Takeshi Kata; Costume Design, Ilona Somogyi; Lighting Design, Matthew Richards; Sound Design, Obadiah Eaves; October 22–November 16, 2003; Cast: Beth Dixon (Amanda Wingfield); Brandon Miller (Tom Wingfield); Jeanine Serralles (Laura Wingfield); Ashley Smith (Jim O'Connor)

A CHRISTMAS CAROL by Charles Dickens; Adapted by Preston Lane and Jonathan Moscone; Director, Jonathan Moscone; Scenic Design, Narelle Sissons; Costume Design, Katherine B. Roth; Lighting Design, York Kennedy; Composer/Sound Design, Kim D. Sherman; Choreographer, David Shimotakahara; Musical Director, Elaine Davidson; November 28–December 24, 2003; Cast: Ron Campbell (Scrooge); James Crawford (Bob Cratchit); Casey Bruce Robinson (Fred); Doug Jackson (Charitable Gentleman); Doug Jackson (Charitable Gentlewoman); Abigail Cartwright (Charitable Girl); Akin Babatunde (Marley's Ghost); Clara Peretz (The Spirit of Christmas Past); Christopher Cartwright (Scrooge as a child); Casey Bruce Robinson (Ali Baba); James Crawford (Snow Man); Taubert Nadalini (Scrooge as an adolescent); Chelsea Erin Jones (Fan); Akin Babatunde (Mr. Fezziwig); Casey Bruce Robinson (Scrooge as a young man); Brian Gonzales (Dick Wilkins); Liz Mikel (Mrs. Fezziwig); Jessica D. Turner (Belle); Liz Mikel (The Spirit of Christmas Present); Sally Nystuen Vahle (Mrs. Cratchit); Ian Flanagan (Peter Cratchit); Clara Peretz (Belinda Cratchit); Abigail Cartwright (Sarah Cratchit); Taubert Nadalini (James Cratchit); Chelsea Erin Jones (Martha Cratchit); Christopher Cartwright (Tiny Tim); Jessica D. Turner (Lily); Sally Nystuen Vahle (Cynthia); Brian Gonzales (Topper); Christopher Cartwright (Ignorance); Victoria Lennox (Want); Sally Nystuen Vahle, James Crawford, Clara Peretz (Rich Men); Liz Mikel (Mrs. Dilber); Amy Mills (Charwoman); Doug Jackson (Joe the Keeper); Brian Gonzales (Debtor); Ashley Gonzales (Debtor's Wife); Ian Flanagan (Turkey Boy)

ACCIDENTAL DEATH OF AN ANARCHIST by Dario Fo; Director, Richard Hamburger; Scenic Design, Leiko Fuseya; Costume Design, Linda Cho; Lighting Design, Stephen Strawbridge; Sound Design, David Budries; January 14–February 8, 2004; Cast: Mary Bacon (Journalist); Craig Bockhorn (Deputy Police Chief); Robert Dorfman (The Maniac); Doug Jackson & Marcus Neely (Police Officers); Sean Runnette (Inspector Bertozzo); and Jerry Russell (Commissioner)

Todd Freeman, David Rainey in *TopDog/Underdog* PHOTO BY LINDA BLASÉ

TOPDOG/UNDERDOG by Suzan-Lori Parks; Director, Amy Morton; Associate Director, Ann C. James; Scenic Design, Loy Arcenas; Costume Design, Nan Cibula-Jenkins; Lighting Design, Kevin Rigdon; Sound Design, Michael Bodeen and Rob Milburn; February 25–March 21, 2004; Cast: K. Todd Freeman (Booth) and David Rainey (Lincoln)

AIN'T MISBEHAVIN' conceived and originally directed by Richard Maltby, Jr.; Director, Greg Ganakas; Scenic Design, Dex Edwards; Costume Design, Clare Henkel; Lighting Design, Kirk Bookman; Sound Design, David Stephen Baker; April 7–May 9, 2004; Cast: Dwayne Clark (Dwayne), Dioni Michelle Collins (Dioni), Janeece Aisha Freeman (Janeece), Liz Mikel (Liz) and Ken Prymus (Ken)

The Company in *Ain't Misbehavin'* PHOTO BY MICHAEL BROSILOW

GEORGIA SHAKESPEARE

Atlanta, Georgia
EIGHTEENTH SEASON

Producing Artistic Director, Richard Garner; Managing Director, Robert A. Fass

MUCH ADO ABOUT NOTHING by William Shakespeare; Director, Kenny Leon; Scenic Design, Vicki Davis; Costume Design, Vicki Davis; Lighting Design, Mike Post; Composer, Dwight Andrews; Sound Design, Lauren Gale; June 11–August 10, 2003; Cast: Brad Sherrill (Don Pedro), Chris Kayser (Benedick), Joe Knezevich (Claudio), Clifton Duncan (Balthasar), Adam Holder (A Boy), Chris Ensweiler (Don John), Rob Cleveland (Borachio), Daniel May (Conrad), Bruce Evers (Leonato), Tracey Copeland (Hero), Carolyn Cook (Beatrice), Hudson Adams (Antonio), Karan Kenrick (Margaret), Carena Crowell (Ursula), Allen O'Reilly (Friar Francis), John Ammerman (Dogberry)

THE SCHOOL FOR WIVES by Molière; translated by Ranjit Bolt; Director, Karen Robinson; Scenic Design, Rochelle Barker; Costume Design, Christine Turbitt; Lighting Design, Mike Post; Composer/Sound Design, Clint Thorton; June 26–August 8, 2003; Cast: Chris Kayser (Arnolphe), Hudson Adams (Chrysalde), Courtney Patterson (Georgette), Tracey Copeland (Alain), Karan Kendrick (Agnes), Daniel May (Horace), Chris Ensweiler (A Notary), Allen O'Reilly (Oronte), Rob Cleveland (Enrique)

THE TALE OF CYMBELINE by William Shakespeare; Director, Nancy Keystone; Scenic Designer, Nancy Keystone; Costume Design, Leon Wiebers; Lighting Design, Justin Townsend; Composer, Klimchack; Sound Designer, Lauren Gale. July 10–August 10, 2003. Cast: John Ammerman (Cymbeline), Carolyn Cook (Queen), Damon Boggess (Arviragus), Daniel May (Guiderius), Courtney Patterson (Imogen); Joe Knezevich (Cloten/Posthumus); Chris Kayser (Belarius), Tracey Copeland (Cornelius), Karan Kendrick (Helen), Allen O'Reilly (Pisanio), Rob Cleveland (Philario/Jupiter), Brad Sherrill (Iachimo), Hudson Adams (Casius Lucius), Chris Ensweiler (Jailer), Carena Crowell (Lady), Jesse Hinson (Soldier), Clifton Duncan (Soldier), Julie Sharbutt (Lady)

THE TEMPEST by William Shakespeare; Director, Richard Garner; Scenic Designer, Rochelle Barker; Costume Designer, Sydney Roberts; Lighting Designer, Liz Lee; Composers, Kendall Simpson & Klimchack; Sound Design, Lauren Gale. October 9–November 2, 2003. Cast: Bruce Evers (Alonso); Joe Knezevich (Sebastian); Tess Malis Kincaid (Antonia), Damon Boggess (Ferdinand), Michele McCullough (Gonzala), Isma'il ibn Conner (Caliban), Chris Ensweiler (Trinculo); Tim McDonough (Stephano), Sarah Hankins (Miranda), Kelly O'Neil (Ariel), Janice Akers (Prospera)

GEVA THEATRE CENTER

Rochester, New York
THIRTY-FIRST SEASON

Artistic Director, Mark Cuddy (on sabbatical)
Acting Artistic Directors, Marge Betley and Skip Greer; Managing Director, John Quinlivan

BILOXI BLUES by Neil Simon; Director, Tim Ocel; Scenic Design, Gary Jacobs; Costume Design, B. Modern; Lighting Design, Kendall Smith; Sound Design, Andrew Hopson, Ph.D.; September 2–October 5; Cast: Michael Hogan (Roy Selridge), Coleman Zeigen (Joseph Wykowski), Sam Misner (Don Carney), Dennis Staroselsky (Eugene Morris Jerome), Fred Berman (Arnold Epstein), Lou Sumrall (Sgt. Merwin J. Toomey), Jim Butz (James Hennesey), Helen Mutch (Rowena), Ivy Vahanian (Daisy Hannigan)

Fred Berman, Lou Sumrall in *Biloxi Blues* PHOTO COURTESY OF GEVA THEATRE CENTER

COPENHAGEN by Michael Frayn; Director, Michael Donald Edwards; Scenic Design, Andrew Lieberman; Costume Design, Kaye Voyce; Lighting Design, Les Dickert; Sound Design, Jonathan Herter; October 14–November 16; Cast: Pat Nesbit (Margrethe), Robert Grossman (Niels Bohr), Christopher Gurr (Werner Heisenberg)

AND THEN THEY CAME FOR ME: REMEMBERING THE WORLD OF ANNE FRANK by James Still; Director Patrick Elkins-Zeglarski; Scenic Design, Rob Koharchik; Costume Design, Amanda Doherty; Lighting Design, Derek Madonia; Sound Design, David R. Pisani; October 7–November 2; Cast: Erin Kate Howard (Anne, Mutti), Sam Misner (Young Ed, Pappy), Mick Mize (Hitler Youth, Heinz, Ed's Father), Maria Ryan (Eva, Ed's Mother)

PYRETOWN by John Belluso; Director, Tim Farrell; Scenic Design, Rob Koharchik; Costume Design, Meghan E. Healey; Lighting Design, Andrew Hill; Sound Design, Dan Roach; November 12–December 7; Cast: Jan Leslie Harding (Louise Josephson), Sue-Anne Morrow (Dr. Rebecca Abbott), Christopher Thornton (Harry Weston) World Premiere

A CHRISTMAS CAROL by Charles Dickens; Adaptation by Richard Hellesen; Director, Mark Booher; Scenic Design, Ramsey Avery; Costume Design, B. Modern; Lighting Design, Kendall Smith; Sound Design, Dan Roach; November 28–December 28; Cast: Robin Chadwick (Ebenezer Scrooge), Mitchell Canfield, Collin Jones (Ebenezer the Child, Edward Cratchit), John Gardiner (Ebenezer the Apprentice, Tailor), Tom Frey (Ebenezer the Young Man, Fred, Music Teacher, The Undertaker's Man), Robert B. Kennedy (Bob Cratchit), Jenna Cole (Mrs. Cratchit, The Ghost of Christmas Past), Karissa Vacker (Martha Cratchit, Belle), Scott Scaffidi (Peter Cratchit, Dick Wilkins), Allison Lynch, Emily Putnam (Belinda Cratchit, Belle's Daughter), Rebecca Rand, Alice Wilder (Timothy Cratchit), Melinda Parrett (Fred's Wife, Mrs. Fezziwig), Rene Thornton, Jr. (Topper, The Ghost of Christmas Yet to Come), Elizabeth Stuart (The Wife's Sister, First Miss Fezziwig, The Charwoman), Catherine McNally (Female Guest at Fred's Party, Tailor's Wife, Belle the Matron, The Laundress), Guy Bannerman (Male Guest at Fred's Party, First Subscription Gentleman, Fezziwig, Belle's Husband), Julia Ann Devine, Rebecca Elizabeth Isenhart (The Beggar Child), Emma Xuxu Marshall, Allie Waxman (Want), Jeremy Ehlinger, Clay Thomson (Ignorance, Turkey Boy), Neil Barclay (Second Subscription Gentleman, The Ghost of Christmas Present), J.G. Hertzler (The Ghost of Jacob Marley, Old Joe), Katie Germano, Gianina Spano (Fan), Alexandra Blazey, Devin Dunne Cannon (Second Miss Fezziwig), Sara Lynn Ianni, Megan Rast (Third Miss Fezziwig), Nick Mannix (First Suitor), Adam Rath (Second Suitor)

THE SMELL OF THE KILL by Michele Lowe; Director, Tim Ocel; Scenic Design, Ramsey Avery; Costume Design, B. Modern; Lighting Design, Kirk Bookman; Sound Design, Dan Roach; January 6–February 8; Cast: Barbara Sims (Nicky), Mhari Sandoval (Molly), Brigitt Markusfeld (Debra), Ray Salah (Jay), Robert Rutland (Danny, Marty)

DEATH OF A SALESMAN by Arthur Miller; Director, Skip Greer; Scenic Design, Erhard Rom; Costume Design, B. Modern; Lighting Design, Kendall Smith; Sound Design, Dan Roach; February 17–March 21; Cast: James Edmondson (Willy Loman), Jeanne Paulsen (Linda), Stephen Key (Happy), Christian Kohn (Biff), Joe Hickey (Bernard), Stacia Fernandez (The Woman), Munson Hicks (Charley), J.G. Hertzler (Uncle Ben), Matt D'Amico (Howard Wagner), Joanna Schmitt (Jenny), Glenn Wein (Stanley), Karyn Casl (Miss Forsythe), Marcy J. Savastano (Letta), Mark Casey (Waiter), Connor Greer, Madison Russell (Children's Voices)

BLUE by Charles Randolph-Wright; Director, Kenny Leon; Scenic Design, Marjorie Bradley Kellogg; Costume Design, Susan E. Mickey; Lighting Design, Tom Sturge; Sound Design, Marc Gwinn; April 13–May 16; Cast: Yusef Miller (Reuben Clark), Denise Burse (Peggy Clark), Darnell Smith, Jr. (Young Reuben, Baby Blue), Kevyn Morrow (Blue Williams), Rashad J. Anthony (Samuel Clark, III), Tinashe Kajese (LaTonya Dinkins), Peter Jay Fernandez (Samuel Clark, Jr.), Brenda Thomas (Tillie Clark)

ALL IS WELL IN THE KINGDOM OF NICE by Kira Obolensky; Director, Karen Coe Miller; Scenic Design, John King, Jr.; Costume Design, Faye Fisher Ward; Lighting Design, Derek Madonia; Sound Design, Dan Roach; April 27–May 9; Cast: Nick Mannix (James), Sandy Oian (A Woman), Marcy J. Savastano (Emily), Edwin Strout (A Man) World Premiere

CAMELOT by Alan Jay Lerner; Director, Christopher Gurr; Scenic Design, G.W. Mercier; Costume Design, John Carver Sullivan; Lighting Design, Marcus Doshi; Sound Design, Lindsay Jones; May 26–July 11; Cast: Remi Sandri (King Arthur), Brigid Brady (Guenevere), Robin Chadwick (Merlyn, King Pellinore), Gerritt VanderMeer (Lancelot), David B. Heuvelman (Squire Dap), Michael Bunce (Sir Dinadan), William Mulligan (Sir Sagramore), Rob Richardson (Sir Lionel), Blaine Hogan (Mordred), Katherine Harber (Lady Anne), Linda Nourie Foster (Lady Sybil), Collin Jones (Clarius), Laura Jean Smillie (Nimue, Woman of the Court), Patti Perkins (Morgan Le Fey, Woman of the Court), Brett Jones (Tom of Warwick), Anne Lourice Barr, Lara Ianni, Kristen Joy Salico, Allyn Van Dusen (Women of the Court), Andrew Arrow, David Autovino, Evan Harrington, Jens Hinrichsen, Rob Johansen, Nick Mannix, Don Rey, Matt Tappon (Men of the Court)

FIVE-COURSE LOVE by Gregg Coffin; Director, Emma Griffin; Scenic/Costume Design, G.W. Mercier; Lighting Design, Ann Wrightson; Sound Design, Lindsay Jones; June 16–July 11; Cast: Heather Ayers (Barbie, Sofia, Gretchen, Rosalinda, Kitty), John Bolton (Matt, Gino, Klaus, Guillermo, Clutch), Jeff Gurner (Dean, Carlo, Heimlich, Ernesto, Pops) World Premiere

THE GOODMAN THEATRE

Chicago, Illinois
SEVENTY-NINTH SEASON

Artistic Director, Robert Falls; Managing Director, Roche Schulfer

IN THE ALBERT:

THE GOAT, OR, WHO IS SYLVIA? by Edward Albee; Director, Robert Falls; Set Design and Lighting Design, Michael Philippi; Costume Design, Nan Cibula-Jenkins; Sound Design, Richard Woodbury; Production Dramaturg, Tom Creamer; Production Stage Manager, Joseph Drummond; Stage Manager, T. Paul Lynch; September 27–November 2, 2003; Cast: Patrick Clear (Martin), William Dick (Ross), Barbara Robertson (Stevie), Michael Stahl-David (Billy)

THE LIGHT IN THE PIAZZA Book by Craig Lucas; Music and Lyrics by Adam Guettel; Based on the novel by Elizabeth Spencer; Director, Bartlett Sher; Music Director, Ted Sperling; Choreography, Marcela Lorca; Set Design, Michael Yeargan; Costume Design, Catherine Zuber; Lighting Design, Christopher Akerlind; Sound Design, Acme Sound Partners; Orchestrations, Ted Sperling & Adam Guettel; Production Dramaturg, Rick DesRochers; Production Stage Manager, Joseph Drummond; Stage Manager, T. Paul Lynch; January 10–February 22, 2004; Cast: Victoria Clark (Margaret Johnson), Celia Keenan-Bolger (Clara Johnson); Wayne Wilcox (Fabrizio Naccarelli), Mark Harelik (Signor Naccarelli); Patti Cohenour (Signora Naccarelli); Glenn Seven Allen (Guiseppe Naccarelli); Kelli O'Hara (Franca); Andrew Rothenberg (Roy Johnson); Amy Arbizzani (Ensemble), Stephen Rader (Ensemble), Jonathan Raviv (Ensemble), Brooke Sherrod (Ensemble)

CROWNS Written and Directed by Regina Taylor, Adapted from the book by Michael Cunningham & Craig Marberry; Choreography, Dianne McIntyr; Set Design, Riccardo Hernandez; Costume and Hat Design, Emilio Sosa; Lighting Design, Scott Zielinski; Soundscape, Darron L. West; Music Director, William F. Hubbard; Original Arrangements, Linda Twine; Additional Arrangements, David Pleasant & William Hubbard; Dramaturg, Megan Monaghan; Production Stage Manager, Pat. A. Flora; Stage Manager, Anjali Bidani; March 5–April 18, 2004; Cast: John Steven Crowley (Preacher/Man), Desiré Dubose (Yolanda), Tina Fabrique (Mother Shaw), Gail Grate (Wanda), Karan Kendrick (Jeanette), Barbara D. Mills (Mabel), Bernadine Mitchell (Velma), Musicians: e'Marcus Harper (Piano), David Pleasant (Percussion, Traps, Guitar, Harmonica)

HEARTBREAK HOUSE by George Bernard Shaw; Director: Kate Whoriskey; Set Design, Walt Spangler; Costume Design, Catherine Zuber; Lighting Design, Michael Philippi; Original Music and Sound Design, Rob Milburn and Michael Bodeen; Choreographer, Randy Duncan; Dramaturg, Tom Creamer; Production Stage Manager, Joseph Drummond; Stage Manager, T. Paul Lynch; May 1–June 6, 2004; Cast: Alyssa Bresnahan (Hesione Hushabye), Matt DeCaro (Alfred "Boss" Mangan), Mary Beth Fisher (Lady Utterwood); Marin Ireland (Ellie Dunn), Ernest Perry, Jr. (Burglar), Don Reilly (Hector Hushabye), Jerry Saslow (Randall Utterwood),

Catherine Smitko (Nurse Guinnes), Jack Wetherall (Captain Shotover), Will Zahrn (Mazzini Dunn)

ELECTRICIDAD by Luis Alfaro; Director Henry Godinez; Set Design, Riccardo Hernández; Lighting Design, Christopher Akerlind; Sound Design, Ray Nardelli & Joshua Horvath; Original Music, Gustavo Leone; Chorographer, Wilfredo Rivera; Production Dramaturg, Rick DesRochers; Production Stage Manager, Alden Vasquez; Stage Manager, Rolando Linares; June 19–July 25, 2004; Cast: Sandra Marquez (Clemencia), Cecilia Suárez (Electricidad), Charin Alvarez (Ifigenia), Maximino Arciniega Jr. (Orestes), Ivonne Coll (Abuela), Edward Torres (Nino), Laura E. Crotte, Sandra Delgado, Tanya Saracho, Marisabel Suarez (Las Vecincas)

IN THE OWEN

THE PLAY ABOUT THE BABY by Edward Albee; Director, Pam Mackinnon; Set Design, Todd Rosenthal; Costume Design, Birgit Rattenborg Wise; Lighting Design, Robert Christen; Sound Design, André Pluess & Ben Sussman; Production Dramaturg, Rick DesRochers; Production Stage Manager, Kimberly Osgood; Stage Manager, Ellen Hay; September 20–November 2, 2003; Cast, Julie Granata (Girl), Scott Antonucci (Boy), Matt DeCaro (Man), Linda Kimbrough (Woman)

PROOF by David Auburn; Director, Chuck Smith; Set Design, Davis Swayze; Costume Design, Birgit Rattenborg Wise; Lighting Design, Robert Christen; Original Music & Sound Design, Ray Nardelli & Joshua Horvath; Dramaturg, Rick DesRochers; Production Stage Manager, Kimberly Osgood; Stage Manager, Rolando Linares; March 27–April 25, 2004; Cast: Karen Aldridge (Catherine), Ora Jones (Claire), Dwain A. Perry (Hal); Phillip Edward VanLear (Robert)

MOONLIGHT AND MAGNOLIAS by Ron Hutchinson; Director, Steven Robman; Set and Lighting Design, Michael Philippi; Costume Design, Birgit Rattenborg Wise; Sound Design, Richard Woodbury; Dramaturg, Tom Creamer; Production Stage Manager, Kimberly Osgood; Stage Manager, Ellen Hay; May 15–June 13, 2004; Cast: Ron Orbach (David O. Selznick), William Dick (Ben Hecht), Mary Seibel (Miss Poppenghul), Rob Riley (Victor Fleming)

Marin Ireland, Don Reilly, Mary Beth Fisher in *Heartbreak House* PHOTO BY LIZ LAUREN

SPECIAL EVENTS EDWARD ALBEE FESTIVAL
Program One: October 21, October 26 and November 1, 2003

THE ZOO STORY by Edward Albee; Director, Lynn Bernatowicz; Set Design, Todd Rosenthal; Lighting Design, Robert Christen; Costume Design, Rachel Ann Healy; Sound Design, André Pluess & Ben Sussman; Production Dramaturg, Rick DesRochers; Production Stage Manager, Ellen Hay; Stage Managers, Margaret Cangelosi & Deya Friedman; Cast: Steve Key (Jerry), Bradley Armacost (Peter)

THE DEATH OF BESSIE SMITH by Edward Albee; Director, Chuck Smith; Set Design, Todd Rosenthal; Lighting Design, Robert Christen; Costume Design, Rachel Ann Healy; Sound Design, André Pluess & Ben Sussman; Production Dramaturg, Tom Creamer; Production Stage Manager, Ellen Hay; Stage Managers, Margaret Cangelosi & Deya Friedman; Cast: Scott Duff (Intern), Michael A. Torrey (Bernie), Senuwell L. Smith (Jack), Bill McGough (Father), Terrance J. Watts (Orderly), Kati Brazda (Nurse), Jamie Virostko (Second Nurse)

Program Two: October 23, October 26 and November 1, 2003

BOX by Edward Albee; Director, Eric Rosen; Set Design, Todd Rosenthal; Lighting Design, Robert Christen; Costume Design, Rachel Rattenborg Wise; Sound Design, André Pluess & Ben Sussman; Production Dramaturg, Rick DesRochers; Production Stage Manager, Ellen Hay; Stage Managers, Margaret Cangelosi & Deya Friedman; Cast: Linda Kimbrough (Woman)

THE SANDBOX by Edward Albee; Director, Eric Rosen; Set Design, Todd Rosenthal; Lighting Design, Robert Christen; Costume Design, Rachel Rattenborg Wise; Sound Design, André Pluess & Ben Sussman; Production Dramaturg, Rick DesRochers; Production Stage Manager, Ellen Hay; Stage Managers, Margaret Cangelosi & Deya Friedman; Cast: Ted Hoerl (Daddy), Brad Burton (Young Man), Jason McDermott (Musician), Rondi Reed (Mommy), Mary Seibel (Grandma)

FINDING THE SUN by Edward Albee, Director, Eric Rosen; Set Design, Todd Rosenthal; Lighting Design, Robert Christen; Costume Design, Rachel Rattenborg Wise; Sound Design, André Pluess & Ben Sussman; Production Dramaturg, Rick DesRochers; Production Stage Manager, Ellen Hay; Stage Managers, Margaret Cangelosi & Deya Friedman; Cast: Gary Wingert (Henden), Benjamin Newton (Benjamin), James Immekus (Fergus), Scott Duff (Daniel), Caitlin Hart (Gertrude), Tiffany Scott (Abigail), Kati Brazda (Cordelia), Patricia Kane (Edmee)

Program Three: October 25, October 29 and November 2, 2003

MARRIAGE PLAY by Edward Albee; Director, Lou Contey; Set Design, Todd Rosenthal; Lighting Design, Robert Christen; Costume Design, Rachel Ann Healy; Sound Design, André Pluess & Ben Sussman; Production Dramaturg, Tom Creamer; Production Stage Manager, Ellen Hay; Stage Managers, Margaret Cangelosi & Deya Friedman; Cast: Linda Reitner (Gillian), Scott Rowe (Jack)

Wayne Wilcox, Celia Keenan-Bolger in *The Light in the Piazza* PHOTO BY LIZ LAUREN

A CHRISTMAS CAROL by Charles Dickens; Adapted by Tom Creamer; Director, Kate Buckley; Set Design, Todd Rosenthal; Costume Design, Heidi Sue McMath; Lighting Design, Robert Christen; Sound Design, Lindsay Jones; Original Music Composed and Traditional Carols Arranged by Joe Cerqua; Production Stage Manager, Alden Vasquez; Stage Manager, Rolando Linares; November 22–December 27, 2003; Cast: Moshe R. Adams (Dick Wilkins, Young Man); Allen Alvarado (Tiny Tim); Justin Amolsch (Musician); LaShawn Banks (Chestnut Seller, Percy, Gravedigger); William Brown (Ebenezer Scrooge); Christine Bunuan (Martha Cratchit); Lisa Dodson (Ghost of Christmas Past, Mrs. Cratchit); Ray Grae (Fan, Emily Cratchit, Want); Zach Grae (Peter Cratchit, Boy Scrooge); Ricardo Guitierrez (Mr. Crumb); Steven Hinger (Topper, Undertaker); Gregory Hirte (Fiddler, Mr. Sawyer); Hai Tao Huang (Musician); Gregory Isaac (Wreath Seller, Young Scrooge, Ghost of Christmas Future); Regina Leslie (Musician); John Lister (Bob Cratchit, Schoolmaster); Bradley Mott (Mr. Blodget, Mr. Fezziwig, Ghost of Christmas Present); Stefanie Neuhauser (Belle, Young Woman); William J. Norris (Jacob Marley, Old Joe); Robby O'Connor (Pratt, Turkey Boy, Newsboy, Ignorance); Sharon Sachs (Mrs. Fezziwig, Philomena, Charwoman); Robert Schleifer (Mr. Adams, Gravedigger); Kevin Theis (Fred); Estelle Nora de Vendegies (Johnston, Belinda Cratchit), Genevieve VenJohnson (Mrs. Adelle Ortle), Nancy Voigts (Abby, Mrs. Dilber)

GOODSPEED MUSICALS

East Haddam, Connecticut

FORTIETH SEASON

Executive Director: Michael P. Price; Associate Producer: Sue Frost; Music Director: Michael O'Flaherty; General Manager: Harriett Guin-Kittner

ME AND MY GIRL by L. Arthur Rose and Douglas Furber and Music by Noel Gay; Director, Scott Schwartz; Scenic Design, Anna Louizos; Costume Design, David C. Woolard; Lighting Design, Jeff Croiter; April 25–July 5, 2003; Cast: Hunter Bell (Bill Snibson), Bob Dorian (Sir John Tremayne), M'el Dowd (Maria, Duchess of Dene), Ian Knauer (The Hon. Gerald Bolingbrooke), Michele Ragusa (Lady Jacqueline Carstone), Stephen Temperley (Charles Hethersett, the Butler), Becky Watson (Sally Smith), Ron Wisniski (Mr. Parchester, the Family Solicitor), Ken Alan (Ensemble), Todd Anderson (Ensemble), Scott Barnhardt (Ensemble/Understudy for Bill), Sara Braslow (Ensemble), George Cavey (Sir Jasper Tring/Ensemble/Understudy for Sir John), Tammy Colucci (Lady Diss/Ensemble), Peter Cormican (Lord Battersby/Constable/Understudy for Parchester and Hethersett), Christianne Davis (Lambeth Girl/Ensemble), Margot de la Barre (Mrs. Worthington-Worthington/Ensemble/Understudy for Sally), Warren Freeman (Bob Barking/Ensemble/Understudy for Gerald), Marci Reid (Lady Brighton/Ensemble/ Understudy for Jacquie), Marian Steiner (Lady Battersby/Mrs. Brown/Ensemble/ Understudy for Maria, Duchess of Dene), Adam Michael (Telegram Boy)

VERY GOOD EDDIE by Philip Bartholomae and Guy Bolton, Music by Jerome Kern, Lyrics by Schuyler Greene; Director, BT McNicholl; Scenic Design, John Coyne; Costume Design, Suzy Benzinger; Lighting Design, Richard Pilbrow; July 11–October 4, 2003; Cast: Patrick Boll (Percy Darling), Donna Lynne Champlin (Mme. Matroppo), Jay Douglas (Frenchman), Ann Kittredge (Georgina Kettle), Perry Ojeda (Dick Rivers), Randy Rogel (Eddie Kettle), Christianne Tisdale (Elsie Lilly), Gerry Vichi (Clerk & Ship Steward), Alison Walla (Elsie Darling), Jacqueline Bayne (Gay Anne Giddy), James Compton (Fullern A. Goat), Kurt Domoney (Wat Pumkyns), Jennifer Evans (Lily Pond), Paul Lincoln (Dyer Thurst), Gregory Lofts (Tayleurs Dummee), Louise Madison (Alwys Innit), Karen Sieber (Chrystal Poole), Sarah Anders (Swing), Chris Murrah (Swing)

A TREE GROWS IN BROOKLYN by George Abbott and Betty Smith, Music by Arthur Schwartz, Lyrics by Dorothy Fields; Director, Elinor Renfield; Scenic Design, James Noone; Costume Design, Pamela Scofield; Lighting Design, Jeff Croiter; October 10–December 14, 2003; Cast: Adam Heller (Harry), Deven May (Johnny Nolan), Kerry O'Malley (Katie), Steve Routman (Max/Mr. Swanson/Understudy for Harry), Tom Souhrada (Aloysius Moran), Sari Wagner (Cissy), Megan Walker (Hildy), Remy Zaken (Francie), Michael Buchanan (Ensemble/Understudy for Petey and Willie), Todd Buonopane (Willie/Ensemble), Leslie Marie Collins (Della/Ensemble/Understudy for Katie/Hildy/Miss McShane), Zachary Halley (Petey/Ensemble/Understudy for Johnny Nolan), Leslie Klug (Neighborhood Woman/Ensemble), Kevin Loreque (Allie/Ensemble), Mary Jo McConnell (Miss McShane/Ensemble/Understudy for Nellie), Danny Rothman (Ensemble/Understudy for Aloysius Moran), Adam Shonkwiler (Ensemble/Understudy for Allie), Frank Stancati

The Company in *A Tree Grows in Brooklyn* PHOTO BY DIANE SOBOLEWSKI

(Moriarty/Ensemble/ Understudy for Max/Swanson), Amber Stone (Nellie/ Understudy for Cissy), Katy Lin Persutti (Maudie/Ensemble), Nicole Poulter (Understudy for Francie and Maudie)

STAND BY YOUR MAN by Mark St. Germain; Director, Gabriel Barre; Scenic Design, Dennis C. Maulden; Costume Design, Bridget R. Bartlett; Lighting Design, Todd O. Wren; Sound Design, Jay Hilton; May 15–June 8, 2003; Cast: Nicolette Hart (Tammy Wynette), Jim Wann (George Jones), Miles Aubrey (Euple Bryd/Ensemble), Galen Butler (Burt Reynolds/ Ensemble/Music Director), Kevin Fox (Dr. Chapel/Ensemble), Jim Herrernan (Michael Tomlin/Ensemble), Jenny Littleton (Young Tammy/Ensemble), Susan Mansur (MeeMaw/Ensemble), Jim Price (George Richey/Ensemble), Louis Tucci (Billy Sherrill/Ensemble)

CAMILLE CLAUDEL by Nan Knighton, Music by Frank Wildhorn; Director, Gabriel Barre; Scenic Design, Walt Spangler; Costume Design, Constance Hoffman; Lighting Design, Howell Binkley; Sound Design, Acme Sound Partners; August 14–September 7, 2003; Cast: Matt Bogart (Paul Claudel), Linda Eder (Camille Claudel), Rita Gardner (Madame Claudel), Michael Nouri (Auguste Rodin), Milo O'Shea (Monsieur Claudel), John Paul Almon (Ensemble), Timothy W. Bish (Ensemble), Nick Cavarra (Ensemble), Margaret Ann Gates (Ensemble), Natalie Hill (Ensemble), Antonia L. Kitsopoulos (Young Camille), Mayumi Miguel (Ensemble), Tracy Miller (Ensemble), Tricia Paoluccio (Ensemble), Darren Ritchie (Ensemble), Shonn Wiley (Ensemble)

O. HENRY'S LOVERS by Joe DiPietro, Music by Michael Valenti; Director, Gordon Greenberg; Scenic Design, Neil Patel; Costume Design, Catherine Zuber; Lighting Design, Jeff Croiter; Sound Design, Jay Hilton; November 13–December 7, 2003; Cast: John Braden (Porter), Emily Rabon Hall (Johnsy), Celia Keenan-Bolger (Nevada), Megan Lawrence (Sue), Amanda Naughton (Barbara), Richard Roland (Gilbert), Joe Vincent (Jerome)

INDIANA REPERTORY THEATRE
2003–2004 SEASON

Indianapolis, Indiana

THIRTY-FIRST SEASON

Artistic Director: Janet Allen; Managing Director: Daniel Baker

ARCADIA by Tom Stoppard, Director: Peter Amster, Scenic Designer: Russell Metheny, Costume Designer: Gail Brassard, Lighting Designer: Michael Lincoln, Composer: Andrew Hopson, Dialect Coach: Matt Harding. September 23–October 18, 2003. Cast: Elizabeth Ledo (Thomassina Coverly), Jason Bradley (Septimus Hodge), Frederick Marshall (Jellaby), Patrick Dollymore (Ezra Chater), Mark Goetzinger (Richard Noakes), Mary Beth Fisher (Lady Croom), Robert Neal (Captain Edward Brice), Laura T. Fisher (Hannah Jarvis), Maragret Murray (Chloë Coverly), Ben Werling (Bernard Nightingale), Matt Zeigler (Valentine Coverly), Blaine Hogan (Gus Coverly, Augustus Coverly)

THE TURN OF THE SCREW by Jeffrey Hatcher adapted from the book by Henry James, Director: John Green, Scenic Designer: Robert M. Koharchik, Costume Designer: Joel Ebarb, Lighting Designer: Ryan Koharchik, Composer: Frank Felice. October 22–December 13, 2003. Cast: Robert K Johansen (the Man), Jenny McKnight (the woman)

A CHRISTMAS CAROL by Charles Dickens, adapted for the stage by Tom Haas, Director: Priscilla Lindsay, Scenic Designer: Russell Metheny, Costume Designer: Murell Horton, Lighting Designer: Michael Lincoln, Composer: Andrew Hopson, Choreographer: David Hochoy, Associate Lighting Designer: Betsy Cooprider-Bernstein, Musical Director: Charles Manning. November 5–December 24, 2003. Cast: Scott Boulware (Bob Cratchit, Undertaker), Charles Goad (Scrooge), Gerson Dacanay (Fred, Ghost of Christmas Past, Broker), Emily Ristine (Felicity, Fan), Mark Goetzinger (Portly Gentleman, Fezziwig, Topper), Adrienne Cury (Sister of Mercy, Mrs. Fezziwig, Plump Sister), Calvin Smith (Waif, Ignorance, Turkey Boy), Collier Huntley (Waif, Ignorance, Turkey Boy), Lynne Perkins (Mrs. Cratchit, Charwoman), Lorne Batman (Belinda Cratchit), Hannah Kennedy (Belinda Cratchit), Price Suddarth (Peter Cratchit, Adolescent Scrooge, Dick Wilkins), Andrew Flockhart (Peter Cratchit, Adolescent Scrooge, Dick Wilkins), Larry Williams (Tiny Tim, Boy Scrooge), Connor Avery (Tiny Tim, Boy Scrooge), Michael Shelton (Waiter, Young Scrooge, Broker), Robert Neal (Marley, Young Marley, Ghost of Christmas Future), David Alan Anderson (Schoomaster, Old Joe, Ghost of Christmas Present), Ben Ayres (Wilful Smackers, Belle's Husband, Nutley, Broker), Jose Antonio Garcia (Lamplighter, Postboy, Broker, Poulterer's Man), Jennifer Kern (Belle, Roses Sister), Tara Celeste Morton (Betsy Cratchit), Ridley Morgan (Betsy Cratchit), Lauren Morris Bertram (Martha Cratchit, Maid, Laundress)

THE DRAWER BOY by Michael Healey, Director: Janet Allen, Scenic Designer: Ann Sheffield, Costume Designer: Kathleen Egan, Lighting Designer: Ann G. Wrightson, Composer: Greg Coffin, Sound Designer: Todd M. Reischman. January 7–31, 2004. Cast: Mark Goetzinger (Angus), Robert Elliott (Morgan), Jason Bradley (Miles)

MOST VALUABLE PLAYER conceived by Gayle Cornelison, written by Mary Hall Surface, Director: David Alan Anderson, Scenic Designer: Robert M. Koharchik, Costume Designer: Martin Chapman-Bowman, Lighting Designer: Ryan Koharchik, Sound Designer: Todd M. Reischman. January 15–February 28, 2004. Cast: Bryant Bentley (Jackie Robinson), Robert Neal (Leo Durocher, Kevin, Time-keeper, Enos Blackwell, Al Campanis), Robert K Johansen (Pee Wee Reese, Joe, Basketball Player, Larry, McPhail, Clay Hopper), Jeff Keel (Branch Rickey, Chuckie), Kathi Ridley (Mallie Robinson, Rachel Isum Robinson), Jennifer Bohler (Ruth Warton, Helen, Phyllis Hunt, Waitress, Cashier)

JITNEY by August Wilson, Director: Timothy Douglas, Scenic Designer: Tony Cisek, Costume Designer: Tracy Dorman, Lighting Designer: Michael Gilliam, Sound Designer: Vincent Olivieri. February 10–March 6, 2004. Cast: Shane Taylor (Youngblood), Michael W. Howell (Turnbo), Ernest Perry, Jr. (Fielding), Cortez Nance, Jr. (Doub), David Alan Anderson (Shealy), Adrian Bethea (Philmore), Chuck Patterson (Becker), Tymberlee Chanel (Rena), Darryl Theirse (Booster)

ROMEO AND JULIET by William Shakespeare, Director: Priscilla Lindsay, Scenic Designer: Robert M. Koharchik, Costume Designer: Linda Pisano, Lighting Designer: Betsy Cooprider-Bernstein, Sound Designer: Todd M. Reischman, March 10–April 24, 2004. Cast: Andrew C. Ahrens (Romeo), Kailey Bell (Juliet), Charles Goad (Friar Laurence, Servant), Blaine Hogan (Tybalt, Paris), Robert k Johansen (Capulet), Andrew Navarro (Mercutio, Montague), Wendy Rader (Lady Capulet, Apothecary), Ben Tebbe (Benvolio), Milicent Wright (Nurse, Prince)

PRIVATE LIVES by Noël Coward, Director: Michael Donald Edwards, Scenic Designer: Andrew Lieberman, Costume Designer: David Zinn, Lighting Designer: Lenore Doxsee, Sound Designer: Todd M. Reischman. March 23–April 17, 2004. Cast: Naomi Peters (Sybil Chase), Ted Deasy (Elyot Chase), Jay Stratton (Victor Prynne), Lise Bruneau (Amanda Prynne), Sara Locker (Louise)

PLAZA SUITE by Neil Simon, Director: James Still, Scenic Designer: Russell Metheny, Costume Designer: Joyce Kim Lee, Lighting Designer: Michael Lincoln, Sound Designer: Todd M. Reischman. April 27–May 23, 2004. Cast: Christian Stolte (Bellhop, Jesse Kiplinger, Waiter, Borden Eisler), Priscilla Lindsay (Karen Nash, Norma Hubley), Patrick Clear (Sam Nash, Roy Hubley), Jennifer Kern, (Jean McCormack, Muriel Tate, Mimsey Hubley)

Kristin Flanders, Laurence Ballard in *Homebody/Kabul* PHOTO BY CHRIS BENNION

INTIMAN THEATRE

Seattle, Washington
THIRTY-FIRST SEASON

Artistic Director, Bartlett Sher; Managing Director, Laura Penn

NORA, based on **A DOLL'S HOUSE** by Henrik Ibsen; Stage Version by Ingmar Bergman; English Translation by Frederick J. Marker and Lise-Lone Marker; Director, Bartlett Sher; Scenic Design, Matthew Smucker; Costume Design, Deb Trout; Lighting Design, Greg Sullivan; Original Music, Peter John Still; Sound Design, Joseph Swartz; April 18–May 18, 2003; Cast: Laurence Ballard (Doctor Rank), Kristin Flanders (Nora Helmer), Mari Nelson (Mrs. Linde), John Procaccino (Nils Krogstad), Stephen Barker Turner (Torvald Helmer), Olivia Spokoiny (Emmy Helmer)

THE LIGHT IN THE PIAZZA by Craig Lucas (book) and Adam Guettel (music and lyrics) based on the novel by Elizabeth Spencer; Director, Craig Lucas; Choreographer, Pat Graney; Music Director, Ted Sperling; Scenic Design, Loy Arcenas; Costume Design, Catherine Zuber; Lighting Design, Christopher Akerlind; Sound Design, Acme Sound Partners; Orchestrations, Ted Sperling and Adam Guettel; Associate Scenic Designer, John McDermott; Dialect Coach, Deena Burke; May 31–July 19, 2003; Cast: Victoria Clark (Margaret Johnson), Celia Keenan-Bolger (Clara Johnson), Steven Pasquale (Fabrizio Naccarelli), Mark Harelik (Signor Naccarelli), Patti Cohenour (Signora Naccarelli), Glenn Seven Allen (Guiseppe Naccarelli), Kelli O'Hara (Franca), Robert Shampain (Roy Johnson), Jeffrey Froome (Ensemble), Fae Phalen (Ensemble)

BLUE/ORANGE by Joe Penhall; Director, Kate Whoriskey; Scenic Design, Matthew Smucker; Costume Design, Tesse Crocker; Lighting Design, Scott Zielinski; Composer/Sound Design, Matthew McQuilken; July 25–August 24, 2004; Cast: Laurence Ballard (Robert), Ian Brennan (Bruce), Sylvester Foday Kamara (Christopher)

HOMEBODY/KABUL by Tony Kushner; Director, Bartlett Sher; Scenic Design, John Arnone; Costume Design, Elizabeth Caitlin Ward; Lighting Design, Justin Townsend; Sound Design, Peter John Still; Dramaturg,

Mame Hunt; Dialect/Language Coach, Judith Shahn; September 12–October 11, 2003; Cast: Jacqueline Antaramian (Mahala), Laurence Ballard (Milton Ceiling), Ismail Bashey (Khwaja Aziz Mondanabosh), Ed Chemaly (Mullah Ali Aftar Durranni, Zai Garshi), Kristin Flanders (Priscilla Ceiling), Ellen McLaughlin (The Homebody), Simeon Moore (Quango Twistleton), Shanga Parker (Doctor Qari Shah, A Munkrat, A Border Guard), Zaki Abdelhamid (Ensemble), Onkar Meno Sharma (Ensemble)

21 DOG YEARS: DOING TIME @ AMAZON.COM by Mike Daisey; Director, Jean-Michele Daisey; Scenic Design, Edie Whitsett; Lighting Design, Greg Sullivan; Directing Consultant, Dan Fields; October 24–November 22, 2003; Cast: Mike Daisey

BLACK NATIVITY: A GOSPEL SONG PLAY by Langston Hughes; Director, Jacqueline Moscou; Scenic Design, Dana Perreault; Costume Design, Doris E. Landolt Black; Lighting Design, Rick Paulsen; Sound Design, Stephen LeGrand; Musical Direction and Arrangements, Pastor Patrinell Wright; Choreographer, Kabby Mitchell III; November 29–December 28, 2003; Cast: Shannon Davis (Joseph), Cynthia Jones (Narrator), Sylvester Foday Kamara (Narrator), Reverend Dr. Samuel B. McKinney (Narrator), Erricka S. Turner (Mary), Pastor Patrinell Wright (The Woman), The Total Experience Gospel Choir, The Black Nativity Choir, Sonny Byers (Piano), Thaddeus Turner (Lead Guitar), Gerald Turner Jr. (Bass Guitar), Tony Coleman (Drums), Jessica Howard (Percussion)

THIRTY-SECOND SEASON

CROWNS by Regina Taylor, adapted from the book by Michael Cunningham and Craig Marberry; Director, Jacqueline Moscou; Music Direction, Pastor Patrinell Wright; Choreographer, Donald Byrd; Scenic Design, Carey Wong; Costume Design, Catherine Hunt; Lighting Design, Edward P. Bartholomew; Sound Design, Stephen LeGrand; Hat Consultant and Milliner, Henrietta Price; April 30–May 28, 2004; Cast: Gretha Boston (Velma); Doug Eskew (Preacher/Man); Deidrie N. Henry (Mabel); Josephine Howell (Wanda); Cynthia Jones (Mother Shaw), Felicia V. Loud (Yolanda); Shaunyce Omar (Jeanette); Mark Sampson (Musician); Bill Sims Jr. (Musician)

Victoria Clark, Celia Keenan-Bolger in *The Light in the Piazza* PHOTO BY CHRIS BENNION

LA JOLLA PLAYHOUSE

La Jolla, California
FIFTY-SIXTH SEASON

Artistic Director, Des McAnuff; Managing Director, Steven B. Libman

FRÄULEIN ELSE translated and adapted by Francesca Faridany; from the Novella by Arthur Schnitzler; Director, Stephen Wadsworth; Scenic Design, Thomas Lynch; Costume Design, Anna Oliver; Lighting Design, Joan Arhelger; Sound Engineer, Bill Williams; June 10–July 13, 2003; Cast: Francesca Faridany (Fräulein Else), Michael Tisdale (Paul), Lauren Lovett (Cissy), Mary Baird (Mother), Julian López-Morillas (Herr Von Dorsday), Garrett Neergaard (Porter)

THE BURNING DECK by Sarah Schulman; Director, Kirsten Brandt; Inspired by the novel, *Cousin Bette* by Honoré de Balzac; Scenic Design, Ryan Palmer; Costume Design, Ivy Chou; Lighting Design, David Lee Cuthbert; Sound Design, Casi Pacilio; Dramaturg, Carrie Ryan; Fight Director, Colleen Kelly; July 15–August 3, 2003; Cast: Diane Venora (Bette), Lionel Mark Smith (Earl), José Chavarry (Joseph Cadine), Christine Albright (Hortense), Alex Cranmer (Hector Tibbs), Makela Spielman (Valerie Korie), José Chavarry and D.W. Jacobs (Delivery Men), Sandra Ellis-Troy (Crevel), D.W. Jacobs (Frederick)

THE COUNTRY by Martin Crimp; Director, Lisa Peterson; Scenic Design, Rachel Hauck; Costume Design, Joyce Kim Lee; Lighting Design, Christopher Akerlind; Sound Design, Mark Bennett; Dramaturg, Carrie Ryan; July 29–August 31, 2003; Cast: Gary Cole (Richard), Catherine Dent (Corinne), Emily Bergl (Rebecca)

BEAUTY by Tina Landau; Director, Tina Landau; Scenic Design, Riccardo Hernandez; Costume Design, Melina Root; Lighting Design, Scott Zielinski; Original Music and Sound Design, Rob Milburn and Michael Bodeen; Production Dramaturg, Heidi Coleman; September 16–October 19, 2003; Cast: David Ari (Ensemble/Prince), Corey Brill (Ensemble, King Bertrand), Jason Danieley (James), Lisa Harrow (Constance), Simone Vicari Moore (Ensemble/Madeleine), Kelli O'Hara (Rose), Adam Smith (Ensemble/Prince), Amy Stewart (Ensemble/Queen Marguerite), Richard Tibbitts (Musician)

COMEDY OF ERRORS by William Shakespeare; Adapted by Robert Richmond; Created by Peter Meineck and Robert Richmond; Director, Robert Richmond; Producer, Peter Meineck; Production Design, Robert Richmond and Peter Meineck; Composer, Anthony Cochrane; October 14–November 16, 2003; Cast: Alex Webb (Egeon), Andrew Schwartz (Solinus, Duke of Ephesus; Angelo, a goldsmith; Gaoler; Pinch, a doctor), Richard Willis (Antipholus of Syracuse), Louis Butelli (Dromio of Syracuse), John Butelli (Dromio of Ephesus), Lisa Carter (Adriana, wife of Antipholus of Ephesus), Lindsay Rae Taylor (Luciana, sister of Adriana), Heather Murdock (Nell, a kitchen maid), Sheridan Willis (Antipholus of Ephesus), Alex Webb (Balthasar, a merchant), Heather Murdock (Courtesan and Emilia, an abbess)

700 SUNDAYS…BILLY CRYSTAL…A LIFE IN PROGRESS by Billy Crystal; Director, Des McAnuff; Scenic Design, David F. Weiner; Lighting Design, David Lee Cuthbert; Sound/Projection Design, Chris Luessmann; April 20–May 2, 2004; Cast: Billy Crystal

CONTINENTAL DIVIDE: MOTHERS AGAINST by David Edgar; Director, Tony Taccone; Scenic Design, William Bloodgood; Costume Design, Deborah M. Dryden; Lighting Design, Alexander V. Nichols; Sound Design, Jeremy J. Lee; May 25–August 1, 2004; Cast: Michael Elich (Don D'Avanzo), Bill Geisslinger (Sheldon Vine), Paul Vincent O'Connor (Mitchell Vine), Robynn Rodriguez (Connie Vine), Christina Rouner (Lorianna Weiner), Vilma Silva (Caryl Marquez), Derrick Lee Weeden (Vincent Baptiste) Christine Williams (Deborah Vine)

CONTINENTAL DIVIDE: DAUGHTERS OF THE REVOLUTION by David Edgar; Director, Tony Taccone; Scenic Design, William Bloodgood; Costume Design, Deborah M. Dryden; Lighting Design, Alexander V. Nichols; Sound Design, Jeremy J. Lee; May 25–August 1, 2004; Cast: Michelle Duffy (Abby/Beth/Branflake), Michael Elich (Bill/Troy/Zee/Don D'Avanzo), Lynnda Ferguson (Rebecca McKeene), Bill Geisslinger (Ted/Jimmy/Nighthawk/Sheldon Vine), Marielle Heller (Dana/Nancy/Trina/Aquarius), Lorri Holt (Blair Lowe), Terry Layman (Michael Bern), Craig W. Marker (Jack/Darren/Sam/No Shit), Paul Vincent O'Connor (Arnie/Ira/Eddie/Mitchell), Jacob Ming-Trent (Jools/J.C./Rainbow/Bob LeJeune), Robynn Rodriguez (Elaine/Ash/Connie Vine), Christina Rouner (Lorianna Weiner/Firefly), Vilma Silva (Kate/Therese/Yolande/Hoola Hoop), Derrick Lee Weeden (Kwesi Ntuli), Christine Williams (Ryan/Pat/Snowbird)

SUITCASE OR, THOSE THAT RESEMBLE FLIES FROM A DISTANCE by Melissa James Gibson; Director, Daniel Aukin; Scenic Design, Louisa Thompson; Costume Design, Maiko Matsushima; Lighting Design, Matt Frey; Sound Design, Shane Rettig; Projection Design Elaine J. McCarthy; April 20–May 2, 2004; Cast: Christina Kirk (Sallie), Thomas Jay Ryan (Lyle), Colleen Werthmann (Jen)

PARIS COMMUNE by Steven Cosson and Michael Friedman; Music and Lyrics Adapted by Michael Friedman; Director, Steven Cosson; Scenic Design, Kevin Judge; Costume Design, Emily Pepper; Lighting Design, Jennifer Setlow; Sound Design, Walter Trarbach; Choreographer, Jean Isaacs; July 27–August 15, 2004; Cast: Aysan Celik (Mignon), Brad Fleischer (Bakery Owner/Militiaman/others), Stacey Fraser (Soprano), Bruce McKnzie (Pére Duchene), Geno Monteiro (Militiaman/others), Katie Sigismund (Milliner/others), Brian Slaten (Baker/others), Andrew William Smith (Priest/Militiaman/others), Dale Soules (Baker's Mother/others), Lisa Velten (Schoolteacher/others)

THE LOVE OF THREE ORANGES Freely Adapted by Nona Ciobanu; Adapted from a Scenario by Carlo Gozzi; American Adaptation by James Magruder; Director, Nona Ciobanu; Scenic and Costume Design, Iulian Baltatescu and Nona Ciobanu; Lighting Design, and Composer, Iulian Baltatescu; Romanian Adaptation Translated into English. Mihnea Mircan; September 14–October 17, 2004; Cast: John Altieri (Truffaldino/A Clown), Pascale Armand (Ninetta/Mouth/Creonta/A Clown/Morgana's Kid/Dove), Colette Beauvais (Girl 1/Squit/A Clown/Morgana's Kid), Tina Benko (Smeraldina/Celio/Tit/A Clown), Donald Corren (Pantalone/Fata Morgana/Zit), Carmen Gill (A Clown/Morgana's Kid), Owiso Odera (Leandro/Nose/2nd Cowboy/A Clown/Creonta/Morgana's Kid), Jim Parsons (Tartaglia), Time Winters (Silvio/Farfarello/Creonta/1st Cowboy)

JERSEY BOYS Book by Marshall Brickman and Rick Elice; Music by Bob Gaudio; Lyrics by Bob Crewe; Director, Des McAnuff; Choreographer, Sergio Trujillo; Music Director, Ron Melrose; Orchestrator, Steve Orich; Scenic Design, Klara Zierglerova; Costume Design, Jess Goldstein; Lighting Design, Howell Binkley; Sound Design, Steve Canyon Kennedy; Projection Design Michael Clark; October 5–November 21, 2004; Cast: Sarah Avery (Girl Singer/Church Lady/Royal Teen/Angel #1/Lorraine/Ensemble), Tituss Burgess (Yannick/Royal Teen/Hal Miller/Berry Belson/Ohio Officer/Walter/Ensemble), Marisa Echeverría (Girl Singer/Frankie's Mom/Nick's Girlfriend/Miss Frankie Nolan/Angel #2/Francine/Ensemble), Steve Gouveia (Cop/Joey/Dick Clark/Bob Crewe's Production Assistant/New Season 1/Ensemble), Peter Gregus (Bob Crewe/Vince/ Davis/Ensemble), Christian Hoff (Tommy DeVito), Donnie Kehr (Gyp DeCarlo/Royal Teen/Nick DeVito/Billy Dixon/New Season 2/Ensemble), Jennifer Naimo (Girl Singer/Mary/Royal Teen/Angel #3/Ensemble), David Noroña (Frankie Vallie), Joe Payne (Hank), Daniel Reichard (Bob Gaudio), Sean Smith (Judje/Stosh/Royal Teen/Engineer/Norm/Finney/Priest/ Ensemble), J. Robert Spencer (Nick Massi)

MARK TAPER FORUM

Los Angeles, California
THIRTY-SEVENTH SEASON

Artistic Director, Gordon Davidson; Managing Director, Charles Dillingham

HOMEBODY/KABUL by Tony Kushner; Director; Scenic Design, James Schuette; Costume Design, Mara Blumenfeld; Lighting Design, Christopher Akerlind; Original Composition and Sound Design, Joe Cerqua; Casting, Amy Lieberman, CSA, and Erica Daniels; Presented in association with the Steppenwolf Theatre Company; September 21–November 9, 2003; Cast: Firdous Bamji (Khwaja Aziz Mondanabosh), Reed Birney (Milton Ceiling), Bill Camp (Quango Twistleton), Linda Emond (The Homebody), Rahul Gupta (A Munkrat, Border Guard), Maggie Gyllenhaal (Priscilla Ceiling), Maz Jobrani (Dr. Qari Shah)), Dariush Kashani (Zai Garshi), Aasif Mandvi (Mullah Ali Aftar Durranni), Rita Wolf (Mahala, Woman in Burqa), Mueen Jahan Ahmad, Gillian Doyle, Laura Kachergus, John Rafter Lee, Kamal Maray, Shaheen Vaaz (Ensemble).

Viola Davis, Russell Hornsby in *Intimate Apparel* PHOTO BY CRAIG SCHWARTZ

LIKE JAZZ Music, Cy Coleman; Lyrics, Alan and Marilyn Bergman; Writer, Larry Gelbart; Musical Staging and Choreography, Patricia Birch; Director, Gordon Davidson; Scenic Design and Lighting, D Martyn Bookwalter; Costume Design, Judith Dolan; Sound Design, Jon Gottlieb and Philip G. Allen; Projection Design, Marc I. Rosenthal; Music Director, Tom Kubis; Casting, Amy Lieberman, CSA; Presented in association with Transamerica; World Premiere; November 21, 2003–January 25, 2004; Cast: Patti Austin, Bill Cantos, Jennifer Chada, Cleavant Derricks, Katy Durham, Harry Groener, Dameka Hayes, Rick Jarrett, Tom Kubis, Greg Poland, Margo Reymundo, Nicki Richards, Jack Sheldon, Timothy Ware, Lillias White, Carlton Wilborn, Natalie Willes; Chuck Berghofer, Ray Brinker, Rich Bullock, Stu Blumberg, Pete Christlieb, Keith Fiddmont, Ramon Flores, Jennifer Hall, Gary Halopoff, Tamir Hendelman, Michael Higgins, Rusty Higgins, Alan Kaplan, Wendell Kelly, Sal Lozano, Warren Luening, Charlie Morillas (Musicians)

TOPDOG/UNDERDOG by Suzan-Lori Parks; Director, George C. Wolfe; Assistant Director, Raelle Myrick-Hodges; Scenic Design, Riccardo Hernández; Costume Design, Emilio Sosa; Lighting Design, Scott Zielinski; Sound Design, Dan Moses Schreier; Casting, Jordan Thaler and Amy Lieberman, CSA; Presented in association with Seattle Repertory Company; February 1–March 28, 2004; Cast: Larry Gilliard, Jr. (Booth) and Harold Perrineau (Lincoln)

THE TALKING CURE by Christopher Hampton; Director, Gordon Davidson; Scenic Design and Projected Images, Peter Wexler; Costume Design, Durinda Wood; Lighting Design, Paulie Jenkins; Sound Design, Philip G. Allen; Original Music, Kark Fredrik Lundeberg; Casting, Amy Lieberman, CSA; Fight Director, Steve Rankin; Wigs and Hair Design, Carol F. Doran; American premiere; April 4–May 23, 2004; Cast: Abby Brammell (Sabina Spielrein), Sue Cremin (Emma Jung), Taylor Daubens (Agathe Jung), John Hansen (Orderly), Bruce Katzman (S.S. Officer), Henri Lubatti (Otto Gross), P.J. Marino (Orderly), Shiva Rose McDermott (Nurse), Emily Rose Morris (Russian Girl/Gret Jung), Sam Robards (Carl Gustav Jung), Libby West (Nurse), Harris Yulin (Sigmund Freud)

STONES IN HIS POCKETS by Marie Jones; Director, Neel Keller; Scenic Design, Richard Hoover; Costume Design, Candice Cain; Lighting Design, Rand Ryan; Sound Design, Jon Gottlieb; Musical Staging, Ken Roht; Casting, Amy Lieberman, CSA; May 29–July 18, 2004; Cast: JD Cullum (Jake) and Barry McEvoy (Barry McEvoy)

INTIMATE APPAREL by Lynn Nottage; Director, Dan Sullivan; Scenic Design, Derek McLane; Costume Design, Catherine Zuber; Lighting Design, Allen Lee Hughes; Sound Design, Marc Gwinn; Music, Harold Wheeler; Casting, Mele Nagler and Amy Lieberman, CSA; the Roundabout Theatre Company production; July 27–September 12, 2004; Cast: Arija Bareikis (Mrs. Van Buren), Viola Davis (Esther), Lynda Gravátt (Mrs. Dickson), Russell Hornsby (George), Corey Stoll (Mr. Marks), Lauren Velez (Mayme)

MCCARTER THEATRE

Princeton, New Jersey
SEVENTY-FOURTH SEASON

Artistic Director, Emily Mann; Managing Director, Jeffrey Woodward

ANNA IN THE TROPICS by Nilo Cruz; Director, Emily Mann; Set Design, Robert Brill; Costume Design, Anita Yavich; Lighting Design, Peter Kaczorowski; Sound Design, Dan Moses Schreier; September 9–October 19, 2003; Cast: Victor Argo (Santiago), Vanessa Aspillaga (Marela), John Ortiz (Eliades/Palomo), Jimmy Smits (Juan Julian), Priscilla Lopez (Ofelia), Daphne Rubin-Vega (Conchita), David Zayas (Cheché)

WINTERTIME by Charles Mee; Director, David Schweizer; Set Design, Andrew Lieberman; Costume Design, David Zinn; Lighting Design, Kevin Adams; Sound Design, Eric Shim; October 14-November 2, 2003; Cast: McCaleb Burnett (Jonathan), Brienin Bryant (Ariel), Marsha Mason (Maria), Michael Cerveris (Francois), Nicholas Hormann (Frank), T. Scott Cunningham (Edmund), Carmen deLavallade (Bertha), Lola Pashalinski (Hilda), Danny Mastrogiorgio (Bob), Tina Benko (Jacqueline)

David Zayas, Jimmy Smits, John Ortiz, Daphne Rubin-Vega, Vanessa Aspillaga in
Anna in the Tropics PHOTO BY T. CHARLES ERICKSON

A CHRISTMAS CAROL by Charles Dickens; Adaptation by David Thompson; Director, Michael Unger, Scenic Design, Ming Cho Lee; Costume Design, Jess Goldstein; Lighting Design, Stephen Strawbridge; Sound Design, Brian Ronan; Original Music & Lyrics, Michael Starobin; Choreography, Rob Ashford, Musical Director, Charles Sundqvist; Choreography supervisor, Casey Nicholaw; December 9–28, 2003; Cast: Jason Bowcutt (Young Scrooge/Mr. Bonds), Nora Cole (Christmas Present), Aloysius Gigl (Marley/Mr.Stocks), Grace Hsu (Lily/Belle), John Jellison (Mr.Fezziwig/Old Joe), John Christopher Jones (Scrooge), Susan Knight (Mrs. Cratchit), James Ludwig (Fred), Doan Ly (Fan/Mrs. Bonds), Anne O'Sullivan (Mrs. Fezziwig/Mrs. Stocks/Laundress), Daniel Pearce (Mr. Cratchit), Susan Pelligrino (Mrs. Dilber), Danny Hallowell (Tiny Tim), Jesse Girard (Peter Cratchit), Ben Schindel (Young Marley), Ben Taub (Young Scrooge), Mackenzie King (Belinda Cratchit), Sheridan Gates (Martha Cratchit), Hilary Zipperstein (Christmas Past 1), Kimaya Abreu (Christmas Past 2), Sara-Kate Levy (Christmas Past 3), Amy Hallowell (Begger Girl), Desmond Confoy (Begger Boy), Rachael Haber (Fezziwig Party Girl), Abby Mycek (Alice the Cook), Esther Ammon (Charlotte Fezziwg), Chorus: Derek Travis Collard, Molly A. Curry, Abby Feldman, Michael Francis, Joshua Furr, Patrick Pastor, Brian Pollack, Oron Stenesh, Randi Lynn Strong, Sarah Zeitler

FRÄULEIN ELSE, an adaptation by Francesca Faridany from the novella by Arthur Schnitzler; Director, Stephen Wadsworth; Set Design, Thomas Lynch; Costume Design, Anna Ruth Oliver; Lighting Design, Joan Arhelger; Sound Design, Bill Williams; January 6–February 15, 2004; Cast: Francesca Faridany (Else), Michael Tisdale (Paul), Lauren Lovett (Cissy), Mary Baird (Mother), Julian López-Morillas (Herr von Dorsday), Omid Abtahi (Porter)

CANDIDA by George Bernard Shaw, Director, Lisa Peterson; Set Design, Neil Patel; Costume Design, Michael Krass; Lighting Design, David Weiner; Sound Design, Mark Bennet; Vocal Consultant, Ralph Zito; March 23–April 11, 2004; Cast: Polly Lee (Proserpine), Michael Siberry (Morell), Michael Milligan (Lexy), Robert Langdon Lloyd (Burgess), Kate Forbes (Candida), Jeffrey Carlson (Marchbanks)

MY FAIR LADY, Book and Lyrics by Alan Jay Lerner, Music by Frederick Loewe, Director, Gary Griffin; Musical Director, Thomas Murray; Set Design, John Culbert; Costume Design, Nan Cibula-Jenkins; Lighting Design, Chris Binder; Sound Design, Dan Moses Schreier; Dialect Coach, Stephen Gabis; May 4–June 27, 2004; Cast: Jane Connell (Mrs. Higgins), Michael Cumpsty (Professor Henry Higgins), Jeff Edgerton (Harry/Charles/Prince of Transylvania), Kate Fry (Eliza Doolittle), Stephen Mo Hanan (Jamie/Butler/Lord Boxington/Zoltan Karpathy), Simon Jones (Colonel Hugh Pickering), Patricia Kilgarriff (Mrs. Pearce), Brenda Martindale (Mrs. Eynsford-Hill, Mrs. Hopkins), Michael McCarty (Alfred P. Doolittle), Jim Stanek (Freddy Eynsford-Hill)

THE OLD GLOBE

San Diego, California
SIXTY-NINTH SEASON

Artistic Director, Jack O'Brien; Executive Director, Louis G. Spisto

ROUGH CROSSING by Tom Stoppard; Director, Stan Wojewodski; Scenic Design, John Coyne; Costume Design, Katherine Roth; Lighting Design, David F. Segal; Sound Design, Paul Peterson; September 13–October 23, 2003; Cast: Alan Coates (Ivor), Christian Clemenson (Gal), Adam Greer (Adam), Mark Nelson (Dvornichek), Jennifer Roszell (Natasha), Marc Vietor (Turai), Deborah Annette Heinig, Bethany Smith, Emmelyn Thayer (Ladies of the Chorus)

BLUE/ORANGE by Joe Penhall; Director, Richard Seer; Scenic Design, Robin Sanford Roberts; Costume Design, Charlotte Devaux; Lighting Design, Chris Rynne; Sound Design, Paul Peterson; September 19–October 26, 2003; Cast: Teagle F. Bougere (Christopher), Brian Hutchison (Bruce), Ned Schmidtke (Robert)

HOW THE GRINCH STOLE CHRISTMAS! by Timothy Mason; Music, Mel Marvin; Director, Jack O'Brien; Scenic Design, John Lee Beatty; Costume Design, Robert Morgan; Lighting Design, Pat Collins; Sound Design, Paul Peterson; Choreography, John DeLuca; Musical Direction, Phil Reno; Conductor, Lisa LeMay; November 9–December 31, 2003; Cast: David Brannen (Grinch), Rusty Ross (Young Max), Ken Page (Old Max), Steve Gunderson (J.P. Who), Melinda Gilb (Mama Who), Robert MacAulay (Grandpa Who), Eileen Bowman (Grandma Who), Shawn Sullivan/Natalie Verhulst (Cindy Lou Who alternate parts), David Cabinian (Boo Who), Nicholas Felizardo (Danny Who), Jennica Vargas (Annie Who), Alexa Haley Bergman, Mary Frances McClay (Betty Who), Alex Apostolides, Danielle Forsgren, Phil Johnson,Warren G. Nolan, Jr., James Vasquez, Jessa Watson (Grown-up Who Ensemble), Alejandra Jimenez, Charlotte Mary Wen (Teen Who), Ari Lerner, Anna Strickland, Kathleen Sullivan, Joy Newbegin, Gina Holslag, Caroline Hyatt, Steven Jones, Rebecca Lauren Meyers, Corey Hable, Anita Deshea Lewis, Shanna McCue (Children's Ensemble)

STRIKING 12 by Brendan Milburn, Rachel Sheinkin, Valerie Vigoda; Director, Ted Sperling; Scenic Design, David Ledsinger; Costume Design, Shelly Williams; Lighting Design, Michael Gilliam; Sound Design, Rob Killenberger; December 7–December 31, 2003; Cast: Gene Lewin (Gene), Brendan Milburn (Brendan), Valerie Vigoda (Valerie)

LA PASTORELA DE FELICIDAD by Max Branscomb; Director, William Virchis; Music Director, Don Higginbotham; Music Arranger, Michael Campos; Scenic Design, Anna Louizos, Costume Design, April Lowry-Leon; Lighting/Sound Design, Keoni; December 12–December 28, 2003; Cast: Paul Araujo (Chivera), Bob Bartholomew (Gaspar), Oriana Clark (Maria), Sylvia Enrique (Menga), Timothy Paul Evans (Satan), Michelle Ezroj (Arminda), Goyo Flores (Soledad), Christine Marie Rose Gonzales (Corazón), Melody Gonzales (Archangel Gabriel), Rhys Green (Moloch), Willie Green (Archangel Michael), José Herrera, Arturo Medina (Bato), Anthony Moya (Bartolo), Jaime Orphanos (Jose), Megan Orphanos (Michaela), John Padilla (Lucifer), Monique Padilla (Chantal), Erica Yazdan Parast (Envy), Hector Rivera (Crespo), Evita Rodriguez (Veruta), Sandra Ruiz (Gila), Geneva Stroh-Melton (Estrella/Star of Belen), Gail Teran (Popo), Larry Trouba (Raul); Band: Michael Campos (Guitar), Don Higginbotham (Guitar/Keyboards), Patrick Noyes (Bass), Juan Sanchez (Percussion)

Sarah Rafferty, Kristin Fiorella in *SkyGirls* PHOTO BY CRAIG SCHWARTZ

SKY GIRLS by Jenny Laird; Director, Brendon Fox; Scenic Design, Russell Metheny; Costume Design, Holly Poe Durbin; Lighting Design, Jennifer Setlow; Sound Design, Lindsay Jones; January 10–February 15, 2004; Cast: Kristin Fiorella (DeLang), Judith Hawking (Jackie Cochran), Breean Julian (Lil), Jennifer Lynn McMillan (Breeny), Sarah Rafferty (Mags), Carolyn Stone (Bishop); West Coast premiere

BUS STOP by William Inge; Director, Joseph Hardy; Scenic Design, Robin Sanford Roberts; Costume Design, Robert Morgan; Lighting Design, Aaron Copp; Sound Design, Paul Peterson; January 24–February 29, 2004; Cast: DeAnna Driscoll (Grace), Ben Fox (Bo), Christian Kauffman (Will Masters), Kevin Mahoney (Carl), Johnathan McMurtry (Dr. Lyman), Stephen Payne (Virgil Blessing), Kate Steele (Cherie), Karen Zippler (Elma Duckworth)

TWO SISTERS AND A PIANO by Nilo Cruz; Director, Karen Carpenter; Scenic Design, Kris Stone; Costume Design, Charlotte Devaux; Lighting Design, Chris Rynne; Sound Design, Paul Peterson; March 6–April 11, 2004; Cast: Gloria Garayua (Sofia), Phillip Hernandez (Lt. Portuondo), Jesse Ontiveros (Victor Manuel), Socorro Santiago (Maria Celia)

RESURRECTION BLUES by Arthur Miller; Director, Mark Lamos; Scenic Design, Riccardo Hernandez; Costume Design, Lewis Brown; Lighting Design, York Kennedy; Sound Design, Paul Peterson; March 20–April 25, 2004; Cast: Bruce Bohne (Stanley), Chris Henry Coffrey (Skip L. Cheeseboro), Daniel Davis (Henri Schultz), John de Lancie (General Felix Barriaux), Michael Doyle (Phil, a cameraman), Jenni-Lynn McMillan (Sarah, a soundwoman), Mike Newman (Soldier), Jennifer Regan (Emily Shapiro), Neil Shah (Police Captain), Dana Slamp (Jeanine), Jennifer Stewart (Nurse), Karen Zippler (2nd Soldier); West Coast premiere

THE FOOD CHAIN by Nicky Silver; Director, Matt August; Scenic Design, James Noone; Costume Design, Holly Poe Durbin; Lighting Design, Chris Rynne; Sound Design, Paul Peterson; April 24–May 30, 2004; Cast: Paolo Andino (Serge), Rod Brogan (Ford), Michael Lluberes (Otto), Christa Scott-Reed (Amanda), Marilyn Sokol (Bea)

DON JUAN by Molière; Directed and adapted by Stephen Wadsworth; Scenic Design, Kevin Rupnik; Costume Design, Anna Oliver; Lighting Design, Joan Arhelger; Sound Design, Chris Walker; Choreographer, Danny Pelzig; May 8–June 13, 2004; Cast: Mary Bacon (Charlotte/Ragotin), Gilbert Cruz (Gusman/The Statue), M. Burton Curtis (Pierrot/Pauper/La Violette), Francesca Faridany (Donna Elvira/Don Alonso), Laura Kenny (Mathurine/Mr. Dimanche), Laurence O'Dwyer (Prologue Player/Don Luis), Adam Stein (Don Juan), Bruce Turk (Don Carlos/La Remee), Andrew Weems (Sganarelle), Ross Hellwig, Edelen McWilliams, Jon A. Sampson (Multiple Roles)

SUMMER FESTIVAL 2004

ANTONY AND CLEOPATRA by William Shakespeare; Director, Darko Tresnjak; Scenic Design, Ralph Funicello; Costume Design, Linda Cho; Lighting Design, York Kennedy; Sound Design, Christopher Walker; June 25–August 3, 2004; Cast: Brian Bielawsky (Canidius/Pompey's Soldier), Rod Brogan (Dercetas/Pompey's Soldier), Liam Craig (Thydias/Menas), Bree Elrod (Iras), Matthew Gaydos (Antony's Soldier), Graham Hamilton (Taurus/Varrius), Charles Janasz (Agrippa), Katie MacNichol (Octavia), Jenni-Lynn McMillan (Cleopatra's Maid/Whore/Clown), Jonathan McMurtry (Lepidus/Old Soldier), Edelen McWilliams (Caesar's Soldier), Michael Newman (Mardian), James Joseph O'Neill (Octavius), Gregor Paslawsky (Maecenas), Jon Sampson (Procelius/Menercetas), Brian Sgambati (Pompey/Scarus), Neil Shah (Alexas), Daniel Jay Shore (Dolabella/Pompey's Soldier), Dan Snook (Antony), Jennifer Stewart (Caesar's Soldier), Carolyn Stone (Antony's Soldier), Sara Surrey (Cleopatra), Greg Thornton (Enobarbus), Deborah Taylor (Charmian), Bruce Turk (Soothsayer/Euphronius), Michael Wrynn (Diomedes), Zura Young (Cleopatra's Maid)

AS YOU LIKE IT by William Shakespeare; Director, Karen Carpenter; Scenic Design, Ralph Funicello; Costume Design, Lewis Brown; Lighting Design, York Kennedy; Sound Design, Christopher Walker; Composer, Karl Fredrik Lundberg; June 29–October 1, 2004; Cast: Daniel Jay Shore (Orlando), Jonathan McMurtry (Adam/Corin), James Joseph O'Neil (Oliver), Neil Shah (Dennis/William), Rod Brogan (Charles the Wrestler), Katie MacNichol (Rosalind), Edelen McWilliams (Celia), Gregor Paslawsky (Touchstone), Bruce Turk (Le Beau/Amiens), Greg Thornton (Duke Frederick/Duke Senior), Ross Hellwig (Lord/Hymen), Matthew Gaydos/Brian Bielawski (Lords), Michael Wrynn (Silvius), Charles Janasz (Jaques), Deborah Taylor (Audrey), Michael Newman (Sir Oliver Martext/Priest/Jaques de Boys), Jennifer Stewart (Phebe/Hisperia), Zura Young/Jon A. Sampson (Servants)

THE TWO NOBLE KINSMEN by William Shakespeare and John Fletcher; Director, Darko Tresnjak; Scenic Design, Ralph Funicello; Costume Design, Linda Cho; Lighting Design, York Kennedy; Sound Design, Christopher Walker; July 2–September 24, 2004; Cast: Brian Bielawsky (Soldier), Rod Brogan (Pirithous), Liam Craig (Wooer), Bree Elrod (Jailer's Daughter), Matthew Gaydos (Valerius/Countryman), Graham Hamilton (Palamon), Charles Janasz (Doctor), Jenni-Lynn McMillan (Amazon/Flavina/Venus), Michael Newman (Soldier), Gregor Paslawsky (Jailer), Brian Sgambati (Arcite), Dan Snook (Theseus), Carolyn Stone (Amazon/Diana), Sara Surrey (Hippolyta), Karen Zippler (Emilia)

Adam Stein, Mary Bacon in *Don Juan* PHOTO BY CRAIG SCHWARTZ

PASADENA PLAYHOUSE
STATE THEATRE OF CALIFORNIA

Pasadena, California

EIGHTY-FIRST SEASON

Artistic Director, Sheldon Epps; Executive Director, Lyla White; Managing Director, Brian Colburn

TALLEY'S FOLLY by Landford Wilson; Director, Andrews J. Traister; Scenic Design, D. Martyn Bookwalter; Costume Design, Alex Jaeger; Lighting Design, Dennis Parichy; Sound Design, Matthew Spiro; January 9–February 15, 2004; Cast: Michael Santo (Matt Friedman), Angela Reed (Sally Talley)

DIRTY BLONDE by Claudia Shear; Director, James Lapine; Scenic Design, Douglas Stein; Costume Design, Susan Hilferty; Lighting Design, David Lander; Sound Design, Dan Moses Schreier; February 27–April 4, 2004; Cast: Claudia Shear (Joe/Mae), Tom Riis Farrell (Charlie), Bob Stillman (Man)

ENCHANTED APRIL by Matthew Barber (From the Novel by Elizabeth Von Arnim); Director, Michael Wilson; Scenic Design, Tony Straiges; Costume Design, Alejo Vietti; Lighting Design, Rui Rita; Music and Sound Design, John Gromada; Casting, Julia Flores; April 16–May 23, 2004; Cast: Marriette Hartley (Mrs. Graves), Nancy Bell (Lotty Wilton), Chris Conner (Antony Wilding), Blake Lindsley (Rose Arnott), Monette Magrath (Lady Cariline Bramble), Michael James Reed (Mellersh Wilton), Daniel Reichert (Frederick Arnott), Jayne Taini (Constanza)

110 IN THE SHADE by N. Richard Nash, Music by Harvey Schmidt, Lyrics by Tom Jones; Scenic Design, Roy Christopher; Costume Design, Randy Gardell; Lighting Design, Michael Gilliam; Sound Design, Frederick W. Boot; Casting, Bruce H. Newberg C.S.A.; June 18–July 25, 2004; Cast: Marin Mazzie (Lizzie Curry), Jason Danieley (Starbuck), Stuart Ambrose (Joe Copeland), Jessica Burrows (Beverly Copeland), Christopher Callen (Maurine Toops), Ben Davis (File), Lyle Kanouse (H.C. Curry), Brad Keating (George Curtis), Adam Lambert (Phil Mackey), Bob Lauder Jr. (Gil Demby), Alli Mauzey (Snooky Updegraff), Rachel Strutt (Sammie-Sue Miller), Mary Van Arsdel (Hannah Curtis), Tom Wilson (Noah Curry), Adam Wylie (Jimmy Curry)

VINCENT IN BRIXTON by Nicholas Wright; Director, Elina de Santos; Scenic Design, John Iacovelli; Costume Design, Maggie Morgan; Lighting Design, Leigh Allen; Sound Design, Pierre Dupree; august 13–September 19, 2004; Cast: Tracie Lockwood (Anna Van Gogh), Graham Miller (Vincent Van Gogh), Trevor Murphy (Sam Plowman), Carolyn Palmer (Eugenie Loyer), Stephanie Zimbalist (Ursula Loyer)

The Company in *110 In the Shade* PHOTO BY CRAIG SCHWARTZ

SIDE BY SIDE BY SONDHEIM with Music & Lyrics by Stephen Sondheim, Music by Leonard Berstein, Mary Rodgers, Richard Rodgers, Jule Styne & Continuity by Ned Sherrin; Director, Nick DeGruggio; Musical Director, Dean Mora; Choreographer, Lee Martino; Scenic Design, Tom Giamario; Costume Design, Alex Jaeger; Lighting Design, Steven Young; Sound Design, Pierre Dupree; October 8–November 21, 2004; Cast: Davis Gaines, Juli Dixon Jackson, Teri Ralston.

PLAID TIDINGS by Stuart Ross; Original Musical Continuity, Supervision & Arrangements, James Raitt; Director and Musical Staging, Stuart Ross; Musical Director, David Snyder; Scenic Design, Neil Peter Jampolis; Costume Design, Debra Stein; Lighting Design, Jane Reisman; Sound Design, Frederick W. Boot; December 3–23, 2004; Cast: Stan Chandler (Jinx), David Engel (Smudge), Larry Raben (Sparky), Michael Winther (Frankie).

Michael Winther, Stan Chandler, David Engel, Larry Raben in *Plaid Tidings*
PHOTO BY CRAIG SCHWARTZ

PITTSBURGH PUBLIC THEATER

Pittsburgh, Pennsylvania
TWENTIETH SEASON

Ted Pappas, Artistic & Executive Director

THE MIKADO by Gilbert and Sullivan. Director and choreographer, Ted Pappas. Scenic Design, James Noone. Musical Director, F. Wade Russo. Costume Design, Howard Tsvi Kaplan. Lighting Design, Dennis Parichy. Sound Design, Zach Moore. Orchrestrator, Dan Delange. September 25–October 26, 2003. Cast: Kenneth Kantor (Mikado). John Matthew Morgan (Nanki-Poo). Frederick Reeder (Ko-Ko). Dennis Jesse (Pooh-Bah). Larry Daggett (Pish-Tush). Catrina Lennon (Yum-Yum). Sarah Anne Lewis (Pitti-Sing). Haviland Stillwell (Peep-Bo). Melissa Parks (Katisha). Will Erat, Amy Fitts, Zanna Fredland, Laura Gersh, Ellen Victoria Graham, Yugo Ikach, Daniel Krell, Erik Nelson, Laura Yen Solito, Lou S. Valenzi, John Whitney, Michael Zegraski (Chorus).

THE CHIEF (WORLD PREMIERE) by Rob Zellers and Gene Collier. Directed by Ted Pappas. Scenic and Costume Designer, Anne Mundell. Lighting Designer, Phil Monat. Sound Designer, Zach Moore. November 6–December 14, 2003. Cast: Tom Atkins (Art Rooney).

THE SUBJECT WAS ROSES by Frank D. Gilroy. Directed by Rob Ruggiero. Scenic Designer, Michael Schweikardt. Costume Designer, Jess Goldstein. Lighting Designer, John Lasiter. Sound Designer, Fitz Patton. January 22–February 22, 2004. Cast: Ross Bickell (John Cleary). Carole Monferdini (Nettie Cleary). Joe Delafield (Timmy Cleary).

ACCIDENTAL DEATH OF AN ANARCHIST by Dario Fo. Directed by Richard Hamburger. Scenic Designer, Leiko Fuseya. Costume Designer, Linda Cho. Lighting Designer, Stephen Strawbridge. Sound Designer, David Budries. March 4–April 4, 2004. Cast: Robert Dorfman (The Maniac). Sean Runnette (Inspector Bertozzo). Marcus Neely (Police Officer). Doug Jackson (Police Officer). Craig Bockhorn (Deputy Police Chief). Jerry Russell (Commissioner). Patricia Hodges (Journalist)

THINGS OF DRY HOURS (world premiere) by Naomi Wallace. Directed by Israel Hicks. Scenic Designer, James Noone. Costume Designer, Gabriel Berry. Lighting Designer, Phil Monat. Sound Designer and Original Music, Fitz Patton. April 15–May 16, 2004. Cast: Rosalyn Coleman (Cali Hogan). Roger Robinson (Tice Hogan). Robert Sedgwick (Corbin Teel).

MARY STUART by Friedrich Schiller. Directed by Ted Pappas. Scenic Designer, James Noone. Costume Designer, Paul Tazewell. Lighting Designer, Kirk Bookman. Composer, Michael Moricz. Sound Designer, Zach Moore. May 27–June 27, 2004. Cast: Jill Tanner (Hannah Kennedy). Edward James Hyland (Sir Amias Paulet). Deirdre Madigan (Mary Stuart, Queen of Scots). Adam Ludwig (Sir Edward Mortimer). Ross Bickell (Lord Burleigh). Doug Mertz (Earl of Kent). Douglas Harmsen (Sir William Davison). Lisa Harrow (Elizabeth I, Queen of England). John Shepard (Count L'Aubespine).

Kenneth Boys (Count Bellievre). Robert Haley (Earl of Shrewsbury). John Feltch (Earl of Leicester). Corey Rieger (O'Kelly). David Crawford (Sir Andrew Melvil). Elena Alexandratos (Margaret Curl). David W. Dietz, III (Page). Ross A. Donaldson (Officer of the Guard)

THE PEOPLE'S LIGHT & THEATRE CO.

Malvern, Pennsylvania
TWENTY-NINTH SEASON

Artistic Director, Abigail Adams; Managing Director, Grace E. Grillet

ONCE IN A LIFETIME by George S. Kaufman & Moss Hart; Director, Lou Jacob; Scenic Design, James F. Pyne, Jr.; Costume Design, Ilona Somogyi; Lighting Design, Thomas Hase; Sound Design, Lindsay Jones; Mainstage: May 21–June 15, 2003; Cast: David Ingram (Jerry), Mary Elizabeth Scallen (May), Benjamin Lloyd (George), Erin Brese (Page/Bridesmaid), Peter DeLaurier (Headwaiter/Fulton/Flick/Cameraman), Mark Del Guzzo (Chauffer/Policeman/Schlepkin/Page), Jennie Eisenhower (Florabel/Script Girl), Lenny Haas (Bellboy/Sullivan/Leading Man/Tieman), Mark Lazar (1st Man/Schlepkin/Kammerling/Reporter), Larry Grant Malver (Lawrence Vail/Chauffer/Light man/Biographer), Paul Meshejian (Glogauer/Porter), Karen Elizabeth Peakes (Phyllis Fontaine/Office Girl/Secretaries), Roslyn Ruff (Cigarette Girl/Miss Leighton/Bridesmaid), Marcia Saunders (Helen Hobart/Mrs. Walker), Amanda Schoonover (Coat Check Girl/ Miss Chasen), Tom Teti (2nd Man/Schlepkin/Meterstein/Weisskopf/Bishop), Elizabeth Webster (Susan Walker/1st Girl)

THE LITTLE RED RIDING HOOD SHOW [world premiere] by Russell Davis; Director, Abigail Adams; Scenic Design, Scott Weldin; Costume Design, Marla J. Jurglanis; Lighting Design, Dennis Parichy; Sound Design, Charles T. Brastow; Steinbright Stage June 18–July 27, 2003; Cast: Anne Berkowitz (Jennifer-Little Red), Jan Lucas (her Mother), John Lumia (Malarkey, a wolf), Alda Cortese (a Grandmother)

LOOKING OVER THE PRESIDENT'S SHOULDER Written and Directed by James Still; Scenic Design, Russell Methany; Costume Design, Kathleen Egan; Lighting Design, Darren McCroom; Sound Design, Michael Keck; Mainstage July 9–August 3, 2003; Cast: David Alan Anderson (Alonzo Fields)

MIDONS—OR THE OBJECT OF DESIRE (world premiere) Written and Directed by Lillian Groag; Scenic Design, John Conklin; Costume Design, Tracy Dorman; Lighting Design, Russell Champa; Sound Design, Charles T. Brastow; Mainstage September 17–October 12, 2003; Cast: Susan McKey (the Lady/the Falcon/the Moon), Marcia Saunders (the Countess of Montfort/the Pigboy), Kathryn Petersen (the Duchess of Castelnau/Fanette), Kevin Bergen (the Troubadour/Vidal/Jehan), Tom Teti (the Lord/Archbishop of Foix/Capet), Stephen Novelli (the Abbott/Montfort/Master Aubin/Andreas), David Ingram (the Knight/theFalconer), Scott Boulware (Servant/Falconer's Man/Visored Knight/Monk/Herald)

(CONTINUED ON NEXT PAGE)

(CONTINUED FROM PREVIOUS PAGE)

THE FANTASTICKS by Tom Jones & Harvey Schmidt; Director, Tazewell Thompson; Scenic Design, Donald Eastman; Costume Design, Marla J. Jurglanis; Lighting Design, Jorge Arroyo; Musical Direction, Charles Gilbert; Steinbright Stage October 15–December 14, 2003; Cast: Forest McClendon (El Gallo), Shelley Thomas (Luisa), John Wernke (Matt), Jim Bergwall (Hucklebee), Paul Kuhn (Bellamy), Lenny Haas (Henry, the Old Actor), Mark Del Guzzo (Mortimer).

ARTHUR'S STONE, MERLIN'S FIRE: THE MAKING OF A KING (world premiere) by Kathryn Petersen; Director, Abigail Adams; Scenic Design, Lewis Folden; Costume Design Rosemarie E. McKelvey; Lighting Design, Dennis Parichy; Sound Design, Charles T. Brastow; Composer, Robert Maggio; Mainstage November 19–December 28, 2003; Cast: Kevin Bergen (Llewellynn/Cardoc/Saxon), Kamal Bostic-Smith (Bedwyr), Séan Camoni (Accolon/Kurdon), Joyce Cohen (Ludmilla/Lady of the Lake), Alda Cortese (Enid/Birch Tree Spirit), Michael Cruz (Gydric/Saxon Priest), Cat Haas (Praydn), Aisha Hobbs (Ceiwynn/Briton Druid Priest), Mark Lazar (Chief Ector/Old Caledonian Pine Tree Spirit), Aubie Merrylees (Garr/Little Pine Tree Spirit), Joseph Nevin (Kei), Stephen Novelli (Father Sansum), Mary Elizabeth Scallen (Queen Morgaine), Tobias Segal (Arthur), Josh Shaffer (Dawg of the One Eye), Cathy Simpson (Norwenna/Ash Tree Spirit), Graham Smith (Torag/Merlin), Elizabeth Webster (Nimue), David Whalen (Maximus).

HOLES by Louis Sachar; Director, David Bradley; Scenic Design, James F. Pyne, Jr.; Costume Design, Marla J. Jurglanis; Lighting Design, John Hoey; Sound Design & Composer, Fabian Obisbo; Mainstage January 15–February 16, 2004*; Cast: Robert Beatty (Police Officer/Sam/Atty. General), Jake DeLaurier (Magnet), Peter DeLaurier (Mr. Sir/Igor), Mark Del Guzzo (Zero), David Good (Zigzag), PJ McCabe (Stanley Yelnats), Antoine McClary (X-ray), Susan McKey (Stanley's Mom/Sarah/Kate Barlow), Kathryn Petersen (Myra/Warden/Linda), Ceal Phelan (Mme. Zeroni/Mrs. Collingswood/Ms. Morengo/Zero's Mom), Pete Pryor (Police Officer/Mr. Pendanski/Myra's Dad/Trout Walker), Patrick Ellison Shea (Stanley's Dad/Elya/Jesse/Sheriff), Julian N. Swiggett (Armpit).

*Re-mounted at Philadelphia academy of Music in January, 2005

Julian N. Swiggett, Jake DeLaurier, Mark Del Guzzo, Kathryn Petersen in *Holes*

PRETTY FIRE by Charlayne Woodard; Director, David Bradley; Lighting Design, Gregory S. Miller; Sound Design, Dominic Chacon; Steinbright Stage February 11–February 22, 2004; Cast: Cathy Simpson (Charlayne)

JULIUS CAESAR by William Shakespeare; Director, Lou Jacob; Scenic Design, James F. Pyne, Jr.; Costume Design, G. W. Mercier; Lighting Design, Thomas C. Hase; Sound Design & Original Music, Lindsay Jones; Mainstage March 10–May 2, 2004; Cast: Pearce Bunting (Brutus), Tom Byrn (Cinna/Titinius/Ensemble), Séan Camoni (Trebonius/Lucilius/Ensemble), Michael Cruz (Octavius/Metellus/Ensemble), Joe Guzmán (Decius/Messala/Ensemble), John Lumia (Marc Antony), Forest McClendon (Marullus/Soothsayer/Ensemble), Christopher Patrick Mullen (Casca/Pindarus/Ensemble), Stephen Novelli (Cassius), Kathryn Petersen (Portia/Ensemble), Mary Elizabeth Scallen (Calphurnia/Artemidora/Ensemble), Alvah Smith (Lucius/Ensemble), Tom Teti (Caesar)

Pearce Bunting (front), Joe Guzmán, Séan Camoni, Stephen Novelli, Michael Cruz, Tom Byrn in *Julius Ceasar* PHOTOS BY MARK GARVIN

THE FORGIVING HARVEST by Y York; Director, Shannon O'Donnell; Scenic Design, Lewis Folden; Costume Design, Rosemarie E. McKelvey; Lighting Design, Dennis Parichy; Sound Design, Charles T. Brastow; Steinbright Stage April 16–May 23, 2004; Cast: Anne Berkowitz (Myka), Kevin Bergen (Uncle Ted), David Corenswet (Great), Peter DeLaurier (Addison), Ray Lorini (Teddy), David Whalen (Mr. Nelson)

BORN YESTERDAY by Garson Kanin; Director, Ken Marini; Scenic Design, Scott Weldin.; Costume Design, Marla J. Jurglanis; Lighting Design, Dennis Parichy; Sound Design, Charles T. Brastow; Mainstage May 26–June 20, 2004; Cast: Trice Baldwin (Manicurist), Carla Belver (Mrs. Hedges), Mark Del Guzzo (Bellboy/Bootblack), Peter DeLaurier (Asst. Manager/Barber), Lenny Haas (Paul Verrall), Mark Lazar (Harry Brock), Lou Lippa (Senator Hedges), Stephen Novelli (Ed Devery), Karen Peakes (Billie Dawn), Marcia Saunders (Helen), Graham Smith (Eddie Brock)

PLAYMAKERS REPERTORY COMPANY

Chapel Hill, North Carolina
TWENTY-EIGHTH SEASON

Artistic Director, David Hammond; Executive Director, Donna Bost Heins; Jason T. Prichard, Production Manager

A PRAYER FOR OWEN MEANY, a play for the stage after the novel by John Irving, adapted by Simon Bent; Director, David Hammond; Scenic Design, Bill Clarke; Costume Design, Bill Clarke; Lighting Design, Mary Louise Geiger; Sound Design, M. Anthony Reimer; October 15–November 8, 2003; Cast: Tandy Cronyn (Mrs. Meany/Mitzi Lish); Joan Darling (Grandma Wheelwright); Jeffrey Blair Cornell (Reverend Merrill), Ray Dooley (Mr. Meany/Dr. Dolder), Julie Fishell (Lydia/Nun); Jeff Gurner (Owen Meany), Matthew Floyd Miller (John Wheelwright), Gregory Northrop (Dan Needham), Jessica K. Peterson (Barb Wiggins/Jarvit Mother); Kenneth P. Strong (Rector Wiggins/Major Rawls); Vicki Van Tassel (Tabitha Wheelwright)

HOBSON'S CHOICE by Harold Brighouse; Director, Blake Robison; Scenic Design, McKay Coble; Costume Design, Russell Parkman; Lighting Design; Peter West; Sound Design, M. Anthony Reimer; November 26–December 21, 2003; Cast: David Adamson (Timothy "Tubby" Wadow); Robert Breuler (Henry Horatio Hobson); Jeffrey Blair Cornell (William Mossop), Ray Dooley (Dr. MacFarlane), Julie Fishell (Mrs. Hepworth); Rachel Fowler (Maggie Hobson); Kenneth P. Strong (Jim Heeler)

KING LEAR by William Shakespeare; Director, Mark Wing-Davey; Scenic Design, Narelle Sissons; Costume Design, Marina Draghici; Lighting Design, Mary Louise Geiger; Sound Design, M. Anthony Reimer; January 14–February 8, 2004; Cast: Michael Babbitt (Duke of Cornwall); Carolyn Baeumler (Regan); Jeffrey Blair Cornell (Duke of Albany); Ray Dooley (Fool); John Feltch (Edgar); Charles Parnell (Edmond); Kenneth P. Strong (Earl of Kent); Karen Walsh (Cordelia); Jeffrey West (Oswald); Michael Winters (Lear, King of Britain); Rebecca Wisocky (Gonerill)

Melissa Hickey, Bjorn Thorstad in *Luminosity* PHOTO BY JON GARDINER

Jeffrey Blair Cornell, Rachel Fowler in *Hobson's Choice* PHOTO BY JON GARDINER

THE SUBJECT WAS ROSES by Frank R. Gilroy; Director, Drew Barr; Scenic Design, Russell Parkman; Costume Design; Russell Parkman; Lighting Design, Peter West; Sound Design, M. Anthony Reimer; February 25–March 21, 2004; Cast: Tandy Cronyn (Nettie Cleary), J.R. Horne (John Cleary); Brandon Michael Smith (Timmy Cleary)

LUMINOSITY by Nick Stafford; Director, David Hammond; Scenic Design, Bill Clarke; Costume Design, Bill Clarke; Lighting Design, Peter West; Sound Design, M. Anthony Reimer; April 67–May 2, 2004; Cast: Earl Baker, Jr. (Saul Mercer); members Jeffrey Blair Cornell (Dalton); Tandy Cronyn (Margaret Mercer); Ray Dooley (John Gardner); Charity Henson (Debra Mercer), Melissa Hickey (Victoria Cotton); Kenneth P. Strong (Forbes); Bjorn Thorstad (James Mercer); Chandler Williams (Robert)

PORTLAND CENTER STAGE

Portland, Oregon
SIXTEENTH SEASON

Artistic Director, Chris Coleman; Managing Director, Edith H. Love

ANOTHER FINE MESS by Steven Drukman; Director, Cliff Fannin Baker; Set Design, Russell Parkman; Costume Design, Jeff Cone; Lighting Design, Don Crossley; Sound Design, Jen Raynak; Dramaturg, Mead Hunter; Stage Manager, Marcella Y. Crowson; Production Assistant, Jamie Hill; September 23rd–November 8th, 2003; Cast: David Cromwell (Gordon), Sharonlee McLean (Marge), Michael O'Connell (Roger), Ted Roisum (Dennis), Zach Shaffer (Bobby), Erin Way (The Boy)

BAT BOY: THE MUSICAL Story and Book by Keythe Farley and Brian Flemming; Music and Lyrics by Laurence O'Keefe; Director, Chris Coleman; Assistant Director, Eric Skinner; Musical Director, Rick Lewis; Set Design, Dex Edwards; Costume Design, Susan E. Mickey; Lighting Design, Diane Ferry Williams; Sound Design, Jen Raynak; Fight Choreographer, John Armour; Stage Manager, Mark Tynan; Production Assistant, Ellie Sturgill;

(CONTINUED ON NEXT PAGE)

(CONTINUED FROM PREVIOUS PAGE)

October 28th–November 23rd, 2003; Cast: Michael Abbott, Jr. (Rick Taylor/Lorraine/Mr. Dillon), Amy Jo Arrington (Ruthie Taylor/Ned), Dominic Bogart (Bud/Daisy/Pan), Susannah Mars (Meredith Parker), Kelley McCollum (Sheriff), Wade McCollum (Bat Boy), Victor Morris (Reverend Hightower/Mrs. Taylor/Roy), Charlie Parker (Maggie/Ron Taylor), Dan Sharkey (Dr. Thomas Parker), Rena Strober (Shelley Parker)

THE SANTALAND DIARIES by David Sedaris adapted by Joe Mantello, with **A CHRISTMAS MEMORY** by Truman Capote; Director, Neel Keller; Set Design, Allen Moyer; Costume Design, Jeff Cone; Lighting Design, Don Crossley; Sound Design, Jen Raynak; Stage Manager, Marcella Y. Crowson; Production Assistant, Jamie Hill; December 2nd–December 23rd, 2003; Cast: Steve Wilkerson

THE MERCHANT OF VENICE by William Shakespeare; Director, Róbert Alföldi; Dramaturg/Translator, Anikó Szűcs; Set Design, Robert Pyzocha; Costume Design, Miranda Hoffman; Lighting Design, Daniel Ordower; Sound Design, Jen Raynak; Video/Projection Designer, Tom Frisch; Text & Dialect Coach, Christine Menzies; Fight & Movement Designer, Attila Király; Fight Coordinator, John Armour; Stage Manager, Mark Tynan; Production Assistant, Ellie Sturgill; January 13th–February 1st, 2004; Cast: Charles Borland (Antonio), Joshua M. Bott (Gratiano), Camille E. Cettina (Nerissa), Scott Coopwood (Shylock), Kasey Mahaffy (Salarino), Douglas Mace (Old Gobbo/Tubal/Receptionist/The Duke), Wade McCollum (Lancelot Gobbo), Michael A. Newcomer (Lorenzo), Cody Nickell (Bassanio), Jennifer Erin Roberts (Portia), Mark Schwahn (TV Moderator/Policeman/Gang Member), Kelly Talent (Jessica), Róbert Alföldi & Joseph Fisher & Kristan Seemel & Michael O'Connell (Suitors), Kari Michele Bortolussi & Steven Gregory Brian & Alisa Glembotski (Ensemble)

36 VIEWS by Naomi Iizuka; Director, Chay Yew; Set Design, Dan Ostling; Costume Design, Lydia Tanji; Lighting Design, Mary Louise Geiger; Composer, Nathan Wang; Stage Manager, Marcella Y. Crowson; Production Assistant, Jamie Hill; February 10th–February 29th, 2004; Cast: Melody Butiu (Claire Tsong), Sean Haberle (Darius Wheeler), Maile Holck (Setsuko Hearn), Gregory Patrick Jackson (John Bell), Alan Nebelthau (Owen Matthiassen), Camillia Sanes (Elizabeth Newman-Orr)

CAT ON A HOT TIN ROOF by Tennessee Williams; Director, Chris Coleman; Set Design, William Bloodgood; Costume Design, Jeff Cone; Lighting Design, Kirk Bookman; Sound Design, Jen Raynak; Stage Manager, Mark Tynan; Assistant Stage Manager, Marcella Y. Crowson; Production Assistant, Ellie Sturgill; March 9th–April 4th, 2004; Cast: Tobias Anderson (Reverend Tooker), Amanda Child (Trixie), Clara Bach Deweese (Dixie), Gray Eubank (Doctor Baugh), Joann Johnson (Big Mama), Kevin E. Jones (Sookie), Dario Oman (Buster), Jim Peck (Big Daddy), Jeff Portell (Brick), Maureen Porter (Mae), Alex Schultz (Sonny), Tim True (Gooper), Brandy Zarle (Maggie)

FULLY COMMITTED by Becky Mode; Director, Mark Setlock; Set Design, Jeff Seats; Costume Design, Jeff Cone; Lighting Design, Don Crossley; Sound Design, Jen Raynak; Musical Arrangement, Michael Friedman; Stage Manager, Marcella Y. Crowson; Production Assistant, Jamie Hill; April 13th–May 30th, 2004; Cast: Mark Setlock

THE REPERTORY THEATRE OF ST. LOUIS

St. Louis, Missouri

THIRTY-SEVENTH SEASON

Artistic Director, Steven Woolf; Managing Director, Mark Bernstein

METAMORPHOSES by Mary Zimmerman, based on the *Myths of Ovid*; Director, Mary Zimmerman; Staging, Eric Rosen; Scenic Design, Daniel Ostling; Costume Design, Mara Blumenfeld; Lighting Design, T.J. Gerckens; Sound Design, Andre Pluess & Ben Sussman; Composer, Willy Schwarz; Casting, Rich Cole (New York) & Claire Simon (Chicago); Stage Manager, Glenn Dunn; Assistant Stage Manager, Shannon B. Sturgis; Associate Director, Anjali Bidani; Associate Scenic Designer, Brenda Sabatka; Associate Costume Designer, Jessica Chaney; Associate Lighting Designer, Jonathan Spencer; September 10-October 10, 2003; Cast: Cherise Boothe (Alcyone & others), Sun Mee Chomet (Myrrha & others), Joe Dempsey (Erysichthon & others), Anne Fogarty (Eurydice & others), Antony Hagopian (Hermes & others), Andrew Long (Midas & others), James McKay (Phaeton & others), Manu Narayan (Orpheus & others), Lisa Tejero (Therapist & others), Tamilla Woodard (Aphrodite & others)

MY FAIR LADY, book & lyrics by Alan Jay Lerner, music by Frederick Loewe; Adapted from George Bernard Shaw's play and Gabrial Pascal's motion picture *Pygmalion*; Director, Susan V. Booth; Choreographer, Daniel Pelzig; Musical Director, Steven Gross; Scenic Design, Michael Philippi; Costume Design, Linda Roethke; Lighting Design, Dawn Chiang; Dialect Coach, Rocco Dal Vera; Casting, Rich Cole; Stage Manager, T.R. Martin; Assistant Stage Manager, Tony Dearing; Assistant Lighting Designer, Jim Primm; Sound Consultant, Clay Benning; October 15–November 14, 2003; Cast: Neal Benari (Henry Higgins), Keith Howard (Busker, George, Higgins' Butler, Zoltan Karpathy, Vendor), Howard Kaye (Busker, Selsey Man, Harry, Charles, The Royal Footman, Vendor), Jeffrey Kuhn (Lord Tarrington, Vendor), Russell Leib (Colonel Pickering), Crista Moore (Eliza Doolittle), Alan Souza (Freddy Eynsford-Hill), Rebecca Spencer (Mrs. Eynsford-Hill, Busker, Higgins' Maid, Angry Woman, Servant, Lady Tarrington, Queen of Transylvania, Mrs. Higgins' Maid), Linda Stephens (Mrs. Higgins, Mrs. Pearce), Peter Van Wagner (Alfred P. Doolittle)

THE GOAT, OR WHO IS SYLVIA? by Edward Albee; Director, Steven Woolf; Scenic Design, John Ezell; Costume Design, Garth Dunbar; Lighting Design, Peter E. Sargent; Casting, Rich Cole; Stage Manager, Champe Leary; October 22–November 9, 2003; Cast: Anderson Matthews (Martin), Carolyn Swift (Stevie), Bruce Longworth (Ross), Clint Zugel (Billy)

TEN LITTLE INDIANS by Agatha Christie; Director, Susan Gregg; Scenic Design, John Ezell; Costume Design, James Scott; Lighting Design, Michael Philippi; Casting, Rich Cole; Stage Manager, Glenn Dunn; Assistant Stage Manager, Shannon B. Sturgis; December 3, 2003–January 2, 2004; Cast: Jerry Vogel (Thomas Rogers), Susie Wall (Ethel Rogers), Beau Speer (Fred Narracott), Chandler Vinton (Vera Claythorne), Rob Krakovski (Philip Lombard), Paul Hufker (Anthony Marston), David Heuvelman (William Blore), Whit Reichert (General John Mackenzie), Richard Ramos (Sir Lawrence Wargrave), David McCann (Dr. Edward Armstrong), Darrie Lawrence (Emily Brent)

THE IMPORTANCE OF BEING EARNEST by Oscar Wilde; Director, John Going; Scenic Design, James Wolk; Costume Design, Elizabeth Covey; Lighting Design, Dennis Parichy; Casting, Rich Cole; Stage Manager, T.R. Martin; Assistant Stage Manager, Tony Dearing; January 7–February 6, 2004; Cast: Thomas Carson (Lane), Erik Steele (Algernon Moncrieff), Jeffries Thaiss (John Worthing, J.P.) Jill Tanner (Lady Bracknell), Brandy Zarle (Hon. Gwendolen Fairfax), Thomas Carson (Merriman), Ashley West (Cecily Cardew), Darcy Pulliam (Miss Prism), Max Robinson (Rev. Canon Chasuble, D.D.)

LIFE (X) 3 by Yasmina Reza; Translated by Christopher Hampton; Director, Thom Sesma; Scenic Design, John Roslevich, Jr.; Costume Design, Elizabeth Eisloeffel; Lighting Design, Glenn Dunn; Casting, Rich Cole; Stage Manager, Champe Leary; Fight Choreography, Kim Bozark; January 21–February 8, 2004; Cast: Mark Jacoby (Henry), Bridget Ann White (Sonia), Mary Gordon Murray (Inez), Michael Rupert (Hubert)

BLUE/ORANGE by Joe Penhall; Director, Steven Woolf; Scenic Design, Narelle Sissons; Costume Design, Marie Ann Chiment; Lighting Design, Mary Jo Dondlinger; Casting, Rich Cole; Stage Manager, Glenn Dunn; Assistant Stage Manager, Shannon B. Sturgis; February 11–March 12, 2004; Cast: Rashaad Ernesto Green (Christopher), Jeremy Webb (Bruce), Anderson Matthews (Robert)

MISTER ROBERTS by Thomas Heggen & Joshua Logan; Director, Edward Stern; Scenic Design, Paul Shortt; Costume Design, Kristine Kearney; Lighting Design, Peter E. Sargent; Fight Director, Drew Fracher; Casting, Rich Cole; Stage Manager, Glenn Dunn; Assistant Stage Manager, Tony Dearing; March 17–April 16, 2004; Cast: John Ahlin (Chief Johnson), Bill Doyle (Lieutenant (j.g) Roberts), Joneal Joplin (Doc), Gary McGurk (Dowdy), Robert Elliott (The Captain), Jim Holdridge (Insigna), Mark Mineart (Mannion), Josh Renfree (Lindstrom), André Marrero (Stefanowski), Matthew F. Morgan (Wiley), Greg McFadden (Ensign Pulver), Geoffrey Molloy (Dolan), Christopher Gottschalk (Gerhart), Cristin Mortenson (Lieutenant Ann Girard), David Webb (Shore Patrol Officer), Blake Anthony (Military Policeman), Jeremy Sher (Shore Patrolman), Michael Hammack (Sailor), Matt Kutz (Sailor), Jeremy Roberts (Sailor), Percy Rodriguez (Sailor)

THE LAST FIVE YEARS written & composed by Jason Robert Brown; Director, John Ruocco; Musical Director, David Geist; Scenic Design, Narelle Sissons; Costume Design, Curtis Hay; Lighting Design, Mary Jo Dondlinger; Casting, Rich Cole; Stage Manager, Champe Leary; March 24–April 18, 2004; Cast: Kate Baldwin (Kathy), Anthony Holds (Jamie); Musicians: David Geist, Piano; Adrian Walker, Violin; Natasha Rubinstein, Cello

THE IMAGINARY THEATRE COMPANY

LEWIS AND CLARK: A BICENTENNIAL OF DISCOVERY by Kathryn Schultz Miller; Director, Jeffery Matthews; Scenic Design, John Roslevich, Jr.; Costume Design, Betsy Krausnick; Sound Design, Bob Wotawa; Stage Manager, Daryl Vaughan; Director of Education, Marsha Coplon; Associate Director of Education, Kim Allen Bozark; Artistic Supervisor, Jeffery Matthews; 2003–2004; Cast: Gwendolyn Wotawa (Shannon, Sacagawea, Martha, Ellicott, Citizen, Bostonian, Old Dorion, Big White, Watkuweis), Alan Knoll (Captain William Clark, Jefferson, Napoleon, Charbonneau, Blackfoot 2), Sharon Hunter (Ordway, Paper Boy, York, Arcawechar, Black Buffalo, Twisted Hair, Cameahwait, Blackfoot 1), Nick Choksi (Captain Meriwether Lewis)

THE SNOW QUEEN by Hans Christian Andersen; Adapted for the stage by Kim Esop Wylie; Music by Joe Dreyer; Lyrics by Kim Esop Wylie & Joe Dreyer; Director, Kathleen Singleton; Scenic Design, John Roslevich, Jr.; Costume Design, Bonnie Kruger; Stage Manager, Daryl Vaughan; Director of Education, Marsha Coplon; Associate Director of Education, Kim Allen Bozark; Artistic Supervisor, Jeffery Matthews; 2003–2004; Cast: Alan Knoll (Evil Imp, River, Rose, Prince, Old Woman 1 & 2), Nick Choksi (Kade, Crow, Reindeer), Gwendolyn Wotawa (Gerda), Sharon Hunter (Grandmother, Snow Queen, Witch, Princess, Robber Girl)

RIKKI TIKKI TAVI by Rudyard Kipling; Adapted for the stage by Lynne Alvarez; Director, Andrea Urice; Music & Lyrics by Joe Dreyer; Scenic & Costume Design, Lou Byrd; Stage Manager, Daryl Vaughan; Director of Education, Marsha Coplon; Associate Director of Education, Kim Allen Bozark; Artistic Supervisor, Jeffery Matthews; 2003–2004; Cast: Nick Choksi (Rikki-Tikki-Tavi), Gwendolyn Wotawa (Darzee, Chuchundra), Alan Knoll (Nag, Father's Voice), Sharon Hunter (Nagaina, Mother's Voice), Hal Matthews (Teddy's Voice); Musicians: Saurabh Gayen & Shauvik Gayen

SAN JOSE REPERTORY THEATRE

San Jose, California

TWENTY-THIRD SEASON

Artistic Director, Timothy Near; Managing Director, Alexandra Urbanowski

NOISES OFF by Michael Frayn; Director, Richard Seyd; Scenic Design, John Iacovelli; Costume Design, Beaver Bauer; Lighting Design, York Kennedy; Sound Design, Jeff Mockus; Stage Manager, Donna Rose Fletcher; Casting Director, Bruce Elsperger; Los Angeles Casting, Julia Flores; Dialect Coach, Deborah Sussel, Stunt Coordinator, Will Leong; September 6–October 5, 2003; Cast: Jane Carr (Dotty Otley), Adrian Neil (Lloyd Dallas), Ben Livingston (Garry Lejeune), Jamie Day (Brooke Ashton), Ali Taylor (Poppy Norton-Taylor), Dan Hiatt (Fredrick Fellowes), Maura Vincent (Belinda Blair), Liam Vincent (Tim Allgood), Edward Sarafian (Selsdon Mowbray)

Cody Nickell, Julie Jesneck in *Mary's Wedding*

MARY'S WEDDING by Stephen Massicotte; Director, Michael Butler; Scenic Design, Alexander V. Nichols; Costume Design, B. Modern; Lighting Design, Alexander V. Nichols; Sound Design, Jeff Mockus; Original Music, Michael Butler, Jeff Mockus; Production Stage Manager, Jenny R. Friend; Stage Manager, Bruce Elsperger; Casting Director, Bruce Elsperger; New York Casting, Harriet Bass; October 18–November 16, 2003; Cast: Cody Nickell (Charlie Edwards), Julie Jesneck (Mary Chalmers/Sgt. Flowerdew)

WINTERTIME by Charles L. Mee; Director, Timothy Near; Scenic Design, Giulio Cesare Perrone; Costume Design, Shigeru Yaji; Lighting Design, Lap-Chi Chu; Sound Design, Steve Schoenbeck; Stage Manager, Jenny R. Friend; Casting Director, Bruce Elsperger; New York Casting, Harriet Bass; Choreography, Timothy Near, Ellie Klopp; Additional Choreography, Erica Smith; Musical Consultant, Craig Bohmler; Social Dance Instructor, Quinn Van Antwerp; Dialect Coach, Lynne Soffer; November 29, 2003–January 4, 2004; Cast: Soraya Broukhim (Ariel), Joseph Parks (Jonathan), Suzan Hanson (Maria), Michael Butler (Francois), James Carpenter (Frank), Perry Ojeda (Edmund), Wilma Bonet (Bertha), Catherine E. Coulson (Hilda), Charles Dean (Bob), Mari-Esther Magaloni (Dr. Jaqueline Benoit)

Jane Carr in *Noises Off*

Charles Dean, Joseph Parks, James Carpenter, Catherine E. Coulson, Suzan Hanson, Perry Ojeda in *Wintertime*

A MIDSUMMER NIGHT'S DREAM by William Shakespeare; Director, Anne Bogart; Created and Performed by SITI Company; Set Design, Neil Patel; Costume Design, Gabriel Berry; Lighting Design, Christopher Akerlind; Original Music and Sound Design, T. Griffin; Production Stage Manager, Elizabeth Moreau; Set and Lighting Associate Designer, Brian Scott; Assistant Set Designer, Timothy Mackabee; Assistant Stage Manager (California), Nicole Olson; Assistant Stage Manager (New York), Maria Goyanes; January 24–February 22, 2004; Cast: J. Ed Araiza (Lysander, Flute/Thisbe, Cobweb), Ellen Lauren (Hippolyta, Titania), Kelly Maurer (Helena, Snug (Lion), Mustardseed), Tom Nelis (Theseus, Oberon, Quince), Barney O'Hanlon (Puck), KJ Sanchez (Hermia, Starveling, Moonshine, Moth), Stephen Webber (Demetrius, Snout/Wall), Peaseblossom, Chris Spencer Wells (Egeus, Bottom)

ROUNDING THIRD by Richard Dresser; Director, John McCluggage; Scenic Design, Scott Weldin; Costume Design, B Modern; Lighting Design, Rick Paulsen; Sound Design, Jeff Mockus; Stage Managers, Nicole Olson & Jenny R. Friend; March 20–April 18, 2004; Cast: Charles Dean (Don), Remi Sandri (Michael)

Remi Sandri, Charles Dean in *Rounding Third*

Carol Halstead in *Bad Dates*

BAD DATES by Theresa Rebeck; Director, Timothy Near; Scenic Design, Robert Mark Morgan; Costume Design, B. Modern; Lighting Design, Peter Maradudin; Sound Design, Steve Schoenbeck; Production Stage Manager, Jenny R. Friend; Stage Manager, Nicole Olson; Casting Director, Bruce Elsperger; Dialect Coach, Lynne Soffer; L.A. Casting, Julia Flores; N.Y. Casting, Harriet Bass; May 8–June 6, 2004; Cast: Carol Halstead (Haley Walker)

THE UNDERPANTS by Carl Sternheim & adapted by Steve Martin; Director, Jon Jory; Scenic Design, Robert A. Dahlstrom; Costume Design, David Murin; Lighting Design, Rick Paulsen; Composition, Peter Ekstrom; Sound Design, Brian Jerome Peterson; Production Stage Manager, Bruno Ingram; Stage Manager, Jenny R. Friend; June 19-July 18, 2004; Cast: Conan McCarty (Theo Maske), Julia Dion (Louise Maske), Peggity Price (Gertrude Deuter), Jim Lorio (Frank Versati), Jarion Moore (Professor Klinglehoff)

Conan McCarty, Jarion Moore in *The Underpants* PHOTOS COURTESY OF SAN JOSE REPERATORY THEATRE

YALE REPERTORY THEATRE

New Haven, Connecticut
THIRTY-EIGHTH SEASON

Artistic Director, James Bundy; Managing Director, Victoria Nolan

THE BLACK DAHLIA adapted by Mike Alfreds from the novel by James Ellroy; Director, Mike Alfreds; Scenic Design, Peter McKintosh; Costume Design, Anne Kenney; Lighting Design, Stephen Strawbridge; Sound Design, Daniel Baker; Projections, Blythe Quinlan. American Premiere, October 17–November 8, 2003. Cast: David Bardeen (Club Stan Owner, Conventioneer), Amanda Cobb (Kay Lake, Marjorie Graham), Frank Deal (Emmett Sprague, Sergeant Bill Koenig, Chief Green, Fight Announcer, Cecil Durkin), Mike Dooly (Officer Dwight "Bucky" Bleichert), Marcus Dean Fuller (Sergeant Leland "Lee" Blanchard, Bobby DeWitt), Mercedes Herrero (Ramona Sprague, Jane Chambers, Barmaid at LaVerne's Hideaway, Aggie Underwood), Matt Hoverman (Deputy District Attorney Ellis Loew, Johnny Vogel, Robert Manley), Allen E. Read (Sailor in Motel, Sid Man), Christina Rouner (Madeleine Sprague, Betty Short), Sara Surrey (Sheryl Saddon, Linda Martin, Sally Stinson, Martha Sprague, Lorraine), Graham Winton (Sergeant Fritz Vogel, Milton Dolphine, Dr. Newbarr, Braven Dyer, Baxter Fitch), Jeffrey Withers (Charles Issler, Parole Clerk), Mark Zeisler (Lieutenant Russ Millard, Cleo Short, Bevo Means, Loren Bidwell)

CULTURE CLASH IN AMERICCA created, written and performed by Culture Clash: Richard Montoya, Ric Salinas and Herbert Siguenza; Director, Tony Taccone; Scenic Design and Lighting Design, Alexander V. Nichols; Costume Design, Donna Marie. November 14-December 6, 2003

ROTHSCHILD'S FIDDLE adapted by Kama Ginkas from the story by Anton Chekhov; Director, Kama Ginkas; Scenic Design and Costume Design, Sergei Barkhin, Lighting Design, Gleb Filshtinsky, Sound Operator, Maria Bacharnikova. World Premiere January 14-31, 2004. Cast: Valerii Barinov [Yakov (Bronza)], Igor Yasulovich (Rothschild), Arina Nesterova (Marfa), Alexei Dubrovsky (Doctor's Assistant)

Gavin Creel, Scott Ferrara in *The Mystery Plays* PHOTO BY CAROL ROSEGG

Richard Montoya, Ric Salinas, Herbert Siguenza in *Culture Clash in AmeriCCa*

KING LEAR by William Shakespeare; Director, Harold Scott; Music Composer, Anthony Davis; Scenic Design, Blythe R.D. Quinlan; Costume Design, Jessica Ford; Lighting Design, S. Ryan Schmidt; Sound Design, Philip Scott Peglow. February 13–March 13, 2004. Cast: Giovanni Adams (Ensemble), Che Ayende (Oswald), Baub R.J. Bidon (Ensemble), Avery Brooks (King Lear), Johnny Lee Davenport (Kent), Justin Emeka (Edgar), Larry W. Floyd (Ensemble), Ray Ford (Fool), Mark Sage Hamilton (Ensemble), Albert Lawrence (Ensemble), Kobi Libii (Ensemble), Wiley Moore (France, Ensemble), Petronia Paley (Regan), Jovan Rameau (Burgundy, Ensemble), John Livingston Rolle (Albany), Roslyn Ruff (Cordelia), Marie Thomas (Goneril), John Douglas Thompson (Edmund), David Toney (Cornwall), Charles Turner (Gloucester), Lakai Worrell (Ensemble)

THE KING STAG by Carlo Gozzi; Adaptors, Evan Yionoulis, Mike Yionoulis and Catherine Sheehy; Music and Lyrics, Mike Yionoulis; Director and Choreographer, Evan Yionoulis, Scenic Design, Sergio Villegas; Costume Design, Camille Assaf; Lighting Design, Stephen Strawbridge; Sound Design, Sabrina McGuigan. March 26–April 17, 2004. Cast: Opal Alladin (Angela), Chad Callaghan (Sphinx, Ensemble), Bryan Terrell Clark (Dr. Phat, Ensemble), Matthew Cowles (Cigolotti), B.J. Crosby (Durandarte), Timothy Gulan (Brighella), Lisa Jolley (Smeraldina), David Matranga (Leandro), Les J.N. Mau (Pantalone), Jim Noonan (Mos'ly Deaf, Ensemble), Ryan Quinn (Li'l Moo Moo, Ensemble), Jeremy Rabb (Truffaldino), Daina Schatz (Mother, Ensemble), Jeanine Serralles (Clarice), Alexander K. Sfakianos (Young Boy), Bill Thompson (Deramo), Mark Zeisler (Tartaglia)

THE MYSTERY PLAYS by Roberto Aguirre-Sacasa; Director, Connie Grappo; Scenic Design, Sandra Goldmark; Costume Design, Amanda Walker; Lighting Design, S. Ryan Schmidt; Sound Design and Original Music, Keith Townsend Obadike. World Premiere April 30-May 22, 2004. Cast: Gavin Creel (Joe Manning and Others), Scott Ferrara (Nathan West and Others), Leslie Lyles (Amanda Urbane and Others), Mark Margolis (Mister Mystery and Others), Heather Mazur (Abby Gilley and Others), Peter Stadlen (Ben Gilley and Others)

AWARDS

2004 THEATRE WORLD AWARD WINNERS

Shannon Cochran of *Bug*

Stephanie D'Abruzzo of *Avenue Q*

Mitchel David Federan of *The Boy From Oz*

Alexander Gemignani of *Assassins*

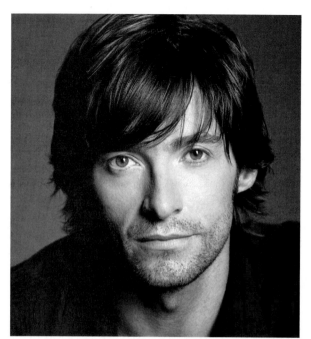

Hugh Jackman of *The Boy From Oz*

Isabel Keating of *The Boy From Oz*

Sanaa Lathan of *A Raisin in the Sun*

Jefferson Mays of *I Am My Own Wife*

Euan Morton of *Taboo*

Anika Noni Rose of *Caroline, or Change*

John Tartaglia of *Avenue Q*

Jennifer Westfeldt of *Wonderful Town*

SPECIAL THEATRE WORLD AWARD

Sarah Jones, for outstanding writing and solo performance
in the Off-Broadway presentation of *bridge and tunnel*

60TH ANNUAL
THEATRE WORLD AWARDS PRESENTATION

Studio 54; Monday, May 31, 2004

Created in 1944 by Theatre World founders Daniel Blum, Norman MacDonald, and John Willis to coincide with the first release of Theatre World, the now sixty-year-old definitive pictorial and statistical record of the American theatre, the Theatre World Awards are the oldest awards given for debut performances in New York City, as well as one of the oldest honors bestowed on New York actors.

A committee of New York drama critics currently joins longtime Theatre World editor John Willis in choosing six actors and six actresses for the Theatre World Award, who have distinguished themselves in Broadway and Off-Broadway productions during the past theatre season. Occasionally, Special Theatre World Awards are also bestowed on performers, casts, or others who have made a particularly lasting impression on the New York theatre scene.

The Theatre World Award "Janus" statuette is an original bronze sculpture in primitive-modern style created by internationally recognized artist Harry Marinsky. It is adapted from the Roman myth of Janus, god of entrances, exits, and all beginnings, with one face appraising the past and the other anticipating the future. It is cast and mounted on marble in the Del Chiaro Foundry in Pietrasanta, Italy.

Theatre World Awards Board members:

Tom Lynch, President
Marianne Tatum, Vice President
Patricia Elliott, Secretary
Peter Filichia, Treasurer
David Birney
Ben Hodges
Walter Willison

The Theatre World Awards are voted on by the following committee of New York drama critics:

Clive Barnes (*New York Post*), Peter Filichia (*Theatermania.com*), Harry Haun (*Playbill*), Ben Hodges (*Theatre World*), Frank Scheck (*The Hollywood Reporter*), Michael Sommers (*Newark Star Ledger*), Douglas Watt (*The Daily News*), John Willis (*Theatre World*), and Linda Winer (*Newsday*).

Master of Ceremonies, Peter Filichia

Executive Producer, Ben Hodges

Theatre World editor John Willis and *Theatre World* associate editor and Theatre World Awards executive producer Ben Hodges

1996 Theatre World Award winner and 2004 presenter Viola Davis

Master of Ceremonies and Theatre World Awards Treasurer Peter Filichia with 2004 Theatre World Award winner John Tartaglia

1968 Theatre World Award winner and 2004 presenter Bernadette Peters with 1959 winner Tammy Grimes

Theatre World editor John Willis with 2004 Theatre World Award winner Jennifer Westfeldt

2004 Theatre World Award winner Jefferson Mays

2004 Theatre World Award winner Euan Morton

1982 Theatre World Award winner and 2004 performer Karen Akers

2004 Theatre World Award winner Sanaa Lathan

Karen Akers, *Theatre World* editor John Willis, staff photographer Michael Viade, and associate editor and Theatre World Awards executive producer Ben Hodges

Theatre World editor John Willis and previous winner and 2004 presenter Linda Hart

2004 Special Theatre World Award
winner Sarah Jones

1991 Theatre World Award winner LaChanze presents a Theatre World
Award to 2004 winner Shannon Cochran

2004 Theatre World Award winner
Hugh Jackman

1980 Theatre World Award winner and
2004 presenter Lonny Price

Previous winner Karen Akers; 2004 award winners Anika Noni Rose and Isabel Keating; *Theatre World* editor John
Willis; Previous winners and 2004 presenters, Jarrod Emick and Alice Playten; 2004 award winner John Tartaglia

1966 Theatre World Award winner John Cullum with
1959 winner Tammy Grimes

Previous winner and 2004 presenter Audra McDonald, Master of Ceremonies Peter Filichia, Previous winners and 2004
presenters Michael Cerveris and Lonny Price

1981 Theatre World Award winner Amanda Plummer with Broadway producers Fran and Barry Weissler

Theatre World editor John Willis

1994 Theatre World Award winner and 2004 presenter Jarrod Emick

Previous Award winners LaChanze and Ralph Carter with 2004 Theatre World Award winner Anika Noni Rose

1993 Theatre World Award winner and 2004 presenter Michael Cerveris

1982 Theatre World Award winner and 2004 performer Karen Akers with Theatre World editor John Willis

Theatre World editor John Willis and 2004 Theatre World Award winner Mitchel David Federan

Previous Theatre World Award winners John Cullum and Theatre World Awards Secretary Patricia Elliott

Blythe Danner

Joanna Gleason

Jonathan Kaplan

John Mahoney

PREVIOUS THEATRE WORLD AWARD RECIPIENTS

1944–45: Betty Comden, Richard Davis, Richard Hart, Judy Holliday, Charles Lang, Bambi Linn, John Lund, Donald Murphy, Nancy Noland, Margaret Phillips, John Raitt

1945–46: Barbara Bel Geddes, Marlon Brando, Bill Callahan, Wendell Corey, Paul Douglas, Mary James, Burt Lancaster, Patricia Marshall, Beatrice Pearson

1946–47: Keith Andes, Marion Bell, Peter Cookson, Ann Crowley, Ellen Hanley, John Jordan, George Keane, Dorothea MacFarland, James Mitchell, Patricia Neal, David Wayne

1947–48: Valerie Bettis, Edward Bryce, Whitfield Connor, Mark Dawson, June Lockhart, Estelle Loring, Peggy Maley, Ralph Meeker, Meg Mundy, Douglass Watson, James Whitmore, Patrice Wymore

1948–49: Tod Andrews, Doe Avedon, Jean Carson, Carol Channing, Richard Derr, Julie Harris, Mary McCarty, Allyn Ann McLerie, Cameron Mitchell, Gene Nelson, Byron Palmer, Bob Scheerer

1949–50: Nancy Andrews, Phil Arthur, Barbara Brady, Lydia Clarke, Priscilla Gillette, Don Hanmer, Marcia Henderson, Charlton Heston, Rick Jason, Grace Kelly, Charles Nolte, Roger Price

1950–51: Barbara Ashley, Isabel Bigley, Martin Brooks, Richard Burton, Pat Crowley, James Daley, Cloris Leachman, Russell Nype, Jack Palance, William Smithers, Maureen Stapleton, Marcia Van Dyke, Eli Wallach

1951–52: Tony Bavaar, Patricia Benoit, Peter Conlow, Virginia de Luce, Ronny Graham, Audrey Hepburn, Diana Herbert, Conrad Janis, Dick Kallman, Charles Proctor, Eric Sinclair, Kim Stanley, Marian Winters, Helen Wood

1952–53: Edie Adams, Rosemary Harris, Eileen Heckart, Peter Kelley, John Kerr, Richard Kiley, Gloria Marlowe, Penelope Munday, Paul Newman, Sheree North, Geraldine Page, John Stewart, Ray Stricklyn, Gwen Verdon

1953–54: Orson Bean, Harry Belafonte, James Dean, Joan Diener, Ben Gazzara, Carol Haney, Jonathan Lucas, Kay Medford, Scott Merrill, Elizabeth Montgomery, Leo Penn, Eva Marie Saint

1954–55: Julie Andrews, Jacqueline Brookes, Shirl Conway, Barbara Cook, David Daniels, Mary Fickett, Page Johnson, Loretta Leversee, Jack Lord, Dennis Patrick, Anthony Perkins, Christopher Plummer

1955–56: Diane Cilento, Dick Davalos, Anthony Franciosa, Andy Griffith, Laurence Harvey, David Hedison, Earle Hyman, Susan Johnson, John Michael King, Jayne Mansfield, Sara Marshall, Gaby Rodgers, Susan Strasberg, Fritz Weaver

1956–57: Peggy Cass, Sydney Chaplin, Sylvia Daneel, Bradford Dillman, Peter Donat, George Grizzard, Carol Lynley, Peter Palmer, Jason Robards, Cliff Robertson, Pippa Scott, Inga Swenson

1957–58: Anne Bancroft, Warren Berlinger, Colleen Dewhurst, Richard Easton, Tim Everett, Eddie Hodges, Joan Hovis, Carol Lawrence, Jacqueline McKeever, Wynne Miller, Robert Morse, George C. Scott

1958–59: Lou Antonio, Ina Balin, Richard Cross, Tammy Grimes, Larry Hagman, Dolores Hart, Roger Mollien, France Nuyen, Susan Oliver, Ben Piazza, Paul Roebling, William Shatner, Pat Suzuki, Rip Torn

1959–60: Warren Beatty, Eileen Brennan, Carol Burnett, Patty Duke, Jane Fonda, Anita Gillette, Elisa Loti, Donald Madden, George Maharis, John McMartin, Lauri Peters, Dick Van Dyke

1960–61: Joyce Bulifant, Dennis Cooney, Sandy Dennis, Nancy Dussault, Robert Goulet, Joan Hackett, June Harding, Ron Husmann, James MacArthur, Bruce Yarnell

1961–62: Elizabeth Ashley, Keith Baxter, Peter Fonda, Don Galloway, Sean Garrison, Barbara Harris, James Earl Jones, Janet Margolin, Karen Morrow, Robert Redford, John Stride, Brenda Vaccaro

1962–63: Alan Arkin, Stuart Damon, Melinda Dillon, Robert Drivas, Bob Gentry, Dorothy Loudon, Brandon Maggart, Julienne Marie, Liza Minnelli, Estelle Parsons, Diana Sands, Swen Swenson

1963–64: Alan Alda, Gloria Bleezarde, Imelda De Martin, Claude Giraud, Ketty Lester, Barbara Loden, Lawrence Pressman, Gilbert Price, Philip Proctor, John Tracy, Jennifer West

1964–65: Carolyn Coates, Joyce Jillson, Linda Lavin, Luba Lisa, Michael O'Sullivan, Joanna Pettet, Beah Richards, Jaime Sanchez, Victor Spinetti, Nicolas Surovy, Robert Walker, Clarence Williams III

1965–66: Zoe Caldwell, David Carradine, John Cullum, John Davidson, Faye Dunaway, Gloria Foster, Robert Hooks, Jerry Lanning, Richard Mulligan, April Shawhan, Sandra Smith, Leslie Ann Warren

1966–67: Bonnie Bedelia, Richard Benjamin, Dustin Hoffman, Terry Kiser, Reva Rose, Robert Salvio, Sheila Smith, Connie Stevens, Pamela Tiffin, Leslie Uggams, Jon Voight, Christopher Walken

1967–68: David Birney, Pamela Burrell, Jordan Christopher, Jack Crowder (Thalmus Rasulala), Sandy Duncan, Julie Gregg, Stephen Joyce, Bernadette Peters, Alice Playten, Michael Rupert, Brenda Smiley, Russ Thacker

1968–69: Jane Alexander, David Cryer, Blythe Danner, Ed Evanko, Ken Howard, Lauren Jones, Ron Leibman, Marian Mercer, Jill O'Hara, Ron O'Neal, Al Pacino, Marlene Warfield

1969–70: Susan Browning, Donny Burks, Catherine Burns, Len Cariou, Bonnie Franklin, David Holliday, Katharine Houghton, Melba Moore, David Rounds, Lewis J. Stadlen, Kristoffer Tabori, Fredricka Weber

1970–71: Clifton Davis, Michael Douglas, Julie Garfield, Martha Henry, James Naughton, Tricia O'Neil, Kipp Osborne, Roger Rathburn, Ayn Ruymen, Jennifer Salt, Joan Van Ark, Walter Willison

1971–72: Jonelle Allen, Maureen Anderman, William Atherton, Richard Backus, Adrienne Barbeau, Cara Duff-MacCormick, Robert Foxworth, Elaine Joyce, Jess Richards, Ben Vereen, Beatrice Winde, James Woods

1972–73: D'Jamin Bartlett, Patricia Elliott, James Farentino, Brian Farrell, Victor Garber, Kelly Garrett, Mari Gorman, Laurence Guittard, Trish Hawkins, Monte Markham, John Rubinstein, Jennifer Warren; Special Award: Alexander H. Cohen

1973–74: Mark Baker, Maureen Brennan, Ralph Carter, Thom Christopher, John Driver, Conchata Ferrell, Ernestine Jackson, Michael Moriarty, Joe Morton, Ann Reinking, Janie Sell, Mary Woronov; Special Award: Sammy Cahn

1974–75: Peter Burnell, Zan Charisse, Lola Falana, Peter Firth, Dorian Harewood, Joel Higgins, Marcia McClain, Linda Miller, Marti Rolph, John Sheridan, Scott Stevensen, Donna Theodore; Special Award: Equity Library Theatre

1975–76: Danny Aiello, Christine Andreas, Dixie Carter, Tovah Feldshuh, Chip Garnett, Richard Kelton, Vivian Reed, Charles Repole, Virginia Seidel, Daniel Seltzer, John V. Shea, Meryl Streep; Special Award: *A Chorus Line*

1976–77: Trazana Beverley, Michael Cristofer, Joe Fields, Joanna Gleason, Cecilia Hart, John Heard, Gloria Hodes, Juliette Koka, Andrea McArdle, Ken Page, Jonathan Pryce, Chick Vennera; Special Award: Eva LeGallienne

1977–78: Vasili Bogazianos, Nell Carter, Carlin Glynn, Christopher Goutman, William Hurt, Judy Kaye, Florence Lacy, Armelia McQueen, Gordana Rashovich, Bo Rucker, Richard Seer, Colin Stinton; Special Award: Joseph Papp

1978–79: Philip Anglim, Lucie Arnaz, Gregory Hines, Ken Jennings, Michael Jeter, Laurie Kennedy, Susan Kingsley, Christine Lahti, Edward James Olmos, Kathleen Quinlan, Sarah Rice, Max Wright; Special Award: Marshall W. Mason

1979–80: Maxwell Caulfield, Leslie Denniston, Boyd Gaines, Richard Gere, Harry Groener, Stephen James, Susan Kellermann, Dinah Manoff, Lonny Price, Marianne Tatum, Anne Twomey, Dianne Wiest; Special Award: Mickey Rooney

1980–81: Brian Backer, Lisa Banes, Meg Bussert, Michael Allen Davis, Giancarlo Esposito, Daniel Gerroll, Phyllis Hyman, Cynthia Nixon, Amanda Plummer, Adam Redfield, Wanda Richert, Rex Smith; Special Award: Elizabeth Taylor

1981–82: Karen Akers, Laurie Beechman, Danny Glover, David Alan Grier, Jennifer Holliday, Anthony Heald, Lizbeth Mackay, Peter MacNicol, Elizabeth McGovern, Ann Morrison, Michael O'Keefe, James Widdoes; Special Award: Manhattan Theatre Club

1982–83: Karen Allen, Suzanne Bertish, Matthew Broderick, Kate Burton, Joanne Camp, Harvey Fierstein, Peter Gallagher, John Malkovich, Anne Pitoniak, James Russo, Brian Tarantina, Linda Thorson; Special Award: Natalia Makarova

1983–84: Martine Allard, Joan Allen, Kathy Whitton Baker, Mark Capri, Laura Dean, Stephen Geoffreys, Todd Graff, Glenne Headly, J.J. Johnston, Bonnie Koloc, Calvin Levels, Robert Westenberg; Special Award: Ron Moody

1984–85: Kevin Anderson, Richard Chaves, Patti Cohenour, Charles S. Dutton, Nancy Giles, Whoopi Goldberg, Leilani Jones, John Mahoney, Laurie Metcalf, Barry Miller, John Turturro, Amelia White; Special Award: Lucille Lortel

1985–86: Suzy Amis, Alec Baldwin, Aled Davies, Faye Grant, Julie Hagerty, Ed Harris, Mark Jacoby, Donna Kane, Cleo Laine, Howard McGillin, Marisa Tomei, Joe Urla; Special Award: Ensemble Studio Theatre

1986–87: Annette Bening, Timothy Daly, Lindsay Duncan, Frank Ferrante, Robert Lindsay, Amy Madigan, Michael Maguire, Demi Moore, Molly Ringwald, Frances Ruffelle, Courtney B. Vance, Colm Wilkinson; Special Award: Robert DeNiro

1987–88: Yvonne Bryceland, Philip Casnoff, Danielle Ferland, Melissa Gilbert, Linda Hart, Linzi Hately, Brian Kerwin, Brian Mitchell, Mary Murfitt, Aidan Quinn, Eric Roberts, B.D. Wong; Special Awards: Tisa Chang, Martin E. Segal

1988–89: Dylan Baker, Joan Cusack, Loren Dean, Peter Frechette, Sally Mayes, Sharon McNight, Jennie Moreau, Paul Provenza, Kyra Sedgwick, Howard Spiegel, Eric Stoltz, Joanne Whalley-Kilmer; Special Awards: Pauline Collins, Mikhail Baryshnikov

1989–90: Denise Burse, Erma Campbell, Rocky Carroll, Megan Gallagher, Tommy Hollis, Robert Lambert, Kathleen Rowe McAllen, Michael McKean, Crista Moore, Mary-Louise Parker, Daniel von Bargen, Jason Workman; Special Awards: Stewart Granger, Kathleen Turner

1990–91: Jane Adams, Gillian Anderson, Adam Arkin, Brenda Blethyn, Marcus Chong, Paul Hipp, LaChanze, Kenny Neal, Kevin Ramsey, Francis Ruivivar, Lea Salonga, Chandra Wilson; Special Awards: Tracey Ullman, Ellen Stewart

1991–92: Talia Balsam, Lindsay Crouse, Griffin Dunne, Larry Fishburne, Mel Harris, Jonathan Kaplan, Jessica Lange, Laura Linney, Spiro Malas, Mark Rosenthal, Helen Shaver, Al White; Special Awards: *Dancing at Lughnasa* Company, Plays for Living

1992–93: Brent Carver, Michael Cerveris, Marcia Gay Harden, Stephanie Lawrence, Andrea Martin, Liam Neeson, Stephen Rea, Natasha Richardson, Martin Short, Dina Spybey, Stephen Spinella, Jennifer Tilly. Special Awards: John Leguizamo, Rosetta LeNoire

1993–94: Marcus D'Amico, Jarrod Emick, Arabella Field, Adam Gillett, Sherry Glaser, Michael Hayden, Margaret Illman, Audra Ann McDonald, Burke Moses, Anna Deavere Smith, Jere Shea, Harriet Walter

1994–95: Gretha Boston, Billy Crudup, Ralph Fiennes, Beverly D'Angelo, Calista Flockhart, Kevin Kilner, Anthony LaPaglia, Julie Johnson, Helen Mirren, Jude Law, Rufus Sewell, Vanessa Williams; Special Award: Brooke Shields

1995–96: Jordan Baker, Joohee Choi, Karen Kay Cody, Viola Davis, Kate Forbes, Michael McGrath, Alfred Molina, Timothy Olyphant, Adam Pascal, Lou Diamond Phillips, Daphne Rubin-Vega, Brett Tabisel; Special Award: *An Ideal Husband* Cast

1996–97: Terry Beaver, Helen Carey, Kristin Chenoweth, Jason Danieley, Linda Eder, Allison Janney, Daniel McDonald, Janet McTeer, Mark Ruffalo, Fiona Shaw, Antony Sher, Alan Tudyk; Special Award: *Skylight* Cast

1997–98: Max Casella, Margaret Colin, Ruaidhri Conroy, Alan Cumming, Lea Delaria, Edie Falco, Enid Graham, Anna Kendrick, Ednita Nazario, Douglas Sills, Steven Sutcliffe, Sam Trammel; Special Awards: Eddie Izzard, *Beauty Queen of Leenane* Cast

1998–99: Jillian Armenante, James Black, Brendan Coyle, Anna Friel, Rupert Graves, Lynda Gravatt, Nicole Kidman, Ciaran Hinds, Ute Lemper, Clarke Peter, Toby Stephens, Sandra Oh; Special Award: Jerry Herman

1999–2000: Craig Bierko, Everett Bradley, Gabriel Byrne, Ann Hampton Callaway, Toni Collette, Henry Czerny, Stephen Dillane, Jennifer Ehle, Philip Seymour Hoffman, Hayley Mills, Cigdem Onat, Claudia Shear

2000–2001: Juliette Binoche, Macaulay Culkin, Janie Dee, Raúl Esparza, Kathleen Freeman, Devin May, Reba McEntire, Chris Noth, Joshua Park, Rosie Perez, Joely Richardson, John Ritter; Special Awards: Seán Campion, Conleth Hill

2001–2002: Justin Bohon, Simon Callow, Mos Def, Emma Fielding, Adam Godley, Martin Jarvis, Spencer Kayden, Gretchen Mol, Anna Paquin, Louise Pitre, David Warner, Rachel Weisz

2002-2003: Antonio Banderas, Tammy Blanchard, Thomas Jefferson Byrd, Jonathan Cake, Victoria Hamilton, Clare Higgins, Jackie Hoffman, Mary Stuart Masterson, John Selya, Jochum ten Haaf, Daniel Sunjata, Marissa Jaret Winokur; Special Awards: Peter Filichia, Ben Hodges

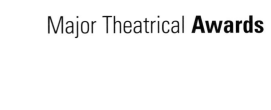

Major Theatrical **Awards**

AMERICAN THEATRE WING'S ANTOINETTE PERRY "TONY" AWARDS

The 58th annual Tony Awards are presented in recognition of distinguished achievement in the Broadway theater. The 2003–2004 Tony Awards Nominating Committee (appointed by the Tony Awards Administration Committee), included: Maureen Anderman, actor; Ira Bernstein, manager; Stephen Bogardus, actor; Schulyer G. Chaplin, executive; Kristen Childs, musical theatre writer; Veronica Claypool, manager; Betty Corwin, archivist; Gretchen Cryer, composer; Jacqueline Z. Davis, executive; Merle Debuskey, press; Edgar Dobie, manager; Nancy Ford, composer; David Marshall Grant, actor; Micki Grant, composer; Julie Hughes, casting; Betty Jacobs, consultant; Geoffrey Johnson, casting; David Lindsay-Abaire, playwright; Enid Nemy, journalist; Gilbert Parker, agent; Shirley Rich, casting; Judith O. Rubin, executive; Bill Schelble, press; Rosemarie Tichler, casting; William Tynan, journalist; Jon Wilner, producer

BEST PLAY (award goes to both author as well as producer): *I Am My Own Wife* by Doug Wright; produced by Delphi Productions, Playwrights Horizons

Nominees: *Anna in the Tropics* by Nilo Cruz; produced by Roger Berlind, Daryl Roth, Ray Larsen, Robert G. Bartner, The McCarter Theatre Center; *Frozen* by Bryony Lavery; produced by MCC Theatre, Robert LuPone, Bernard Telsey, William Cantler, John G. Shultz, Hal Newman, Zollo/Paleologos and Jeffrey Sine, Roy Gabay, Lorie Cowen Levy and Beth Smith, Peggy Hill, Thompson H. Rogers, Swinsky/Filerman/Hendel, Sirkin/Mills/Baldassare, Darren Bagert; *The Retreat from Moscow* by William Nicholson; produced by Susan Quint Gallin, Stuart Thompson, Ron Kastner, True Love Productions, Mary Lu Roffe, Jam Theatricals

BEST MUSICAL (award goes to producer): *Avenue Q* produced by Kevin McCollum, Robyn Goodman, Jeffrey Seller, Vineyard Theatre, The New Group

Nominees: *Caroline, or Change* produced by Carole Shorenstein Hays, HBO Films, Jujamcyn Theaters, Freddy DeMann, Scott Rudin, Hendel/Morten/Wiesenfeld, Fox Theatricals/Manocherian/Bergére, Roger Berlind, Clear Channel Entertainment, Joan Cullman, Greg Holland/Scott Nederlander, Margo Lion, Daryl Roth, Zollo/Sine, The Public Theater; *The Boy From Oz* produced by Ben Gannon, Robert Fox; *Wicked* produced by Marc Platt, Universal Pictures, The Araca Group, Jon B. Platt, David Stone

BEST BOOK OF A MUSICAL: Jeff Whitty, Avenue Q

Nominees: Tony Kushner, *Caroline, Or Change*; Martin Sherman/Nick Enright, *The Boy From Oz*; Winnie Holzman, *Wicked*

BEST ORIGINAL SCORE (music and/or lyrics): Robert Lopez and Jeff Marx, *Avenue Q*

Nominees: Jeanine Tesori and Tony Kushner, *Caroline, or Change*; Boy George, *Taboo*; Stephen Schwartz, *Wicked*

BEST REVIVAL OF A PLAY (award goes to producer): Henry IV produced by Lincoln Center Theater, André Bishop, Bernard Gersten

Nominees: *Jumpers* produced by Boyett Ostar Productions, Nederlander Presentations Inc., Freddy DeMann, Jean Doumanian, Stephanie McClelland, Arielle Tepper, The National Theatre of Great Britain; *King Lear* produced by Lincoln Center Theater, André Bishop, Bernard Gersten, Stratford Festival of Canada; *A Raisin in the Sun* produced by David Binder, Vivek J. Tiwary, Susan Batson, Carl Rumbaugh, Ruth Hendel, Arielle Tepper, Jayne Baron Sherman, Dede Harris, Barbara Whitman, Cynthia Stroum

BEST REVIVAL OF A MUSICAL (award goes to producer): Assassins, produced by Roundabout Theatre Company, Todd Haimes, Ellen Richard, Julia C. Levy

Nominees: *Big River*, produced by Roundabout Theatre Company, Todd Haimes, Ellen Richard, Julia C. Levy, Deaf West Theatre, Ed Waterstreet, Bill O'Brien, Center Theatre Group/Mark Taper Forum; *Fiddler on the Roof*, produced by James L. Nederlander, Stewart F. Lane/Bonnie Comley, Harbor Entertainment, Terry Allen Kramer, Bob Boyett/Lawrence Horowitz, Clear Channel Entertainment; *Wonderful Town*, produced by Roger Berlind, Barry and Fran Weissler, Edwin W. Schloss, Allen Spivak, Clear Channel Entertainment, Harvey Weinstein

BEST PERFORMANCE BY A LEADING ACTOR IN A PLAY:
Jefferson Mays, *I Am My Own Wife*

Nominees: Simon Russell Beale, *Jumpers*; Kevin Kline, *Henry IV*; Frank Langella, *Match*; Christopher Plummer, *King Lear*

BEST PERFORMANCE BY A LEADING ACTRESS IN A PLAY:
Phylicia Rashad, *A Raisin in the Sun*

Nominees: Eileen Atkins, *The Retreat from Moscow*; Tovah Feldshuh, *Golda's Balcony*; Anne Heche, *Twentieth Century*; Swoosie Kurtz, *Frozen*

BEST PERFORMANCE BY A LEADING ACTOR IN A MUSICAL:
Hugh Jackman, *The Boy From Oz*

Nominees: Hunter Foster, *Little Shop of Horrors*; Alfred Molina, *Fiddler on the Roof*; Euan Morton, *Taboo*; John Tartaglia, *Avenue Q*

BEST PERFORMANCE BY A LEADING ACTRESS IN A MUSICAL:
Idina Menzel, *Wicked*

Nominees: Kristin Chenoweth, *Wicked*; Stephanie D'Abruzzo, *Avenue Q*; Donna Murphy, *Wonderful Town*; Tonya Pinkins, *Caroline, or Change*

BEST PERFORMANCE BY A FEATURED ACTOR IN A PLAY: Brian F. O'Byrne, *Frozen*

Nominees: Tom Aldredge, *Twentieth Century*; Ben Chaplin, *The Retreat from Moscow*; Aidan Gillen, *The Caretaker*; Omar Metwally, *Sixteen Wounded*

BEST PERFORMANCE BY A FEATURED ACTRESS IN A PLAY:
Audra McDonald, *A Raisin in the Sun*

Nominees: Essie Davis, *Jumpers*; Sanaa Lathan, *A Raisin in the Sun*; Margo Martindale, *Cat on a Hot Tin Roof*; Daphne Rubin-Vega, *Anna in the Tropics*

(CONTINUED FROM PREVIOUS PAGE)

BEST PERFORMANCE BY A FEATURED ACTOR IN A MUSICAL:
Michael Cerveris, *Assassins*

Nominees: John Cariani, *Fiddler on the Roof*; Raul Esparza, *Taboo*; Michael McElroy, *Big River*; Denis O'Hare, *Assassins*

BEST PERFORMANCE BY A FEATURED ACTRESS IN A MUSICAL: Anika Noni Rose, *Caroline, or Change*

Nominees: Beth Fowler, *The Boy From Oz*; Isabel Keating, *The Boy From Oz*; Jennifer Westfeldt, *Wonderful Town*; Karen Ziemba, *Never Gonna Dance*

BEST SCENIC DESIGN: Eugene Lee, *Wicked*

Nominees: Robert Brill, *Assassins*; Ralph Funicello, *Henry IV*; Tom Pye, *Fiddler on the Roof*

BEST COSTUME DESIGN: Susan Hilferty, *Wicked*

Nominees: Jess Goldstein, *Henry IV*; Mike Nicholls and Bobby Pearce, *Taboo*; Mark Thompson, *Bombay Dreams*

BEST LIGHTING DESIGN: Jules Fisher and Peggy Eisenhauer, *Assassins*

Nominees: Brian MacDevitt, *Fiddler on the Roof*; Brian MacDevitt, *Henry IV*; Kenneth Posner, *Wicked*

BEST CHOREOGRAPHY: Kathleen Marshall, *Wonderful Town*

Nominees: Wayne Cilento, *Wicked*; Jerry Mitchell, *Never Gonna Dance*; Anthony Van Laast and Farah Khan, *Bombay Dreams*

BEST DIRECTION OF A PLAY: Jack O'Brien, *Henry IV*

Nominees: Doug Hughes, *Frozen*; Moisés Kaufman, *I Am My Own Wife*; David Leveaux, *Jumpers*

BEST DIRECTION OF A MUSICAL: Joe Mantello, *Assassins*

Nominees: Kathleen Marshall, *Wonderful Town*; Jason Moore, *Avenue Q*; George C. Wolfe, *Caroline, or Change*

BEST ORCHESTRATIONS: Michael Starobin, *Assassins*

Nominees: Paul Bogaev, *Bombay Dreams*; William David Brohn, *Wicked*; Larry Hochman, *Fiddler on the Roof*

SPECIAL TONY AWARD FOR LIFETIME ACHIEVEMENT IN THE THEATRE: James M. Nederlander

REGIONAL THEATRE TONY AWARD: Cincinnati Playhouse in the Park, Cincinnati, Ohio

Past Tony Award Winners

Awards listed are Best Play followed by Best Musical, and as awards for Best Revival and the subcategories of Best Revival of a Play and Best Revival of a Musical were instituted, they are listed respectively.

1947: No award given for musical or play **1948:** Mister Roberts (play) **1949:** Death of a Salesman, Kiss Me, Kate (musical) **1950:** The Cocktail Party, South Pacific **1951:** The Rose Tattoo, Guys and Dolls **1952:** The Fourposter, The King and I **1953:** The Crucible, Wonderful Town **1954:** The Teahouse of the August Moon, Kismet **1955:** The Desperate Hours, The Pajama Game **1956:** The Diary of Anne Frank, Damn Yankees **1957:** Long Day's Journey into Night, My Fair Lady **1958:** Sunrise at Campobello, The Music Man **1959:** J.B., Redhead **1960:** The Miracle Worker, Fiorello! tied with The Sound of Music **1961:** Becket, Bye Bye Birdie **1962:** A Man for All Seasons, How to Succeed in Business Without Really Trying **1963:** Who's Afraid of Virginia Woolf?, A Funny Thing Happened on the Way to the Forum **1964:** Luther, Hello, Dolly! **1965:** The Subject Was Roses, Fiddler on the Roof **1966:** The Persecution and Assassination of Marat as Performed by the Inmates of the Asylum of Charenton Under the Direction of the Marquis de Sade, Man of La Mancha **1967:** The Homecoming, Cabaret **1968:** Rosencrantz and Guildenstern Are Dead, Hallelujah Baby! **1969:** The Great White Hope, 1776 **1970:** Borstal Boy, Applause **1971:** Sleuth, Company **1972:** Sticks and Bones, Two Gentlemen of Verona **1973:** That Championship Season, A Little Night Music **1974:** The River Niger, Raisin **1975:** Equus, The Wiz **1976:** Travesties, A Chorus Line **1977:** The Shadow Box, Annie **1978:** Da, Ain't Misbehavin', Dracula (innovative musical revival) **1979:** The Elephant Man, Sweeney Todd **1980:** Children of a Lesser God, Evita, Morning's at Seven (best revival) **1981:** Amadeus, 42nd St., The Pirates of Penzance **1982:** The Life and Adventures of Nicholas Nickelby, Nine, Othello **1983:** Torch Song Trilogy, Cats, On Your Toes **1984:** The Real Thing, La Cage aux Folles, Death of a Salesman **1985:** Biloxi Blues, Big River, Joe Egg **1986:** I'm Not Rappaport, The Mystery of Edwin Drood, Sweet Charity **1987:** Fences, Les Misérables, All My Sons **1988:** M. Butterfly, The Phantom of the Opera, Anything Goes **1989:** The Heidi Chronicles, Jerome Robbins' Broadway, Our Town **1990:** The Grapes of Wrath, City of Angels, Gypsy **1991:** Lost in Yonkers, The Will Rogers' Follies, Fiddler on the Roof **1992:** Dancing at Lughnasa, Crazy for You, Guys and Dolls **1993:** Angels in America: Millenium Approaches, Kiss of the Spider Woman, Anna Christie **1994:** Angels in America: Perestroika (play), Passion (musical), An Inspector Calls (play revival), Carousel (musical revival) **1995:** Love! Valour! Compassion!, Sunset Boulevard, Show Boat, The Heiress **1996:** Master Class, Rent, A Delicate Balance, King and I **1997:** Last Night of Ballyhoo, Titanic, A Doll's House, Chicago **1998:** Art, The Lion King, View from the Bridge, Cabaret **1999:** Side Man, Fosse, Death of a Salesman, Annie Get Your Gun **2000:** Copenhagen, Contact, The Real Thing, Kiss Me, Kate **2001:** Proof, The Producers, One Flew Over the Cuckoo's Nest, 42nd Street **2002:** Edward Albee's The Goat, or Who Is Sylvia?, Thoroughly Modern Millie, Private Lives, Into the Woods **2003:** Take Me Out, Hairspray

VILLAGE VOICE OBIE AWARDS

49th annual; For outstanding achievement in Off- and Off-Off-Broadway theater:

Performance: Viola Davis, *Intimate Apparel*; Lisa Emery, *Iron*; Jayne Houdyshell, *Well*; Sarah Jones, *Bridge and Tunnel*; Jefferson Mays, *I Am My Own Wife*; Zilah Mendoza, *Living Out*; Maude Mitchell, *Mabou Mine's Dollhouse*; Brían F. O'Byrne, *Frozen*; Tonya Pinkins, *Caroline, or Change*; Lili Taylor, *Aunt Dan and Lemon*; Shannon Cochran, Michael Shannon, Michael Cullen, Amy Landecker and Reed Birney, *Bug*; Ana Reeder, Mary Shultz, Rob Campbell, Daniel Eric Gold, Lee Pace and Rosemarie DeWitt, *Small Tradgedy*

Direction: Lee Breuer, *Mabou Mine's Dollhouse*; Moisés Kaufman, *I Am My Own Wife*

Best American Play: *Small Tragedy*, Craig Lucas

Scenic Design: Lauren Helpern, *Bug*

Lighting Design: Tyler Micoleau, *Bug*

Costume Design: Kim Gill, *Bug*

Sound Design: Brian Ronan, *Bug*

Props Design: Faye Armon, *Bug*

Scenic Design: Derek McLane, *I Am My Own Wife*, *Aunt Dan and Lemon* and *Intimate Apparel*

Music: Robert Een, *Hiroshima Maiden*

Lifetime Achievement: Mark Russell

Special Citations: Pieter-Dirk Uys, *Foreign AIDS*; Tony Kushner and Jeanine Tesori, *Caroline, or Change*; Soho Rep for *Molly's Dream*; The Builders Association and motiroti, *Alladeen*; Kyle Jarrow and Alex Timbers, *A Very Merry Unauthorized Children's Scientology Pageant*; George C. Wolfe, for his stewardship of the Public Theatre; Martin Moran, *The Tricky Part*; Terry Nemeth for play publishing at Theatre Communications Group

Grants: The Civilians, Musicals Tonight, THAW (Theaters Against War)

Ross Wetzsteon Award: St. Ann's Warehouse (Susan Feldman, artistic director)

Past Obie Best New Play Winners

1956: Absalom, Absalom **1957:** A House Remembered **1958:** no award given **1959:** The Quare Fellow **1960:** no award given **1961:** The Blacks **1962:** Who'll Save the Plowboy? **1963:** no award given **1964:** Play **1965:** The Old Glory **1966:** The Journey of the Fifth Horse **1967:** no award given **1968:** no award given **1969:** no award given **1970:** The Effect of Gamma Rays on Man-in-the-Moon Marigolds **1971:** House of Blue Leaves **1972:** no award given **1973:** The Hot L Baltimore **1974:** Short Eyes **1975:** The First Breeze of Summer **1976:** American Buffalo, Sexual Perversity in Chicago **1977:** Curse of the Starving Class **1978:** Shaggy Dog Animation **1979:** Josephine **1980:** no award given **1981:** FOB **1982:** Metamorphosis in Miniature, Mr. Dead and Mrs. Free **1983:** Painting Churches, Andrea Rescued, Edmond **1984:** Fool for Love **1985:** The Conduct of Life **1986:** no award given **1987:** The Cure, Film Is Evil, Radio Is Good **1988:** Abingdon Square **1989:** no award given **1990:** Prelude to a Kiss, Imperceptible Mutabilities in the Third Kingdom, Bad Benny, Crowbar, Terminal Hip **1991:** The Fever **1992:** Sight Unseen, Sally's Rape, The Baltimore Waltz **1993:** no award given **1994:** Twilight: Los Angeles 1992 **1995:** Cyrptogram **1996:** Adrienne Kennedy **1997:** One Flea Spare **1998:** Pearls for Pigs and Benita Canova **1999:** no award given **2000:** no award given **2001:** The Syringa Tree **2002:** no award given **2003:** no award given **2004:**

DRAMA DESK AWARDS

49th annual; For outstanding achievement in the 2003–2004 season, voted on by an association of New York drama reporters, editors and critics from nominations made from a committee:

New Play: *I Am My Own Wife*

New Musical: *Wicked*

Revival of a Play: *Henry IV*

Revival of a Musical: *Assassins*

Book: Winnie Holzman, *Wicked*

Composer: Jeanine Tesori, *Caroline, or Change*

Lyricist: Stephen Schwartz, *Wicked*

Actor in a Play: Kevin Kline, *Henry IV*

Actress in a Play: (tie) Viola Davis, *Intimate Apparel*; Phylicia Rashad, *A Raisin in the Sun*

Featured Actor in a Play: Ned Beatty, *Cat on a Hot Tin Roof*

Featured Actress in a Play: Audra McDonald, *A Raisin in the Sun*

Actor in a Musical: Hugh Jackman, *The Boy From Oz*

Actress in a Musical: Donna Murphy, *Wonderful Town*

Featured Actor in a Musical: Raúl Esparza, *Taboo*

Featured Actress in a Musical: Isabel Keating, *The Boy From Oz*

Solo Performance: Jefferson Mays, *I Am My Own Wife*

Director of a Play: Jack O'Brien, *Henry IV*

Director of a Musical: Joe Mantello, *Wicked*

Choreography: Kathleen Marshall, *Wonderful Town*

Orchestrations: Michael Starobin, *Assassins*

Set Design of a Play: John Lee Beatty, *Twentieth Century*

Set Design of a Musical: Eugene Lee, *Wicked*

Costume Design: Susan Hilferty, *Wicked*

Lighting Design: Jules Fisher and Peggy Eisenhauer, *Assassins*

Sound Design: Dan Moses Schreier, *Assassins*

Unique Theatrical Experience: Toxic Audio in *Loudmouth*

Distinguished Achievement: Dakin Matthews, adaptation of William Shakespeare's *Henry IV*, parts 1 and 2; The Flea Theatre; The Classical Theatre of Harlem

OUTER CRITICS CIRCLE AWARDS

54th annual; For outstanding achievement in the 2003–2004 season, voted on by critics in out-of-town periodicals and media:

Broadway Play: *I Am My Own Wife*

Off-Broadway Play: *Intimate Apparel*

Revival of a Play: *Henry IV*

Actor in a Play: Frank Langella, *Match*

Actress in a Play: Eileen Atkins, *The Retreat From Moscow*

Featured Actor in a Play: Ned Beatty, *Cat on a Hot Tin Roof*

Featured Actress in a Play: Audra McDonald, *A Raisin in the Sun*

Director of a Play: Jack O'Brien, *Henry IV*

Broadway Musical: *Wicked*

Off-Broadway Musical: (tie) *Johnny Guitar* and *The Thing About Men*

Revival of a Musical: *Wonderful Town*

Actor in a Musical: Hugh Jackman, *The Boy From Oz*

Actress in a Musical: Donna Murphy, *Wonderful Town*

Featured Actor in a Musical: (tie) John Cariani, *Fiddler on the Roof*; Michael Cerveris, *Assassins*

Featured Actress in a Musical: Karen Ziemba, *Never Gonna Dance*

Director of a Musical: Joe Mantello, *Wicked*

Choreography: Kathleen Marshall, *Wonderful Town*

Scenic Design: Eugene Lee, *Wicked*

Costume Design: Susan Hilferty, *Wicked*

Lighting Design: Jules Fisher and Peggy Eisenhauer, *Assassins*

Solo Performance: Jefferson Mays, *I Am My Own Wife*

John Gassner Playwriting Award: Lynn Nottage, *Intimate Apparel*

Special Achievement Award: Ensemble performance and puppet artistry, the cast of *Avenue Q*

PULITZER PRIZE AWARD WINNERS FOR DRAMA

1918: *Why Marry?* by Jesse Lynch Williams **1919:** no award **1920:** *Beyond the Horizon* by Eugene O'Neill **1921:** *Miss Lulu Bett* by Zona Gale **1922:** *Anna Christie* by Eugene O'Neill **1923:** *Icebound* by Owen Davis **1924:** *Hell-Bent for Heaven* by Hatcher Hughes **1925:** *They Knew What They Wanted* by Sidney Howard **1926:** *Craig's Wife* by George Kelly **1927:** *In Abraham's Bosom* by Paul Green **1928:** *Strange Interlude* by Eugene O'Neill **1929:** *Street Scene* by Elmer Rice **1930:** *The Green Pastures* by Marc Connelly **1931:** *Alison's House* by Susan Glaspell **1932:** *Of Thee I Sing* by George S. Kaufman, Morrie Ryskind, Ira and George Gershwin **1933:** *Both Your Houses* by Maxwell Anderson **1934:** *Men in White* by Sidney Kingsley **1935:** *The Old Maid* by Zoe Atkins **1936:** *Idiot's Delight* by Robert E. Sherwood **1937:** *You Can't Take It with You* by Moss Hart and George S. Kaufman **1938:** *Our Town* by Thornton Wilder **1939:** *Abe Lincoln in Illinois* by Robert E. Sherwood **1940:** *The Time of Your Life* by William Saroyan **1941:** *There Shall Be No Night* by Robert E. Sherwood **1942:** no award **1943:** *The Skin of Our Teeth* by Thornton Wilder **1944:** no award **1945:** *Harvey* by Mary Chase **1946:** *State of the Union* by Howard Lindsay and Russel Crouse **1947:** no award **1948:** *A Streetcar Named Desire* by Tennessee Williams **1949:** *Death of a Salesman* by Arthur Miller **1950:** *South Pacific* by Richard Rodgers, Oscar Hammerstein II, and Joshua Logan **1951:** no award **1952:** *The Shrike* by Joseph Kramm **1953:** *Picnic* by William Inge **1954:** *The Teahouse of the August Moon* by John Patrick **1955:** *Cat on a Hot Tin Roof* by Tennessee Williams **1956:** *The Diary of Anne Frank* by Frances Goodrich and Albert Hackett **1957:** *Long Day's Journey into Night* by Eugene O'Neill **1958:** *Look Homeward, Angel* by Ketti Frings **1959:** *J.B.* by Archibald MacLeish **1960:** *Fiorello!* by Jerome Weidman, George Abbott, Sheldon Harnick, and Jerry Bock **1961:** *All the Way Home* by Tad Mosel **1962:** *How to Succeed in Business Without Really Trying* by Abe Burrows, Willie Gilbert, Jack Weinstock, and Frank Loesser **1963:** no award **1964:** no award **1965:** *The Subject Was Roses* by Frank D. Gilroy **1966:** no award **1967:** *A Delicate Balance* by Edward Albee **1968:** no award **1969:** *The Great White Hope* by Howard Sackler **1970:** *No Place to Be Somebody* by Charles Gordone **1971:** *The Effect of Gamma Rays on Man-in-the-Moon Marigolds* by Paul Zindel **1972:** no award **1973:** *That Championship Season* by Jason Miller **1974:** no award **1975:** *Seascape* by Edward Albee **1976:** *A Chorus Line* by Michael Bennett, James Kirkwood, Nicholas Dante, Marvin Hamlisch, and Edward Kleban **1977:** *The Shadow Box* by Michael Cristofer **1978:** *The Gin Game* by D.L. Coburn **1979:** *Buried Child* by Sam Shepard **1980:** *Talley's Folly* by Lanford Wilson **1981:** *Crimes of the Heart* by Beth Henley **1982:** *A Soldier's Play* by Charles Fuller **1983:** *'night, Mother* by Marsha Norman **1984:** *Glengarry Glen Ross* by David Mamet **1985:** *Sunday in the Park with George* by James Lapine and Stephen Sondheim **1986:** no award **1987:** *Fences* by August Wilson **1988:** *Driving Miss Daisy* by Alfred Uhry **1989:** *The Heidi Chronicles* by Wendy Wasserstein **1990:** *The Piano Lesson* by August Wilson **1991:** *Lost in Yonkers* by Neil Simon **1992:** *The Kentucky Cycle* by Robert Schenkkan **1993:** *Angels in America: Millenium Approaches* by Tony Kushner **1994:** *Three Tall Women* by Edward Albee **1995:** *Young Man from Atlanta* by Horton Foote **1996:** *Rent* by Jonathan Larson **1997:** no award **1998:** *How I Learned to Drive* by Paula Vogel **1999:** *Wit* by Margaret Edson **2000:** *Dinner with Friends* by Donald Margulies **2001:** *Proof* by David Auburn **2002:** *Topdog/Underdog* by Suzan Lori-Parks **2003:** *Anna in the Tropics* by Nilo Cruz **2004:** *I Am My Own Wife* by Doug Wright

NEW YORK DRAMA CRITICS' CIRCLE AWARD WINNERS

2003 New York Drama Critics' Circle Committee: President, Charles Isherwood (*Variety*), Clive Barnes (*The New York Post*), Jeremy Carter (*The New York Sun*), David Cote (*Time Out New York*), Michael Feingold (*The Village Voice*), Robert Feldberg (*The Bergen Record*), John Heilpern (*The New York Observer*), Howard Kissel (*Daily News*), Michael Kuchwara (*The Associated Press*), Jacques le Sourd (Gannett *Journal News*), Ken Mandelbaum (*Broadway.com*), David Sheward (*Back Stage*), Michael Sommers (*The Star-Ledger*/Newhouse Papers), Donald Lyons (*The New York Post*), Frank Scheck (*The Hollywood Reporter*), John Simon (*New York*), Linda Winer (*Newsday*), Jason Zinoman (*Time Out New York*), Richard Zoglin (*Time*)

Awards listed are in the following order: Best American Play, Best Foreign Play, Best Musical, and Best Regardless of Category, which was instituted during the 1962–1963 award season:

1936: Winterset **1937:** High Tor **1938:** Of Mice and Men, Shadow and Substance **1939:** The White Steed **1940:** The Time of Your Life **1941:** Watch on the Rhine, The Corn Is Green **1942:** Blithe Spirit **1943:** The Patriots **1944:** Jacobowsky and the Colonel **1945:** The Glass Menagerie **1946:** Carousel **1947:** All My Sons, No Exit, Brigadoon **1948:** A Streetcar Named Desire, The Winslow Boy **1949:** Death of a Salesman, The Madwoman of Chaillot, South Pacific **1950:** The Member of the Wedding, The Cocktail Party, The Consul **1951:** Darkness at Noon, The Lady's Not for Burning, Guys and Dolls **1952:** I Am a Camera, Venus Observed, Pal Joey **1953:** Picnic, The Love of Four Colonels, Wonderful Town **1954:** Teahouse of the August Moon, Ondine, The Golden Apple **1955:** Cat on a Hot Tin Roof, Witness for the Prosecution, The Saint of Bleecker Street **1956:** The Diary of Anne Frank, Tiger at the Gates, My Fair Lady **1957:** Long Day's Journey into Night, The Waltz of the Toreadors, The Most Happy Fella **1958:** Look Homeward Angel, Look Back in Anger, The Music Man **1959:** A Raisin in the Sun, The Visit, La Plume de Ma Tante **1960:** Toys in the Attic, Five Finger Exercise, Fiorello! **1961:** All the Way Home, A Taste of Honey, Carnival **1962:** Night of the Iguana, A Man for All Seasons, How to Succeed in Business without Really Trying **1963:** Who's Afraid of Virginia Woolf? **1964:** Luther, Hello Dolly! **1965:** The Subject Was Roses, Fiddler on the Roof **1966:** The Persecution and Assassination of Marat as Performed by the Inmates of the Asylum of Charenton under the Direction of the Marquis de Sade, Man of La Mancha **1967:** The Homecoming, Cabaret **1968:** Rosencrantz and Guildenstern Are Dead, Your Own Thing **1969:** The Great White Hope, 1776 **1970:** The Effect of Gamma Rays on Man-in-the-Moon Marigolds, Borstal Boy, Company **1971:** Home, Follies, The House of Blue Leaves **1972:** That Championship Season, Two Gentlemen of Verona **1973:** The Hot L Baltimore, The Changing Room, A Little Night Music **1974:** The Contractor, Short Eyes, Candide **1975:** Equus, The Taking of Miss Janie, A Chorus Line **1976:** Travesties, Streamers, Pacific Overtures **1977:** Otherwise Engaged, American Buffalo, Annie **1978:** Da, Ain't Misbehavin' **1979:** The Elephant Man, Sweeney Todd **1980:** Talley's Folley, Evita, Betrayal **1981:** Crimes of the Heart, A Lesson from Aloes, Special Citation to Lena Horne, The Pirates of Penzance **1982:** The Life and Adventures of Nicholas Nickleby, A Soldier's Play, (no musical) **1983:** Brighton Beach Memoirs, Plenty, Little Shop of Horrors **1984:** The Real Thing, Glengarry Glen Ross, Sunday in the Park with George **1985:** Ma Rainey's Black Bottom, (no musical) **1986:** A Lie of the Mind, Benefactors, (no musical), Special Citation to Lily Tomlin and Jane Wagner **1987:** Fences, Les Liaisons Dangereuses, Les Misérables **1988:** Joe Turner's Come and Gone, The Road to Mecca, Into the Woods **1989:** The Heidi Chronicles, Aristocrats, Largely New York (special), (no musical) **1990:** The Piano Lesson, City of Angels, Privates on Parade **1991:** Six Degrees of Separation, The Will Rogers Follies, Our Country's Good, Special Citation to Eileen Atkins **1992:** Two Trains Running, Dancing at Lughnasa **1993:** Angels in America: Millenium Approaches, Someone Who'll Watch Over Me, Kiss of the Spider Woman **1994:** Three Tall Women, Anna Deavere Smith (special) **1995:** Arcadia, Love! Valour! Compassion!, Special Award: Signature Theatre Company **1996:** Seven Guitars, Molly Sweeny, Rent **1997:** How I Learned to Drive, Skylight, Violet, Chicago (special) **1998:** Pride's Crossing, Art, Lion King, Cabaret (special) **1999:** Wit, Parade, Closer, David Hare (special) **2000:** Jitney, James Joyce's The Dead, Copenhagen **2001:** The Invention of Love, The Producers, Proof **2002:** Edward Albee's The Goat, or Who is Sylvia?, Special

citation to Elaine Stritch for Elaine Stritch at Liberty **2003:** Take Me Out, Talking Heads, Hairspray **2004:** *Intimate Apparel* (Special citation to Barbara Cook for her contribution to the musical theatre)

LUCILLE LORTEL AWARDS

Presented by the League of Off-Broadway Theatres and Producers

The 2004 awards committee consisted of Mark Dickerman, Susan Einhorn, Adam Feldman, George Forbes, Charles Isherwood, Walt Kiskaddon, Gerald Rabkin, Mark Rossier, Marc Routh, Donald Saddler, Tom Smedes, Anna Strasberg, Barbara Wolkoff

Play: *Bug*, by Tracy Letts

Musical: *Caroline, or Change*, book and lyrics by Tony Kushner, music by Jeanine Tesori

Outstanding Solo Show: *I Am My Own Wife*, by Doug Wright, starring Jefferson Mays

Actor: Brían F. O'Byrne, *Frozen*

Actress: Tonya Pinkins, *Caroline, or Change*

Featured Actor: Will McCormack, *The Long Christmas Ride Home*

Featured Actress: Anika Noni Rose, *Caroline, or Change*

Direction: Dexter Bullard, *Bug*

Choreography: Hope Clarke, *Caroline, or Change*

Scenery: Derek McLane, *I Am My Own Wife*

Costumes: Catherine Zuber, *The Beard of Avon*

Lighting: Tyler Micoleau, *Bug*

Sound: Brian Ronan, *Bug*

Body of Work: The Public Theater

Playwrights' Sidewalk: Tony Kushner

Edith Olivier Award: Kathleen Chalfant

Unique Theatrical Experience: *Noche Flamenca*

Past Lucille Lortel Award Winners

Awards listed are Outstanding Play and Outstanding Musical, respectively, since inception

1986: *Woza Africa!*; no musical award **1987:** *The Common Pursuit*; no musical award **1988:** no play or musical award **1989:** *The Cocktail Hour*; no musical award **1990:** no play or musical award **1991:** *Aristocrats*; *Falsettoland* **1992:** *Lips Together, Teeth Apart*; *And the World Goes 'Round* **1993:** *The Destiny of Me*; *Forbidden Broadway* **1994:** *Three Tall Women*; *Wings* **1995:** *Camping with Henry & Tom*; *Jelly Roll!* **1996:** *Molly Sweeney*, *Floyd Collins* **1997:** *How I Learned to Drive*; *Violet* **1998:** (tie) *Gross Indecency* and *The Beauty Queen of Leenane*; no musical award **1999:** *Wit*; no musical award **2000:** *Dinner With Friends*; *James Joyce's The Dead* **2001:** *Proof*; *Bat Boy. The Musical* **2002:** *Metamorphoses*; *Urinetown* **2003:** *Take Me Out*, *Avenue Q*

AMERICAN THEATRE CRITICS/STEINBERG NEW PLAY AWARDS AND CITATIONS

New Play Citations

1977: *And the Soul Shall Dance* by Wakako Yamauchi **1978:** *Getting Out* by Marsha Norman **1979:** *Loose Ends* by Michael Weller **1980:** *Custer* by Robert E. Ingham **1981:** *Chekhov in Yalta* by John Driver and Jeffrey Haddow **1982:** *Talking With* by Jane Martin **1983:** *Closely Related* by Bruce MacDonald **1984:** *Wasted* by Fred Gamel **1985:** *Scheherazade* by Marisha Chamberlain

New Play Awards

1986: *Fences* by August Wilson **1987:** *A Walk in the Woods* by Lee Blessing **1988:** *Heathen Valley* by Romulus Linney **1989:** *The Piano Lesson* by August Wilson **1990:** *2* by Romulus Linney **1991:** *Two Trains Running* by August Wilson **1992:** *Could I Have This Dance* by Doug Haverty **1993:** *Children of Paradise: Shooting a Dream* by Steven Epp, Felicity Jones, Dominique Serrand, and Paul Walsh **1994:** *Keely and Du* by Jane Martin **1995:** *The Nanjing Race* by Reggie Cheong-Leen **1996:** *Amazing Grace* by Michael Cristofer **1997:** *Jack and Jill* by Jane Martin **1998:** *The Cider House Rules, Part II* by Peter Parnell **1999:** *Book of Days* by Lanford Wilson

ATCA/Steinberg New Play Awards and Citations

2000: *Oo-Bla-Dee* by Regina Taylor; Citations: *Compleat Female Stage Beauty* by Jeffrey Hatcher; *Syncopation* by Allan Knee **2001:** *Anton in Show Business* by Jane Martin; Citations: *Big Love* by Charles L. Mee; *King Hedley II* by August Wilson **2002:** *The Carpetbagger's Children* by Horton Foote; Citations: *The Action Against Sol Schumann* by Jeffrey Sweet; *Joe and Betty* by Murray Mednick **2003:** *Anna in the Tropics* by Nilo Cruz; Citations: *Recent Tragic Events* by Craig Wright; *Resurrection Blues* by Arthur Miller **2004:** *Intimate Apparel* by Lynn Nottage; Citations: *Gem of the Ocean* by August Wilson; *The Love Song of J. Robert Oppenheimer* by Carson Kreitzer

ASTAIRE AWARDS

23rd annual; For excellence in dance and choreography, administered by the Theatre Development Fund and selected by a committee comprising Douglas Watt (Chairman), Clive Barnes, Howard Kissel, Michael Kuchwara, Donald McDonagh, Richard Philip, Charles L. Reinhart, and Linda Winer:

Choreography: Kathleen Marshall, *Wonderful Town*
Female Dancer: Donna Murphy, *Wonderful Town*
Male Dancer: Hugh Jackman, *The Boy From Oz*

CARBONELL AWARDS

29th annual; For outstanding achievement in South Florida theater during the 2003–2004 season.

New Work: *Running with Scissors*, by Michael McKeever
Ensemble: *Tracers*, produced by Juggerknot Theatre Company
Production of a Play: *The Goat, or Who Is Sylvia?*
Director of a Play: Joseph Adler, *The Goat, or Who Is Sylvia*
Actor in a Play: David Kwiat, *QED*
Actress in a Play: Laura Turnbull, *The Goat, or Who Is Sylvia?*
Supporting Actor in a Play: Paul Tei, *Running with Scissors*
Supporting Actress in a Play: Lorena Diaz, *Betty's Summer Vacation*
Production of a Musical: *Jacques Brel Is Alive and Well and Living in Paris*, produced by Palm Beach Dramaworks
Director of a Musical: J. Barry Lewis, *Jacques Brel Is Alive and Well and Living in Paris*
Actor in a Musical: E.L. Losada, *Bat Boy*
Actress in a Musical: Jeanne Lynn, *The Life*
Supporting Actor in a Musical: Terrel Hardcastle, *Annie*
Supporting Actress in a Musical: Morgot Moreland, *Annie*
Musical Direction: Craig D. Ames, *Jacques Brel Is Alive and Well and Living in Paris*
Choreography: Chrissi Ardito, *West Side Story*
Scenic Design: Rich Simone, *The Goat, or Who Is Sylvia?*
Lighting: Jeff Quinn, *The Goat, or Who Is Sylvia?*
Costumes: Mary Lynne Izzo, *Return to the Forbidden Planet*
Sound: Steve Shapiro, *Take Me Out*

Non Resident Productions

Production: *The Producers*
Actress: Kate Mulgrew, *Tea At Five*
Actor: Lewis J. Stadlen, *The Producers*
Director: Susan Stroman, *The Producers*
George Abbott Award: Sherron Long
Howard Kleinberg Award: Mark Nerenhausen
Ruth Foreman Award: Lawrence E. Stein
Bill Hindman Award: Meredith Lasher

CLARENCE DERWENT AWARDS

59th annual; Given to a female and male performer by Actors Equity Association, based on work in New York that demonstrates promise.
Anika Noni Rose; John Tartaglia

CONNECTICUT CRITICS' CIRCLE AWARDS

14th annual; For outstanding achievement in Connecticut theater during the 2003–2004 season:

Production of a Play: Yale Repertory Theatre, *The Mystery Plays*

Production of a Musical: Goodspeed Musicals, *Very Good Eddie*

Actress in a Play: Jill Clayburgh, *All My Sons*

Actor in a Play: (tie) Hamish Linklater, *Hamlet*; Cody Nickell, *Visiting Mr. Green*

Actress in a Musical: Julia Kiley, *Follies*

Actor in a Musical: Randy Rogel, *Very Good Eddie*

Direction of a Play: Oskar Eustis, *The Long Christmas Ride Home*

Direction of a Musical: Gary John LaRosa, *La Cage aux Folles*

Choreography: Dan Siretta, *Very Good Eddie*

Set Design: Adrian W. Jones, *The Dazzle*

Lighting Design: (tie) T.J. Gerckens, *Metamorphoses*; S. Ryan Schmidt, *The Mystery Plays*

Costume Design: Suzy Benzinger, *Very Good Eddie*

Sound Design: (tie) Keith Townsend Obadike, *The Mystery Plays*; Asa F. Wembler, *Route 66*

Ensemble Performance: Antoinette Broderick, Sun Mee Chomet, Anne Fogarty, Raymond Fox, Kyle Hall, Chris Kipiniak, Erika LaVonn, James McKay, Paul Oakley Stovall, Gabra Zackman, *Metamorphoses*

Road Show: Hartford Stage, Hedwig and the Angry Inch

Debut Award: (tie) Zack Griffiths, *The Goat, or Who Is Sylvia?*; Remy Zaken, *A Tree Grows in Brooklyn*

Special Award: Donald Margulies

Tom Killen Memorial Award: Bert Bernardi, artistic director of Downtown Cabert Children's Company

DRAMA LEAGUE AWARDS

70th annual; For distinguished achievement in the American theater:

Play: *I Am My Own Wife*

Musical: *Wicked*

Revival of a Play or Musical: *Henry IV*

Performance: Hugh Jackman, *The Boy From Oz*

Julia Hansen Award for Excellence in Directing: George C. Wolfe

Achievement in Musical Theatre: Donna Murphy

Unique Contribution to Theater: City Center Encores!: Jack Viertel, Arlene Shuler and Rob Fisher

DRAMATIST GUILD AWARDS

Elizabeth Hull-Kate Warriner Award (to the playwright whose work deals with social, political or religious mores of the time): Doug Wright, *I Am My Own Wife*

Frederick Loewe Award for Dramatic Composition: Jerry Bock

Flora Roberts Award: William Finn

Lifetime Achievement: John Kander and Fred Ebb

ELLIOTT NORTON AWARDS

22st annual; For outstanding contribution to the theater in Boston, voted by a Boston Theater Critics Association selection committee comprising Terry Byrne, Carolyn Clay, Iris Fanger, Joyce Kullhawik, Jon L. Lehman, Bill Marx, Ed Siegel and Caldwell Titcomb:

Sustained Excellence: Paula Plum

Visiting Company: *As You Like It*, produced by Theatre Royal Bath, Sir Peter Hall Company, Broadway in Boston and Huntington Theatre Company at the Wilbur Theatre

Large Resident Company: *The Long Christmas Ride Home*, produced by Trinity Repertory Company

Small Resident Company: *Collected Stories*, produced by Gloucester Stage Company

Local Fringe Company: (two awards) *Jesus Hopped the "A" Train*, produced by Company One; *Pussy on the House*, produced by The Gold Dust Orphans

(Musical) Large Resident Company: *Pacific Overtures*, produced by North Shore Music Entertainment

(Musical) Small Resident Company: *Sweeney Todd*, produced by New Repertory Theatre

Actor: Large company: Paxton Whitehead, *What the Bulter Saw*; Small company: Vincent E. Siders, *Jesus Hopped the "A" Train, Monticel* and *Our Lady of 121st Street*

Actress: Large company: Julie White, *Bad Dates*; Small company: Leigh Barret, *Jacques Brel, Sweeney Todd, The Threepenny Opera*, and *Follies*

Director: Large company: Kevin Moriarty, *The Merry Wives of Windsor* Small company: Rick Lombardo, *Sweeney Todd*

Set design: Yi Li Ming, *Snow in June*

Special Citations: Overture Productions for *Follies* concert; Puppet Showplace Theatre for 30 years of dedication to the ancient art of puppetry

Guest of Honor: Edward Albee

GEORGE FREEDLEY MEMORIAL AWARD

For the best book about live theater published in the United States the previous year; 2003 winner:
A History of African American Theatre, by Errol G. Hill and James V. Hatch
Special Jury Prize: *Everything Was Beautiful: The Birth of the Musical Follies*, by Ted Chapin

GEORGE JEAN NATHAN AWARD

For dramatic criticism; 2003–2004 winner:
Hilton Als

GEORGE OPPENHEIMER AWARD

To the best new American playwright, presented by *Newsday*; 2004 winner:
Will Eno, *The Flu Season*

HELEN HAYES AWARDS

20th annual; Presented by the Washington Theatre Awards Society in recognition of excellence in Washington, D.C., theater.

Resident Productions

Play: *The Drawer Boy*, produced by Round House Theatre
Musical: *Crowns*, produced by Arena Stage
Lead Actress, Musical: Jacquelyn Piro, *110 in the Shade*
Lead Actor, Musical: Tom McKenzie, *Ragtime*
Lead Actress, Play: Nancy Robinette, *The Rivals*
Lead Actor, Play: (tie) Ted van Griethuysen, *The Life of Galileo*; Bruce Nelson, *The Dazzle*
Supporting Actress, Musical: Lynda Gravátt, *Crowns*
Supporting Actor, Musical: Stephen Gregory Smith, *110 in the Shade*
Supporting Actress, Play: Emily Donahoe, *Shakespeare in Hollywood*
Supporting Actor, Play: Everett Quinton, *Shakespeare in Hollywood*
Director, Play: Kasi Campbell, *The Dazzle*
Director, Musical: Regina Taylor, *Crowns*
Set Design, Play or Musical: James Kronzer, *The Drawer Boy*
Costume Design, Play or Musical: Paul Tazewell, *Camelot*
Lighting Design, Play or Musical: Danie MacLean Wagner, *The Drawer Boy*
Sound Design, Play or Musical: Martin Desjardins, *A Midsummer Night's Dream*

Musical Direction, Play or Musical: William F. Hubbard, *Crowns*
Choreography: Ilona Kessel, *Ragtime*

Non-Resident Productions

Production: (tie) *Chicago*, produced by the National Theatre; *Lackawanna Blues*, produced by the Studio Theatre
Lead Actress: Bianca Marroquin, *Chicago*
Lead Actor: Ruben Santiago-Hudson, *Lackawanna Blues*
Supporting Performer: Patti Mariano, *42nd Street*
Charles MacArthur Award for Outstanding New Play: *Shakespeare in Hollywood*, by Ken Ludwig

HENRY HEWES DESIGN AWARDS

For outstanding design originating in the U.S., selected by a committee comprising Jeffrey Eric Jenkins (chair), Tish Dace, Glenda Frank, Mario Fratti, Randy Gener, Mel Gussow, Henry Hewes, Joan Ungaro; 2004 winners:
Scenic Design: David Korins, *Blackbird*
Lighting Design: Jules Fisher and Peggy Eisenhauer, *Assassins*
Costume Design: Catherine Zuber, *Intimate Apparel*
Notable Effects: James Schuette (scenery and costumes), Brian H. Scott (lighting) and Darron L. West (sound), *bobrauschenbergamerica*

JOSEPH JEFFERSON AWARDS

35th annual; For achievement in Chicago theater during the 2003–2004 season, given by the Jefferson Awards Committee in 26 competitive categories.

Resident Productions

New Work: (three-way tie): Theatre District, by Richard Kramer; Only the Sound, by Jenny Laird; We All Went Down to Amsterdam, by Bruce Norris
New Adaptation: Crime and Punishment, by Marilyn Campbell and Curt Columbus
Production of a Play: Famous Door Theatre, The Cider House Rules: Parts I and II
Production of a Musical: Drury Lane Theatre, Singin' in the Rain
Prodution of a Revue: (tie) The Second City e.t.c., Curious George Goes to War and Pants on Fire
Director of a Play (Michael Maggio Award): David Cromer and Marc Grapey, *The Cider House Rules: Parts I and II*
Director of Musical: Marc Robin, *Singin' in the Rain*
Director of a Revue: Ron West, *Curious George Goes to War*

Actor in a Principal Role, Play: Larry Neumann Jr., *The Cider House Rules: Parts I and II*

Actress in a Principal Role, Play: Kymberly Mellen, *Rocket to the Moon*

Actor in a Supporting Role, Play: Maury Copper, *Judgement at Nuremberg*

Actress in a Supporting Role, Play: Jennifer Pompa, *The Cider House Rules: Parts I and II*

Actor in a Principal Role, Musical: Richard Kind, *Bounce*

Actress in a Principal Role, Musical: Joyce Faison, *Lady Day at Emerson's Bar and Grill*

Actor in a Supporting Role, Musical: Richard Strimer, *Singin' in the Rain*

Actress in a Supporting Role, Musical: Deanna Dunagan, *James Joyce's The Dead*

Actor in a Revue: Keegan-Michael Key, *Curious George Goes to War*

Ensemble: *The Cider House Rules: Parts I and II,* produced by Famous Door Theatre

Scenic Design: Elizabeth E. Schuch, *Journey's End*

Costume Design: Nancy Missimi, *Cats*

Lighting Design: A. Cameron Zetty, *Journey's End*

Sound Design: Josh Schmidt, *Journey's End*

Choreography: Marc Robin, *Cats*

Original Music: Joseph Fosco, *The Cider House Rules: Parts I and II*

Musical Direction: Jeff Lewis, *James Joyce's The Dead*

Citations Wing Awards

31st annual; For outstanding achievement in professional productions during the 2003–2004 season of Chicago theaters not operating under union contracts:

Productions (plays): *Detective Story,* produced by Strawdog Theatre Company; *Hannah and Martin,* produced by TimeLine Theatre Company

Production (musical): *Dr. Sex,* produced by Bailiwick Repertory

Ensembles: *Angus, Thongs and Full Frontal Snogging,* Griffin Theatre Company; *Detective Story,* Strawdog Theatre Company

Directors: (play): Jeremy B. Cohen, *Hannah and Martin*; Shade Murray, *Detective Story* (musical): David Zak, *Dr. Sex*

New Work: Larry Bortniker and Sally Deering, *Dr. Sex*; Sharon Evans, *Blind Tasting*; Kate Fodor, *Hannah and Martin*

New Adaptation: Christina Calvit, *Angus, Thongs and Full Frontal Snogging*; Michael Murphy, *Sin: A Cardinal Deposed*

Actress in a Principal Role: (play): Kate Harris, *Misery*; Donna McGough, *Happy Days*; Katherine Nawocki, *Angus, Thongs and Full Frontal Snogging*; Elizabeth Rich, *Hannah and Martin* (musical): Sarah Laue, *Dr. Sex*

Actor in a Principal Role: (play): Darrell W. Cox, *Blackbird*; Jim Sherman, *Sin: A Cardinal Deposed* (musical): Jamie Axtell, *Dr. Sex*

Actress in a Supporting Role: (play): Danica Ivancevic, *Hannah and Martin*; Kelly Schumann, *Steel Magnolias* (musical): Rebecca Finnegan, *A Kurt Weill Review: Songs of Darkness and Light*

Actor in a Supporting Role: (play): Scott Aiello, *Broadway Bound*; Marco Verna, *Blind Tasting*

(musical): David Heimann, *Kurt Weill Review: Songs of Darkness and Light*; Scott O'Brien, *Pinafore!*

Scenic Design: Tom Burch, *Misery*; Robert A. Knuth, *Steel Magnolias*; Ray Vlcek, *Detective Story*

Costume Design: Carol J. Blanchard, *Amadeus*

Lighting Design: Brian Sidney Bembridge, *Hannah and Martin*; Jared Moore, *Misery*

Sound Design: Victoria Delorio, *The Shadow*

Choreography: Brigitte Ditmars, *Pinafore!*; Kristen Folzenlogen, *Dr. Sex*

Original Music: Poh'ro, *Kiwi Black*

Musical Direction: Alan Bukowiecki, *Dr. Sex*; Eugene Dizon, *Amadeus*

JOSEPH KESSELRING PRIZE

National Arts Club member Joseph Otto Kesselring was born in New York in 1902. He was an actor, author, producer, and playwright. Mr. Kesselring died in 1967, leaving his estate in a trust which terminated in 1978 when the life beneficiary died. A bequest was made to the Nation Arts Club "on condition that said bequest be used to establish a fund to be known as the Joseph Kesselring Fund, the income and principal of which shall be used to give financial aid to playwrights, on such a basis of selection and to such as the National Arts Club may, in it's sole discretion, determine."

A committee appointed by the president and the governors of the National Arts Club administers the Kesselring Prizes. It approves monetary prizes annually to playwrights nominated by qualified production companies whose dramatic work has demonstrated th ehighest possible merit and promise and is deserving of greater recognition, but who as yet has not received prominent national notice or acclaim in the theater. The winners are chosen by a panel of judges who are independent of the Club. In addition to a cash prize, the first prize winner also receives a staged reading of a work of his or her choice. The Kesselring Prize Committee: O. Aldon James, Stanley Morton Ackert III, Arnold J. Davis, Michael Parva, Jason deMontmorency, Dary Derchin, Alexandra Roosevelt Dworkin, John T. James, Raymond Knowles.

2004: Tracey Scott Wilson **2003:** Bridget Carpenter **2002:** Melissa James Gibson **2001:** David Lindsay-Abaire **2000:** David Auburn **1999:** Heather McDonald **1998:** Kira Obolensky **1997:** No Award **1996:** Naomi Wallace **1995:** Amy Freed, Doug Wright **1994:** Nicky Silver **1993:** Anna Deavere Smith **1992:** Marion Isaac McClinton **1991:** Tony Kushner **1990:** Elizabeth Egloff, Mel Shapiro **1989:** Jo Carson **1988:** Diane Ney **1987:** Paul Schmidt **1986:** Marlane Meyer **1985:** Bill Elverman **1984:** Philip Kan Gotanda **1983:** Lynn Alvarez **1982:** No Award **1981:** Cheryl Hawkins **1980:** Susan Charlotte

(CONTINUED ON NEXT PAGE)

(CONTINUED FROM PREVIOUS PAGE)

Honorable Mentions

2004: John Borello **2003:** Lynn Nottage **2002:** Lydia Diamond **2001:** Dael Orlandersmith **2000:** Jessica Hagedorn **1999:** Stephen Dietz **1998:** Erik Ehn **1997:** Kira Obolensky, Edwin Sanchez **1996:** Nilo Cruz **1993:** Han Ong **1992:** José Rivera **1991:** Quincy Long, Scott McPherson **1990:** Howard Korder **1989:** Keith Reddin **1988:** JosE Rivera, Frank Hogan **1987:** Januzsz Glowacki **1986:** John Leicht **1985:** Laura Harrington **1983:** Constance Congdon **1981:** William Hathaway **1980:** Carol Lashof

KENNEDY CENTER

Honors

26th annual; For distinguished achievement by individuals who have made significant contributions to American culture through the arts:
James Brown, Carol Burnett, Loretta Lynn, Mike Nichols, Itzhak Perlman

Mark Twain Prize

7th annual; For American humor:

Lorne Michaels

M. ELIZABETH OSBORN AWARD

Presented to an emerging playwright by the American Theatre Critics Association; 2004 winner:

Rolin Jones, *The Intelligent Design of Jenny Chow*

MUSICAL THEATRE HALL OF FAME

This organization was established at New York University on November 10, 1993.

Harold Arlen; Irving Berlin; Leonard Bernstein; Eubie Blake; Abe Burrows; George M. Cohan; Betty Comden; Dorothy Fields; George Gershwin; Ira Gershwin; Adolf Green; Oscar Hammerstein II; E.Y. Harburg; Larry Hart; Jerome Kern; Burton Lane; Alan Jay Lerner; Frank Loesser; Frederick Loewe; Mary Martin; Ethel Merman; Cole Porter; Jerome Robbins; Richard Rodgers; Harold Rome

NATIONAL MEDALS OF THE ARTS

For individuals and organizations who have made outstanding contributions to the excellence, growth, support, and availability of the arts in the United States, selected by the President of the United States from nominees presented by the National Endowment; 2003 winners:

Austin City Limits, Beverly Cleary, Rafe Esquith, Suzanne Farrell, Buddy Guy, Ron Howard, Mormon Tabernacle Choir, Leonard Slatkin, George Strait, Tommy Tune

NEW DRAMATISTS LIFETIME ACHIEVEMENT AWARD

To an individual who has made an outstanding artistic contribution to the American theater; 2004 winner:

Meryl Streep

OVATION AWARDS

Established in 1989, the L.A. Stage Alliance Ovation Awards are Southern California's premiere awards for excellence in theatre; 2004 winners:
World Premiere Play: *Exits and Entrances*, Athol Fugard, produced by Fountain Theatre
World Premiere Musical: *The Shaggs: The Philosophy of the World*, Joy Gregory and Gunnar Madsen, produced by Powerhouse Theatre Company at Inside the Ford, with Andrew Barrett-Weiss and Tess Skorczewski
Lead Actor in a Play: Morlan Higgins, *Exits and Entrances*
Lead Actress in a Play: Viola Davis, *Intimate Apparel*
Lead Actor in a Musical: Steve Glaudini, *1776*
Lead Actress in a Musical: Yvette Freeman, *Dinah Was*
Featured Actor in a Play: Joseph Fuqua, *All My Sons*
Featured Actress in a Play: Carolyn Hennesy, *The Fan Maroo*
Featured Actor in a Musical: Nils Anderson, *1776*
Featured Actress in a Musical: Jill Van Velzer, *1776*
Solo Performance: Gigi Bermingham, *Non-Vital Organs (redux)*
Ensemble Performance: Cast of Baz Luhrman's production of *La Bohème*; Cast of *Caught in the Net*
Director of a Play: Ray Cooney, *Caught in the Net*; Stephen Sachs, *Exits and Entrances*; Daniel Sullivan, *Intimate Apparel*
Director of a Musical: Nick DeGruccio, *1776*
Choreographer: Dana Solimando, *Swing!*
Musical Direction: Dean Mora, *Lady Macbeth Sings the Blues*

Production from a Touring Company: *The Phantom of the Opera*, Center Theatre Group: Ahmanson Theatre, Cameron Mackintosh and Really Useful Theatre Company, Inc.

Play (smaller theatre): *Master Class*; (larger theatre): *All My Sons*

Musical (smaller theatre): *Hedwig and the Angry Inch*; (larger theatre): *1776*

Set Design (smaller theatre): Joel Daavid, *Ma Rainey's Black Bottom*; (larger theatre): Catherine Martin, *Baz Luhrmann's production of La Bohème*

Lighting Design: (smaller theatre): Mike Durst, *Nocturne* (larger theatre): Nigel Levings, *Baz Luhrmann's production of La Bohème*

Sound Design: (smaller theatre): Steve Goodie, *Cold/Tender*, Julie Ferrin, Martin Carrillo, Paul Hepker, *Romeo and Juliet: Antebellum New Orleans, 1836* (larger theatre): Acme Sound Partners, *Baz Luhrmann's production of La Bohème*

Costume Design: (smaller theatre): Alex Jaeger, *Romeo and Juliet: Antebellum New Orleans, 1836*; (larger theatre): Catherine Zuber, *Intimate Apparel*

James A. Doolittle Award for Leadership in the Theatre: Paula Holt

The Career Achievement Award: Betty Garrett

RICHARD RODGERS AWARDS

For staged readings of musicals in nonprofit theaters, administered by the American Academy of Arts and Letters and selected by a jury including Stephen Sondheim (chairman), Lynn Ahrens, Jack Beeson, John Guare, Sheldon Harnick, Richard Maltby, Jr., Jeanine Tesori and Francis Thorne. 2004 winners: **Richard Rodgers Production Award** *The Tutor*, Maryrose Wood and Andrew Gerle; **Richard Rodgers Awards for Staged Readings** *To Paint the Earth*, Daniel Frederick Levin and Jonathan Portera; *Unlocked*, Sam Carner and Derek Gregor

ROBERT WHITEHEAD AWARD

For outstanding achievement in commercial theatre producing, bestowed on a graduate of the fourteen-week Commercial Theatre Institute Program who has demonstrated a quality of production exemplified by the late producer, Robert Whitehead.

The Commercial Theater Institute, Frederic B. Vogel, director, is the nation's only formal program which professionally trains commercial theater producers. It is a joint project of the League of American Theatres and Producers, Inc., and Theatre Development Fund.

2001–2004: No Award **2000:** Anne Strickland Squadron **1999:** Eric Krebs **1998:** Liz Oliver **1997:** Marc Routh **1996:** Randall L. Wreghitt **1995:** Kevin McCollum **1994:** Dennis Grimaldi **1993:** Susan Quint Gallin; Benjamin Mordecai

SUSAN SMITH BLACKBURN PRIZE

26th annual; For women who have written works of outstanding quality for the English-speaking theater:

Sarah Ruhl, The Clean House

WILLIAM INGE THEATRE FESTIVAL AWARD

23nd annual; For distinguished achievement in American theater: Arthur Laurents

New Voice: Mary Porster

THE THEATER HALL OF FAME

The Theater of Hall of Fame was created in 1971 to honor those who have made outstanding contributions to the American theater in a career spanning at least twenty-five years, with at least five major credits.

The following were honorees inducted January 26, 2004:
Julian Beck; Jane Greenwood; Madeline Kahn; Kevin Kline; Judith Malina; Patricia Neal; Peter Stone; Richard Wilbur

George Abbott; Maude Adams; Viola Adams; Stella Adler; Edward Albee; Theoni V. Aldredge; Ira Aldridge; Jane Alexander; Mary Alice; Winthrop Ames; Judith Anderson; Maxwell Anderson; Robert Anderson; Julie Andrews; Margaret Anglin; Jean Anouilh; Harold Arlen; George Arliss; Boris Aronson; Adele Astaire; Fred Astaire; Eileen Atkins; Brooks Atkinson; Lauren Bacall; Pearl Bailey; George Balanchine; William Ball; Anne Bancroft; Tallulah Bankhead; Richard Barr; Philip Barry; Ethel Barrymore; John Barrymore; Lionel Barrymore; Howard Bay; Nora Bayes; John Lee Beatty; Samuel Beckett; Brian Bedford; S.N. Behrman; Norman Bel Geddes; David Belasco; Michael Bennett; Richard Bennett; Robert Russell Bennett; Eric Bentley; Irving Berlin; Sarah Bernhardt; Leonard Bernstein; Earl Blackwell; Kermit Bloomgarden; Jerry Bock; Ray Bolger; Edwin Booth; Junius Brutus Booth; Shirley Booth; Philip Bosco; Alice Brady; Bertolt Bercht; Fannie Brice; Peter Brook; John Mason Brown; Robert Brustein; Billie Burke; Abe Burrows; Richard Burton; Mrs. Patrick Campbell; Zoe Caldwell; Eddie Cantor; Morris Carnovsky; Mrs. Leslie Carter; Gower Champion; Frank Chanfrau; Carol Channing; Stockard Channing; Ruth Chatterton; Paddy Chayefsky; Anton Chekhov; Ina Claire; Bobby Clark; Harold Clurman; Lee. J. Cobb; Richard L. Coe; George M. Cohan; Alexander H. Cohen; Jack Cole; Cy Coleman; Constance Collier; Alvin Colt; Betty Comden; Marc Connelly; Barbara Cook; Katherine Cornell; Noel Coward; Jane Cowl; Lotta Crabtree; Cheryl Crawford; Hume Cronym; Russel Crouse; Charlotte Cushman; Jean Dalrymple; Augustin Daly; E.L. Davenport; Gordon Davidson; Ossie Davis; Ruby Dee; Alfred De Liagre Jr.; Agns DeMille; Colleen Dewhurst; Howard Deitz; Dudley Digges; Melvyn Douglas; Eddie Dowling; Alfred Drake; Marie Dressler; John Drew;

(CONTINUED ON NEXT PAGE)

(CONTINUED FROM PREVIOUS PAGE)

Mrs. John Drew; William Dunlap; Mildred Dunnock; Charles Durning; Eleanora Duse; Jeanne Eagles; Fred Ebb; Florence Eldridge; Lehman Engel; Maurice Evans; Abe Feder; Jose Ferber; Cy Feuer; Zelda Fichandler; Dorothy Fields; Herbert Fields; Lewis Fields; W.C. Fields; Jules Fischer; Minnie Maddern Fiske; Clyde Fitch; Geraldine Fitzgerald; Henry Fonda; Lynn Fontanne; Horton Foote; Edwin Forrest; Bob Fosse; Rudolf Friml; Charles Frohman; Robert Fryer; Athol Fugard; John Gassner; Larry Gelbart; Peter Gennaro; Bernard Gersten; Grace George; George Gershwin; Ira Gershwin; John Gielgud; W.S. Gilbert; Jack Gilford; William Gillette; Charles Gilpin; Lillian Gish; John Golden; Max Gordon; Ruth Gordon; Adolph Green; Paul Green; Charlotte Greenwood; Joel Grey; Tammy Grimes; George Grizzard; John Gaure; Otis L. Guernsey Jr.; Tyrone Guthrie; Uta Hagan; Lewis Hallam; T. Edward Hambleton; Oscar Hammerstein II; Walter Hampden; Otto Harbach; E.Y. Harburg; Sheldon Harnick; Edward Harrigan; Jed Harris; Julie Harris; Rosemary Harris; Sam H. Harris; Rex Harrison; Kitty Carlisle Hart; Lorenz Hart; Moss Hart; Tony Hart; June Havoc; Helen Hayes; Leland Hayward; Ben Hecht; Eileen Heckart; Theresa Helburn; Lillian Hellman; Katherine Hepburn; Victor Herbert; Jerry Herman; James A. Herne; Henry Hewes; Al Hirschfeld; Raymond Hitchcock; Hal Holbrook; Celeste Holm; Hanya Holm; Arthur Hopkins; De Wolf Hopper; John Houseman; Eugene Howard; Leslie Howard; Sidney Howard; Willie Howard; Barnard Hughes; Henry Hull; Josephine Hull; Walter Huston; Earle Hyman; Henrik Ibsen; William Inge; Bernard B. Jacobs; Elise Janis; Joseph Jefferson; Al Jolson; James Earl Jones; Margo Jones; Robert Edmond Jones; Tom Jones; Jon Jory; Raul Julia; John Kander; Garson Kanin; George S. Kaufman; Danny Kaye; Elia Kazan; Gene Kelly; George Kelly; Fanny Kemble; Jerome Kern; Walter Kerr; Michael Kidd; Richard Kiley; Sidney Kingsley; Florence Klotz; Joseph Wood Krutch; Bert Lahr; Burton Lane; Frank Langella; Lawrence Langner; Lillie Langtry; Angela Lansbury; Charles Laughton; Arthur Laurents; Gertrude Lawrence; Jerome Lawrence; Eva Le Gallienne; Ming Cho Lee; Robert E. Lee; Lotte Lenya; Alan Jay Lerner; Sam Levene; Robert Lewis; Beatrice Lillie; Howard Lindsay; Frank Loesser; Frederick Loewe; Joshua Logan; Pauline Lord; Lucille Lortel; Alfred Lunt; Charles MacArthur; Steele MacKaye; David Mamet; Rouben Mamoulian; Richard Mansfield; Robert B. Mantell; Frederic March; Nancy Marchand; Julia Marlowe; Ernest H. Martin; Mary Martin; Raymond Massey; Siobhan McKenna; Terrence McNally; Helen Menken; Burgess Meredith; Ethel Merman; David Merrick; Jo Mielziner; Arthur Miller; Marilyn Miller; Liza Minnelli; Helena Modjeska; Ferenc Molnar; Lola Montez; Victor Moore; Robert Morse; Zero Mostel; Anna Cora Mowatt; Paul Muni; Tharon Musser; George Jean Nathan; Mildred Natwick; Nazimova; James M. Nederlander; Mike Nichols; Elliot Norton; Sean O'Casey; Cliiford Odets; Donald Oenslager; Laurence Olivier; Eugene O'Neill; Jerry Orbach; Geraldine Paige; Joseph Papp; Osgood Perkins; Bernadette Peters; Molly Picon; Harold Pinter; Luigi Pirandello; Christopher Plummer; Cole Porter; Robert Preston; Harold Prince; Jose Quintero; Ellis Rabb; John Raitt; Tony Randall; Michael Redgrave; Ada Rehan; Elmer Rice; Lloyd Richards; Ralph Richardson; Chita Rivera; Jason Robards; Jerome Robbins; Paul Robeson; Richard Rodgers; Will Rogers; Sigmund Romberg; Harold Rome; Lillian Russell; Donald Saddler; Gene Saks; William Saroyan; Joseph Schildkraut; Harvey Schmidt; Alan Schnider; Gerald Shoenfeld; Arthur Schwartz; Maurice Schwartz; George C. Scott; Marian Seldes; Irene Sharaff; George Bernard Shaw; Sam Shepard; Robert F. Sherwood; J.J. Shubert; Lee Shubert; Herman Shumlin; Neil Simon; Lee Simonson; Edmund Simpson; Otis Skinner; Maggie Smith; Oliver Smith; Stephen Sondheim; E.H. Sothern; Kim Stanley; Jean Stapleton; Maureen Stapleton; Frances Sternhagen; Roger L. Stevens; Isabelle Stevenson; Ellen Stewart; Dorothy Stickney; Fred Stone; Tom Stoppard; Lee Strasburg; August Strindberg; Elaine Stritch; Charles Strouse; Jule Styne; Margaret Sullivan; Arthur Sullivan; Jessica Tandy; Laurette Taylor; Ellen Terry; Tommy Tune; Gwen Verdon; Robin Wagner; Nancy Walker; Eli Wallach; James Wallack; Lester Wallack; Tony Walton; Douglas Turner Ward; David Warfield; Ethel Waters; Clifton Webb; Joseph Weber; Margaret Webster; Kurt Weill; Orson Welles; Mae West; Robert Whitehead; Oscar Wilde; Thorton Wilder; Bert Williams; Tennessee Williams; Landford Wilson; P.G. Wodehouse; Peggy Wood; Alexander Woollcott; Irene Worth; Teresa Wright; Ed Wynn; Vincent Youmans; Stark Young; Florenz Zeigfeld; Patricia Zipprodt.

Founders Award

Established in 1993 in honor of Earl Blackwell, James M. Nederlander, Gerald Oestreicher and Arnold Weissberger, the Theater Hall of Fame Founders Award is voted by the Hall's board of directors to an individual for his of her outstanding contribution to the theater:

1993: James M. Nederlander **1994:** Kitty Carlisle Hart **1995:** Harvey Sabinson **1996:** Henry Hewes **1997:** Otis L. Guernsey Jr. **1998:** Edward Colton **1999:** no award **2000:** Gerard Oestreicher, Arnold Weissberger **2001:** Tom Dillon **2002:** No Award **2003:** Price Berkley

Margo Jones Citizen of the Theater Medal

Presented annually to a citizen of the theater who has made a lifetime commitment to theater in the United States and has demonstrated an understanding and affirmation of the craft of playwriting:

1961: Lucille Lortel **1962:** Michael Ellis **1963:** Judith Rutherford Marechal; George Savage (university award) **1964:** Richard Barr, Edward Albee & Clinton Wilder; Richard A. Duprey (university award) **1965:** Wynn Handman; Marston Balch (university award) **1966:** Jon Jory; Arthur Ballet (university award) **1967:** Paul Baker; George C. White (workshop award) **1968:** Davey Marlin-Jones; Ellen Stewart (workshop award) **1969:** Adrian Hall; Edward Parone & Gordon Davidson (workshop award) **1970:** Joseph Papp **1971:** Zelda Fichandler **1972:** Jules Irving **1973:** Douglas Turner Ward **1974:** Paul Weidner **1975:** Robert Kalfin **1976:** Gordon Davidson **1977:** Marshall W. Mason **1978:** Jon Jory **1979:** Ellen Stewart **1980:** John Clark Donahue **1981:** Lynne Meadow **1982:** Andre Bishop **1983:** Bill Bushnell **1984:** Gregory Mosher **1985:** John Lion **1986:** Lloyd Richards **1987:** Gerald Chapman **1988:** no award **1989:** Margaret Goheen **1990:** Richard Coe **1991:** Otis L. Guernsey Jr. **1992:** Abbot Van Nostrand **1993:** Henry Hewes **1994:** Jane Alexander **1995:** Robert Whitehead **1996:** Al Hirschfield **1997:** George C. White **1998:** James Houghton **1999:** George Keathley **2000:** Eileen Heckart **2001:** Mel Gussow **2002:** Emilie S. Kilgore

Longest Running Shows on **Broadway**

LONGEST RUNNING SHOWS
ON BROADWAY

When the musical or play version of a production is in question, it is so indicated, as are revivals. *Still playing as of June 1, 2004.

CATS
7,485 performances
Opened October 7, 1982; Closed September 10, 2000

PHANTOM OF THE OPERA*
6,814 performances
Opened January 26, 1988

LES MISÉRABLES
6,680 performances
Opened March 12, 1987; Closed May 18, 2003

A CHORUS LINE
6,137 performances
Opened July 25, 1975; Closed April 28, 1990

OH! CALCUTTA! (REVIVAL)
5,959 performances
Opened September 24, 1976; Closed August 6, 1989

BEAUTY AND THE BEAST*
4,143 performances
Opened April 18, 1994

MISS SAIGON
4,097 performances
Opened April 11, 1991; Closed January 28, 2001

42ND STREET
3,486 performances
Opened August 25, 1980; Closed January 8, 1989

GREASE
3,388 performances
Opened February 14, 1972; Closed April 13, 1980

RENT*
3,370 performances
Opened April 29, 1996

FIDDLER ON THE ROOF
3,242 performances
Opened September 22, 1964; Closed July 2, 1972

LIFE WITH FATHER
3,224 performances
Opened November 8, 1939; Closed July 12, 1947

TOBACCO ROAD
3,182 performances
Opened December 4, 1933; Closed May 31, 1941

CHICAGO (MUSICAL, REVIVAL)*
3,138 performances
Opened November 19, 1996

HELLO, DOLLY!
2,844 performances
Opened January 16, 1964; Closed December 27, 1970

THE LION KING*
2,768 performances
Opened November 13, 1997

MY FAIR LADY
2,717 performances
Opened March 15, 1956; Closed September 29, 1962

ANNIE
2,377 performances
Opened April 21, 1977; Closed January 22, 1983

CABARET (REVIVAL)*
2,377 performances
Opened March 19, 1998

Austin Pendleton, Zero Mostel, Joanna Merlin in *Fiddler on the Roof* PHOTO BY FRIEDMAN-ABELES

MAN OF LA MANCHA
2,328 performances
Opened November 22, 1965; Closed June 26, 1971

ABIE'S IRISH ROSE
2,327 performances
Opened May 23, 1922; Closed October 21, 1927

OKLAHOMA!
2,212 performances
Opened March 31, 1943; Closed May 29, 1948

SMOKEY JOE'S CAFÈ
2,036 performances
Opened March 2, 1995; Closed January 16, 2000

PIPPIN
1,944 performances
Opened October 23, 1972; Closed June 12, 1977

SOUTH PACIFIC
1,925 performances
Opened April 7, 1949; Closed January 16, 1954

THE MAGIC SHOW
1,920 performances
Opened May 28, 1974; Closed December 31, 1978

DEATHTRAP
1,793 performances
Opened February 26, 1978; Closed June 13, 1982

GEMINI
1,788 performances
Opened May 21, 1977; Closed September 6, 1981

HARVEY
1,775 performances
Opened November 1, 1944; Closed January 15, 1949

DANCIN'
1,774 performances
Opened March 27, 1978; Closed June 27, 1982

LA CAGE AUX FOLLES
1,761 performances
Opened August 21, 1983; Closed November 15, 1987

HAIR
1,750 performances
Opened April 29, 1968; Closed July 1, 1972

AIDA*
1,740 performances
Opened March 23, 2000

THE WIZ
1,672 performances
Opened January 5, 1975; Closed January 29, 1979

BORN YESTERDAY
1,642 performances
Opened February 4, 1946; Closed December 31, 1949

THE BEST LITTLE WHOREHOUSE IN TEXAS
1,639 performances
Opened June 19, 1978; Closed March 27, 1982

CRAZY FOR YOU
1,622 performances
Opened February 19, 1992; Closed January 7, 1996

AIN'T MISBEHAVIN'
1,604 performances
Opened May 9, 1978; Closed February 21, 1982

MARY, MARY
1,572 performances
Opened March 8, 1961; Closed December 12, 1964

EVITA
1,567 performances
Opened September 25, 1979; Closed June 26, 1983

THE VOICE OF THE TURTLE
1,557 performances
Opened December 8, 1943; Closed January 3, 1948

John Rubinstein and the Company in *Pippin* PHOTO BY CHERYL SUE DOBEY

JEKYLL & HYDE
1,543 performances
Opened April 28, 1997; Closed January 7, 2001

BAREFOOT IN THE PARK
1,530 performances
Opened October 23, 1963; Closed June 25, 1967

BRIGHTON BEACH MEMOIRS
1,530 performances
Opened March 27, 1983; Closed May 11, 1986

DREAMGIRLS
1,522 performances
Opened December 20, 1981; Closed August 11, 1985

MAME (MUSICAL)
1,508 performances
Opened May 24, 1966; Closed January 3, 1970

GREASE (REVIVAL)
1,503 performances
Opened May 11, 1994; Closed January 25, 1998

SAME TIME, NEXT YEAR
1,453 performances
Opened March 14, 1975; Closed September 3, 1978

ARSENIC AND OLD LACE
1,444 performances
Opened January 10, 1941; Closed June 17, 1944

THE SOUND OF MUSIC
1,443 performances
Opened November 16, 1959; Closed June 15, 1963

ME AND MY GIRL
1,420 performances
Opened August 10, 1986; Closed December 31, 1989

HOW TO SUCCEED IN BUSINESS WITHOUT REALLY TRYING
1,417 performances
Opened October 14, 1961; Closed March 6, 1965

HELLZAPOPPIN
1,404 performances
Opened September 22, 1938; Closed December 17, 1941

THE MUSIC MAN
1,375 performances
Opened December 19, 1957; Closed April 15, 1961

Vanessa Townsell, Loretta Devine, Sheryl Lee Ralph in *DreamGirls* PHOTO BY MARTHA SWOPE

FUNNY GIRL
1,348 performances
Opened March 26, 1964; Closed July 15, 1967

MUMMENSCHANZ
1,326 performances
Opened March 30, 1977; Closed April 20, 1980

ANGEL STREET
1,295 performances
Opened December 5, 1941; Closed December 30, 1944

THE PRODUCERS*
1,294 performances
Opened April 19, 2001

LIGHTNIN'
1,291 performances
Opened August 26, 1918; Closed August 27, 1921

PROMISES, PROMISES
1,281 performances
Opened December 1, 1968; Closed January 1, 1972

42ND STREET (REVIVAL)*
1,268 performances
Opened May 2, 2001

THE KING AND I
1,246 performances
Opened March 29, 1951; Closed March 20, 1954

CACTUS FLOWER
1,234 performances
Opened December 8, 1965; Closed November 23, 1968

SLEUTH
1,222 performances
Opened December 8, 1965; Closed October 13, 1973

TORCH SONG TRILOGY
1,222 performances
Opened June 10, 1982; Closed May 19, 1985

1776
1,217 performances
Opened March 16, 1969; Closed February 13, 1972

EQUUS
1,209 performances
Opened October 24, 1974; Closed October 7, 1977

SUGAR BABIES
1,208 performances
Opened October 8, 1979; Closed August 28, 1982

GUYS AND DOLLS
1,200 performances
Opened November 24, 1950; Closed November 28, 1953

AMADEUS
1,181 performances
Opened December 17, 1980; Closed October 16, 1983

CABARET
1,165 performances
Opened November 20, 1966; Closed September 6, 1969

MISTER ROBERTS
1,157 performances
Opened February 18, 1948; Closed January 6, 1951

ANNIE GET YOUR GUN
1,147 performances
Opened May 16, 1946; Closed February 12, 1949

GUYS AND DOLLS (REVIVAL)
1,144 performances
Opened April 14, 1992; Closed January 8, 1995

THE SEVEN YEAR ITCH
1,141 performances
Opened November 20, 1952; Closed August 13, 1955

BRING IN 'DA NOISE, BRING IN 'DA FUNK
1,130 performances
Opened April 25, 1996; Closed January 19, 1999

BUTTERFLIES ARE FREE
1,128 performances
Opened October 21, 1969; Closed July 2, 1972

PINS AND NEEDLES
1,108 performances
Opened November 27, 1937; Closed June 22, 1940

MAMMA MIA!*
1,102 performances
Opened October 12, 2001

PLAZA SUITE
1,097 performances
Opened February 14, 1968; Closed October 3, 1970

FOSSE
1,092 performances
Opened January 14, 1999; Closed August 25, 2001

THEY'RE PLAYING OUR SONG
1,082 performances
Opened February 11, 1979; Closed September 6, 1981

GRAND HOTEL (MUSICAL)
1,077 performances
Opened November 12, 1989; Closed April 25, 1992

KISS ME, KATE
1,070 performances
Opened December 30, 1948; Closed July 25, 1951

DON'T BOTHER ME, I CAN'T COPE
1,065 performances
Opened April 19, 1972; Closed October 27, 1974

THE PAJAMA GAME
1,063 performances
Opened May 13, 1954; Closed November 24, 1956

SHENANDOAH
1,050 performances
Opened January 7, 1975; Closed August 7, 1977

ANNIE GET YOUR GUN (REVIVAL)
1,046 performances
Opened March 4, 1999; Closed September 1, 2001

THE TEAHOUSE OF THE AUGUST MOON
1,027 performances
Opened October 15, 1953; Closed March 24, 1956

DAMN YANKEES
1,019 performances
Opened May 5, 1955; Closed October 12, 1957

CONTACT
1,010 performances
Opened March 30, 2000; Closed September 1, 2002

NEVER TOO LATE
1,007 performances
Opened November 26, 1962; Closed April 24, 1965

BIG RIVER
1,005 performances
Opened April 25, 1985; Closed September 20, 1987

THE WILL ROGERS FOLLIES
983 performances
Opened May 1, 1991; Closed September 5, 1993

ANY WEDNESDAY
982 performances
Opened February 18, 1964; Closed June 26, 1966

SUNSET BOULEVARD
977 performances
Opened November 17, 1994; Closed March 22, 1997

URINETOWN*
965 performances
Opened September 20, 2001

A FUNNY THING HAPPENED ON THE WAY TO THE FORUM
964 performances
Opened May 8, 1962; Closed August 29, 1964

THE ODD COUPLE
964 performances
Opened March 10, 1965; Closed July 2, 1967

ANNA LUCASTA
957 performances
Opened August 30, 1944; Closed November 30, 1946

KISS AND TELL
956 performances
Opened March 17, 1943; Closed June 23, 1945

SHOW BOAT (REVIVAL)
949 performances
Opened October 2, 1994; Closed January 5, 1997

DRACULA (REVIVAL)
925 performances
Opened October 20, 1977; Closed January 6, 1980

BELLS ARE RINGING
924 performances
Opened November 29, 1956;Closed March 7, 1959

THE MOON IS BLUE
924 performances
Opened March 8, 1951; Closed May 30, 1953

BEATLEMANIA
920 performances
Opened May 31, 1977; Closed October 17, 1979

PROOF
917 performances
Opened October 24, 2000; Closed January 5, 2003

THE ELEPHANT MAN
916 performances
Opened April 19, 1979; Closed June 28, 1981

KISS OF THE SPIDER WOMAN
906 performances
Opened May 3, 1993; Closed July 1, 1995

LUV
901 performances
Opened November 11, 1964; Closed January 7, 1967

THE WHO'S TOMMY
900 performances
Opened April 22, 1993; Closed June 17, 1995

CHICAGO (MUSICAL)
898 performances
Opened June 3, 1975; Closed August 27, 1977

APPLAUSE
896 performances
Opened March 30, 1970; Closed July 27, 1972

CAN-CAN
892 performances
Opened May 7, 1953; Closed June 25, 1955

CAROUSEL
890 performances
Opened April 19, 1945; Closed May 24, 1947

I'M NOT RAPPAPORT
890 performances
Opened November 19, 1985; Closed January 17, 1988

HATS OFF TO ICE
889 performances
Opened June 22, 1944; Closed April 2, 1946

FANNY
888 performances
Opened November 4, 1954; Closed December 16, 1956

CHILDREN OF A LESSER GOD
887 performances
Opened March 30, 1980; Closed May 16, 1982

FOLLOW THE GIRLS
882 performances
Opened April 8, 1944; Closed May 18, 1946

KISS ME, KATE (MUSICAL, REVIVAL)
881 performances
Opened November 18, 1999; Closed December 30, 2001

THOROUGHLY MODERN MILLIE
879 performances
Opened April 18, 2002

CITY OF ANGELS
878 performances
Opened December 11, 1989; Closed January 19, 1992

CAMELOT
873 performances
Opened December 3, 1960; Closed January 5, 1963

I LOVE MY WIFE
872 performances
Opened April 17, 1977; Closed May 20, 1979

THE BAT
867 performances
Opened August 23, 1920; Closed September 1922 [date unknown]

MY SISTER EILEEN
864 performances
Opened December 26, 1940; Closed January 16, 1943

NO, NO, NANETTE (REVIVAL)
861 performances
Opened January 19, 1971; Closed February 3, 1973

RAGTIME
861 performances
Opened January 18, 1998; Closed January 16, 2000

SONG OF NORWAY
860 performances
Opened August 21, 1944; Closed September 7, 1946

CHAPTER TWO
857 performances
Opened December 4, 1977; Closed December 9, 1979

A STREETCAR NAMED DESIRE
855 performances
Opened December 3, 1947; Closed December 17, 1949

BARNUM
854 performances
Opened April 30, 1980; Closed May 16, 1982

COMEDY IN MUSIC
849 performances
Opened October 2, 1953; Closed January 21, 1956

RAISIN
847 performances
Opened October 18, 1973; Closed December 7, 1975

BLOOD BROTHERS
839 performances
Opened April 25, 1993; Closed April 30, 1995

YOU CAN'T TAKE IT WITH YOU
837 performances
Opened December 14, 1936; Closed December 1938 [date unknown]

LA PLUME DE MA TANTE
835 performances
Opened November 11, 1958; Closed December 17, 1960

THREE MEN ON A HORSE
835 performances
Opened January 30, 1935; Closed January 9, 1937

THE SUBJECT WAS ROSES
832 performances
Opened May 25, 1964; Closed May 21, 1966

BLACK AND BLUE
824 performances
Opened January 26, 1989; Closed January 20, 1991

THE KING AND I (REVIVAL)
807 performances
Opened April 11, 1996; Closed February 22, 1998

INHERIT THE WIND
806 performances
Opened April 21, 1955; Closed June 22, 1957

ANYTHING GOES (REVIVAL)
804 performances
Opened October 19, 1987; Closed September 3, 1989

TITANIC
804 performances
Opened April 23, 1997; Closed March 21, 1999

Glenn Close, Jim Dale in *Barnum* PHOTO BY MARTHA SWOPE

NO TIME FOR SERGEANTS
796 performances
Opened October 20, 1955; Closed September 14, 1957

FIORELLO!
795 performances
Opened November 23, 1959; Closed October 28, 1961

WHERE'S CHARLEY?
792 performances
Opened October 11, 1948; Closed September 9, 1950

THE LADDER
789 performances
Opened October 22, 1926; Closed May 1928 [date unknown]

FORTY CARATS
780 performances
Opened December 26, 1968; Closed November 7, 1970

LOST IN YONKERS
780 performances
Opened February 21, 1991; Closed January 3, 1993

THE PRISONER OF SECOND AVENUE
780 performances
Opened November 11, 1971; Closed September 29, 1973

M. BUTTERFLY
777 performances
Opened March 20, 1988; Closed January 27, 1990

THE TALE OF THE ALLERGIST'S WIFE
777 performances
Opened November 2, 2000; Closed September 15, 2002

OLIVER!
774 performances
Opened January 6, 1963; Closed November 14, 1964

THE PIRATES OF PENZANCE (REVIVAL, 1981)
772 performances
Opened January 8, 1981; Closed November 28, 1982

THE FULL MONTY
770 performances
Opened October 26, 2000; Closed September 1, 2002

WOMAN OF THE YEAR
770 performances
Opened March 29, 1981; Closed March 13, 1983

MY ONE AND ONLY
767 performances
Opened May 1, 1983; Closed March 3, 1985

SOPHISTICATED LADIES
767 performances
Opened March 1, 1981; Closed January 2, 1983

BUBBLING BROWN SUGAR
766 performances
Opened March 2, 1976; Closed December 31, 1977

INTO THE WOODS
765 performances
Opened November 5, 1987; Closed September 3, 1989

STATE OF THE UNION
765 performances
Opened November 14, 1945; Closed September 13, 1947

STARLIGHT EXPRESS
761 performances
Opened March 15, 1987; Closed January 8, 1989

THE FIRST YEAR
760 performances
Opened October 20, 1920; Closed August 1922 [date unknown]

BROADWAY BOUND
756 performances
Opened December 4, 1986; Closed September 25, 1988

YOU KNOW I CAN'T HEAR YOU WHEN THE WATER'S RUNNING
755 performances
Opened March 13, 1967; Closed January 4, 1969

TWO FOR THE SEESAW
750 performances
Opened January 16, 1958; Closed October 31, 1959

JOSEPH AND THE AMAZING TECHNICOLOR DREAMCOAT (REVIVAL)
747 performances
Opened January 27, 1982; Closed September 4, 1983

HAIRSPRAY
743 performances
Opened August 15, 2002

DEATH OF A SALESMAN
742 performances
Opened February 10, 1949; Closed November 18, 1950

FOR COLORED GIRLS WHO HAVE CONSIDERED SUICIDE/WHEN THE RAINBOW IS ENUF
742 performances
Opened September 15, 1976; Closed July 16, 1978

SONS O' FUN
742 performances
Opened December 1, 1941; Closed August 29, 1943

CANDIDE (MUSICAL VERSION, REVIVAL)
740 performances
Opened March 10, 1974; Closed January 4, 1976

GENTLEMEN PREFER BLONDES
740 performances
Opened December 8, 1949; Closed September 15, 1951

THE MAN WHO CAME TO DINNER
739 performances
Opened October 16, 1939; Closed July 12, 1941

NINE
739 performances
Opened May 9, 1982; Closed February 4, 1984

CALL ME MISTER
734 performances
Opened April 18, 1946; Closed January 10, 1948

VICTOR/VICTORIA
734 performances
Opened October 25, 1995; Closed July 27, 1997

WEST SIDE STORY
732 performances
Opened September 26, 1957; Closed June 27, 1959

HIGH BUTTON SHOES
727 performances
Opened October 9, 1947; Closed July 2, 1949

FINIAN'S RAINBOW
725 performances
Opened January 10, 1947; Closed October 2, 1948

Deborah Kerr, John Kerr in *Tea and Sympathy*

CLAUDIA
722 performances
Opened February 12, 1941; Closed January 9, 1943

THE GOLD DIGGERS
720 performances
Opened September 30, 1919; Closed June 1920 [date unknown]

JESUS CHRIST SUPERSTAR
720 performances
Opened October 12, 1971; Closed June 30, 1973

CARNIVAL!
719 performances
Opened April 13, 1961; Closed January 5, 1963

THE DIARY OF ANNE FRANK
717 performances
Opened October 5, 1955; Closed June 22, 1955

A FUNNY THING HAPPENED ON THE WAY TO THE FORUM (REVIVAL)
715 performances
Opened April 18, 1996; Closed January 4, 1998

I REMEMBER MAMA
714 performances
Opened October 19, 1944; Closed June 29, 1946

TEA AND SYMPATHY
712 performances
Opened September 30, 1953; Closed June 18, 1955

JUNIOR MISS
710 performances
Opened November 18, 1941; Closed July 24, 1943

FOOTLOOSE
708 performances
Opened October 22, 1998; Closed July 2, 2000

LAST OF THE RED HOT LOVERS
706 performances
Opened December 28, 1969; Closed September 4, 1971

THE SECRET GARDEN
706 performances
Opened April 25, 1991; Closed January 3, 1993

COMPANY
705 performances
Opened April 26, 1970; Closed January 1, 1972

SEVENTH HEAVEN
704 performances
Opened October 30, 1922; Closed July 1924 [date unknown]

GYPSY (MUSICAL)
702 performances
Opened May 21, 1959; Closed March 25, 1961

THE MIRACLE WORKER
700 performances
Opened October 19, 1959; Closed July 1, 1961

THAT CHAMPIONSHIP SEASON
700 performances
Opened September 14, 1972; Closed April 21, 1974

THE MUSIC MAN (MUSICAL, REVIVAL)
698 performances
Opened April 27, 2000; Closed December 30, 2001

DA
697 performances
Opened May 1, 1978; Closed January 1, 1980

CAT ON A HOT TIN ROOF
694 performances
Opened March 24, 1955; Closed November 17, 1956

LI'L ABNER
693 performances
Opened November 15, 1956; Closed July 12, 1958

THE CHILDREN'S HOUR
691 performances
Opened November 20, 1934; Closed July 1936 [date unknown]

PURLIE
688 performances
Opened March 15, 1970; Closed November 6, 1971

DEAD END
687 performances
Opened October 28, 1935; Closed June 12, 1937

THE LION AND THE MOUSE
686 performances
Opened November 20, 1905; Unknown closing date

Alfonso Ribeiro, Hinton Battle, and the Company in *The Tap Dance Kid.* PHOTO BY MARTHA SWOPE

WHITE CARGO
686 performances
Opened November 5, 1923; Closed November 1924 [date unknown]

DEAR RUTH
683 performances
Opened December 13, 1944; Closed July 27, 1946

EAST IS WEST
680 performances
Opened December 25, 1918; Closed August 1920 [date unknown]

COME BLOW YOUR HORN
677 performances
Opened February 22, 1961; Closed October 6, 1962

THE MOST HAPPY FELLA
676 performances
Opened May 3, 1956; Closed December 14, 1957

DEFENDING THE CAVEMAN
671 performances
Opened March 26, 1995; Closed June 22, 1997

THE DOUGHGIRLS
671 performances
Opened Dec. 30, 1942; Closed July 29, 1944

THE IMPOSSIBLE YEARS
670 performances
Opened October 13, 1965; Closed May 27, 1967

IRENE
670 performances
Opened November 18, 1919; Closed June 1921 [date unknown]

BOY MEETS GIRL
669 performances
Opened November 27, 1935; Closed July 1937 [date unknown]

THE TAP DANCE KID
669 performances
Opened December 21, 1983; Closed August 11, 1985

BEYOND THE FRINGE
667 performances
Opened October 27, 1962; Closed May 30, 1964

MOVIN' OUT*
664 performances
Opened October 24, 2002

WHO'S AFRAID OF VIRGINIA WOOLF?
664 performances
Opened October 13, 1962; Closed May 16, 1964

BLITHE SPIRIT
657 performances
Opened November 5, 1941; Closed June 5, 1943

A TRIP TO CHINATOWN
657 performances
Opened November 9, 1891; Unknown closing date

THE WOMEN
657 performances
Opened December 26, 1936; Closed July 1938 [date unknown]

BLOOMER GIRL
654 performances
Opened October 5, 1944; Closed April 27, 1946

THE FIFTH SEASON
654 performances
Opened January 23, 1953; Closed October 23, 1954

RAIN
648 performances
Opened September 1, 1924; Closing date unknown

WITNESS FOR THE PROSECUTION
645 performances
Opened December 16, 1954; Closed June 30, 1956

CALL ME MADAM
644 performances
Opened October 12, 1950; Closed May 3, 1952

JANIE
642 performances
Opened September 10, 1942; Closed January 16, 1944

THE GREEN PASTURES
640 performances
Opened February 26, 1930; Closed August 29, 1931

AUNTIE MAME (PLAY VERSION)
639 performances
Opened October 31, 1956; Closed June 28, 1958

A MAN FOR ALL SEASONS
637 performances
Opened November 22, 1961; Closed June 1, 1963

JEROME ROBBINS' BROADWAY
634 performances
Opened February 26, 1989; Closed September 1, 1990

THE FOURPOSTER
632 performances
Opened October 24, 1951; Closed May 2, 1953

THE MUSIC MASTER
627 performances
Opened September 26, 1904; Closed September 1906 [date unknown]

TWO GENTLEMEN OF VERONA (MUSICAL VERSION)
627 performances
Opened December 1, 1971; Closed May 20, 1973

THE TENTH MAN
623 performances
Opened November 5, 1959; Closed May 13, 1961

THE HEIDI CHRONICLES
621 performances
Opened March 9, 1989; Closed September 1, 1990

IS ZAT SO?
618 performances
Opened January 5, 1925; Closed July 1926

ANNIVERSARY WALTZ
615 performances
Opened April 7, 1954; Closed September 24, 1955

THE HAPPY TIME (PLAY VERSION)
614 performances
Opened January 24, 1950; Closed July 14, 1951

SEPARATE ROOMS
613 performances
Opened March 23, 1940; Closed September 6, 1941

AFFAIRS OF STATE
610 performances
Opened September 25, 1950; Closed March 8, 1952

OH! CALCUTTA!
610 performances
Opened June 17, 1969; Closed August 12, 1972

STAR AND GARTER
609 performances
Opened June 24, 1942; Closed December 4, 1943

THE MYSTERY OF EDWIN DROOD
608 performances
Opened December 2, 1985; Closed May 16, 1987

THE STUDENT PRINCE
608 performances
Opened December 2, 1924; May 18, 1926

SWEET CHARITY
608 performances
Opened January 29, 1966; Closed July 15, 1967

BYE BYE BIRDIE
607 performances
Opened April 14, 1960; Closed October 7, 1961

RIVERDANCE ON BROADWAY
605 performances
Opened March 16, 2000; Closed August 26, 2001

IRENE (REVIVAL)
604 performances
Opened March 13, 1973; Closed September 8, 1974

SUNDAY IN THE PARK WITH GEORGE
604 performances
Opened May 2, 1984; Closed October 13, 1985

ADONIS
603 performances
Opened ca. 1884; Unknown closing date

BROADWAY
603 performances
Opened September 16, 1926; February 11, 1928

PEG O' MY HEART
603 performances
Opened December 20, 1912; Closed May 1914 [date unknown]

MASTER CLASS
601 performances
Opened November 5, 1995; Closed June 29, 1997

STREET SCENE (PLAY)
601 performances
Opened January 10, 1929; Closed June 1930 [date unknown]

FLOWER DRUM SONG
600 performances
Opened December 1, 1958; Closed May 7, 1960

KIKI
600 performances
Opened November 29, 1921; Unknown closing date

A LITTLE NIGHT MUSIC
600 performances
Opened February 25, 1973; Closed August 3, 1974

ART
600 performances
Opened March 1, 1998; Closed August 8, 1999

AGNES OF GOD
599 performances
Opened March 30, 1982; Closed September 4, 1983

DON'T DRINK THE WATER
598 performances
Opened November 17, 1966; Closed April 20, 1968

WISH YOU WERE HERE
598 performances
Opened June 25, 1952; Closed November 28, 1958

SARAFINA!
597 performances
Opened January 28, 1988; Closed July 2, 1989

A SOCIETY CIRCUS
596 performances
Opened December 13, 1905; Closed November 24, 1906

ABSURD PERSON SINGULAR
592 performances
Opened October 8, 1974; Closed March 6, 1976

A DAY IN HOLLYWOOD/A NIGHT IN THE UKRAINE
588 performances
Opened May 1, 1980; Closed September 27, 1981

THE ME NOBODY KNOWS
586 performances
Opened December 18, 1970; Closed November 21, 1971

THE TWO MRS. CARROLLS
585 performances
Opened August 3, 1943; Closed February 3, 1945

KISMET (MUSICAL VERSION)
583 performances
Opened December 3, 1953; Closed April 23, 1955

GYPSY (MUSICAL VERSION, REVIVAL)
582 performances
Opened November 16, 1989; Closed July 28, 1991

BRIGADOON
581 performances
Opened March 13, 1947; Closed July 31, 1948

DETECTIVE STORY
581 performances
Opened March 23, 1949; Closed August 12, 1950

NO STRINGS
580 performances
Opened March 14, 1962; Closed August 3, 1963

BROTHER RAT
577 performances
Opened December 16, 1936; Closed May 1938 [date unknown]

BLOSSOM TIME
576 performances
Opened September 29, 1921; Closed October 1921 [date unknown]

PUMP BOYS AND DINETTES
573 performances
Opened February 4, 1982; Closed June 18, 1983

SHOW BOAT
572 performances
Opened December 27, 1927; Closed May 4, 1929

THE SHOW-OFF
571 performances
Opened February 5, 1924; Closed June 1925 [date unknown]

SALLY
570 performances
Opened December 21, 1920; Closed April 22, 1922

JELLY'S LAST JAM
569 performances
Opened April 26, 1992; Closed September 5, 1993

GOLDEN BOY (MUSICAL VERSION)
568 performances
Opened October 20, 1964; Closed March 5, 1966

ONE TOUCH OF VENUS
567 performances
Opened October 7, 1943; Closed February 10, 1945

THE REAL THING
566 performances
Opened January 5, 1984; Closed May 12, 1985

HAPPY BIRTHDAY
564 performances
Opened October 31, 1946; Closed March 13, 1948

LOOK HOMEWARD, ANGEL
564 performances
Opened November 28, 1957; Closed April 4, 1959

MORNING'S AT SEVEN (REVIVAL)
564 performances
Opened April 10, 1980; Closed August 16, 1981

THE GLASS MENAGERIE
561 performances
Opened March 31, 1945; Closed August 3, 1946

I DO! I DO!
560 performances
Opened December 5, 1966; Closed June 15, 1968

WONDERFUL TOWN
559 performances
Opened February 25, 1953; Closed July 3, 1954

THE LAST NIGHT OF BALLYHOO
557 performances
Opened February 27, 1997; Closed June 28, 1998

ROSE MARIE
557 performances
Opened September 2, 1924; Closed June 1925 [date unknown]

STRICTLY DISHONORABLE
557 performances
Opened Sept. 18, 1929; Closed January 1931 [date unknown]

SWEENEY TODD, THE DEMON BARBER OF FLEET STREET
557 performances
Opened March 1, 1979; Closed June 29, 1980

THE GREAT WHITE HOPE
556 performances
Opened October 3, 1968; Closed January 31, 1970

A MAJORITY OF ONE
556 performances
Opened February 16, 1959; Closed June 25, 1960

THE SISTERS ROSENSWEIG
556 performances
Opened March 18, 1993; Closed July 16, 1994

SUNRISE AT CAMPOBELLO
556 performances
Opened January 30, 1958; Closed May 30, 1959

TOYS IN THE ATTIC
556 performances
Opened February 25, 1960; Closed April 8, 1961

JAMAICA
555 performances
Opened October 31, 1957; Closed April 11, 1959

STOP THE WORLD—I WANT TO GET OFF
555 performances
Opened October 3, 1962; Closed February 1, 1964

FLORODORA
553 performances
Opened November 10, 1900; Closed January 25, 1902

NOISES OFF
553 performances
Opened December 11, 1983; Closed April 6, 1985

ZIEGFELD FOLLIES (1943)
553 performances
Opened April 1, 1943; Closed July 22, 1944

DIAL "M" FOR MURDER
552 performances
Opened October 29, 1952; Closed February 27, 1954

GOOD NEWS
551 performances
Opened September 6, 1927; Closed [date unknown]

PETER PAN (REVIVAL)
551 performances
Opened September 6, 1979; Closed January 4, 1981

HOW TO SUCCEED IN BUSINESS WITHOUT REALLY TRYING (REVIVAL)
548 performances
Opened March 23, 1995; Closed July 14, 1996

LET'S FACE IT
547 performances
Opened October 29, 1941; Closed March 20, 1943

MILK AND HONEY
543 performances
Opened October 10, 1961; Closed January 26, 1963

WITHIN THE LAW
541 performances
Opened September 11, 1912; Closed December 1913 [date unknown]

PAL JOEY (REVIVAL)
540 performances
Opened January 3, 1952; Closed April 18, 1953

THE SOUND OF MUSIC (REVIVAL)
540 performances
Opened March 12, 1998; Closed June 20, 1999

WHAT MAKES SAMMY RUN?
540 performances
Opened February 27, 1964; Closed June 12, 1965

THE SUNSHINE BOYS
538 performances
Opened December 20, 1972; Closed April 21, 1974

WHAT A LIFE
538 performances
Opened April 13, 1938; Closed July 8, 1939

CRIMES OF THE HEART
535 performances
Opened November 4, 1981; Closed February 13, 1983

DAMN YANKEES (REVIVAL)
533 performances
Opened March 3, 1994; Closed August 6, 1995

THE UNSINKABLE MOLLY BROWN
532 performances
Opened November 3, 1960; Closed February 10, 1962

THE RED MILL (REVIVAL)
531 performances
Opened October 16, 1945; Closed January 18, 1947

RUMORS
531 performances
Opened November 17, 1988; Closed February 24, 1990

A RAISIN IN THE SUN
530 performances
Opened March 11, 1959; Closed June 25, 1960

GODSPELL
527 performances
Opened June 22, 1976; Closed September 4, 1977

FENCES
526 performances
Opened March 26, 1987; Closed June 26, 1988

THE SOLID GOLD CADILLAC
526 performances
Opened November 5, 1953; Closed February 12, 1955

BILOXI BLUES
524 performances
Opened March 28, 1985; Closed June 28, 1986

IRMA LA DOUCE
524 performances
Opened September 29, 1960; Closed December 31, 1961

THE BOOMERANG
522 performances
Opened August 10, 1915; Closed November 1916 [date unknown]

FOLLIES
521 performances
Opened April 4, 1971; Closed July 1, 1972

ROSALINDA
521 performances
Opened October 28, 1942; Closed January 22, 1944

THE BEST MAN
520 performances
Opened March 31, 1960; Closed July 8, 1961

CHAUVE-SOURIS
520 performances
Opened February 6, 1922; Unknown closing date

BLACKBIRDS OF 1928
518 performances
Opened May 9, 1928; Closed August 1929 [date unknown]

THE GIN GAME
517 performances
Opened October 6, 1977; Closed December 31, 1978

SIDE MAN
517 performances
Opened June 25, 1998; Closed October 31, 1999

SUNNY
517 performances
Opened September 22, 1925; Closed December 11, 1926

VICTORIA REGINA
517 performances
Opened December 26, 1935; Closed June 1936 [date unknown]

FIFTH OF JULY
511 performances
Opened November 5, 1980; Closed January 24, 1982

HALF A SIXPENCE
511 performances
Opened April 25, 1965; Closed July 16, 1966

THE VAGABOND KING
511 performances
Opened September 21, 1925; Closed December 4, 1926

THE NEW MOON
509 performances
Opened September 19, 1928; Closed December 14, 1929

THE WORLD OF SUZIE WONG
508 performances
Opened October 14, 1958; Closed January 2, 1960

THE ROTHSCHILDS
507 performances
Opened October 19, 1970; Closed January 1, 1972

ON YOUR TOES (REVIVAL)
505 performances
Opened March 6, 1983; Closed May 20, 1984

SUGAR
505 performances
Opened April 9, 1972; Closed June 23, 1973

SHUFFLE ALONG
504 performances
Opened May 23, 1921; Closed July 15, 1922

UP IN CENTRAL PARK
504 performances
Opened January 27, 1945; Closed January 13, 1946

CARMEN JONES
503 performances
Opened December 2, 1943; Closed February 10, 1945

SATURDAY NIGHT FEVER
502 performances
Opened October 21, 1999; Closed December 30, 2000

THE MEMBER OF THE WEDDING
501 performances
Opened January 5, 1950; Closed March 17, 1951

PANAMA HATTIE
501 performances
Opened October 30, 1940; Closed January 13, 1942

PERSONAL APPEARANCE
501 performances
Opened October 17, 1934; Closed December 1935 [date unknown]

BIRD IN HAND
500 performances
Opened April 4, 1929; Closed June 1930 [date unknown]

ROOM SERVICE
500 performances
Opened May 19, 1937; Closed July 1938 [date unknown]

SAILOR, BEWARE!
500 performances
Opened September 28, 1933; Closed December 1934 [date unknown]

TOMORROW THE WORLD
500 performances
Opened April 14, 1943; Closed June 17, 1944

Longest Running Shows **Off-Broadway**

LONGEST RUNNING SHOWS
OFF-BROADWAY

*Still playing as of June 1, 2004.

THE FANTASTICKS
17,162 performances
Opened May 3, 1960; Closed January 13, 2002

PERFECT CRIME*
7,089 performances
Opened April 5, 1987

TUBES*
6,393 performances
Opened November 17, 1991

TONY N' TINA'S WEDDING
4,914 performances
Opened May 1, 1987; Closed May 18, 2003

STOMP*
4,298 performances
Opened February 27, 1994

NUNSENSE
3,672 performances
Opened December 12, 1985; Closed October 16, 1994

I LOVE YOU, YOU'RE PERFECT, NOW CHANGE*
3,255 performances
Opened August 1, 1996

THE THREEPENNY OPERA
2,611 performances
Opened September 20, 1955; Closed December 17, 1961

DE LA GUARDA*
2,356 performances
Opened June 16, 1998

FORBIDDEN BROADWAY 1982–87
2,332 performances
Opened January 15, 1982; Closed August 30, 1987

LITTLE SHOP OF HORRORS
2,209 performances
Opened July 27, 1982; Closed November 1, 1987

GODSPELL
2,124 performances
Opened May 17, 1971; Closed June 13, 1976

NAKED BOYS SINGING*
2,031 performances
Opened July 22, 1999

VAMPIRE LESBIANS OF SODOM
2,024 performances
Opened June 19, 1985; Closed May 27, 1990

JACQUES BREL
1,847 performances
Opened October 1, 1992; Closed February 7, 1997

FOREVER PLAID
1,811 performances
Opened May 20, 1990; Closed June 12, 1994

VANITIES
1,785 performances
Opened August 6, 1928; Unknown closing date

YOU'RE A GOOD MAN, CHARLIE BROWN
1,597 performances
Opened March 7, 1967; Closed February 14, 1971

Mark Martino, Roxie Lucas, Craig Wells in *Forbidden Broadway* 1986 PHOTO BY HENRY GROSSMAN

THE BLACKS
1,408 performances
Opened May 4, 1961; Closed September 27, 1964

THE VAGINA MONOLOGUES
1,381 performances
Opened October 3, 1999; Closed January 26, 2003

ONE MO' TIME
1,372 performances
Opened October 22, 1979; Closed 1982–83 season

GRANDMA SYLVIA'S FUNERAL
1,360 performances
Opened October 9, 1994; Closed June 20, 1998

LET MY PEOPLE COME
1,327 performances
Opened January 8, 1974; Closed July 5, 1976

LATE NITE CATECHISM
1,268 performances
Opened October 4, 1995; Closed May 18, 2003

THE DONKEY SHOW*
1,225 performances
Opened January 26, 1999

DRIVING MISS DAISY
1,195 performances
Opened April 15, 1987; Closed June 3, 1990

THE HOT L BALTIMORE
1,166 performances
Opened September 8, 1973; Closed January 4, 1976

I'M GETTING MY ACT TOGETHER AND TAKING IT ON THE ROAD
1,165 performances
Opened May 16, 1987; Closed March 15, 1981

LITTLE MARY SUNSHINE
1,143 performances
Opened November 18, 1959; Closed September 2, 1962

STEEL MAGNOLIAS
1,126 performances
Opened November 17, 1987; Closed February 25, 1990

EL GRANDE DE COCA-COLA
1,114 performances
Opened February 13, 1973; Closed April 13, 1975

THE PROPOSITION
1,109 performances
Opened March 24, 1971; Closed April 14, 1974

OUR SINATRA
1,096 performances
Opened December 8, 1999; Closed July 28, 2002

BEAU JEST
1,069 performances
Opened October 10, 1991; Closed May 1, 1994

TAMARA
1,036 performances
Opened November 9, 1989; Closed July 15, 1990

ONE FLEW OVER THE CUCKOO'S NEST (REVIVAL)
1,025 performances
Opened March 23, 1971; Closed September 16, 1973

THE BOYS IN THE BAND
1,000 performances
Opened April 14, 1968; Closed September 29, 1985

FOOL FOR LOVE
1,000 performances
Opened November 27, 1983; Closed September 29, 1985

OTHER PEOPLE'S MONEY
990 performances
Opened February 7, 1989; Closed July 4, 1991

Dana Ivey, Morgan Freeman in *Driving Miss Daisy* PHOTO BY BOB MARSHAK

CLOUD 9
971 performances
Opened May 18, 1981; Closed September 4, 1983

SECRETS EVERY SMART TRAVELER SHOULD KNOW
953 performances
Opened October 30, 1997; Closed February 21, 2000

SISTER MARY IGNATIUS EXPLAINS IT ALL FOR YOU & THE ACTOR'S NIGHTMARE
947 performances
Opened October 21, 1981; Closed January 29, 1984

FORBIDDEN BROADWAY: 20TH ANNIVERSARY CELEBRATION*
944 performances
Opened March 20, 2002

YOUR OWN THING
933 performances
Opened January 13, 1968; Closed April 5, 1970

CURLEY MCDIMPLE
931 performances
Opened November 22, 1967; Closed January 25, 1970

LEAVE IT TO JANE (REVIVAL)
928 performances
Opened May 29, 1959; Closed 1961–62 season

MENOPAUSE THE MUSICAL*
927 performances
Opened April 4, 2002

THE MAD SHOW
871 performances
Opened January 9, 1966; Closed September 10, 1967

HEDWIG AND THE ANGRY INCH
857 performances
Opened February 14, 1998; Closed April 9, 2000

FORBIDDEN BROADWAY STRIKES BACK
850 performances
Opened October 17, 1996; Closed September 20, 1998

WHEN PIGS FLY
840 performances
Opened August 14, 1996; Closed August 15, 1998

SCRAMBLED FEET
831 performances
Opened June 11, 1979; Closed June 7, 1981

THE EFFECT OF GAMMA RAYS ON MAN-IN-THE-MOON MARIGOLDS
819 performances
Opened April 7, 1970; Closed June 1, 1973

OVER THE RIVER AND THROUGH THE WOODS
800 performances
Opened October 5, 1998; Closed September 3, 2000

A VIEW FROM THE BRIDGE (REVIVAL)
780 performances
Opened November 9, 1965; Closed December 11, 1966

THE BOY FRIEND (REVIVAL)
763 performances
Opened January 25, 1958; Closed 1961–62 season

TRUE WEST
762 performances
Opened December 23, 1980; Closed January 11, 1981

Guy-Paris Thompson, Elizabeth Franz in *Sister Mary* PHOTO BY SUSAN COOK

FORBIDDEN BROADWAY CLEANS UP ITS ACT!
754 performances
Opened November 17, 1998; Closed August 30, 2000

ISN'T IT ROMANTIC
733 performances
Opened December 15, 1983; Closed September 1, 1985

DIME A DOZEN
728 performances
Opened June 13, 1962; Closed 1963–64 season

THE POCKET WATCH
725 performances
Opened November 14, 1966; Closed June 18, 1967

THE CONNECTION
722 performances
Opened June 9, 1959; Closed June 4, 1961

THE PASSION OF DRACULA
714 performances
Opened September 28, 1977; Closed July 14, 1979

LOVE, JANIS
713 performances
Opened April 22, 2001; Closed January 5, 2003

ADAPTATION & NEXT
707 performances
Opened February 10, 1969; Closed October 18, 1970

OH! CALCUTTA!
704 performances
Opened June 17, 1969; Closed August 12, 1972

SCUBA DUBA
692 performances
Opened November 11, 1967; Closed June 8, 1969

THE FOREIGNER
686 performances
Opened November 2, 1984; Closed June 8, 1986

THE KNACK
685 performances
Opened January 14, 1964; Closed January 9, 1966

FULLY COMMITTED
675 performances
Opened December 14, 1999; Closed May 27, 2001

THE CLUB
674 performances
Opened October 14, 1976; Closed May 21, 1978

THE BALCONY
672 performances
Opened March 3, 1960; Closed December 21, 1961

PENN & TELLER
666 performances
Opened July 30, 1985; Closed January 19, 1992

DINNER WITH FRIENDS
654 performances
Opened November 4, 1999; Closed May 27, 2000

AMERICA HURRAH
634 performances
Opened November 7, 1966; Closed May 5, 1968

OIL CITY SYMPHONY
626 performances
Opened November 5, 1987; Closed May 7, 1989

THE COUNTESS
618 performances
Opened September 28, 1999; Closed December 30, 2000

THE EXONERATED
608 performances
Opened October 10, 2002; Closed March 7, 2004

HOGAN'S GOAT
607 performances
Opened March 6, 1965; Closed April 23, 1967

BEEHIVE
600 performances
Opened March 30, 1986; Closed August 23, 1987

CRISS ANGEL MINDFREAK
600 performances
Opened November 23, 2001; Closed January 6, 2003

THE TROJAN WOMEN
600 performances
Opened December 23, 1963; Closed May 30, 1965

THE SYRINGA TREE
586 performances
Opened September 14, 2000; Closed June 2, 2002

THE DINING ROOM
583 performances
Opened February 24, 1982; Closed July 17, 1982

KRAPP'S LAST TAPE & THE ZOO STORY
582 performances
Opened August 29, 1960; Closed May 21, 1961

THREE TALL WOMEN
582 performances
Opened April 13, 1994; Closed August 26, 1995

THE DUMBWAITER & THE COLLECTION
578 performances
Opened January 21, 1962; Closed April 12, 1964

FORBIDDEN BROADWAY 1990
576 performances
Opened January 23, 1990; Closed June 9, 1991

DAMES AT SEA
575 performances
Opened April 22, 1969; Closed May 10, 1970

THE CRUCIBLE (REVIVAL) (TRANSFER)
571 performances
Opened March 14, 1990; Closed May 13, 1990

THE ICEMAN COMETH (REVIVAL)
565 performances
Opened May 8, 1956; Closed 1957–58 season

FORBIDDEN BROADWAY 2001: A SPOOF ODYSSEY
552 performances
Opened December 6, 2000; Closde February 6, 2002

THE HOSTAGE (REVIVAL) (TRANSFER)
545 performances
Opened October 16, 1972; Closed October 8, 1973

WIT
545 performances
Opened October 6, 1998; Closed April 9, 2000

WHAT'S A NICE COUNTRY LIKE YOU DOING IN A STATE LIKE THIS?
543 performances
Opened July 31, 1985; Closed February 9, 1987

FORBIDDEN BROADWAY 1988
534 performances
Opened September 15, 1988; Closed December 24, 1989

GROSS INDECENCY: THE THREE TRIALS OF OSCAR WILDE
534 performances
Opened September 5, 1997; Closed September 13, 1998

FRANKIE AND JOHNNY IN THE CLAIRE DE LUNE
533 performances
Opened December 4, 1987; Closed March 12, 1989

SIX CHARACTERS IN SEARCH OF AN AUTHOR (REVIVAL)
529 performances
Opened March 8, 1963; Closed June 28, 1964

ALL IN THE TIMING
526 performances
Opened November 24, 1993; Closed February 13, 1994

OLEANNA
513 performances
Opened October 3, 1992; Closed January 16, 1994

MAKING PORN
511 performances
Opened June 12, 1996; Closed September 14, 1997

THE DIRTIEST SHOW IN TOWN
509 performances
Opened June 26, 1970; Closed September 17, 1971

HAPPY ENDING & DAY OF ABSENCE
504 performances
Opened June 13, 1965; Closed January 29, 1967

GREATER TUNA
501 performances
Opened October 21, 1982; Closed December 31, 1983

A SHAYNA MAIDEL
501 performances
Opened October 29, 1987; Closed January 8, 1989

THE BOYS FROM SYRACUSE (REVIVAL)
500 performances
Opened April 15, 1963; Closed June 28, 1964

BIOGRAPHICAL DATA

Stephanie D'Abruzzo   Robert Hock   Deborah Lew   David Zayas

Alexander, Leslie Born Dec. 1 in Lubbock, TX. Attended Texas Technical U. Bdwy debut 2001 in *Mamma Mia!*, followed by *The Boy From Oz*.

Alfonso, Ioana Born May 17, 1978 in New York, NY. Graduate NYU, New World School of the Arts. Bdwy debut 2000 in *Saturday Night Fever*, followed by *Wicked*.

Barnes, Ezra Born January 22 in Brooklyn, NY. Graduate Amherst College, National Theatre Conservatory. OB debut 1998 in *Richard II*, followed by *Far and Wide*.

Barnett, Ken Born in Memphis, TN Graduate Wesleyan U. Bdwy debut 2000 in *Green Bird*, followed by *Wonderful Town*. OB in *My Life With Albertine*, *Imperfect Chemistry*, *A Christmas Carol*, *Debbie Does Dallas*.

Barnhardt, Scott Born March 19, 1979 in Orange, CA. Graduate Wagner College. Bdwy debut 2003 in *Big River*.

Blythe, Domini Born Aug. 28, 1947 in Cheshire, England. Graduate Central School of Speech and Drama. Bdwy debut 2004 in *King Lear*.

Charles, Walter Born April 4, 1945 in East Stroudsburg, PA. Graduate Boston U. School for the Arts. Bdwy debut 1973 in *Grease*, followed by *1600 Pennsylvania Avenue*, *Prince of Grand Street*, *Sweeney Todd*, *Cats*, *La Cage Aux Folles*, *Me & My Girl*, *Aspects of Love*, *A Christmas Carol*, *Kiss Me Kate*, *Boys From Syracuse*, *Big River*. OB in *Anna Karenina*, *Circle-In-The-Square*, *110 In The Shade*, *Call Me Madam*, *Wit*, *MCC* & *Union Square*, *The Immigrant*.

Ciulla, Celeste Born in New York, NY. Graduate Northwestern U. OB debut 1992 in *Othello*, followed by *The Good Natur'd Man*, *Phaedra*, *Andromache*, *A Will of His Own*, *Exit the King*, *Iphegenia at Aulis*, *Romeo and Juliet*, *Phantom Lady*, *Much Ado About Nothing*, *Nathan the Wise*, *She Stoops to Conquer*, *The Tempest*, *The Rivals*, *The Merchant of Venice*.

Collins, Patrick Born in New York, NY. Graduate Manhattan College. Bdwy debut 2003 in *Cat on a Hot Tin Roof*. OB in *Mass Appeal*, *Joan of Lorraine*, *A Funny Thing Happened On the Way to the Forum*.

Crandall, Kelly Born July 25 in Orlando, FL. Graduate U. of Michigan. Bdwy debut 2001 in *Dirty Dancing*, followed by *A Christmas Carol*, *The Boy From Oz*.

D'Abruzzo, Stephanie Born Dec. 7, 1971 in Pittsburgh, PA. Graduate Northwestern U. Bdwy debut 2003 in *Avenue Q* (also OB).

Deakin, Ian Born April 9, 1950 in Eyesham, England. Graduate Dalhousie U. Bdwy debut 2004 in *King Lear*. OB in Stratford Festival of Canada, *The Miser*, *Much Ado About Nothing*.

Federan, Mitchel David Born Dec. 17, 1991 in Cleveland, OH. Bdwy debut 2001 in *The Music Man*, followed by *The Boy From Oz*.

Federer, Michelle Born Dec. 5, 1972 in Cleveland, OH. Graduate Ithaca College. Bdwy debut 2003 in *Wicked*. OB in *A Man of No Importance*, *Mrs. Patrick*, *In The Absence of Spring*.

Hawks, Colleen Born in Oakdale, CA. Bdwy debut 1999 in *Smokey Joe's Café*, followed by *The Boy From Oz*. OB in *Shake That Thing!*, *The Wild Party*.

Heslin, George C. Graduate Trinity College, Dublin. Bdwy debut 2002 in *Stones In His Pockets*. OB in *The Colleen Bawn*, *Mister Man*, *Flaherty's Window*.

Hock, Robert Born May 20, 1931 in Phoenixville, PA. Graduate Yale U., Yale School of Drama. Bdwy debut in *Some Americans Abroad*. OB in *Daisy Mayme*, *Heartbreak House*, *The Tempest*, *Much Ado About Nothing*, *Romeo and Juliet*, *Iphegenia in Aulis*, *Exit the King*, *The Cherry Orchard*, *The Oresteia*, *The Way of the World*, *The Seagull*, *The Country Wife*, *The Miser*, *The Chairs*, *Venice Preserved*, *Misalliance*, *Life Is A Dream*, *A Doll's House*, *Antigone*, *King Lear*, *The Beaux Stratagem*, *Oedipus At Colonus*, *Mrs. Warren's Profession*, *Twelfth Night*, *The Game of Love and Chance*, *Oedipus*, *The King*, *Phaedra*, *The Good Natur'd Man*, *The Rivals*.

Hohn, Amy Born in Royal Oak, MI. Graduate Syracuse U. Bdwy debut 2003 in *Cat On a Hot Tin Roof*. OB in *June Moon*, *The Country Club*, *Dream True*, *A Few Stout Individuals*.

Jullien, Claire Born Oct. 4, 1972 in Ontario, Canada. Graduate U. of Windsor. Bdwy debut 1998 in *Much Ado About Nothing*.

Kanouse, Lyle Born July 12, 1952 in Ft. Worth, TX. Graduate Texas Wesleyan, Indiana U. Bdwy debut 1983 in *Chaplin*, followed by *Big River*. OB in *The Miser*.

Lew, Deborah Born May 7, 1978 in Grand Rapids MI. Graduate Calvin College. OB debut 2003 in *Cupid and Psyche*.

Lipton, Logan Born Aug. 6, 1981 in Kalamazoo, MI. Graduate U. of Michigan. OB debut 2003 in *Cupid and Psyche*.

Leamy, Deborah Born Aug. 30, 1969 in Providence, RI. Graduate Emerson College. Bdwy debut 1999 in *Fosse*, followed by *Sweet Smell of Success*, *Never Gonna Dance*. OB in *The Green Heart*.

Lemenager, Nancy Born June 1, 1970. Bdwy debut in *Meet Me In St. Louis*, followed by *Guys & Dolls*, *How To Succeed In Business Without Really Trying*, *Dream*, *Kiss Me Kate*, *Never Gonna Dance*.

MacGregor, Barry Born Sept. 10, 1936 in Herts, Gt. Britain. Bdwy debut 1964 in *King Lear*, followed by *Flea In Her Ear*, *King Lear* (2004). OB in *Don't Shoot Mabel It's Your Husband*.

Marx, Peter Born April 17, 1958 in New York, NY. Graduate U. of Michigan School of Music. Bdwy debut 1983 in *On Your Toes*, followed by *Singin' in The Rain*, *Annie Get Your Gun*, *Imaginary Friends*, *42nd Street*. OB in *No Way To Treat a Lady* and *The Cocoanuts*.

McCourt, Sean Born January 19, 1971 in MI. Graduate NYU. Bdwy debut 1997 in *Titanic*, followed by *It Ain't Nothin' But the Blues*, *Wicked*. OB in *Honky Tonk Highway*, *June and Jean In Concert*, *Woody Guthrie's American Song*, *Portable Pioneer*, *Yiddle With a Fiddle*, *Bat Boy*, *The Castle*, *A Man of No Importance*.

McNall, Sean Born Oct. 1, 1974 in Whittier, CA. Graduate Juilliard School of Drama. OB debut in *Hamlet*, followed by *Julius Caesar*, *The Rivals*, *Daisy Mayme*, *The Tempest*.

Mehiel, Isabella Born June 16, 1992 in New York, NY. Bdwy debut 2003 in *Cat on a Hot Tin Roof*. OB in *Miracle Worker*.

Ojeda, Perry Born April 25, 1968 in Tecumseh, MI. Graduate U. of Michigan. Bdwy debut in *Blood Brothers*, followed by *On The Town*, *Imaginary Friends*. OB in *Babes In Arms*, *Johnny Johnson*, *Wish You Were Here*.

Orbach, Ron Born March 23, 1952 in Newark, NJ. Graduate Rider College, American Conservatory Theatre. OB debut 1993 in *Laughter on the 23rd Floor*, followed by *Dance of the Vampires*, *Never Gonna Dance*. OB in *Lies and Legends: The Musical Stories of Harry Chapin*, *Pal Joey*, *Chicago* (1997), *The Job*, *Hotel Suite*.

Ortiz, John Born Nov. 21, 1969 in Brooklyn, NY. Bdwy debut in *Anna in the Tropics*.

Prosky, Andy Born June 27, 1965 in Washington D.C. Graduate Rutgers U. Bdwy debut 2004 in *King Lear*. OB in *Titus Andronicus*, *Much Ado About Nothing*, *The Tempest*, *The Merchant of Venice*.

Saxton, Charlie Born Nov. 7, 1989 in Bristol, PA. Bdwy debut 2003 in *Cat on a Hot Tin Roof*. OB in *To Kill A Mockingbird*.

Schlecht, Ryan Born March 11, 1976 in Bellevue, WA. Graduate Bellevue Community College, National Theatre of the Deaf Professional Theatre School, National Theatre of the Deaf Actor's Academy. Bdwy debut 2003 in *Big River*.

Schultz, Carol Born Feb. 12 in Chicago, IL. Bdwy debut in *Abe Lincoln In Illinois*. OB in *Marvin's Room*, *Hard Times*, *John Gabriel Borkman*, *The Way of the World*, *Merry Wives of Windsor*, *Angel Street*, *King Lear*, *Peer Gynt*, *The Ghost Sonata*, *The Cherry Orchard*.

Shew, Timothy Born Feb. 17, 1959 in Grand Forks, ND. Graduate Millikan U. Bdwy debut 1988 in *Les Miserables*, followed by *Guys & Dolls*, *Sunset Boulevard*, *The Scarlet Pimpernel*, *Les Miserables* (1999), *Radio City Music Hall Christmas Spectacular*, *Wonderful Town*. OB in *Captains Courageous*, *Tenderloin*, *Promised Land*, *The Knife*.

Sheffer Stevens, Eric Born June 19, 1972 in Sacramento, CA. Graduate Wheaton College, U. of Alabama. Bdwy debut 2004 in *King Lear*. OB in *Romeo & Juliet*, *Much Ado About Nothing*.

Verhoest, P.J. Born Dec. 23, 1991 in Wayne, NJ. Bdwy debut 2000 in *Beauty & the Beast*, followed by *Oklahoma!*, *The Boy From Oz*. OB in *James and the Giant Peach*, *White Widow*.

Vlastnik, Frank Born May 30, 1969 in Peru, IL. Graduate Illinois Wesleyan U. Bdwy debut 1996 in *Big*, followed by *Sweet Smell of Success*, *A Year With Frog and Toad*. OB in *Oy!*, *Saturday Night*.

Wong, Eunice Born May 19, 1977 in Ontario, Canada. Graduate Juilliard School of Drama. OB in *House of Bernarda Alba*, *Free Market*, *Howling*, *Twelfth Night*, *She Stoops to Conquer*, *Nathan the Wise*, *The Rivals*, *The Merchant of Venice*.

Youmans, William Born Sept. 18, 1957 in Englewood, NJ. Graduate SUNY Purchase. Bdwy debut 1981 in *Little Foxes*, followed by *Big River* (1985), *Titanic*, *La Boheme*, *Wicked*. OB in *Henry V*, *Flux*, *Widow Claire*, *1,2,3,4,5*, *Weird Romance*, *Orphan of Zhao*.

Zayas, David Born Aug. 15 in Bronx, NY. Bdwy debut 2003 in *Anna in the Tropics*. OB in *Tony and Son*, *Den of Thieves*, *Cutting Open Wings*, *In Arabia We'd All Be Kings*, *Jesus Hopped the A Train*, *Our Lady of 121st Street*.

OBITUARIES
June 1, 2003–May 31, 2004

Sheldon Abend, 74, New York, New York-born theatre executive, died August 24, 2003 in New York City. He made his mark as a representative of author estates including those of Damon Runyon, G.B. Shaw, Shirley Jackson, Somerset Maugham, and Tennessee Williams. He was an owner of American Play Company, and the executive producer for both the movie *Original Sin* and the television version of *Rear Window*. He is responsible for the Supreme Court's "Abend Rule" which involves copyright renewal infringements. He established the Author's Research Co. and was a literary and rights negotiator for RKO, 7 Arts, United Artists, Warner Bros., and others. Survivors include a son, grandson, longtime friend Renee Stewart and her son.

Lewis Allen, 81, Berryville, Virginia-born producer, died December 8, 2003, in New York City, of pancreatic cancer. He was considered to be one of the last "gentleman producers." His prolific career as a theatrical and movie producer includes the productions of: *Annie, Master Class, I'm Not Rappaport, A Few Good Men, The Iceman Cometh, My One and Only, Billy Bishop Goes to War, Half a Sixpence, Slow Dance on the Killing Ground, The Physicists, Ballad of the Sad Café, Tru, The Prime of Miss Jean Brodie, Big Fish, Little Fish, The Man in the Dog Suit* and *The Big Love*. His Off-Broadway plays include *A Lie of the Mind* and *Vita and Virginia*." He is survived by his wife, writer Jay Presson Allen, his daughter Brooke, two brothers, Howard and Douglas, and two grandchildren.

Rosalie Allen, 79, Old Forge, Pennsylvania-born singing cowgirl, yodeler, and country disc jockey, died September 23, 2003, in Palmdale, California, of heart failure. In 1947 she was part of the first country concert at Carnegie Hall, performing with Ernest Tubb and Minnie Pearl among others. By the late 1940s she had her own country radio show on NBC. She retained the moniker Queen of Country Radio until her death. She is survived by her daughter, Dorothy Bunch.

Carl Anderson, 58, Lynchburg, Virginia-born actor/singer, died February 23, 2004, in Los Angeles, California, of leukemia. His Broadway credits include *Play On!* and the role of Judas in *Jesus Christ Superstar*. He received two Golden Globe nominations for his portrayal of Judas in the 1973 film version of Jesus Christ Superstar, and played the role on numerous national tours of the show as late as 2002, logging in an estimated 1200 performances of the role. Throughout the '80s and '90s he sang on albums of the band Earth, Wind, & Fire and recorded with pop hits with singing stars Gloria Loring, Skip Yarborough, and Nancy Wilson. His 1986 duet with Loring, "Friends and Lovers" hit Number 1 on the pop charts. Anderson appeared in the film *The Color Purple* and on the television series *Hill Street Blues*. He is survived by his wife, Veronica, a son from a previous marriage, Khalil McGhee-Anderson, stepdaughters Hannah and Laila, and several sisters.

Hy Anzell, 79, New York, New York-born actor, died August 24, 2003, in Fresno, California, of natural causes. He debuted on Broadway in 1946 in Duke Ellington's musical *Beggar's Holiday*. His other Broadway credits included *Checking Out* and *Oklahoma*. Off-Broadway credits include *Little Shop of Horrors, Kvetch, Manny, Yentl, Seidman & Son*, and *Blood, Sweat and Stanley Poole*. Anzell appeared in several of Woody Allen's films, most notably *Annie Hall, Bananas*, and *Deconstructing Harry*.

Victor Argo, 69, New York, New York-born actor, died April 7, 2004, in New York City, of lung cancer. He appeared in many Broadway and Off-Broadway productions including Nilo Cruz's Pulitzer prize-winning drama *Anna in the Tropics* this season. His other stage credits include *Clean, The Dog Problem, Animals, Breaking Legs*, and *Floating Islands*. Argo also appeared in several films including *Taxi Driver, King of New York, The Last Temptation of Christ, Ghost Dog*, and *Crimes and Misdemeanors*. Survivors include two sisters.

George Axelrod, 81, New York, New York-born playwright, died June 21, 2003, in Los Angeles, of heart failure. He was both a prolific Hollywood screenwriter and playwright of such classics as Broadway's *The Seven Year Itch*, the somewhat autobiographical *Will Success Spoil Rock Hunter?*, and *Goodbye Charlie*; all three of which were adapted into movies. He adapted for the stage the novels *My Face for the World to See* and Gore Vidal's *Visit to a Small Planet*. His Broadway directing credits include: *Once More, With Feeling, Small Wonder*, and Neil Simon's *Star Spangled Girl*. He had a long, prolific life in Hollywood writing screenplays, including *Breakfast at Tiffany's* and *The Manchurian Candidate*. He shared his Hollywood producing duties with colleague Richard Quine. Axelrod is survived by daughter Nina, sons Peter, Steven, and Jonathan, seven grandchildren, and a sister.

Etta Moten Barnett, 102, Texas-born actress and contralto, died January 2, 2004, of cancer. Her first starring role was in the 1942 Broadway revival of *Porgy and Bess*. Other stage credits are *Fast and Furious* and *Zombie*. She worked in Hollywood dubbing voices for Barbara Stanwyck, Ginger Rogers, and others. It was in 1934 that Eleanor Roosevelt invited her to sing for President Roosevelt's birthday and this invitation made her the first black woman to be asked to the White House. She is survived by a daughter, several grandchildren and great-grandchildren.

Alan Bates, 69, Derbyshire, England-born actor, died December 27, 2003, in London, of cancer. Bates had an illustrious, long career as an international leading man both on stage and in film. He won two Tony Awards for his roles in *Fortune's Fool* (2002) and *Butley* (1972). He also appeared Off-Broadway in the 2002 production of *The Unexpected Man*. He began his career in 1955 when he studied at the English Stage Company, where his critically-acclaimed performance as Cliff in *Look Back in Anger* was followed by a role in both the London and New York productions of *The Caretaker*. His 1958 role in *Long Day's Journey Into Night* garnered more great reviews. He was a master of Chekhov and a revered Shakespearean actor, appearing in *Hamlet, Richard III*, and *Anthony and Cleopatra*. He worked steadily in film until 2002, and is best known for his roles in *Women in Love, Zorba the Greek*, and *An Unmarried Woman*. Bates is survived by actor son Benedict, a granddaughter, and two brothers.

Richard Bauman, 79, Sandusky, Ohio-born actor, dancer, and talent agent, died July 31, 2003, in Sherman Oaks, California, of undisclosed causes. He acted in local theatres until his teens and then worked on Broadway and Off-Broadway as a dancer and actor in the 1950s. He started his own talent agency, the Richard Bauman agency, in 1960. His roster of clients included Jean Stapleton, Bette Midler, Robert De Niro, and James Earl Jones. Bauman later partnered with Walter N. Hiller and formed Bauman-Hiller & Associates.

Rudolph Bennett, 78, musical director and conductor, died September 22, 2003, in Marshfield, Massachusetts, of Parkinson's disease. He was a prolific theatrical musical director and conductor. He conducted more than sixty musicals on Broadway including: *The Secret Affairs of Mildred Wilde, High Spirits, Man of La Mancha, La Cage aux Folles,* and revivals of *Oklahoma* and *My Fair Lady*. He is survived by his wife, Barbara, and a daughter.

Lyle Bettger, 88, Philadelphia, Pennsylvania-born actor, died September 24, 2003, in Atascadero, California, of natural causes. He began his career on Broadway in the 1940 production of *The Flying Girados*. His other legit credits include *The Moon is Down, John Loves Mary,* and *Oh, Brother*. He appeared in over 30 films and several television series. Bettger is survived by his wife Sue, a sister, two sons, a daughter, and three grandchildren.

True Boardman, 94, Seattle, Washington-born actor and screenwriter, died July 28, 2003, in Pebble Beach, California, of cancer. Boardman made his legitimate acting debut with his parents when he was only a few weeks old. He appeared on stage in *Gang War* in 1928, but his work was mostly concentrated in movies, television, and radio. In 1942 he helped form Armed Forces Radio, and stood up to Joseph McCarthy during the 1954 "witch hunts;" eventually clearing his name of slander. He was married to actress Thelma Hubbardd for 43 years until her death in 1978. He is survived by second wife Kathleen Gilmour, two daughters, and six grandchildren.

Frederick Bradlee, 84, New York, New York-born actor-writer, died July 12, 2003, in New York City, of Alzheimer's disease. His Broadway, Off-Broadway, touring, and regional credits include: *Dame Nature* (1938), *Fledgling* (1940), *Theatre, The Happy Days,* (1941), *A Winter's Tale, The Man Who Came to Dinner, Arms and the Man, The First Mrs. Fraser, The Browning Version,* and *The Second Threshold*. He contributed articles and verse to several publications and was a published novelist and editor. Bradlee is survived by his brother Benjamin.

Dana Broccoli, 82, New York, New York-born actress, novelist and producer, died February 29, 2004, in Los Angeles, of cancer. She studied at Cecil Clovelly's Academy of Dramatic Arts in Carnegie Hall and was a member of the Pasadena Playhouse. Along with second husband Albert "Cubby" Broccoli she parlayed Ian Fleming's James Bond character into filmdom's most enduring franchise. Her association with Fleming led to piloting the film version and later the stage version of *Chitty Chitty Bang Bang*, which opened in London's West End in 2002 and is set to open on Broadway in 2005. Broccolli is survived by four children and five grandchildren.

Charles Brown, 57, Talladega, Alabama-born actor, died January 8, 2004, in Cleveland, Ohio, of cancer. The prolific actor worked with the Negro Ensemble Theatre Company where he received a Tony nomination for his performance in Samm-Art Williams' *Home*. He earned his second Tony nomination and a Drama Desk award in 2001 for his role in August Wilson's *King Hedley II*. His other stage credits include: *Fences, The Mighty Gents, First Breeze of Summer, Nevis Mountain Dew,* Charles Fuller's Pulitzer prize-winning *A Soldier's Play,* Neil Simon's *Rumors,* and Ronald Ribman's *The Poison Tree*. In 2002 he appeared in *The Exonerated* at New York City's Culture Project. Brown is survived by his wife, Renee Lescook, his father, Mack, two brothers, and one sister.

Mary Bryant, 71, Apopka, Florida-born theatrical press agent and publicist, died February 22, 2004, in Hillsdale, New York, of a stroke. She did press for over fifty plays and musicals in her long career. She frequently represented the shows of Stephen Sondheim and Hal Prince. She was an actor at the Hedgerow Theatre in Moylan, Pennsylvania, but she saw that her skills were in the written word. Her client roster included: *Fiorello!, Toys in the Attic, The Aspern Papers, Flora, the Red Menace, Cabaret, Evita, Candide, Company, Side by Side by Sondheim, A Touch of the Poet, A Little Night Music, Zorba, Pacific Overtures, Kiss of the Spider Woman, Show Boat, Never Too Late,* and *Follies,* among many others.

Norman Burton, 79, New York, New York-born actor, died November 29, 2003, in Ajijic, Mexico, of injuries sustained in a car accident. He studied with Lee Strasberg and appeared on Broadway in *The Wedding Breakfast, Sound of Hunting, Anna Christie, Sweet Bird of Youth,* and Jose Quintero's production of Behan's *The Quare Fellow in New York City*. He was also seen in over 40 feature films and was a frequent guest star on several television series. Burton is survived by a daughter, a niece, a nephew, and two grandsons.

Virginia Capers, 78, Sumpter, South Carolina-born singer and actress, died May 6, 2004, in Los Angeles, of pneumonia. She began her stage career in 1950 as an actor in Yiddish theatre after graduating from Julliard. She won a 1974 Tony Award for the role of Lena Younger in *Raisin,* the musical adaptation of *A Raisin in the Sun*. Previously Capers was featured in the Broadway productions of *Saratoga* and *Jamaica*. While pursuing her career in film and television in Los Angeles she founded the Lafayette Players West, a performing arts repertory group. She made notable appearances in many films and television shows, including *Lady Sings the Blues, What's Love Got to Do With It,* and *The Great White Hope*. Her honors include the National Black Theatre Festival Living Legend Award, the Paul Robeson Pioneer Award, and the NAACP's first Image Award for theatrical excellence. She is survived by her son, Gary, and a brother.

Art Carney, 85, actor and comedian, Mount Vernon-born, died November 9, 2003, in Connecticut, of a long-term illness. Carney began his career as comedian and impersonator. His fame as Ed Norton on *The Honeymooners* might never wane, but his Broadway credits from the 1950s through the 1980s are significant. He appeared in *The Rope Dancers, Flora, the Red Menace, The Prisoner of Second Avenue, Lovers,* and *Take Her, She's Mine*. In 1965 he originated the role of Felix Unger in Neil Simon's *The Odd Couple* opposite Walter Matthau. His performance in the film *Harry and Tonto* garnered him an Oscar in 1974. Carney made significant appearances in many other television series including *Studio One, Kraft Television Theatre,* and *The Twilight Zone*. Other film credits include *The Late Show* and *The Greatest Show on Earth*. Carney is survived by his wife, Jean Myers, and children Eileen, Bryan, and Paul.

Gene Casey, 70, Fort Sills, Oklahoma-born composer/lyricist and musical arranger, died September 28, 2003, in Los Angeles, of liver failure. He and his brother Jan co-wrote numerous musical theatre shows including *Hubba Hubba* for the Goodspeed Opera House, *An Original Jimmy Shine,* the children's musical *The Magic Weave,* and *The Orphan's Revenge*. His last musical revue "Gene Casey's Theatresongs" was produced at Lonny Chapman's Group Repertory Theatre in the spring of 2003. He also served as an accompanist to a wide range of talents including Barbra Streisand and Liza Minnelli, and wrote for television shows. He is survived by his writing partner and best friend of 42 years, Richard Alan Woody; and his sister.

Alan Bates

Virginia Capers

Hume Cronyn

Buddy Hackett

Malonga Casquelourd, 55, Congo Republic-born drummer, dancer, and choreographer, died June 15, 2003, in Oakland California, in a car accident. At the Alice Arts Center in Oakland, California he taught both the music and moves of his native land. By 1965 he was touring with the National Congolese Dance Company as principle dancer. He toured Africa, Europe, and the United States and later moved to Paris to work as choreographer and principle performer with Le Ballet Diaboua. In New York City he co-founded Tanawa which was the first central African dance company in the United States. It was in the 1970s when he moved to California and founded the Fua Dia Congo dance troupe.

Joseph Chaikin, 67, Brooklyn, New York-born avant-garde theatre director and actor, died June 22, 2003, at his home in New York City, of heart failure. Chaikin collaborated with both Sam Shepard and Samuel Beckett and is best known for founding the Open Theatre in 1963. In 1959 he joined the Living Theatre; this gave him the foundation for his own free-wheeling, avant-garde ideas. He respected and taught method acting, as well as more traditional concepts. Some of his credits include: *The Connection*, Brecht's *Man is Man*, his own *Texts for Nothing*, and Sam Shepard's *Savage Love* and *Tongues*. He directed many plays including *Endgame*, *The Bald Soprano*, *The Dybbuk* at the Public Theatre, *The Leader*, *Medea*, and Arthur Miller's *Broken Glass*. He won five Obies and two Guggenheim Fellows. Chaikin also authored the book *The Presence of the Actor*. His sister, actress Shami Chaikin, survives him.

David Clarke, 95, Chicago, Illinois-born actor, died April 18, 2004, in Arlington, Virginia, of natural causes. His career spanned more that 60 years and he appeared in over 12 Broadway productions and many film noir and action movies of the 1940s to the 1960s, though rarely played the lead. Mr. Clark made his Broadway debut in 1936 in *200 Were Chosen* with his friend, actor Will Geer. He was also seen in the original casts of Abe *Lincoln in Illinois*, *A View from the Bridge*, *The Visit*, and The *Ballad of the Sad Café*, and 1975's revival of *Of Mice and Men*. He and Geer remained life-long friends and appeared with him in the film *Intruder in the Dust* as well as on television's *The Waltons*. Clark is survived by his daughters, K.C. Ligon and Susan Bennett, and two grandchildren.

Hume Cronyn, 91, London, Ontario-born actor, writer, and director, died June 15, 2003, at his home in Fairfield, Connecticut, of prostate cancer. Cronyn and his wife of 52 years, Jessica Tandy, were one of the theatre world's most formidable pairings, and his career spanned seven decades. His first role on Broadway was as a janitor in *Hipper's Holiday*, a flop, but he then went on to portray roles in the early hits *Three Men on a Horse*, *Room Service*, *Boy Meets Girl*, *High Tor*, and 1939's production of *Three Sisters*. He would later go on to win a best featured actor Tony Award for his performance as Polonius in the 1964 production of *Hamlet*. His distinguished stage career included the productions of: *There's Always a Breeze*, *Escape This Night*, *Off to Buffalo*, *The Weak Link*, *Retreat to Pleasure*, *Mr. Big*, *The Survivors*, *The Physicists*, *Slow Dance on the Killing Ground*, *Noel Coward in Two Keys*, *Now I Lay Me Down to Sleep*, *Hilda Crane*, *The Little Blue Light*, *The Egghead*, *The Man in the Dog Suit*, *Triple Play*, *Promenade Al*, and *Big Fish, Little Fish* (Tony nomination). Many of his most notable roles came with his equally famous wife. After he spotted her in a production of the 1940 play *Juniper Laughs*, he pursued her until she agreed to marry him. Together they moved to Los Angeles where Cronyn worked as a contract player for MGM. While there he directed her in the young Tennessee Williams one-act *Portrait of a Madonna*, prompting Williams to cast her in *A Streetcar Named Desire*. In later years the pair appeared together in such productions as *The Fourposter*, *The Honeys*, *A Day by the Sea*, *Triple Play*, *Noel Coward in Two Keyes*, *The Petition* (Tony nomination), and Edward Albee's *A Delicate Balance* (Tony nomination).They most notably appeared together in Mike Nichols' 1977 production of the Pulitzer–prize winning play, *The Gin Game*, which garnered Tony nods for both. In 1983 they also appeared together in *Foxfire*, which Cronyn co-wrote with Susan Cooper, who later would become his wife after Tandy's passing. *Foxfire* was also adapted into a teleplay, in which Cronyn and Tandy recreated their roles. Together they received the first Lifetime Achievement Tony Awards in 1994. Cronyn appeared in over 40 films including 1944's *The Seventh Cross* which earned him a supporting Oscar nomination. He appeared with Tandy in 1985's *Cocoon*. In 1994 Cronyn received an Emmy Award for his role in the CBS/Hallmark Hall of Fame telepic, *To Dance With the White Dog*, in which Tandy made one of her final appearances before her death. Cronyn also loved to work in the regional theatre where he was able to play the classics more often. The actor published his biography in 1991, entitled *A Terrible Liar*. Cronyn is survived by his wife, Susan, two children, three stepchildren, eight grandchildren, and five great-grandchildren.

Joan Cullman, 72, Far Rockaway, New York-born producer, died March 18, 2004, in Tryall, Jamaica, of heart failure. She was a producer of at least nine Broadway shows including Yasmina Riza's *Art*, which won the Tony and the New York Drama Critics Circle Award for best play in 1998. She also produced *Sweet Smell of Success, One Night Stand, Oh, Brother!, The Play what I Wrote, The Rink, Judas Kiss, Caroline, or Change, Carmelina*, and David Hare's *Skylight*. Ms. Cullman was a Vice-Chairwoman on the board of the Lincoln Center Theatre, where she had served since 1985. There she founded the Joan Cullman Award for Extraordinary Creativity, a cash prize that has been given to Tom Stoppard, Stockard Channing, Julie Taymor, Spalding Gray, and others. She is survived by her husband, Joseph Cullman, a son and daughter, a brother, and one grandson.

Richard Cusack, 77, New York, New York-born actor and playwright, died June 2, 2003, in Evanston, Illinois, from pancreatic cancer. His stage credits include *The Man in 605*. He also appeared in various small roles in over 20 films. A former ad executive, he turned his passion into playwriting and scribed the plays *The Night They Shot Harry Lindsey With a 155 Millimeter Howitzer and Blamed it on Zebras, Punto*, and *The Last Word of the Bluebird*. He was an Emmy award winner for his documentary *The Committee*. All of his five children, John, Joan, Susie, Ann, and Bill have become actors. He appeared in films with John and Joan, and wrote and acted in the 1999 HBO film *The Jack Bull* in which John starred. Besides his children, he is survived by his wife of 43 years, Nancy, and two grandchildren.

Eileen Darby, 87, Portland, Oregon-born theatrical photographer, died March 30, 2004, at her home in Long Beach, New York, of a fall from which she never recovered. Her photographs live in the collective consciousness and help define the memory of major stage productions, including some 500 Broadway shows. Her work includes photographs of the original productions of both *Death of a Salesman* and *A Streetcar Named Desire*. Her photographs of actors include Tallulah Bankhead, the Lunts, Helen Hayes, Gregory Peck, Katharine Hepburn, and Paul Robeson.

Buddy Ebsen, 95, Belleville, Illinois-born actor, playwright, and song-and-dance man, died July 6, 2003 in Torrance, California, of natural causes. He started his performing career as a dancer in the chorus of *Whoopee*, and danced in *Flying Colors* and *The Ziegfeld Follies of 1934*. During WWII he wrote sketches and staged variety shows and musicals. After the war he wrote plays that were produced in regional theatres. He performed in nightclubs and vaudeville, and then advanced on the stage and film. He performed on Broadway in the musical *Yokel Boy* in 1939, and toured in the plays *The Male Animal* and *Good Night Ladies*. Ebsen appeared in the 1947 revival of *Show Boat*. He co-wrote songs including "Handsome Stranger," "Whispering Pines," and "Squeezin' Polka." As a writer he penned the plays *Champagne General* and *Honest John*. He then turned to a lucrative and long-term life in television, and is most-remembered for his roles as Barnaby Jones and the patriarch Jed Clampett in *The Beverly Hillbillies* for nine seasons. Ebsen is survived by his third wife, Dorothy, six daughters, and one son.

Marianna Elliott, 72, China Grove, North Carolina-born theatrical costume designer, died on June 21, 2003, in Beverly Hills California, after a long bout with cancer. She designed the world premieres of the musicals *Play On* and *QED*. She collaborated on Tom Stoppard's *The Real Thing* and Ibsen's *Hedda Gabler*. She was resident designer of Washington D.C.'s Arena Stage Theatre and she worked at the Seattle Repertory Theatre., the Arizona Theatre

Company, and the Pittsburgh Playhouse. At the Mark Taper Forum in Los Angeles her design work included *Floating Island, Green Card*, and Tom Stoppard's *Arcadia* for which she won the 1998 Los Angeles Drama Critics Award. At San Diego's Old Globe, she worked on *Private Lives, Dancing at Lughnasa* and *Blues in the Night*. She is survived by her husband, actor Alan Oppenheimer, two daughters, Jane Bergeron and Jennifer Oppenheimer, a son, Michael, and four grandchildren.

Hal England, 71, North Carolina-born actor, died November 6, 2003, in Burbank, California, of heart failure. He starred on Broadway in *Love Me a Little, Say Darling, Conversations at Midnight*, and understudied Robert Morse in *How to Succeed in Business Without Really Trying*. He was a member of Joseph Papp's first season of Shakespeare in the Park in New York's Central Park where he appeared in *Romeo and Juliet, Two Gentlemen of Verona*, and *Macbeth*. England also had numerous television credits.

Jenifer Estess, 40, Moline, Illinois-born theatrical producer, died December 16, 2003, in New York City, of Lou Gehrig's disease. She worked as an actor after graduating from NYU with a drama degree. She co-founded the theatre company Naked Angels for which she was producing director until 1993. She helped found the Nantucket Film Festival and the New York Women's Film Festival. Her biopic memoir "Tales From the Bed: On Living, Dying, and Having It All" was published in 2004. She also started the Project A.L.S and had raised over $17 million for research on Lou Gehrig's disease. She is survived by three sisters, a brother, and her mother.

David Dylan Evans, 83, England-born actor, died March 21, 2004, in Rosendale, New York, after a short illness. He made his Broadway debut in John Gielgud's 1950 production of *The Lady's Not for Burning*. He also appeared in *The School for Scandal* in 1962. In 1964 he played opposite Richard Burton in the acclaimed Broadway production of "*Hamlet*," and then appeared both with Vivian Leigh in *Ivanov* and with Frank Langella in *Dracula*. Evans was a graduate of the Royal Academy of Dramatic Art. He is survived by his wife, Karin, three sisters, and a brother.

Don Evans, 65, Philadelphia, Pennsylvania-born playwright, died October 16, 2003, in Merchantville, New Jersey, of heart failure. He was a member of the Black Arts Movement of the '60s and '70s. His plays were performed in repertory theatres and campuses both in the United States and Europe. Original productions were mounted at the Crossroads Theatre Company in Brunswick, New Jersey and the New Federal Theatre in New York City. His works include *It's Showdown Time, One Monkey Don't Stop No Show, A Love Song for Miss Lydia, Sugar-mouth Sam Don't Dance No More*, and *Orrin* which was his New York debut. He was director of the college theatre at Cheney University of Pennsylvania and then joined the faculty at the College of New Jersey where he was department chairman of African-American Studies. He was adjunct professor at Princeton University and professor of theatre arts at Rutgers University. He was a board member of the National Shakespeare Company and founder of the Players Company of Trenton (New Jersey). His two sons, Todd and Orin, daughter, Rachel Marianno, and mother, Mary Evan, and seven grandchildren survive him.

Patricia Falkenhain, 77, Atlanta, Georgia-born actress, died January 5, 2004, in Newcastle, Maine, of heart failure. She was a mainstay of ensembles at the Phoenix Repertory Theatre, The Public Theatre in New York, and the Long Wharf in New Haven, Connecticut. Her first Broadway role was with Melvyn Douglas in *Waltz of the Toreadors*. She appeared in *Once a Catholic* and *The*

Utter Glory of Morrissey Hall. Her last Broadway role was in the 1986 production at Lincoln Center of John Guare's *House of Blue Leaves.* In 1960 she won two Obies during the same season for her roles in the Phoenix Repertory Theatre's production of *Henry IV, Part 2* and in Ibsen's *Peer Gynt.* She was awarded her third Obie for cast citation for *The Marriage of Bette and Boo* at the Public. She won a Drama Critics Award for her role in Shaw's *Heartbreak House* at the Loeb Theatre at Harvard University.

Tommy Farrell, 82, Hollywood, California-born actor and comedian, died May 9, 2004, in Los Angeles, California, of natural causes. His Broadway debut was with Keenan Wynn in *Strip for Action.* He appeared in *Winged Victory* and *Barefoot Boy with Cheek.* He headlined as a comic for thirteen years at hotels, nightclubs, and in vaudeville; and he was primarily known for playing "sidekick" roles in Hollywood westerns. He also appeared in over 235 television shows. Mr. Farrell is survived by his wife of 43 years, Bobbi, a son, Mark, three daughters, Erin, Ellen, and Kathy, and three grandchildren.

Harold Fielding, 86, Woking, Surrey, England-born theatre impresario, died September 27, 2003, in Kingston-Upon-Thames, England, after a series of strokes. He produced over thirteen stage musicals in Britain including *Half a Sixpence, The Great Waltz,* and *Charlie Girl.* He exported many shows from the U.S. including *Mame, Sweet Charity, The Music Man, Showboat, Barnum,* and *You're a Good Man Charlie Brown.* He introduced Elaine Stritch to British audiences in Noel Coward's *Sail Away.* In 1958 he brought Rodgers and Hammerstein's *Cinderella* to London where it received great acclaim. In 1996 he received the Gold Badge of Merit from the British Academy of Songwriters, Composers & Authors.

Pauline Flanagan, 77, Sligo County, Ireland-born actress, born June 29, 1926, died June 28, 2003, in New York, New York, of lung cancer. She drew on her Irish heritage when acting in plays by Brian Friel and Sean O'Casey. She appeared often in Off-Broadway's Irish Repertory Theatre in plays including *Philadelphia, Here I Come, Summer,* and *Grandchild of Kings.* In 1994 she appeared again in *Philadelphia, Here I Come* when it moved to Broadway. Her Main Stem debut was in the 1957 production of Dylan Thomas' *Under the Milkwood.* Other Broadway credits include *God and Kate Murphy, Step on a Crack, Antigone, The Crucible, The Plough and the Stars, The Innocents, The Father, Medea, Steaming, Corpse!,* and *Lost in Yonkers.* In 2001 she won an Olivier Award for her performance in Frank McGuiness' *Dolly West's Kitchen.*

Nina Fonaroff, 89, New York, New York-born dancer, died August 14, 2003, in London, of undisclosed causes. She studied the Isadora Duncan method with Michel and Vera Fokine. She later studied dance at the School of American Ballet, and both acting and dance at the Cornish School in Seattle. It was there where she met Martha Graham and composer Louis Horst. She joined the Graham company and created roles in Graham productions including *American Document, Every Soul is a Circus, Letter to the World, Punch and the Judy, Deaths and Entrances* and *Appalachian Spring.* She began to choreograph on her own in 1946. She presented new pieces by new choreographers at the 92nd Street YMCA's program, a program that was one of the first of its kind. In 1949 she participated in forming the modern dance repertory company at City Center. She played both violin and piano and showed talent in both costume and set design. She studied fine art with George Grosz in New York. She taught at Bennington College, Teachers College at Columbia University, and movement for actors at the Neighborhood Playhouse in New York. She formed the Nina Fonaroff and Company troupe and headed it from 1946 to 1953. There were no known survivors.

Gant Gaither, 86, Hopkinsville, Kentucky-born Broadway producer, died February 16, 2004, in Palm Springs, California, of undisclosed causes. He made one attempt at acting, appearing during WWII in the all-military musical *Winged Victory.* He became a producer shortly thereafter. His work included *Craig's Wife, Seventh Heaven, The First Mrs. Fraser, The Shop at Sly Corner, Gayden,* and *Dear Barbarians.* He revived *Craig's Wife* with Grace Kelly's uncle, George, who was also a producer. His association with the Kelly family later led him to author a biography of her life. He left no immediate survivors.

Herb Gardner, 68, Brooklyn, New York-born playwright, died September 24, 2003, in New York, of lung disease. He is most noted for his whimsical, eccentric, and quirky characters that grew out of his youth in New York. He first gained notoriety with the 1962 production of *A Thousand Clowns,* starring Jason Robards. He was hailed as the year's most promising playwright, and three years later he was nominated for an Oscar for the film adaptation of the play that also starred Robards. His other plays included *The Goodbye People* (1968), *Who is Harry Kellerman and Why Is He Saying Those Terrible Things About Me?* (1971), *Thieves* (1974), *I'm Not Rappaport* (1986 Tony Award for best play), and *Conversations With My Father* (1992). Actor Judd Hirsch who starred in both *Rappaport* and *Conversations* won lead actor Tony awards for both performances in those shows. During his college years he created the cartoon strip "The Nebbishes" which ran for many years in syndication in over sixty newspapers. He retired the cartoon to work on his plays. In 1958 he authored the book *A Piece of the Action.* He is survived by his wife, Barbara Sproul, and two sons, Jake and Rafferty.

John Gleason, 62, New York, New York-born lighting designer, died October 28, 2003, of undisclosed causes. Gleason had over 600 Broadway and Off-Broadway design credits, and was the resident designer of the Lincoln Center's Vivian Beaumont Theatre. His first Broadway production was the flop musical *La Grosse Valise.* Many more productions followed, including *The Great White Hope* (1968), *We Bombed in New Haven* (1968), *In the Matter of J. Robert Oppenheimer* (1969), the Richard Rodgers musical *Two by Two* (1970), *Lorelei* (1974), *Over Here!* (1974), a hit revival of George S. Kaufman and Edna Ferber's *The Royal Family* (1975), the 20th anniversary revival of *My Fair Lady* (1976), and *An Evening With Diana Ross* (1976). His last Broadway show was *The Guys in the Truck* (1983). Gleason also worked at resident theatres, such as the Mark Taper Forum, American Shakespeare Festival, and Cincinnati Playhouse in the Park. His longest-running job was at New York University, where he taught lighting design for a quarter of a century, from 1971–97.

Ram Gopal, age uncertain but guessed to be late 80s, Bangalore, India-born dancer, died October 9, 2003, in London, England, of undisclosed causes. He was invited by La Meri, an American dancer who specialized in non-Western forms, to come tour the West with her. He made his solo debut in New York in 1938 at the 46th Street Theatre. He toured extensively and appeared at the New York Golden Anniversary International Dance Festival at City Center in 1948, the Jacobs Pillow Festival, and the Edinburgh Festival in the 1950s. His creation "Radha Krishna" was based on Hindu Myths. In 1999 he received the Order of the British Empire. There are no immediate survivors.

Harry Goz, 71, St. Louis, Missouri-born actor and singer, died September 6, 2003, of cancer. He is best known for playing the role of Tevye in the original Broadway production of *Fiddler on the Roof*. He made his Broadway debut as an understudy for Herschel Bernardi in the 1963 production of *Bajour*. He appeared in Richard Rodgers' *Two by Two*, Neil Simon's *Prisoner of Second Avenue*, and *Chess*. Goz had an extensive career as a voice-over actor as well as in television and film. Besides his wife, Margaret, he is survived by three children and nine grandchildren.

Charles J. Grant, Jr., 79, died June 28, 2005, his seventy-ninth birthday, at St. Vincent's Hospital in the West Village of New York, New York, of complications from surgery to repair a neck fracture he sustained two weeks prior. The dedication of this volume of Theatre World reads "In memory of Zan Van Antwerp and Charles J. Grant, Jr. Without their steadfast encouragement of the associate editor for the past seven years, this series would not have continued to have been published. Their unwavering and enthusiastic support of the arts and artists in all respects is surpassed only by their inspirational devotion to one another and those they loved. They will forever be remembered and honored by the editors of these volumes, as well as by all who were lucky enough to have known them." Charlie was born and raised in Brooklyn, NY, the son and only child of Charles J. Grant, Sr. and Ella Croft Grant. His great stalwart growing up was his "Auntie" Helen (Henrietta H. Grant), who maintained her independence in the family home at 605 Hemlock Street well into her nineties, and Charlie would make dutiful pilgrimages out to the wilds of East New York, dressed in mufti and listening for the following footsteps of muggers (not always successfully). Auntie Helen could also be found visiting with Zan and Charlie, her tiny presence lost among the welter of stuffed toys on the couch in the living room at 55 Morton St. Known as "Buddy" to his family and close friends growing up, Charlie enlisted in the Infantry toward the end of World War II. After his honorable discharge, he enrolled at New York University where he completed his undergraduate degree work. He married Joyce Rogerson Perkins at Duane-Metropolitan Church in 1955 and became a doting step-father to Joyce's daughter, Joy, from her earlier marriage. Charlie was devastated by Joyce's death from esophogeal cancer in 1973, but remained a loving step-father to Joy, venturing out with Zan to the strange menagerie on Long Island kept by Joy and her husband, until Joy's untimely death in 1995. The last twenty-two years of his life were spent with the incomparable Zan, whom he showered with utmost devotion through years of declining health and through her final illness and death earlier in 2005. Charlie was a journalist, perhaps more of the soft boiled than the hard boiled variety, but utterly tenacious, as those who heard him hold forth on any topic could attest. He labored for many years as a promotion copywriter at the Journal-American until its demise as the World Journal Tribune in 1967. The capstone of his career were the years he spent with King Features Syndicate doing all the research and writing for Ripley's *Believe It Or Not*. His domain was the great Main Reading Room of the New York Public Library at 42nd Street. It was entirely in keeping with the wide range of his interests that the vast archives of that venerable instiution were his "office." Perhaps his greatest personal interest was film, and his cinematic knowledge qualified him as considerably more than just a movie buff. Charlie sought a copyright in 1950 for a film and script entitled "Tel-O-Movie Game." It was a quiz game in which certain letters and pictures were flashed on the screen followed by or preceded by an addition or subtraction sign. These pictures and symbols, when correctly interpreted, would reveal the name of a film star. Hardly suprising, therefore, that his favorite toast to Zan, on any occasion,

was Humphrey Bogart's "Here's looking at you, kid" from *Casablanca*. Charlie's death came just four months after the death of his most beloved companion, Zan E. Van Antwerp, and it was impossible for his friends to think of Charlie as someone apart from Zan. Now, in death, we can once again think of them as an inseparable unity.

Spalding Gray, 62, Barrington, Rhode Island-born writer, actor, and monologist, died on or about January 11, 2004, in New York, New York, of a suicide. He was primarily known for his trenchant, personal narratives delivered on sparse, unadorned sets with a dry, WASP, quiet mania. His works include: *Terrors of Pleasure, Sex and Death to the Age 14, Booze, Cars and College Girls, India (and After), Swimming to Cambodia, It's a Slippery Slope, Monster in a Box, Gray's Anatomy*, and *Black Spot;* the last of which was never produced. He also portrayed the Stage Manager in the 1988 Tony nominated revival of *Our Town* and in the 2001 Tony nominated revival of Gore Vidal's *The Best Man*. Gray began his career in regional theatre, moved to New York in 1967 and three years later joined Richard Schechner's experimental troupe, the Performance Group. He co-founded the Wooster Group ensemble in 1975 where he first performed a trilogy of plays about growing up in Rhode Island and began to explore using the monologue as a type of performance art. Gray also appeared in over 40 films including film versions of his plays. He is survived by his wife, Kathleen Russo; her daughter, Marissa; their sons, Forrest and Theo; and two brothers, Rockwell and Channing.

Raymond J Greenwald, 81, a theatrical producer and real-estate entrepreneur, died October 18, 2003, after a lengthy illness. Greenwald studied acting and directing with Lee Strasberg at the American Theatre Wing in the early 1950s. After a number of stage efforts on the Off Broadway scene, he pursued a real estate career and became a co-owner of a group which owned several Manhattan office buildings. He returned to the theatre as a producer with the 1986 Broadway revival of *Oh, Coward!* Other producing efforts included *Gore Vidal's The Best Man, Things You Shouldn't Say Past Midnight, The Cocoanuts, A Thousand Clowns, Songs of Paradise, The Complete Works of William Shakespeare Abridged* and the 2003 production of *Enchanted April*, which garnered a Tony nomination for best play. Greenwald was on the boards of the Hudson Guild Theatre and the American Jewish Theatre, subsequently renamed the Raymond J. Greenwald Theatre. He is survived by his wife Pearl.

Gerald Gutierrez, 53, Brooklyn, New York-born director, died December 30, 2003, in Brooklyn, New York, of complications from the flu. He began his career as an actor after studying at Julliard with Marian Seldes. He made his Broadway debut in 1975 in the Acting Company's production of *Richard II*. After helming productions at several Off Broadway and regional theatres, he went on to become one of Broadway's most-celebrated directors. His stellar oeuvre includes: For Lincoln Center: *The Heiress*, Albee's *A Delicate Balance, Ivanov, Abe Lincoln in Illinois, The Most Happy Fella, Playboy of the West Indies, Northeast Local, Ring Around the Moon*, and *Dinner at Eight*. His other directorial works are *Edward II, The Time of Your Life, Life In the Theatre, Three Sisters, Curse of an Aching Heart, Little Johnny Jones, White Liars & Black Comedy*, and *Honour*. For Playwrights Horizons he staged *Meetings, Geniuses, Rise and Rise of Daniel Rocket, Isn't It Romantic*, and *Boys and Girls*. On Broadway he directed the 1996 revival of *Once Upon a Mattress* and *Curse of the Aching Heart*. He won back to back Tony Awards for 1995's *A Delicate Balance* and for 1996's production of *The Heiress*. Gutierrez is survived by a brother, two nieces, and a nephew.

Buddy Hackett, 78, Brooklyn, New York-born actor and comedian, died June 30, 2003, at his home in Malibu, California, of undisclosed causes. He was a much-beloved figure on television, in nightclubs and dinner theatres, movies, and on the stage. He began his show business career as a stand-up comedian and toured the Borscht Belt and the Catskills while still in high school. After serving three years in the army during World War II he returned to New York and studied method acting, but failed to ignite his nightclub career. His act fared well in California and Las Vegas and he eventually returned East to better success. In 1954 he was featured in the Broadway production of Sidney Kingsley's farce *Lunatics and Lovers*. His performance garnered great reviews. In 1964 he starred in the musical *I Had A Ball*, which became a hit primarily because of his comic gifts and popularity. In addition, he starred in *Viva Madison Avenue!* by George Panetta. As a producer he mounted "Eddie Fisher and Buddy Hackett at the Palace," a variety/comedy review. Hackett was also known for his portrayal of Marcellus Washburn in the 1963 film version of *The Music Man*. On television he was a staple of the *The Tonight Show with Jack Parr, Rowan & Martin's Laugh-In,* and *The Hollywood Squares*; and he starred in the 1956 sitcom *Stanley* opposite Carol Burnett. He was married to the former Sherry Dubois, and they had three children, Ivy, Lisa, and Sandy, who often did the opening act for his father's appearances.

Uta Hagen, 84, Gottingen, Germany-born actress, died January 14, 2004, at her home in Manhattan, New York. She was a formidable and wide-ranging actress who riveted audiences with her second Tony award-winning performance as Martha in the 1962 Broadway production of Edward Albee's *Who's Afraid of Virginia Woolf?* Over a career spanning almost seventy years she acted in plays by Shakespeare, Chekhov, Tennessee Williams, and George Bernard Shaw. She co-founded and taught with her husband Herbert Berghof at the HB Studios in Greenwich Village. Hagen made her debut in 1937 playing Ophelia in *Hamlet*. Other acclaimed roles were Nina in *The Seagull*, Desdemona in *Othello*, and Blanche DuBois in *A Streetcar Named Desire* along with her roles in the productions of *St. Joan* and Clifford Odets' *The Country Girl*, for which she won the 1951 Tony Award for best actress in a play. After devoting herself to her students for many years, it was in the 1960s and the years following she ventured back into the theatre. She played roles in *The Island of Goats, The Magic and the Loss, In Any Language, The Whole World Over, Vickie, Key Largo, The Cherry Orchard, Charlotte, Mrs. Warren's Profession, Mrs. Klein, You Never Can Tell,* and Donald Margulies' *Collected Stories*. In 1999 she returned to *…Virginia Woolf* in a single performance benefiting the HG Studios, playing opposite Jonathan Pryce, Matthew Broderick and Mia Farrow. In 2001 she appeared at the Geffen Playhouse in Los Angeles with David Hyde Pierce in *Six Dance Lessons in Six Weeks*. Hagen was also the author of the book, *Respect for Acting*, which many consider the actor's bible on performing. She also received a 1999 lifetime achievement Tony Award and a 2002 National Medal of the Arts. Hagen is survived by her daughter, Letitia Ferrer (from previous marriage to José Ferrer), a granddaughter, and a great-granddaughter.

Bill Hargate, 68, St. Louis, Missouri-born costume designer, died September 12, 2003, in Los Angeles, of leukemia. He began his career at the St. Louis Municipal Opera. He went on to design costumes for the 1979 Broadway revivals of *Peter Pan* and *Oklahoma* and the shows *Skyscraper, Doug Henning and his World of Magic*, and *Barefoot in the Park*. His Off-Broadway work includes *The Golden Apple, Anything Goes*, and *Black Nativity*. He received four Emmy Awards out of eleven nominations for his work in the television industry, most notably for *Murphy Brown*. Survivors include his companion of 43 years, Ted Sprague, his mother, brother, sister-in-law, and nephew.

Jeff Harris, 68, Brooklyn, New York-born writer, composer/lyricist, died February 2, 2004, in East Hampton, New York, of emphysema. He first appeared on the stage in the Broadway production of *Winesburg, Ohio*, and then appeared in *Tall Story*. He wrote sketches, music, and lyrics for cabaret performers and two Off-Broadway revues *That Thing at the Cherry Lane*, and *Another Evening With Harry Stoones*, the latter of which starred a 19-year-old Barbra Streisand. Harris wrote, directed and produced television shows for Steve Allen, Pat Boone, Jimmy Durante, the Everly Brothers, Milton Berle, and Roseanne Barr, and co-created the sit com *Diff'rent Strokes*. He is survived by his wife of 40 years, Judy, a son, a daughter, and two grandchildren.

Luther Henderson, 84, Kansas City, Missouri-born music arranger and conductor, died July 29, 2003, in Manhattan, New York of cancer. His deft hand at arranging was deeply prized by Duke Ellington, and during his career he worked on more than fifty Broadway musicals. He was twice awarded Tony Award nominations for *Jelly's Last Jam* and *Play On!* He worked with Richard Rodgers, Jule Styne, Lena Horne, and Ellington, among others. His skill was in transforming the rhythms of jazz written for small ensembles into orchestrations for the much larger Broadway pit orchestra. He created the musical arrangements for many hits including: *Ain't Misbehavin', Purlie, Good News, Doctor Jazz, Rodgers & Hart, So Long, 174th Street, The American Dance Machine, Black and Blue, Happy New Year, Lena Horne: The Lady and her Music, The First, Ol' Man Satan, Do Re Mi, Bravo Giovanni, Flower Drum Song, Hot Spot, Funny Girl, I Had a Ball, Hallelujah, Baby!, No, No Nanette,* and *Golden Rainbow*. He arranged the music for Duke Ellington's only Broadway show, *Beggar's Holiday* in 1946, and began a close association with Ellington on through the 1950s. Henderson was a graduate of Julliard, arranged for the U.S. Navy jazz band, and also worked in television from the 1950s to the 1980s. Shortly before his death he was chosen by the National Endowment for the Arts as a recipient of a Jazz Masters fellowship. Besides his wife, theatre director and actor Billie Allen, he is survived by two sons, Denson and Luther III, daughter Melanie, two grandchildren, and one great-grandchild.

Eben Henson, 81, Danville, Kentucky-born actor and playhouse founder, died April 25, 2004, at home, of undisclosed causes. In 1950 he established the Pioneer Playhouse which is Kentucky's oldest outdoor theatre and still operates to this day. Pioneer Playhouse has mounted over 300 productions under Henson's reign, and aided the careers of John Travolta, Lee Majors, and Lee Varney, to name a few. He claimed that he was bringing "Broadway to Bluegrass." He performed in plays at the New School for Social research in New York where he acted with young thespians Tony Curtis, Bea Arthur, and Harry Belafonte. He served on numerous arts boards and was named a Kentucky Colonel by several governors of the state.

Uta Hagen

Katharine Hepburn

Bob Hope

Hope Lange

Katharine Hepburn, 96, Connecticut-born actress, died June 29, 2003, at her home in Old Saybrook, Connecticut, of natural causes. Her seventy-year-long career was defined by her independent, strong-willed personality which made her a role model for generations of women. After attending Bryn Mawr college she made her professional debut in Baltimore in *The Czarina* in 1928. That same year she made her Broadway bow in *These Days*. In 1932 she was cast as Antiope in *The Warrior Husband*, a role which led to a Hollywood screen test. A year later and in her third film *Morning Glory* she won her first Academy Award. She became a movie star quickly but never let it eclipse her love for the theatre as she consistently returned to the New York stage in plays and even one musical. Amidst her 12 Academy Award nominations with 4 wins from over 50 films, her stage work included: *The Lake* (1933), *Jane Eyre* (1937), *The Philadelphia Story* (1939), *Without Love* (1942), *As You Like It* (1950), *The Millionairess* (1952) *The Merchant of Venice* (1957), *Much Ado About Nothing* (1957), *Twelfth Night* (1960), *Antony and Cleopatra* (1060), *Coco* (1969), *A Matter of Gravity* (1976), and *The West Side Waltz* (1981).

John Hess, 85, playwright, died April 15, 2004, in Bucks County, Pennsylvania, of natural causes. He began his professional career writing for radio, magazines, and television, but supplemented this with work in the theatre. He served a playwright in residence at the Bucks County Playhouse after World War II where many of his plays had their premieres. In 1953 he wrote the controversial play *The Gray-Eyed People* which ran on Broadway and starred Walter Matthau. He had a prolific television career writing for dozens of series, and created the soap opera *Love of Life*. He is survived by wife Mary Ann, two sons, a brother, and two grandsons.

Earl Hindman, 61, Bisbee, Arizona-born actor, died December 2003, in Stamford, Connecticut, of lung cancer. He made his name in Off-Broadway theatre appearing in *Dark of the Moon*, *The Basic Training of Pavlo Hummel*, *The Lincoln Mask*, and *The Love Suicide at Schofield Barracks*. Hindman was best known for playing the mysterious neighbor Wilson who was hidden behind the fence in the long-running sitcom *Home Improvement*. Hindman is survived by his wife of 27 years, Molly McGreevey, his mother, a brother, and a sister.

Gregory Hines, 57, New York, New York-born actor, singer, and dancer, died August 9, 2003, in Los Angeles, California, of cancer. The suave, genial showman personified the art of classical tap dance and was responsible for resurrecting the art form in the 1980s. He began studying dance before the age of three. He made his debut in New York at age five with his brother Maurice in an act called the Hines Kids. They made appearances often at the Apollo Theatre in Harlem. In 1954 at the age of six he and Maurice were cast in the Broadway musical *The Girl in Pink Tights* starring the French ballerina Jeanmaire. Later they became "Hines, Hines and Dad" when their father, Maurice, Sr. joined them. He received his first Tony nomination for *Eubie* in 1978, in which his brother also appeared after the two had parted ways for almost a decade. Two more nominations followed for *Comin' Uptown* and *Sophisticated Ladies*. In 1992 he won a Tony Award for his role as Jelly Roll Morton in *Jelly's Last Jam*. He co-hosted the Tony Awards telecast twice, appeared in his own Emmy nominated television special "Gregory Hines: Tap Dance in America," starred in his own self-titled sitcom, and received a Daytime Emmy for his voice work in the Bill Cosby animated series, *Big Bill*. Hines tapped danced with his brother in the film *The Cotton Club* and shared the screen with Mikhail Baryshnikov in the 1985 film *White Nights*. Hines is survived by his fiancé, Negrita Jade, his father, his brother, his daughter, Daria, his son, Zach, and his step-daughter, Jessica.

Bob Hope, 100, Eltham, London, England-born comedian, actor, singer, died July 27, 2003, at home in Toluca Lake, California, of complications from pneumonia. He was a man of many talents, and he proved this over his seven-decade career: hoofer, stand-up comic, vaudevillian, screen and stage actor, dancer. He made his debut in vaudeville with Lloyd Durbin in a 1924 revue headlined by Fatty Arbuckle. It was Arbuckle who recommended Hope for a job in the 1925 *Hurley's Jolly Follies* where he partnered with George Byrne. He and Byrne worked their way west through the theatre circuit on bills with Siamese twins and trained seals. After moving to New York he worked on the RKO circuit and in 1927 he landed a part in *The Sidewalks of New York*. He soon went solo and formed his own Chicago company with acts including Edgar Bergen and Charlie McCarthy. His Broadway roles include *Ballyhoo of 1932* and the 1933 Jerome Kern musical *Roberta*. He joined the 1936 *Ziegfeld Follies*, then later starred in and earned great reviews in Broadway's *Red, Hot and Blue* with Jimmy Durante and Ethel Merman. His other stage work includes: *Say When*,

Bob Hope at the Palace, and *Ups-a-Daisy*. Hollywood soon discovered him and he proceeded to make over fifty movies. He was a living legend from his work with the USO during WWII where he entertained and built the morale of millions of soldiers with his variety shows which involved major stars of the moment. One columnist called him, "Santa Claus, Uncle Sam and a letter from home, all wrapped up in one package." Survivors include wife of 69 years, Dolores and their four children, Linda, Tony, Kelly, and Nora.

Larry Hovis, 67, A Yakima Indian reservation, Washington-born actor, writer, and teacher, died September 9, 2003, in Austin, Texas, after a long battle with cancer. He began his professional on-stage career while a young man. He wrote plays and songs and eventually moved to Hollywood where his screenplays were well received. He toured in the road production of *The Best Little Whorehouse in Texas* and appeared in New York in *From A to Z*. After many years in Hollywood he went back home to Texas and taught acting at Texas State University and appeared in numerous stage productions in his home state. He was best known for playing the role of Sgt. Carter on the 1960s television series, *Hogan's Heroes*. Hovis is survived by four children.

Ellen Idelson, 42, Los Angeles, California-born writer and actress, died September 19, 2003, in Los Angeles, after a long battle with Crohn's disease. Before making her mark as a television producer and writer she performed on stage at the Mark Taper Forum, in the Los Angeles Shakespeare Festival, Theatre West, and Magic Theatre in San Francisco. She was co-artistic director of Theatre Sports Los Angeles.

Avraham Inlender, 70, Zamose, Poland-born playwright and director, died July 24, 2003, in his Manhattan home, of bladder cancer. In 1955 Inlender was awarded "observer status" while Elia Kazan worked on *Cat on a Hot Tin Roof*. He then studied with Lee Strasberg at the Actor's Studio and with Erwin Piscator in Berlin. In Israel he served as dramaturge with the Cameri Theatre's Repertory company. His play *On an Open Roof* was produced there and was brought to Broadway in 1962. His one-person plays *Mrs. Davidson's Story*, *Jerusalem Spy Story*, and *Shadows* collectively explored the Jewish experience. Under his direction, these productions starred his wife, the Obie award-winning actress Rosina Fernhoff. His play *Snow People* premiered in Israel and is still produced across the United States and in Europe. During the last years of his life he worked with his friend and colleague Milton Kastelas as dramaturge at Kasteleas' Beverly Hills Playhouse. Survivors include his wife, two daughters, and two grandsons.

Marshall Jamison, 85, Boston, Massachusetts-born actor, director, and playwright, died September 2, 2003, in Orlando, Florida, of heart failure. His Broadway debut was in *Mister Roberts* in 1948. This was followed by *The Cure for Matrimony*. He branched out into stage directing and producing, and moved into television for the rest of his professional life. His oeuvre as a director and casting agent includes *Point of No Return*, *Wish You Were Here*, *On Borrowed Time*, *Picnic*, *Kind Sir*, *By the Beautiful Sea*, and *The Young and the Beautiful*. Jamison was also the producer of the 1960s satirical review "That Was the Week that Was" on American television. He is survived by wife Janet, four daughters, a son, six grandchildren, and three great-grandchildren.

David Jiranek, 45, Broadway producer, writer, and photographer, died August 17, 2003, in Quebec, of a swimming accident. After graduating from NYU he teamed up with producer-friends David Weil and John Houseman to co-produce 1981's *Curse of an Aching Heart*. In 1982 he co-produced David Mamet's *Edmond* at the Provincetown Playhouse; this production won two Obies. In 2000 he, Weil, and Jiranek's wife Cricket Hooper formed CTM Productions and co-produced the Broadway revue *Ain't Nothin' But the Blues*. Later that year they produced the revival of *Fool Moon* which won the Tony for best theatrical event. He produced Bill Maher's one-man *Victory Begins at Home*. At the time of his death he was slated to direct *Lysistrata* for the Jean Cocteau Repertory. He was a member of the League of American Theatres and Producers. Jiranek is survived by his wife, two daughters, his mother, and four half-brothers.

Elia Kazan, 94, Constantinople, Turkey-born director, author, and actor, died September 28, 2003, in New York, New York, at his home in Manhattan, of natural causes. He was one of the most preeminent directors in the history of both Broadway and motion pictures. When he was a young man he joined the Group Theatre in New York City as an actor and assistant stage manager. He acted in dozens of plays including *Waiting for Lefty* (1935), *Golden Boy* (1937), *The Gentle People*, *Chrysalis*, *Men in White*, *Gold Eagle Guy*, *Till the Day I Die*, *The Young Go First*, *Paradise Lost*, *The Case of Clyde Griffiths*, *Johnny Johnson*, *Golden Boy*, *The Gentle People*, *Night Music*, *Lilliom*, and *Five Alarm Waltz*. He began directing plays in 1935 and won raves for his direction of *Café Crown*. More encomiums followed with his direction of Thornton Wilder's *The Skin of Our Teeth*. The Production won a Pulitzer Prize and earned Kazan a New York Drama Critics Circle award. In 1947 he founded the Actor's Studio with Lee Strasburg, Cheryl Crawford and Robert Lewis. It was that year that his extraordinary talent was firmly established from his direction of *A Streetcar Named Desire* and Arthur Miller's *All My Sons*. These were followed by Miller's *Death of a Salesman*. His astounding oeuvre includes: *Café Crown*, *The Strings*, *Harriet*, *Jacobowsky and the Colonel*, *Deep are the Roots*, *Truckline Café*, *Sundown Beach*, *The Shadow of a Gun*, *Marathon '33*, *After the Fall*, *Marco Millions*, *Blues for Mr. Charlie*, *But for Whom Charlie*, *Baby Want a Kiss*, *The Changling*, *Tartuffe*, *Salome*, *Cat on a Hot Tin Roof*, *Sweet Bird of Youth*, *The Dark at the Top of the Stairs*, *Tea and Sympathy*, *One Touch of Venus*, *J.B.*, *Camino Real*, and *Incident at Vichy*. Kazan earned best director Tony Awards for *All My Sons*, *Death of a Salesman*, and *J.B.* Five of the plays he directed earned Pulitzer Prizes for Drama. In 1972 he won the Handel Medallion, New York City's highest award. In 1983 he earned a Kennedy Center Citation. He won five Tony awards. Dustin Hoffman said that he doubts that he, Robert De Niro, and Al Pacino would have had careers without the influence of Kazan.

Alan King, 76, New York, New York-born actor, comedian, singer, and Broadway producer, died May 9, 2004, in New York, New York, of lung cancer. His long, prolific career includes stand-up comedy, myriad appearances on television specials, variety shows, movie roles, nightclub performances, and work as a producer. In 1968 he co-produced the Broadway productions of *A Lion in Winter*, *Something Different*, *Dinner at Eight*, and *The Investigation*. He was an executive producer of the Toyota Comedy Festival in New York from 1992 to 2002. His Broadway roles include: *Guys and Dolls*, *The Impossible Years*, *Applause*, and *Judy Garland: A Concert*. He earned excellent reviews for his 2002 performance in the Off-Broadway production of the one-man play *Mr. Goldwyn* about movie mogul Sam Goldwyn. King is survived by his wife, Jeanette; two sons; a daughter; and seven grandchildren.

Hope Lange, 70, Redding Ridge, Connecticut-born, died December 19, 2003, in Santa Monica, California, of complications from acute colitis. She made her Broadway debut at age 12 in Sidney Kingsley's *The Patriots*. She appeared in both 1977's *Same Time Next Year* and 1981's *Supporting Cast*. Her active career in movies brought her to Hollywood where she made an indelible mark in motion pictures, including the role of Emma in the film version of the play *Bus Stop*. She also appeared in several early television drama programs including *Playhouse 90* and *Kraft Television Theatre*. She is survived by third husband, theatrical producer Charles Holerith, a son, actor Christopher Murray, daughter Patricia Murray, two grandchildren, a brother, and two sisters.

Basil Langton, 91, Bristol, England-born actor and director, died June 5, 2003, in Santa Monica, California, of undisclosed causes. During WWII he founded the Traveling Repertory Theatre which performed in bombed-out cities and for war-weary troupes. He taught acting at St. Dennis' London Theatre Studio. He appeared in the London premiere of Odets' *Awake and Sing*. He moved to the States after the War and appeared in numerous Broadway plays including *The Affair, Camelot, French Without Tears, Sing Till Tomorrow, 13 rue de l'Amour, and Soldiers*. In 1948 he directed a production of *The Devil's Disciple*. In 1951 he produced the first Shaw festival in America on Martha's Vineyard. In 1957 he created the "Poets and Playwrights" series where actors and writers read plays and poems at the Public Library. He also had a prolific photography career. Surviving Langton is his daughter from his first marriage, Jessica Andrews.

Jerome Lawrence, 88, Cleveland, Ohio-born playwright and director, died February 29, 2004, in Malibu, California, of natural causes. He was best known for writing the Broadway hits *Auntie Mame* and *Inherit the Wind*. *Auntie Mame* inspired the Broadway musical *Mame* ten years after it debuted on Broadway in 1956. Lawrence wrote thirty-nine plays, many in collaboration with writing partner Robert E. Lee, including: *Look Ma, I'm Dancin'!, The Night Thoreau Spent in Jail, The Madwoman of Chaillot, The Gang's All Here, Shangri La, Only in America, A Call on Kuprin, Diamond Orchid, Dear World, First Monday in October, The Incomparable Max,* and *Whisper in the Mind*. He taught playwriting for fifteen years at USC's Master of Professional Writing program. He also taught at NYU, Baylor University, and the Salzburg seminars. He was a longtime member of the Dramatists Guild, the Writers Guild of America West, and ASCAP. In 1990 he was named to the Theatre Hall of Fame. He is survived by his companion, Will Willoughby, his nieces, Paula and Deborah Robison, and nephew, Joshua Robison.

James Mitchell Lear, 80, St. Paul, Minnesota-born actor and writer, died July 14, 2003, in Deerfield Beach, Florida, of undisclosed causes. He was an alumnus of Chicago's Goodman Theatre and the Pasadena Playhouse. His roles on and Off Broadway include: *Othello, Macbeth, The Caine Mutiny, Threepenny Opera, Great Day in the Morning, Enemy of the People,* and *Never Too Late*. He was best known for his one-man play *Hemingway Reminisces*, which he performed in many parts of the world.

Donald Leight, 80, musician, born in the Bronx, New York, died on January 3, 2004, in Manhattan, New York, of pneumonia and complications from Parkinson's disease. He was the inspiration for the Tony Award winning play *Sideman*, about a trumpet player living the anonymous life in the music business. His son Warren wrote the Pulitzer Prize-nominated play. He was a featured player in many big bands in the '40s, '50s, and '60s. He worked in nightclubs and in the orchestra pit for the Broadway musical *Hair*, performing its entire four-year run. Leight is survived by his son, a brother, and daughter, Jody.

Arthur Lithgow, 88, Dominican Republic-born actor and director, died March 24, 2004, in Amherst, Massachusetts, of heart failure. Lithgow, the father of actor John Lithgow, was a pioneer in the regional theatre movement, and the founder of two Shakespearean festivals. In 1952 he founded and served as the artistic director of the Antioch Shakespeare Festival in Ohio. All of Shakespeare's works were produced there in six years time, and Lithgow directed and acted in several of the productions. In 1962 he founded the Great Lakes Shakespeare Festival in Lakewood, Ohio, which continues today as the Great Lakes Theatre Festival in Cleveland. As a performer his roles on the Broadway stage included: *Lorelei, A Cure for Matrimony,* and *Steel*. In 1963 he became artistic director of the McCarter Theatre at Princeton University until 1972 when he and his family moved to Boston where he was a visiting professor at the University of Massachusetts. He served as administrative director of the Brattleboro Center for the Performing Arts in Vermont. In addition to his son John, he is survived by his wife, Sarah, his son David, two daughters, Robin and Sarah Jane, two sisters, and 13 grandchildren.

Philip Locke, 76, United Kingdom-born actor, born March 29, 1928, died April 19, 2004. He received a Tony Award nomination for his portrayal of Professor Moriarity in the 1974 production of *Sherlock Holmes*. He won the Plays and Players Awards Best Supporting Actor award for his portrayal of Horatio in *Hamlet*. He appeared twice on Broadway in *A Midsummer Night's Dream*, once in 1954 and then in 1971.

Harold Loeb, 84, New London, Connecticut-born actor, director, and producer, died May 17, 2003, in Los Angeles, California, of cancer. He directed summer stock at the Robin Hood Theatre in Delaware, and studied acting with Sanford Meisner, Wynn Handman, and Lee Strasberg. In 1968 he produced the Sidney Poitier-directed *Carry Me Back to Morningside Heights*. Loeb also worked as a casting director, and was involved with several Warner Brothers East Coast productions in the film business. He is survived by three children and two grandchildren.

Dorothy Loudon, 70, Boston, Massachusetts-born actress and comedian, died November 15, 2003, in New York, New York, of cancer. She was known best for creating the role of Miss Hannigan in the hit musical *Annie*, which earned her the 1977 Tony Award, Drama Desk Award and the Outer Critics Circle Award for best actress in a musical. She was nominated for two Tonys for her roles in *Ballroom* (1979) and *The Fig Leaves are Falling* (1969). She established herself in the New York cabaret scene in the early '60s, headlining with friends Mike Nichols and Elaine May, and made her Broadway debut in 1962 in *Nowhere to Go But Up*. She became well-known around the country when she replaced Carol Burnett on *The Gary Moore Show*, but she knew her real talents lay in the theatre. She had roles in *Noel Coward's Sweet Potato, The Women, Jerry's Girls, Comedy Tonight*, and a musical based on Nabakov's *Lolita* called *Three Men on a Horse*. She replaced Angela Lansbury in original production of *Sweeney Todd*. She starred in both *West Side Waltz* and *Noises Off*. In 2002 she was forced by deteriorating health to withdraw from the Broadway revival of *Dinner at Eight*. Loudon is survived by two step-daughters.

Giselle MacKenzie, 76, Winnipeg, Canada-born actress and singer, died September 5, 2003, in Burbank, California, of colon cancer. As a child she showed precocious talent for the violin, piano, and voice. She joined Robert Shuttleworth's band during WWII, playing the piano and singing. Once she chose singing as her primary instrument she never lacked work thereafter. She toured with Jack Benny and he became her biggest booster, bringing her on his

Dorothy Loudon

Mercedes McCambridge

Ann Miller

Jan Miner

television show many times. She was most known as the singing star of the 1950s television show *Your Hit Parade*. She appeared in regional theatre productions of *Mame, Gypsy, Hello, Dolly!*, and *The King and I*. She is survived by her daughter, son, brother, sister, and two grandchildren.

Thalia Mara, 92, Chicago, Illinois-born ballerina, died October 8, 2003, in Jackson, Mississippi, of natural causes. She made her professional debut in Chicago with the Ravinia Park Opera Ballet in 1926 and then went to Paris to dance with the Carina Ari Ballet. In the 1930s she appeared on Broadway in *The Great Waltz* and *Virginia*. In 1947 she directed the Jacob's Pillow Dance Festival. In 1962 she and her husband co-founded the National Academy of Ballet and Theatre Arts in New York in 1962. In the '70s, she moved to Jackson and founded the Jackson Ballet Guild's first professional troupe. She also founded the non-profit Thalia Mara Arts International Foundation in Jackson. She wrote eleven books on ballet.

William Marshall, 78, Gary, Indiana-born actor, died June 11, 200, in Los Angeles, of Alzheimer's disease. He was a member of the Actor's Studio and the Neighborhood Playhouse in New York. He traveled Europe to pursue his acting career and won accolades from the London press for his *Othello*. At the age of 8, Marshall's backstage visit to the original production of *The Green Pastures* inspired him to be an actor. In 1951 he played the lead part of DeLawd in a Broadway revival. He was also noted for his portrayal of notable African-American figures. He played Paul Robeson on stage and spent a decade touring colleges and regional theatres with his one-man show *Enter Frederick Douglass*. Marshall was also a teacher and director at UC Irvine and the Mufandi Institute. He is survived by his life partner of 42 years, Sylvia Jarrico, three sons, and a daughter.

Davey Martin-Jones, 71, Winchester, Indiana-born professor of theatre, died March 2004, of cancer. He toured the country as a magician at age 13 and went on to become an actor, director, and theatre critic. In 1930 he appeared on Broadway in *The Second Little Show*. He reviewed theatre for newspapers in Washington, D.C. and Detroit. He spent the last fifteen years of his life teaching directing and playwriting at the University of Nevada at Las Vegas.

Mercedes McCambridge, 87, Joliet, Illinois-born actress, died March 2, 2004, in San Diego, California, of natural causes. She debuted on Broadway in *A Place of Our Own* in 1945. Other Broadway credits include *Woman Bites Dog, The Young and Fair, The Love Suicides at Schofield Barracks*, and she was a stand-by for *Who's Afraid of Virginia Woolf?* In 1990 she was asked to play the grandmother in Neil Simon's *Lost in Yonkers*, a role which she performed over 500 times both in New York and on the road. McCambridge's raspy voice and great vocal versatility earned her much work in radio dramas, and she had a sporadic film career. She won an Oscar for the 1949 film *All the King's Men*. She might be most-famous Linda Blair's terrifying voice-over of the Devil in *The Exorcist*.

Joseph McCaren, 58, Los Angeles, California-born actor and novelist, died October 14, 2003, in New York, New York, of cancer. He made his Broadway debut opposite Mary Tyler Moore in *Who's Life is it Anyway?* He appeared in *Brothers* with Carroll O'Connor and opposite Lauren Bacall in *Sweet Bird of Youth*. He was also in the international touring company of "West Side Story." His novel *The Devil's Lottery* was published in 2004. He is survived by his companion, Patricia Nehaus, and a sister.

Ann Miller, believed to be 80, Chireno, Texas-born actress and dancer, died January 22, 2004, in Los Angeles, California, of lung cancer. In her heyday she was America's premiere female tap star. She began her career at age 12 as a dancer, and her mother took her to California at age 14 where she landed roles in movies. Her stage career began in 1939 in *George White's Scandals* on Broadway. She landed a studio contract with MGM after she replaced Cyd Charisse in *Easter Parade*, leading to other movie musicals *On the Town, Kiss Me, Kate*, and *Hit the Deck*. Besides her flourishing film work in the '50s she worked in nightclubs and was featured on several television variety shows. In 1969 Miller was cast to replace Angela Lansbury in the Broadway production of *Mame*. She went on the road with the touring companies of *Can-Can, Panama Hattie, Blithe Spirit*, and *Hello, Dolly*. But it was her 1979 Tony-nominated role in *Sugar Babies* with Mickey Rooney that she scored her biggest comeback. She played the show for over 1700 performances during three-year run and took the show on the road.

Betty Miller, 79, Boston, Massachusetts-born actress, died July 3, 2004, in Manhattan, New York, after a long illness. She had a sixty-year career on the stage. Her roles include *The Girl on the Via Flaminia, Summer and Smoke, La Ronde, Desire Under the Elms, The School for Scandal, Right You Are if You Think You Are, The Misanthrope, Cock-A-Doodle-Dandy, The Au Pair Man, Dance of Death, Who's Afraid of Virginia Woolf?*, and *The Balcony*. At the New York Shakespeare Festival she played in *Richard III, Hamlet*, and *King Lear*. She appeared on Broadway in *Three Sisters, You Can't Take It With You, Eminent Domain, The Queen and the Rebels*, and *A Touch of the Poet*. She performed for four seasons with the Phoenix Rep in The *Cherry Orchard, The Wild Duck*, and *War and Peace*. Her last performance was in the Off-Broadway show *Shoppers Carried Up Escalators into Flames* in 2002. She is survived by one son, Frank Askin.

Jan Miner, 86, Boston, Massachusetts-born actress, died February 15, 2004, in Bethel, Connecticut, of undisclosed causes. Miner is best known for her commercial television work as Palmolive's "Madge the Manicurist." She began her career on the stage and worked from the 1940s through the 1980s. She appeared at the American Shakespeare Festival in Stratford, Connecticut for six seasons and often shared the stage with her husband Richard Merrell. In 1973 she played in the revival of *The Women* and in 1980 was in Lillian Hellman's *Watch on the Rhine*. She performed in Circle in the Square's 1983–84 production of *Heartbreak House*. Her other Broadway credits include: *Street Scene, Viva Madison Avenue!, The Lady of the Camelias, The Freaking Out of Stephanie Blake, Romeo and Juliet, The Heiress, Othello, Butterflies Are Free, The Milk Train Doesn't Stop Here Anymore*, and *Major Barbara*. Miner is survived by a brother.

Remus [Lex] Monson, 77, Grindstone, Pennsylvania-born actor, died February 12, 2004. In 1961 he played in the original New York cast production of Jean Genet's *The Blacks: A Clown Show* at the St. Mark's Playhouse. It ran for an amazing 1,408 performances. He acted on Broadway in *Moby Dick, Trumpets of the Lord*, and the 1990 Steppenwolf production of *The Grapes of Wrath*. His regional credits included *Much Ado About Nothing* at the Long Wharf and *God's Trombone* at Ford's Theatre in Washington, D.C.

Michael Moran, 59, New York, New York-born actor, died February 4, 2004, of Guillain-Barre syndrome. He created the role of Pap in the Off Broadway show *Hank Williams: Lost Highway*, performing in its full run after it moved to the Little Shubert. At Ensemble Studio Theatre he appeared in Horton Foote's *The Prisoners, Everything That Rises Must Converge*, and *The Belmont Avenue Social Club*. He is survived by his wife, Sandy, and two daughters.

Barry Morell, 75, Long Island, New York-born opera singer, died December 4, 2003, at his home in Cape Cod, Massachusetts of cancer. He made his debut singing "Ol' Man River" for the New York Actor's Fund benefit. In his first year with the Metropolitan Opera he sang seven leading roles in twenty-two performances. He had a particular affinity for the operas of Puccini, appearing frequently in *Madama Butterfly, Tosca*, and *La Boheme*. He moved to Rome with his family and sang in various houses all over Europe including Covent Garden, the Vienna Staatsoper, Berlin, Barcelona and the Rome Opera. His last Met appearance was in 1979 in *Madame Butterfly*.

LeRoy Myers, 84, Philadelphia, Pennsylvania-born tap dancer, died April 26, 2004, in Manhattan, New York, of undisclosed causes. He was one of the last surviving members of the venerable Copasetics Tap group. He performed his first act "Pops and LeRoy" with William Rogers at age 15. He then joined Sinclair Rogers, a trumpet player, and they formed the team "Sinclair and LeRoy" where they featured ventriloquism, dancing, singing, and impersonation. He performed with James Walker who was known as Chuckles. When Bill Robinson (the famous Mr. Bojangles) died in 1949, Myers was drawn into management, and a tap club was formed called The Copasetics. Later in life he served as road manager for the Supremes and manager for B.B. King until the 1970s. He then acquired the Wonder Garden in Atlantic City; which he sold in 2001. Through the '80s he was business manager for the Copasetics ensemble.

Steven Eric Nelson, 52, Chicago, Illinois-born actor and playwright, died January 7, 2004, in New York, New York, of lung cancer. In 1976 he formed his own troupe called the Fourth E Company which produced the plays that he wrote including *The Object of the Game, Most Powerful Piece*, and *Their Towers Kissed the Sky*. He appeared in *Kennedy's Children* and *Michelangelo's Models* both by playwright Robert Patrick.

David Newman, 66, Brooklyn, New York-born stage and screen writer, died June 26, 2003, in New York, of a stroke. While working as an editor at Esquire magazine in 1960s, he befriended fellow editor Robert Benton. Together they penned the book for Hal Prince's Broadway musical *It's a Bird...it's a Plane...it's Superman!* in 1966. A year later Newman and Benton landed their three-year-old screenplay for *Bonnie and Clyde*, which earned them an Academy Award nomination. In 1971 British critic Kenneth Tynan asked him to collaborate on a then-untitled stage play about sex. *Oh! Calcutta!* opened to smash, albeit controversial, reviews and was the first show to feature full frontal nudity on stage. He focused on screenwriting during most of the 1970s, and with his wife and frequent collaborator, Leslie, wrote the screenplays for the first three *Superman* films that starred Christopher Reeve. He returned to the stage to write the book for Cy Coleman's *The Life* in 1997, earning him a Tony nomination for best book of a musical. Newman is survived by his wife, children Catherine and Nathan, and two grandchildren.

Elliot Norton, 100, Boston, Massachusetts-born theatre critic, died July 20, 2003, in Ft. Lauderdale, Florida, of natural causes. He became the pre-eminent pre-Broadway critic in a career that stretched from 1932 to 1982; from *Porgy and Bess* to *Dreamgirls*. Norton reviewed over 6000 productions in his career and contributed reviews and columns to the *Boston Herald*, the *Boston Post*, and the *Boston Record-American*. His television talk show *Elliot Norton Reviews* on WGBH in Boston featured interviews with writers, actors, and directors from the shows that he had reviewed. Neil Simon credited Norton for inspiring a successful re-write of *The Odd Couple* when Norton revealed he missed the Pigeon Sisters at the end of the play, who were not originally in the scene. Norton was awarded a special Tony Award for his writing in 1971, and since 1983 the Elliot Norton Awards have been given for theatre achievement in Boston. In 1988 he was inducted into the Theatre Hall of Fame. He is survived by a son, two daughters, three grandchildren, and three great-grandchildren.

Donald O'Connor, 78, Chicago, Illinois-born actor, singer, dancer, and composer, died September 27, 2003, in Woodland Hills, California, of heart failure. He was born into a show business family, and made his debut at age 3 days in their act, "The O'Connor Family: The Royal Family of Vaudeville." They played the top houses in the country. He went on to make a huge motion picture career for himself. His movie career declined in the '50s but his talents were recognized on TV specials and variety shows. He also composed pieces for an orchestra and conducted his symphony "Reflections d'un Comique" with the L.A Philharmonic. The Brussels Philharmonic recorded an album of his compositions. He made his debut on Broadway in 1981 in *Bring Back Birdie* and two years later appeared as Cap'n Andy in *Show Boat*. Still a brilliant song and dance man far into his 70s, he headlined in Las Vegas and stayed busy with guest spots in TV and in nightclubs.

May O'Donnell, 97, Sacramento, California-born modern dancer and choreographer, died February 1, 2004, in New York, New York, of natural causes. She began her professional career with Martha Graham, and she served as a model for the Pioneer Woman in Graham's *Appalachian Spring* in 1943. She choreographed a modern dance classic *Suspension* inspired by a low-flying airplane she saw during WWI. In the 1940s, she danced with Graham's company and created roles including the Attendant in *Herodiade*, the Earth in *Dark Meadow*, and the Chorus in *Cave of the Heart*. Her other principal roles were in *Letter to the World*, *Deaths and Entrances*, *Every Soul is a Circus,* and *Primitive Mysteries*. In 1949 she founded a New York-based company that performed into the 1980s. She received the Martha Hill Lifetime Achievement Award in 1982. Some of her students included Gerald Arpino, Robert Joffrey, Ben Vereen, and Dudley Williams.

Ron O'Neal, 66, Utica, New York-born actor, died January 14, 2004, in Los Angeles, of pancreatic cancer. In Ohio, he joined the Karamu House, a theatre company that presented plays with interracial casts, starring in productions of *A Raisin in the Sun* and *A Streetcar Named Desire* during his six years with that company. He taught acting in the '60s in New York, and appeared in Joe Papp's production of *No Place to Be Somebody* at the Public Theatre. His work won him Obie, Drama Desk, Clarence Derwent, and Theatre World Awards. He gained fame when he starred in the legendary movie *Superfly*. Other stage credits included *Othello* at the Stratford Festival in Ontario, Canada. He is survived by his wife, Audrey and a sister.

John Orrell, 68, Maidstone, England-born theatrical historian, died September 12, 2003, in Edmonton, Canada, of melanoma. His historical detective work led to the reconstruction of the Old Globe Theatre in England in 1997. The Shakespearean scholar's calculations were done through trigonometric methods and determined the size, seating and proportions within small percentages of error. He received his education at Oxford and then his PhD at University of Toronto. He wrote the book *The Quest for Shakespeare's Globe* in 1983, which provided the first blueprint for the Globe's reconstruction.

Carlos Orta, 60, Caracas, Venezuela-born choreographer and dancer, died May 15, 2004 in Manhattan, New York, of heart failure. He was a disciple of Jose Limon and taught at the Limon Company in New York. He studied in Paris and Germany with Pina Bausch. When he joined the Limon Company in 1979, he soon starred in dances including *Moor's Pavane*. His own choreography drew on his South American heritage. In 1985 he received the Prize of Dance form the Venezuelan government and awards at the International Academy of Dance in Cologne.

Fraydele Oysher, 90, Lipkon, Russia-born actress and singer, died January 5, 2004, of natural causes. She was a star of the Yiddish theatre and made her mark as the first Yeshiva "boy," where the boy is revealed at the end to be a girl. She had a magnificent basso profundo voice and sang with the Metropolitan Opera chorus for 40 years, as well as appearing on Broadway in several Gershwin musicals. She toured the U.S. and South America and Europe performing folk songs, theatre songs and liturgical chants. She starred in musicals written for her such as *The Little Queen*, *The Golden Girl*, and *Fraydele's Wedding*. Her daughter is Marilyn Michaels, the comedian and singer, who survives her. In addition to Michaels, she is survived by her son and two grandchildren.

Julie Parrish, 62, Middlesboro, Kentucky-born actress, died October 1, 2003, in Los Angeles, California, of cancer. She received a Los Angeles Drama Critics Award for the role of Maggie in Arthur Miller's *After the Fall*. She worked extensively in movies and television as an actor and writer, including appearances in films with Elvis Presley and Jerry Lewis. Parrish actively worked in Los Angeles in battered women's shelters and served on the board of the Los Angeles Commission on Assaults Against Women. She is survived by two sisters and two brothers.

Robert Pastorelli, 49, New Jersey-born actor, died March 8, 2004, in Los Angeles, California, of an apparent drug overdose. He began his stage career in New York in the early 1970s, appearing in *Rebel Without a Cause* followed by regional productions of *Death of a Salesman* and *The Rainmaker*. Most recently, he appeared in *Act One*, a series of one-act plays at the Met Theatre in Los Angeles. He perfected his craft at the New York Academy of Theatrical Arts and The Actor's Studio, before participating in programs at the Performing Arts Gallery. He moved to Hollywood in 1982, where he worked prolifically in television.

William Paterson, 84, Buffalo, New York-born actor, died September 3, 2003, in his San Francisco, California home, of lung cancer. He began his regional theatre career in 1947 at the Cleveland Playhouse, staying with them for twenty seasons. He made his debut there in *Joan of Lorraine*. In 1967, he joined the American Conservatory Theatre in San Francisco where he performed until 1998. There he played James Tyrone in *Long Days Journey into Night*. He was in the Broadway revival of *Three Sisters* in 1969. His other credits at A.C.T. include *Buried Child, The Gin Game, Painting Churches, Saint Joan, Gaslight, A Christmas Carol,* and *Mary Stuart*. He served for nine years on the San Francisco Arts Commission. He earned numerous awards including Drama-Logue and Bay Area Theatre Critics' Circle Awards. Paterson is survived by a step-daughter and a sister.

Albert Paulsen, 78, Guayaquil, Ecuador-born actor, died April 25, 2004, in Los Angeles, California, of natural causes. As a young thespian, he studied at the Actor's Studio in New York. He made his Broadway debut in 1964 in *The Three Sisters*. His other Broadway credits include *Night Circus*, and *The Only Game in Town*. He starred at the American Place Theatre in *Papp* and *Fingernails as Blue as Flowers*. A long time admirer of Vladimir Nabokov, he wrote and starred in a one-man show *Nabokov* at Los Angeles' Odyssey Theatre and on the road. Paulsen is survived by a brother and sister-in-law, three nieces, and two nephews.

Gregory Peck, 87, La Jolla, California-born actor, died June 12, 2003, in his Los Angeles, California home, of natural causes. Along with Dorothy McGuire and Mel Ferrer, he was a founder of the La Jolla Playhouse. He spent the summer of 1940 at the Barter Theatre in Virginia, the summers of 1941 and 1942 in stock companies at Suffern and White Plains in New York, and on Massachusetts' Cape Cod. He had done more than twenty shows when he was spotted by the leading Broadway director Guthrie McClintic, who cast him in a small role for the tour of George Bernard Shaw's *The Doctor's Dilemma*, starring McClintic's famous wife, Katharine Cornell. His Broadway debut was as a brilliant, young physician in Emlyn Williams' wartime drama *Morning Star*, with Gladys Cooper and Wendie Barrie. His next play was John Patrick's *The Willow and I* with Martha Scott as his leading lady. That show lasted 28 performances, six more than his third and final show of the season, Irwin Shaw's drama *Sons and Soldiers*, with Max Reinhardt directing a cast that included Stella Adler and Karl Malden. In 1992, his recorded voice was used for the role of Florence Ziegfeld in the 1991 Tony Award winning production of *The Will Rogers' Follies*. On his 82nd birthday, he performed his one-man show *A Grand Evening With Gregory Peck* presented by the La Jolla Playhouse. Peck made over 50 films, including his Oscar winning performance in 1961's *To Kill a Mockingbird.*

Dennis Quilley, 75, Great Britain-born actor, died October 5, 2003, in London, England, of cancer. His prolific career began at the Birmingham Repertory Theatre in 1945. He had long runs on London's West End during the '50s in *Wild Thyme* and *Grab Me a Gondola*. He was at the National Theatre in the '70s in plays that include *Macbeth, Hamlet, The Tempest,* and *Long Day's Journey Into Night* alongside Laurence Olivier. In 1977, he won his first Society of West End Theatre Awards for his role in the play-with-music *Privates on Parade*. In 1978 he starred in the London premiere of *Deathtrap*. In 1980, he won a second Society of West End Theatres Award for his eponymous role in *Sweeney Todd*. In 1990, he appeared in the National revival of the show playing Judge Turpin, and eventually the title role again. In 1986, he was in the London premiere of *Les Cages aux Folles,* portraying the role of Georges. In 1990–91, he appeared in the National revivals of *The School for Scandal* and *The White Devil*. In his final years he played opposite Simon Russell Beale in Bernstein's *Candide* and Diana Rigg's suitor in *Humble Boy*. His final appearance was in the National's recent revival of *Anything Goes,* in which he became ill and was not able to perform when the show transferred to the West End. Quilley is survived by his wife, Stella, a son, and two daughters.

J.C. Quinn, 63, Philadelphia-born actor, died February 10, 2004, in Juarez, Mexico, in an automobile accident. He began his career as a stage actor, and appeared on Broadway with Sean Penn in *Heartland* in 1981. He moved to Hollywood and was featured in more than 50 feature films and several television shows. He is survived by his wife and two daughters.

Jason Raize (Rothenberg), 28, Oneonta, New York-born actor, died February 3, 2004, in Yass, Australia, of a suicide. He made his Broadway debut as Simba in the original production of Julie Taymor's *The Lion King*. His other stage work includes roles in the touring companies of *The King and I, Jesus Christ Superstar, Miss Saigon,* and Kopit and Yeston's *Phantom*. He was appointed Goodwill Ambassador by the United Nations for his "furthering the cause of the environment through the use of his creative talents." Raize is survived by his father and stepmother, and his mother.

Tony Randall, 84, actor, Tulsa, Oklahoma-born actor, director, and producer, died May 18, 2004, in New York, after a long illness. Randall was a versatile actor whose career spanned 60 years in the theatre, television, and film. He made his stage debut in 1941 in *A Circle of Chalk*. He then appeared with Ethel Barrymore in *The Corn is Green* and with Jane Cowell in *Candida*. He was featured in *Antony and Cleopatra* and *Caesar and Cleopatra* during the mid-1940s. After WWII, he became a popular movie and TV star, but at heart, he considered himself a theatre actor. Randall is best known for his Emmy-winning role of the persnickety, fastidious Felix Unger opposite Jack Klugman's Oscar Madison in the television series of *The Odd Couple*, based on the hit Neil Simon play. Years later, after the show went off the air, he and Klugman would tour the United States and London in revivals of the play. Randall had previously played the stage role in an early tour of the show in the 60s, and from that production was approached about doing the television series. In 1955, he appeared in the original Broadway production of *Inherit the Wind*. In 1958, he was nominated for a Tony for his work in the musical *Oh, Captain!* He appeared on Broadway in *UTBU* in 1966 and in *M. Butterfly* in 1989. He also toured in the national company of *The Music Man*. As he entered his 60s, his focus was on how to bring classic theatre back to Broadway. He formed the National Actor's Theatre in 1991. It began as a repertory group and its first work was Arthur Miller's *The Crucible*. It then became more of a producing company, mounting more than fifteen productions including revivals of *Inherit the Wind, Three Men on a Horse, Timon of Athens, The Government Inspector, The Flowering Peach, Gentlemen Prefer Blondes, The School for Scandal, The Gin Game, The Sunshine Boys, The Seagull, Saint Joan, Night Must Fall,* and *Judgment at Nuremberg*. In a bow to changing Broadway economics, Randall moved NAT to Pace University in downtown Manhattan, where it mounted *The Resistible Rise of Arturo Ui, The Persians,* and *Right You Are*, the latter marking his final stage appearance. Randall is survived by his wife, Heather Harlan, and their two children.

John Randolph, 88, the Bronx, New York-born actor, died February 24, 2004, in Hollywood, California, of natural causes. He was a veteran of dozens of Broadway productions and was one of the founding members of the Actor's Studio. He made his Broadway debut in 1938 in *Coriolanus*. In 1986, he received Tony and Drama Desk Awards for his work in Neil Simon's *Broadway Bound*. His oeuvre includes *Mother Courage and Her Children, No More Peace, Captain Jinks of the Horse Marines, Medicine Show, Hold on to Your Hats, Command Decision, The Golden State, The Grey-Eyed People, Seagulls Over Sorrento, Room Service, All Summer Long, House of Flowers, The Wooden Dish, Miss Isobel, A Case of Libel, Conversations at Midnight, My Sweet Charlie, An American Clock, The Sound of Music, Paint Your Wagon,* and *Come Back, Little Sheba* as well as revivals of *Our Town* and *Peer Gynt*. He made his last Broadway appearance in 1991 in *Prelude to a Kiss*.

Donald O'Connor

Gregory Peck

Tony Randall

John Randolph

John Henry Redwood III, 60, Brooklyn, New York-born actor turned playwright, died June 17, 2003, in Philadelphia, Pennsylvania, of heart disease. A prolific writer, actor, Redwood amassed a body of work that included roles on Broadway in *Guys and Dolls* and *The Piano Lesson*, as well as television and film. He spent the last year and a half touring the country in the one-man show, *Looking Over the President's Shoulder*, about a White House butler that served under four presidents. He appeared in the one-man show *Paul Robeson* and provided the voice of Robeson in the PBS special *I'll Make Me a World*. His play *The Old Settler* was cited by American Theatre magazine as one of 10 most produced plays in the 1998–99 and 1999–00 seasons. His other plays include *No Niggers, No Jews, No Dogs* (which was nominated for a 2001 Barrymore New Play Award and played Off Broadway in 2001), and *Mark VIII: xxxvi, Acted Within Proper Departmental Procedure* and *Sunbeam*. In 2000, he appeared in *A Lesson Before Dying*. He was most proud of his one-act *What If You're the One*, which encouraged women to have mammograms. He was invited to write a play in remembrance of 9/11, and *We Never Knew Their Names* appeared at Town Hall in New York City. He is survived by four children and two grandchildren.

Leonard Reed, 97, Lightning Creek, Oklahoma-born tap dancer, died April 8, 2004, in Covina, California, of heart failure. Reed's career spanned an amazing 80 years. He began his career partnering with Willie Bryant in their vaudeville act *Brains As Well As Feet*. He produced shows at the Cotton Club in Manhattan and was master of ceremonies at the Apollo Theatre for 20 years. He was also a songwriter, bandleader and comedian. In 2000, he received a Lifetime Achievement Award from the American Music Awards. In 2002, he received an honorary doctor of performing arts degree from Oklahoma City University. When not tap dancing, he was a songwriter, bandleader, and comedian. He is noted for creating the famous "Shim Sham Shimmy" dance routine.

Alan Reisner, 80, actor and director, died April 8, 2004 at his home in Beverly Hills, California, of Alzheimer's disease. He began his stage career in New York and appeared on Broadway in *Junior Miss*, *No Exit*, and *Home of the Brave*. He then became an acclaimed television director for Playhouse 90, GE Theatre, and Desilu Playhouse. For the next three decades, he directed movies and television, becoming known as someone who keenly understood the needs of stage actors transitioning from theatre to television.

John Ritter, 54, Burbank, California-born actor died September 11, 2003, in Burbank, California, of an aortic dissection. Ritter is best remembered for his role as Jack Tripper in the hit television show *Three's Company*, and proved his wide range of acting skills in feature movies and over 50 made-for-TV miniseries and dramas. His made his Broadway debut with his friend and television star Henry Winkler in 2000 in Neil Simon's *The Dinner Party* for which he won a Theatre World Award. Ritter was starring in the series *8 Simple Rules for Dating My Teenage Daughter* at the time of his unexpected death. He is survived by his wife, Amy Yasbeck, and four children.

Carlos Rivas, 78, El Paso, Texas-born actor, died June 16, 2003 in Beverly Hills, California, of prostate cancer. He was a leading man in Mexico appearing in more than twenty movies there, and in over forty movies after he moved to California. He frequented Los Angeles stages as well, appearing in Matt Crowley's *Remote Asylum* at the Ahmanson as well as in Fernando Arrabal's *Ceremony for an Assassinated Black Man* at the Nosotro Theatre. In 1969, he was a founding member of the Nosotros organization to improve the image of Latinos and Hispanics in the entertainment industry. Rivas is survived by his wife, a daughter, and granddaughter.

Rex Robbins, 68, Pierre, South Dakota-born actor, died September 23, 2003, in Pierre, South Dakota, of a brain aneurysm. He appeared in 18 Broadway shows from 1963 to 2000. His work includes the role of Herbie opposite Angela Lansbury in the 1974 revival of *Gypsy*, the 1979 production of *Richard III* with Al Pacino, *The Sisters Rosensweig*, *One Flew Over the Cuckoo's Nest*, *Scratch*, *The Changing Room*, *The Magic Show*, *A Memory of Two Mondays*, *27 Wagons Full of Cotton*, *They Knew What They Wanted*, *Secret Service*, *Boy Meets Girl*, *Comedians*, *An Almost Perfect Person*, *Players*, *King Richard III*, *You Can't Take it With You*, *Noises Off*, *Play Memory*, *All My Sons*, *Six Degrees of Separation*, and James Joyce's *The Dead*. He performed at the Williamstown Theatre Festival in Massachusetts for 17 seasons, and in 15 productions at the Long Wharf Theatre in New Haven. He toured nationally in *Gypsy, Hello, Dolly!* with Carol Channing, and *Into the Woods* with Cleo Lane. He is survived by his wife, Patricia, their daughters, Margaret and Mary Victoria, and a son, Timothy, and a brother, Bill.

William Roy, 75, Detroit, Missouri-born actor, songwriter, singer, and music director, died September 2, 2003, in West Palm Beach, Florida, of respiratory failure. As a child he had roles in 20 films including *The Corn is Green*. During his youth, he started composing music. In 1953, he wrote the music and lyrics for a Broadway show *Maggie* and later wrote the book, music and lyrics for the Off-Broadway show *The Penny Friend* starring Bernadette Peters. He wrote the music and lyrics for the revue, *New Faces of '62*. He also worked as a nightclub arranger and musical director for the Julius Monk revues at the Upstairs at the Downstairs and at Plaza 9 in the Plaza Hotel in New York City. He was the writer, arranger and conductor for Ms. Peters' nightclub act, and also was musical director and pianist for Julie Wilson, performing with her on several numbers in her act. Roy also worked with Rosemary Clooney, Dorothy Dandridge, Dolores Gray, Celeste Holm, Linda Lavin, Carol Lawrence, Portia Nelson, Ginger Rogers, and countless others.

Janice Rule, 72, Norwood, Ohio-born actress, died October 17, 2003, in New York, New York, of undisclosed causes. She made her Broadway debut in William Inge's *Picnic* playing opposite Paul Newman. Among her other Broadway shows were *Miss Liberty*, *Great to Be Alive*, *The Flowering Peach*, *The Happiest Girl in the World*, and *Night Circus*. After roles in several films, she eventually got her doctorate in psychoanalysis in 1973. She practiced in New York and Los Angeles and continued to act occasionally.

Carl Samuelson, 77, the Bronx, New York-born theatre founder and producer, died April 20, 2004, in Delray Beach, Florida, of undisclosed causes. He founded the Stagedoor Manor Performing Arts Training Center in upstate Loch Sheldrake, New York in 1975, which served as the inspiration for the 2004 film *Camp*, directed by former Stagedoor Manor student and Broadway actor, Todd Graff. Samuelson was featured in a small role in the film. Other famous theatre folk who attended the camp as youngsters include Jon Cryer, Danny Gurwin, Natalie Portman, Robert Downey, Jr., Nicky Silver, Mary Stuart Masterson, and Julia Murney. Besides running his camp in the 1990s, he produced several shows in southern Florida including, *Me and My Girl* and *Annie Warbucks*.

Lesley Savage, 90, actress, director, and producer, died October 8, 2003, in New York, New York, of natural causes. Savage founded the Bellport Summer Theatre in Long Island, NY, in 1947, introducing Long Island to professional Equity theatre. She later sold the company and it became the Gateway Playhouse. In 1949 she founded the Theatre-Go-Round in Virginia Beach, Virginia where she produced, directed, and acted in over 100 plays between 1949 and 1958. For the New York stage, she produced *Musical Chairs* and *The American Way*. She also appeared in several Broadway and regional plays and toured with the USO productions during WWII. Until her death, she remained active in the League of American Theatre Producers. She is survived by two daughters, a son, and two grandsons.

Lynn L. Seidler, 67, New Brunswick, New Jersey-born Shubert Arts Foundation director, died March 23, 2004, in Turks and Caicos Islands while on vacation, of lung cancer. She became the organization's first director in 1975, turning it into one of the largest grant-making institutions in the country. She set up funds for non-profit theatres, drama schools and dance companies to aid in their operating expenses. In 2003, the foundation awarded over $13 million in grants. She also founded the Shubert Archive in 1976, after finding a trove of dusty boxes, papers and files tucked away in various Shubert theatres. With over 6 million items, it is now one of the largest collections of theatre memorabilia in the country. Seidler is survived by her husband, Lee, her father, a daughter, and a grandson.

Herbert Senn, 78, Ilion, New York-born set designer, died August 3, 2003, Yarmouthport, Massachusetts, after a brief illness. He designed many Broadway shows including *What Makes Sammy Run?*, *Noel Coward's Sweet Potato*, *A Musical Jubilee*, *Macbeth*, *Roar Like a Dove*, *Oh, Coward!*, *No Sex Please, We're British*, and the revivals of *Show Boat* and *The Boys from Syracuse*. He and his wife, Helen Pond, also a set designer, collaborated on over 50 operas for the Opera Company of Boston including *Aida*, *Mass*, and the American premieres of *War and Peace* and *Russlan and Ludmilla*. They also spent thirty-five summers designing sets for the Cape Playhouse in Dennis, Massachusetts. Senn and Pond co-designed for the New York City Opera, The Houston Grand Opera, Lincoln Center's Vivian Beaumont Theatre, the Paper Mill Playhouse in New Jersey, the Boston Ballet's Nutcracker Suite for 25 years. In 1993 Senn and Pond became the first recipients of the Elliot Norton-Robert Edmund Jones prize for outstanding Boston designer. Two years later they received the Balletic Medal of Honor. Besides Pond, Senn is survived by two cousins.

Marvin Sims, 55, educator and head of Black Theatre Network, died December 25, 2003, in Gainesville, Florida, of heart failure. He was a pioneer in the theatre community, becoming the first African-American president of the Association for the Theatre in Higher Education. Concurrently, he was serving a two-year term as the president of BTN, a group that strives to preserve black theatre nationwide. Also a professor, he taught at the University of Illinois and Eastern Michigan University before becoming head of performance at Virginia Commonwealth University in Richmond.

Penny Singleton, 95, Philadelphia, Pennsylvania-born actress, died November 12, 2003, in Los Angeles, California, of natural causes. She was a radio and movie star for decades and toured in vaudeville. Singleton brought the comic strip Blondie to life in a popular series of 28 films and was the voice of Jane on television's animated series, *The Jetsons*. Before her radio and film career she made her Broadway debut in the 1927 musical, *Good News*. She went on to appear on Broadway in *Sky High*, *The Great Temptations*, *Hey, Nonny Nonny!*, and *No, No, Nannette*.

Edna Skinner, 82, Washington, D.C.-born actress and singer, died in North Bend, Oregon, of heart failure. Skinner sang in vaudeville and clubs in Manhattan. She made her mark as Ado Annie, replacing Celeste Holm, in the legendary original run of *Oklahoma!*, after Rodgers and Hammerstein hired her to sing scores for them. During WWII, she organized rallies for the Treasury Department featuring such stars as Fanny Brice, Bea Lillie and Gertrude Lawrence. Skinner played neighbor Kay Addison on the television series *Mr. Ed*.

John Ritter

Isabelle Stevenson

Peter Ustinov

Paul Winfield

Florence Stanley, 79, Chicago, Illinois-born actress, died October 3, 2003, in Los Angeles, California, of complications from a stroke. Known for her distinct, raspy voice she made her mark in the legit theatre, movies, and television. She began her stage career on Broadway in the original production of *Fiddler on the Roof* and in the 1965 revival of *The Glass Menagerie*. She also had roles in *The Secret Affairs of Mildred Wild*, *Fools*, and *The Apple Doesn't Fall…*. She was also in the original cast production of Neil Simon's *The Prisoner of Second Avenue*. She appeared in productions at the Manhattan Theatre Club including *What's Wrong With This Picture?*, and acted with the New York Shakespeare Festival. She was a long-time member of the League of Professional Theatre Women. Television audiences remember her for her role as Bernice Fish on *Barney Miller*, and that show's subsequent spin-off series *Fish*, starring as Abe Vigoda's wife. Stanley is survived by her husband, two children, and two grandchildren.

Ray Stark, 88, New Jersey-born producer died January 17, 2004, in Los Angeles, California, of complications from a stroke. He was a legendary Hollywood power broker, producing many award-winning movies, and brought several of Neil Simon's comedies to the screen. Before he began his producing career, he developed his eye as a literary and talent agent in the 1940s and '50s. In 1957 he and Elliot Hyman formed Seven Arts, a company that dealt mainly with television, purchasing the rights to stage and literary properties. His marriage to Frances Brice in 1939 gave him the retaining rights to the life of his mother-in-law, Fanny Brice, and he began his legit producer career with the Broadway musical *Funny Girl* based on her life, and boosted Barbra Streisand's career. His other Broadway productions include: *The World of Suzie Wong*, *Everybody Loves Opal*, *Any Wednesday*, and *The Owl and the Pussycat*. He continued to work as an independent producer with his company Rastar Productions, which he later sold to Columbia pictures and made him one of the wealthiest producers in Hollywood. Stark is survived by daughter, Wendy Stark Morrisey; and a granddaughter.

Jan Sterling (Jane Sterling Adriance), 82, New York, New York-born actress, died March 26, 2004, in Woodland Hills, California, after several strokes. As a young woman, she studied acting in England and made several appearances on the London stage. She made her Broadway debut in 1938 at the age of 15 in *Broadway Born*. Her other Broadway credits include, *Grey Farm*, *Bachelor Born*, *When We Are Married*, *This Too Shall Pass*, *Small War on Murray Hill*, *Born*

Yesterday, *Present Laughter*, *Two Blind Mice*, *The Perfect Setup*, *Once For the Asking*, *The Front Page*, and *The November People*. Sterling appeared in more than 40 films between 1948 and 1980, usually in supporting roles. She earned an Oscar nomination and a Golden Globe Award for her role in the film, *The High and the Mighty*.

Isabelle Stevenson, 90, Vineland, New Jersey-born chairwoman of the American Theatre Wing, died December 28, 2003, in Manhattan, New York, after a brief illness. She was president of the organization for 33 years and became chairman of the board in 1998. The Theatre Wing began as the Stage Women's War Relief Fund, founded in 1917, renamed the American Theatre Wing War Service Theatre in 1939. The Wing was famous for its Stage Door Canteens. After WWII, the Wing established the Tony Awards and also the Professional Training School for returning soldiers, which existed from 1946 to 1965. In her positions with the Wing, Stevenson oversaw a diverse range of programs designed to bring theatre to the community and nurture new theatregoers. She was a familiar face to the public as the doyenne of the Tony Awards, appearing every year at the telecast in her tenure. Stevenson also inaugurated the series of "Working in the Theatre" seminars, held twice a year at the Graduate Center of CUNY and shown on cable television. The seminars brought together leading performers, playwrights, directors, producers, and designers. She also began a program of grants and fellowships to Off and Off Off Broadway Theatres. Stevenson nurtured the Hospital Program, which takes plays and cabaret shows to hospitals, nursing homes, and AIDS centers. Theatre for Children, another program she developed, produced plays for thousands of New York public school children each year. Her Introduction to Broadway provided theatre tickets for as low as $2.50 to high school audiences. As a performer, she made her debut in Earl Carroll's *Vanities*, an annual musical which rivaled the *Ziegfeld Follies*. She also appeared in George White's *Scandals*. She toured the U.S. as a dancer and performed at the London Palladium for the Queen. She was known in Paris as the "blond Josephine Baker." She joined the ATW in 1954. She received a special Tony for Lifetime Achievement in 1999. In 2001, she was inducted into the Theatre Hall of Fame. Stevenson is survived by two daughters.

William Swetland, 90, Kalispell, Montana-born actor, died October 31, 2003, in Branford, Connecticut, of natural causes. He was one of country's premiere regional theatre actors, and was in the original company at the Long Wharf in New Haven, CT. He appeared in over seventy-five plays there, through the '90s. Swetland began acting in Cleveland, and was an actor and director at the Cleveland Playhouse for ten years. He also acted at the Hartford Stage in *On Borrowed Time*, at the McCarter Theatre in Princeton, NJ, and at the Williamstown Theatre Festival. His Broadway debut was in 1936 in *Parnell*. Other credits include: *The National Health*, the revival of O'Neill's *Ah, Wilderness! Having Wonderful Time, Ring Two, Goodbye in the Night, Who Was That Lady I Saw You With? A Call on Kuprin, Solitaire/Double Solitaire, The Changing Room, The National Health, The Philadelphia Story, Major Barbara,* and *Borak*. Among his survivors are two sons and two stepsons.

John Taras, 84, New York, New York-born dancer and choreographer, died April 2, 2004, in Manhattan, New York, of undisclosed causes. He was an internationally known ballet master, who worked with the New York City Ballet and the American Ballet Theatre. From 1940, his work was linked to George Ballanchine and his companies. He created *Design for Strings* to the music of Tchaikovsky for the Metropolitan Ballet of Edinburgh in 1948. In 1952, he presented *Peige de Lumiere* for the Grand Ballet du Marquis de Cuevas in Paris. It was restaged in 1964 for the City Ballet. He choreographed *Arcade* specifically for Suzanne Farrell, a star in Ballanchine's company at the time. His more enduring works at City Ballet include *Ebony Concerto* to Stravinsky's music, *Souvenir de Florence* in 1981, and *Graziana* for the American Ballet Theatre in 1945. For the Dance Theatre of Harlem, he choreographed *Firebird* to spectacular reviews. He was artistic director for the Paris Opera Ballet and for the Berlin Ballet in the late 1960s through the early 1970s. After Ballanchine's death 1983, he became associate director of the American Ballet Theatre for six years. As a young man, he danced with the Philadelphia Ballet and the American Ballet Caravan, a precursor to the City Ballet. He created *Camille* for the Original Ballet Russe and its guest star, Alicia Markova. He also created the *Tchaikovsky Waltz* for the Markova-Dolin Ballet. He created the ballet *Fanfare for a Prince* for the wedding of Grace Kelly to Prince Rainier of Monaco. In 1966, he choreographed his version of Nijinsky's *Jeux* for the City Ballet.

June Taylor, 86, Chicago, Illinois-born dancer and choreographer, died May 16, 2004, in Miami, Florida, of natural causes. She was a seasoned nightclub dancer until a bout with tuberculosis forced her to turn to choreography. She made a name for herself creating dances for variety TV shows in the 1950s and 1960s, including routines on *The Jackie Gleason Show*. Each week 16 high-kicking young women called the June Taylor Dancers would open his show with an intricate, expensive, wholesome-looking chorus line, often shot from above, resulting in a kaleidoscopic pattern reminiscent of the films of Busby Berkeley. When the Gleason show moved to Miami in 1964, she relocated to Florida. After the show ended, she remained in Florida and went on to choreograph for the Miami Dolphins cheerleaders from 1978 until her retirement in 1990. She is survived by her sister, Marilyn Gleason (Jackie's widow) and a nephew.

Markland Taylor, 67, Adelaide, Australia-born theatre critic and reporter, died July 6, 2003, in Southbury, Connecticut, of a heart attack. Taylor covered New England theatre—from pre-Broadway tryouts in New Haven and Boston to many regional and summer festivals—for more than two decades for *Variety*, providing an invaluable part of the paper's legit coverage. After graduating from college he worked in Australia as a theatre critic in Adelaide and Melbourne, and then as an associate editor of Plays & Players in London. He moved to New York in the early '60s to study criticism under New York Herald Tribune drama critic Judith Crist at Columbia University. Taylor later became the head of publicity at the William Morris Agency in New York. He returned to writing and became the theatre critic for the New Haven Register. While working at the Register, he began filing reviews for *Variety*. He is survived by partner Hartney Arthur, a former theatre producer and agent, and a brother.

Ludmilla Tcherina, 79, Paris, France-born ballerina, died March 21, 2004, in Paris, France, of undisclosed causes. She began dancing with the Nouveaux Ballets de Montecarlo. In 1942, she dances the role of Juliet in Lifar's *Romeo et Juliette* in Paris. In 1957, she danced in Debussy's *Martyrdom of St. Sebastian* to great acclaim, combining music, dance and drama. In the 1980s, she also published two novels and a screenplay.

Leon Uris, 79, Baltimore, Maryland-born author and lyricist, died June 21, 2003, on Shelter Island, New York. Best known for his non-fiction novels, he made his Broadway debut writing the book and the lyrics for *Ari*, the musical adaptation of his best-seller, *Exodus*.

Peter Ustinov, 82, London, England-born actor, playwright, and raconteur, died March 28, 2004, in Geneva, Switzerland, of heart failure. He was a multi-faceted theatre man, who in addition to acting, also often directed and performed in the plays he wrote. Sir Ustinov's career spanned more than 60 years. His first play was produced on the London stage when he was 21. His best known work, *Romanoff and Juliet*, was a hit in London, and went on to earn Tony nominations for the Broadway production for best actor and play. He also composed music for the show. His other Broadway credits include: *The Love of Four Colonels* (playwright), *Photofinish* (actor, playwright, director), *The Unknown Soldier and His Wife* (playwright), *Halfway Up the Tree* (playwright, director), *Who's Who in Hell* (playwright, actor), and *Beethoven's Tenth* (playwright, actor). During his career, he wrote more than a dozen books, spoke numerous languages and was admired as a raconteur and humorist. He supported many charities, was rector of the University of Scotland in Dundee and was an impassioned advocate of UNESCO and UNICEF for which he served as goodwill ambassador. Ustinov earned two Oscars for *Spartacus* and *Topkapi*, a Golden Globe for *Quo Vadis?*, three Emmy Awards, and a Grammy Award for his narration in *Peter and the Wolf*. He is survived by his third wife and four children.

Zan Ericson Van Antwerp, 70, died peacefully on February 26, 2005, at the Village Nursing Home in the West Village of New York, NY, following a long illness. The dedication of this volume of *Theatre World* reads "In memory of Zan Van Antwerp and Charles J. Grant, Jr. Without their steadfast encouragement of the associate editor for the past seven years, this series would not have continued to have been published. Their unwavering and enthusiastic support of the arts and artists in all respects is surpassed only by their inspirational devotion to one another and those they loved. They will forever be remembered and honored by the editors of these volumes, as well as by all who were lucky enough to have known them." She was survived by her beloved companion of twenty-three years, Charles J. Grant, Jr. ("Mr. Charlie Bear"), her sister-in-law Helen C. Van Antwerp, her nephew William M. Van Antwerp, wife Margaret and their children, William, Jr., Scott, Autumn, and Peter Terenzi; her nephew Bradley P. Van Antwerp, wife Janine, and their children, Michaela, Sarah, Emily, and Meredith; together with many Ericson, Van Antwerp, and Van Rensselaer cousins, and special friends Linda Adler, Lori Batdorf, Bill Bush, Stanley Ackert, Brad Hampton, Ben Hodges, David Plank, and Robert Rems. Born in Albany, New York, she was the daughter of the late Colonel William M. Van Antwerp and Marian Ericson Van Antwerp. Her adored brother, Captain William M. Van Anterp, Jr., died in Viet Nam. The Albany Academy, high school years in Waynesboro, Virginia, a year at Mount Holyoke and a year living in Turkey when her father was posted there with the military formed the backdrop of her life. She exhibited her signature powers as a legal secretary, able to cosset crotchety partners, to rewrite briefs in better English, and to speak with federal judges on a first-name basis (but then, she never bothered knowing anyone except on a first-name basis). Zan had retired as an executive legal secretary, and is fondly remembered as a longtime (forty-six year) West Village resident and activist, having served for many years as the Treasurer of the Morton Street Block Association. It was Zan's second nature (some would say her first) to be a caregiver, and her extended family encompassed all those whose needs and problems were as much Zan's concern as theirs. She was never without a good report on the two ring-tailed wonders who were her nephews, whose love redoubled for the loss of her brother Bill. We remember especially her unique devotion to her dear neighbor "Weegie," Louise Suhr, sho was able to spend her final years in comfort in her apartment at 55 Morton Street thanks to the ministrations of Zan and her neighbor, Bill Bush. Bill, in turn, was for many years the recipient of Zan's special care as a regular Saturday night dinner companion. "The Annex" to 55 Morton Street was the home of Zan's mother, Marian, at Pendennis Mount in Annapolis, MD. Through an extraordinary long-distance network of neighbors, Zan oversaw Marian's final years, confronting her own mounting infirmities to make the necessary pilgrimages with Charlie to Annapolis. Her greatest project through all of this remained "Mr. Charlie Bear," whose devotion bore up through increasing adversity, and whose constancy kept time with her until at last she slipped away. Zan kept a gray metal box with index cards on her office desk. On the inside of its lid was taped a quotation from an old golfer, which enjoined that we should go through life, always "taking time to smell the flowers." Zan lived that advice, and in good weather, she and Charlie could often be found in the garden at St. Luke-in-the-Fields, We cannot doubt that she will be found there again, where the bricks and flowers and vines bear indelible witness to her memory, and the Gardener will speak her name once more.

Kelly Waymire, 36, Columbus, Ohio-born actress, died November 24, 2003, in Los Angeles, California, of an undisclosed medical condition. She had a prolific career in regional theatres including South Coast Repertory, the Pasadena Playhouse and the La Jolla Playhouse. She was a member of the Circle X Theatre and the Antaeus Theatre in Los Angeles and was a founding member of the Rogue Theatre in New York City. She received a Drama-Logue Award for her starring role in *Sylvia* at the Old Globe Theatre in San Diego. Waymire appeared on many television series including *Six Feet Under, Friends, Seinfeld, The Practice, NYPD Blue, The X-Files, and Ally Mc Beal,* in addition she worked in feature films. She is survived by her partner, Gary Judson Smoot, her mother, father, brother, and sister.

Bernard "Bernie" Weiss, 78, Cleveland, Ohio-born set designer, died March 24, 2003, in Las Vegas, Nevada, of undisclosed causes. He was a skilled designer and worked on and Off Broadway for over 40 years. He was house carpenter and manager of technical activities for the Shuberts, closely supervising productions at the Cort Theatre. He also participated in renovations and design work of theatres in Mexico City and the Soviet Union. In 2002, he was honored as a Fellow of the U.S. Institute for Theatre Technology. Survivors include his wife of 48 years, Joyce, a daughter, son, and brother.

Elizabeth Welch, 99, New York, New York-born actress and singer, died July 15, 2003, in London, England, of natural causes. Her Broadway debut was at age 17 in *Running Wild*. She is credited for introducing the song and the dance "Charleston" to US audiences. She appeared with Bill "Bojangles" Robinson in *Blackbirds of 1928*, which toured to Paris and introduced her to Europe. In 1933, Cole Porter asked her to open in his show in London, *Nymph Errant*. While in London, she sang "Stormy Weather" in the show *Dark Doings*, the song's British debut. Her oeuvre includes Cole Porter's *The New Yorkers* (1931), *Black Broadway* (1980), *Jerome Kern Goes to Hollywood* (1986—Tony nomination), and her one-woman show *Time to Start Living* (Obie Award). Her other London credits include *Glamorous Night, The Crooked Mile, Ciny-Ella, A Marvelous Party*, and *Pippin*.

Beatrice Winde (Beatrice Lucille Williams), 79, Chicago, Illinois-born actress, died January 3, 2004, in New York, New York, of cancer. She received a Theatre World Award and a best supporting Tony nomination for her role in the 1972 musical by Melvin Van Peebles', *Ain't Supposed to Die a Natural Death*. She won an Audelco Award for her role as the godmother in *Lesson Before Dying* at the Signature Theatre Company. In 1997, she appeared again on Broadway in *The Young Man From Atlanta,* and in that year, she received the Living Legend Award from the National Black Theatre. She also acted in plays mounted by the Manhattan Theatre Club, the Jean Cocteau Repertory, the Negro Ensemble Theatre Company, and Playwrights Horizons. She had roles in more than a dozen films and popular television series. Winde is survived by two brothers.

Paul Winfield, 62, Los Angeles, California-born actor, died March 7, 2004, in Los Angeles, California, of heart failure. Before embarking on a long, Oscar and Emmy-nominated career in movies and TV, Winfield made his stage debut in two controversial plays, *The Dutchman* and *The Toilet*. Burgess Meredith cast him personally. After a short stint as a contract player for Columbia Pictures, he joined the Stanford Repertory in San Francisco and Los Angeles' Inner City Cultural Center Theatre. He made his Broadway debut with Denzel Washington in the play *Checkmates*. At the Goodman Theatre in Chicago, he played in Ibsen's *Enemy of the People*. Concurrent with his burgeoning movie career, he continued to appear on stage at the Mark Taper Forum and other area theatres. Winfield received a NAACP Image Award for best actor and was inducted to the Black Filmmakers Hall of Fame. He is survived by his sister.

Jessica Grace Wing, 31, composer, died July 19, 2003, in Brooklyn, New York, of colon cancer. Her full length musical *Lost,* based on the fairy tale "Hansel and Gretel," was completed 36 hours before her death, and opened one week after at New York's International Fringe Festival. She was founder of the Inverse Theatre in New York City, a troupe devoted to performing "in verse." She wrote the music for several productions for the troupe including 1998's *Othello* and *Midnight Brainwash Revival*. Wing is survived by her parents, a brother, and three stepsisters.

George Wojtasik, 69, Equity Library Theatre director, died April 30, 2004, at his home in Old Town, Maine, of cancer. He served from 1967 to 1989 as the managing director of the New York-based Equity Library Theatre, a showcase for emerging professional actors. While there, he produced 196 plays and received numerous awards including a special Tony Award (1977), a Special Theatre World Award (1975), and an Outer Critics Circle Award (1972). In 1991, he became director of the Grand Auditorium in Ellsworth, Maine until he retired in 1996.

Mel Wong, 64, Oakland, California-born dancer, choreographer, and teacher, died July 17, 2003, in Santa Cruz, California, of heart failure. As a young man he studied at the School of American Ballet and with Merce Cunningham. He performed with the Merce Cunningham Dance Company from 1968 to 1972 and was in the original casts of *Canfield, Tread, Second-Hand*, and *Signals*. An accomplished visual artist as well, he incorporated dance and visual arts in his own choreography. A program of solos, "Growing Up Asian-American in the 1950s" was touring the country at the time of his death. He taught at the State University of New York at Purchase, University of Colorado, New York University, and at the American Dance Festival. Wong is survived by his wife, Connie Kreemer, three daughters, his mother, Louise, and a brother, Maurice.

Lesley Woods, 90, actress, died August 2, 2003 in Los Angeles, California, of natural causes. She made her Broadway debut in *Double Dummy* in 1936. She continued her stage career on Broadway in plays including *Excursion, Comes the Revelation* and *A Case of Libel*. She was a long-time member and supporter of Theatre West. Her last stage role there was in *Tom Tom on a Rooftop* with Betty Garrett and Philip Abbott. She also donated the marquee that adorns the theatre. She worked extensively as a series regular or continuing character primarily in soap operas, and appeared in several feature films. She is survived by stepson, actor Sam McMurray.

Brian Wright, 43, Shoreline, Washington-born dancer and figure skater, died July 29, 2003, of AIDS. He helped choreograph winning routines for Olympic gold medalists and was credited with opening the door for lesbian and gay ice skaters infected with HIV to encourage honesty about alternative lifestyles. After graduating from high school he toured with the Ice Capades and appeared on Broadway in *A Chorus Line*.

Philip Yordan, 89, Chicago, Illinois-born playwright, died March 24, 2003, San Diego, California. In 1944, he made his Broadway debut with his play *Anna Lucasta* produced by the American Negro Theatre with an all-black cast. It ran 957 performances. It was followed by his work *Any Day Now*. During the McCarthy era, he served as a front for many blacklisted writers.

INDEX

JOHN WILLIS | Editor

John Willis has been editor-in-chief of both *Theatre World* and its companion series *Screen World* for forty-two years. *Theatre World* and *Screen World* are the oldest and definitive pictorial and statistical records of the American theatrical and foreign and domestic film seasons, respectively, referenced by theatre devotees, industry professionals, students, and historians worldwide.

Mr. Willis has also served as editor of *Dance World*, *Opera World*, *A Pictorial History of the American Theatre 1860–1985*, and *A Pictorial History of the Silent Screen*. Previously, he served as assistant to *Theatre World* founder Daniel Blum on *Great Stars of the American Stage*, *Great Stars of Film*, *A Pictorial History of the Talkies*, *A Pictorial History of Television*, and *A Pictorial Treasury of Opera in America*.

For the past forty-two years he has also presided over the presentation of the annual Theatre World Awards. Founded in 1945, they are the oldest awards given to actors for an Outstanding Broadway or Off-Broadway debut, and one of the oldest awards bestowed on actors in any regard. On behalf of *Theatre World*, Mr. Willis has received the Special 2001 Tony Honor for Excellence in the Theatre, as well as lifetime achievement awards from the Broadway Theater Institute, Drama Desk, Lucille Lortel, National Board of Review, Marquis Who's Who Publications Board, and Milligan College. He has served on the nominating committees for the Tony Awards and the New York University Hall of Fame, and is currently on the board of the University of Tennessee Clarence Brown Theatre.

BEN HODGES | Associate Editor

As an actor, director, and/or producer, Ben has appeared in New York with the Barrow Group Theatre Company, Origin Theatre Company, Daedalus Theatre Company, Monday Morning Productions, the Strawberry One-Act Festival, and Coyote Girls Productions. Additionally, he has appeared in numerous productions presented by theatre companies that he founded, the Tuesday Group and Visionary Works. On film, he can be seen in *Macbeth: The Comedy*.

In 2001, he became a director of development, then served as executive director for Fat Chance Productions, Inc. and the Ground Floor Theatre, a New York-based nonprofit theatre and film production company. *Prey for Rock and Roll* was developed by Fat Chance from their stage production into a critically acclaimed feature film starring Gina Gershon, Drea de Matteo, and Lori Petty. Additionally, Fat Chance conducted numerous readings, workshops, and productions in their Ground Floor Theatre, the mission statement being to present new works by new artists.

In 2003, frustrated with the increasingly daunting economic prospects involved in producing theatre on a small scale in New York, Ben organized NOOBA, the New Off-Off- Broadway Association, an advocacy group dedicated to representing the concerns of expressly Off-Off-Broadway producers in the public forum and in negotiations with other local professional arts organizations. He also serves on the New York Innovative Theatre Awards Committee, selecting outstanding individuals for recognition Off-Off-Broadway.

Ben served as an editorial assistant for many years on the 2001 Special Tony Honor Award-winning *Theatre World*, becoming the associate editor to John Willis in 1998. Also an assistant for many years to Mr. Willis for the prestigious Theatre World Awards, Ben was elected to the Theatre World Awards Board in 2002 and currently serves as an executive producer for the 2005 LAMBDA Literary Foundation "Lammy" Awards, held in New York City.

Forbidden Acts, the first collected anthology of gay and lesbian plays from the span of the twentieth century, edited and with an introduction by Ben, was published by Applause Theatre & Cinema Books in 2003 and was finalist for the 2004 LAMBDA Literary Award for Drama.

In 2005, Ben founded and currently serves as executive director of the Learning Theatre, a 501(c)(3) nonprofit organization incorporating theatre into the development of autistic and learning disabled children.

He lives in New York City.

SCOTT DENNY | Assistant Editor

Scott Denny is an actor and currently resides in New York. His credits include national tours of *1776*, *Footloose*, and *The Music Man*. He has appeared at over 25 regional, stock, and dinner theatre companies across the country, including Houston's Theatre Under the Stars, Stage One Wichita, Prince Street Players, and the Prather Family of Theatres in Fort Myers, Florida and Lancaster, Pennsylvania. Scott is originally from Terre Haute, Indiana and holds a BFA in Performing Arts from Western Kentucky University. He also works part-time as a cruise travel agent.

VICTORIA V. GUELI | Assistant Editor

Victoria V. Gueli worked on *Theatre World* while an interning editorial assistant at Applause Theatre & Cinema Books. A former journalist for the *Staten Island Advance*, she is a student at the College of Staten Island and a managing editor of the school's *Serpentine Literary Magazine*. Currently, she is collaborating with Peter Marsh and Patrick Montero on the development of *Cynosure*, a Staten Island-based literary magazine. A freelance writer and poet, Victoria is also a member of the Staten Island Writers Group.

LUCY NATHANSON | Assistant Editor

Lucy Nathanson grew up in Manhattan, during a more heroic and innocent time. She studied fine arts at the High School of Music & Art, ballet at the School of American Ballet, and sculpture and painting at the Arts Students League. The genesis of her love of musical theatre, plays, and cultural performances of all kinds began at home, nurtured by her theatrical/motion picture press-agent father and classical pianist mother. She freelances as an editor and personal assistant. Working for John Willis, Ben Hodges, and *Theatre World* has reinforced her belief that Art, beautifully shaped, can reshape lives.

ZACHARY DAVID PALMER | Assistant Editor

Zachary David Palmer holds a degree in English-Creative Writing from Ohio University. He was an assistant in the production of the 2005 Theatre World Awards and the 2005 Lambda Literary Awards, and assisted in the creation of the Learning Theatre, Inc., a nonprofit organization founded by Hodges that incorporates theatre into the development of autistic and learning disabled children. Zachary is the nightlife editor and an editorial assistant for *The L Magazine*, and is both a poet and an artist. He lives and works in New York City.

RACHEL WERBEL | Assistant Editor

Rachel assisted on *Theatre World* and the Theatre World Awards from 2001–2005. She is a graduate of the American Academy of Dramatic Arts and is currently attending the New School as a bachelor candidate.